INTERNATIONAL FINANCE

V. A. AVADHANI

M.A., Ph.D. (U.S.A.), M.A., LL.B., C.A.I.I.B

* Retired Adviser in the Reserve Bank of India,
* Former Director of Research and Training in Bombay Stock Exchange,
* Former Adviser in Hyderabad Stock Exchange,
* Former visiting faculty in many Management Institutions

Himalaya Publishing House

ISO 9001:2015 CERTIFIED

Second Revised and Updated Edition	:	**1996**
Third Revised Edition	:	**1998**
Fourth Revised and Enlarged Edition	:	**2000**
Fifth Revised Edition	:	**2004**
Reprint	:	**2004**
Sixth Revised Edition	:	**2006**
Seventh Edition	:	**2008**
Reprint	:	**2009**
Seventh Revised Edition	:	**2011**
Eight Revised Edition	:	**2012**
Reprint	:	**2015, 2017, 2018, 2020**
Reprint	:	**2022**
Reprint	:	**2023**

Published by : Mrs. Meena Pandey
for **HIMALAYA PUBLISHING HOUSE PVT. LTD.,**
"Ramdoot", Dr. Bhalerao Marg, Girgaon, Mumbai - 400 004.
Phone: 022-23860170, 23863863; **Fax:** 022-23877178
E-mail: himpub@bharatmail.co.in; **Website:** www.himpub.com

Branch Offices :

New Delhi : "Pooja Apartments", 4-B, Murari Lal Street, Ansari Road, Darya Ganj, New Delhi - 110 002.
Phone: 011-23270392, 23278631; Fax: 011-23256286

Nagpur : Kundanlal Chandak Industrial Estate, Ghat Road, Nagpur - 440 018.
Phone: 0712-2721215, 2721216

Bengaluru : Plot No. 91-33, 2nd Main Road, Seshadripuram, Behind Nataraja Theatre,
Bengaluru - 560 020. Phone: 080-41138821; Mobile: 09379847017, 09379847005

Hyderabad : No. 3-4-184, Lingampally, Besides Raghavendra Swamy Matham, Kachiguda,
Hyderabad - 500 027. Phone: 040-27560041, 27550139

Chennai : No. 34/44, Motilal Street, T. Nagar, Chennai - 600 017. Mobile: 09380460419

Pune : "Laksha" Apartment, First Floor, No. 527, Mehunpura,
Shaniwarpeth (Near Prabhat Theatre), Pune - 411 030.
Phone: 020-24496323, 24496333; Mobile: 09370579333

Cuttack : Plot No. 5F-755/4, Sector-9, CDA Markat Nagar, Cuttack - 753 014,
Odisha. Mobile: 09338746007

Kolkata : 3, S.M. Bose Road, Near Gate No. 5, Agarpara Railway Station,
North 24 Parganas, West Bengal - 700 109. Mobile: 09674536325

DTP by : HPH, Editorial Office, Bhandup (Megha S.)

Printed at : M/s. Sri Sai Art Printer, Hyderabad. On behalf of HPH.

Preface to the Eighth Revised Edition

The present revision of this book has to be viewed in the background of the basics on which it was built. Any book on International Finance has to deal with all the components of the International Financial System. So this book started with the present International Financial System *vis-à-vis* the domestic system — financial system as against the real system and the International Monetary Fund, and New International Economic order, etc. The new order should bring out the role of emerging market economies like China and India and their new role among the developing countries. These relations among countries are undergoing changes which have to be brought out in this revision. The emerging market economies and among them the Asian developing countries have been called upon to play a more dynamic role in the world economic order. The components and institutions in the International Financial System (IFS) are changing and their role and operations particularly, in relation to India are bound to change with the changing socio-political and economic conditions in the real world. These are incorporated in this revision.

Since, the last publication of this book, in 2007-2008, there were two major developments in the Global economy:

Firstly, there was financial turmoil in the sub-prime mortgage market in the U.S. and increased unemployment in the U.S. These have diverse effects on the world economies particularly in the fields of growth, trade and capital flows. The Financial crisis led to slowdown in the U.S and other major developed countries and developing countries including India.

Second, there were reports of debt default by Greece and sagging financial markets and slowdown in the European economies. Since, Early 2008, there were reports of global crisis leading to reduced trade and slowdown in the capital flows to emerging market economies like India. Accordingly there was first a slowdown in the growth of GDP in India from 9% in 2007-2008 to 7% in 2008-2009 and to 7.5% in 2009-2010.

The export growth rate decelerated from 29% in 2007-2008, 3.4% in 2008-2009 and imports were also lower at 1.4% in 2008-2009 as against 30% in the previous year. This position deteriorated further in 2009-2010.

The IMF had estimated that global growth rate would go down from 5% in 2007 to 4.1 % in 2008 and to 3.9% in 2009. The capital flows also came down to the EMEs and India. It is reported that the net capital flows to the EMEs fell from U.S dollars 618 billion dollars in 2007 to around 109 billion dollars in 2008. During the years 2008 and 2009, the financial flows into India were also lower and this led to depressed market conditions in the stock markets in this period.

There was recession in the Indian economy and Industrial growth rates were lower and export and imports was also lower these global factors led to a rise in inflationary pressures at above 10% by June 2010. India has deal with a situation of recession and higher inflationary expectations in 2009-10. The Government has come out with stimulus measures or incentives for investment growth and curtailment of inflationary pressures. This is the background in the external sector of India in 2010.

More recently, BPO service is also growing at a fast rate along with IT enabled services (ITES). Another chapter on OUTSOURCING was therefore added at the end of the book, not to disturb the earlier order in this revision. Besides, the needed changes are made to emphasize the growth of Free Trade Agreements (FTAs) and importance of SEZs and STPs in the latest EXIM policy in India. The importances given to growth of exports and globalisation of the economy have been brought out in the respective chapters. Exports of merchandise and in particular of the invisibles, trade are rising at a faster rate than before. The present financial scenario has to be viewed in the context of the GDP growth at about 8%, and a targeted growth of the manufacturing at 12% on top of a growth of the services sector at more than 9%. International Finance is part of the Financial sector which is growing rapidly at present. Another development is the road map drawn up for the full capital account convertibility. Already, a number of steps were taken to liberalise the capital outflows for investment, mergers and acquisitions, joint ventures, etc., and permission was given for external commercial borrowings and ADRs and GDRs, etc. The Government has also allowed capital inflows liberally through the FDI route in selected sectors and FII for portfolio investments in the capital market and NRI inflows at free market rates-along with investments by Persons of Indian Origin and Overseas Corporate Bodies.

Trade and aid are related and an important component of international financial flows. As such trade theory and practices have found a place in this book, along with other parts of international financial systems.

The present revision has incorporated all the latest changes in policies and practices and tried to present a correct picture of the contents as much as possible within the constraints of space and context. The current policies of trade and commercial policy and our compliance with the WTO requirements are all brought out.

This revision has benefited from the comments and suggestions from the teaching faculty. The author gratefully acknowledges the help and co-operation from the teaching faculty and the Publishers, namely Himalaya Publishing House.

AUTHOR

Contents

Part - I

International Financial System

Part - II

International Trade — Theory and Practice

Part – III

Balance of Payments and Restrictive Policies

Part – IV

International Marketing and Trade Practices and Procedures

Part – VI

Foreign Exchange Risks Management

PART – I

INTERNATIONAL FINANCIAL SYSTEM

1

Introduction to International Finance

Scope of the Book

The object of this book is to develop linkages between the domestic economic and financial system and international financial system and to provide theoretical and analytical inputs necessary for a student of international financial system. The corporate executives have before them the corporate goals for implementing the management function, finance function or marketing function. All these functions are interrelated and connected with the international financial system. The finance manager or the production manager operates at the corporate level in both domestic and foreign markets corresponding to the domestic and foreign sectors. If we start with the production function of a corporate entity and analyse the finance function of the manager, his operations in the foreign sector provide the link between the corporate sector, on the one hand, and the foreign sector, on the other. The mutual interactions between foreign sectors of various countries lead to the emergence of the international financial system. The foreign sectors are the cementing blocks of the international financial system and institutions operating in the international financial system are closely connected with the foreign sectors of the various economies. In this book an attempt has been made to trace back the operations in the international finance system from the international level to the national level through various financial institutions and banks and at the national level, from these institutions to the corporate units and the company executives.

There are various facets of the international financial system (IFS) which are analysed in depth in the book. To start with, an important aspect of international financial system is international trade which accounts for the largest chunk of international commercial and financial relations and payments. Thus, a part of the treatment of this book is on the theory and practice of international trade followed by a discussion on Balance of Payments and related aspects of international economic relations. Another aspect is the institutions and organisations in it under which banks, national and international financial institutions have all found a place in this book.

The sub-markets in the financial system such as in foreign currency, corresponding to short term flow of funds as between countries' investments in foreign money markets and in foreign claims, etc., are reflected in financial flows as between countries through the flows of money payments and receipts. Thus, both international trade and international currency and exchange markets are closely connected and are dealt with. Yet another aspect of the international financial system is the role of term lending and foreign aid in the flows of trade as between countries, corresponding to long term flows as between countries. It is in this context that foreign trade and aid are discussed as important components of the international financial system as short-term and long-term wings of the operations of the International Financial System.

Relevance to Management

As this book is intended for students and corporate executives, we should set out in the beginning itself the relevance of international finance to their day-to-day work. Domestic finance and international finance are next-door neighbours — both complementary and competitive — viewed either as sources or uses of funds. Firstly, in a fast-growing world economy and world markets, it would be naive for a corporate executive to confine himself to the domestic markets and domestic finance alone. The days of national autarky have gone by and we are in a world of interdependence. With a fast growing network of transport and communications, the world is getting closer and a finance executive can hardly ignore the forces operating on him from the international plane as much as from the domestic plane. Secondly, as the operations and systems in domestic and international finance are different, the factors influencing them need to be studied separately. Thirdly, in a world of competition and survival of the fittest, the managerial function involves choosing the right input mix both from home and abroad and the right output mix suitable for home and foreign markets and expose oneself to the winds of competition both at national and international levels. These aspects are clearly noticed in India, with the opening up of the economy since July 1991 through Economic and Financial Reforms.

It is to be conceded that the impact of the foreign sector on the activities of the corporate executive is more keenly felt in some lines than in others. Such lines are in exportable goods and services, shipping, airways, tourism, etc. If the corporate entity belongs to the sector of multinational companies, foreign-owned companies, subsidiaries or branches of foreign companies etc., international forces are relatively more important. At any rate, any management executive can ill-afford to be blind to the international economic and financial scene even if he is not directly involved in it as these forces operate on him in the modern world.

Finance Function

The objective of the finance function of a manager may be set out in different ways. He may aim at optimising the value of his assets or minimising the worth of his liabilities. Put in differently, he may maximise his gross profits or net profits or aim at optimising the market value of his company's shares. Looked at from any angle, the management basically aims at economy, efficiency and productivity leading to greater profitability. For this purpose, he concentrates on the efficient management of cash and credit so far as the financial aspect is concerned. But more importantly, he has to consider the production function of which cash and credit are inputs. The finance function is closely related to marketing function also, as the latter involves the use of cash and credit. The manager has to take into account the international forces in the preparation of plans and budgets for resource inflows and outflows and in input and output markets. In the raising of funds and use of such funds, the cost of alternative uses and sources have to be considered both at home and abroad. Finance Function is all pervading being related to all activities of the firm.

In terms of the real sector or the financial sector, he has to observe the criteria of efficiency and productivity etc., in the input market and output market and in allocation of physical resources or financial resources. In the input and output markets as well as in financial markets, both domestic and foreign forces have to be reckoned with.

Input Market

In the input market, physical and financial inputs are fed into the productive system. Physical inputs relate to physical capital equipment, plant and machinery, raw materials, spare parts and intermediate (semi-finished) products, etc. They may come from domestic or foreign markets. Financial inputs relate to project outlays or moneys spent on wages for labour or cash kept for current liabilities or contingencies. Such inputs can be secured both from domestic markets and foreign markets. As such, a cost calculus has to be made for the right mix of inputs and the right sources of supply of such inputs so as to minimise the costs for a given product mix. It is possible that some raw materials or spares are more cheaply available abroad than at home and due to free access to such markets the manager may plan for a mix of inputs at the least cost, subject to the technical feasibilities in the production process. The markets, both domestic and foreign, have to be assessed for these inputs in terms of costs and prices and alternative sources of supply explored. This is an area in international economics and finance. In the supply of financial inputs for production purposes one has to take into account the need for cash and credit and the relative proportions of each both from home and abroad and to assess their relative costs. Marginal costing of cash and credit is part of the wider subject of cash management. The cash component as an input in the production function is part of the subject of production management, while the overall management of all funds — is in the domain of financial management.

In a subsidiary or branch of a foreign company, foreign sources play a more important role even in financial inputs. Such exercises relating to financial inputs have to be made after an assessment of cash inflows and outflows, both on current and capital accounts. On the capital account, sources and uses of funds for investment also become an important pre-requisite for planning for credit. These will be discussed below under sources and uses of funds.

Output Market

In the output market, the sale of final and intermediate products can be made both in domestic and foreign markets. International marketing and international finance are closely interlinked and flows of finance follow the flows of trade. Marketing is an important pre-requisite for trade. International trade and international finance are close complements. The costs of production and selling costs and the available margins both on domestic sales and foreign sales have to be considered. Here again, it is assumed that there is a free market in India and abroad or trading is possible subject to satisfying all the requirements of the government policy in this regard. A cost calculus has to be made for planning for the right mix of sales at home and abroad. For an assessment of the demand prospects abroad, we need to know the alternative sources of supply in such markets, costs and prices of such alternative sources, transport and selling costs, etc., which are the subject of international economics and finance. In India due to premium put on export sales by government policy the cost calculus has to take into account this aspect also.

Sources and Uses

At the micro level of a company, an analysis of the sources of funds reveals that broadly there are three categories of sources: (i) Savings of the company which are its retained earnings, (ii) External sources (domestic) from the capital and money markets such as banks, all-India or State-level financial institutions, government or the public and (iii) Foreign sources, namely, institutions and persons abroad. The last category can in turn be specified as follows:

(a) Credit from private parties, viz., trade credit, buyer's credit, etc.;

(b) Foreign government credit, viz., government to government line of credit, foreign aid or grants or loans;

(c) Resources from international or inter-regional bodies such as IFC, IBRD, foreign banks or Euro-currency markets, etc.; and

(d) Non-resident individuals and institutions.

The same analysis holds good at the sectoral and national level. In fact, the emergence of international financial markets can be traced to this sectoral interdependence, including the foreign sector and intranational dependence. Basically, as no country is self-sufficient or autarkic but is dependent on other countries for something or the other, international economic and commercial relations emerge. These are referred to later in this chapter.

In a similar fashion, it would be appropriate to set out the pattern of use of funds of any company into various sectors of the economy, including the foreign sector. Dispensation of funds for current or capital expenditures in domestic markets and international markets can be separately set out. Such an analysis is particularly more relevant to multinational corporations and branches or subsidiaries of foreign companies in whose case foreign markets and foreign sources of supply play an important part. The head office or the holding company may spend a part of its funds in investment in the host country, make inward remittances for working capital or investment purposes and outward remittances for royalty and dividend, payments or technical fees.

Macro View of Foreign Flows

RBI Company Finance Studies throw light on the macro-view of foreign inflows and outflows in the Corporate Sector. These are published in RBI Bulletins regularly. A large number of smaller companies contribute larger foreign exchange earnings to the country. It is true that both expenditure and earnings on foreign account are concentrated in a small number of large foreign controlled Indian companies and multi-national corporations, but they may not add much to the net accrual of foreign exchange. But a large number of small companies do not operate on such a large scale, but add substantially to our net accrual of foreign exchange.

Sectoral Interdependence

International financial markets emerged out of the felt need to facilitate operations of nations arising out of the commercial and financial transactions with the rest of the world. This emergence can be attributed logically to: *(a)* Sectoral interdependence, and *(b)* National interdependence.

It would be apt to set out here the inter-relations between the micro-level operations of a finance manager with the macro-level working of the corporate sector and foreign sector. A finance manager is a micro unit in the corporate sector. The environment he faces is competition from other similar units in the corporate sector and as suppliers of inputs or as consumers of output. Besides, the corporate sector, in turn, is interlinked with all other sectors of the economy. The micro-level manager is thus faced with a total environment of the economy which includes foreign sector, and it is thus relevant to him to be familiar with the international financial system, which is the product of developments in the foreign sectors of all the world economies.

The corporate sector is a part of the total business sector having trading and manufacturing activities. The corporate sector or business sector is also connected with all sectors of the economy, namely government sector, household sector and foreign sector either as suppliers of inputs or as consumers of output. Besides, all these domestic and foreign sectors are interconnected through the flow of funds and savings from one sector to the other. In each sector, there are both savers and investors. Only the household sector is a net saver in India. Besides, the household sector is a supplier of factors of production such as labour, management, enterprise, etc. For some time in the past, foreign sector was a net saver, as there was a net balance on current account of our balance of payments leading to the accretion to our foreign exchange reserves. We are running huge deficits in merchandise trade account for a long time which was offset by positive balance on the invisible trade account. This would mean a negative savings in the foreign sector leading to a loss of our foreign exchange reserves. If there is a net inflow of funds from abroad either as foreign credits, grants, etc., or borrowings from foreign governments, international bodies, etc., there may be a positive balance in the balance of payments and foreign savings would accrue. The surplus savings in some sectors would flow into other sectors with deficit. In the corporate sector where investment is invariably more than their available savings, the units have to depend on other sectors to finance them. These savings may flow directly from the government sector or household sector or indirectly through financial institutions, banks, NBFCs and other agencies. It would thus be clear that the corporate sector is intricately connected with all other sectors of the economy either as suppliers of inputs of production or suppliers of factors of production, including land, labour, capital or enterprise or consumers of their products or services. They are also connected with other sectors of the economy through inflow or outflow of funds or savings or financial assets — moneys or near money assets or financial flows.

Another aspect of interdependence of the various sectors of the economy is foreign private investment in the domestic economy or Indian investment abroad. The investment may take the form of — (i) Equity participation in Indian enterprises, (ii) Investment in bonds or debentures, (iii) Granting of loans or credits either on government to government basis or party to party basis in the private sector, (iv) Joint ventures in third countries and (v) Technical consultancy or know-how participation etc. Transfer of technology is also one of the aspects of the international commercial and financial relations which is necessary for a sustained rate of growth at the lowest possible cost and the highest level of productivity.

All the inputs of the corporate sector come either from the household sector as labour, capital or enterprise or from Government sector as infrastructure, land, electricity, water, etc., or from agriculture or industry (business sector) as raw materials, intermediate products, spares parts, etc.

Particularly more relevant for our discussion is the contribution of foreign sector towards inputs of the corporate sector in the form of physical capital, plant, machinery, spares, raw materials, etc., or financial inputs in the form of short-term credits or investment in financial assets, etc.

Such interdependence between the corporate sector and other sectors is also noticed in the field of outputs. The main consumers of some products may in fact be the foreigners. Either in respect of consumer goods or capital goods, there is a good element of foreign demand, particularly from the less developed countries. In view of the vastness of our domestic markets in India, the executives of the corporate sector rarely explore the foreign markets, unless the products are export-oriented. With the projected expansion of the industry and limitations in the domestic markets, the present executives may have to think more in terms of foreign markets than of domestic markets. More recently, export-oriented industries and 100 per cent export units are being encouraged by the government in the light of the prevailing balance of payments difficulties of the country and increasing export shortfalls. Besides, the philosophy of the government is also veering round to the view of making our economy more competitive with a greater role allocated to the private sector. The recent trend to globalisation and opening up of the economy to free market forces make the foreign sector more relevant than before. The cost consciousness and competitiveness has increased in the Indian enterprise. In such an environment, the role of foreign sector can be hardly overemphasised when the chill winds of competition and cost consciousness make the present executives of the corporate enterprise more alert and informed on both the domestic and external sectors. The foreign environment would be equally important and more challenging than the domestic market due to the ever changing scene of demand and supply forces, competition and cost price factors operating from all sides of the world. These may hopefully improve the efficiency of factors and lower the costs of production.

There is another reason why the foreign sector is more important to India, namely, the limits are already reached in the domestic markets and the scope for further expansion of markets lie abroad. Besides, there is the debt service burden which we carry due to our reliance on foreign credits during the last few decades of our planning. This burden can be discharged by a continuous flow of goods and services outside the country leading to an export surplus for the nation.

In the output market, the domestic household sector has been the main consumer in India, followed by the government sector which needs the output of the corporate sector both for capital formation and current consumption. Besides, the government with its contracting role in the economy has got less say in the affairs of the corporate sector today and is likely to become lesser in future due to their avowed policy of a greater role for the private sector in the years to come. The business sector comprising industry and agriculture continue to consume the products of the corporate sector as intermediates or raw materials for manufacture or further processing. These facts are brought out in any analysis of input-output matrix tables for the economy, brought out by the ISI and CSO.

Intra-National Dependence

We have seen that national economy of a country is composed of a number of sectors, including the foreign sector and the interdependence of these sectors either as suppliers of savings or of factors of production, or of other inputs in the productive process or as consumers of their output leads to economic, commercial and financial transactions as between these sectors. It is such transactions between the domestie sectors and foreign sector that give rise to the international financial system.

An extension of this principle of mutual interdependence to the case of national economy of one country depending upon that of others lends further support to our thesis that emergence of international financial markets is the result of such interdependence. Thus, no modern nation/state is self-sufficient nor is it closed to external forces from other nations and states. This dependence is the result of the expanding civilisation and modern socio-economic systems. It is now well recognised that countries are interdependent in various degrees resulting in economic commercial and financial transactions among them. Such interdependence is a necessary but not a sufficient condition for the emergence of international financial markets. But the conquering of the distance and time by revolution in Telecommunications, electronic media and information Technology has brought the world together and led to a sufficient condition for emergence of International Financial System.

The interdependence of nations can be ascribed to the following factors:

(1) Differential factor endowments and natural endowments in different countries, leading to different production functions.

(2) Different stages of growth of industry, agriculture and other sectors in the economies of these countries, and different levels of savings and investment.

(3) Differentials in technological advancement.

(4) Differences in habits tastes and consumer preferences, leading to different demand functions.

(5) Differences in standards of living and incomes, leading to flow of funds through grants, loans, etc.

(6) Differences in wealth are leading to differences in asset performances and the demonstration effects that these differences produce on the consumption function.

It would thus be seen that the origin and emergence of the international financial system can be traced to the sectoral and national interdependence which leads to international economic, commercial and financial relations as between countries. International trade, aid and financial flows account for the bulk of such transactions as between nations. The basic economic principles of efficiency, productivity and least cost optimisation process necessitate the use of inputs both domestic and foreign and flow of goods and services across national borders, provided there are no barriers to such flows. The result is the exchange of goods and services involving payments and receipts as between countries and exchange of one currency for another and borrowing and lending of money or near money assets across borders. These transactions and trading in foreign currencies, foreign assets or liabilities and foreign claims constitute the international financial system.

2

International Trade and International Finance

India has commercial and financial relations with almost all foreign countries except for a few African countries. These relations take the form of bilateral or multilateral trade — imports and exports of goods and services and financial flows. Corresponding to the physical movement of goods and services, and of men and talent there are corresponding monetary payments into and outside the country. Short-term funds move in to finance trade or for working capital purposes and other productive activities or as gifts, unilateral transfers, etc. Speculative capital flows are also possible although not in India to take advantage of the differentials in interest rates or exchange rates. There may be remittances in and out towards dividend payments, royalties, technical fees, penalties, etc., or payments for services such as banking insurance shipping and other transport.

If the funds are moving in and out for investment purposes, they may take the form of investment in working capital (inventories or trade credits). It is also possible that some short-term working capital flows along with capital investment in plant and machinery or purchase of shares, debentures, bonds, etc. These investments may also be in consultancy or technical know-how or in project export such as construction projects, turnkey projects, engineering and capital goods on deferred payments. Some of the above flows are of current or income nature and constitute trade items in goods and services. Thus, trade is an important constituent of international economic relations and thus assumes pre-eminent position in any study of international finance. Trade accounts for about two-thirds of the financial transactions as between the countries. Aid, credits and grants, finance, trade and constitute the other components of international financial relations. All these items are directly relevant to the corporate executive not only in terms of supply or sources of funds but as inputs or outputs and as part of the environmental forces that operate on the corporate sector. These environmental forces are to be reckoned with in corporate planning and budgeting to start with and subsequently in actual operations of the company, namely investment, production, sales and or financing of such operations, exports, imports, etc.

Trade and Balance of Payments

In terms of our model of providing interlinkages between the micro level finance manager and macro level financial system, the avenues of linking the corporate executive to the international finance markets are to be set out. Basically, the origin and source of international finance are the various economic, commercial and financial transactions as between countries, recorded as balance of payments of a country. Any resident individual firm or company may be an exporter or importer, can receive remittances from abroad, gifts, charities, etc., or he may sell financial assets like shares, debentures etc., to foreigners. The origin of the international financial system can be traced to such transactions in which either funds come into or funds go out to foreigners.

Current Items

Basically, there are three types of transactions which lead to the emergence of international finance of a current nature: *(i)* Economic and commercial transactions which involve exchange of goods for goods or goods for money abroad: this would constitute trade of merchandise items of a tangible nature. When an exporter sends goods abroad, it is a credit item for the country exporting as money is received from abroad. This is a source of foreign funds for the country exporting; *(ii)* Trade in invisible items: A country can also export services in the form of shipping, banking and insurance, tourism, hospitality, I.T. communications, multi-media, technical consultancy or emigrant labour services, etc. It is also possible that the country can receive remittances from abroad in the form of profits, dividends, interest etc., on capital invested abroad and royalties on patents, trade marks or the technical know-how exported abroad; and *(iii)* Yet another category of inflow of funds is unilateral transfers in the form of gifts, charities, donations, free samples, etc., to the residents or companies inside the country from abroad.

The above categories of exports of goods in the form of tangible merchandise items or intangible services or unilateral transfers or normal non-monetary gold would constitute the so-called current items of the balance of payments of a country. The term "balance of payments" and related issues are discussed in a separate chapter. All these items would add to the supply of funds from abroad to the country in question or to the inflow from abroad.

Corresponding to the current inflows, there are also out-flows in the form of imports of tangible merchandise goods or intangible services. There can also be outward transfers of funds unilaterally in the form of gifts, charities etc., to foreigners. These items constitute the supply of domestic funds in the international markets. Any export of goods or services has to be paid for by the foreigners in terms of foreign exchange or foreign currency, just as any import of goods or services has to be paid for in terms of domestic currency to be exchanged for foreign currencies. It would thus be apparent that in the international finance markets, there is an exchange of currencies in supply with the currencies in demand. This constitutes the foreign exchange market where one currency is exchanged for another. Similarly when a unilateral transfer takes place in the form of gifts, remittances, charities, etc., there is an exchange of one currency for another. This exchange transaction involves two currencies and arises out of the prevailing system of national currencies and lack of any internationally acceptable currency for all countries. Each country is sovereign and has its own national currency useful for its domestic transactions. But international transactions are to be settled by exchange of one currency with the currencies of other countries. In case where such exchanges do not tally and result in excess of supply or demand of any currency, this would lead to claim in financial forms of one country over another, leading to foreign assets or liabilities of a country. The above transactions in foreign currencies would thus result in various forms of financial claims — assets and liabilities denominated in foreign currencies.

For a long time, gold has been internationally accepted as a medium of exchange and the inflows and outflows of gold used to settle the excess supply or excess demand position of currencies or meet the deficits in the trade balance of the countries. In view of the recent developments in the gold market leading to the sky-rocketting of its price and changes in strength of the currency, gold is no longer used as an international medium of exchange. On the other hand, a number of convertible currencies like the US dollar, Pound sterling, Japanies yen, etc., are being used as an international medium of exchange. Foreign claims are denominated and exchanged in these currencies because of their convertibility into gold and because of their greater acceptability by the comity of nations. It would thus appear that the current transactions involving export and import of goods and services and unilateral transfers and movement of non-monetary gold would account for the bulk of the international commercial and financial transactions.

Capital Items

There are transactions of a capital nature affecting the foreign assets and liabilities of the various countries. These transactions take the form of short-term capital movements out of one country into another for working capital or for speculative purposes to take advantage of interest rate differentials or exchange rate discrepancies. There are also long-term capital flows for investment in physical assets like plant, machinery, etc., construction projects or in consultancy or other services. The investment from abroad can also take the form of purchases of financial assets at home by non-resident individuals, companies or foreign governments. These investments may be in shares, debentures, bonds, etc., of domestic companies or governments or purchases of real estate, gold and silver, etc., at home by foreigners. Some of these investments as in real estate, buildings etc., are not allowed freely in all countries. However, assuming a free exchange market the residents of one country can have financial transactions with the residents of another country through various forms of capital investment of either short-term or long-term duration, either at governmental level or in private sector, such inflows and outflows of funds would result in transactions in the foreign exchange market in terms of exchange of one currency against another, such exchanges also lead to the demand for foreign exchange or supply of foreign currency *vis-a-vis* the domestic currency. In the foreign exchange market, these supply and demand forces generated by the current account and capital account transactions of one country against others would affect the exchange rate of the currency if it is allowed to fluctuate freely. The exchange rate and the mechanics of foreign exchange market are discussed in a separate chapter.

The combined account of current transactions and capital transactions constitute the balance of payments between one country and the rest of the world, involving economic, commercial and financial transactions between the residents of one country and the rest of the world. Demand for and supply of one currency against other currencies would emerge from each of the items of balance of payments, leading to the so called foreign exchange market. This market involves the exchange of currencies or deposit of one currency against borrowings of other currencies. It would thus be seen that international economic and financial transactions result in counter-claims of a financial nature. Trading in these financial claims or currencies of one country against another leads to what is termed as international currency market and international exchange market. The distinction between these markets is referred to later. But all these transactions would result in a net accretion or depletion of foreign assets or liabilities of the country. If it is accretion, it would result in an increase in foreign assets or lead to an addition to the foreign exchange reserves. A depletion of funds from India would lead to an increase in our foreign liabilities, fall in our foreign exchange reserves and a decline in our balances held abroad or foreign investments in other countries. Thus, all the transactions on current account would end up in either an increase or a fall in foreign assets of the country. Similarly, any changes in capital account of our balance of payments in the form of foreign credits, loans, grants, etc., would result in an increase in our foreign assets or a decrease in foreign liabilities or vice-versa. The changes in foreign assets and foreign liabilities on account of foreign receipts and payments are reflected in the international financial markets and are recorded in the balance of payments of a country. The institutions and bank which operate in the international financial markets carry out the transactions on behalf of the residents, individuals, companies and the government at home with the corresponding foreign individuals and foreign companies and governments abroad.

Components of International Financial System

International financial system relates to the management of and trading in international money and monetary assets. These monetary assets are claims on foreign currency, foreign deposits and investments and/or foreign assets. The claims may be denominated in various foreign currencies purchased and sold and involve exchange as between various currencies. Thus, these transactions give rise to: *(i)* Borrowing and lending operations in foreign currencies or trading in financial assets denominated in foreign currencies and *(ii)* A foreign exchange transaction involving an exchange of one currency for another. The first is called the foreign currency market and the second is the foreign exchange market.

Foreign Exchange Market

International economic and commercial relations between countries involve exchange of goods and services and payments for these exchanges. The payments lead to conversion of one currency into another. Each country has its own financial system and its own currency and financial assets. Exchanges between the money and financial assets of one country for money or financial assets of another country constitutes international financial transactions. These transactions are put through the foreign exchange market. The demand for any currency as against its supply in such markets determines the exchange rate. These financial assets could be money or near-money assets, cheques, drafts, mail transfers and other negotiable instruments.

The difference between the domestic financial system and international financial system lies in the introduction of exchange of one currency for another or exchange of one instrument in one currency for another denominated in a different currency. In the process of such exchange, the transfer problem arises in the international markets which relates to the problem of finding the proper source of supply to suit demand for any foreign currency. This leads to an adjustment process in the balance of payments of the various countries which in turn depends upon the type of international monetary system in vogue. These will be dealt with in another chapter.

The basic principle involved is that economic and commercial transactions between one country and another are adjusted by the corresponding purchase and sale of financial assets, including money and near-money by one country for that of another country. The prices of goods and services of one country vis-a-vis the prices of the corresponding goods and services of another country will determine the purchasing power of each currency. Exchange rate is primarily a reflection of the purchasing power of the currency domestically. Exchange rate fluctuations on a day-to-day basis will depend, however upon the competitive forces of demand for and supply of any currency in these markets. In the long run, exchange rates would depend upon the relative degrees of inflation in the domestic economies and changes in the purchasing power of currencies. Exchange standard and the international monetary system would facilitate such adjustment of exchange rates to changes in supply and demand and to changes in purchasing power parities. Speculative purchases and sales of currencies and hedge trading in these currencies would also take place daily and would depend upon their relative strengths in international markets, market confidence in those currencies and intrinsic strength of the domestic economies.

The International Monetary Fund was established to facilitate transactions as between the member-countries and impart an element of stability in the international monetary scene. Each country can purchase and sell its currency from the International Monetary Fund for another currency of the member country to meet its requirements of international payments for goods and services.

International Currency Markets

As an adjunct to the exchange markets, there are international currency markets where internationally-accepted currencies, namely, the so-called reserve currencies, are traded. These relate to the deposits of such currencies with international banks at an agreed rate of interest. The excess funds in these reserve currencies owned by countries, institutions and governments having surplus receipts over payments would be lent out to banks and other financial institutions for various durations at a rate of interest. The currencies are in demand for meeting the balance of payments deficits or for investment in fixed capital or for working capital purposes. The borrowing and lending for short term constitute the international money markets.

The other components of the international financial system are international capital markets and bonds markets. The international capital markets such as London, New York, Zurich etc., have lost much of their popularity due to national restrictions and scarcity of funds in those centres. Bond markets in these centres are still operating and international banks are arranging these issues on a selective basis. Now, Euro-currency and Euro-bond markets are the most popular international means of medium and long-term financing.

The relations between the foreign exchange market and international currency markets are not difficult to comprehend. The trade and other economic and commercial transactions involve receipts and payments as between countries. These will lead to exchange of one currency for others. The demand for and supply of each of the currencies against an alternative currency determines the rate at which two currencies are exchanged. This is called the exchange rate and the market is the foreign exchange market. In the process of such economic and commercial transactions, a country can be a net creditor or a debtor. If a country is a net creditor or has a positive trade surplus or receives more than it pays out, it has net foreign claims on others. Such claims are held in the form of deposits, balances, etc., abroad or investments in Treasury Bills, Government and Private securities etc. Such claims would lead to international currency holdings which are generally held in convertible currencies by the creditor countries for reasons of facilitating subsequent use and conversion for international payments. Any market representing the demand for and supply of such currencies is called the international currency market. While thus the foreign currency market refers to trading in external dollars or other currencies held abroad, foreign exchange market refers to the conversion of such dollars into other currencies. The obvious inter-relations between those two segments in the international financial system need no elaboration. The details of how they originate and the factors of supply and demand, etc., are discussed in a later chapter.

Institutions in International Financial System

There are a number of institutions who are part of the international financial system. These institutions can be classified into the following categories and are discussed in later chapters.

(a) National banks and domestic financial institutions which are authorised to deal in foreign currencies and foreign credits.

(b) International brokers and security firms of repute.

(c) Regional or multi-national banks or corporations dealing in international markets and borrowing/lending in these markets.

(d) Regional Finance and Development Corporations and banks such as the Asian Development Bank, Commonwealth Finance Corporation, Latin American Development Bank, African Development Bank, etc.

(e) International financial organisations like International Monetary Fund (IMF), International Bank for Reconstruction and Development (IBRD), International Finance Corporation (IFC), and International Development Agency (IDA).

To sum up, international trade is the basis for international finance and constitutes the bulk of the transaction in international finance. The constituents of the international finance are the components of balance of payments, both on current account and capital account. The markets constituting the international finance are international exchange markets and international currency markets. The main agencies operating in them are FIs banks, brokers and the apex bodies are the IMF for the short-term wing and World Bank (IBRD) for the long-term wing.

3 The International Monetary System

The International Monetary System is the short term wing of the international financial system. It encompasses all relations as between the national market systems. I.M.F is the Apex body for this system and acts as a central bank of central banks of the nations.

The establishment of the International Monetary Fund (IMF) in 1945 was a landmark in the international monetary field. Before 1945 there was international monetary disorder, exchange restrictions and a host of other undesirable trade and exchange practices. The need for international monetary co-operation and understanding was felt soon after the war, and the Bretton Woods Conference resulted in the establishment of IMF and the World Bank. Originally 44 member countries met at the Conference and the IMF was set up as per the agreement reached among them in December 1945. It had an original membership of 29 countries and now, it covers almost all the countries, namely about 192 as in March 2010.

The IMF is governed by a policy-making body, viz., the Board of Governors but the day-to-day affairs are looked into by the Board of Executive Directors consisting of the representatives of 16 elected countries and 6 nominated countries. The Board of Executives Directors meets as often as is necessary to decide on all matters pertaining to the role of the Fund. The Managing Director is the chief executive of the Fund and is appointed by the Board of Executive Directors. It has a secretariat in Washington.

Objectives of IMF

The IMF is primarily a short-term financial institution — a lender and a borrower — and a central bank of central banks and secondarily, aims at promoting a code of conduct among members for orderly exchange arrangements and international monetary management. The objectives of the Fund as laid down in its Articles may be briefly set out as follows:

(1) To promote international monetary co-operation through consultation and mutual collaboration.

(2) To promote exchange stability and maintain orderly exchange arrangements and avoid competitive exchange depreciation.

(3) To help members with temporary balance of payments difficulties to tide over them without resort to exchange restrictions.

(4) To promote growth of multilateralism in trade and payments and thus expand world trade and aid.

(5) To help achieve the balance of payments equilibrium shorten the duration of disequilibrium and promote orderly international relations.

The main object of the Fund is to promote exchange stability and encourage multilateral trade and payments. It is also a financing institution and has schemes for provision of short-term finance for meeting the balance of payments purposes. It provides international liquidity in tune with the requirements of world trade and fosters the growth of world trade and freer system of payments. Gold was originally the unit of account in which the various currencies were denominated. This was subsequently replaced by Special Drawing Rights (SDRs) which is a standard unit of account whose value is fixed in terms of a basket of currencies. These functions of the Fund are reviewed briefly below.

Fund's Role of Consultation

In all matters of exchange rate changes, imposition of restrictions on current account, use of discriminatory practices, members are obliged to consult the Fund. Failing this, the members could be ineligible to have recourse to financial resources of the Fund. Such consultations may take the form of supply of economic and financial data to the Fund by the member country. Secondly, the staff of the Fund can call for various types of data from a member country as and when they require on an ad hoc basis. Thirdly, the staff teams visit member countries at least once a year for a first-hand study of economic and financial conditions in the member country. At the time of annual general meeting or at the time of negotiating a credit arrangement, representatives of member countries hold consultations and discussions with the Board of Executive Directors. Many times informal consultations also take place between the member's Governor or Executive Director with the IMF staff, particularly at a time when the member country approaches the Fund for a standby arrangement or a credit drawal.

Sources of Funds — Quotas

Every member country is given a quota in the Fund. These quotas were fixed originally on a formula: (a) 2 per cent of the national income; (b) 5 per cent of gold and dollar balances; (c) 10 per cent of average annual imports; (d) 10 per cent of maximum variation in annual exports. The sum of the above, increased by the percentage ratios of average annual exports to national income of a member, is used as the basis for fixing the quotas.

Each member's quota was thus fixed as their initial contribution to the Fund. A member had to contribute its quota to the Fund in the form of gold upto 25 per cent of its quota or 10 per cent of its net gold holdings or US dollars on September 12, 1946, whichever was less and the rest of the quota was payable in member's own currency. Since 1980, the clause of 25 per cent of the quota in gold or US dollar was replaced by contribution of SDR and convertible currencies. At the time, gold was valued at $ 35 per fine ounce and India paid $ 27.5 million in gold for a quota of $ 400 million. The quota of India stood at 3056 million SDRs after the 10th General Quota increase in 1995. IMF holds substantial gold reserves which were received as part of members' contribution towards their quotas, and liquid reserves in the form of convertible currencies of member countries.

The total of quotas of 44 nations which gathered at Bretton Woods in 1944 was fixed at $ 8800 million. By end December 1994, the membership rose to 178 with a total of quotas at SDRs 144,620 million after the 9th General Review of quotas made in 1990. The work of Tenth general Review of Quotas was undertaken in 1994-95, and Eleventh quota review was completed in 1998 and the quota increase of 45% was effected in 1999. The Twelfth Quota Review was completed in 2005 and as in March 2005, total quotas stood at SDR 213.5 billion, gold holdings at SDR 585.2 million and SDR holdings at 574 million.

Share Capital of IMF

In January 1999, the increase of share capital or total quota of IMF from SDR 145.6 billion (US $ 204 billion) to SDR 212 billion (US $ 297 billion) took effect, with the consent given by the requisite 85% of the memberships. The Fund's usable resources rose by SDR 45 billion or US. $ 63 billion. India' s quota was SDR 3055.5 million, which comes to about 2.098 per cent of the total IMF quota. This quota is now increased to SDR 4158.2 million which comes to about 1.961 per cent as in March 2005. Thus, in relative terms, the position of India came down considerably in the fund. Width the quota increases in September 2008, to all members of the fund, India's quota increased to 582, Indian SDR which increased the share of India in fund form 1.96 per cent to 2.44 per cent as from 2008. India was allocated SDR 3082 million under general allocation in August 2009 and SDR 214.6 under special allocation in September 2009, by the IMF, which are now included in India's forex reserves.

When it was set up, India was among the top five quota holders. Now she has been pushed down to 13th position in the list. The current top countries are U.S.A. Japan, Germany, France, U.K, Italy, Saudi Arabia, Canada, Russia, Netherlands, China Belgium and India.

The increase of IMF quotas has been effected by conventional calculations for determining the quotas of countries, referred to earlier. But, if economic strength of a country is determined by relative purchasing power parity, it is understood that China would be number two or three and India number five or six.

Other Sources of Funds

The IMF has, in addition to member's quotas, other sources of funds. In 1962 IMF concluded a General Agreement to borrow (GAB) under which IMF could borrow from the participating members (Group of Ten Developed Countries) specified amounts of their currencies. The amounts which the Ten Countries (Belgium, Canada, France, West Germany, Italy, Japan, Netherlands, Sweden, U.K. and USA) undertook to provide was set in the agreement. Interest and service charges were payable on such loans in agreed terms (upto 5 years) in gold, later replaced by SDR. The IMF borrowed not only from above countries but also from others such as Saudi Arabia on similar terms. The IMF can also acquire any member's currency, as desired, in exchange for the gold, which it holds.

Since August 1975, as agreed by the members in the Interim Committee to reduce the role of gold, about one-sixth of its gold holdings was sold in auctions and in non-competitive bids and the proceeds realised amounted to US $ 5.7 billion of which $ 1.1 billion representing the capital value of the original gold was added to Trust Fund. About one-sixth of the gold out of the Fund holdings has been distributed to members so far. The Fund has still two-third of the original quantity of gold with it. Sale of gold by IMF is another source of funds, as it is sold at current market values. India has purchased 200 metric tones of gold from IMF in Nov., 2009 at a value of $ 6609 million. In Feb., 2010, again IMF announced a sale in open market of 191 tones of gold. The IMF has thus, opened on market sales of gold to augment its resources.

Fund's Lending Operations

As a financial institution, the Fund provides temporary financial assistance for balance of payments purposes in the form of sale of currencies. When a member borrows from the Fund it purchases foreign currencies against its own currency. When it repays loans, it is repurchasing its own currency against foreign currency. The Fund's exchange operations are classified into four categories as follows:

(1) Gold Tranche is upto the amount of gold paid by the member towards its quota plus its credit position with the Fund (which is the same thing as other countries' borrowings of its currency). If a country has 25 per cent of its quota in gold, then upto this limit this member can draw upon the Fund automatically. If that country has also a credit position of 10 per cent of its quota as borrowings by other countries, then that country can borrow automatically upto 35 per cent of its quota (gold tranche of 25 per cent plus super gold tranche of 10 per cent).

(2) Four Credit Tranches: There are four credit tranches, each equivalent to 25 per cent of its quota. If gold payment is 25 per cent of the quota and the rest of the 75 per cent is paid in own currency, the Fund can hold upto 200 per cent of a member's quota in its currency and credit tranches would aggregate to 100 per cent of quota.

(3) Compensatory financing facility was started in February 1963 to provide credit in connection with any shortfalls in export proceeds below some average annual figure. The member was permitted credit upto 50 per cent of the member's quota which was raised in stages to 100 per cent of the quota in 1980.

(4) The international buffer stock financing facility was established in June 1969 in respect of any primary commodity that the member country produces. The credit is upto a limit of 50 per cent of its quota for special stocks of sugar, tin, cocoa, etc., under various international commodity agreements.

The above facilities, except in the case of gold tanche which is automatic, are subject to the following conditions:

(1) No member should draw in any 12 month period more than 25 per cent of its quota.

(2) No member should draw in total beyond a point where the Fund's holdings of the member's currency reaches 200 per cent of its quota which it will have if it has borrowed upto 125 per cent of its quota with a gold subscription of 25 per cent and its own currency upto 75 per cent.

(3) The combined drawal under compensatory financing and buffer stock financing should not exceed 75 per cent of the member's quota.

(4) Total holding of IMF of any member's currency under all the above facilities should not exceed 275 per cent of the quota of that member, and this condition was waived many times.

The conditionality of drawings under various credit tranches and other financial facilities will vary according to the state of the country and the economic and financial policies pursued. Requests for drawings beyond the first credit tranche require substantial justification and the conditions laid down would be more rigorous in terms of policies to be pursued by the member country in fiscal, monetary any foreign exchange fields so as to provide quick corrective programme of action for remedying the balance of payments disequilibrium. These conditions are imposed with a fair degree of flexibility.

Standby Arrangements

When a member feels that the need for credit might arise during any year, it may enter into standby arrangements with the Fund. This will give an assurance of financial support from the Fund in time of need. This facility was introduced in 1952 to meet a felt need for it although there was no specific provision for it in the Fund's Articles of Agreement. Since then, such facility was frequently used by the members and both the Fund and the members are happy for such prior arrangement in the nature of an overdraft limit. The standby facility is repayable generally in three years, while other types of borrowings are repayable in 3 to 5 years. A member's obligation to repurchase also arises if its exchange reserves rise beyond a limit. The repurchase is made in terms of the currency borrowed or in any convertible currency or a currency which is in demand and the Fund's holdings of it are less than 75 per cent of that country's quota. A member's indebtedness to the IMF can be repaid in three ways: (1) Repurchase with gold and convertible currencies; (2) The drawings of its currency by other countries; and (3) The offset of an earlier creditor position.

IMF Charges

The schedule of IMF charges on the member's drawings is such that the rate varied with the period for which it is outstanding and the tranche position of the country. For a long time the maximum rate of interest was 5 per cent and now it varied from time to time. The rates for supplementary financing facility were higher at 10-11.5 per cent or even more, as these rates depended on the rates at which the Fund borrowed from the lender countries and on the money market conditions of the major creditor countries. The margin kept by the IMF is about 0.2 to 0.325 per cent. Since May 1, 1981, IMF had adopted a uniform charge of 7.0 per cent per annum on outstanding borrowings of members from the Fund's own resources and a higher rate for those resources borrowed from outside. The Fund makes a service charge of 0.5 per cent on all purchases other than those in reserve tranche and 0.25 per cent on all standby and extended Fund facilities.

These charges are payable normally in gold or US dollars or SDRs but as in the case of other provisions of the Fund which are operated with flexibility, this may be waived if the nation's external reserves are below half of its quota. Thus, Fund's charges were paid by India in rupees only. These charges are very nominal in view of the fact that Fund does not pay any interest on currencies held by it. Since 1969, IMF was paying about 1½ per cent per annum to a creditor position of a member that is, when its currency held by the Fund fell below 75 per cent of its quota.

Other Facilities

The oil facility was originally designed in 1974. These funds were lent to countries in balance of payments difficulties due to oil price escalation during 1970-73. Arrangements to borrow SDR 6.9 billion for this Fund from 17 member countries with a strong external payments position were made in 1974. This facility was extended from year to year and by 1982 borrowing members have repaid most of the outstanding debt.

In 1974, the Fund also established an Extended Fund facility to provide special medium-term loans to meet the balance of payments deficits over a longer period and to help correct the structural imbalances in the economy of a member country. This assistance is up to three years and in amounts larger than that permitted by the member's quota.

In August 1975, a Subsidy Account was set up with contributions from 24 members for an amount of SDR 160 million to assist the member countries in balance of payments difficulties due to a rise in oil prices and to provide subsidy to interest payments on the use of resources made available to them through the oil facility. The effective interest rate to borrowing members which include India is 2.7 per cent as against the original rate of 7.7 per cent. The final payment under this Account was completed in August 1983.

In May 1976, a Trust fund was started for providing special balance of payments assistance to developing countries at highly concessional rates. The sources of funds for this Trust are the realisations from the sale proceeds of one-sixth of IMF gold holding, income from investment and loans and proceeds of repayment and donations. Only about 60 member countries (including India) which are developing were eligible for this assistance. The first auction sale of gold by the Fund took place in June 1976.

A Supplementary Financing Facility was established in August 1977 (Wittaveen Facility) with the objective of extending financial assistance to members with large payments difficulties which are larger in relation to their incomes and quotas with the Fund. This is usable by members under a standby or under an extended arrangement for a period of 1 to 3 years. Some 14 member countries agreed to provide SDR 7.8 billion for this facility. The borrowings on this Fund by members were started in May 1979 and IMF has in turn borrowed from the lending members at a rate calculated for each of the six months on the basis of yield on US Government securities of 5-year maturity. A subsidy account was also started in December 1980 for subsidising the interest rate on the borrowings of the low-income developing members under this Wittaveen facility. This facility could not be extended beyond 1982 due to further non-committal of funds by lender-members.

A new Structural Adjustment Facility (SAF) was established in October 1985 and became operative in March 1986 financed out of SDR 2.7 billion that are available during 1985-91 from repayment of Trust Fund loans and interest dues. This facility is confined to the lowest income countries with protracted balance of payments problems needing a structural adjustment programme. This loan carries a rate of ½ of 1 per cent with a grace period of 5 years and subsequent semi-annual repayments extending over five years. The programme of adjustment is expected to be of about three years during which the country's balance of payments position would be strengthened and its debt repayment capacity revived.

Enhanced structural adjustment facility was continued upto 1993 for helping the low income countries, in strengthening their payments position.

Many additional facilities were created from time to time to suit to the changing conditions. Thus, in April 1993, the Fund created a new temporary facility called systemic transformation assistance to members with, systemic disruption of economies moving from planned economies to private market-oriented economies. In December 1997 the fund had set up the supplementary Reserve Facility to provide additional finance to members facing exceptional balance of payments problems due to loss of funds following the loss of market confidence.

Exchange Rates and Par Values

An important aspect of IMF activities is to maintain orderly exchange arrangements. The exchange rate system set up by the Articles of Agreement was called par value system. Each member is required to express the par value of its currency in terms of gold as a common denominator or in US dollar at a value of $ 35 per fine ounce of gold. Thus, gold was the basis of valuation and exchange rate fluctuations were to be kept within a narrow margin of 1 per cent on either side. While the USA performed this by buying and selling gold for US dollar, other countries did it through an intervention currency, such as US dollar of UK sterling.

The par value can be changed at the initiative of the country but with the concurrence of the IMF. For any change up to 10 per cent in the par value, to make adjustments in the balance of payments, the Fund would not raise any objection. For any change beyond 10 per cent, the country has to justify to the Fund that it would be needed to correct a "fundamental disequilibrium" — a concept which has not been defined by the Fund but relates to a structural change in the economies and in cost price parities.

Besides, members are obligated to avoid control on current account except under Article XIV which permits member countries to have such restrictions on a temporary basis. Some members who opted for this clause continue to have these restrictions in some form or the other. Article VIII enjoins on the members to free current transactions from all restrictions which was adopted by the major developed countries in the sixties. About 60 members have accepted Article VIII of the Fund so far and India is one of them since 1994. But a majority of members are still following Article XIV provisions, under which some forms of control on Current Account transactions were permitted.

The stable par value system has broadly served the purpose of larger trade and greater international co-operation. This system continued to prevail up to August 1971 during which time there was international monetary stability and orderly growth in world trade.

So long as the dollar convertibility into gold was maintained, IMF served the purpose and dollar and gold shared the honour of serving as an international medium of exchange. While the surplus countries have not been adjusting their economies, the burden of adjustment fell on the deficit countries. When the US was one of such deficit countries and found it difficult to adjust the domestic economies to the requirements of the IMF system and its role as an international banker, the fixed parity system lost its credibility.

The Bretton Woods system in respect of exchange rates was formally abandoned in August 1971 when convertibility of the US dollar into gold was withdrawn. The continued inflation at home, deficits in balance of payments and persistent pressure on the US dollar by its creditor countries along with speculative attacks on the dollar particularly in Euro-currency market, led to the suspension of its convertibility. The US abandoned its obligation to buy and sell gold in international settlements since August 1971. This was followed by a system of floating rates and a temporary regime of central rates and wider margins since December 1971.

The Smithsonian Agreement of December 1971 put back the broken pieces of the system together into a new shape, based on (i) A realignment of currency value against the dollar with a small devaluation of $ (revaluation of gold $ 38 = 1 fine ounce) and (ii) A return to fixed parity system by December 1971. But this system was short-lived and UK sterling was the first to abandon the fixed parity system in June 1972, followed by others in favour of a floating system of exchange rates. In February 1973, there was a further devaluation of dollar by 10 per cent in terms of gold in the midst of rampant speculation in dollar. A Committee of Twenty and subsequently the Interim Committee took up to formulate in 1972 a package of reforms in the international monetary system concerning exchange rates, role of gold, SDRs etc. After years of deliberation, they agreed on the following measures, in 1978.

International Monetary Reforms

In respect of exchange rates it was agreed that the floating exchange system which was a fait accompli should be legalised. But members are still under an obligation to collaborate with the Fund to ensure orderly exchange arrangements and promote a system of stable exchange rates. It was also provided that countries may return to a stable but adjustable par value system at a future date. Meanwhile, floating rates with a wider band of fluctuations of 2.25 per cent on either side which was prevailing since the Smithsonian Agreement would continue.

A new concept of "international surveillance of the exchange rate systems" was developed and accepted as a new approach to the exchange rate systems. Of the 149 members in the Fund, as at end December 1986, there were about 14 countries independently floating 8 countries in a joint float and 32 countries linked to the US dollar, 14 to the French Franc, 12 to SDR, 31 to a currency basket and the rest linked to other currencies. The fixed parity system had disappeared completely.

As regards gold, it would no longer function as an international unit of value or medium of exchange for the purpose of the Fund. The official price for gold is abolished and obligatory payments and receipts in gold between the Fund and members were withdrawn. Members are free, however, to deal in gold among themselves, SDR will be the unit and medium of exchange in future. The existing gold stocks of the fund are to be disposed of by returning to members half of their original contributions and by selling the other half in the market through auctions and to use the proceeds for the Trust Fund. Provisions are made for greater use and resort to SDRs, referred to later.

Two amendments were made to the Articles of Agreement, in connection with the reforms. Firstly, in 1969 an amendment was made to create a system of SDRs which will be referred to later. Secondly, Articles were amended in 1978 to introduce reforms in the international monetary system referred to earlier.

The principle of surveillance of the Fund over the members' exchange rate systems was embodied in the Second Amendment. So also was the abandonment of gold as an international unit of account or a medium of exchange for which SDR is redesigned.

Surveillance involves the following principles:

(1) A member shall avoid manipulating exchange rates to its advantage or prevent effective balance of payments adjustment.

(2) A member shall intervene in the exchange market if necessary to counter disorderly conditions.

(3) Members should take into account the interests of other members of the Fund in their intervention policy.

Members are free to choose their exchange rate arrangements except to maintain values in terms of SDR and co-operate with the Fund in the orderly exchange arrangements.

International Liquidity

International liquidity is defined to include all the assets gold and currencies that are freely and unconditionally usable in meeting the balance of payments deficits and other international obligations of countries. Gold has for long served as a unit of account, measure of value and medium of exchange. In the narrow official sense, the liquid assets used to meet balance of payments deficit by governments or monetary authorities include gold, convertible foreign exchange assets and reserve position with the IMF. In a sense, all owned and potential borrowings should be included as liquidity. These potential borrowings are vast and the scope for them is expanding with the passage of time. Besides, in a wider sense, all currencies and currency deposits and credits, actual and potential are part of the liquidity whether available to the governments and monetary authority or private parties. But since reserves held by private parties are not available to monetary authorities for meeting balance of payments requirements, only gold, official reserves, gold tranche and super-gold tranche (creditor position) with the IMF are considered as freely usable liquid assets by the authorities. Gold and super-gold tranche positions are drawable without conditions like the current account position with banks. SDRs which have been created by the IMF since 1969 are also included as liquid assets. In a narrow sense, thus, the official foreign exchange assets include gold, foreign currency deposits and investments in currencies which are freely convertible if that country has accepted Article VIII of the IMF Articles of Agreement, whereby no current account restrictions are used. India has accepted this position in March 1994.There are about 150 members under this Article as in 2009.

Need for Reserves

With the growth of world trade and payments, the need for reserves increases to meet the payments and deficit requirements. Just as in the case of domestic cash requirements for transactions, precautionary and speculative motives, international reserves also serve these three motives. Under a system of fixed par values adopted by the IMF and operative upto 1971, intervention in the markets to maintain the exchange rates stable used to require a large volume of liquid assets by the authorities. However, under the system of floating rates with a wider band of fluctuations, a larger need for reserves exists for various reasons. Firstly, the larger the balance of payments deficits, the larger is the need for reserves, and these deficits are growing. Secondly, then existing exchange rate system called "managed float" requires a larger official intervention which depends on the official holding of reserves. Thirdly, the IMF has put an obligation on members to return to the fixed par value system as and when conditions permit, for which a comfortable stock of reserves is necessary. Fourthly, increasing deficits in balance of payments of non-oil producing countries in more recent years require to be financed by reserves. Fifthly, a large number of poor countries have their exchange rates pegged to a currency or basket of currencies for which central bank's intervention in the market is necessary, particularly when their deficits are growing. The demand for reserves for precautionary motives emerges out of the need for contingencies and to maintain their credit standing. The speculative demand for reserves may not be felt in a country where all exchange dealings are strictly controlled and supervised by the authorities.

Composition and Level

The official reserve composition of India in 1971 and the latest position are presented below. The composition includes Reserve Tranche Position in IMF. As at end April 2010, India's foreign exchange reserves stood in terms of US dollars at US $ 200 billions, which covers more than 90 per cent of import bill in the year 2008-09.

(Rs. crores)

	End March 1971	*End March 1981*	*Jan. 1994*	*Dec. 1999*	*June 2002*	*End March 2006*	*March 2010*	*March 2012*
Gold*	182	226	12,665	12,790	16,272	25,674	81,188	1,38,300
Foreign Exchange Assets	438	4,822	61,440	1,39,134	2,67,333	6,40,732	11,49,650	13,30,500
SDR Units	112	497	233	18	47	12	22,596	22,900
Total	732	5,545	74,338	1,51,942	2,83,652	6,73,013	12,53,434	14,91,700

* Valued at London market price.

Source: RBI Bulletins. (Reserve Tranche Position with IMF is igonred).

@Inclusive of Reserve Tranche Position in IMF. In the totals, but not shown separately in the table.

Historically, the role of gold was taken by the US dollar and UK Sterling in inter-war and post-war periods and was replaced by SDR in the seventies. Gold is now completely replaced by SDR in the international monetary system.

Adequacy of Reserves

The currency composition of foreign exchange has also undergone substantial changes since 1975. The role of the US dollar was replaced partly by other currencies such as DM, Swiss franc and Japanese yen and partly by SDR.

If reserves are important, the adequacy of reserves of international liquidity is equally important. Firstly, adequacy of reserves may be judged by the relationship of reserves to imports, secondly, by the rate of growth of world trade as compared to the rate of growth of reserves and thirdly, by the magnitude of balance of payments deficit today as against a base year. Reserves as percentage of imports for all countries stood at 85 per cent in 1950 but declined to 38 per cent by 1966. By 1970 when SDR allocation was started, the inadequacy of reserves in relation to imports was glaring.

The adequacy of reserves is also assessed sometimes with reference to the degree of fluctuations in exports earnings. The problem of in adequacy is more patent if only deficit countries are considered.

There is a maldistribution of reserves, with the rich holding a larger proportion and the poor countries holding a small of proportion of total resources. The symptoms of inadequacy include increased restrictions on current account transactions such as imports, efforts to curtail foreign aid, depreciation of currency and greater reliance on trade credits, etc. With increased access to international capital markets, more recently by creditworthy countries like India, the question of adequacy of reserves became less important to them.

At end March 2012 total reserves of India totalled about Rs. 15,061 billion which covers an import bill for about nine months. (RBI Bulletin, June 2012)

Problems of Liquidity

The basic problems of international liquidity are as follows:

1. Inadequacy of Growth: Compared to the growth of world trade and increased deficits in balance of payments or judged by any other criteria, the inadequacy of reserves was felt more in the sixties and seventies than before. This was the justification for the creation of SDRs by the IMF.

2. Unsatisfactory Distribution of Reserves: The bulk of the reserves, namely, around 60 per cent, was held by the developed world and more recently by the combined groups of developed countries and oil-producing developing countries. The poor developing countries and non-oil producing countries are left with inadequate reserves.

3. Unsatisfactory Composition of Reserves: The proportion of gold to total reserves in 1952 was 68 per cent which fell to 53 per cent in 1968 and further to 23 per cent in 1973. Since then gold was completely replaced in official transactions by the SDRs. Gold, however, continued to play an important role with some countries because of its intrinsic worth, despite its demonetisation by IMF in 1973. Gold was revalued in terms of the US dollar from $ 35 to $ 38 per fine ounce in 1971 and again to $ 42.2 per fine ounce in February 1973.

In December 1997, the fund established the supplementary Reserve Facility to provide additional financial assistance to countries in financial crisis due to balance of payments difficulties and loss of market confidence. From time to time many facilities were added while some have lapsed.

Augmentation of Liquidity

The methods of augmenting the liquidity adopted by the Fund are the quota increase, borrowing from members under GAB and creation of SDRs. Increase, in quotas of all members with the IMF would improve global liquidity as their borrowing operations could simultaneously increase. Normally, quota reviews are held at intervals of not more than 5 years. Then the Fund would consider the growth of world economies, growth of international transactions and world trade and judge the adequacy of existing international liquidity. The quotas of members would determine their existing subscriptions to the Fund, their drawing rights on the Fund under both regular and special facilities and their share of allocation of SDRs and their voting power in the Fund.

So far thirteen quota reviews took place in the past. The eighth General Review of quotas made in 1984 raised the total quotas with the Fund by 47.5 per cent to 90 billion. Under the ninth quota increase, in 1990, total quotas increased further by 51.7% to SDR 136.7 billion. Even so, the ratio of Fund quotas to world imports is still lower at 4 per cent as compared to 9 per cent in 1970 and 12 per cent in 1965. Such general increases in quotas had taken place earlier in addition to some special increases of quotas of a few members whose currencies were supposed to be lower than the general requirements.

Special Drawing Rights (SDR)

The Special Drawing Rights (SDRs) are another source of augmenting international liquidity. This is an asset specially intended to take the place of gold and as such called paper gold. Each SDR is equal to 0.88671 grms. of fine gold, equivalent to one US dollar prior to devaluation in 1971. The value of SDR was changed with the devaluation of dollar in 1971 and 1973. During 1974 to 1980 the value of SDR was fixed on a daily basis as a weighted average value of a basket of 16 currencies of countries with more than 1 per cent of world trade. In 1981 these 16 were replaced by 5 major currencies, namely US $ DM, UK £, French Franc and Yen. As in 2005, the value of SDR=US $1.51678 and it is a weighted average of Euro, Japanese Yen, UK £, and US $.

These reserve assets have been created by the Fund since 1969 as and when required as part of the long-term strategy of augmenting world liquidity to keep pace with the requirements of a growing world economy and world trade. The actual allocation of SDRs to members would depend on the then quotas with the Fund. The acceptability of the SDR as an international liquid asset would depend upon the unconditional acceptance of this asset by the members of the Fund. The Fund members have been given the option to join the SDR scheme and those who have joined are bound to abide by the rules of unconditional acceptance for international payments, conversion into reserve currencies, payment and receipt of interest, etc. About 115 members had joined it originally in 1970 but now all its members have accepted and are allotted the SDRs.

SDR accounts are kept separate from the General Account of the Fund. The SDR is like a coupon or a credit facility which can be exchanged for reserve currency as needed by the user and approved by the Fund. The governments of the countries are holders of the SDR and their accounts in SDRs are maintained by the Fund through book entries. If a member wants to use the SDR, it requests the Fund to designate another member to accept them in exchange for a reserve currency to use in international payments and the latter member is obliged to accept as designated by the Fund. This would then tantamount to a credit granted by the latter member to the former for which an interest rate of 1½ per cent is paid to the creditor by the debtor through the Fund. In this sense, SDRs are better than gold as no interest was received on gold. In order to encourage acceptability of these SDRs, a member country may be required to hold in all 300 per cent of the cumulative allocations — 100 per cent representing the original allocation and 200 per cent representing the part received from others as designated by the Fund. These SDRs are the liability of the member borrowing currencies in exchange for SDRs and not of the Fund which keeps only the accounts with a surveillance over the operations. The members are not expected to transfer SDRs for changing the composition of its international reserves. The Fund may also acquire SDRs in the process of its operations on General Account as the members may repurchase in SDRs or pay interest or service charges in SDRs. Further, with a view to put a limit on the use of this facility by deficit countries, the principle of "reconstitution" is laid down under which a member's net use of SDRs must be such that the average of its daily holdings over a five year period should be not less than 30 per cent (reduced to 15 per cent and later removed altogether) implying thereby, that it could use only 70 per cent of the allocation on average. This puts an obligation on the members using SDRs to repurchase them also.

SDR Allocation

Starting with January 1970, SDRs were allotted to all member countries of the IMF who accepted the SDR scheme. The first SDR allocations were made during each of the years 1970-72 totalling SDR 9.3 billion. Further allocations were made for each of the years during 1979-81, totalling SDR 12 billion. The cumulative allocations since the beginning of the scheme were SDR 21,433 million. Such cumulative allocations amounted to only 5-7 per cent of the total world reserves other than gold. In timing of the allocations, the Fund kept in view the global need to supplement the existing reserve assets. Since then, in September 1997, a special one time allocation of SDR 21.4 billion was made which raised all participants' cumulative allocations to a common bench mark ratio of 29.3157 88813 per cent of the quotas based on the Ninth General Review. The Eleventh quota increase was effected in 2005. The total quotas of IMF stood in 2005 at SDR 213.5 billion of which India's quota was SDR 4158 million. Of the IMF holdings, SDRs stood at 574 million and gold holdings at 585.2 millions in addition to currencies of SDR 213.5 billion. India's quota in SDRs after quota increases in 2009, stood at 5821 million SDRs.

Limitations

The SDRs cannot be used directly as reserves as they have to be converted into reserves of one or other currency before use for payments. They can be used by official agencies and for designated purposes only. These are not money as such, but are comparable to near money or credit instruments. The fact that interest is payable on SDRs used by the debtors to the creditors would indicate that the SDRs are credit facilities.

Uses

Countries have made considerable use of these facilities since their first allocation in 1970. These transfers were partly designations by the IMF or by voluntary agreements among the members or in transactions with the Fund by members and partly in transactions by other international bodies who are holders of SDRs. Since, then gold has been replaced by SDR in the Fund's transactions as well as in the international transactions of members. The SDRs cannot, however, be exchanged for gold or for changing the composition of reserves of a country.

There are charges payable for use of SDRs. The charge for a creditor position in SDRs with the Fund is paid to the member holding excess SDRs than allocated. This charge of 1½ per cent was raised to 5 per cent in June 1974. Subsequently, the interest rate on borrowings in SDRs is determined quarterly by reference to a combined market interest which is weighted average rate on specified short-term instruments in the money markets of the same five countries in whose currencies the SDR value is determined, namely, the USA, West Germany, UK, France and Japan. The interest rates in the money markets of these five countries are weighted according to the same weights as used for SDR valuation. The IMF rate of remuneration to creditor countries was fixed in terms of SDR interest rate.

SDRs can also be used in swap arrangements and in forward operations, as a unit of account or measure of value or a means of payment. The SDR is used as a currency peg by some countries and as security or pledge. The Asian Currency Union and a number of international and inter-regional bodies are using SDRs in the above applications.

SDRs in India

India was allocated SDRs in the name of the Government of India since January 1970. These SDRs do not enter into the accounts of the RBI. During 1979-81, India was given further allocations on the basis of its quota with the Fund beginning with January 1979. India had a total allocation of about SDR 681 million during 1970-81.

India has used the SDRs in a very active manner since their inception and as at end March 1994, SDRs stood at Rs. 339 crore and as at end April 2012, SDRs stood at Rs. 22,900 crore. SDR was used by India for payment of interest and repurchases from the Fund. India has also accepted them under the "Designation" Plans of the Fund. India has very comfortable exchange reserve position due to economic reforms effected since July 1991. As referred to earlier IMF has made general and special allocation of SDRs to India in 2009.

India's IMF Net Position

India actively participated in IMF operations since 1947 when they were started. India has drawn IMF credits under most of its schemes. Any country can count as its reserves its IMF position in gold and super-gold tranches. Similarly, its repurchase obligations with the IMF are to be deducted from its official gross reserves. It is in this context that India's IMF position becomes relevant. India's repurchase obligations were nil in 1970-71, when it had repaid Rs. 154 crore due to IMF. But India had a major drawal of about Rs. 815 crore in August 1980 under two credits, namely, Rs. 540 crores from the Special Trust Fund and Rs. 275 crore from the compensatory financing facility. Our gold tanche position was about 25 per cent of the quota which stood at 2207 million SDRs taking into account the 8th General Quota increase granted in January 1984. India has drawn into its credit tranches and stand by credit arrangement, Extended Fund Facility also the compensatory and contingency financing facility, oil facility and special Trust Fund facility. In June 2002, we have a reserve position in the IMF at $ 651 million and outstanding use of IMF credit (net) stood at nil SDR; our net debt position to IMF was zero as at end June 2003, and remained zero since then.

Additional SDRs

SDRs allocation to India was increased in 1997 by an additional 240 million SDRs due to special one time SDR allocation amounting to 21.4 billion to all.

The principle of equitable share of cumulative SDR allocation to member countries as against the earlier principle of allocation as a ratio of quotas benefited India.

As against the earlier share of 22%, it has now got 29%, which secured for India an additional 240 million SDR in 1997.

Besides in the 11th general quota review, the quota funds were increased by 45%, in which India also benefitted. The total of IMF quotas was increased and 75% of the overall increase was distributed in proportion to the present quotas of member countries, as against the earlier proportion of 60%. India stood to gain in this respect also. India's quota is now SDR 5821 million, of which India's present holdings are SDR 2,885 million as in April 2012.

4

New International Economic Order

Economic System and financial system are inter-linked and a discussion on new Economic order in the world is relevant in this context. The recent trends in world trade and aid revealed highly disturbing features. Although, world trade has grown rapidly over the last three decades, growth was biased in favour of the industrialised developed countries (called here the "North") and against the less developed countries (the "South"). Secondly, the flow of aid from the developed to developing countries has been stagnating and frozen in recent years. Thirdly, the restrictive and protectionist measures of the developed countries have further reduced the export growth of the developing countries. As a result of the above trends, the gap between the rich and the poor countries has been widening, reflecting the slow-down in the growth of developing countries, partly due to the policies of the North.

Dependence on Aid has come down due to drying up of these sources. Nineties has seen the growth of commercial borrowing and Euro-currency markets. It is in this context the investment by MNCs in LDCs has assumed greater importance for their growth of output and incomes. For this market oriented economies and opening up of the economies is necessary.

World Trade Trends

The present problems of the South are mainly due to the world trade trends. Exports of the world grew at a rate of 8.3 per cent in the fifties, 9.7 per cent in the sixties and 21.1 per cent in the seventies. But the growth rate in exports of non-oil developing countries was lower except in the latest decade; at 4.9 per cent in fifties, 7.8 per cent in the sixties and 21.4 per cent in the seventies. During the eighties, world trade (in volume) stagnated at around 3 per cent due to a recession in industrialised countries. World trade grew by 4.2% in 1990, 2.3% in 1991, 4.5% in 1992 and 2.4% in 1993. The volume of world trade grew by 9.1% in 1994, 9.6% in 1995 but growth slowed down to 3.4% in the later half of nineties. Trade in Asian Region grew faster. The share of the non-oil developing countries in world trade declined sharply during the last two decades. The balance of current account continued to show deficits for developing countries which had also widened during the last two decades. There was world trade recession during 1997 to 1999 and export growth rate was 3.3% in 1998 and 3.8% in 1999. The recession continued in 2000 to 2002 and world trade volume infact declined in 2001 and recovered modestly to 2.5% in 2002. Against during 2008 to 2010, the world trade had stagnated or declined due to global recession and decline in world output.

On top of these, the commodity composition of world trade also changed against the interest of the less-developed countries. The share of manufactured products which is the major domain of developed countries increased while that of primary products which is the concern of the less-developed countries declined. Thus, the share of manufactured products in world trade shot up while that of primary agricultural products declined sharply. The terms of trade have also become more adverse to developing countries because of the declining demand for their products with the growth of synthetics and because of the fall or fluctuations in international prices (as per the recent FAO Survey) of 15 major primary products. The problems of the "South" have been accentuated due to these factors, coupled with the unfavourable trading environment in the eighties and nineties due to industrial recession in the developed countries and growth of tariff and non-tariff barriers in the trading system. The Generalised System of Preferences (GSP) introduced by some developed countries did not help the "South" due to inherent restrictive clauses. The antidumping measures and quota restrictions imposed by the US and EEC countries have virtually blocked the exports of developing countries, including India. The non-tariff barriers apart from quotas, which reduced the exports of developing countries, are arbitrary customs valuations, rigid consumer formalities, labelling and packaging restrictions, health and sanitary regulations and rigorous tests and inspections. The state of affairs continued to persist over the decades despite all pious resolutions of the UNCTAD and GATT. The Table in the next page presents the data of world output and trade for illustration.

World Aid Trends

For historical and economic reasons, the South is heavily dependent on the North, both in respect of trade and aid. While world trade trends referred to earlier showed that the interests of the developing world are undermined, world aid trends accentuated these problems.

World Output and Trade

(Percentage changes)

Output	*Industrial Countries*	*Developing Countries*	*Asia*
1990	2.5%	4.3%	5.9%
1996	3.0%	6.5%	8.3%
2000	3.8%	5.8%	6.5%
2004	3.4%	7.2%	8.2%
2005	2.6%	6.3%	7.4%
2009	–3.8%	1.5%	5.5%
2010	3.0	7.4	4.5

				Percentages
Advanced Countries		*Developing Countries*		
Trade (volume)	*Exports*	*Imports*	*Exports*	*Imports*
1990	6.8	5.0	6.2	7.9
1996	6.4	6.4	9.6	9.6
2000	11.7	11.6	15.0	16.0
2004	8.1	8.5	17.1	15.8
2005	5.9	6.5	7.2	7.3
2009	–15.5	–13.6	–6.5	–9.6
2010-11	4.2	2.2	(EMEs) 4.0	3.0

Source: *RBI Publications, World Economic Outlook, IMF.*

Note: Sources changed in 2009 and data became non-comparable. • EME: Emerging Market Economics

Over the past two decades, two major shifts in the flow of international capital took place — one shift from equity to debt and the other from official to private sources of finance. Both accentuated the debt burden of the South. The official supplies of aid declined due to balance of payments problems of donor countries and poor utilisation of aid by donee countries. There was a corresponding increase in the commercial borrowing by the developing countries. Consequently, there was a shortening of the maturity periods and an increase in interest rates.

Official concessional lending declined, while official non-concessional aid and commercial lending increased in the eighties and nineties as compared with that in the seventies. The rapid growth of commercial borrowing and the sharp rise in interest rates contributed to the mounting debt problems of the developing countries in the early eighties and ninetees. The ratio of debt servicing to exports of goods and services of all the developing capital importing countries rose to 50% and more in some countries. The ratio of debt of GDP in these countries also rose. (See world Bank's Debt Tables of member countries). In view of the continued balance of payments deficits of these countries due to adverse trading conditions, debt payments have to be rescheduled for a number of countries. The ODA (Official Development Assistance) has stopped growing and IDA credit remained choked. Similarly, private investment inflow into developing countries is lagging far behind the outflow of profits and returns on earlier capital investment with the result that the flow of funds started moving in the reverse direction since 1983 from the developing countries to developed countries.

Foreign investment flows reached a peak of $ 62 billion in 2007-08 but declined to $ 24 billion in 2008-09 but rose again to US $ 70 dollar in 2009-10. The bulk of this is in non-debt creating nature, following the policy guidelines of the government to discourage FDI inflows, in debt forms. These developments are due to world economic recession in 2008 and 2009, and recovery thereafter.

The oil price shocks during the seventies have brought about heavy borrowing and restructuring of the economies of many developing countries. These involved heavy expenditures on agriculture and energy sectors for the purpose of promoting their export rehabilitation and import substitution programmes. These trends led to fresh structural imbalances and increased governmental deficits which in turn resulted in higher rates of inflation in a number of developing countries.

Some of the International monetary developments have also contributed to the accentuation of the problems of the South. The post-Smithsonian monetary arrangement led to a greater uncertainty in international exchange markets, higher inflation and rising interest rates. The major pre-requisites of sustained growth and stable economic order, namely, price stability and balance of payments equilibrium, were lacking in this period. The floating exchange rate system and managed currencies, and continued balance of payments deficits, coupled with domestic budgetary deficits, led to inflation in the developed countries which in turn increased the strains on the international economic order. The disparate rates of inflation and postponement of corrective domestic economic policies in some developed countries also led to greater adjustment problems in international economic relations. The gap between the North and South widened and the traditional links between the developed and developing countries were strained. The increasing resentment of the South and disillusionment of the North has resulted in an estrangement between the North and the South. There was a move to greater South-South co-operation, regional economic arrangements and vocal preference for a South-South bank exclusively for the developing countries. the growth rate of the South stood at 4.8% in 2002 as against 4.0% in 2001, which were lower than the rate in the nineties. The growth rates priced up except in the years 2008 to 2010 due global recessions. Net Official Capital inflows to developing countries in 2000 — 2005 were much lower than in the nineties and turned negative in many years, (2003 to 2008) due to larger repayments than fresh inflows into EMEs.

Role of MNCs

Given the current debt problems of the South and attenuating soft loans of the multilateral agencies, the LDCs have perforce to depend more on direct foreign investment in their economies. More recently the LDCs have increased their reliance on commercial borrowings and free market forces. The role of Multinational Corporations (MNC) has increased in this context due to this changed attitude of the LDCs to foreign direct investment and the adaptation of MNCs to the concerns and needs of the host countries. The LDCs have come to realise the importance of resource and technology transfers for their growth, which foreign direct investment would bring in. They permit private foreign investment either through joint ventures, technical collaboration or equity participation, subject to the overall needs of the economy, safeguards and security for the host country and some sectoral or geographical restrictions. Accordingly, the attitude of suspicion, fear of political intervention and of monopoly and restrictive practices have given way to more open-door policies and even invitation to foreign direct participation to companies from developed countries such as transnational companies. These companies are, however, choosey in the selection of avenues and the countries for investment based on the extent of political and economic stability, right policies and the extent of the market, etc.

World Monetary Trends

As referred to earlier, some developments in the international monetary system have also adversely affected the North-South relations. The Bretton Woods System and originally designed in 1945 did not take into account the special disabilities of the LDCs. In respect of both the role of gold as well as the distribution of international liquidity, the developing countries continued to stand at a disadvantage. Despite thirteen general reviews of quotas, increasing the liquidity of members, the disparities between the North and the South in the distribution of reserves continued to persist. The new liquidity created was regressive in the sense that the rich developed countries got the bulk of the additional liquidity (around 80 per cent) of the SDRs allocated during the past, not to speak of the then existing maldistribution of reserves.

The reforms in the international monetary system that took place during 1976-78 also did not benefit the developing world. The freely fluctuating exchange rates adopted by many countries led to inflation in the developed countries and rising interest rates as a result of which the growth in the LDCs was adversely affected. Similarly, the oil price shocks experienced during the seventies also adversely influenced the balance of payment position of the non-oil producing developing countries. The various facilities of the IMF, although intended to benefit the primary-producing developing countries, did not significantly benefit the balance of payments position of these countries. Exchange rate volatility, uncertainty and hot money flow make the strong currencies stronger and weak currencies weaker. Besides, the Fund's surveillance authority does not extend to influence the policies of surplus member countries, throwing undue burdens on the borrowing members which are mostly the developing countries. The main drawback was the limited resources of the IMF and the huge magnitude of the deficits of the LDCs. Similarly, the role of the LDCs in the decision-making process of the IMF and affiliated bodies has been insignificant and the place of India, for example, had in fact gone down in the list of member countries in terms of their quotas and role in decision-making. The liquidity and assistance provided to LDCs has also not grown significantly as compared with their requirements or as compared with the growth of liquidity of the developed countries. The creation of additional liquidity or the flow of foreign aid has not been linked to the requirements of the LDCs. The South have, therefore, expressed their disillusionment at the existing international monetary system and hence the demand for South-South Bank exclusively for the developing countries.

Role of GATT

The rules and principles embodied in the Havana Charter signed in March 1948 were the result of protracted negotiations in trade matters among the developed and developing countries since the Second World War. The countries recognised the need for removal of restrictive practices in trade, tariffs and other barriers and discrimination in trade. The GATT is a multilateral treaty which embodied some of the principles and the reciprocal rights and obligations of member countries as set out in the Havana Charter. The GATT agreement as amended from time to time provided for reciprocal tariff concessions, liberalisation and removal of restrictions and to adopt positive measures to facilitate trade of less developed countries and their economic growth.

It was felt that the exceptions to the GATT non-discriminatory rules were very general and allowed protectionist measures in developed countries, particularly in respect of agriculture. These did not help the developing countries and the principle of reciprocity in granting tariff concessions benefited only the developed countries. The less-developed countries continued to face problems of inadequate exports and fluctuations in export earnings due to discrimination and barriers to trade imposed by the developed countries. The objectives of GATT could not, therefore, be achieved fully. This led to the establishment W.T.O in 1995.

Role of UNCTAD

The General Assembly of the U.N. designated the sixties as the U.N. Development decade and called for a conference on trade problems of developing countries. This was the origin of the United Nations Conference on Trade and Development (UNCTAD). The first meeting of UNCTAD was held in Geneva in 1964. Some general principles and special principles were embodied in the resolutions calling for greater trade and aid to meet the growth needs of the developing countries. The meeting held in Columbia in 1992 agreed to revitalise the UNCTAD and meet atleast once in four years and constituted many ad-hoc committees to deal with trade problems.

This conference has become a permanent organ of the General Assembly of the U.N. to be convened at intervals of three to five years. At the same time, the Group of '77' developing countries emerged out of the first meeting as a common forum. The first ministerial meeting of the group was held at Algiers in 1967 and called for greater self-help and mutual co-operation among the developing countries to be pursued along with programme of action for removal of all trade barriers and the general system of preferences by the developed countries.

Origin in NIEO

The basis for launching the movement of New International Economic Order (NIEO) is the existing deficiencies in the present order and the failure of both GATT and UNCTAD to achieve their objectives set for them. There are asymmetries in the working of the present system, such as undue dependence of the South on the North, bias in favour of the rich developed countries and a trend to make the rich richer and the poor poorer. Besides, the decision-making process is highly concentrated in the rich developed countries, based on their control on finance. These asymmetries are inherent in the present system due to the dependence of the South on the North for trade aid, investment and technological flows. This dependence was exploited by the rich to continue the existing gaps between the two groups. The demand for a new economic order has, therefore, emerged following the growth of independent sovereign nations from out of the erstwhile colonial countries. The new movement of the non-aligned nations was against politicalisation of development and trade issues. The developing countries began to assert their right to participate in the decision-making process of the world bodies such as World Bank, IMF, GATT, etc.

Emergence of North-South Dialogue

The first vocal reference to a new economic order was made sixty years ago at the Afro-Asian Conference at Bandung (1955). The new system which they wanted was to be based on equity, justice and common participation of all countries including the poor developing countries. The same sentiments were expressed at the subsequent conferences of non-aligned nations at Belgrade, Cairo,

Lusaka and Algiers, not to speak of the various 'UNCTAD Conferences' where similar resolutions on matters of trade and aid were passed.

The Idea of NIEO was formally mooted in the Algiers Conference of non-aligned countries in 1973 and formally ratified by the Group of '77' of the UNCTAD in the Arusha meeting in 1979. In the Sixth Special Session of the Group held in May 1975, they adopted a declaration and programme of action of the establishment of NIEO. The declaration emphasised the right of every state to full sovereignty over its natural resources and the programme of action proposed some measures on all aspects of international economic and financial relations.

The Paris talks in 1977 led to negotiations between the North and the South and achieved an agreement on the need for the setting up of a common fund for development and a pledge on the part of the rich to provide an additional US $ 1 billion to aid the poorest countries. At present, the aid flows of developed countries to developing countries were not near to the target of even 1 per cent GNP of the developed countries.

The Willy Brandt Commission — a body of 18 members with Brandt as Chairman was set-up to go into all issues of international economic development in December 1977 and submitted its report in February 1980. The report emphasised the need for North-South co-operation and endorsed the demands of the Group '77' and UNCTAD resolutions on trade and aid with respect to developing countries. The report is a true statement of what the South should have in terms of the NIEO. It recommended the establishment of a common development fund, for strengthening the structure of development lending, a code of conduct for MNCs and inter-governmental co-operation in monetary and fiscal matters as much as in trade matters. The Commission adopted a radical resolution proposing increased participation of developing countries in the decision-making process of international bodies also.

Objectives

The NIEO suggests more equitable allocation of resources of the world, larger flow of aid from the rich to the poor and positive discrimination and preferences in favour of the poor developing countries of the world. Some more topics were discussed in the South-South Conference held in New Delhi in February 1982 such as global negotiations between North and South, greater regional and South and South co-operation, increasing food and energy production in the South etc. The NIEO also envisages that the developing countries be given a voice in matters of trade, aid and other international economic affairs. The Brandt Report recommended" the establishment of a new international currency, the implementation of SDR-aid linkage, the increased stabilisation of international floating exchange system and the use of IMF fund as interest subsidy on loans to the poorest developing countries".

The NIEO aims at economic development through self-help and South-South co-operation. According to the Brandt Commission Report, "the call for the day is now to overcome world hunger, mass misery and alarming disparities between the living conditions of the rich and the poor". In this effort, the North has a role as much as the South. The North and South have more common interests in the medium and long-run than are recognised prima facie. If the South is developed, free from hunger and mass poverty, the trade between developed countries can grow and aid utilised by the developing countries can be repaid to developed countries. The quicker development and rising standards of living of the poor countries would be a sure way to greater stability and growth in the developed world as well. The narrow view of protection and tariff barriers and reduction in the aid flows by developed countries are, therefore, suicidal to both developed and developing countries. All problems of the South such as of balance of payments adjustment process, debt crisis, inadequate foreign resources and unsuitable exchange systems should be resolved by the N.I.E.O.

Elements

The various resolutions adopted by UNCTAD and its subsidiary organs since 1964 contained the elements of the programme of action for establishing a N.I.E.O. At its sixth special session held in April-May 1974, the UN General Assembly adopted a declaration and a programme of action for the establishment of New International Economic order. The strong feelings of resentment by the developing countries were manifested in passing this declaration. The LDCs called for a system based "on equity, sovereign equality, common interest and co-operation among all states, irrespective of their social and economic systems, which shall correct inequalities and redress existing injustices, make it possible to eliminate the widening gap between the developed and developing countries and ensure steadily accelerating economic and social development and peace and justice for present and future generations".

The basic elements of N.I.E.O. are more equitable allocation of financial resources and just and favourable terms of interdependence so far as the developing countries are concerned. The basic philosophy of N.I.E.O. is interventionist and biased in favour of the LDCs as opposed to the existing system of free market orientation and biased in favour of DCs.

The N.I.E.O. emphasises the need for a more rapid development of LDCs for which larger international trade and aid for the LDCs is necessary for increasing their import capacity. That would mean freer international trade devoid of all quantitative and qualitative restrictions of the DCs. The existing GATT rules of MFN treatment and reciprocity in trade negotiations are not suitable to increase the share of LDCs in world trade. A more positive boost to exports of LDCs is needed by giving favourable treatment by DCs, and flow of aid and financial resources from DCs to LDCs to finance the flows of trade and technology to LDCs. There should be a shift of emphasis from non-discrimination in trade to discrimination in favour of LDCs.

As regards the flow of financial resources there should not only be larger flows from DCs but such flows should be free from any restrictions or ties as to their use or policies adopted by the recipient countries. There should be depoliticalisation in the flow of private direct investment and the official flows. Aid should be in a multilateral form to a larger extent, which would help in facilitating the structural adjustments in the developing countries which is a pre-requisite for their growth.

There is need for restructuring the international monetary system as well. Recognising that trade and aid alone cannot bring about a significant improvement in the position of the LDCs, there is a demand from LDCs for increasing the volume of trade and improve the terms and conditions of balance of payments support made available by the IMF. Similarly, the creation of additional liquidity should be linked to aid to LDCs needed for the growth. The major elements in the N.I.E.O., are the linking of the creation of SDRs to development assistance to LDCs, depoliticalisation of all assistance and greater role for South countries in the decision-making process in the I.M.F. and World Bank.

Similar proposals were made with regard to transfer of technology. What the South wanted was freer transfer of technology at lower costs from DCs, effective control on restrictive business practices by the MNCs and to enhance the technological capabilities of the LDCs.

Implementation of N.I.E.O. Action Programme

The implementation of the Action Programme was rather disappointing. The main reason was the opposition from the capitalistic developed world. There are powerful vested interests in the world polity which discredited the N.I.E.O. Action Programme. They blamed the respective countries for their poverty and mis-management and pleaded their inability to help in view of their overwhelming domestic problems.

Another weakness in the implementation of the Action Programme is the poor bargaining power of the LDCs *vis-a-vis* the rich developed countries. The interests of LDCs are heterogeneous and the oil-producing developing countries do not have unity among themselves, not to speak of any cohesion with non-oil producing developing countries. Among the socialist countries barring Russia, there were no major trading partners who would sympathise or take up the cause of the LDCs. The economic relations between the LDCs and the socialists bloc were not powerful enough to break the position of eminence enjoyed by the capitalist western countries in the world trade and aid. The support that these LDCs got from the socialist bloc was, therefore, poor or inadequate.

On top of these hurdles, there was the powerful lobby among the intellectuals in the world who advocate free and perfect markets and oppose all interventionist policies. They are all neo-classical economists with a belief in laissez-faire philosophy. The world bodies are fully encompassed by such economists and intellectuals. There were only a few exceptions to this general rule such as Raul Presbisch and Willy Brandt.

The theoretical justification for the N.I.E.O. was sought in the second best considerations in the allocation of resources and factors of production due to market imperfections, risk, uncertainty and imperfect information, etc. A large bulk of international trade takes place on oligopolistic lines, particularly in manufactures and semi-manufactures, and in respect of trade by multinationals. Similarly, aid flows are made on negotiated settlement and on bilateral basis and free market forces do not operate. Where they operate as in agriculture, they operate against the interests of the LDCs. There is therefore, a case for interventionist philosophy as advocated by N.I.E.O. in favour of weaker sections of international polity, namely the LDCs. There was also an intellectual defence for the philosophy behind N.I.E.O. and it was supported strongly by the Report of the Brandt Commission. The oil crisis and the resultant problems of non-oil producing LDCs have proved beyond doubt that the structural problems are more pressing for the LDCs rather than any mismanagement of the economies by wrong policies pursued by the respective countries themselves. It would thus appear that the theoretical justification for the N.I.E.O. is strong enough but it has to be brought to light more widely. Besides the empirical support to the N.I.E.O. although based on strong grounds, is not well propagated by intellectual circles and international economists.

There is, therefore, undoubtedly a case for greater co-operation among the South countries through regional bodies like S.A.R.C. (South Asian Regional Conferences) for freer exchange of information flow, technology and greater trade and aid; there is also need to encourage inflow of FDI and the role of MNCs.

GROWTH OF REGIONALISM

In 1960, East Asia accounted for only 4% of the World Economic output whereas in 1999 it worked to about 25% - 30%. While GNP in Europe and USA grew 2.5% - 3% p.a. over the last decade, many East Asian Countries grew by 6.5%-7.5% p.a. and this trend is likely to continue in the 21st Century. Thus, the East Asian Region is showing a better growth as also is the case with Latin America and Africa with the result that the centre of economic power shifts away to regions other than Europe and U.S.

In this context, the voice of developing countries is heard through in the establishment of W.T.O following Uruguay Agreement. It is an achievement in that it covers under the GATT for the first time agricultural exports, services, investment and intellectual properly rights which were not covered earlier. The most useful benefit from the WTO is that it would add 300-400 billion dollars to 3.6 trillion annual volume of world trade. The tariff barriers and trade wars as between the trading partners and tensions due to trade will considerably come down. The developing regions would mainly benefit from this development. The earlier trend of discrimination against developing countries, and the possibility of rich becoming richer will be considerably reduced due to the trend towards globalisation of markets and trade in the developing East Asian Region. Thus, East Asian intra-regional trade and financial flows are showing fastest growing share of the regions. During nineties almost 70% of foreign investment in east Asia came from within region, while 10.3% came from Europe and 10.9% came from US. This development is comparable to what has happened in Western Europe where intra-regional trade accounted for 70% of the total and a similar trend was noticed in North America with the implementation of NAFTA. In this changing scenario, each region is becoming independent of the developments in other regions and the growth seems to be fastest in the East Asian Region.

The new world economic order will result in *ad-hoc* Alliances in international trade. The trend towards privatisation and globalisation in South Korea, Taiwan and India would provide new opportunities for Multi National Corporations of US and Europe to operate in these countries. During

1980-1990 total imports of Industrialising countries of East Asia increased by about 250% and this trend accelerated during the 90's and later. Countries in East Asia namely Thailand, Indonesia, Taiwan and North Korea, etc., are showing the larger growth of trade, and India's trade with Asia has increased over the decade ending in 2010 from about 20% to 30% in value terms.

In the changing trade and economic conditions in the world and the establishment of WTO and regionalisation of trade and investments, a new economic order is emerging on the world scene.

The new world economic order will contain the following new developments. Firstly, the trend towards market oriented economies and privatisation will grow faster which will result in a faster rate of growth along with accompanying tensions.

Secondly, the trend towards regionalism in the international trade and investment will increase and the present balance of power in favour of Western Europe will be tilted against US and in favour of Japan.

Thirdly, the trade and growth of developing countries will exhibit an acceleration and the balance of power between developed and developing countries will also change in favour of developing countries. This trend is already noticed in the concessions gained by developing countries in Uruguay Round of trade negotiations and in setting up of WTO.

Lastly, the development of East Asian Region with many opening their economies and liberalisation of policies, will be faster and the dependence of the region on trade and investment on other regions particularly Western Europe and USA would decline and the balance of power may tilt in favour of the East Asian Region. The Asian Currency crisis of 1997 has affected many nations and flow of FDI slowed down. The future hope of development lay in the role of MNCs through their control on funds, R&D and technology. The necessary conditions are already created for this.

As noted earlier, WTO was set up in 1995. India supported WTO resolution on Information Technology, transparency in government procurement and trade facilitation. In fact, India is opposed to competitive policy on Investment and Labour standards. Free International Competition will not be acceptable as mandatory for India.

India did not benefit from uruguay Round. India lost due to U.S. curbs on the Indian Textiles, as in rubber, footwear, travel goods, readymade fabrics and foodstuffs. No worthwhile imports of personnel were allowed and freeing of services, did not materialise. It is hoped that India would benefit in services, textiles, dairy products; agricultural products, patents, etc., would also benefit from the policy of WTO.

Even in the Doha ministerial conference of WTO (2001) India voiced many concerns about increased protection to trade in agriculture by developed countries, and on WTO's attention to non-trade related issues, like labour standards and environment. The TRIPs Agreement is to be interpreted in a manner supportive to member's right to protect public health and ensure medicines to all. There should not be any misuse of biological and generic resources and traditional knowledge of the developing countries. The granting of patent rights to intellectual property and freer flow of knowledge based services from India aided the Indian interests. The freer trade in Agriculture and food based industries did not however materialise in the WTO conferences.

India supported the role of greater regional co-operation among the SAARC countries. Many Asian Economies have shown larger savings and investment rates than India, but there was a slow down in their growth rates of output and trade since 2000, which is likely to continue due to global slow down and U.S. Gulf War and lagged recovery of Technology Sector. The capital inflow has also fallen during 2003 to 2009, as compared to mid-Ninetees.

The WTO conference held in Concum in Mexico in Sept. 2003, did not benefit India and other developing countries. More details on WTO are available in Chapter 18.

5

Globalisation Forces

Definition

Globalisation refers to the expansion of economic and financial activity across national boundaries and encompasses all operations in a globally competitive environment. This translates itself in actual practice into free and unfettered movement of goods, services and factors of production across national and regional boundaries. As a pre-requisite for such free flows, the barriers to trade and services have to be reduced and eliminated. Besides, structural adjustments have to be made in the economy in the form of privatisation with market forces of competition and efficiency as the judge of success on the one hand and elimination of inefficiency and monopoly on the other side. Technology and R&D have to be the hall-marks of improving productivity, quality and efficiency, to internationally prevalent standards.

The economic and financial reforms initiated since July 1991 in India aimed at achieving such an environment necessary for globalisation. The IMF and World Bank have been assisting India in this direction. The WTO has been directing its efforts at free movement of goods and services including patent rights across national boundaries. Technology flows also play an important part in this process. Foreign technology is being adopted to suit Indian conditions along with an effort at import substitution of the Technology requirements. Indian tariffs are being drastically reduced, with quantitative and quota restrictions being reduced to the minimum levels. From more than 100% of customs duties, they are now reduced to a maximum of 40% and further down to 10%. The goods under OGL have been expanded enormously over the last few years. Freer import of technology and technical personnel has been allowed by the Government during these reforms since 1991.

Hurdles to Globalisation

Globalisation in the Indian context faces many hurdles. Having had a semi-protective government policy for years in the past, dismantling all of them simultaneously will create chaotic conditions in the Indian corporate polity. Besides with monopoly and semi-monopoly conditions in a number of industries, Indian corporate sector is not yet ready for facing global forces all at one stretch. Foreign technology adopted and adjusted to Indian conditions have created problems of socio-cultural discontent Pollution of air and water and exploitation without replenishment of the natural resources of the country and hurdles to the labour intensive economy of India. The obstruction to changes is common and more so in Indian conditions due to the following macro-environmental forces.

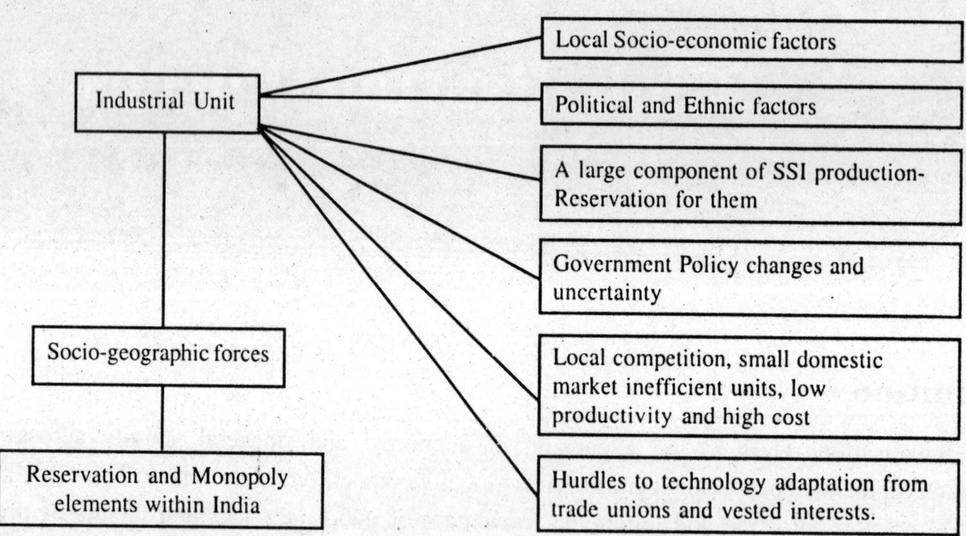

Leaving aside these hurdles, which have to be overcome by co-operation from all corners namely Government, labour, and Management, Technology is a single key to success of globalisation. As India will find it costly to develop its own technology from the scratch, it has to start with imported technology. Its adaptation to Indian conditions and its improvement is an exercise of the R&D efforts and the management's involvement in it. The human resource development, training and change in attitudes of all concerned appears to be one of the ways of reaping the benefits of foreign technology. Simultaneously efforts have to be made to produce improvements in Technology and evolve new Technology, suitable to the Indian conditions, through R&D in Indian Industry.

Management of Change to Globalisation

The environmental forces commonly facing the corporates going global are to be overcome by successful strategies. Strategy changes and internal management's dynamism and management of changes through HRD are all necessary pre-requisites for Indian corporates to go global. The major factors influencing the management of change are government policy changes (such as deregulation, liberalisation and free markets), human resource development (labour component) and changes in systems and procedures. For globalisation, the first essential requirement is the inherent strength of management, human resources and available technology.

Government policy changes since 1992 have been aimed at helping competition with foreign enterprise and improve internal intrinsic strengths of the corporates to fight for survival. Mere changes in laws have found to have little effect on increasing efficiency and productivity of the corporates, essential for globalisation. Government policy changes and environmental changes and the operations of Global players from abroad have all forced the corporates to fight for survival and the weak units have been the targets for takeover and mergers. The Indian Companies if they survive and strengthen themselves to face the competition of foreign MNCs in India, they should be able to fight them not only in our country but in other countries as well through proper change in strategies. The operations of MNCs in India have increased since 1992 and the FFIs and foreign security firms have all offered tough competition in the financial sector in India. The Indian banks have learned to live with foreign banks and Indian security firms with foreign security firms and Indian Institutional Investors with foreign institutional investors. This is only a first step to globalisation; as a next step the Indian firms should compete on equal terms with them on foreign soil as well.

Strategic Planning

Globalisation is both a challenge and opportunity for the Indian corporates, who are forced to make changes in strategies and strengthen their intrinsic competitive power. Some good reputed companies have successfully adapted to change in environment and showed their capacity to go global, as in the case of Reliance, Ranbaxy, Birlas, Bajaj Auto, etc. Many top ranking companies listed in top 500 by the "Business Today" have shown their inherent strengths to change and adapt to changing environment. Their single unique answer is adoption of strategic planning and making changes in them to suit the changing environment. The role of strategic planning in the present corporate scenario cannot be over emphasised, in this context.

Recent Environmental Changes

(1) FERA Relaxation and introduction of a new law of FEMA in 1999, deleting the regulatory aspect of the Act.

(2) Rupee Convertibility on Current Account in 1994 and the steps taken since 1997 towards limited Capital Account Convertibility.

(3) Increasing Foreign Direct Investment and Portfolio Investment, providing keener competition to Indian financial institutions.

(4) Greater Autonomy to banks and Authorised dealers and Restructuring of banking system and their practices and greater FDI in banks.

(5) Reduction of customs and Excise duties and Rationalisation and simplification of tax structure.

(6) Import liberalisation in the direction of eliminating the negative list, subject to controls.

(7) Increased role of MNCs from abroad and opening up the economy to multinationals.

(8) Improved quality and acceptance standards of ISO 9000/ISO 14000.

(9) Rapid changes in emerging technological standards and growth of interna-tional competition in the domestic markets as well as foreign markets.

(10) Freer import of technology and open invitation to foreign collaborators, with both foreign finance and foreign technology.

(11) Weakening trade with rupee payment areas and increasing trade with developing world.

(12) Increasing access to foreign currency markets by both banks, FIs and corporates.

(13) Exporters allowed to keep some funds abroad and forward cover allowed to exporters and NRIs for their foreign currency deposits.

(14) Indian Joint Ventures are allowed to take funds abroad, without RBI's prior permission subject to some limit.

(15) Indian mutual funds are allowed to invest abroad upto a limit.

(16) Indian corporates are allowed to borrow abroad upto $ 3 million and EOUs to borrow upto $ 15 million.

(17) ADs are allowed to borrow abroad and invest abroad and do forfeiting business which will help exporters with foreign currency loans.

(18) Free inflow of funds and limited outflow of funds are allowed under reforms.

(19) RBI policy acted as a facilitator to integrate domestic financial markets with foreign markets, as a step in the direction of globalisation in the financial sector.

(20) Foreign MNCs operating in India and Indian Corporates going abroad with joint ventures are designed to link foreign markets with Indian markets and are given greater freedom to operate through their branches or subsidiaries.

Macro Environment

The Government can only provide macro economic and financial environment necessary for Indian corporates to go global. The measures taken so far have only touched a fringe of the problem and more so, when there is a hiatus between the policy statements and their implementation, so far as the Government is concerned. Even in its efforts to encourage regional co-operation and regional trade much success is not achieved through SAARC, ASEAN etc. Government procedures and practices are time consuming and breed corruption. Our economy is not competitive in the comity of nations, as reflected in lower growth of exports than imports, continued trade-deficits and balance of payments pressures. Productivity and efficiency is not the hall-mark of our economy. Many industries have thrived for decades with high unit costs and protected domestic markets.

The present economic growth rate of 6% to 8% or so, along with an inflation rate of about 8% is a satisfactory performance, but large chunks of capital are tied up as unproductive assets in PSUs and infrastructure projects. The bane of the Indian economy is low productivity of capital, along with inefficient labour entrenched in strong trade union movement and poor performance of infrastructure sector, which is the backbone of all other sectors and industrial growth.

Requisites for Globalisation

Normally, global corporates emerge out of strong economies, stable policies and sound environment forces. They have the vision and leadership qualities supported by muscle power of money. They are the achievers and their management philosophy is dynamic and result-oriented. The "globo-corps" have high credit rating. Quality is the watch word and their strength is their technology and productivity.

"Globo-corps" have production facilities in many countries, international network of distribution centres or subsidiaries in many countries, access to low cost funds anywhere in the world and their profit margins vary from country to country but over all margins are high due to efficient low cost production, varying marketing strategies and good information systems and technology. Their R&D expenditure is high and innovation is their driving force to success. Most important, they think global but act local.

Corporates going global, called here "globo-corps" should have global perspective of the markets, products and designs suitable to the markets. The have set-up production capacity in various countries where inputs and spares are cheaply available and suitable labour and infrastructure is present. The relations of local Government with the host Government, the policies adopted and their stability and certainty in the concerned countries are the other relevant factors, considered by "Globo-corps" in their expansion to globalisation. They secure the inputs from one country, spares from another, labour in the country where the production capacities are built and obtain the low cost finance from wherever possible as all international financial markets are open to them.

Their R&D effort is very strong and technology is continuously upgraded to keep it as low cost as possible. Their marketing strategy is such that their sales are consumer-oriented and designs are developed to suit each market separately and profit margins vary from country to country, but the basic objective of globalisation, namely maximisation of profits is achieved for the total sales as a whole. Their studies of various countries with open economies are very crucial to develop an updated informative system and their strategies are based on the information system that they built. They produce in one country, bring finance from another and market their products in another set of countries. That is the quintessence of the globalisation policy. Not many Indian corporates can play this role on a global basis.

Among the Indian global players, Reliance is a market leader with a vision and both with horizontal and vertical integration, large-scale operation with built in production capacities, leveraged technology, project engineering to control costs and customer-oriented sales strategies. Sundaram fasteners used the innovation strategy along with insistence on quality standards, wide product range and operations on global scale. Bajaj Auto has strong fundamentals and quality with cost controls has made it a global player with world scale operation, production capacities and marketing strategies. There are a number of other global players in India who already made a mark like I.T.C., Ranbaxy, Hero Honda, Infosys, Wipro, etc.

Despite this existence of a few global players in India and Indian MNCs, operating abroad, environmental factors in India are not still conductive to growth of larger number of such players. The major hurdles continued to persist in the form of poor infrastructure, Government policy changes, high cost economy, huge domestic market and incomplete openness of the economy The most important hurdle is the rampant corruption and red-tapism in administration and bureaucracy. But the pace is set and measures taken so far are in the direction of globalisation like opening of the financial markets and integration of domestic markets with foreign markets, etc. Joint Ventures, mergers and acquisitions, and foreign investment in India and Indian investment abroad, wholly owned and partly owned subsidiaries are some of the modes of emergence of global players.

Inevitable Forces of Globalisation

World trade is growing faster than world output in general. This is more particularly noticed in the case of developing countries. World exports of merchandise and services grow by about 6% during the decade of Nineties. The developing continues showed a growth rate of output of 4.5% in Nineties while their merchandise exports (volume) grew by 9% during the same period. Despite the fact that the growth slowed down during 2001 to 2003 and again in 2008 and 2009 due to world recession, the main trend of continued growth of trade in the world and of developing countries in particular evinces greater thrust on globalisation.

The globalisation of business depend in particular on trade, aid flows or foreign investment and cross border mergers and acquisitions. All these factors are more pronounced during the period after 1996 in the case of India. Removal of Quantitative restrictions on trade, reduction of tariff barriers on imports and increased limits to FDI flows in some sectors in India led to enhanced globalisation trends.

According to UNCTAD data, the annual growth rate of FDI inflows was higher at 41% during 1996-2000 than that of 21% during 1991-95. Net capital flows to Emerging market economies reached a low of US $ 7.7 billion in 2000 but picked up in the later years despite continued world economic recession, to US $ 58 billion in 2002; according to world Economic outlook. During 2003 to 2008, private direct and portfolio investments continued to grow while the other private capital flows and official flows were negative in net terms. In 2009-10 it was 51 billion US $ but fell to US $ 37 billion in 2010-11.

Globalisation Models

The current theme is adaptation to globalisation — Techniques and Models. Although the whole organisation is to be involved in this process, the Top Management represented by what we call the "Management" is basically responsible to choose the model suitable to his line of activity, the dynamics of immediate environment, government policy and economies or diseconomies involved, culture of the organisation and the basic philosophy propelling the promoters, etc. No unique solution suitable to all organisations or even of those in the same business or activity can be prescribed. Similarly, the model suitable may undergo changes with the change of environment from time to time. Two basic questions which the management has to face in this process may be mentioned here.

(1) Have the investor members of the company a role or say in the matter.

(2) Have the employees of the company a choice in the techniques to be adopted.

Obviously, no organisation worth the name can ignore the majority opinion of the investors of the Company and of employees of the company. The management has to take with them the promoters, investors involved, financial institutions including banks, creditors and the employees of the organisation. Some models for adaptation to globalisation are set out below:

(1) Reorientation and HRD Plan: This is the normal retraining and Retirement Scheme for staff on a voluntary basis. The existing staff is retrained to meet the new challenges and new tasks. This is coupled with an incentive package for some to retire on voluntary basis paving of the way for the needed restructuring of the organisation. This is the most common and simplest model, suitable to Indian conditions.

(2) Managerial Adaptative Model: In this model, the managerial talents are used to build a strong organisation to become a global player. This depends on the ability vision and willingness of the top management to meet the challenges of globalisation, through strategic planning process. Managers use their vision as in the case of Ambanis to become top global players.

(3) Open Entry and Exit Model: We have in India open entry and freedom to enter into many industries without a licence and raise funds freely from the capital market and go ahead for business of manufacture or trading or provision of services. But the exit policy is difficult and time consuming. If the government is willing to have an exit policy also, the model can be applied. At the present juncture, winding up of a company or retrenchment of staff and reorganisation are constrained by the law particularly of Labour Laws, Trade unions and government procedures. Hence, the use of this model requires some changes in laws in India. But this model is widely used in developed countries.

(4) Indigenous Adaptation of Foreign Technology: This is something like the import substitution in technology which is adjusted and changed to make it Indian and suitable for Indian conditions. It also involves development of India's own technology as in the case of space and Satellite Telecommunication system which India has developed on her own. But development of own technology is costly and adoptation of existing technology is cheaper.

(5) Quality Upgradation Model on R&D: In this model, the Manager and his staff have to plan a strategy, both short-term and long term, to improve the quality (ISO 9000 or ISO 14000) to international standards and bring about a cost reduction through greater efficiency and productivity. The domestic operations and global operations can be brought on par and can be well planned and integrated into a cohesive whole for the company to expand and grow to global stature. This is based on a strong R&D department to help the company to go global. Ranbaxy and Dr. Reddy Labs are examples in the adoption of this model.

(6) Collaboration for Foreign Technology Model: We have many examples as in the case of Maruti, TVS, Suzuki, Modiluft etc. where Indian and foreign companies join in a Joint Venture to manufacture products or provide services for global markets. We have such collaborations in many steel units, engineering and capital goods plants and machinery, autos, scooters, etc. In this model, foreign technology plays a major role in making Indian companies become global players. Government is freely allowing inflow of foreign technology in most of the industries, where Indian technology is not well developed.

(7) Mergers and Acquisitions: In the context of stiff competition from MNCs who have free access to both manufacturing and trading activity in India, the Indian Corporates have to meet this challenge by improving efficiency and productivity. Besides, their technical upgradation should be the main plank for facing foreign competition.

To meet this competition and to be able to operate on level playing ground with MNCs and foreign companies, Indian corporates can strengthen themselves by mergers and acquisition to augment their resource base, achieve economies of scale and increase their asset size, and scale of operations.

Mergers can be friendly takeovers, like the parent companies merging its subsidiaries with it and achieve vertical and horizontal integration. Reliance Industries has adopted this method to become a large Indian MNC. Sometimes, bail out takeover is made to merge with sick and non-viable undertakings. The examples of horizontal diversification and acquisition are those of ITC, Birla Jute, etc.

Mergers can also be arranged marriages particularly arranged by the BIFR in the case of many sick and non-viable units. Hostile takeovers are controlled by SEBI's Rules for takeovers, clauses 40A and B of listing Agreement and Company Law Provisions.

Examples of mergers of group companies are Nav Bharat Ferro taking over of Nav Chrome, and Rasi Cements taking over of Rasi Ceramics. Hindustan Lever has effected a number of group mergers. Gujarat Ambuja got BIFR nod to acquire the ailing Modi Cement.

Mergers among banks are also common. SBI has taken over a number of small and ailing banks. The New Bank of India was merged with Punjab National Bank. The Oriental Bank of Commerce took over the ailing G.T.B. in 2004.

The Corporates have to build global capacities in the present scenario. The financially weak companies have all to fear. From 1995 onwards there were a number of mergers and takeovers. Some of them are for consolidation, like the merger of the East Coast Breweries and Distilleries and Sica Distilleries into Shaw Wallace.

Some weak companies sold off some of their divisions as in the case of Allwyn Refrigerators to Voltas. Duphar Interfram sold its brand Crocin to the Smithkline Beecham PLC. Ajay Piramal group has taken over Nicholas Laboratories, Sumitra Pharmaceutical and Roche products etc.

(8) Consolidation or Market Sharing Agreement: The objective of consolidation is achieved by agreements with competitors or related companies. Thus, DSP and Merill Lynch have had a joint venture in financial services. ICICI is strategic alliance with South Indian Bank, to share business interests and strategies. French Automobile Major Renault has been planning strategic alliance with ailing pal-Peugeot Ltd. Modilfuft is in strategic alliance with British Airways. Swiss air and Air India have planned to share capacity, etc.

(9) Expand to Go Global Through Joint Ventures Abroad: With the permission given for mutual funds to invest abroad, UTI has announced its plans to go abroad. Many export-oriented Companies are also planning to operate abroad. Bharti Global will be the first Indian Company to set and operate Telecom Services outside India, particularly in Seychelles. Ispat of Laxmi Mutual group has launched a new production unit in Mexico and get this Company listed in New York. Joint Ventures abroad may now increase. In future, as the RBI has freed the ADs from prior RBI permission for releasing funds for Joint Ventures abroad, subject to some limits, Indian Companies can become global giants to compete with similar giants abroad. Things are however not that easy for the average Indian Corporates. They have the threat of foreign competitors and fear of building global capacities, in terms of technology, quality, cost and marketing strategies, etc. The Indian laws, taxation and government procedures and a host of other environmental problems stand as hurdles for the Indian Companies to go global. Only the fittest and the strong companies can succeed in competing effctively abroad and become global players.

In sum, each organisation has to adopt a plan unique to itself to meet the global challenges. The opportunities are galore for the Indian Corporates, particularly those with export market and export potential. Each of the corporates had to plan its own strategies suitable to its structure, culture, tradition and its vision or goals. But the opening of the economies of India and Foreign players actively engaged in Indian markets, both in product markets and financial markets have opened up challenges to meet them on equal ground at home and at the same time go abroad and play in their markets on equal terms.

Environmental Adaption for Globalisation

Globalisation involves adaptation to environmental forces. Today's managers faces more challenges in adaptation to the changing environmental scenario than ever before. The manager has to face the competitors, input suppliers and output marketing outlets, distributors and consumers etc. Corporate manager is part of the corporate sector in India which is now open to new challenges due to deregulation and exposure to market competitive forces and globalisation.

Unfortunately, resistance to change is an obstacle to progress, whether it is in technological field or finance and environmental forces. Managing change is a management task and involves the following steps:

(1) Inform the staff and work force of the current situation and create a dissatisfaction with it, by finding and pointing its weakness, faults and hurdles to progress.

(2) Prepare the attitudes of staff to one of positive reception to change, as desirable for effectiveness and efficiency, in the organisation, in their own interest.

(3) Create a vision of the desirable future state to which they are moving and demonstrate how they will benefit from it.

(4) Prepare a plan and priorities in the scheme of adaptation to change.

(5) Remove the negative attitude and create a positive attitude to the new scheme of things and of action in adaptation to change.

(6) Use Training, workshops and seminars to help them acquire the necessary attitudes, skills and adaptation techniques to change.

The present juncture is one of transition form, a regulated environment to deregulated and free competitive forces. The major move is towards opening of the economy to global competitive forces which has both advantages and disadvantages. The task of taking full advantage only is a matter of challenge on the one hand and an opportunity on the other.

Financial Environment

The environmental factors which showed some positive impact are containment of inflation to around 8% and growth of money supply to around 18%. Easier access to credit and lower interest cost are the other favourable factors. The foreign exchange reserves are growing and the moves to capital account convertibility have added a new dimension to Corporate activity in the recent past, particularly after 2000.

The environmental factors which showed some negative impact are sluggish demand, lower capital investment expenditure, recession abroad and continued high trade deficits and current account deficits. The balance of payments showed none too encouraging picture. Added to this the Government fiscal position continued to cause concern due to large fiscal deficit, larger interest burden and uncertainty of economic policies.

On the export front, Corporates can get hedging products from ADs who are permitted to offer cost effective and risk reduction option strategies like Range forwards and Ratio Range forwards and forward covers. ADs have been authorised to approve the release of funds not only for current account remittances or outflows but also capital account flows for joint ventures, subsidiaries and foreign offices for corporates etc. These are forces opening up new challenges to corporate manager, which if taken up on the tide, leads on to the fortunes.

World Economic Trends

The output growth of developing economies is faster than that of developed countries. During 2000 to 2003, the world output grew by 2%-3%, while the output growth of the developing Asia was around 5-6% per annum. World output and trade was higher during 2004 to 2007 after which there was global recession.

India's trade with Asia and developing countries is rising faster through joint ventures and trade agreements. During 2000 and 2003, our trade growth was lower than in the earlier years, due to recession in some foreign markets and moderate growth in a number of Asian countries.

World Economic Trends (Rate of Growth)

Year	World output	World exports of Advanced economies
2000	4.7%	11.7%
2001	2.5%	–0.7%
2002	2.8%	2.2%
2004	4.9%	9.1%
2005	4.5%	6.2%
2006	5.1%	8.5%
2007	5.1%	6.2%
2008	3.1%	2.0%
2009	0.5%	2.5%
2010	5.1%	3.0%

***Source:** IMF World Economic Outlook.*

Private capital flows to India continued to rise consistently, including the FDI, despite the uncertain political environment. Although the country rating of India was slightly lowered in 1996-97 and again after May 1998, pokhran nuclear Test and follow up sanctions of U.S.A. on India, the impact of this is not felt significantly. Many Indian companies borrowed their requirements from abroad and the net inflows into India continued, albeit at a slower pace. Official flows into India continued to be a negative net inflow due to more repayment of loans, and interest payments from India.

Our export growth rate decelerated to 4% and less in 1996-97 to 1998-99 as compared to 19.7% in 1995-96 in US $ terms. Although it picked up in the next two years it became a negative growth in 2001-02 in US dollar terms. Afterwards exports grew at over 20% in the next few years, the imports also grew at a slower pace during 2000-2002 than that in the previous years in dollar terms. As imports grew faster than exports our trade deficit continued to grow larger and larger during 2003 to 2005. The current account deficit was 1 to 2% of GDP upto 2000-01 after which the Current

Account turned positive for three years, 2001-02 to 2003-04. But our external reserves stood at a robust level of $ 88 billion in 2003, and $ 164 billion in May 2006, and to US $ 262 billion by April 2010, US 293 billion in April 2012. Our GDP growth slowed down due to global recession during 2008 to 2010 at trade levels also fell and the current account deficit widened during this period to reach 2.6% of GDP in 2008-09, 2.8% in 2009-10 and 2.6% in 2010-11.

Policy Changes

Globalisation requires a market oriented economy and towards this end some policy changes were initiated since 1992. Whether it is fiscal policy or monetary and credit policy, they have to be assessed relative to the trends in real variables. As per the latest data available real GDP grew about 8% in 2009-10 as against 7.29% average and the rate 7.2% during 2001 to 2009. Of the components of GDP, service sector is showing a faster growth of above 9% per annum and constitutes 65% of GDP. Of the services sector, the fastest growth is seen in financial services. The sectors of agriculture and industries lagged behind. of the number of new issues coming into the capital market for raising funds from public, through prospectus, financial institutions and financial companies dominated the market with a share of around 30% of the total issues.

Fiscal state in India is none too encouraging. The centre is financing even current expenditure by capital revenues. Gross fiscal deficit was as high as 7.4% in 1993-94 but fell to 6.5% in 1995-96 and rose to 10% of GDP in 2001-02. Revenue deficit, as per cent of gross fiscal deficit was as high as 50%, during the recent past. Centre's Interest Burden Constitutes about 38% of the total revenue receipts while subsidies and defence works out to another 38% of the revenue receipts. Fiscal profligacy and inefficiency is seen in huge current account deficit and growth of non-plan expenditure more than the plan expenditure. Interest payments as per cent of revenue receipts was around 50% during 2003-05. Administration and subsidies are the other items accounting for the largest share in total revenue receipts. After passage of Fiscal responsibility and Budgetory Management Act of 2003, the fiscal deficit is being brought down in stages to 4% of GDP borrowing in 2008-09 when the fiscal deficit shot up to 4.5% of GDP; it was around 1 to 2% after 2003.

Fiscal Reforms initiated since 1992 were continued. Fiscal deficit is to be contained to less than 4%-5% over a period of time. RBI credit to government is declining and that of banks is increasing. As the government borrowing is at market related rates, the gilts have become attractive on the one hand but increased the interest burden of the government on the other hand. The creation of ad-hocs which will lead to creation of currency has been replaced in 1997-98 by ways and means of advances to the centre, from the RBI.

The Central Budgets during the recent years aimed at fiscal consolidation by reducing the gross fiscal deficit, reduction of reliance on RBI to limit the monetisation of government debt and proposed continued changes in Direct and Indirect Tax measures. The maximum personal income tax rate is 30% plus a surcharge and Corporate Tax rate is also about 30 plus surcharge and there was abolition of double taxation of dividend income by taxing it only in the hands of Companies. The MAT has been modified by excluding export profits and lowering the tax rate. Voluntary disclosure of income and wealth (VDIS) scheme was implemented to garner more revenue by legalising the black money or hidden wealth by payment of 30% on the declared hidden income. But it was no success.

Peak import duty was reduced from 50% to 40%., and the duties are rationalised and simplified. The same is the case of excise duties. The interest tax on banks and FIs was reduced from 3% to 2%. But the scope of service tax was widened to include Lorry Service, consultation charges of engineers, contractor fees travel/tour services and many banking and brokerage services etc. The Central Budget aimed at simplification of the tax structure and reduction of tax incidence along with the widening of the tax base.

Monetary and Credit Trends

In the banking and credit area, the latest RBI credit policy announced during the recent years carried further the reforms towards liberalisation, initiated since 1992. These reforms moved towards flexible interest rates, freer banking operations, removal of restrictions on deposit rates and lending rates of banks, freer markets and a move to Capital Account convertibility of the Rupee.

In tune with recession in many sectors of the economy, but controlled inflation at around 4%, interest rates on banks' lending and deposit rates were lowered by signaling through a lowering of Bank rate from 10% to 6% and reduction of CRR from 10% to 5% by stages from October 1977 and reduction of SLR uniformly to 25% on both aggregate deposits and incremental aggregate deposit liabilities. Bridge loans are allowed again to boost the primary market. Trade, housing and auto finance get softer treatment from banks. Interest rates are freed from controls and flexible Bank rate policy was adopted. In sum India moved a step closer to global markets in banking and finance in the latest policy, by which Indian corporates would benefit.

A further step is taken in integrating various financial markets in the domestic field and those domestic markets with the global financial markets. The PLR of banks and FIs for term lending is made uniform and separate from that on short-term lending. MMMFs are allowed to invest in corporate bonds and debentures. Money Market Operations are streamlined by raising all transactions through primary dealers and by reducing minimum size of operations to Rs. 5 crores from Rs. 10 crores. The minimum size of issue of CDs is also reduced from Rs. 10 lakhs to Rs. 5 lakhs.

In the government securities market, 14 day TBs were introduced, in addition to 91 day and 364 day Treasury bill. FFIs are allowed to operate in gilt edged market and the retailing of government securities is allowed by the commercial banks. Auction system for both Treasury bills and dated securities is to be continued and to broaden the market participation, a uniform price auction method is introduced.

To integrate the domestic market with the foreign markets, banks are allowed to borrow abroad and invest upto 15% of Tier I capital or $ 10 million whichever is higher. In addition, to deepen and widen the foreign market, the RBI allowed the forward cover facility to NRI depositors, NRERA and FCNR (B) account holders which was withdrawn later due to lower international rates.

With a view to moving towards capital account convertibility, exporters and exchange earners are now allowed to retain 50% of their earnings abroad. 100% EOUs and EPZ units will continue to keep upto 70% of their earnings abroad. Indian project exporters will not have to go to the RBI and banks are authorised to grant them foreign currency for a variety of purposes in respect of project execution. ADs are now allowed to undertake forfeiting of medium term export receivables. Mutual funds can invest some of their funds abroad. Joint venture projects will now be cleared by ADs only upto some limits. Corporates are now allowed to open offices abroad. Current and capital account expenditures by them will be allowed out of EEFC Accounts.

The recent credit policies have far reaching implications for integration of domestic financial markets and for a move towards globalisation. Yields on corporate debt will also decline with those on gilts. Those who linked their borrowing rates on debt to the bank rate or deposit rate will stand to gain as in the case of IDBI, IFCI and ICICI and UTI. Lower bank lending rate will boost the corporate bottom lines. Core industries such as steel, cement infrastructure and petro-chemicals will be the major gainers. Many giants like SAIL, L & T, Tata Steel, TELCO etc. will benefit by lower interest burden.

The money market is linked to government debt market and these links are now strengthened by the financial reforms. By allowing banks and MMMFs to invest in bonds of the corporate sector, money market and capital market are again linked up. By allowing the Mutual funds to invest abroad and of banks to have foreign investments, the trends to globalisation was initiated. Similarly, the move to Capital Account convertibility was strengthened by allowing exporters to leave funds abroad and corporates to have foreign offices and spend for both current and capital expenditure. Joint venture undertakings are now allowed to be financed by ADs without reference to RBI upto certain limits. ADs are also given discretion in granting foreign currencies to those on current account. Most foreign banks which have tie ups with international Agencies will participate in forfeiting business. Indian banks will have to start such tie ups to do forfeiting business on any worthwhile scale. They have started internet banking and electronic transfer of funds.

Trade Policy and Trends

The period of 1992-97 was that of the eighth plan. This period saw many changes in industrial licensing, freeing of capital issues, SEBI control on all players and procedures in the stock and capital markets and in trade policy and financial reforms.

The exim policy announced for the Ninth Plan 1997-2002 provided for some major changes during 1997-98. One major step is freeing of more imports, as many as 392 items have been placed on OGL. Another 150 items can be imported under SIL. About 18% of the total items have been moved out of the restrictive list. At this rate, it was possible to dismantle all the restrictions on imports by the end of 2007-08. More importantly, over two-thirds of these items removed from restrictions are consumer goods.

Another significant move is the introduction of a new duty entitlement pass book scheme over the value based Advance Licence Scheme and quantity based Advance Licence Scheme. (VABAL and QABAL). The new scheme is transparent, easier to operate and the credit transferable as before.

Payment of duty at the maximum level is brought down to 30%. Duty on EPCG scheme is reduced from 15% to 10%. Deemed export status is widened and exports of agro sector, Hi-Tech exports and of SSI products are given special incentives. Deemed export status is extended to oil and gas sectors to encourage domestic sourcing of inputs.

WTO organisation of which India is a member aims at freer exports of Agro products textiles, readymade fabrics, services and Patented Products. In tune with that, the exim policy aims at encouraging such exports. Anti-dumping mechanism has been strengthened as India has to protect its domestic producers. The export obligation under advance Licence has been increased from 12 to 18 months.

Software units are permitted on line data communications for DTA sales also. Electronic hardware units are allowed to sell upto 50% in DTA. The setting up of a green channel facility for clearance of export and import consignments for exporters with a good track record helps to reduce red tape and delay. The computerisation of the office of DGFT by 1998 helped quickening of the process of application disposal, and acceptance of applications on floppy and through E-Mail.

The corporate executive in this scenario has to tune himself for electronic form of communications for disposal of cases. The regional offices of DGFT will help disposal of cases upto a value of ₹5 crores which will quicken the export procedures to some extent.

Export credit is now cheaper and ADs are now permitted to provide to exporters cheaper and larger funds to promote their export trade, particularly to SEZs, EOUs and EPZs.

Liberalised Access to Foreign Borrowing

All infrastructural projects, Telecom and greenfield projects are permitted access to external commercial borrowing upto 35% of their project cost since June 1996. Besides export-oriented units and EPCG licence holders have been given additional incentives in the form of allowing access to ECBs upto $15 million for meeting even project related rupee expenditure. No restriction on number of Euro-issues to be floated in a year is laid down. Corporates and institutions are allowed to raise ECBs upto $3 million in a year. These GDR issues are not to be used for investment in stock market and real estate. Banks. FIIs and NBFCs registered with RBI are also allowed to raise funds through GDRs which will help their lending to corporates.

The thrust of RBI's global policy is to deregulate interest rates, move to a free market system in the financial area and bring about a more efficient functioning of the financial system to promote globalisation. The lendable resources of banks are augmented and the cost of funds to corporates is lowered. There is an attempt at level playing in lending domestic funds and foreign funds. The banks' operational efficiency and profitability should improve with their freedom to borrow anywhere in India or abroad and face competitiveness both at home and abroad. This should help corporates also by lower interest cost and greater access to bank funds and to global resources. The recent credit policy allowed some liberalisation of transactions on capital account also, and for strengthening of the rupee exchange rate of Rs. 44 from Rs. 48, a dollar in June-July 2009. There was much depreciation of the rupee in 2011-12 to Rs. 54 to 55 per dollar.

Capital and Stock Markets

The operation of FFIs and FIIs and foreign security firms led to large inflows for FDI and portfolio investment. The influence of their investment on the stock market is felt to be perceptible. The inflows and outflows also affect the Domestic money market and FOREX market. The stability of Rupee was upset and rupee depreciated during Sept. 1995-Feb, 96 and again for some period in Nov. 1997 to Aug. 1998 due to these foreign pressures. The fall in Hong kong share prices in a crisis form in Oct. 1997 led to worldwide stock price falls. India has also felt the impact of that albeit to a smaller extent. The foreign forces are thus operating on all the domestic markets. This is particularly more prominent in the episodes of 2008 and 2009 due to global recession and financial crisis in Europe.

The above cross section forces influencing the domestic markets led to greater volatility and higher risk scenario. Risk management has assumed a greater significance than before. The Corporate Manager has to sharpen his tools and expertise to face these changing and transitional forces and adopt techniques suitable to the new situation and new openings.

Conclusion

The alternatives open and the strategies to be adopted are now widened to corporates. The environmental forces and global trends will have deep impact on the Indian Corporates. They have to face an ever changing environment and frequent changes in forces operating on them and their adaptation to these environmental forces which are themselves changing in a dynamic fashion are posing new challenges to the Corporate Manager. It is in this context that he has to weigh the pros and cons of the alternative techniques and models of adaptation, available to him. Globalisation has come to stay and study of environmental trends to corporates confirm increasing role of global operators both in India and abroad. The Indian corporates are now gearing themselves to improve their competitive efficiency and expand to play a global role.

PART – II

INTERNATIONAL TRADE THEORY AND PRACTICE

6

Trade Theory

Domestic and Foreign Trade

Imports and exports are the inputs or outputs of the various sectors of the economy with which Finance Managers are concerned in the government sector or the business sector. In order that they may appreciate why exports and imports take place and to understand the mechanics of such flows, it would be appropriate to set out macro-economic theory behind micro-level exports and imports. Besides, in the accounts of balance of payments, merchandise trade constitutes the bulk of either receipts or payments (about 70 per cent), which explains the importance of trade theory.

Trade takes place within a nation from one state to another or from one centre to another to meet the felt needs of the people and explained by differences in demand and supply and in costs and prices. The reasons are the same for trade across national borders as within borders. But there are some differences between domestic trade and foreign trade. Firstly, in the present-day nation states, currency and credit system differs from country to country leading to problems of payments involving exchange of one currency for another. As imports and exports may not be equal in any given period, deficits or surpluses, and problems of payment in settlement of trade balances would also arise. Secondly, because of geographical distances, transport and insurance costs would be substantial and constitute a major factor in export and import decisions. Thirdly, government policies and regulations differ from country to country and the barriers of customs, exchange and trade controls and other policy regulations have to be observed. These may constitute either an incentive or a hindrance to the promotion of trade across national borders and materially affect costs, prices and time of delivery schedules. The above factors, particularly transport costs, freight, insurance and tariff, would definitely alter the normal equilibrium point in the theory of costless transfers or in any consideration of demand-supply forces internally and internationally.

Besides, across borders and nations, the wage and price systems differ. The factor endowments of states are also different leading to comparative cost differences due to wages paid to labour, interest on capital and rent on land and buildings etc. In particular, cost differentials in respect of labour and relative abundance or scarcity of capital play a more important part in international trade than in internal trade. There is a higher degree of immobility of factors across nations than within a nation. Despite some emigration and brain drain, labour cannot move freely as between nations, nor can capital flow freely in view of government regulations. Natural endowments of mines and minerals, land, oil, etc., also differ significantly from country to country. The international immobility of factors of production tend to perpetuate differences in return to them and in costs of production of goods and services. These differences are the basic causes of international trade.

Across the borders, there are also differences in economic and political systems, in language, customs and traditions. The system of measurement and pricing may be different. Such differences make trading across nations difficult, and calls for a separate treatment of the subject. Inter-regional and international trade is concerned with overcoming problems of space, differences in monetary exchange, trade, wage and payment system across nations. These are some of the reasons why international trade is studied separately.

International trade is a branch of a wider subject of international finance, as the latter deals not only with exports and imports but with financing of all economic and commercial relations of nations, including loans, grants and flow or capital across nations, relations between banking and financial systems of countries, international markets in commodities, services and factors of production, etc.

Barter Trade vs. Money Trade

If trade takes place as between commodities or services without the intervention of money or any medium of exchange, it is called barter. Historically, for a number of years in the past, international trade used to take place on a barter basis such as the spices of the Far East exchanging for muslin cloth of Dacca. Subsequently, goods were exchanged for precious stones, gold, silver, etc., after which regular paper money had come into vogue in all the national currency systems. Even today some foreign trade of India takes place on a barter basis with some East European countries and Russia. Such trade takes place in inconvertible rupees, which will be studied in a later chapter. But growth of international trade is not possible if each country attempts to balance its trade with the other on a bilateral basis and all its requirements cannot be met nor can it get its supplies at the least cost from the cheapest sources.

As such, it is to the advantage of all countries and in the interests of expansion of world trade that multilateral trade is encouraged which is the objective of international institutions like the IMF and IBRD. In this type of trade, payment is to be made in an acceptable international medium of exchange, namely, gold or convertible foreign currencies, such as dollar, sterling, etc.

Classical Trade Theories — Absolute Advantage

Any trade theory should explain why trade takes place as between countries, what are the gains from trade and what goods or services each country would export or import and at what costs and prices, etc. The Classical economists, namely, Adam Smith, Ricardo, Mill, etc., believed in the labour theory of value which implies that the value of a product in a country is determined by its labour content. As labour cannot move internationally, differences in the labour content of goods and in returns to labour, namely, wage rates, cannot be equalised. As such, those writers held that some countries have absolute advantage in the production of some goods as the labour value is the lowest for those goods in those countries. Their goods can be exchanged with other countries in return for goods which have a higher labour value in so far as the first country is concerned. Let us take the following example of absolute advantage for trade to take place as between India and the USA:

Production of One Man in One Week

Product	In the USA	In India
Wheat	8 kg	2 kg.
Cloth	2 yards	6 yards

India has an absolute advantage in the production of cloth vis-a-vis USA as the former can produce 6 yards per week as against 2 yards per week in the USA. Similarly, the USA has an absolute advantage in the production of wheat. In India, the exchange ratio between wheat and cloth is 1:3 while in the USA it is 4:1. If wheat of USA is exchanged for cloth of India, trade can take place at any ratio lying between 1:3 and 4:1. For example, a ratio of 2:2 will benefit both the countries. In India, two units of cloth cannot secure more than 1/3 rd unit of wheat while in USA two unit of wheat cannot secure more than 1/4th unit of cloth.

Another possibility is that the labour content of both the commodities is less in the USA than in India, evidencing the fact that labour is more efficient in the USA than in India. Even then trade can take place so long as there is a comparative advantage for any one country over another in the production of any commodity. Consider the following production possibilities.

Production of One Man in One Week

Product	USA	India
Wheat	6 kg.	2 kg.
Cloth	10 yards	6 yards

Comparative Advantage

The principle developed by David Ricardo is the theory of comparative advantage, according to which, a country would export that commodity in which it had a greater comparative advantage and import a commodity in which it has a greater comparative disadvantage. Normally, if no trade takes place in the above example, India can have only 2 kg. of wheat and 6 yards of cloth. With trade taking place, India can produce 12 yards of cloth, keep for itself 6 yards and exchange the other 6 yards for wheat from the USA. They may be able to get probably as much as 3 kg. of wheat even at the domestic exchange ratio in the USA. The assumptions on which the theory is developed is that the commodities are produced only with labour, that value of products is determined by their labour content, and that there is unrestricted flow of trade without tariffs and duties etc., and that costs of transport, insurance etc., are ignored. Thus, trade can take place so long as all countries are not equally efficient in the production of every commodity.

Once it is established that there are certain conditions under which trade can take place, the next issue is what goods are exported or imported. This is decided on the basis of the labour content of goods at home and abroad, so far as the labour content at home is more than abroad it is advantageous to import the commodity from abroad. The ratio at which the goods are exchanged will depend on the theory of reciprocal demand, developed by J.S. Mill, which will be referred to later. This is the demand aspect of international trade.

Labour Theory of Value — Supply of Goods

On the supply side, production in each country depends on the factor endowments. The basic postulate of classical theory is that labour alone is the cause of production and that the value of output depends on the labour content of goods. This theory has certain weaknesses. Labour is not equally homogeneous throughout the country, not to speak of differences as between the countries. Labour cannot, therefore, command equal wages. Besides goods are not produced by labour alone but by a combination of factor inputs such as land, labour, capital, enterprise, etc.

In view of the inherent weaknesses of labour theory, G. Haberler developed the theory of opportunity costs which takes into account not only labour but all factors of production to produce a given output per week. A technique known as production possibility curve is used to demonstrate how trade takes place as between countries. To simplify, a model of two countries and two commodities is used here. Assuming constant returns to scale, which means that a given increase in inputs would lead to a proportionate increase in output, the production possibility curves of USA and India can be set out as follows:

These curves indicated that with given resources, the country, USA, can either produce 6 units of wheat or 10 units of cloth and the marginal rate of transformation is 6:10. A similar ratio for India is 2:6 which implies a price ratio of 2 units of wheat to 6 units of cloth. Any higher price for cloth will shift resources away from wheat into cloth. Given the above ratios in the USA and India, trade can take place at any ratio between 36 : 60 and 20 : 60, corresponding to their domestic price ratios of 6 : 10 and 2 : 6. The actual ratio will depend upon the demand conditions. Suppose the actual ratio is 30 : 60, India will gain by 10 units of wheat per every 60 units of cloth, produced

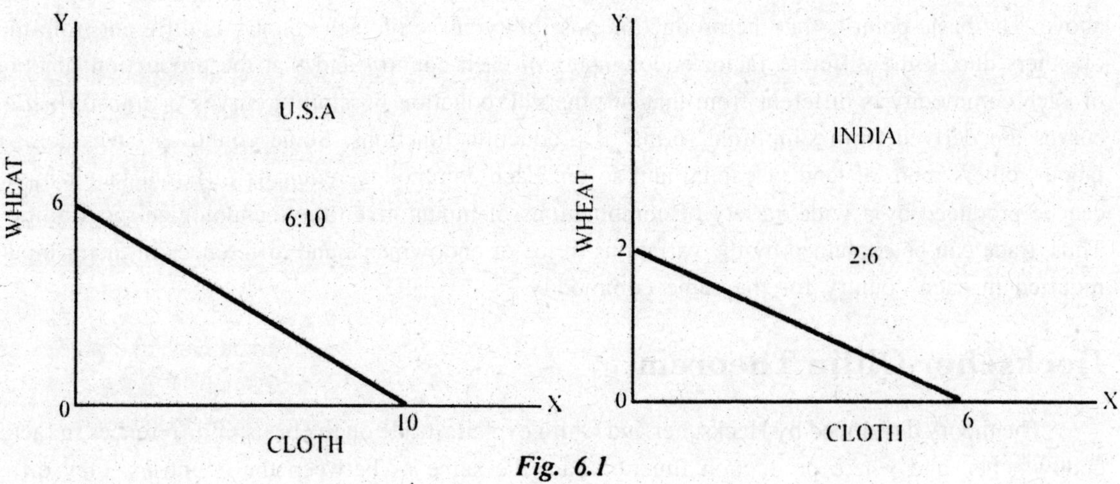

Fig. 6.1

at that ratio. Similarly, USA also gains by having to pay less for cloth, which they now import from India, at a rate of 5 units of wheat (instead of 6 units) for 10 units of cloth. Geometrically, these gains can be represented as follows:

As compared to their domestic ratios of 36:60 and 20:60, international trade can take place in the range of 36 to 20 units of wheat for 60 units of cloth, say at 30 units when both countries will stand to gain. The gain to India, for example, can be a shift of their consumption from C to C1 in Fig. 2.

A similar demonstration of trade and gains can be made with increasing opportunity costs of production or decreasing opportunity costs, as in the case of constant opportunity costs demonstrated

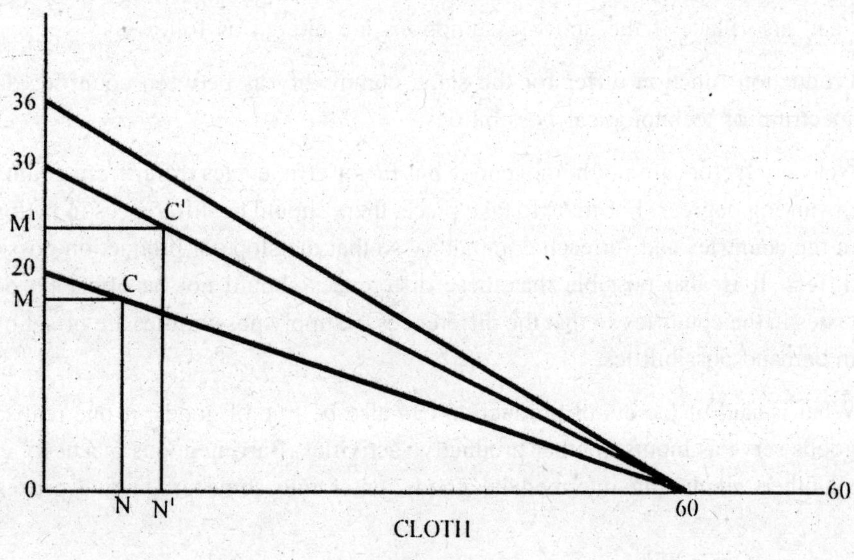

Fig. 6.2

above. The basic point is that the production possibility curve of each country is different from that of others due to the different factor endowments of each country and that the production function of each commodity is different from that of others. Production possibility curves or transformation curves are derived from simplified forms of production functions. Some countries have more of labour, others more of land or capital and so on. Each commodity requiring different factor inputs can be produced by a wide variety of combinations of inputs given the technological possibilities. Thus, trade can be explained by the variations in factor endowments and differences in factor inputs required in each country for the same commodity.

Heckscher-Ohlin Theorem

The theory developed by Heckscher and Ohlin explains trade on the basis of differences in factor endowments, and where production functions are the same as between the countries, they differ as between commodities. Due to differences in factor endowments, countries produce the same commodity at different costs and prices. According to this theory, a country with capital abundance would export capital-intensive goods while a country with labour abundance would export labour intensive goods. The term "capital-intensive" is to be interpreted in a relative sense. The abundance or scarcity can be understood either in a physical sense or in money value, both of which would uphold the Heckscher-Ohlin theory. Thus, capital abundance would cheapen the reward to capital, and cost of the product produced by the use of more capital would also be lower in the country with capital abundance than that with labour abundance. Specific factors or non-competing groups of factors such as mines, minerals, oil, etc., also explain the presence of comparative cost advantage. Thus, trade can take place if the US goods are more capital-intensive in exchange for Indian goods which are more labour-intensive.

Trade can also place if the above assumptions are altered as follows:

(1) Production function differ for the same commodity as between countries due to a wide spectrum of technological possibilities.

(2) Not only factors are not homogenous but factor efficiencies differ from country to country in varying degrees. For trade to take place, there should be differences in factor efficiencies in the countries and for each commodity so that the slope of production possibility curves differs. It is also possible that these differences should not be offset by differences in tastes in the countries so that the differences in supply possibilities are offset by differences in demand possibilities.

(3) What is said of factors of production can also be true of goods, if one realises that many goods serve as inputs in other productive activities. Barring goods meant for consumption, all others, including intermediate goods, enter into some productive process or other.

Theory of Commodity and Factor Price Equalisation

Trade is possible under certain conditions referred to above. Advantages accrue to both the exporting and importing countries in varying degrees. What goods are to be exported and what goods are to be imported and in what order will be decided upon on the basis of relative cost price parities in the respective countries which in turn depend on the factor endowments of countries and relative mix of factor inputs used in the production of each commodity.

Trade will continue until relative price differences for each commodity as between countries disappear, leaving aside transportation and other costs. Following commodity price equalisation, trade brings about factor price equalisation as between countries under conditions of perfect competition and free market forces, free mobility with marginal costs equal to prices and rewards to factors equal to their marginal products. In real world, such equalisation is not brought about as trade potentialities are vast.

Leontief Paradox

Under conditions of perfect competition and no transport costs, international trade is expected to lead to changes in commodity prices and factor prices so as to equalise commodity prices and factor prices at home and abroad. Transport costs and imperfections in the market, however, stand in the way of the operation of Heckscher-Ohlin theorem in the above sense. Not only prices of goods would not be equalised but factor prices would also not be equalised. The Ohlin thesis that a capital-rich country would export capital-intensive goods and labour-rich country would export labour-intensive goods was disproved by Leontief in respect of the U.S.A. First, it is possible that Ohlin-Heckscher assumptions such as perfect competition and absence of transport costs may not hold good. The other assumptions that production functions differ as between commodities but are the same for each commodity as between countries and that production functions are homogeneous of the first degree may not be realistic. These assumptions lead to different factor intensities for different products. Secondly, in the real world, factors not being homogeneous, a capital-intensive country like the USA may really be labour-intensive due to the embodiment of capital in labour. Thirdly, there could be factor reversals in the sense that there need not be one to one correspondence between factor intensities and factor prices. There is thus possibilities that the Leontief paradox can be explained away and Heckscher-Ohlin theorem can still hold good, given its assumptions.

Reciprocal Demand (J.S. Mill)

While the law of comparative costs determines the supply of goods in foreign trade, the law of reciprocal demand sets the prices at which trade will take place. More correctly, it is both demand and supply together which determine the prices. The demand aspects are explained in terms of what J.S. Mill called "the law of reciprocal demand" which reflects the strength of US demand for Indian cloth and Indian demand for US wheat. As in an auction system, quantities offered for sale are cleared by bids and counter-bids, with the price emerging as a result. Such offers and bids in the auctioneering system of international trade are represented by offer curves by Marshall and Edgeworth. These curves can be regarded as demand curves, representing various amounts of cloth which USA would demand in exchange for a unit of wheat and of units of wheat which India would demand in exchange for one unit of cloth.

Indifference Curves

The factors which operate behind the offer curves are the utility or satisfaction represented by a set of indifference curves which are the points of indifference as between various combinations of wheat and cloth in the consumption pattern of an individual. As for individuals, a set of community indifference curves for India and the USA are drawn, despite the limitations of lack of aggregation of individual satisfactions (welfare) differences in the tastes and habits of individuals and lack of a possible stability in their tastes and habits. The indifference curves for each country are drawn and superimposed on the production possibility curve of the country to determine the point of equilibrium between production and consumption for each country. A tangent (TT) to the indifference curve represents the marginal rate of substitution in consumption and one to the production possibility curve represents the marginal rate of transformation in production.

If these two tangents are identical, equilibrium is set between production and consumption at home as shown in Fig. 3. The tangent to ICo is also tangent to the production possibility curve at point C. This tangent has a double meaning as it represents the exchange ratio between two commodities and the marginal transformation ratio of the two goods in production.

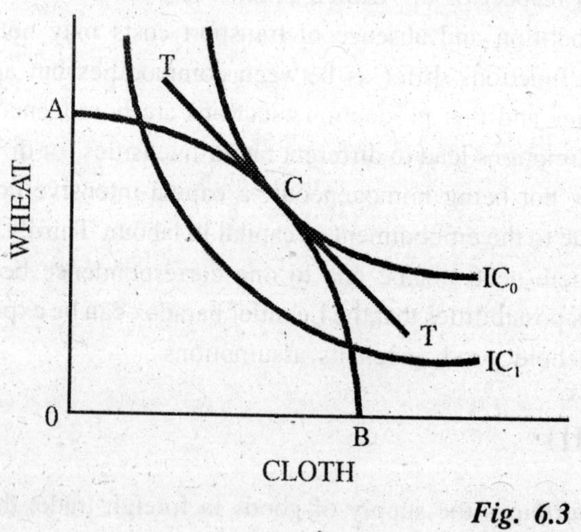

AB= Production Possibility Curve.
IC_0 and IC_1 = Community Indifference Curves.
TT = Tangent to both AB and IC_0 and C is the equilibrium point.

Fig. 6.3

A similar equilibrium can be seen in the USA before trade. These equilibria will be disturbed once trade starts and a new and higher level of equilibrium representing greater welfare is set in.

The equilibrium conditions are as follows:

The marginal rate of transformation in production should be the same as the marginal rate of substitution in consumption:

$$\frac{MC_1}{MC_2} = \frac{MRS_1}{MRS_2}$$

Production:

MC = MRT = Price (Marginal cost = Marginal Rate of transformation in Production = MRP)

Consumption:

MU = MRS = Price (Marginal utility = Marginal Rate of substitution in Consumption = MRC)

General Equilibrium:

MRT = MRS or MC = MU

MRC = MRP

Diagrammatic representation of the new equilibrium after trade is shown in Fig. 4 and Fig. 5.

USA specialises in wheat.

$R_1 R_2$ of wheat exchanged for MN of cloth. After trade the country will be on a higher IC_2 with equilibrium point at C'.

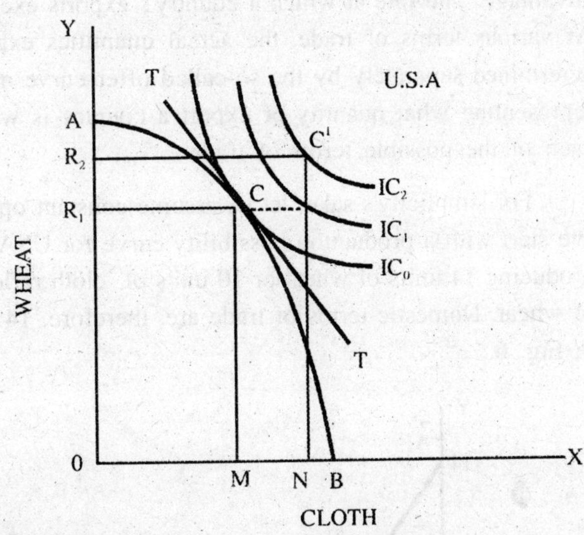

Fig. 6.4

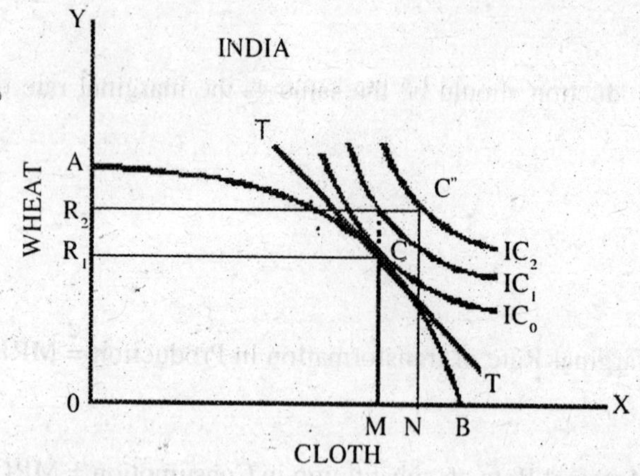

India specialises in cloth. India will also be on a higher IC at the point of equilibrium of C" after trade.

Fig. 6.5

Offer Curves

The nations trade with each other due to the differences in comparative costs or advantages in production possibilities. Both the countries stand to gain by trading due to cost advantages as well as by specialisation by each country in the production of the good, in which it has a comparative advantage. The rate at which a country's exports exchange for imports is called the terms of trade. At various terms of trade, the actual quantities exported vis-a-vis quantities imported would be determined separately by the so-called offer curve mechanism. Offer curves are the loci of points representing what quantity of export a country is willing to make for what quantity of import at each of the possible terms of trade.

For simplicity's sake, let us assume constant opportunity costs and construct the offer curves. We start with a production possibility curve for USA for wheat and cloth showing its capability of producing 14 units of wheat or 10 units of cloth reflecting its comparative advantage in production of wheat. Domestic terms of trade are, therefore, 14:10 if there is no trade. This is represented as in Fig. 6.

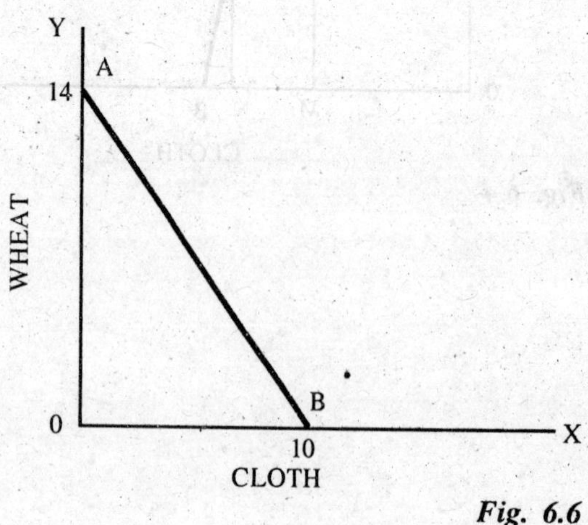

USA can either produce 14 units of wheat of 10 units of cloth.

A B Domestic Terms of Trade.

Fig. 6.6

The above price or exchange ratio can also be shown as a straight line running from the origin, each with a particular angle representing the ratio of exchange between wheat and cloth. This is shown in Fig. 7.

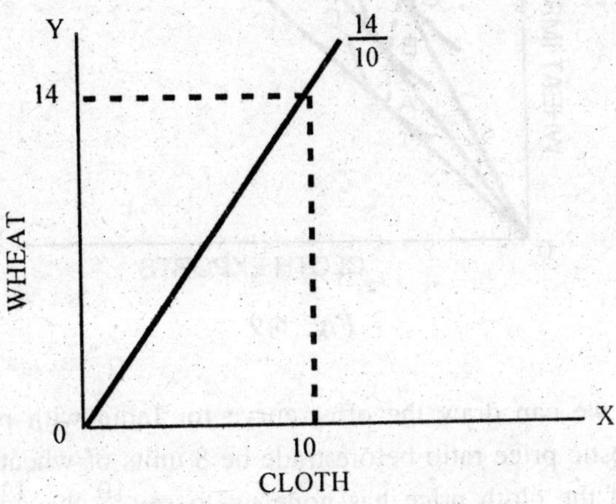

Fig. 6.7: Domestic Price Rate

If the price ratio is different from the above ratio, implying that wheat in USA has become dearer, say 14:12, trade would take place as USA would buy cloth from India in exchange for wheat. The USA offer curve can be drawn as in Fig. 8 with 'O' as the production point and the axes as depicting exports and imports.

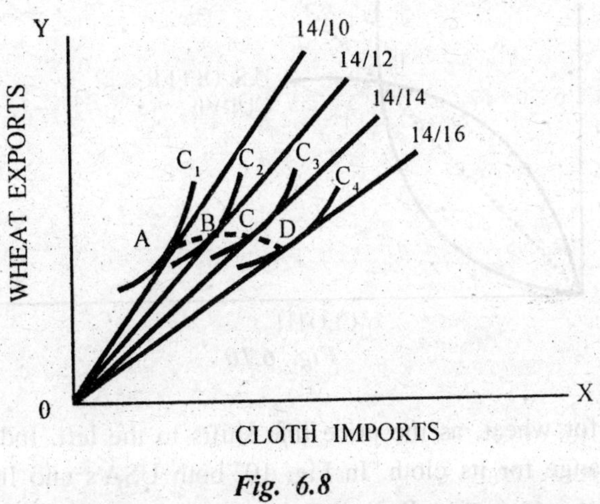

Fig. 6.8

Each of the lines from the origin depicts the various terms of trade depending upon the slope of the line. The points A, B, C, etc., are the points of tangency between the production possibility lines and community indifference curves, C1, C2, C3, etc. At point B, USA will offer more wheat to get more cloth but not quite as much as it was willing to give up earlier. At point C, this trend was more pronounced with the result that this offer curve becomes concave to the origin, reflecting the decreasing marginal satisfaction derived from increasing quantities of the same commodity.

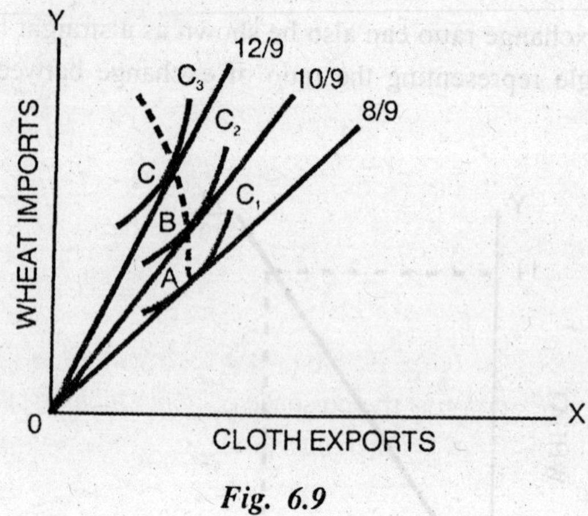

Fig. 6.9

On the same basis, we can draw the offer curve for India with respect to cloth and wheat as in Fig. 9. Let the domestic price ratio before trade be 8 units of wheat for 9 units of cloth. India would buy more wheat if the cloth price has gone up to say $\frac{10}{9}$ or $\frac{12}{9}$.

Thus, with trade, the offer curve shifts counter-clockwise, convex to the origin for the same reason that USA offer curve becomes concave.

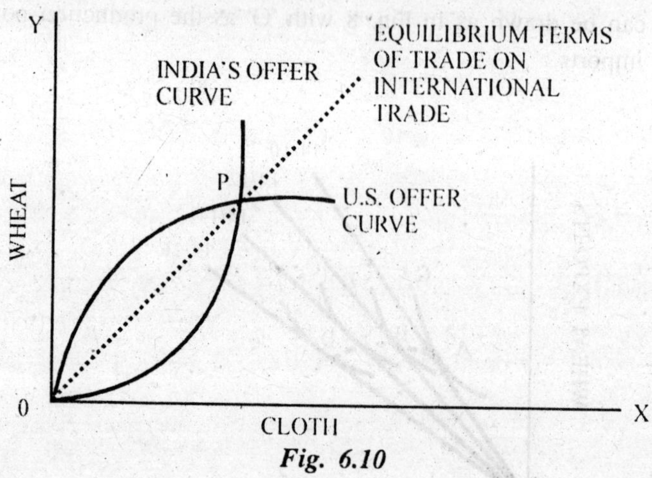

Fig. 6.10

At a lower price for wheat, as the price line shifts to the left, India would buy more wheat from the USA in exchange for its cloth. In Fig. 10, both USA's and India's offer curves are put together and the point of intersection P depicts the equilibrium terms of trade at which both USA and India would be willing to trade as India would want to export just that quantity of cloth which the USA would like to import and USA would like to export just that quantity of wheat which India would like to import. Then trade would be mutually advantageous and gains from trade emerge.

The above is a simple two-country-two-commodity model depicted under conditions of constant opportunity costs. A similar analysis has to be made for increasing opportunity costs or decreasing opportunity costs. Multi-country and multi-commodity models require mathematical application which is beyond the scope of this book.

Changes in Demand

If there is a shift in the offer curve due to, say, an increase in Indian demand for US wheat, it will no doubt result in improved terms of trade for USA but it is doubtful whether it will lead to a higher level of welfare. The reason is the presence of many indeterminates and subjective factors. The USA may move to a higher indifference curve because India would now be offering a larger quantity of cloth for a given unit of American wheat due to a rise in its demand for wheat. Similarly, technological progress may shift the offer curve to the left, in the sense that more wheat can now be offered by USA for the same amount of Indian cloth. The resulting change in the terms of trade may not necessarily improve the level of welfare in USA due to trade taking place. The ability of a country to improve the terms of trade will depend on its size of the share in the world trade and relative elasticities of supply and demand for internationally-traded goods.

Trade Gains

Trade results in gains in consumption and welfare and leads to greater specialisation and larger production. Trade also produces effects on income distribution. Larger production and larger consumption do not necessarily lead to greater welfare of all the sections of the people. In some countries trade may increase wages, while in others the returns to capital may rise. The export sector and merchant community may gain at the expense of producers or other sections of the population. If the gains to the former sections are larger than those to the latter, the former should be able to compensate the latter to conclude that the welfare of the community as a whole has increased. Introduction of distributional effects of trade on a nation would alter the conclusions arrived at through production and consumption effects of trade. Thus, trade is expected to alter savings and investment in such a way as to promote growth of the economy, if the gains to those benefited are greater than the losses to others. Gains and losses would also depend on the relative average propensities and marginal propensities to consume and save of the respective sections of the community.

Generalised Trade Theory

The theory of international trade has been generalised by Prof. Gray to include the role of multi-national corporations (MNC). Traditional theories depend on the different resource endowments of different countries and their international immobility. Once these assumption are invalidated by the MNCs through trade and private foreign direct investment, we have to introduce other variables and trade barriers for the purpose of trade theory.

If the resources are specific and immobile but their services are transferable through MNCs, we have a theory of foreign direct investment through MNCs. What Prof. Gray[1] has done is to link international trade with international production and foreign direct investment. Harry Johnson and Bertil Ohlin had introduced the various trade barriers and locational factors into the theory of international trade. The specific barriers to trade incorporated into the trade theory were: (1) Transportation costs; (2) Psychic distance factors; and (3) Government policy variables like tariffs and subsidies.

The orthodox theory is based on the multi-factor and multi-commodity approach to the factor proportions theory and emphasises gains from trade through larger consumption and greater specialisation in production in line with the comparative cost theory. The change needed for the Generalised Theory is to incorporate factors like specific goods used as input and firm-specific factors of production and product-specific inputs, and integrate the theory of international production with w[illegible]de and foreign direct investment. John H. Dunning's approach in his eclectic theory of "Trade Location of Economic Activity and MNC" involved three sets of determinants of international production, viz., ownership-specific advantages of enterprises of one nationality over those of another, internationalisation of incentives and location specific advantages. Gray's theory adopts Dunning's approach and takes into account the transferability of proprietary technology and services of other specific natural resources or endowments of some countries into others through the MNCs.

The short-run analysis assumes constant global factoral supplies. These supplies are distributed among countries so as to maximise international production and to achieve the lowest costs of production, thanks to the foreign direct investment and the activities of MNCs. The new international allocation of resources could maximise the rates of return to factors of production which are both internationally mobile and immobile and product specific factors are spread out across borders so as to optimise international production. A proper allocation of resource inputs to maximise production and to determine the optimum pattern of trade across national boundaries is simultaneously determined to set an equilibrium according to this theory. Any disturbance in factoral inputs in production and resource allocation would change the pattern of production internationally and thus of trade accordingly.

The proprietary technology, know-how and product specific capital may not allow substitution of such factors in the input-mix of a product. This would then result in a quasi-rent payable to that specific factor. The MNCs would achieve the maximum feasible net value added and quasi-rent for their specific factors by achieving optimum geographical distribution of their assets and their sales and earnings. The MNCs may use such factors and distribute the products or services involving the use of such inputs among nations so as to lower costs of production through better specialisation and increased scales of production. The MNCs may transfer such specific factors of production or their services from one country to another if such relocation would lower the costs and enable the company to make their goods available in the market at a price lower than any other source of supply, namely, through trade or through import substitution measures in the domestic economy.

---

1. Prof. H. Peter Gray: "A Generalised Theory of International Trade" and "Towards a Unified Theory of International Trade, International Production and Direct Foreign Investment" (The Macmillan Press, 1976).

The only countervailing factors to be considered from the point of the LDCs are the alternatives to foreign direct investment, namely, imports through trade or domestic production in substitution of products available through the MNCs. As quasi-rent or the monopoly element of the MNCs is not desirable for promoting strict competition in any economy, MNCs are not prima facie desirable unless the other alternatives are not feasible in the existing set-up. It is in this context that the role of MNCs in international division of labour and in trade has to be carefully assessed in respect of the LDCs.

In the Generalised Theory of International Trade, the changes necessitated by introduction of multi-nationals and foreign direct investment are: (i) The assumptions for a two-country and two-commodity model are to be changed; (ii) There are five categories of inputs, viz.. capital, land, skilled labour and unskilled labour, enterprise and technology, some of which are firm specific and some product specific; (iii) The principal resource endowments, tastes and production functions are supposed to be known and fixed and trade is balanced by means of free exchange rates.

The international transfer of resources and factors of production wherever possible is in substitution for international trade for goods and services. Such migration can be in respect of product specific factors, or firm specific technology and can either be trade creating or trade supplanting or trade diverting. The factors for and against any proposal for foreign direct investment are complex and each case is to be studied separately. Given the assumption that the MNC could make a direct investment and transfer their proprietary specific inputs and product specific inputs to another country, this could create markets and expand trade on a global basis which would be in the interests of the host country or not depending on the alternatives available to the host country.

If the potential for investment by MNC exist through expected higher quasi-rents in the host country, the short-term equilibrium is disturbed and foreign direct investment takes place. A reverse position can be visualised when foreign direct investment will leave the country due to changes in the pattern of costs and prices or of demand to lower the quasi-rents.

The effects of impediments to trade through commercial policies, transportation costs and other psychological barriers would get reflected in the pattern of costs and prices of foreign goods versus domestic goods. The ranking of importable goods versus domestic country and of exportable goods in the foreign country would change. Psychic distance impediments to trade would get reflected through changes in cost and prices of tradable commodities.

The generalised theory of international trade would also incorporate the location specific factors through foreign direct investments by MNCs as also country specific and product specific factors of production. The final outcome of international trade would depend upon the changes introduced in the production patterns in the two countries under consideration and in the costs and prices, including the factor prices in the respective countries and a host of other factors including tastes, habits, technological levels, etc.

7

Haberler's Opportunity Cost Theory

Introduction

Ricardo's theory of comparative cost advantage suffers from a number of limitations. In particular, labour is not the only factor of production, nor is it homogeneous. Different factors are combined in the production process and the proportion in which they are combined also varies from country to country and from goods to goods. It is, therefore, unrealistic to value goods in terms of labour only and to apply the comparative cost advantage to determine the extent of international trade. Prof. G. Haberler[1] tried to salvage this theory by reformulating it in terms of opportunity costs, which dispenses with the need for labour theory of value. He replaced labour costs of goods by opportunity costs.

What is Opportunity Cost?

Opportunity cost relates to opportunities of alternatives foregone to produce one more unit of a good. Thus, if production of one unit of commodity A is possible by foregoing two units of commodity B, then the opportunity cost of commodity A is two units of commodity B. The opportunity cost of one commodity is measured in terms of another commodity. It refers to the alternatives foregone or opportunities given up.

---

1. Gottfried Von Haberler, "The Theory of International Trade". Also read, "A Survey of International Trade Theory", 1955.

Representation Of Opportunity Costs

Since opportunity costs are measured in terms of one commodity against the other, the thesis of Haberler can be explained in terms of two commodities and two countries for simplicity. The opportunity costs of two commodities is the exchange ratio of these two, expressed in the form of a production possibilities curve or production transformation curve. Thus, a country's exchange ratio for two commodities is represented by its production possibility curve. This is constructed on the basis of the following assumptions:

(1) Two commodities only are produced.

(2) Supply of factors is fixed and they are perfectly substitutable.

(3) Perfect competition in factors and in commodities.

(4) Price is equal to the marginal cost of producing each product.

(5) Similarly, factor price is equal to the marginal cost of the factor.

(6) There is full employment to all given resources.

(7) Production function in the sense of relation between inputs and outputs is different for different commodities and the production possibility curve is a simplified form of production function.

Position Under Constant Returns (Costs)

Under conditions of constant returns to scale, the production transformation curve is a straight line for two commodities, namely, wheat and cloth. The slope of the curve, representing the ratio of exchange, is constant. It also reflects the ratio of marginal opportunity cost of wheat and cloth. This would mean that the marginal rate of transformation of one commodity into another is constant, which is a condition for constant returns. This is represented in the diagram below.

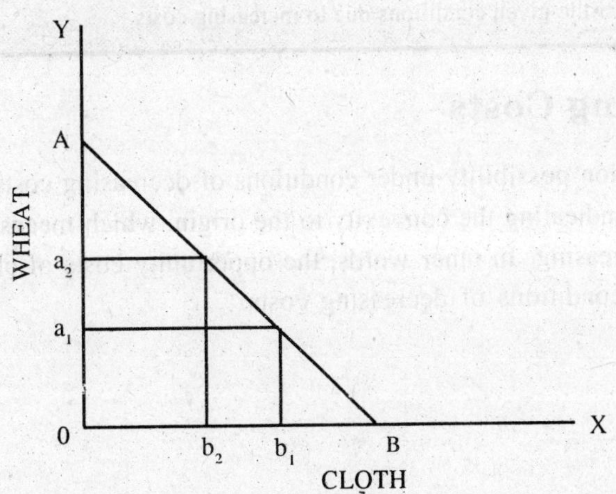

Fig. 7.1: Production Transformation Curve under C R

AB is the production possibility or transformation curve under constant returns. Given the resources of the country, it can either produce OA of wheat or OB of cloth or both commodities in different combinations like $Oa_1 + Ob_1$ or $Oa_2 + Ob_2$. The slope of the curve denotes the marginal rate of transformation, namely, how much of one commo-dity is to be sacrificed for securing one more unit of another commodity. This would thus represent also the exchange ratio between wheat and cloth.

Position Under Increasing Costs

Given the above assumptions, the production possibility curve will be concave to the origin, if the law of increasing costs (or diminishing returns) operates. The concavity of the curve shows that if the production of cloth is substituted for wheat, for every additional unit of cloth, more and more of wheat is to be sacrificed. The marginal rate of transformation or exchange is increasing. The curve is represented as follows:

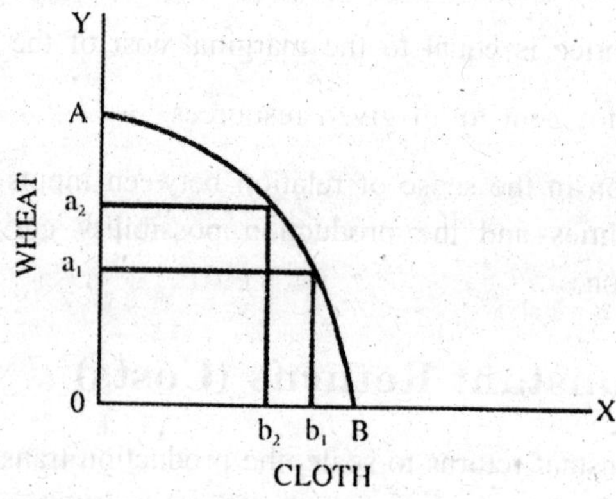

Fig. 7.2: Production Transformation Curve under D R

AB is the production transformation curve, which is concave to the origin. a_1 a_2 of wheat is to be given up to get b_1 b_2 more of cloth. This indicates increasing costs or decreasing returns.

As we move along the curve AB, for each additional unit of cloth sacrificed, a larger and larger quantity of wheat will be exchanged under the given conditions due to increasing costs.

Case of Decreasing Costs

The curve of production possibility under conditions of decreasing costs is shown below. The curve is negative-sloping, indicating the convexity to the origin, which means that the marginal rate of substitution will be decreasing. In other words, the opportunity costs of cloth in terms of wheat will be decreasing under conditions of decreasing costs.

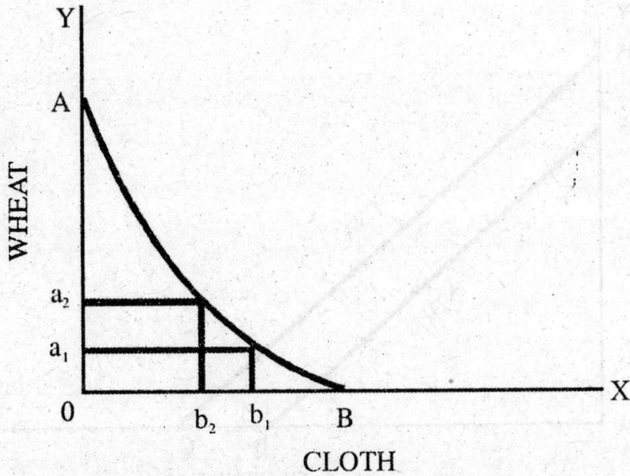

Fig. 7.3: Production Transformation Curve under IR

> AB is the production transformation curve which is convex to the origin. a_1 a_2 of wheat is to be given up to get b_1 b_2 of cloth. For every additional unit of cloth sacrificed, a smaller quantity of wheat will be exchanged due to decreasing costs. In the real world, both the assumptions of constant costs and decreasing costs are rare. What really obtains is a case of increasing costs in the production of goods.

International Trade Possibilities

As in the case of Ricardo's labour theory of value, there are possibilities of gainful trade if the production possibility curves in the two countries are of different slopes. The domestic rate of exchange between any two commodities is given by the slope of its production possibility curve, which expresses the relative commodity prices in the two countries. The opportunity costs of producing a commodity at the margin is given by the relative values of different factors of production, required for producing a unit of that commodity at the margin.

The international trade possibilities can be set out under three heads, namely: (1) Conditions of constant returns or constant rate of transformation; (2) Conditions of increasing costs; and (3) Conditions of decreasing costs.

Trade Under Conditions of Constant Costs

The transformation curves under constant costs are straight lines. If the slope of these two curves is the same, then no gainful trade can take place as the exchange ratios represented by the slope of the two curves are the same in both the countries. This means that prices are the same in both countries and hence no trade can take place. This can be represented by the following diagram.

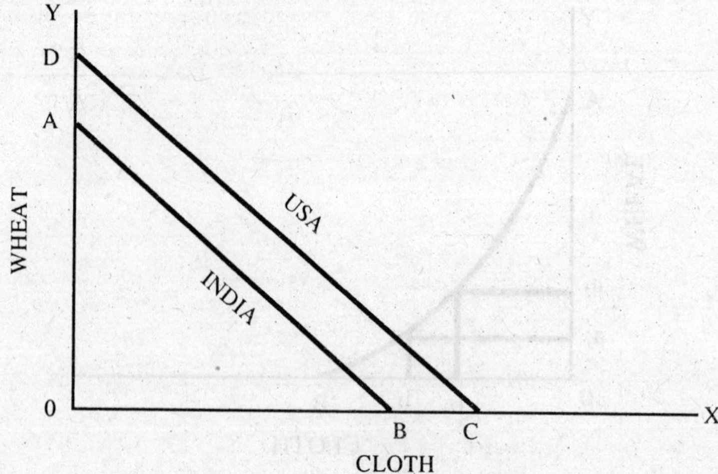

Fig. 7.4: PP Curves of Two Countries under C R - No Trade

AB and CD are the production possibility curves (PP curves) of two countries which are parallel and have the same slope.

The possibility of trade arises when the slopes of these two curves are different. These possibilities are discussed graphically as follows. Take, for example, that the graph AB is that of the production possibility curve of India and CD is that of USA.

Case I: USA can produce both wheat and cloth cheaper than India but it has a comparative cost advantage in the production of wheat as reflected in the slope of the curve. India produces both less efficiently but has a less comparative disadvantage in the production of cloth relative to wheat. The graphs are as follows:

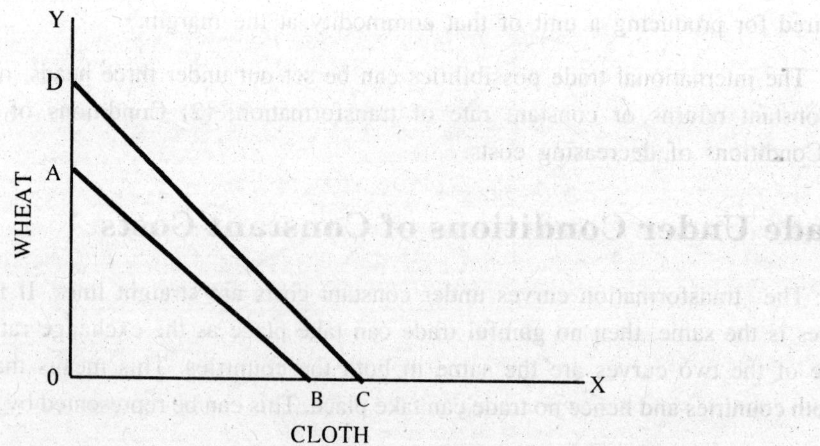

Fig. 7.5: PP Curves of Two Countries when Trade can take Place

AB is PP Curve of India and CD is PP Curve of USA. AB curve shows that although India has a cost disadvantage in both commodities relative to USA, it has less cost disadvantage in the case of cloth. Hence, trade can take place.

Case II: India and USA can produce cloth at equal cost, while in the production of wheat, USA has a comparative cost advantage. This can be depicted as follows:

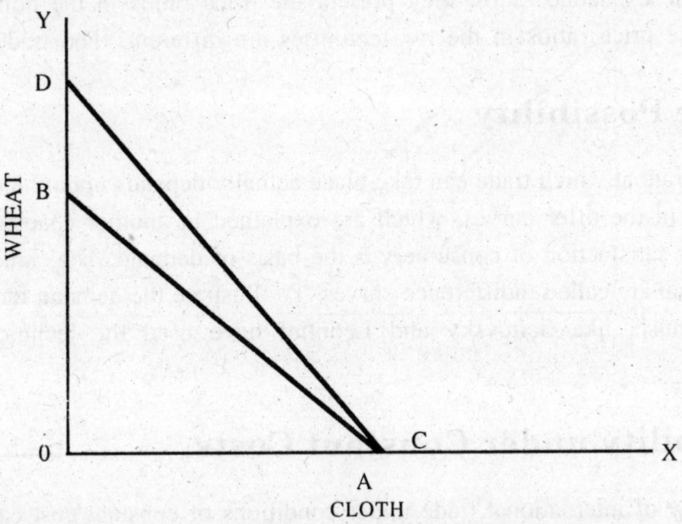

Fig. 7.6: PP Curves of Two Countries when Trade can take Place

AB and CD curves are drawn to show that on the X-axis, the common point of A and C implies that costs in the production of cloth are equal in both countries. But CD is higher than AB, depicting a comparative cost advantage of USA in wheat. Hence, trade can still take place.

Case III: USA can have absolute cost advantage in wheat while India can have absolute cost advantage in cloth. This can be depicted as follows:

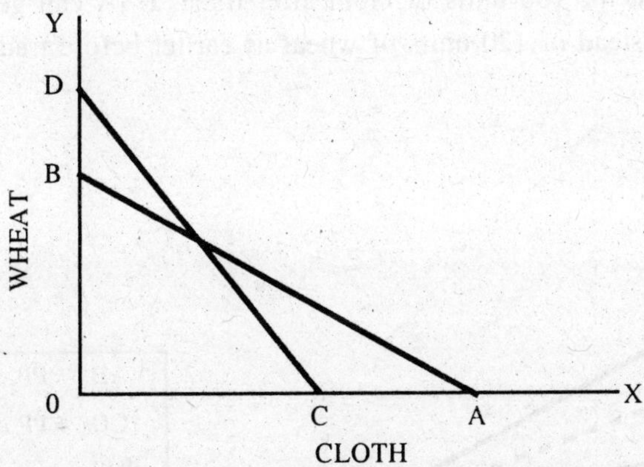

Fig. 7.7: PP Curves of Two Countries when Trade can take Place

CD transformation curve shows more comparative advantage in wheat while AB shows more comparative advantage in cloth. In this case also trade can take place.

As there is absolute cost advantage in wheat in USA, it can specialise in wheat while India can specialise in cloth and gainful trade can take place in this case also. As the production possibility curves show also the exchange ratios, they present the price ratios in the domestic economy. In other words, if these price ratios in the two countries are different, then trade can take place.

Actual Trade Possibility

The exchange rate at which trade can take place actually depends upon the demand conditions, which are reflected in the offer curves, which are explained in another chapter. Behind the offer curves, the utility or satisfaction of consumers is the basis of demand. The amount of satisfaction is represented by what are called indifference curves. To illustrate the demand factor in international trade, many economists like Scitovsky and Leontief have used the technique of community indifference curves.

Trade Possibility under Constant Costs

The actual flow of international trade under conditions of constant cost can be demonstrated with the help of price ratios or exchange ratios. Let us assume for simplicity's sake that production possibility curves of USA and India are juxtaposed in one diagram with exchange ratios of 100 : 60 for India, and 100 : 120 for USA. Under constant costs, these curves are straight lines. When trade takes place between wheat of USA and cloth of India, the exchange ratio to be gainful to both, should be in between the domestic exchange ratios of 100 : 60 and 100 : 120. Thus, it may be around 100 : 90 which is shown below:

Thus, while domestically, India can get only 60 units of wheat for 100 units of cloth, it can now get 90 units of wheat for 100 units of cloth after trade. USA can get 100 units of cloth for 90 units of wheat only, instead of 120 units of wheat as earlier before trade. So both the countries stand to gain by trade.

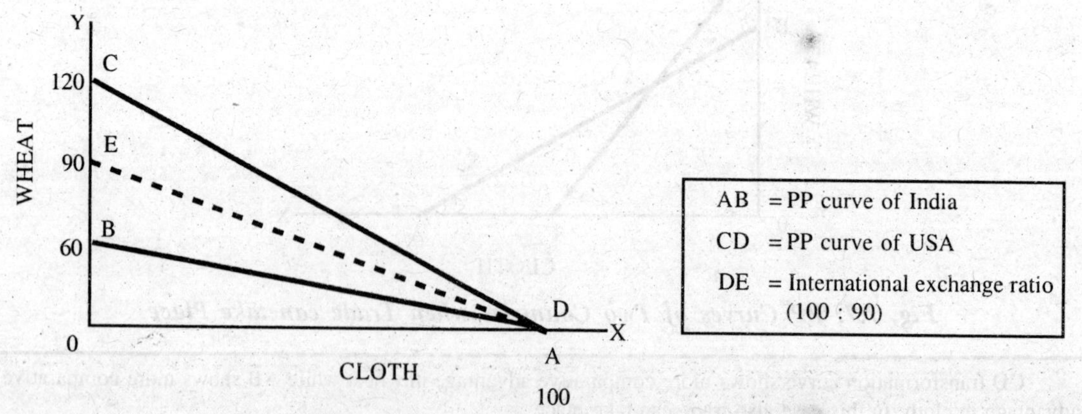

Fig. 7.8: PP Curves under CR and Exchange Ratios

Case of Increasing Costs

In actual world, constant costs are an unrealistic assumption. There will be mostly increasing costs following an increase in production. Even decreasing costs is a rarity and a short-run phenomenon. The case of increasing costs can be demonstrated by the production possibility curve for increasing costs which is concave to the origin and by juxtaposing it with the price line reflecting the domestic demand conditions. This is shown below:

AB is the PP curve while CD is the domestic price line, based on internal demand, drawn as a tangent to AB, to touch it at E, which is the equilibrium point where the supply of output equals demand. Under increasing cost conditions, there can be no complete specialisation in any one commodity but there will be partial specialisation and both domestic production and imports will be there for each good. After trade, the demand line changes to MN, which is the international price line, giving a new equilibrium point E_1 where output coincides with the new demand for both wheat and cloth. It will be seen that after trade, India can consume more of both commodities than that it could produce with its own resources before trade.

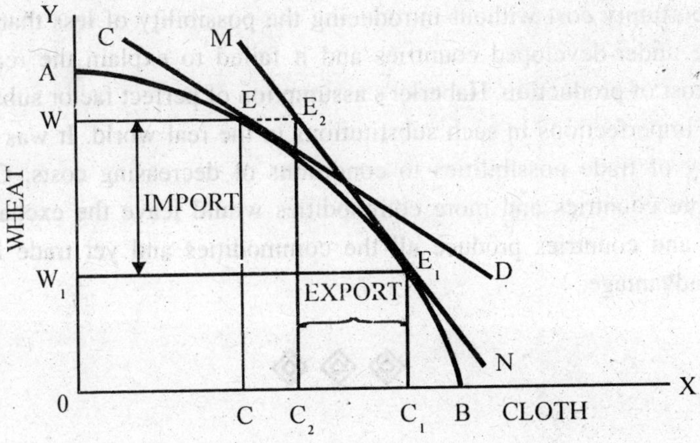

Fig. 7.9: PP Curves under DR - Trade Possibility

> At the old equilibrium point (E), consumption was OW of wheat and OC of cloth. At the new equilibrium point (E1), consumption would be OW of wheat and OC2 of cloth which is possible due to specialisation. OC2 is larger than OC. (E1) is the new equilibrium in production and E2 is the new equilibrium in consumption, which is possible due to trade. Production of wheat was OW1 and of cloth OC1 but the country (India) exports C1C2 of cloth and imports WW1 of wheat. By specialisation in cloth, there will be more production. Accordingly, consumption of cloth can also increase as well as exports of cloth to maintain the domestic level of consumption of wheat at OW. Thus, trade leads to more consumption and larger gains and greater welfare.

India continues to produce both wheat and cloth after trade also but due to specialisation in cloth, it can produce more of cloth and less of wheat. The production of cloth can increase more than necessary to compensate for wheat production foregone through imports from USA, which is specialising in wheat. Thus, under conditions of increasing cost, specialisation would lead to producing more of the same commodities in which the country has a comparative cost advantage. There will still be gain from trade through specialisation but not as much as under complete specialisation, which is possible under conditions of constant costs.

Evaluation

Haberler's contribution was an improvement upon the classical version of labour theory of value. While the classical theory explained mainly under constant costs the opportunity cost approach explains the theory under varying cost conditions. The use of more than one factor and the application of equilibrium analysis with the price ratio of commodities have been demonstrated in Haberler's opportunity cost doctrine. The gains from trade are more clearly brought out under varying cost conditions and the possibility of partial specialisation under increasing cost conditions, which is more realistic has been explained, above.

Criticism

On the other hand, even Haberler's theory suffers from many limitations. It simply replaced labour cost by opportunity cost without introducing the possibility of less than full employment as is prevalent in the under-developed countries and it failed to explain the reasons underlying the differences in the cost of production. Haberler's assumption of perfect factor substitutability is subject to question due to imperfections in such substitutions in the real world. It was graham who applied the classical theory of trade possibilities to conditions of decreasing costs. Graham said that the introduction of more countries and more commodities would leave the exchange ratio less at the mercy of demand and countries produce all the commodities and yet trade in the order of their comparative cost advantage.

8

Heckscher – Ohlin Theorem

Introduction

Modern economists were critical of the classical theory of international trade on various grounds. Although they accepted that comparative cost differences are the basis of trade, that was considered not adequate as they have not explained why comparative cost differences take place. The real basis of trade is something what modern economists have explained. In particular, Heckscher and Ohlin have applied the general equilibrium tools to the analysis of international trade. According to them, international trade is but a special case of inter-local or inter-regional trade. E.F. Heckscher first wrote his book, "The Effects of Foreign Trade on the Distribution of Income" in 1919. Bertil Ohlin,[1] his disciple, perfected the new approach to the analysis of international trade in his book, "Inter-regional and International Trade" published in 1933.

Is there any Need for a Separate Theory?

Heckscher, Ohlin and other modern economists have argued that there is no need for a separate theory of international trade for the following reasons:

(1) Factor mobility among the countries is as restricted as among the regions within the country and some factor mobility exists among the countries as in Europe or Latin America.

(2) The differences in the currencies among nations do not stand in the way of trade due to the existence of arrangements for exchange of currencies in the foreign exchange market.

(3) The existence of transport costs is not a unique factor in international trade as transport costs exist in domestic trade also.

1. Bertil Ohlin (1899-1979) is recipient of the Nobel Prize for economics, awarded in 1977 by the Royal Swedish Academy for his contributions to the theory of international trade. He shared the prize with Prof. J. E. Meade. Bertil Ohlin published his book. "Inter-regional and International Trade" in 1933.

(4) The comparative cost differentials can exist even in internal trade within the regions as in international trade.

(5) The other differences alleged to exist between internal and international trade like national frontiers, tariff and other restrictions, differences in customs and habits of people of different nations are not insurmountable obstacles and at the most, constitute differences in degree rather than in kind so far as internal and international trades are concerned.

Basis of Ohlin's Theory

Ohlin started with the comparative cost theory of the classical writers but built into it the general theory of value and the mutual interdependence in price theory between commodity prices and factor prices and analysed the demand and supply factors to arrive at the fundamental equilibrium, under the general theory of value. While the classical theory is a single market theory based only on time dimension. Ohlin's theory is a multi-market theory based on time and space dimensions to explain the phenomenon of international trade.

Elements of Ohlin's Theory

In its simplest terms, Ohlin's model is also a two-factor and two-commodity and two-country model as that of classical writers but the latter had based only on one factor. The basis of trade is the relative cost differentials of commodities as between countries. These cost differences are the same thing as price differences in the classical theory, as price is equal to the marginal cost of the commodity.

These price differences are explained by Ohlin by differences in factor prices resulting from differences in factor endowments in the different countries. Thus, in the final analysis, differences in factor endowments explain international trade.

That is why Ohlin's theory is also called factor proportions analysis. Some countries have abundance of labour, they are labour rich, and others have abundance of capital, they are capital rich. The labour rich countries have lower wage rates and specialise in the production of labour-intensive goods, which will necessarily be produced at lower costs and lower prices; while the capital rich countries specialise in the production of capital-intensive goods which will be produced at relatively lower costs and prices.

The labour-rich countries export labour-intensive goods while capital-rich countries export capital-intensive goods and thus international trade takes place.

Assumptions

The above theory assumes the following points:

(1) There is perfect competition in commodity and factor markets such that the price of a commodity is equal to its marginal cost and the price of a factor is equal to its marginal product.

(2) It is a two-factor (labour and capital) two-commodity (X and Y) and two country model. One country is labour abundant and the other one is capital abundant. Good X is capital-intensive and good Y is labour intensive.

(3) Demand conditions are identical in both countries.

(4) Production functions are homogeneous of the first degree, which results in constant costs of production.

(5) There are no restrictions on trade and no transport costs.

Given the above assumptions, international trade takes place on the basis of differences in factor endowments.

Factor Abundance — Main Factor Explained

This factor abundance can be explained in terms of price criterion and physical criterion.

Abundance of Capital in the USA

Assume that USA produces machine tools using more of capital relative to labour and hence its price is lower as compared to that in India. Under these conditions, USA will specialise in the production of machine tools, because production of this item involves capital-intensive methods and capital is relatively cheaper in USA.

Labour Abundance in India

Similarly, India will specialise in the production of cloth, as its production is labour-intensive and it is labour-abundant and its price is lower relatively.

Thus, a capital-abundant country specialises in capital-intensive goods and a labour-abundant country specialises in labour-intensive goods.

This type of specialisation leads to lower costs and lower commodity prices of the respective commodities. Differences in factor prices and in factor intensities used in the production of goods lead to different costs of production and prices. These differences in prices would cause the international trade to take place. Thus, the capital abundant country exports capital-intensive goods which are relatively cheap and in which it specialises and labour-intensive goods are imported as labour is more expensive, relatively in that country. The reverse is true in the case of a labour-abundant country.

Price Criterion

The labour abundance can be represented in the price ratios as follows:

$$(PK/PL)\ A < (PK/PL)\ B$$

Where P is the price of factors, K and L stand for capital and labour respectively. From the price ratios given above, it is seen that capital is abundant in country A, as its price is lower relatively there than in country B.

Similarly, country B is labour-abundant, and its price is lower than in country A. Let us assume that there are two commodities namely, X (capital intensive) and Y (labour-intensive) produced by both the countries. If X is cheaper in country A, it is due to the use of cheaper factor of capital more in country A; in the case of commodity Y it is cheaper in country B due to the larger use of labour which is relatively cheaper in that country. Thus, the capital-abundant country uses more of capital in the production of goods which are capital-intensive (i.e., they require more capital and less labour), and hence such goods are cheaper there as in the case of commodity X. Similarly, the labour-abundant country uses more of its cheap labour in the production of goods which are labour-intensive (i.e., they require more labour and less capital for their production) and hence such goods are cheaper in country B as in the case of commodity Y.

Factor Proportion Theory

To take a concrete case, India is labour-abundant where the labour price, namely, wage rate, is lower. It produces cloth cheaply by the use of larger quantity of labour relative to capital. On the other hand, in USA capital is abundant and its price, namely, interest cost, is lower. It produces machine tools cheaply, relative to cloth. Trade takes place when USA exports machine tools and imports cloth and when India exports cloth and imports machine tools.

The above theory can be demonstrated diagrammatically as in Fig. 1.

From the above analysis, it is clear that commodity X is relatively cheaper in country A and expensive in country B. X is a capital-intensive good, while Y is a labour-intensive good. Thus, the capital-abundant country like USA has a comparative cost advantage in the production of capital-intensive goods. The capital-abundant country can, therefore, export its cheaper capital-intensive goods to country B, while the latter being a labour abundant country can export its labour-intensive good. Trade can thus take place between country A and country B in the commodities X and Y.

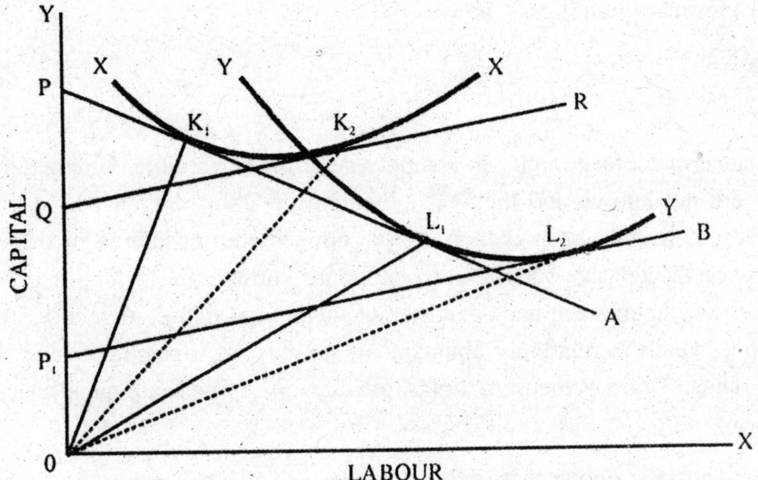

Fig. 8.1 Explanation of International Trade by Ohlin

XX and YY are isoquants, namely, equal product curves, reflecting the factor intensities. Thus, XX is capital-intensive as it falls nearer to the vertical axis Y representing capital. On the same basis, YY is labour-intensive as labour is represented on the horizontal axis 'X'.

Let us assume that both goods can be produced in country A and country B. The price line PA has a slope reflecting the prices of factors, capital and labour, in country A. The points of tangency to the isoquants XX and YY, say, at K1 L1 indicate the equilibrium conditions for factor combinations. Given their price ratio namely (PA) OK1 and OL1 represent equilibrium factor proportions for X and Y commodities in country A. On the same lines, P1 B (price-line for country B) represents the slope of the factor price ratio in country B and QR is parallel to that reflecting the same slope while P1B is tangential to YY isoquant at L2 its parallel QR representing the same factor price ratio as P1B, is tangential to XX isoquant at K2. Thus, the equilibrium factor proportions are OK2 for good X and OL2 for good Y in country B.

In country A, the cost of using capital for both X and Y, is the amount of OP, which is the point at which PA cuts the capital axis Y. In country B, the costs of producing X and Y commodities are OQ and OP1. This means that in country B production of X is more expensive in terms of capital input as OQ (for X commodity) is higher than OP1 (for Y commodity).

The above propositions assume that the demand conditions and factor-endowments are fixed. The data on relative factor price ratios used in the above diagram are derived from the interaction of supply of and demand for factors. The supply relates to factor endowments and demand for factors is a derived demand from the demands for the final products, namely, X and Y.

Physical Criteria

Factor abundance in physical quantities is to be inferred from price ratios used above

$$\left(\frac{PK}{PL}\right) A < \left(\frac{PK}{PL}\right) B$$

Expressed in physical quantities it is =

$$\left(\frac{K}{L}\right)A > \left(\frac{K}{L}\right)B$$

Factor abundance or factor scarcity is a supply determined variable. If demand conditions are not known, prices are not known and the above theorem of Ohlin does not hold good. But Ohlin argued that his theorem would apply even if factor supplies are considered in physical quantities. He asserts that if once the relative supplies of factors are known, the factor price structure can be derived from the relative abundance and scarcities of factors in country A relative to country B. A cheaper factor is one which is relatively abundant in supply and a costlier factor is one which is scarce in supply. Thus, Ohlin's theorem holds good even if physical quantities of factors are considered.

It will be seen from the above that trade takes place due to differences in factor endowments as between the countries and due to factor immobility as between nations. Since factors cannot move between countries, goods move from country to country and trade in goods and services acts as a substitute for factor mobility.

Assumptions of the Theory Given Up

- The extent of trade depends on the conditions of reciprocal demand and the rate of exchange of the respective national currencies.
- Besides, the basic framework of the theory holds if it is extended to more than two commodities and more than two countries.
- The trading countries need not have dissimilar factor supplies as trade can take place due to specialisation and larger markets for any tradable commodity.
- Similarly, if there are qualitative differences in factors as between nations and if factors are not homogeneous, the above trade theory can still apply, as it is based on the general theory of value and the operation of factors of demand and supply.
- The introduction of transport costs and tariff and other barriers to trade will not stand in the way of the theory as they will only increase the costs and reduce the price differential between the countries.
- We had already seen that his theory is applicable under all cost conditions, namely, the law of constant costs, increasing costs and decreasing costs.

Under modern conditions the assumptions of full employment and free trade made under the above theory do not however hold good. There are varying degrees of oligopolistic or imperfect market conditions, both in internal and international trade. Such conditions are particularly marked due to the prevalence of multinational corporations, monopoly big business houses and restrictive trade practices of some of these bodies in the modern world. The Ohlin-Heckscher theory has therefore, been modified by Grey in his restatement of generalised theory, referred to earlier.

THE MODERN THEORY OF INTERNATIONAL TRADE — (EQUILIBRIUM ANALYSIS)

Introduction

The classical theory has failed to explain the ultimate basis of trade, namely, what is the basic cause behind all trade. The classical theory explained only the apparent cause of trade, namely, comparative cost differences which in turn are dependent on the labour or factor efficiencies, whereby a country becomes superior in the production of one or more of the commodities.

The modern theory is also called "The General Equilibrium Theory", which explains why and how much of trade takes place through the application of both supply and demand sides and shows that there is hardly any difference between internal and international trade theory. The value theory which is applicable to trade between two different locations can be extended to cover between two or more nations. The analysis of market forces applicable to a nation through demand and supply forces can be made applicable to trade among nations. The differences in currencies, geographical place, transport costs and barriers to trade do not vitiate the application of value theory to trade but to extension of its application, whereby international trade theory becomes a special case in inter-regional trade.

General Equilibrium Approach

To demonstrate the application of general equilibrium approach to international trade, we require both supply and demand sides of the equation. The supply side is provided by the production possibility curves of Haberler, referred to earlier and demand side by the community indifference curves, which will be explained below.

P-P Curve

As referred to earlier, the production possibility curve presents the loci of points of different combinations of two goods which can be produced in a country with given factor endowments. With the assumption of two commodities and the given factor endowments, the production possibility curves (PP curves) can be drawn to depict the combinations of goods that can be produced. If we assume constant returns to scale, the production possibility curve is a straight line with its slope, indicating the relative cost ratio of producing wheat and cloth respectively. The straight line (shown in Fig. 2) indicates that if we increase production, the ratio of costs of production of wheat to cloth would remain unchanged.

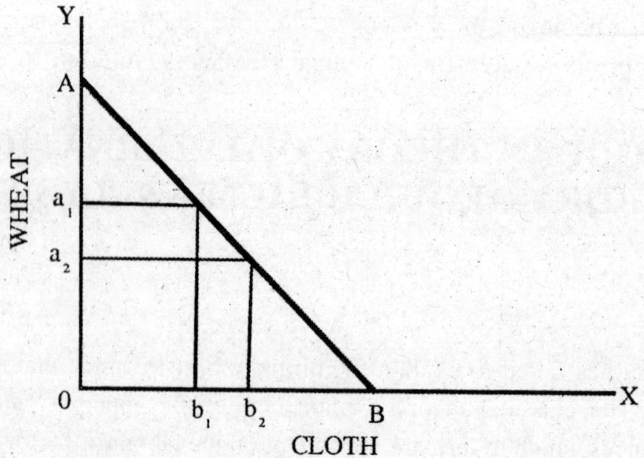

Fig. 8.2 Production Possibility Curve under Constant Costs

AB is the production possibility curve for India. With given factors of production, it can produce either OA of wheat or OB of cloth or various combinations of wheat and cloth such as $Oa_1 + Ob_1$ or $Oa_2 + Ob_2$.

If we further assume increasing cost of production, which is a more realistic assumption, the PP curve is concave to the origin as shown in Fig. 3.

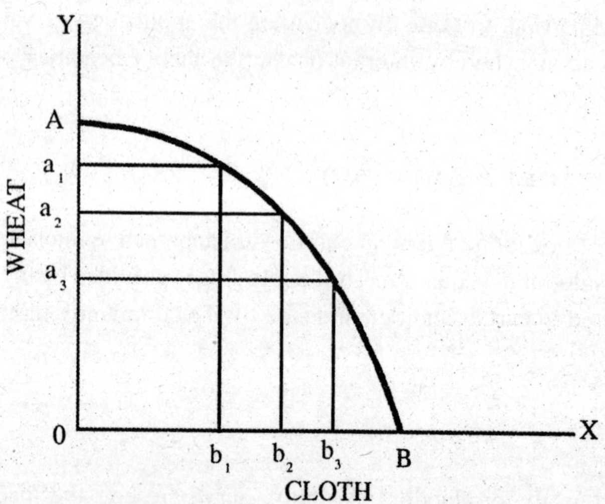

Fig. 8.3 PP Curve for a Country with Increasing Cost of Production

A country can produce either OA of wheat or OB of cloth with the given factor endowments or it can produce both the goods in various combinations, such as $Oa_1 + Ob_1$ or $Oa_2 + Ob_2$, etc. Such PP curves can be drawn for both India and USA in our example and the two commodities considered are wheat and cloth. This PP curve depicts the supply conditions.

Definition of Indifference Curves

For presenting the demand conditions, we have to construct indifference curves. An indifference curve is defined as the locus of points representing alternative combinations of two goods yielding the same amount of satisfaction or utility to the consumer. From the indifference curves of individuals, a community or country indifference curve can also be drawn conceptually. The community indifference curve is a collection of commodity combinations between which the individual consumers of the community are indifferent. The utility or satisfaction is a subjective factor and the summation of subjective factors is not realistic. However, writers like Scitovsky and Vanek have used the concept of community indifference curves as the summation of individual indifference curves for purposes of analysis. A series of indifference curves can thus be drawn for each country, each representing a set of combinations to which the community is indifferent for a given income distribution. If this distribution changes, the indifference curve also changes. A set of such indifferent curves representing various combinations of income is called the indifference map. This is shown diagrammatically in Fig. 4.

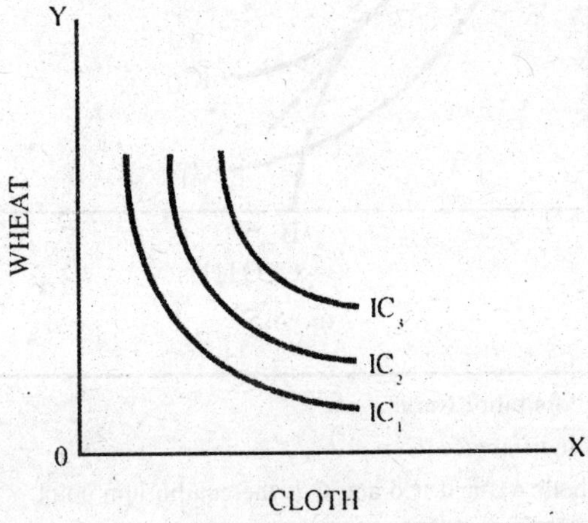

Fig. 8.4: Indifference Map

> On any point on IC_1 curve, the level of satisfaction is the same. On IC_2 the level of satisfaction is higher than on IC_1 and so on.

Application of Indifference Curves

As referred to earlier, the factors which operate behind the demand are the utility and satisfaction represented by a set of indifference curves which are the points of indifference as between various combinations of wheat and cloth in the consumption pattern of an individual. As for individuals, a set of community indifference curves for India and the USA are drawn, despite the limitation of lack of aggregation of individual satisfactions (welfare), differences in the tastes and habits of individuals and lack of possible stability in their tastes and habits. The indifference curves for each country are drawn and superimposed on the production possibility curve of the country to determine the point of equilibrium between production and consumption for each country. A tangent (TT) to the indifference curve represents the marginal rate of substitution in consumption and that (TT) to the production possibility curve represents the marginal rate of transformation in production. TT is also the price or exchange ratio as between the two commodities, wheat and cloth.

If these two tangents are identical, equilibrium is set between production and consumption at home as shown in Fig. 5. The tangent to ICo (TT) is also tangent to the production possibility curve AB at point C. This tangent has a double meaning as it represents the exchange ratio between two commodities in consumption and the marginal transformation ratio of the two goods in production.

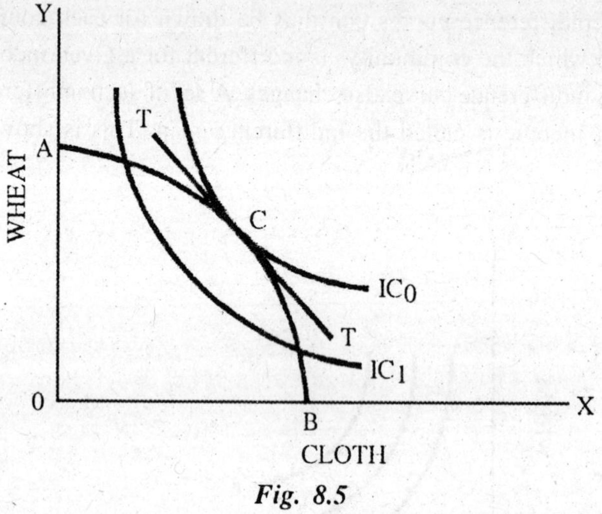

Fig. 8.5

AB	=	Production Possibility Curve
IC_o and IC_1	=	Community Indifference Curves.
TT	=	Tangent to both AB and ICo and C is the equilibrium point.

A similar equilibrium can be seen in the USA before trade. These equilibria will be disturbed, once the trade starts and a new and higher level of equilibrium representing greater welfare is set in.

The equilibrium conditions are as follows:

The marginal rate of transformation (MRT) in production should be the same as the marginal rate of substitution in consumption:

$$\frac{MC_1}{MC_2} = \frac{MRS_1}{MRS_2}$$

Production

MC = MRT = Price (Marginal cost = Marginal rate of transformation in production = MRP)

Consumption

MU = MRS = Price (Marginal utility = Marginal rate of substitution in consumption = MRC)

General Equilibrium

MRT = MRS or MC = MU

MRC = MRP

Diagrammatic representation of the new equilibrium after trade is shown in Figs., 6 and 7, for USA and India respectively.

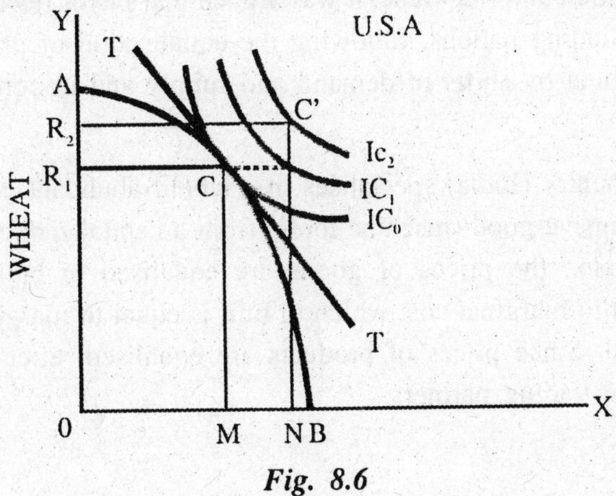

Fig. 8.6

> USA specialises in wheat.
>
> $R_1 R_2$ of wheat exchanged for MN of cloth. After trade the country will be on a higher indifference curve namely, IC_2 with equilibrium point at C'.

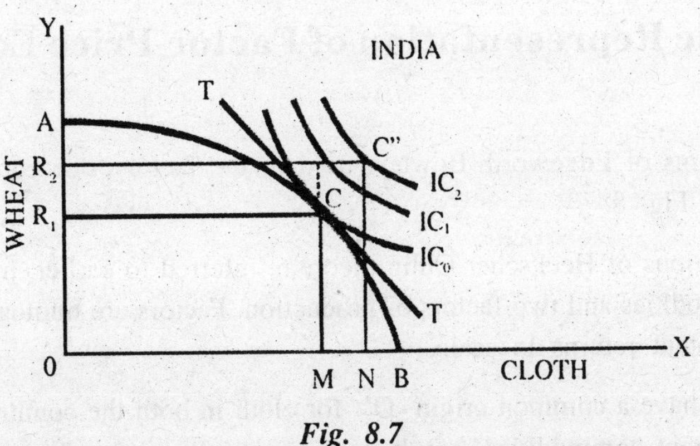

Fig. 8.7

> India specialises in cloth. India will also be on a higher curve IC_2 at the point of equilibrium of C" after trade.

Basic Postulates of Ohlin Theory

The Ohlin theory can be restated in terms of the following two basic postulates.

(1) Factors are immobile internationally and they are the basis for producing goods. The goods produced by the factors can move across the borders or nations leading to international trade. (2) The basis for trade is the differences in factor supplies resulting in differences in factor costs and prices of goods.

Factor-Price Equalisation Theorem

Following Ohlin's theorem, and given the assumptions accompanying the theorem like full employment, free competition and free trade, it was argued that factor rewards or factor prices would be equalised among the trading nations, following the equalisation of prices of traded goods. The equalisation is brought about by shifts of demand and supply and in commodity prices in the two trading countries.

If the labour-rich country (India) specialises in a labour-abundant good (cloth) and exports it in return for a capital-intensive good (machine tools) from a capital-rich country, ignoring transport costs and selling costs, etc., the prices of goods are equalised in both the countries by trade. Commodity price is equal to marginal cost which in turn is equal to marginal product, of the factor, under conditions assumed. Since prices of products are equalised, after trade, factor rewards are also equalised, among the trading partners.

Limitations

There are a number of limiting conditions in the real world, which prevent full factor price equalisation. These limitations are absence of full and free competition and free trade. Besides, the factor supplies are not fixed, nor are the factor proportions in the production of goods, as assumed in Heckscher theorem. As such, full factor price equalisation is not possible in the real world.

Diagrammatic Representation of Factor-Price Equalisation Theorem

The box-diagrams of Edgeworth-Bowley, used in the factor price equalisation theorem, can be represented as in Fig. 8.

All the assumptions of Heckscher-Ohlin theorem, referred to earlier, hold good. Assume two countries, two commodities and two factors of production. Factors are homogeneous and production function shows constant returns to scale.

The two boxes have a common origin 'O' for cloth in both the countries but different factor proportions for different commodities result in two separate origins for wine in Y and Y_1.

As drawn, country A (USA) uses more capital-intensive methods than country B (India) for both wine and cloth. the production functions reflected in the efficiency locus or contract curves, drawn inside the boxes, show constant returns to scale.

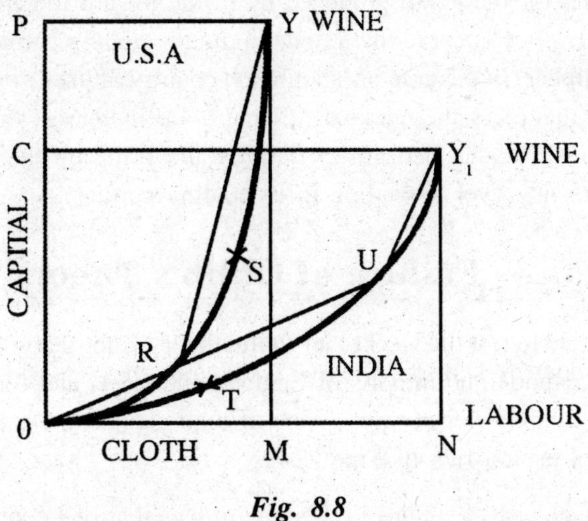

Fig. 8.8

OM YP is the resources diagonal of USA, which is capital-abundant. ONY_1C is the resource diagonal of India, which is labour abundant. ORSY is USA's efficiency locus and its pre-trade equilibrium is S, determined by domestic demand conditions. $OTUY_1$ is India's efficiency locus and its pre-trade equilibrium is T.

Production functions for wine are the same in both the countries as reflected in the slopes of RY and UY1 and similarly, production functions for cloth are the same as reflected in the slopes of OR and OU in the above diagram.

After trade opens up, USA moves from S to R and India from T to U. R and U, on the same line from O, represent equal proportions, in which labour and capital are used in the production of cloth in both the countries. Similarly, there are identical factor proportions which are used in the production of wine also. The fact that R and U are on the same line with the same slope indicates equality of prices, and factor price equalisation is brought about following equalisation of product prices in both the countries.

Under the conditions assumed, payments to factors are rewards equal to their marginal product and under equilibrium-conditions, marginal product = marginal cost, which is equal to the price of the commodity.

Since, marginal cost is equal to the price of a commodity and marginal cost is the factor reward under conditions assumed, it follows that rewards to each factor are the same in both the trading countries after trade, if the prices of commodities produced by them are equal after trade.

How trade brings about factor price equalisation can be explained as follows.

In the capital-rich country, the reward to capital is lower to start with. After it starts exporting the capital-intensive good, the demand for that good increases. As more capital will be demanded to meet increased demand for the good, produced by it, the reward to capital also increases. In the process, it will push up its price equal to that prevailing in the trading partner, where capital is scarce and hence its reward is higher. In the case of labour-rich country, it uses more of labour in production of its goods and export them. As the demand for that good increases, the prices of the good and that of the factor used in it would also go up. This would bring up the reward for labour in the labour surplus country to the level prevailing in its trading partner.

Leontief Paradox — Failure of Ohlin's Theory

Some economists tried to test the Heckscher-Ohlin theory empirically in the real world situation. MacDougall studied the exports and imports of England and USA, and found that England was not exporting goods of low capital intensity but goods of high capital intensity contrary to the general belief that England is not capital-rich like the USA.

One of the premier empirical studies in this regard was that of Leontief. He studied American exports and imports and concluded that though America was capital-rich, her exports were mainly labour-intensive and her imports were capital-intensive. This is known as the Leontief Paradox. This contradicts the theory of Heckscher-Ohlin that a capital-rich country exports capital-intensive goods while a labour-rich country exports labour-intensive goods.

Paradox Explained

Many reasons were attributed to the failure of Ohlin's theory and the appearance of Leontief Paradox. Firstly, all the assumptions made by the Heckscher-Ohlin theory are not found to be true in the real world. Secondly, the quality and efficiency of labour has to be considered in international comparisons. Thus, if USA's labour is more efficient than its trading partner, then it may appear that it is a labour-rich country and not capital-rich. Thirdly, labour skills are to be treated as embodied capital and as such USA although capital-rich, has a labour highly skilled through embodiment of capital, which makes it appear as labour-rich. A number of other reasons were attributed to the failure of Ohlin's theory in its application in the real world, such as tariff barriers, imperfections in markets, etc.

Contribution of Heckscher and Ohlin

The major contribution of Heckscher and Ohlin lies in their enquiry into the ultimate determinants of trade. Their theorem does not reject the Ricardo Theory as such but supplements it. Ricardo's comparative cost theory is the starting point for the general equilibrium theory of Heckscher and Ohlin. While Ricardo's theory is based on single factor approach, the Ohlin's theorem is built on two factors and sets out in detail inter-relations between commodity prices and factor prices.

Ohlin's theorem supplements Ricardo's theory as it is also based on comparative cost and price advantages. For Ohlin, factor supplies constitute a vital determinant of comparative advantage, while Ricardo did not consider factor supplies at all. Differences in factor endowments led to differences in factor prices and in costs of production in different countries. This may be called the necessary condition for international trade. If different factor combinations exist in the production of different goods, there would also be sufficient condition for trade to take place.

Ohlin's theory is an extension of Ricardo's theory as his single factor model is replaced by two factors, two commodities and two countries model. Ohlin considered that international trade is a special case of inter-regional trade. The framework of Casselian general equilibrium theory, which is applied to internal trade has been used to explain the international trade as well. Multi-market theory of pricing is adopted for this purpose.

The Ricardian assumption of constant returns to scale was extended in increasing returns and decreasing returns as well. While Ricardo discussed in terms of relative prices of goods leading to trade between countries, Ohlin's theory emphasises on the relative abundance in factor supplies leading to trade. Ohlin went beyond the limits of Ricardo and extended the theory to modern conditions by supplementing rather than supplanting it through the application of general equilibrium theory to international trade.

Critical Evaluation of Heckscher-Ohlin Model

Heckscher-Ohlin theorem is more elegant and more satisfying than the classical theory in that it connects the international sector with the working of the whole economic system. Unlike the classical theory of Ricardo, it lays emphasis on all the factors and not only labour, and on the scarcity and abundance of them. It also recognises the possibility of a variety of factor combinations which can exist in different countries, which may lead to differences in cost advantages as between countries.

Prof. Lancaster observed that "Heckscher-Ohlin analysis occupies the very centre of international trade theory for reasons unconnected with its realism and indeed strengthened by the very premises which have been subject to so much criticism".[2]

Although this theory is based on some unrealistic assumptions like perfect competition, homogeneity of factor units, absence of product differentiation, identical production functions, etc., these will not be sufficient reasons to undermine the importance of this theory. The simplification of the model with those assumptions has enabled us to concentrate on the essential features of the factor proportions theory, namely international differences in factors prices and differences in technical collaborations of factors.

---

2. K. Lancaster: The Heckscher-Onlin Trade Model-Geometric Treatment, Economica, February 1957.

The main points of criticism against Heckscher-Ohlin theorem are as follows:

(1) Nothing innovative: Vinar has shown that even before Ohlin's writings his points were considered by other writers and Ohlin has only given a cleaner exposition of the same. But Ohlin claimed that he explained the international trade theory in terms of multiple market theory of pricing.

(2) Identical factors in both countries not realistic: The theory assumed that factors of production of identical quality existed in both countries which is not realistic because there are many quality differences in factors as between countries.

(3) Introduction of money costs was not new: Abandonment of labour theory and substitution of money costs for labour costs was nothing new and as Viner has pointed out, the classical writers themselves abandoned it.

(4) Demand factors not given importance: In the determination of factor prices, Ohlin assumed that relative factor supplies determine factor prices and the role of demand was not given due weightage in this process.

(5) Constant returns to scale-assumption unrealistic: Under conditions of increasing returns, costs can be lowered by increasing production due to economies of scale. In such a case, even without comparative cost differences, trade can take place due to economies of scale.

(6) Assumption of same production function in both countries unrealistic: For a given product the production function is assumed to be the same in both countries but it may differ from commodity to commodity. But if production functions differ for the same goods in different countries, trade may not take place. The assumption is unrealistic as technological progress is not uniform among countries and hence the production function for the same goods may differ in different countries.

(7) Unrealistic assumptions of free trade and perfect competition: Ohlin's theory has been criticised for many unrealistic assumptions like free trade, complete immobility of factors, perfect competition, etc.

To sum up, Heckscher–Ohlin Theory of International trade is the basis modern theory and for the generalized theory of Prof. Grey, integrating the trade theory with Aid theory at international level in the modern world.

Modern Theory vs. Classical Theory

A comparison of the two theories may be made as follows:

Classical Theory	Modern Theory
1. It seeks to explain in terms of labour theory of value - a separately developed theory for exploiting the advantages of international trade.	1. It explains international trade in terms of general theory of value or general equilibrium analysis, emphasising that there is no need for a separate theory.
2. It makes international trade theory different from internal trade theory.	2. It makes international trade theory an extension of the internal or inter-regional trade theory.
3. It explains the apparent cause of trade as comparative costs and demonstrates gains from trade.	3. It provides the real basis of international trade as differences in factor endowments. It explains the cause of comparative cost advantages in international trade. It thus, supplements the Ricardian theory.
4. It involves time dimension only.	4. It incorporates both time and space dimensions.
5. It is based on one factor model and on constant returns to scale. It considers labour as the only factor of production.	5. It is built on two factor model and based on differences in factor endowments and considers all types of returns to scale - constant, increasing and decreasing returns.
6. It assumes production function of a commodity is to be different in different countries.	6. It assumes uniform production function for the same commodity in the trading countries.
7. Its approach is in terms of relative prices of goods.	7. Its approach is in terms of relative prices of factors.
8. It mainly rests on the immobility of factors internationally and mobility within the nation.	8. It depends on the available quantity of the factors domestically and mobility or lack of mobility is less material to this theory.
9. It emphasised only the supply side of trade.	9. This incorporates both supply and demand sides of trade.
10. It is a crude statement of international trade theory in terms of costs of production as the basis of trade.	10. It is a refinement of international trade theory in terms of both supply and demand, incorporating equilibrium analysis and general theory of value.
11. It is an improvement of the "Absolute cost advantage" Doctrine of Adam Smith.	11. It is not a new theory, but supplements (and does not supplant) the classical (Ricardo's) doctrine of comparative costs.

9 Recent Theories of International Trade

The classical theories explaining international trade through comparative cost advantage and opportunity costs have been supplemented by the factor endowments theory and factor price equalisation theorem. The changes in technologies and availability of alternative production processes, changes in tastes, habits and problems of heterogeneity in factors etc., have caused differences between theory and actual practice leading to a number of alternative explanations to international trade flows across borders.

The variables involved are many and complex in international trade that the simplified models of two country, two commodity and two factors are unsuitable explanations of the trade flows in real world. For example Prof. I.B. Kravis has argued that availability of factor supply and of commodity supply determine the trade flow rather than comparative cost advantage. In Ohlin's model, commodities flow out in the order of comparative differences based on factor endowments in countries but such flows depend on the supply availability in the countries as argued by Kravis.

Kravis Theory

Kravis has put forward the doctrine of availability as an alternative explanation of trade theory. Under free trade conditions if there are four countries which produce the same commodities, X and Y the countries which have exportable surplus only can export to other countries in need of the commodity X or Y. Here availability theory applies. The consumer preferences for country A product or its brand may also play a role in trade flows. In brief, the domestic supplies and exportable supplies are major determinants of International trade as per Kravis, J.B. Prof. Williams has also offered a similar doctrine namely "vent for surplus" which means that a country exports its surplus after satisfying domestic demand for the commodity, which applies to primary commodities mostly.

Kindleberger's Thesis

Kindleberger has argued that there is factor level disequilibrium which stands in the way of operation of Ohlin theory. He has highlighted the possibility of structural disequilibrium at factor level which will create a problem for the operation of factor proportion theory. "Disequilibrium at the factor level may arise either because a single factor receives different returns in different uses or because the price relationships among factors are out of line with factor availabilities." (Kindleberger; C.P. International Economics).

Kindleberger was arguing the case of LDCs where the trade theory on the basis of factor proportions may face problems due to structural maladjustment at factor level and commodity level. Unsuitable technologies of developed countries applied to LDCs or market imperfections in LDCs will not allow free trade situation as ideal for the LDCs.

Bhagwati's Hypothesis

J.N. Bhagwati has proposed a trade theory for the LDCs, based on export led growth. Based on theory and empirical studies, he has demonstrated that although free trade is not an ideal policy for LDCs, export promoting growth is to be preferred to import substituting growth on the ground that export led growth will lead to greater efficiency and economy in production and consumption of the LDC. Tariffs are better than quota restrictions according to Bhagwati, as the price incentive is maintained and market forces still operate.

The elasticity pessimism has led Prof. Nurkse to argue in favour of import led strategy whereas Haberler, Viner and Bhagwati have argued in favour of export led growth on grounds of encouraging freer play to market forces. Bhagwati in particular has argued on the basis of empirical evidence of growth patterns of countries in the LDC group.

The Metzler Paradox

Metzler's paradox states that only if the trading Partner's demand elasticity for the tariff imposing country's exports is larger than that Country's marginal propensity to consume exportables. will the price of import good increase in the country which has imposed the tariff. But if the country's marginal propensity to consume its export good is larger than the foreign demand elasticity for its exports, the domestic price of imports will fall because of the tariff.

If the price of import good falls in domestic market because of tariff, then the effects on income distribution are the opposite to those suggested by Stolper — Samuelson theorem. As the price of imports falls relatively, price of exports rises; production of exportables will be more profitable and factor reward of the factor used intensively in exports will increase and income distribution will turn in favour of the country's abundant factor of production. The Metzler's result is based on the fact that the foreign country's demand elasticity for the first country's exports is low and hence the demand for this good will not fall much despite the rise in its price. Under these conditions, a tariff can create excessive demand in tariff imposing country's market for its export good. If this happens, the price of imports will fall because of the tariff. (Metzler. L.A. Journal of Political Economy 57: 1-29, Tariffs, the Terms of Trade and the Distribution of National Income).

"Dutch Disease"

The existence of internationally non-traded goods leads to the phenomenan known as 'Dutch Disease'. This means that boom in one traded goods sector might lead to a decline in another traded goods sector or non-traded goods sector. If these declining sectors are in manufacturing these will lead to de-industrialisation, which is termed as 'Dutch Disease' by Forsyth and Kay (Also see Bo. Sodersten). The net effect of the boom in one of the traded goods sector will be to reduce the size of the remaining traded goods sector. This will be effected through reduction in the comparative advantage enjoyed in other export goods and increased the comparative disadvantage in the import competing goods. (Refer Fiscal Studies I, 1-28. Forsyth P.J. and Kay J.A. 1980).

Falvey-Kierzkowski Model

According to this model, capital rich country will export the higher quality goods. Quality enters into the model through improvements in either capital or in higher efficiency of labour. If we assume that high average incomes are positively correlated with high endowment of capital, relative to labour then the outcome is that they will produce higher quality goods due to improved capital equipment or tools.

Lerner Symmetry Theorem

According to this theorem, an advalorem tax on exports has the same effect as an advalorem tax on imports, set at the same rate. Both will have the same effect on the relative price of importables and on the terms of trade. Both will reduce the volume of trade, but if the revenue from export tax is spent in the same way as the revenue from import tariff, the effects of the two policies will be the same.

The symmetry between the export tax and the import tariff also extends to the concept of optimum export tax as similar to optimum import tariff. There is an equivalent symmetry between a subsidy on imports and a subsidy on exports.

Eckaus Theory

R.S. Eckaus has brought forward the Market Imperfections hypothesis as applicable in particular to the LDCs. In his paper "The Factor Proportions Problem in Underdeveloped Areas" published in The American Review, Sept. 1955, he argued that there are large differences in factor returns leading to factor market imperfections. Limitations in technologies adopted may lead to redundancy of labour. Besides, labour surpluses may arise due to imperfect substitutability of labour following differences in quality and efficiency. Labour abundance does not therefore assure that labour intensive goods are produced by them and exported. There can be unemployment of labour and the actual output may be less than optimal. Use of wrong technologies by the LDCs would also produce outputs less than optimal and the technologies may be unsuitable to the factor availabilities.

The following diagram demonstrates the Eckaus theory: The available technology used by the country A may lead to points a, b, and c, as representative of combinations of factors which can be used to produce output, quite irrespective of the relative factor endowments and factor prices. The slope of the line joining these points is equal to the constant capital—labour ratio. This may lead to limited technical substitutability of factors. When the factor endowments of the country is off the line Oabc, say at a point E in the Figure, there will be inevitably some unemployment and production will be less than optimal.

Besides, there can be more than one process for producing the same goods. In reality, the proportions in which the two factors can be used are not confined to one ratio but, may be, the technology will permit many combinations of factors and the one most suitable to the factor endowments of the country may be chosen. Even so, the available technology will set the limits to trade possibilities of the LDCs. (Fig. 9.1)

This is critical analysis of his theory, but not an exact reproduction of his wordings and ideas.

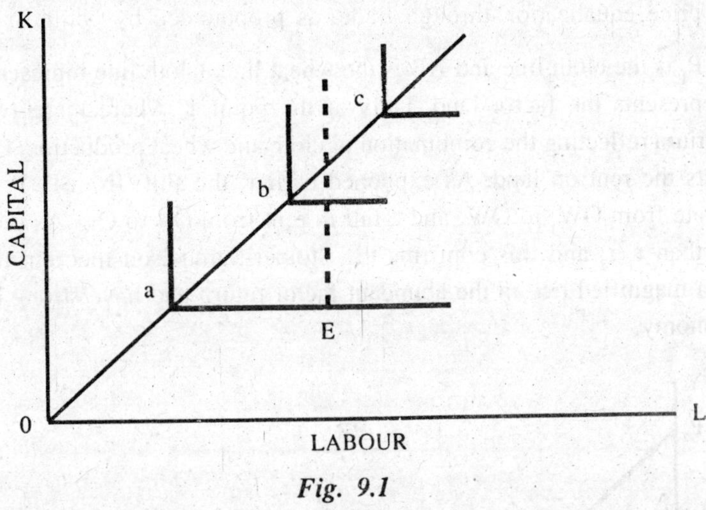

Fig. 9.1

"Oabc" gives the combinations of capital and labour which can be used for production of given levels of output with a certain technology under constant labour capital ratio. Such a technology may be unsuitable to the country, as the country's factor endowments are represented by the point "E". This confirms the statement that available technology sets the limit to trade possibilities as postulated by Prof. Eckaus.

Stolper — Samuelson Theorem

The effect of changes in relative prices of goods on factor prices was first analysed by W. Stolper and P. Samuelson in their paper, "Protection and Real Wages" (Review of Economic Studies

1941). In a two factor economy, changes in relative goods prices have very strong effects on income distribution which means there will be magnified effect of goods prices on factor prices.

The Figure below Fig. 2 explains the magnifying effect. Price of cloth rises relative to wheat and this shifts the cloth line from P_1 to P_2 while the wheat line remains at 'AB', unchanged. Now equilibrium factor price point at 1 shifts to 2. This involves a rise in wage rate from W_1 to W_2 and a fall in rental rate on land from r_1 to r_2. Similarly, a rise in the price of wheat would rise the rental rate on land and lower the wage rate. Because an increase in price of cloth leads to a fall in the rent on land, those who depend upon income from land rent only will find their purchasing power reduced in terms of both goods. At the same time, if the wage rate rises more than proportionately due to the increase in price of cloth, those who derive all their income from wages only, will find that their purchasing power has increased in terms of both goods.

It will be seen from the above, that international trade has strong income distribution effects, as changes in relative prices of goods have strong effects on relative earnings of factors and as trade changes relative prices of goods. The owners of abundant factors will gain from trade while owners of scarce factors will loose. Stolper-Samuelson theorem has thus emphasised the income distribution effects, which make the abundant factors gain more than the scarce factors. This may make it difficult to achieve factor price equalisation through trade, as propounded by Ohlin and his supporters.

In Fig. 2, $P_1 P_1$ is the cloth line and AB is the wheat line. Cloth line represents the factor labour and wheat line represents the factor land. Only at the point 1, where these two lines cut, is the production equilibrium reflecting the combination of cloth and, wheat production: OW represents wage rate and Or reflects the rent on land. As explained earlier, the shift from $P_1 P_1$ line to $P_2 P_2$ leads to a rise in wage rate from OW_1 to OW_2 and a fall in rent from Or_1 to Or_2. As seen from the Figure, $W_1 W_2$ is greater than $r_1 r_2$ and this confirms the Stolper-Samuelson theorem that a rise in goods price will lead to a magnified rise in the abundant factor return and have strong income distribution effects in the economy.

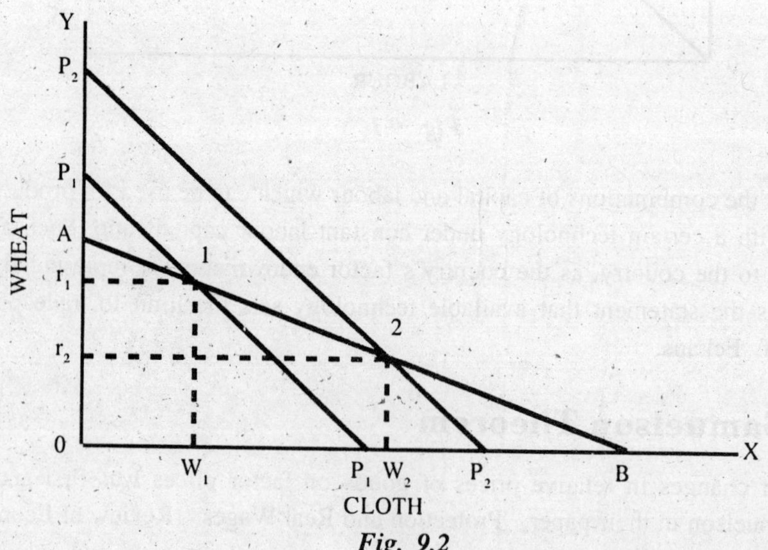

Fig. 9.2

Kuhn's Theorem

It was already seen that Production Possibility curve (PP) moves to right and outward if there is economic growth. If the growth is export biassed, the shift is in favour of export goods and factors used in the export goods would benefit. If the growth is in favour of import goods, PP curve would shift towards and in favour of import goods. Increase in factor supplies or decrease would affect the PP curve. If the technology used is neutral, the shift in PP curve is outward and parallel.

Prof. Kuhn has introduced the possibility of crossing of isoquants when the assumptions of Ohlin and his factor price equalisation theorem would not hold good. He brought in a concept of intensity hypothesis which refers to the intensities in which the factors can be used for producing a given unit of a good. Kuhn has introduced a problem that two isoquants relating to two commodities could cross each other. His intensity hypothesis states that there is a numbering of commodities and factors associating each commodity with its intensive factor. If the first commodity is more intensive in the first factor and second commodity is more intensive in the second factor, then the second commodity is more expensive to produce than the first, when the first factor is free. The first commodity is more expensive to produce than the second commodity when the second factor is free. Crossing of intensities may lead to crossing of isoquants and this is easy to understand in the case of two commodities and two factors. This is sought to be explained with the following diagram.

In Figure 3, the isoquants IC_1 and IC_2 cross at the point T due to the change in factor intensities, and such a situation cannot ensure the factor price and commodity price equalisations.

In this Figure - IC_1 and IC_2 are two isoquants of two commodities where isoquants represent equal product curves representing loci of points of combinations of capital and labour producing one

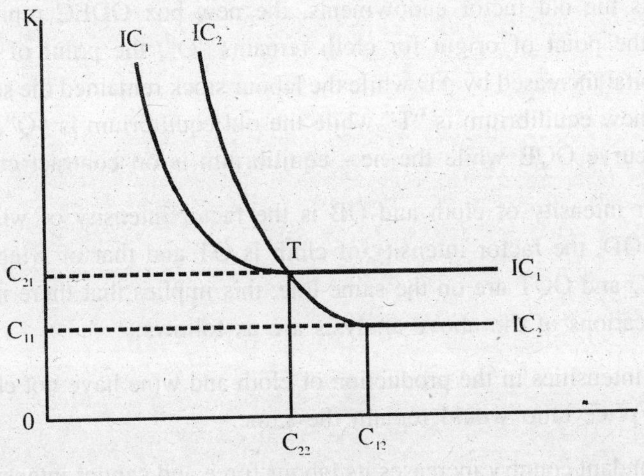

Fig. 9.3

unit of the same output. If one product is capital intensive and the other is labour intensive uniformly, the isoquants do not cross normally. But if the factor intensity varies from segment to segment of the isoquant line, then combinations of factors in which a good is produced will vary and devoid of consistency, the isoquants may cross at more than one point depending on the segments where production is taking place.

The above figure thus demonstrates that Ohlin's hypothesis that factor price equalisation and commodity price equalisation are possible, within the theory of factor proportions and factor endowments of the trading partners, does not hold good. Empirically it was found that there are possibilities of factor intensity reversals and crossing of isoquants of any two commodities.

Rybczynski Theorem

Rybczynski Theorem has elucidated the Ohlin's factor price equalisation theorem by dropping the underlying assumption of constant factor supplies. His theorem tries to examine the effect of a change in factor supplies in one of the two trading partners. He has shown that any change in factor supply in a country comes in the way of factors price equalisation, as postulated by Ohlin. The assumption of constant factor supplies is thus vital for the Ohlin theory, but this is unrealistic in the real world.

The Figure demonstrates the Rybczynski theorem. The box OABC represents the factor supply of labour and capital of country "M". The diagram as drawn shows that the country is capital abundant and labour scarce. It exports cloth which is a capital intensive product and imports labour intensive product, wine, "O" is the point of origin for cloth and "B" is the point of origin for wine. Cloth is exported and wine is imported by country M.

As drawn in Figure 4 capital stock is increased from OA to OD that is by AD. While the old box OABC represents the old factor endowments, the new box ODEC represent the new factor endowments. While the point of origin for cloth remains "O", the point of origin for wine now becomes "E". The capital increased by AD while the labour stock remained the same. After the change in factor supply, the new equilibrium is "T" while the old equilibrium is "Q". The old equilibrium point is on contract curve OQB while the new equilibrium is on contract curve OTE.

OQ is the factor intensity of cloth and QB is the factor intensity of wine. When the capital stock is increased to OD, the factor intensity of cloth is OT and that of wine is TE, but as TE is parallel to QB and OQ and OQT are on the same line, this implies that there is no change in factor intensities. The implications of the above analysis are as follows:

(1) The factor intensities in the production of cloth and wine have not changed. Factor prices and factor price ratio would remain the same.

(2) Labour abundant country increases its labour force and capital intensive country increased its capital stock; the factor price ratio does not change and hence factor price equalisation is not possible. Thus, the Ohlin theorem does not hold good, when the factor supplies change in the trading countries.

(3) When product prices depend on the factor prices and when the latter do not change, the former also do not change. Thus, factor price ratio and product price ratios do not change as a result of changes in factor supplies in the trading countries.

(4) When the factor supply of labour increases, the product produced by the abundant factor will increase but the other product produced by the second factor whose supply has not increased will fall.

It will thus be seen that when the equilibrium position shifts from Q to T, there is only change in the quantity of goods produced, but there is no change in the factor prices and hence in goods prices. As OT is larger than OQ, more cloth is produced. As TE is shorter than QB, less wine is produced, but the factor price ratios do not change and hence product price ratios also do not change. This suggests that if the capital stock increases in capital abundant country indefinitely, the country will tend to have complete specialisation in production of cloth. The same can be said of the labour abundant country. These trends produce changes in terms of trade and not factor prices and product prices and will not allow factor price equalisation among trading partners as visualised by Ohlin. Thus, Rybczynski has showed that Ohlin's theory of factor price equalisation will not hold good when factor supplies change in any of the trading countries.

As QB and TE are parallel, there is no change in factor intensities, goods produced will change, as also exchange ratios or terms of trade.

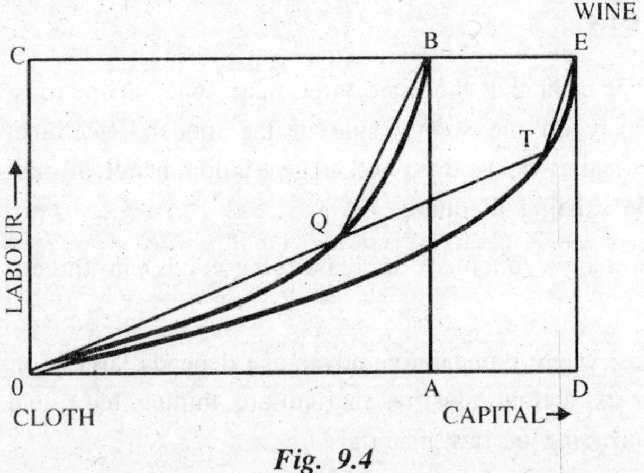

Fig. 9.4

Thus, if the assumption of constant factor supply is dropped, the theorem of factor price equalisation will not hold good. If the factor supply increases, the country tends to increase its exportable good due to its abundant supply, but its terms of trade will deteriorate. There is no possibility of changes in factor prices and when factor prices do not change, product prices also do not change. Thus, Ohlin's theorem does not hold if the assumption of constant factor supplies, is dropped.

(T.M. Rybczynski: Factor Endowment and Relative Commodity Prices, Economica, November 1955).

TECHNOLOGY AND TRADE THEORY

Technological differences may also lead to comparative trade advantages, if we consider that technology as a factor of production. The Hecksher-Ohlin theorem will hold good, if we consider that technology is incorporated in either capital or labour. Country A with technological advantage in the production of Y good, has a comparative advantage in it. Technology will benefit the country and the factor depending upon where it is first introduced and which factor will enjoy the scale economies within that country.

Posner (MV) considers that technological change is a continuous process and that it is a determinant of trade. Introduction of new technology in a good or introduction of a new good based on new technology may lead to trade in that good and from that country, if it leads to price-cost differences as between the countries. Imitation lag will generally be longer than demand lag which will lead to generation of trade due to innovation. This lead the postulation by Posner of what is called 'Imitation Gap model" following the technological changes in the trading countries.

Posner's theory states that the country first introducing new technology will increase its exports and the flow of technology from one country to another will take time due to product-specific and country-specific nature of these innovations. During the time gap, the innovating country will benefit from trade.

Emerging Models

From the above it is clear that there are three main types of theories of inter-industry trade, all of which focus largely on the supply side of the model: Ricardian, Heckscher-Ohlin and technological. The empirical evidence does not suggest a dominance of one set of theories over the others, as seen from the existing literature.

As a consequence, many economists are classifying goods into three classes which match the three theories.

(a) Ricardo goods, where comparative advantage depends largely on production conditions. Examples are extraction industries (agriculture, mining, etc.) and industries which carry out basic processing of raw materials.

(b) Heckscher-Ohlin goods, which have generally, known and relatively stable technologies, with comparative advantage resting largely on factor endowments. Textiles are often cited as the typical Heckscher-Ohlin good.

(c) Technological goods, for which the production process is sophisticated and subject to frequent change, with the most recent technology probably specific to certain countries. I.T computers and pharmaceutical products are examples of such goods.

10 Gains from Trade

Introduction

International trade flows in the direction of where the demand lies. Demand arises out of the felt needs of the consumers and the population of the importing country. The goods emanate from the countries having the necessary excess supplies. Trade taking place between the country supplying the goods and the country demanding the goods will benefit both.

Gains from trade can be explained in terms of benefits to three kinds of people:

(A) For exporting country,

(B) For importing country, and

(C) To the whole world.

A. GAINS TO THE EXPORTING COUNTRY

In the supplying country, larger production and larger incomes are derived from their exports. These may in turn lead to greater specialisation, large-scale production and economies of scale. Larger export income may lead to higher wages or larger profits in the export sector to the disadvantage of other sectors. Or alternatively, these may benefit all the sectors. There are also distributional effects of higher income in the economy, such as making the rich richer, which are not easy to predict but the welfare of the community can be reasonably assumed to grow as a result of trade. The details of their effects may be set out as follows:

(1) Increased Output and Incomes: Increased output as a result of international trade will lead to maximisation of total production, fuller utilisation of resources and the possible lowering of the costs of production, following specialisation in a line suitable to the country producing the commodity.

(2) Greater Specialisation and Better use of Productive Resources: As a result of trade taking place across the borders, each country specialises in the production of goods to which it is well suited or has a comparative advantage. This suitability depends on the availability of natural factors such as land, labour or capital called "factor endowments". Thus, if Taiwan is suited to produce labour-intensive goods and Japan to produce capital-intensive goods, they will specialise in their respective lines of production. This will in turn lead to more optimal use of the productive resources and international division of labour.

(3) Better Growth and Faster Economic Development: By increased world trade, production and consumption will increase in all the participating countries, leading to larger incomes and higher growth rates of national product. All the exporting countries thus stand to gain in varying degrees from foreign trade.

(4) Widened Market and Lower Costs: International trade leads to widened markets and larger production of those goods traded. Due to increase in the volume of production, economies of scale emerge and costs of production and prices could be lowered. Countries gain by larger availability of goods and better wages in the exporting countries.

B. GAINS TO THE IMPORTING COUNTRY

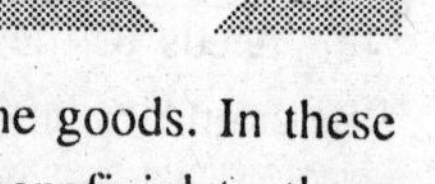

A similar set of benefits would accrue to the countries who are importing the goods. In these countries, there is a felt need for imported goods and hence imports would be beneficial to these countries as well. These benefits can be set out under the following heads:

(1) Trade Leads to Larger Consumption of Goods and Services: This would lead to better satisfaction and improved standard of living of people in general. It is possible that imported goods may not be available internally or could be produced only at higher costs and higher prices, both of which would be less beneficial to the country than importing these goods.

(2) Trade Leads to Greater Satisfaction in Consumption — Increase in the Standard of Living: The commodities imported are valued more than those available domestically, which is one of the reasons why they are imported. Thus, gain from trade arises as this involves an exchange of goods valued less by the exporting country and valued more by the importing country, whereby the total value, of satisfaction for both the countries is higher than before trade took place.

(3) There will be Higher Economic Growth: If imported goods are raw materials or intermediate goods used in production or capital goods used in investment, then domestic investment and production potential would increase, leading to larger output of goods and services and higher economic growth. Imports act as an engine of growth for many developing countries in need of foreign resources and capital goods, including technology. The researches conducted by the author revealed that imports leads to larger capital formation and higher growth.

(4) Enjoying a Variety of Goods: An importing country enjoys a variety of goods which it cannot produce. It gets the advantage of different skills possessed by other countries. For example,

Indian people could enjoy consumption of goods like life saving drugs due to imports which cannot be produced domestically or produced at higher prices.

(5) Learning: An importing country can learn to produce goods imported from abroad, and produce those goods themselves and try to capture international markets by re-exporting the indigenously produced foreign goods. The best example is that of Japan, which initially copied or imitated foreign made goods and Japanese people learnt the art and has today become a powerful competitor in the world market.

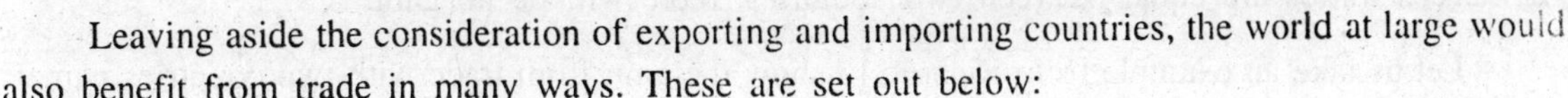

C. OVERALL GAINS TO THE WORLD

Leaving aside the consideration of exporting and importing countries, the world at large would also benefit from trade in many ways. These are set out below:

(1) Inter-country Benefits: Larger international trade leads to larger production, increase in world productivity, larger incomes and higher growth in all participating countries. Economic development of countries is facilitated by trade. This is called export led growth. Similarly, there is import led growth also.

(2) Benefit to All Trade Partners: Large-scale production in some countries leads to increased productivity and lower costs which would benefit all the trading partners and the world at large, either through lower prices or improved quality of products to consumers and larger profits to producers.

(3) Widening of the World Market: Trade widens the market and the scale of operations of the producing countries. This would lead to better utilisation of resources, higher output resulting in larger investment in Research and Development and improved technologies, which would benefit all the countries.

(4) Multiplier Effect of Increase in Trade: Trade results in gains in consumption and welfare in some countries and larger production in other countries. Taking the world as a whole, larger production and consumption may lead to larger incomes and may result in multiplier effects of trade on the growth of the economies.

(5) Better Utilisation of Scarce Resources: Since different countries have different factor endowments, all of them mutually benefit by better utilisation of their scarce resources through international trade.

(6) Higher Wages to Labour: Due to large exports, labour in the exporting countries is benefited in the form of higher wages. Similarly, rewards for other factors may also increase.

(7) Dumping: International trade helps to dump excess supply of domestic goods in the world market and in return can import important scarce goods.

Factors Influencing Gains

The extent of gains to each country would depend on a number of factors. Besides, the net gains may be negative sometimes if the trade has resulted in displacement of domestic industries and misallocation of domestic resources. The gains may also be negative if there are adverse effects of trade on income distribution in any country. The total welfare gained may be positive only if the gains of trade on production and consumption are not offset by losses in distributional effects. Some of the factors influencing the extent of gain are set out below:

(1) Relative Cost and Price Ratios as between the Trading Partners: The larger the differences in the cost of production as between two countries, the larger is the gain from trade. If the cost ratios are equal between two countries, there will be no gain.

Let us take an example from Ricardo to show the gain from trade with two countries namely, England and Portugal and two commodities wine and cloth. The table shows the domestic cost comparisons of the commodities in those countries.

Table: Cost Comparisons Labour Cost of Production (in hours)

	1 Unit of Wine	1 Unit of Cloth	Domestic Exchange Ratio
Portugal	80	90	8:9
England	120	100	12:10

Portugal has absolute advantage while England has absolute disadvantage in respect of both commodities. But Portugal has a comparative advantage in wine and England in cloth. This will be clear if the cost ratios are compared with a common base say 1 unit of cloth. Thus, the cost ratio in Portugal is 0.89: 1 (wine : cloth) and that in England is 1.2:1 (wine : cloth). Portugal can produce wine with less number of hours of labour or at lower cost while England can produce cloth at lower cost relatively. When trade takes place, the terms of trade or exchange ratio would lie anywhere between these two domestic exchange ratios so as to be gainful to both. Let us assume that one unit of cloth exchanges for one unit of wine, in international trade, then Portugal gains by giving less of wine by 0.11 for 1 units of cloth from England, while England gains by getting 0.20 more of wine for giving 1 unit of cloth. Thus, both countries gain from trade and gain depends upon the relative cost and price ratios.

(2) The Differences between Factor Endowments and Factor Rewards: If the differences in factor endowments as between the two trading partners are larger, there will be larger gains from trade. If the two trading partners are non-competing or complementary in factor endowments, the gain from entering into trade would be the highest.

(3) Differences between Production and Consumption Pattern: If the two countries have dissimilar production frontiers or production patters, then the chances of trade gains are more. Similarly, if the consumption patterns of the two countries are also different, relative to their production patterns, trade frontiers are widened and gains would be larger.

(4) Relative Terms of Trade as between Exports and Imports: Terms of trade are the ratio of export prices to import prices. If these terms are favourable to any country, then the gains would be larger to that country. This shows the ratio in which the gains are distributed between the trading partners.

(5) Relative Elasticity of Demand for Different Commodities: The gains from trade would also depend on the relative elasticities of demand as between the trading countries. The country with greater elasticity of demand is more responsive to changes in prices which leads to greater trade and larger gains from trade. The country with inelastic demand may not gain significantly as expansion in trade will be slow to follow from changes in costs and prices.

A number of other factors influence the gains from trade such as the stage of economic development, exchange and trade controls and general trade policy of the countries. Free trade is highly conducive to generate gains while restricted trade leads to distortions in trade pattern and reduced gains. Thus, the gains are dependent and relative to many factors, some of which are not quantifiable.

Measurement of Gains

There are no methods which are accurate and scientific to measure the gains from trade. Some of these gains are notional and subjective while others are qualitative. The quantitative measurement of gains is rather crude and unscientific. Some of these rough measures are set out below:

(1) Expansion in Production or Rise in National Income: Rise in incomes is no doubt indicator of gains from trade, but as incomes and production also rise due to a number of other factors, the rise attributed to trade is difficult to estimate.

(2) Improvement in Terms of Trade: The ratio at which exports exchange for imports, in terms of price or quantum is referred to as "the terms of trade". The more favourable the terms of trade for any country, the greater is the gains to that country. But this has also a limitation in the sense that some improvement in export prices may be due to a rise in costs which may lead to lower trade. Similarly, the larger export quantity for a given amount of import quantity is also not a sign of gain from trade as more real resources are given away by the country than it is getting in the form of imports.

(3) Trade Balance and Net Inflows of Funds on Current Account of Balance of Payments: It is sometimes understood that a positive trade balance is a sign of gains to the country as then exports are more than imports and the country gains an additional income from abroad. But this concept covers up the relative costs involved in exports and imports and hence not a good measure of trade gains.

(4) Relative Costs and Prices of Trading Commodities: If international trade reduces costs due to large-scale production and economies of scale in the traded commodities, this is a positive gain to the trading countries. In the producing country, specialisation and reduction in unit costs of production would take place and is a measure of gain from trade. But this is also an imperfect measure, as it is difficult to isolate the fall in costs due to foreign trade alone. Thus, all the above factors are only rough and crude indicators of gains from trade.

Gains Represented Diagrammatically

Gains from trade can be demonstrated with the help of diagrams, using the production possibility curves (Pp curves). For trade to take place, the only condition is that the slope of PP curves (domestic exchange ratios should be different for different countries. Under conditions of constant costs, consider that USA has an exchange ratio as 100 : 100 for wheat and cloth and the same for Britain is 50 : 100. The PP curves for USA and Britain are presented in Figure 1, under conditions of constant costs.

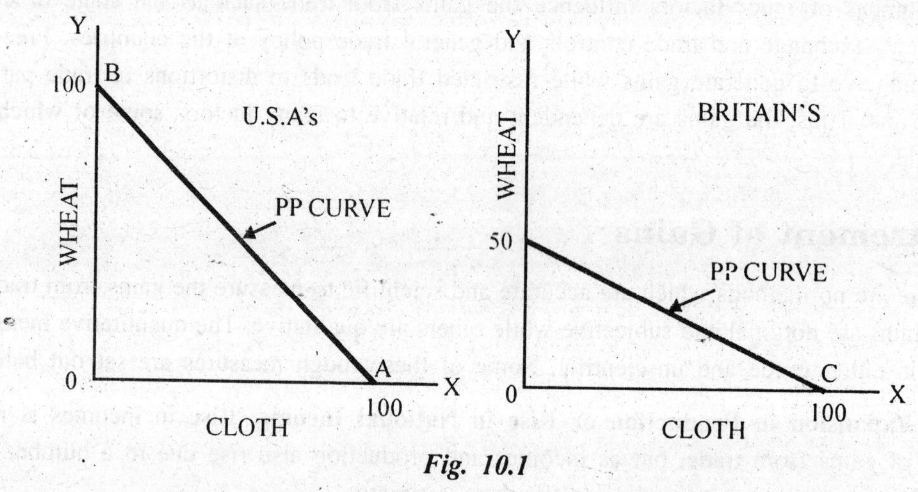

Fig. 10.1

It will be seen from the Fig. 1, that wheat is relatively cheaper in USA where 100 bushels of wheat are exchanged for 100 yards of cloth. But in Britain, cloth is relatively cheaper with 100 yards of cloth exchanging for 50 bushels of wheat. USA has a comparative advantage in production of wheat and Britain in cloth. Naturally, USA exports wheat to Britain and imports cloth from Britain. Assuming no transport costs and no barriers to trade, the prices at which international trade takes place can be represented as follows:

Juxtapose the PP curves of USA and Britain to represent the domestic exchange ratios in those countries. Actual trade takes place at a ratio which is advantageous to both. Britain will specialise in cloth and USA in wheat and they exchange in trade their respective products: The exchange ratio in international trade will lie in between their domestic exchange ratios as shown below:

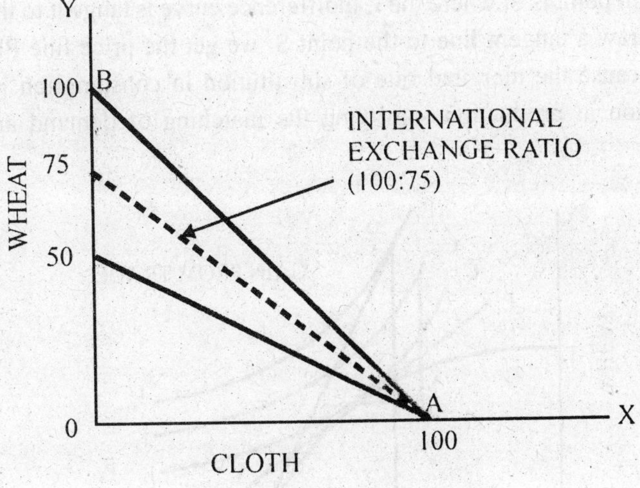

Fig. 10.2 Gain from Trade

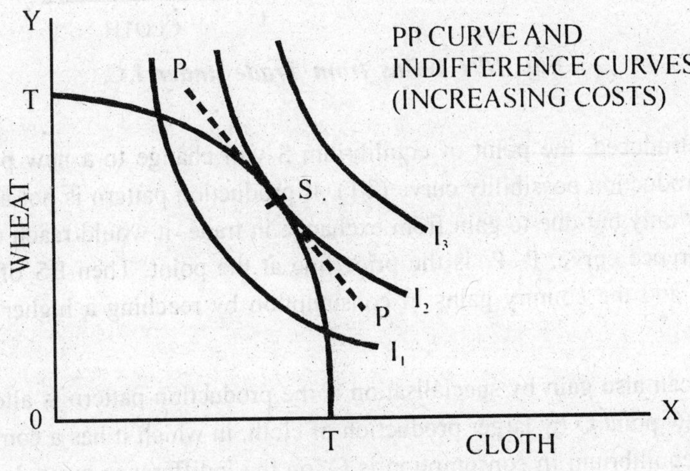

Fig. 10.3 Equilibrium under I.C

The domestic exchange ratios are 100: 50 in Britain and 100 : 100 in USA, and the international exchange ratio may lie anywhere between them at say 100 : 75 when both stand to gain.

Fig. 3, presents the PP curves with increasing cost conditions and concave to the origin. This is juxtaposed with Indifference curves I_1 to I_3; on the I_2 curve the point of equilibrium is shown at fig. 3. The tangent line PP represent exchange ratio.

The above demonstration of gains from trade can also be done with the help of PP curves under increasing cost conditions, which will be more realistic. The PP curve would then be concave to the origin as shown below and juxtapose on it the community indifference curves to represent the demand factors, while PP curve represents the supply factors (Fig.4).

The equilibrium point is S, where the I_2 indifference curve is tangent to the production possibility curve (TT). If we draw a tangent line to the point S, we get the price line PP. At S, the equilibrium point is reached because the marginal rate of substitution in consumption is equal to the marginal rate of transformation in production signifying the matching of demand and supply factors.

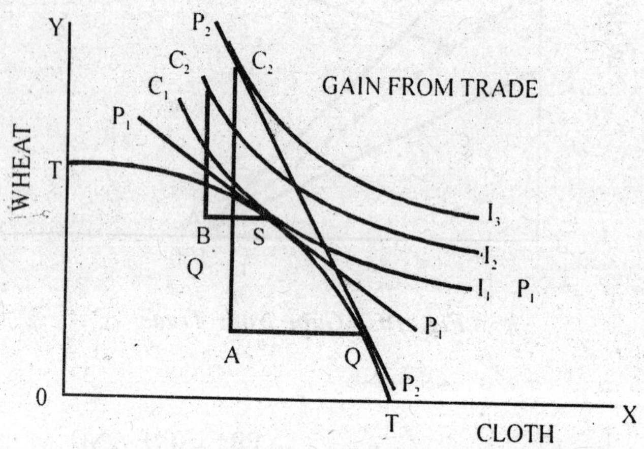

Fig. 10.4 Gains from Trade under I.C.

If trade is introduced, the point of equilibrium S will change to a new point Q, where P_2 P_2 is tangent to the production possibility curve (TT). If production pattern is not alterable, the country could produce at S only but due to gain from exchange in trade, it would reach a consumption point of C_1 on I_1 indifference curve. P_1 P_1 is the price line at the point. Then BS of cloth is exchanged for BC_1, of wheat and the country gains in consumption by reaching a higher I_1C_1, *viz.*, I_2C_2 than before.

The country can also gain by specialisation if the production pattern is alterable and the point S can move to a new point Q by larger production of cloth, in which it has a comparative advantage. Then the point of equilibrium in consumption is C_2 on the indifference curve I_3 where the marginal rate of substitution in consumption is equal to terms of trade represented by P_2 P_2. The AQ of cloth is exchanged for AC_2 of wheat and the point C_2 on the I_3 indifference curve represents the gain in consumption from trade as well as from specialisation in production. This, shows that by introducing trade a country can gain in consumption and reach a higher utility represented by a higher Indifference Curve.

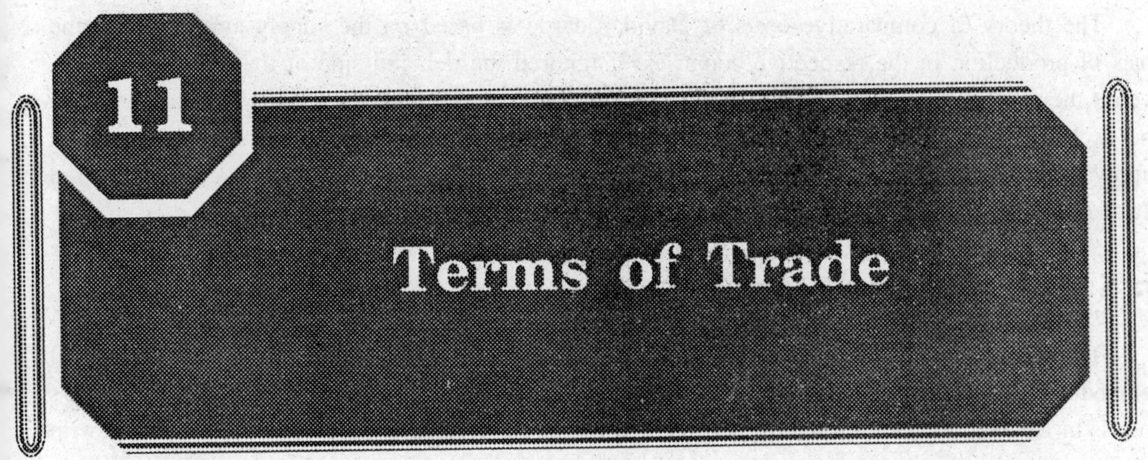

11 Terms of Trade

Definition

Gains from trade depends, inter alia, on the terms of trade of a country. Gains from trade is more a subjective and qualitative factor, while terms of trade is somewhat measureable although both are relative and related subjects.

The concept of terms of trade refers to the rate at which two trading countries exchange goods in trade. It is ratio of export value to import value. There are many variants of this concept, which will be referred to later. In its simplest form, it is the ratio of export price index to the import price index. If these terms of trade are compared with the same base year, improvement or deterioration in the exchange position can be observed.

Favourable and Unfavourable Terms

Normally, if a country can import more for a given level of exports in exchange, the terms of trade are said to be favourable. However, if a country can import less for a given amount of exports, the terms of trade are said to be unfavourable. Taking the above example of export and import prices, if export prices rise more relatively to import prices, the terms of trade are said to become favourable. If, however, import prices rise more relatively to export prices, as compared with a base date, then terms of trade are said to be unfavourable. These terms, "favourable" and "unfavourable" are relative terms and relative to time and space. It has to be compared over two countries or two time periods, in order to examine the movements in terms of trade.

Demand Side of Trade

Terms of trade mostly reflect the demand side of international trade, because the rate of exchange is determined by the relative demands of country A vis-a-vis country B and of country B *vis-a-vis* country A.

The theory of comparative costs of David Ricardo is based on the supply side, namely, the costs of production in the respective countries. It ignored the demand side of the exchange. Thus, even if the two countries have excess supplies of the respective commodities, trade cannot take place and exchange will not occur if there is no demand for these commodities. Thus, both demand and supply should be considered as if these are two blades of the scissors in the example of Alfred Marshall.

J. S. Mill's Thesis

The demand aspects are explained in terms of what J.S. Mill has called "the law of reciprocal demand", which reflects the strength of India's demand for US goods and US's demand for India's goods. In an auction system quantities offered for sale are cleared by bids and counter-bids, with the final price emerging as a result. Such offers and bids in the auction system of international trade are represented by offer curves by Marshall and Edgeworth. These curves can be regarded as demand curves representing various amounts of cloth which USA would demand in exchange for a unit of its good, say, wheat and units of US good, say, wheat which India would demand in exchange for one unit of its good, namely cloth.

RECIPROCAL DEMAND

According to J.S. Mill, the law of reciprocal demand determines the terms of trade. The reciprocal demand refers to the relative strength of demand of country A for the products of country B as against the demand of country B for the products of country A. These demands in turn depend upon the respective elasticities in the countries A and B.

To simplify, let us take a two-country and two-commodity model. The two countries are USA and India and the two commodities are wheat and cloth. Following the Ricardo's labour theory of value, let us assume a given amount of labour, namely, one man per one week, which in USA can produce 40 units of wheat or 20 units of cloth. In India the same labour input can produce 30 units of wheat or 20 units of cloth. The above example indicates that USA has a comparative advantage in the production of wheat and India in cloth. The domestic price ratio in USA is 40 : 20, while the same in India is 30 : 20. There are the ratios before trade took place. The relative prices of wheat and cloth in USA and India are represented in Fig. 1 (A and B).

Exchange Ratios

Domestic ratios of exchange are as follows:

	Wheat		Cloth
USA	4	:	2
India	3	:	2

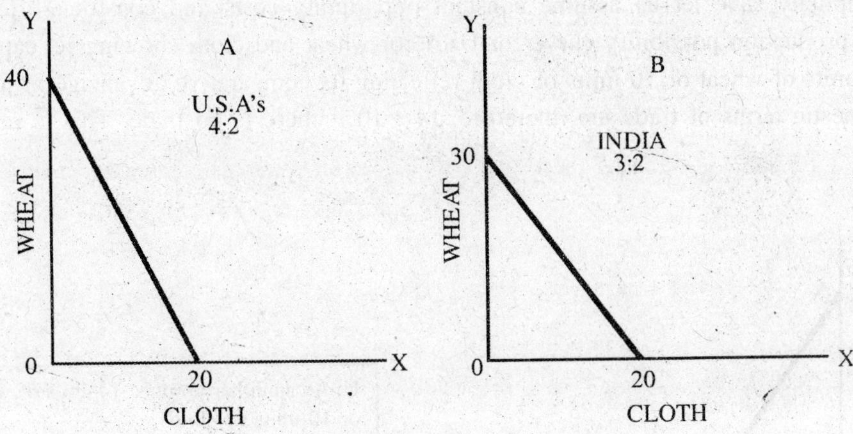

Fig. 11.1 Domestic Exchange Ratios

USA will gain, if it can get more than 2 units of cloth for 4 units of wheat. India will gain, if it can get more than 3 units of wheat for 2 units of cloth. Then both the countries would stand to gain if the ratio of exchange lies between 3 and 4 units of wheat for 2 units of cloth. The actual exchange rate in international trade will depend on the reciprocal demand or relative strengths of their demand. (The ratio lying between 3 and 4 of wheat for 2 units of cloths.)

The terms of trade, which are the ratio of exchange between USA and India in the above example, would thus depend on relative elasticities of demand in the respective countries.

Assumptions

The assumptions in the above analysis are as follows:

(1) Commodities are produced with labour.

(2) Value of commodities is determined by their labour content.

(3) Trade is unrestricted without tariff, duties, etc.

(4) Costs of transport, insurance, etc., are ignored.

Offer Curves (Marshall-Edgeworth Analysis)

Nations trade with each other due to the differences in comparative costs or advantage in production possibilities both the countries stand to gain by trading due to cost advantages as well as by specialisation by each country in the production of the good, in which it has a comparative advantage. The rate at which a country's exports exchange for imports is called the terms of trade. At various terms of trade, the actual quantities exported vis-a-vis the quantities imported would be determined separately by the so-called offer curve mechanism. Offer curves are the loci of points representing what quantity of export a country is willing to make for what quantity of import at each of the possible terms of trade.

For simplicity sake let us assume constant opportunity costs and construct offer curves. We start with production possibility curve for USA for wheat and cloth showing its capability of producing 14 units of wheat or 10 units of cloth reflecting its comparative advantage in production of wheat. Domestic terms of trade are, therefore, 14 : 10 if there is no trade. This is represented as in Fig. 2.

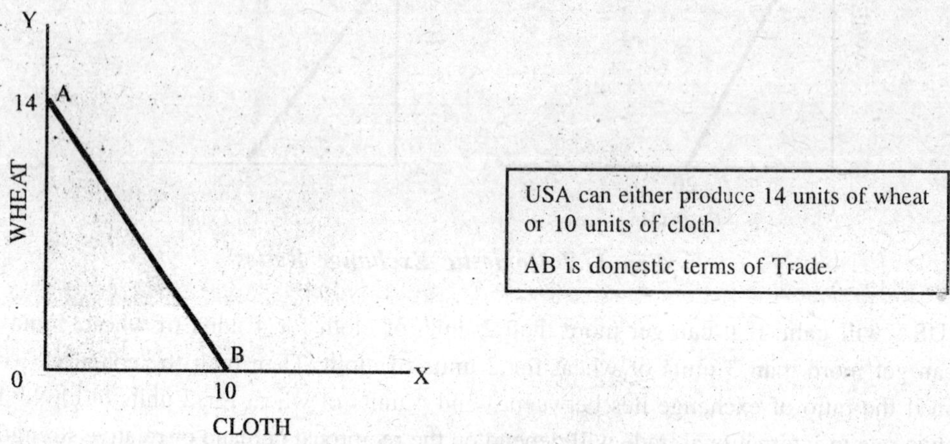

Fig. 11.2 Production Possibility Curve (USA)

The above price or exchange ratio can also be shown as a straight line running from the origin, each with a particular angle representing the ratio of exchange between wheat and cloth as is shown in Fig. 3.

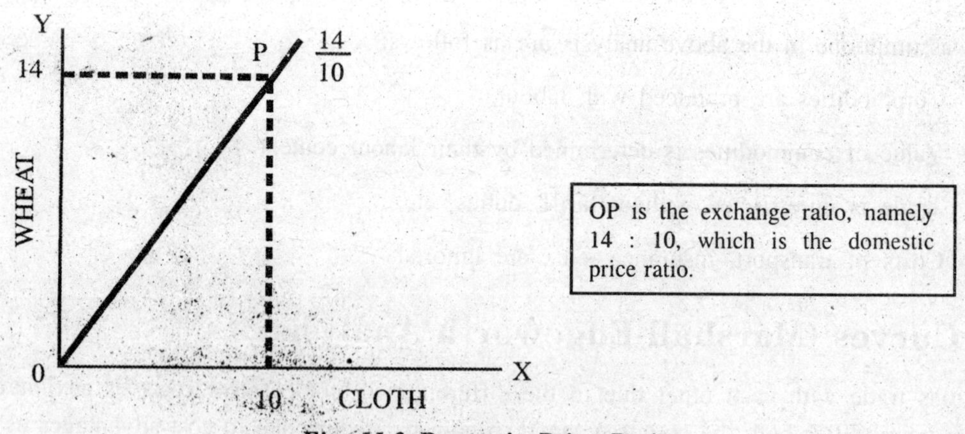

Fig. 11.3 Domestic Price Ratio

If the price ratio is different from the above ratio, implying that wheat in USA has become dearer, say, 14 : 12, trade would take place as USA would buy cloth from India in exchange for wheat. The USA offer curve can be drawn as in Fig. 4 with O as the production point and the axes as depicting exports and imports.

Each of the lines from the origin depicts the various terms of trade, depending upon the slope of the line. The points A, B, C, etc., are the points of tangency between the production possibility lines and community indifference curves, C_1 C_2 C_3 etc. At point 'B' USA will offer more wheat to get more cloth but not quite as much as it was willing to give up earlier at 'A'. At point 'C', this trend was more pronounced with the result that this offer curve becomes concave to the origin, reflecting the decreasing marginal satisfaction derived from increasing quantities of the same commodity.

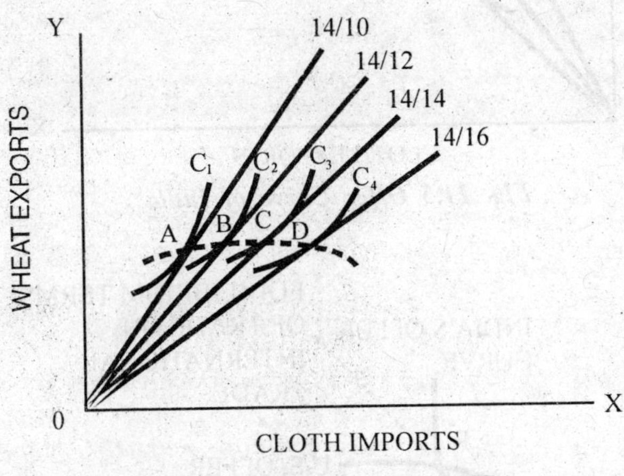

Fig. 11.4 Offer Curve of USA

On the same basis, we can draw the offer curve for India with respect to cloth and wheat as in Fig. 5. Let the domestic price ratio before trade be 8 units of wheat for 9 units of cloth. India would buy more wheat if the cloth price has gone up to say 10/9 or 12/9.

Thus, with trade, the offer curves shifts counter-clockwise, convex to the origin for the same reason that US offer curve becomes concave.

At a lower price, for wheat, as the price line shifts to the left, India would buy more wheat from the USA in exchange for its cloth. In Fig. 6, both USA's and India's offer curves are put together and the point of intersection P depicts the equilibrium terms of trade at which both USA and India would be willing to trade as India would want to export just that quantity of cloth which the USA would like to import and USA would like to export just that quantity of wheat which India would like to import. Then trade would be mutually advantageous and gains from trade emerge.

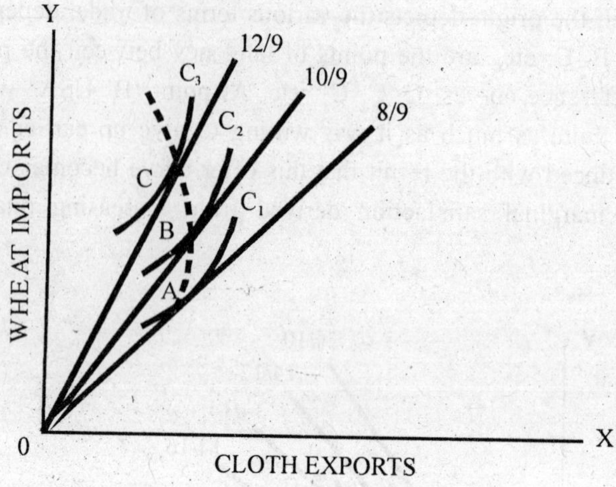

Fig. 11.5 Offer Curve of India

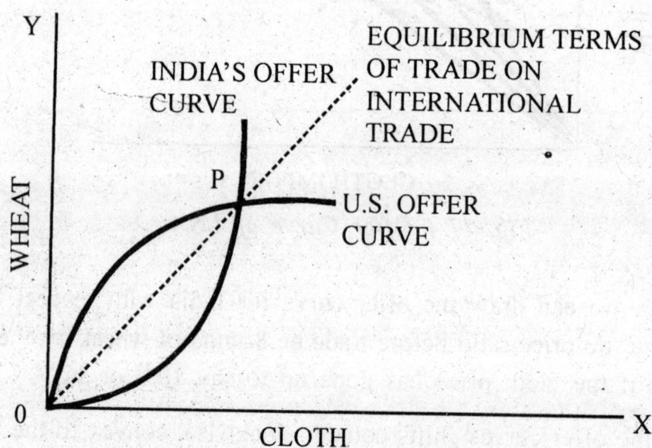

Fig. 11.6 Equilibrium Terms of Trade

The above is a simple two-country-two-commodity model depicted under conditions of constant opportunity costs. A similar analysis has to be made for increasing opportunity costs or decreasing opportunity costs. Multi-country and multi-commodity models require mathematical application which is beyond the scope of this book.

Assumptions in Marshall — Edgeworth Analysis

(1) Ricardo's labour theory of value is used.

(2) There are only two commodities and two countries.

(3) Comparative cost advantage is the basis of trade.

(4) Perfect factor mobility within the country but immobility as between the countries.

(5) Free trade without restrictions.

(6) Costs of transport, insurance, etc., are ignored.

Critical Appraisal

In the real world, the above assumptions do not hold good. But the basic principles of trade possibility and the factors influencing terms of trade would hold good. The Edgeworth-Marshall treatment is criticised for having neglected the supply side, as the offer curves are based on demand conditions only. But Jacob Viner salvaged the above theory by saying that the terms of trade are directly influenced by reciprocal demand and by nothing else, while the demand and cost conditions (supply) together determine the equilibrium position of prices at which all the goods are cleared in trade. **Thus, the offer curves present only the demand side while the supply side is presented by the production possibility curves.**

FACTORS INFLUENCING TERMS OF TRADE

Although the long-term trend in terms of trade is deterioration in the case of less developed countries, the trends in the short run do fluctuate either way. The factors influencing these trends are briefly set out below.

(1) Size of Country and its Population: The larger the size and larger its population as in the case of India, the greater will be the demand for foreign imports which is mostly inelastic. This would lead to adverse terms of trade.

(2) Stage of Economic Development: If a country is underdeveloped and depends upon primary agricultural products for the bulk of its income, its terms of trade will be adverse as foreign demand for its goods will be inelastic.

(3) Rate of Exchange: If a currency is overvalued in terms of foreign currency, it can get more imports for a given value of its exports, and its terms of trade will be favourable.

(4) Trade Policy (tariffs, quotas, etc): If by means of tariffs, quotas and other restrictions, a country can reduce its imports with a given level of exports unchanged, it can improve its terms of trade. This is subject to the condition that the trading partners do not retaliate and impose higher tariffs.

(5) Elasticities of Supply and Demand: The elasticities of supply and demand would depend on the nature of commodities, stage of economic development, habits and customs of people and a host of other factors. The elasticities relevant for this purpose are:

(a) Elasticity of domestic supply of exporting country.

(b) Elasticity of demand for foreign goods.

(c) Elasticity of foreign supply of imported goods.

(d) Elasticity of foreign demand for export goods produced inside the country.

The greater the above elasticities, the greater is the volume of trade and larger are the gains from trade. In fact, the terms of trade of a country are dependent on the relative elasticities of demand and supply of one country vis-a-vis another country, which are referred to above. These are also the elasticities which determine the reciprocal demand of the trading partners and hence their terms of trade.

Effect of Transport Costs

Inclusion of transport cost can create a problem as exports are based on f.o.b. (free on board) and imports on c.i.f. (cost, insurance and freight). If a country carries a part of its exports and a part of its imports, then the net barter terms of trade is not a good measure of exchange terms. In the case of a rise/fall in the cost of transport, real changes in the import and export prices and quantities are not reflected by the above formulations. Transport costs, therefore, create problems in the measurement of terms of trade. Inclusion of c.i.f. in imports and exclusion of them in exports are ideal only if each country is carrying its own imports and have its own ships or aircraft and none of its exports is so carried. Thus, although the terms of trade broadly reflect the gains from trade or welfare, they are not an exact measure which can be depended upon in all circumstances. Terms of trade depend upon the relative elasticities, which are discussed below.

Elasticities

There are two types of elasticities in international trade — income and price elasticities. These cannot be easily separated in their effects. Price elasticity as much as income elasticity may be in respect of demand for or supply of each of the commodities. Price elasticity measures the effect of a unit price change on the quantity of goods exported or imported. A decrease in price will normally lead to a rise in the quantity demanded from abroad. The reverse will be the case in respect of a rise in price. *Income elasticity* similarly measures the changes in the quantity supplied or demanded of exports or imports for a unit change in income. Since income changes may lead to price changes and *vice versa*, it is difficult to isolate their effects.

Unit elasticity refers to a proportionate change in exports or imports for a unit change of price or income. Elasticity may be greater than one (called generally elastic) or less than one (called inelastic). These concepts are applied subject to the assumption of *ceteris paribus*.

Price Elasticity

Thus, elasticity with respect to price is measured as:

$$E = \frac{\text{Percentage change in exports (x)}}{\text{Percentage change in price (p)}} = \frac{dx}{x} \div \frac{dp}{p}$$

Income Elasticity

Elasticity with respect to income is measured in the same way:

$$E = \frac{\text{Percentage change in exports (x)}}{\text{Percentage change in income (y)}}$$

$$E = \frac{dx}{x} \div \frac{dy}{y}$$

Factors Influencing Elasticities

Elasticities may vary with circumstances such as the size of the markets at home and abroad, the amount of production and consumption, the size of price changes, expectations, the time allowed for reaction, market conditions and alternative sources of outlets, etc. Elasticities are generally high under perfectly competitive conditions with a large number of buyer and seller countries for each of the commodities. Each country's demand curve for a product abroad depends on its own production of that commodity or its substitutes or complementaries and elasticities of supply of these products. Generally business conditions, expectations and time elements play an important part in determining the degree of elasticity of products.

Elasticity Pessimism

It is understood that price and income elasticities in foreign trade are generally low. Elasticity pessimism in the post-war period led to a belief that lesser the use of market mechanism, the greater are the benefits from trade. This resulted in greater restriction on trade and payments. It is frequently argued that the general concept of elasticity has no meaning and that what is relevant is elasticity of individual commodities and in any particular segment of the curve of supply or demand. Besides, long-run elasticities are high enough but not so the short-run elasticities when supply adjustments are not possible. It is also argued that average and marginal propensities to import are high in developing countries while the same in respect of exports are low. Such high propensities have also led to the imposition of controls on trade in the developing countries.

Measurement

In the real world, these elasticities of demand and supply are difficult to measure and the methods of measurement are crude and undependable. The factors on which they depend are so numerous that it is difficult to predict them beyond generalised statements of tendencies. They also vary with time, country and commodity and one has to be careful in the use of these concepts.

Concepts of Terms of Trade

As referred to earlier, terms of trade relate to the ratio between the prices of exports and imports. To express this relation, various formulae and variants are used. The more important ones are of the following:

(i) Gross barter terms of trade are quantity of imports (QM) divided by quantity of exports (Qx), Qm/Qx.

(ii) Net barter terms of trade are prices of exports (Px) divided by prices of imports (Pm), Px/Pm. These terms were used originally by Taussig and Viner.

A higher price paid for imports, export price remaining constant, would mean adverse terms of trade in the sense that more will have to be paid for imports in terms of exports. If a larger quantity of exports are required to be made for a given quantity of imports, it is again adverse to the country. This is represented by gross barter terms of trade Qm/Qx.

TERMS OF TRADE AND WELFARE

These concepts do not measure accurately the welfare deriving from foreign trade. Suppose a country has a high export price relative to import price but cannot export much, it cannot obviously increase its welfare. Similarly, a country may have a high capacity to import but its foreign trade is negligible relative to its income, then the country cannot gain much. Besides, one has to consider the productivity gains also. Suppose technology is of neutral type and uniform productivity gains are secured, then terms of trade may worsen but it does not mean that its welfare is reduced; it is only sharing some of its productivity gains with its customers.

Factoral Terms

Taking productivity into account, the concept of "single factoral terms of trade is used in the form of an expression Px/Pm x Zx, where Zx stands for productivity in exports. In actual practice, Zx can be represented by an index number over the base period in terms of output per worker. in a similar way, double factoral terms of trade are represented by Px/Pm x Zx/Zm where Zm is productivity of foreign factors in the import sector. Single factoral terms of trade are more relevant as we are interested in knowing what our factors can earn in terms of goods and not knowing what our factor services can command in terms of services of foreign factors.

Income Terms of Trade

This term was developed by G.S. Dorrance as a measure of the country's capacity to import. It may be expressed as:

$$Ty = \frac{Px.Qx}{Pm}$$

Where Ty is income terms of trade, Px is price of exports, Qx is quantity of exports and Pm is price of imports. This concept measures the quantum of imports that can be secured with a given level of export value. Px.Qx measures the total export value. That is to be divided by unit price of imports given by Pm.

Real Cost Terms of Trade

This concept measures the real gain from international trade. It takes into account the real cost involved in exporting a given quantity of goods through the disutility suffered per unit of a productive factor in the export sector. Real cost terms of trade is expressed in the following form:

$$Tr = \frac{Px}{Pm}.Fx.Rx$$

Where Tr is real cost term of trade, Px/Pm is commodity terms of trade, Fx is productivity in exports and Rx is disutility suffered per unit of productive resources used in the export sector. Thus, Tr is arrived at by multiplying the single factoral terms of trade with the index of disutility incurred per unit of productive factors in the export sector. This concept is subjective and suffers from the neglect of import side and has little practical application.

Utility Terms of Trade

This concept measures the true utility of exports and imports to the economies. Robertson calls it "the true terms of trade". It is arrived by multiplying the index of real cost terms of trade with the index of the relative utility of imports and the commodities foregone. Thus, Tu, the utility terms of trade, is expressed as Tu=Px/Pm. Fx. Rx. u, where u is relative utility of imports as compared with the relative utility lost as a result of exports. The other terms Fx and Rx have been explained earlier in this section.

This concept attempts to rectify the defect of the real cost terms of trade by introducing the import side also. But this concept, like the earlier one, suffers from the same defect of little practical importance.

Usefulness of the Concepts

Of all the above concepts, the gross barter terms of trade and net barter terms of trade are of some practical use, while income terms of trade is more useful for planning in the developing countries. In these countries, the capacity to import is critical for development purposes as imports are necessary for capital formation and productive activities. A country's capacity to import will fall, if the export volume or export prices decline or if import prices rise.

Terms of trade have been deteriorating secularly for the developing countries, as demonstrated by economists like R. Prebisch. The reasons for such a secular deterioration in terms of trade of developing economies are to be sought in the structural features, nature of the export products, tariff and other barriers created by developed countries and host of other factors.

Some other concepts used in this connection are merchandise terms of trade, invisible account terms of trade or current account terms of trade. In actual practice, what is lost in terms of trade on merchandise trade account may be gained on the invisible trade account. So current account terms of trade are a more comprehensive term.

But basically, all these terms are useful for limited purposes of comparison, over time and space, of the effect of trade on the economies of trading partners. Both the gross barter terms of trade and income terms of trade are relatively more frequently used by development economists in planning and forecasting the trends.

TERMS OF TRADE IN INDIA

In view of the low elasticities of supply in developing countries and in foreign demand for their products, there has been a secular stagnation or deterioration in terms of trade according to the studies conducted by UNCTAD and eminent economists like Prebisch, Lewis etc. Net terms of trade, namely, the ratio of the export price to import price deteriorated in India, for a number of years due to the inelasticity in our supplies and demand from abroad.

Gross terms of trade, namely, quantum index of imports divided by quantum index of exports, also deteriorated for several years. Besides, the terms of trade have fluctuated rather unevenly and India has not gained from world trade in terms of value realisation which is more significant for the purpose of exchange reserves. Import prices have gone up by a larger proportion than export prices due to the sharp hikes in the prices of crude oil products during the seventies. India's export earnings are unstable due to her greater dependence on agricultural-based industries, whose supplies and foreign demand for them are inelastic. In the last decade, things have changed due to economic and financial reforms and larger growth of exports following the trend to privatisation and market oriented economy.

The data on terms of trade in India are presented by the D.G.C.I.S., and Reserve Bank of India, under two heads:

$$\text{Gross terms of trade} = \frac{\text{Quantam index for M}}{\text{Quantam index for X}}$$

$$\text{Net terms of trade} = \frac{\text{Quantam index for X}}{\text{Quantam index for M}}$$

Where X stands for exports and M for imports.

The index numbers computed in respect of foreign trade of India are as follows:

(1) Unit value index is constructed according to Paesche's formula:

$$P = \frac{Pn.Qn}{Po.Qo}$$

(2) Quantum index is worked out on the basis of Laspeyre's formula:

$$Q = \frac{Po.Qn}{Po.Qo}$$

Where Pn is the unit value of an article in the current period.

Po the unit value of the article in the base period.

Qn is quantity in the current period and

Qo is quantity in base period

P is price index and

Q is quantity index.

The data on unit value Index, Quantum Index, Gross barter terms of trade, not terms of trade and Income terms of trade are published for the benefit of researchers in the RBI Hand book of Statistics with base year 1978-79 = 100. The same source provides commodity wide Index numbers for all exports and imports (unit value and Quantum) along with the general index for on commodities.

Causes for Deterioration in Terms of Trade

There are several factors to explain why terms of trade deteriorate for less developed countries. Some factors are listed below:

(1) Lack of bargaining power in trade due to poor elasticities of demand and supply;

(2) Lack of technology and development;

(3) Growth of population leading to lower incomes and low purchasing power;

(4) Law of diminishing returns;

(5) Poor mobility of factors of production; and

(6) Non-availability of substitutes.

12

Dynamics of International Trade

It was shown in an earlier chapter that trade leads to greater welfare of trading nations and promotes the growth of production and consumption through greater specialisation and lower costs and prices. Historically, economic growth of some countries was led by exports due to larger markets and larger production and consequential industrial and commercial revolution. In more recent years, however, barring a few smaller nation-states like Taiwan and Korea or oil-producing developing countries in the Middle East, trade was not a major propellant to growth. But the basic proposition remains that growth can be led by exports or exports will expand with growth and that they are inter-related. Theoretically, what is the mechanism that links them? How economic growth influences trade or is influenced by trade will be discussed in this chapter. Static theories were based on assumptions of constancy of tastes, factors of production and technology, perfect markets, etc.

Growth economics introduces an element of dynamics into international trade. The theories presented earlier are based on static equilibrium analysis, assuming other things to remain constant. As these do not remain constant in the real world, the need to introduce elementary dynamics is, therefore, felt. Equilibrium would change under the following conditions:

(a) Changes in factor endowments such as population growth or capital growth, etc.

(b) Technological growth or technological changes.

(c) Structural changes in the economy due to growth of industries, changes in tastes and habits, etc.

Effect of Tastes

Changes in tastes would introduce changes in the available supplies for trade, pattern of consumption and relative costs and prices of commodities and factors. Nurkse spoke of the demonstration effect of trade on tastes and how the demand for goods and services would change with changes in tastes. The indifference curve map would change with changes in tastes and habits and resultant changes in trade may lead to a new equilibrium in production and consumption. Change in tastes may sometimes increase or decrease trade, alter the composition of trade and production structures, etc. The possible degree of disequilibrium from changes in tastes is unpredictable and uncertain.

Changes in Factor Endowments

While labour and capital may expand, land may not change except in a sense that its uses can grow due to technological changes or to the discovery of new mines or minerals. The changes in factor endowments would influence the production possibility curve. A uniform growth of all factors might push the curve outward evenly while the disparate growth in factors with no other changes in the economy can lead either to more exports or less imports depending upon the sector in which the expanding factors are used more. Such growth in factors might lead to export-biased growth if expanding factors are used more in the export sector or import-biased growth in the economy if expanding factors are used more in the import sector or is neutral to both if the goods using the factors expanding in the economy are only for domestic consumption. Not only the quantity of trade might change, but the terms of trade, namely, the ratio of export price to import price, might alter due to changes in costs and prices of goods produced. It is possible that a bias in production due to the growth of factors might be offset by bias in consumption at home or abroad or by changes in cost-price parities.

Technology Changes

Technological growth can be neutral or export-biased or import-biased on the same lines. If it is neutral, only productivity and efficiency might increase, leading to lower costs and prices. Terms of trade will deteriorate for that country. A neutral technological growth is as good as an even growth of all factors of production. An export-biased technological growth will augment the abundant factor and further expand the exports. An import-biased growth in technology will augment the scarce factor in the country and promote the import competing goods resulting in import-based growth. In between such possibilities, there are a host of combinations of growth of technology resulting in growth of the economies. Technological changes may also result in the production of new goods or services which have a market abroad, and it is possible that old goods may be changed in the form and content. These changes take place continuously with the result that pattern, quality and direction of trade flows change in a continuous fashion in the real world. Such changes may result in trade taking place in a fashion unrelated to factor endowments at least in the short run.

Trade and Growth in the LDCs

Whether the LDCs can gain by trade in terms of growth under present-day conditions is controversial. R. Prebisch and a host of other economists have maintained that conditions conducive to growth by trade are not present today due to disadvantage suffered by the LDCs.

(1) Firstly, their terms of trade move adverse to them due to inelasticities in their supply of exportable goods and in foreign demand for their goods.

(2) Their export earnings are unstable due to their greater dependence on a few agricultural products for export which are demand-inelastic abroad. The supply of such products fluctuate widely due to the vagaries of monsoon as they are agricultural products.

(3) The demands for foreign products of LDCs are elastic, while foreign demand for their products is inelastic, leading to a situation adverse to the LDCs in terms of both income and price elasticities.

(4) The tariff and non-tariff barriers of developed countries stand in the way of the export markets of the LDCs.

(5) The high cost price parities in the LDCs due to lower productivity put the LDCs in a disadvantageous position.

(6) The multi-national and monopolistic firms abroad keep out the products of the LDCs in the international markets.

In view of such disadvantages, the LDCs tend to rely on import competing goods or import substitution goods or on domestic markets while only a few countries could have export-led growth. Many LDCs depend on imported growth. The role of imports in capital formation in the LDCs was brought out by the author in his book on, 'Imports and Capital Formation in the LDCs'.@

Linkages — Forward and Backward

The traditional links between trade and growth can be set out in terms of:

(i) Expansion of markets or opening of new markets, (ii) Larger production of export goods and (iii) Specialisation in selected lines of production leading to lower costs, prices, etc. These would lead to forces which will increase the output, income and employment.

The process by which one product stimulates the production of others is called "linkage" by A.O. Hirschman. Both forward and backward linkages operate to promote growth of production. While forward linkages lead to industries which utilise this product as input, backward linkages promote industries which provide ancillaries and inputs to this product. Besides, there is a possibility of growth in terms of "demonstration effect" through a multiplier process. The growth of some industries would accelerate the growth process in general and stimulate the growth of others as in the case of plantations in the LDCs and oil in the Middle East. Such linkages produce changes in production, consumption and distribution in the economy. The use of some goods abroad may lead to the demonstration effect leading to their use domestically also.

@ V.A Avadhani, "*Imports and Capital Formation in LDCs*", Sudhir Prakashan Publications, 1979.

National Income and Trade (Exports)

Trade affects national product and income through changes in production for export markets. In the national income identity in macro terms, domestic product + net inflows from abroad would equal national product. In an open economy National Income = Consumption + Investment + (Exports – Imports).

$$\text{or} \quad Y = C + I + (X - M)$$

In a static situation, trade would increase income through larger exports than imports leading to higher foreign savings (X-M) = If. In a dynamic situation, these savings are invested leading to a further rise in incomes and output of the nation. Such a rise depends on the foreign trade multiplier and accelerator.

Investment = Domestic Savings + Foreign Savings.

$$I = Sd + Sf$$

If leads to Y by a multiple of original *If*, over a period of time, which is called the foreign trade multiplier. Incomes will increase not only by a multiple of domestic investments but of foreign investment (X – M), also.

In general equilibrium models, we have to take both income equation and balance of payments equation and a simultaneous solution is to be sought for both. Balance of payments or trade equation will increase income, which in turn leads to greater investment at home (Id) and greater exports (x) resulting in an accelerator effect on incomes. In the income equation, investments increase income due to operation of the multiplier. Rise in incomes would lead to greater investments and further income growth through the accelerator in operation. Here investment is made a function of increments in income. Both the multiplier and accelerator operate in respect of the foreign sector's impact on the domestic economy.

Imports and Growth

Yet another aspect of the impact of foreign trade is through imports acting as a propeller to growth. Imports of both consumption and capital goods influence the goods market and the factor market and through them, the expenditure and income growth in the economy.[1]

It was shown in the author's model how imports promote growth of capital formation in the LDCs and thus of income and output. Consumption imports add to the goods market and investment imports to the factor market and propel both larger consumption and greater investment, provided imports are used productively and import control channelises the flows into those avenues with growth potential in terms of utilisation of capacity or greater production in the economy.

---

1. *Imports and Capital Formation in LDCs*, V.A. Avadhani, Sudhir Prakashan Publications, 1979.

It would thus be seen that growth of income via foreign trade sector is both feasible and realistic whether conceived in an accounting sense or in a conceptual sense. Both exports and imports have a role to play to promote the economic development, incomes and employment in the country. In the dynamics of the real world, continuous interactions between the foreign sector and domestic sector take place to lead to greater interdependence, mutual benefit and all-round growth of the economies. In this chapter and later chapters, we use some concepts which have a wide application in international trade theory some of which are explained below.

Terms of Trade

As explained in an earlier chapter, terms of trade are the relation between the prices of exports and imports. To express this relation, various formulae and variants are used. Gross barter terms of trade are quantity of imports (Qm) divided by quantity of exports (Qx) = $\frac{Qm}{Qx}$ Net barter terms of trade are price of exports (Px) divided by price of imports (Pm) = $\frac{Px}{Pm}$. These terms were used originally by Taussig and Viner.

A higher price paid for imports export price remaining constant would mean adverse terms in the sense that more will have to be paid for imports in terms of exports. If a larger quantity of exports are required to be sent for a given quantity of imports is again adverse to the country. This is represented by gross barter terms Qm of trade $\frac{Qm}{Qx}$. These concepts are explained in an earlier chapter also.

These concepts do not measure strictly the welfare from foreign trade. Suppose a country has a high export price relative to import price but cannot export much, it cannot obviously increase its welfare. Similarly, a country may have a high capacity to import but its foreign trade is negligible relative to its income, then the country cannot gain much. Besides, one has to consider the productivity gains also. Suppose technology is of neutral type and uniform productivity gains are secured, then terms of trade may worsen but it does not mean that its welfare is reduced; it is only sharing some of its productivity gains with its customers. Taking productivity into account the concept of "single factoral terms of trade" is used in the form of an expression $\frac{Px}{Pm}$ multiplied by Zx, where Zx stands for productivity in exports. In actual practice, Zx, can be represented by an index number over the base period in terms of output per worker. In a similar way, double factoral terms of trade are represented by $\frac{Px}{Pm} \times \frac{Zx}{Zm}$ where Zm is productivity of foreign factors in the import sector. Single factoral terms of trade are more relevant as we are interested in knowing what our factors can earn in terms of goods and not knowing what our factor services can command in terms of services of foreign factors.

Terms of trade have been deteriorating secularly for the developing countries, as demonstrated by economists like R. Prebisch. The reasons for such secular deterioration in terms of trade of a developing economy are to be sought in the structural features, nature of the export products, tariff and other barriers by developed countries and a host of other factors.

Some other concepts used in this connection are merchandise terms of trade, invisible account terms of trade or current account terms of trade. In actual practice, what is lost in terms of trade on merchandise account may be gained on the invisible trade account. So current account terms of trade are a more comprehensive term for measurement of exchange terms.

Inclusion of transport cost can create a problem as exports are on f.o.b (free on board) and imports are on c.i.f. (cost, insurance and freight). If a country carries a part of its exports, and also a part of its imports, then the above is not a good measure of exchange terms. In the case of a rise/fall in the costs of transport, real changes in the import and export prices and quantities are not reflected by the above formalities. Transport costs, therefore, create problems in the measurement of terms of trade. Inclusion of c.i.f. in imports and exclusion of them in exports are ideal only if each country is carrying its own imports and have its own ships or aircraft and none of its exports is so carried. Thus, although the terms of trade broadly reflect the gains from trade or welfare, they are not an exact measure which can be depended upon in all circumstances.

Elasticities @

There are two types of elasticities in international trade: income and price elasticities. These cannot be easily separated in their effects. Price elasticity as much as income elasticity may be in respect of demand for or supply of each of the commodities. Price elasticity measures the effect of a unit price change on the quantity of goods exported or imported. A decrease in price will normally lead to a rise in the quantity demanded from abroad. The reverse will be the case in respect of a rise in price. Income elasticity similarly measures the changes in the quantity supplied or demanded of exports or imports for a unit change in income. Since income changes may lead to price changes and vice-versa, it is difficult to isolate their effects.

Unit elasticity refers to a proportionate change in exports or imports for a unit change of price or income. Elasticity may be greater than one (called generally elastic) or less than one (called inelastic). These concepts are applied subject to the assumption of *ceteris paribus*.

Thus, elasticity with respect to price is measured as:

$$\frac{dx}{x} \div \frac{dp}{p} = \frac{\text{percentage change in exports (x)}}{\text{percentage change in price (p)}}$$

@ This is explained in an earlier Chapter also.

Elasticity with respect to income is measured in the same way as:

$$Ey = \frac{\text{percentage change in exports x}}{\text{percentage change in price y}}$$

$$E = \frac{dx}{x} \div \frac{dy}{y}$$, where "x" is exports and "y" is income

Elasticities may vary with circumstances such as the size of the markets at home and abroad, the amount of production and consumption, the size of price changes, expectations, the time allowed for reaction, market conditions and alternative sources of outlets, etc. Elasticities are generally high under perfectly competitive conditions with a large number of buyer and seller countries for each of the commodities. Each country's demand curve for a product abroad depends on its own production of that commodity or its substitutes or complementaries and elasticities of supply of these products. General business conditions, expectations and time elements play an important part in determining the degree of elasticity of products.

It is understood that price and income elasticities in foreign trade are generally low. Elasticity pessimism in the post-war period led to a belief that lesser the use of market mechanism, the greater are the benefits from trade. This resulted in greater restrictions on trade and payments. It is generally argued that the general concept of elasticity has no meaning and that what is relevant is elasticity of individual commodities and in any particular segment of the curve of supply or demand. Besides long-run elasticities are high enough but not so the short-run elasticities when supply adjustments are not possible. It is also argued that average and marginal propensities to import are high in developing countries while the same in respect of exports are low. Such high propensities have also led to the imposition of controls on trade in the developing countries.

In the real world, these elasticities of demand and supply are difficult to measure and the methods of measurements are crude and undependable. The factors on which they depend are so numerous that it is difficult to predict them beyond generalised statements of tendencies. They also vary with time, country and commodity and one has to be careful in the use of these concepts.

13

India's Foreign Trade

Introduction

Trade policy is an important adjunct of the foreign exchange policy which are parts of International Finance. Trade, aid and exchange policies are interrelated with international politico-economic relations. International trade is basically a reflection, firstly, of the structure and trends in domestic production and secondly, the structure and trends in world production. But more importantly international political forces, regional affinities and socio-economic factors play a vital role in deciding the pattern of aid and trade. In a developing country like India, trade depends on aid and the composition and direction of trade are dictated by aid flows to some extent. Aid was necessary to pay for growing imports in a state of inadequate growth of exports. Planned investment could not be maintained without a minimum component of imports, despite the existence of a wide network of controls. It would thus be vital to promote exports to pay for imports which are themselves growing due to increasing costs and growing requirements of investment. Exports also pay for debt servicing, namely, repayment of old debts and payment of interest, etc. In a country whose exchange reserves are exiguous and exports can meet only part of the requirements of imports and debt servicing liabilities, aid continues to play an important role. In fact, a prudent country has to plan to build up the exchange reserves by a deliberate export strategy to boost export surplus.

The objectives of trade policy in India may be broadly set out as follows:

(a) To promote exports, necessary to pay for imports;

(b) To allow imports which would facilitate planned investment and increased utilisation of capacity; and

(c) Conservation of foreign exchange reserves to aim at maintaining a buffer stock of exchange reserves for debt servicing and for imports of essential requirements at home.

Importance of Foreign Trade

The role of foreign trade in the national economy can be judged by the proportion of foreign trade to national income. As a proportion of national income, exports were about 8 per cent in 1951-52 which fell to 4.4 per cent in 1971-72 but rose again to around 8 per cent in the seventies, and eighties due to faster growth of exports. It was 9.3% in 2002. Imports as a percentage of national income have also declined from 10.7 per cent in 1951-52 to 4.9 per cent in 1971-72 but stood at 9-10 per cent in the seventies. In 2001-02 exports as a percentage of national income stood at 9% per cent while the corresponding percentage for imports was 12% per cent. In 2008-09, exports as percentage of GDP stood at 15% and imports at 23% with the largest trade deficit in recent years. These data would signify that, firstly, India today is less dependent on the world economy than it was three decades ago. Secondly, India's exports did not grow adequately to keep its share in world trade due to the vast domestic market at home and inward-looking growth of the economy. Thirdly, world exports grew much faster than those of India due to the larger share in the growth by developed countries and a few oil rich countries. India's share in world trade fell from 2.2 per cent in 1950 to 0.6 per cent in 1970 and further declined during eighties and nineties to around 0.5%. Although it is undesirable to have a declining share of world trade from the point of international importance of a country, it is not ispo facto an adverse development for two reasons. Firstly, the pattern of growth of Indian economy is not export-oriented. Secondly, the larger the size of a country, the smaller is its share in world trade.

Between 1951 to 2000, world trade grew at a faster rate than India's trade. The declining share in world trade is a common phenomenon for all developing countries which implies thereby that world trade had only benefited developed countries and not others. Not only the share is declining but the terms of trade have also moved adverse to them for a greater part of the period, if the oil-producing developing countries are excluded. In India, exports grew at an average rate of 19.1% during the present decade 2001 to 2010 and imports grew by 21.3% during the same period. During 2010-11 exports grew by 42% and imports by 22% in US dollar terms. As a percentage of GDP exports were 23% in 2010-11 in dollar terms.

Following the Uruguay Round of trade negotiations and the establishment of W.T.O. Indian's share in world trade was expected to go up to 1.0% by 2010 from less than a fraction of one per cent in 2003. This growth rate was achieved except for a setback during 2009 and 2010, due to global recepsion.

Trade Philosophy

Free trade policy adumbrated in the so-called laissez-faire philosophy became today a matter of archaic theoretical interest. Very few countries now allow free and unfettered imports and exports as that would upset all domestic economic plan projections or domestic economic and political interests. Some degree of protection to domestic industry and controls on exports and imports have become the order of the day in the post-war world. These controls took the form of price controls such as tariffs, import and export duties or quantum controls such as quotas, prohibitions, etc. The trade philosophy of India is one of controlled trade expansion in the interest of the nation. Within the broad framework of such a policy of controlled trade, the objectives of export policy and import policy may be set out.

Firstly, export policy is designed to conserve the limited supplies of some essential commodities for domestic consumption and hence their exports are restricted. Secondly, certain types of goods of strategic importance like defence goods are prohibited. Thirdly, exports to certain countries like South Africa and East Africa etc. are now opening up for emerging political reasons. Our country aims at promotion of exports as far as possible consistent with the above limitations so that sufficient foreign exchange is available to pay for the needed imports and facilitate the servicing of foreign debt and to build a buffer stock of reserves.

Import policy is an adjunct to export policy and both are broadly coordinated so as to keep the receipts and payments in balance. While the export policy aims at promotion of exports, import policy attempts at encouraging import substitution so that the drawal on foreign exchange reserves is kept to the minimum and yet encourage domestic production based on imports. Import growth is faster than that of exports in India. We have continuously negative trade balances and current account deficit was 1% to 1.5% of GDP in the nineties and stood at 2.6% in 2010-11.

Import controls aim at restricting unwanted and ostentatious imports to conserve the limited foreign exchange reserves. Of the imports permitted, those of capital goods, not produced at home, spare parts and raw materials get priority. Of the rest, priority among imports goes to foodgrains, scarce consumer goods like oils, sugar, etc., or to agricultural inputs like fertilisers. A substantial chunk of our import bill is accounted for by crude oil and petroleum, imports of which cannot be dispensed with due to inadequate supplies at home. Import controls are widespread in India and both tariff and non-tariff barriers exist. Licence is required for any item of export or import unless it is specifically permitted under the Open General Licence. These restrictions were mostly liberalized in the new millennium, due to our agreement with W.T.O.

Organisational Framework for Trade

Before independence, India had trade surpluses and there was a regular gold inflow on this account to pay for the surplus. But almost the whole of the trade was concentrated in the hands of British companies, and foreign shipping lines facilitated the British colonial interests rather than Indian interests. But during the war period, India accumulated huge sterling balances due to surplus on trade account and war supplies to the U.K. The war-time controls on trade were regularised later by the passing of the Import and Export (Control) Act of 1947 as "Controlled" trade became the order of day in the post-war period. Protection granted to Indian industry necessitated a wide network of controls on trade. With the inception of planning in 1951, trade policy had shifted its emphasis from one of positive trade balance to the immediate needs of development according to plan priorities. Both imports and exports were at a low ebb during 1951-56, due to prevailing trade controls. But some export promotion councils and commodity boards were set up and export quotas were increased and export policy in general was liberalised. During the Second Plan 1956-61, in addition to export promotion, import substitution was also pursued. Import restrictions were tightened and a policy of imports on deferred payment basis was initiated and institutional framework for exports was strengthened by setting up of a Foreign Trade Board in 1957, later replaced by the Board of Trade in 1962. Nineteen Export Promotion Councils with an apex body federation of the export organisations and seven Commodity Boards were set up. Seven Development Councils were also organised to promote exports of heavy and light electrical, leather goods, art silk, drugs and some non-traditional items.

During the Third Plan period (1961-66), export promotion programme was further strengthened in terms of institutional structure, incentives and other policy measures. The Mudaliar Committee (1965) recommended that a selective approach should be adopted in respect of export incentives, fixation of minimum and maximum prices, quality control, inspection etc., designed to promote exports as a long-term strategy.

The institutional support to the export promotion was strengthened during the Fourth to Tenth Plan periods. The Trade Development Authority was set up to induce and organise medium and small-scale entrepreneurs to develop their export potential. Package assistance was provided to them by TDA starting with market information up to execution of export orders. Similar assistance is provided to small-scale entrepreneurs by STC under one window. It may be noted here that STC and MMTC are canalising agencies for a number of import and export items and are entrusted with export promotion activities. A Telephone Regulatory Authority and Insurance Regulatory Authority started operating in the latter half of nineties. Exports of services began to gain more recently. Exim Bank provided one window to help the export units in terms of guarantee, credit information, refinance to banks, etc. The RBI has lowered the interest rates on export credit to BPLR minus 2.5% points.

Trends on Trade

During the First Five-Year Plan, with emphasis on import controls and self-sufficiency, imports were kept low as exports did not grow significantly. But there was an import surplus throughout this period varying from Rs. 29 crores in 1952-53 to Rs. 273 crores in 1951-52. During the Second Plan, there was a change in the strategy of growth to greater capital-intensive industries which required larger imports. As the growth of exports was not adequate, import surplus grew from an average Rs. 101 crores in the First Plan period to Rs. 575 crores in the Second Plan period.

During the Third Plan period, both export promotion and import substitution were pursued simultaneously. But imports grew faster than exports despite controls with the result that the import surplus rose further to an average amount of Rs. 771 crores. Taking the period of two decades 1951-52 to 1970-71 India's export grew at a rate of 2.4 per cent and imports at a rate of 2.3 per cent respectively. Throughout there was an import surplus indicating greater imports than exports, which was planned to finance investment at home.

India's foreign trade in the seventies showed a continuation of deficits except in two years, namely, 1972-73 (with a surplus of Rs. 104 crores) and in 1976-77 (with a surplus of Rs. 72 crores) Exports rose from Rs. 1535 crores in 1970-71 to Rs. 6427 crores in 1979-80 while imports rose from Rs. 1634 crores to Rs. 8684 crores over the same period. The trend rate of growth of exports over the Fourth Plan (1969-74) was 7.7 per cent (at constant prices). This export performance was aided by an international commodity boom, inflation abroad and a consequent rise in world prices of some of our export products and virtual devaluation of rupee due to its link with sterling upto 1975. The growth of our exports during 1974-75 and 1978-79 (Fifth Plan) was at a rate of 9 per cent and in the Sixth Plan (1980-85) at a rate of 2 per cent (in volume). Bulk of the rise in imports is due to petroleum and oil products, fertilisers, etc. The trade deficit was the highest in 1980-81 at about Rs. 5800 crores for any single year, and remained at around the same level in subsequent years, before reaching a peak of Rs. 8735 crores in 1985-86 and Rs. 10,635 crores in 1990-91 and Rs. 34,495 crores in 1998-99. The trade deficit was the lowest at Rs. 3350 crores in 1993-94 during the recent years, and highest at Rs. 5,33,680 crores in 2008-09.

Our import surplus or trade deficit is a chronic feature of our trade picture, partly resulting from a deliberate policy of investment and partly forced by conditions of export stagnancy. It was the result of a deliberate policy in that larger investment outlays were planned in various plan periods depending upon the promised flow of foreign aid. So trade deficit is explained mostly by the availability of aid. In recent years, the foreign aid secured by India was shrinking due to the government's policy of greater self-reliance and reduced availability of funds with international institutions. But foreign grants and foreign credits played an important role in India's foreign trade in the post-war world. Tied aid led to a change of direction in favour of aid giving countries and to bilateral channels or to barter trade. Aid in general has facilitated the growth of our trade by giving the wherewithal for buying abroad. It has also promoted growth of the economy through greater investment than was possible with domestic resources alone. During the recent years in the new millennium, Govt. to Govt. borrowing and bilateral aid fell, while the commercial borrowings by private sector increased. India's trade deficit was made good by the surplus on invisible trade account and partly by resort to drawal on foreign exchange reserves.

Invisible Trade

For a long time, during the planned development, particularly during the fifties and sixties, the net position of invisible trade was negative due to government expenditure abroad, investment income payments and other miscellaneous items of payments for royalties, patents, etc. It was only in the seventies and eighties that some of the items showed a positive balance and recorded substantial inflows. Receipts on account of foreign travel and transfer payments showed sharp increases and miscellaneous items showed a positive balance mainly due to inward remittances in more recent years. Barring one or two years, Invisible Account showed a positive balance during the last decade and in the new millennium.

Direction of Trade

India's foreign trade has undergone structural changes in the post-war world in tune with the structural changes in the economy. During the last few decades, the share of UK fell from 26.3

per cent to 11.2 per cent. The share of other Commonwealth countries like Australia. Canade etc., also fell. On the other hand, our trade with Japan increased over the same period from a negligible percentage to 13.3 per cent and that of USSR from 0.7 per cent to 13.7 per cent. Over the same period, other East European countries has also increased their share in India's trade. Similarly, our trade with Asian and African countries and the Middle East rose significantly. Our trade with bilateral countries, namely, the Soviet Union and other communist countries, was placed at around one-third of our trade.

The share of OECD countries in which Australia and Japan are included rose from under 50 per cent in 1970-71 to about 56 per cent by 1997-98 but fell to 38% in 2007-08. The total share of bilateral trade with East European countries including USSR declined later similarly say to 4% by 1999 and further to 2% in 2007-08. Trade with OPEC (Mid-West countries), on the other hand, rose from 6 per cent in 1990-91 to 11% per cent by 2002 and to 16% in 2007-08. Trade with developing countries rose from 20% in 1991-92 to 30% in 2001-02 and further to 43% by 2007-08. These trends were continued later say up to 2011-12.

Terms of Trade

In view of low elasticities of supply in developing countries and in foreign demand for their products, there has been a secular stagnation or deterioration in terms of trade according to UNCTAD studies and eminent economists like Prebisch, Lewis etc. Net terms of trade, namely, the ratio of the export price to import price deteriorated in India, for example, from a high of 127.8 in 1970-71 (base 1978-79 = 100) to 80.8 in 1981-82 before improving to 145 in 1995-96 but stood at 128 by 2000-01 and at 163.3 in 2007-08. Gross terms of trade, namely quantum index of imports divided by quantum index of exports, deteriorated during eighties and nineties. It was as high as 161 in 1998-99 (Base 1978-79 = 100) but declined to 111 in 2002-03 and stood at 212.1 in 2007-08, as per the RBI data. Thus, the terms of trade have fluctuated rather unevenly and India has not gained from world trade in terms of value of realisation which is more significant for the purpose of exchange reserves. Import prices have gone up by a larger proportion than export prices due to the sharp hikes in prices of crude oil products during the seventies and later also. During nineties, net terms of trade improved upto 1994-95 after which there was a deterioration. As between 1990-91 and 2011-12 export unit reduced by 3½ times, while import unit values rose by 2½ times only while export quantum rose only by 6½ times. But in terms of quantum imports rose faster by 11 times during the same period. The data on terms of trade in India are presented by the RBI under two heads:

(*Source:* RBI:Handbook of Statistics on the India Economy).

$$\text{Gross terms of trade} = \frac{\text{Quantum index for M}}{\text{Quantum index for X}}$$

$$\text{Net terms of trade} = \frac{\text{Unit value index for X}}{\text{Unit value index for M}}$$

where X stands for exports and M for imports.

The index numbers computed in respect of foreign trade of India are as follows:

(1) Unit value index which is constructed according Paesche's formula

$$P = \frac{Pn.Qn}{Po.Qn}$$

(2) Quantum index worked out on the basis of Laspeyre's formula

$$Q = \frac{\Sigma\, Po.Qn}{\Sigma\, Po.Qo}$$

where Pn is the unit value of an article in the current period.

Po the unit value of the article in the base period.

Qn is quantity in the current period and Qo is quantity in base period.

P is price index and

Q is quantity index.

Composition of Trade

In 1947-48 the traditional export items, namely, jute, tea, cotton, hides and skins, oil and oilseeds, coffee, leathers, etc., accounted for 67 per cent of our trade abroad. By 1960 their share came down to 26 per cent. With the growth of industrialisation, exports of traditional agricultural products were replaced by industrial manufactures and processed products. More recently exports of engineering and electronic products and more sophisticated equipments, software products, project exports, etc. had increased in both quantity and value.

It was only in the sixties and seventies that there were major structural changes in India's foreign trade. Thus, machinery and transport equipment, iron and steel products, metal and non-metal manufactures and metalliferous ores whose exports were almost small or negligible in the fifties rose to about one-fourth of the total exports in the seventies. Traditional items of exports, namely, tea, coffee, jute, cotton, leather, spices, tobacco, oils, etc., which accounted for nearly two-thirds to three-fourths of total trade in the fifties declined to about one-third in the seventies. During the more recent years, exports of engineering goods, chemicals, ores, iron and steel, readymade garments, stones, diamonds, jewellery, handicrafts, etc., accounted for about one-half of total exports. Project exports on a turnkey basis have also been undertaken by Indian firms since 1976-77. Appendix I present the principal items of export and imports in Appendix II.

In the import trade also, a similar transformation of the composition has taken place. The share of machinery, iron and steel, non-ferrous metal manufacturers, chemicals, fertilizers, oils and petroleum, etc., had increased substantially in our import bill. During the Seventh Plan period, capital goods accounted for 17-20 per cent, intermediate products and raw materials for 70 per cent. Of the latter category, crude oil and petroleum was responsible for the bulk of the total bill (30-40 per cent) and fertilisers and chemicals for 15 per cent and animal and vegetable oils for about 5-6 per cent.

On the import front, traditional imports were manufactured consumer products, finished and semi-finished consumer and capital goods. Imports of foodgrains which predominated in the first three plans were brought down drastically later by building up of buffer stocks at home. Now the bulk of imports is accounted for by capital equipment, industrial raw materials fertilisers pulses edible oils and petroleum and its products. In view of the escalation in prices of oil in the seventies from about $ 2 per barrel to about $ 70-80 per barrel in the nineteen, the oil import bill came to constitute about 60 per cent of the total export earnings while it constituted only 3 per cent in 1960 and 7 per cent in 1970. Due to growth of domestic oil supply, imports of oil and oil products constituted 33% per cent of the total import bill at present. Bulk imports, under Government account worked out to 39% in 2007-08, of which crude and petroleum products was the most important item followed by fertilisers and consumption goods. Crude oil prices were fluctuations around $ 22 to $ 25 per barrel in 2003 but rose to more than $ 100 per barrel by 2011-12.

Bulk imports of oil fertilisers, capital goods and industrial raw materials came in that order of importance in imports. Imports of services technical know-how, consultancy have also increased with the growth of industrialisation of the country. Appendix II exhibits the proforma in which import data are presented.

Structural Changes

The structural changes in India's foreign trade since independence can be accounted for by the following factors:

(1) Change of hands from foreign nationals to Indian nationals in respect of the export houses and industrial houses and companies.

(2) British and foreign shipping was replaced by Indian shipping lines and importance of foreign shippers has declined in India's trade.

(3) Banking and insurance have been taken over by Indian hands and have since been nationalised in the interests of the country.

(4) Industrialisation of the country and diversification of our industrial base has led to diversification of our trade pattern. Despite the importance of agriculture in our economy, growth of industrialisation in the post-war period had brought about some structural changes in the trade pattern, both in exports and imports.

Government Share in Foreign Trade

Since independence, government has been entering into the foreign sector to an increasing degree. The export and import of goods and services and outflow or inflow of capital on government account have been taking place, particularly in the form of foreign credits, grants and aid. The foreign trade on government account in total import trade has rapidly risen from Rs. 237 crores in 1948-49 to Rs. 35822 crores by 1992-93 and their share stood at 30-35% in 2008-09. Government exports have been negligible throughout the period and accounted for hardly less than 1 per cent of the total. The growing share of the government in import trade is explained, firstly, by the growth of the public sector enterprises in the Indian production system to about one-fourth of GDP and secondly, by domestic requirements of essential commodities such as foodgrains, oils, fertilisers, petroleum and its products, etc. Such imports are facilitated by government-to-government credits, grants and aid from international agencies, which is replaced by Private Sector since the latter half of Nineties.

Trade Policy

The future of India's trade expansion is expected to be with the West Asian and oil rich countries and less developed countries. Prospects of growth of bilateral trade are also good. The Sixth and Seventh Plans have laid emphasis on the expansion of exports in which India has dynamic comparative advantage. The subsequent plans targeted for a larger growth rate of exports of up to 20% of GDP. The domestic saving-investment policy and the process of growth has to be dovetailed with the strategy for exports. Such a strategy is to promote production and export of labour-intensive products or items fetching higher net value added such as precious stones, jewellery, handicrafts, electronics, etc. the dynamic sectors with a long-term comparative advantage have been identified as engineering products, chemical manufactures, readymade garments, leather manufactures handicrafts, marine products, Diamonds, computer software services, I.T. media, etc. These dynamic sectors are called by the Planning Commission the "leading" export sectors, defined as sectors whose share in the expansion of exports exceed 5 per cent and whose export to production ratio is rising. Thus, the export policy is to promote growth of exports at a rate of 20 per cent per annum, widening and deepening the base, and give greater weightage to leading sectors. Export growth rates in dollar terms was 25% in 1995-96, which has since fallen to 2.6% in 2001-02 but has been hovering around 25% in the on average period 2003 to 2010.

Import policy in the latest plan was designed at selective liberalisation of imports and judicious use of foreign exchange reserves for fuller utilisation of capacity in industry and boosting investment and growth. Import substitution methods were streamlined so as to reduce or eliminate costly and inefficient domestic production by giving proper weightage to domestic resources cost vs. Foreign resources cost. Sufficient provision for imports of essential consumer goods was made so as to curb excessive inflation at home and domestic consumption requirements were to be kept in mind in determining the excess supply situation. Contingency provision for crop failures and imports of agricultural products was made. In respect to certain commodities of short supplies such as paper, newsprint, fertilisers, etc., imports were designed to augment the domestic supplies. In the case of oil exploration, telecommunications and shipping, larger imports of capital goods, machinery etc., are needed. So is the need for larger import of technology and foreign knowhow.

At present rapid export promotion is the need of the hour. The national export strategy as recommended by the Tandon Committee (January 1981) aimed at an annual growth rate of 12 per cent in real terms and India's share in world trade at 1 per cent. A series of measures were adopted since 1991-92 to promote exports. These targets were achieved by 2011-12. A few of the important measures are:

(1) Setting up of an Exim Bank to provide all export credit facilities under one window.

(2) Free Trade Zone facilities and other tax concessions to all 100 per cent export-oriented firms and greater fiscal concessions for 100 per cent export-oriented units and for Exports Processing Zones (EPZ) and Special Economic Zones.

(3) Export production to be excluded for consideration of provisions of MRTP Act and for MNCs and for assessing licensed capacity and excess production.

(4) Liberal imports for inputs for export promotion and supply of domestic inputs at international prices for exporters and actual users.

(5) Favourable treatment for import of high technology for export-oriented units, electronic goods, computers, etc.

(6) Ceiling of foreign private investment at 51 per cent to be relaxed for export units and liberalisation of such rules of foreign participation in Indian industry.

(7) Special Thrust to exports of I.T. Software and other services.

Foreign Sector

During the Sixth Plan period 1980-1985 severe balance of payments pressures were noticed with the result that some structural adjustments had to be made to improve the external payments position. India had continuous trade deficits of about Rs. 6 thousand crores per annum which is more than one half of our export earnings. The simple average rate of growth of exports was about 12 per cent while that of imports was 14 per cent at current prices. As against the projected growth rate of 9 per cent in volume, the actual achievement was only 2%. Although the current account deficits were about two-thirds of the projected amount, the pressure persisted due to the shortfall in net aid flowing into India as compared to the projections India borrowed from the IMF 5 billion SDRs under the Extended Fund Facility for the purpose of facilitating structural adjustments. However, successive declines in oil prices and inflow of external resources through non-resident accounts and foreign currency accounts helped India to tide over the external pressures for some time. The improved external payments position in fact helped India forego 1.1 billion of SDR loan in the final year of the Sixth Plan.

The Seventh Plan 1985-90 started with the projections of 7 per cent growth in the volume of exports and 5.8 per cent growth in imports. An export growth of the projected range is expected to be achieved by concentration on "thrust" industries which have a demonstrable and lasting comparative advantage. Some of these "lead industries" have rates of growth of exports higher than that of GDP growth. Such of these commodities, viz., engineering goods, chemicals, garments gem and jewellery, etc., account for nearly half of the increase in exports projected in the Plan. The export of other products may not keep pace with the growth of GDP as in the case of traditional products such as tea, jute, cotton oilcakes, etc., and some non-traditional products like metallic ores, etc.

During 1989 to 1991, there were acute balance of payments problems and we here to draw on IMF loan and devaluation of the rupee. Sub-sequently, we had started structural readjustments leading to Economic and financial reforms from 1992.

The growth rate of exports in US dollar terms was 11.6% in Seventh plan as against 4.5% in Sixth Plan. The growth rate of imports was 8.2% in Seventh plan as against 6.2% in the Sixth plan in dollar terms. Trade deficit was also lower in Seventh plan in dollar terms but was higher in rupee terms. Trade balance deteriorated during 1992-97 which is the Eight plan period. Exports grew by 5.3% in 1996-97, as against 20.8% in 1995-96 and imports rose by 6.7% as against 28% in 1995-96. Imports grew faster than exports during the latter period 2000 to 2009. But in 2010-11 export grew by 37% and import grew by only 27% reversing the trend (in rupee terms).

The rapid growth of export will reduce the need to rely on high cost and inefficient import substitution. The earlier strategy of import substitution was replaced by efficient and competitive levels of domestic production of the import products. Thus, imports of petroleum and its products have declined but still accounted for about one-third of the import bill even in 2009. Imports of fertilisers and other commodities such as steel, cement synthetic fibres, newsprint and non-ferrous metals continued to decline. These measures are expected to contain the current account deficit to manageable limits. In the tenth plan period (2002-2007), exports in rupee terms grew by 25% and imports by 32% as an average per annum.

In the services sector international trade is bound to increase in the years to come. Over the Seventh Plan period, about half of the deficit in merchandise trade was covered by invisible trade earnings as per the Planning Commission's projections. The deficit in the current account during the Seventh Plan period would come to around Rs. 20,000 crores which has to be financed by external borrowings. Our commitment to keep our foreign exchange reserves at a level of around 3 months merchandise trade, necessitated our augmenting the reserves during the period by about Rs. 200 crores as estimated by the Planning Commission.It is also possible that the deterioration in terms our trade might reduce the import power of our exports, and the Plan Document has taken credit for about Rs. 700 crores on this account. Thus, the external borrowings limit would be around Rs. 20,900 crores in total during the Seventh Plan period.

The Tenth Plan Period of 2002-2007 has seen the need for the adoption of right policies on the external front. Import licensing has to be liberalised selectively for giving competition to some industries while, at the same time, improving the availability of inputs for domestic production and for export production. Similarly, import substitution has to be pursued not at any cost but with a view to improving efficiency and productivity and to keep domestic production at the cost price levels obtaining in competing foreign countries.

In the export sector, free trade zones and 100 per cent export units have been strengthened and discrimination against exports in the domestic markets has been removed. This discrimination is due to high costs of inputs leading to uncompetitive conditions in the external markets as against easy availability of markets within the country. All the inputs including credit should be supplied at international cost-price levels in order to counter this bias against foreign markets. Where import restrictions are to be imposed, greater reliance has to be had on tariffs and non-discriminatory assistance to the import substituting sector. Similarly, the policy package for exports consisted of removing the disincentives and handicaps through proper import replenishment schemes — duty drawback, CCS, concessional credits and provision of inputs and intermediates in the production at international prices. Lastly, technological dynamism required for maintaining competitiveness of Indian Industries has got to be ensured. The government has liberalised the imports of technology. Improvement in productivity, lowering of the costs and increase in the competitiveness of our domestic products which have a market abroad should receive the highest priority.

In the nineties, the deceleration in the rate of flow of official aid and multilateral financial resources has forced financial institutions in India to borrow from the commercial markets. Secondly, a number of public sector units and even private corporate units have borrowed from these foreign currency markets and from international banks normally at higher rates. This would lead to a higher debt servicing burden on India in the years to come. However, in view of the sound financial state of the country, after 1992 foreign investment flowed into this country with greater ease than in respect of other developing countries. Besides, the high credit rating of this country has helped us to secure good competitive rates for borrowing in the commercial markets, which the public sector companies and private sector companies took advantage. Barring a couple of years, the commercial borrowing by India grew during the nineties and the first decade of 21st century. Foreign exchange reserves were also built up to cushion up growing trade deficit. There was robust growth of our forex reserves due to larger capital flows during the last decade.

TRADE AS AN ENGINE OF GROWTH

Trade reforms after 1992 placed greater emphasis on improving external competition and greater efficiency in resource allocation. The policy is one of market oriented economy, privatization and globalisation. The economy and markets are opened upto foreign forces leading to freer access to foreign technology and foreign investment in India. This led to greater competition and improved efficiency in the corporate sector: The corporate response has been in terms of increased mergers and acquisitions, survival of fittest, adoption of foreign technologies product differentiation and brand and patent dominance and greater thrust on export markets and production for exports involving cost effectiveness and quality standardization and upgradation.

There was a general paradigm shift in services trade in the nineties decade and the first decade of 21st century. This is in tune with the increasing importance of services in International trade. In the case of India, services sector has been contributing to more than 60% of the GDP in recent years. There was another factor contributing to the importance of services namely the emergence and revolution in information technology, media and entertainment which have become mobile and tradable internationally. The contribution of Services to the GDP grew by 3½ times over the last decade 2001 to 2010.

Service activities like banking and insurance have attracted foreign investment and foreign technology, which have now freer access to India. This led to greater flow of trade across borders, particularly during the last decade. The share of I.T. goods in world trade had increased from 7.5% in 1990 to 11% in 1999. Trade in services was expected to grow in an orderly manner due to the adoption of The General Agreement of trade in Services (GATS) in 1993. Accordingly, there was a sharp rise in trade in I.T. services from India after 1993.

India's share in world trade remained stagnant at around 0.58%, in the nineties despite the growth in services trade. The period upto 1980s was dominated by tourism earnings but the period since the second half of 1990s witnessed an unprecedented jump in India's earnings through software exports and other I.T. related knowledge based service exports. India's share in world trade is now reported to have reached more than 1% of world trade.

The market shift in capital flows from official channels to private sources in the nineties has also contributed to internationalization of skills, technology and related services. At the same time, remittances have continued to be the single most important source of India's invisible earnings, accounting for about 2.7% of GDP in recent years. This also contributed to the growing role of invisible trade in India. The growth of gross invisible earnings has off-set the growth of merchandise trade deficit.

The above trends indicate the relative comparative advantage of India in the provision of services reflecting the role of trade in services as an engine of growth in more recent years and in future. This is to the viewed in the context of increasing barriers to trade in services by developed countries, through the growing restrictions on the grant of visas to professional and I.T. persons. The growth of invisible trade is significant as reflected in the rise in the ratio of invisible earnings to merchandise trade from 40% in 1990-91 to around 90% in 2008-09 as per the Balance of Payments data. The future growth of India's trade lies in the field of services which will act as an engine of growth in India. But during 2009 to 2012, the growth of invisibles was stagnant due to global economic recession.

Project and Consultancy Exports

Since the Seventh Plan period started the emphasis is on promoting exports and in particular exports of services to bridge the deficit in current account. One of the areas of concentration has been the promotion of turn-key projects, civil construction works, capital goods on deferred payments and consultancy in technological and managerial know-how (services contracts).

The Planning Commission has admittedly given priority to the promotion of these exports as India is ranked as the leading exporter in the third-world countries. Our exports in this direction go to Africa, West Asia and the Far East as much as to some developed countries. Some of these are in collaboration with third countries as joint ventures while a few have got sub-contracts. The joint ventures are in operation with advanced countries as also in South East and African countries. The export of capital goods and turn-key projects increased from about Rs. 50 crores in 1971-72 to Rs. 368 crores in 1981-82. In respect of consultancy services, the foreign exchange earnings arising from the services increased multi fold and the studies made by the Indian Institute of Foreign Trade (IIFT) have shown vast potential for these services in the foreign markets, particularly in Indonesia, Malaysia and Singapore. Exports under Turn-key & construction projects as also of Engineering Consultancy grew year after year and constitute an important component of our exports.

All these export contracts require the prior approval of the authorities in the form of Inter-Institutional Working Group comprising representatives of the Reserve Bank of India, Exim Bank, ECGC and the financing banks. In case these contracts are of high value, the consent of the Ministries of Finance and Commerce is also required. The contracts for consultancy services need to be registered with the Working Group although no prior approval is required. The facility of exports of goods on deferred payment basis would be available to engineering goods subject to certain requirements. The ECD of the Reserve Bank would look into the facilities required for such contracts before granting permission for the same. The scrutiny of the RBI and their approval in respect of the execution of the turn-key projects, construction works and services contracts are under the following heads:

(1) Opening and maintaining accounts abroad either at the site in that country or in the third country.

(2) Opening and maintenance of site office or sub-office is one or more places in the importing country or third country.

(3) Payment of agency commission.

(4) Raising of working capital either by borrowing from banks or from Euro-Currency markets abroad.

(5) Purchase of plant and machinery and other equipments from third countries.

(6) Inter-bank transfers and inter-project transfers of funds within the country or as between countries require prior approval.

(7) Investment of excess funds in the importing country or in third countries also require prior permission.

The major problems of these exporters are reported to be inadequacy of finances provided by the banks and the latter's reluctance and delay in granting credit/guarantees and rates of interest higher than in foreign countries. Essentially, Indian banks are alleged to be slow in perceiving the export prospects and helping the exporters. Banks and exporters feel that it is because export credit is not included in the Priority Sector advances. Export credit is cheaper than domestic credit by 2.5 percentage points and it is made a part of priority sector advances. While, on the one hand, the return on export credit is lower than on industrial credit, on the other, the banks are exposed to greater risks and larger work-load in respect of export financing. Also, Exchange Control regulations in India do not allow banks to take any position in currencies or book profits on speculation or hedging.

Briefly, these exporters require guarantees under various heads such as bid bond, performance bond, advance payment guarantee, third country suppliers guarantee, bank guarantee for overseas borrowing and retention guarantee for the maintenance of the plant project. These guarantees carry 3 to 10 per cent commission and involve risk of 10 to 20 per cent of the value of the project.

The Exim Bank provides a host of services to these categories of exporters on the basis of the ECGC guarantee. In some of these, the Exim Bank supplements the bank finances for working capital and term finances for capital and turn-key projects and sharing of bank guarantees for construction contracts. The Exim Bank has been operating a number of schemes suitable for export on deferred payment basis, construction projects and turn-key projects.

In 1981, a Task Force of Project Exports was set up under the chairmanship of Abid Hussain, the then Commerce Secretary. The major findings of the Committee were that India should go ahead to promote these exports and that there are vast potential markets in West Asia, Africa and the Far East. The SBI and its subsidiaries accounted for nearly 50 per cent of the value bids made by Indian exporters in this regard. The percentage of success of securing bids has considerably gone down recently in view of the high costs quoted by Indian firms, lower quality and long delivery periods.

In the case of civil construction work also, Indian contractors have lost the bids due to large time-lags in the processing by banks and high costs quoted by the Indian contractors and the local country preferences for services and technology of the developed countries. It would thus appear that the cost, availability of finances and the time-lags involved play a major role in the quantity of exports in this field.

Exim Policy

Following the earlier policy of dismantling the barriers to trade, as many as 392 items have been placed on free import list (OGL). Another 150 items are put under Special Import Licence (SIL); sixty items have been moved from SIL to OGL. Thus, by removing a total of 542 items (18% of the total) from the restrictive list, the Government has moved in the direction of removing all restrictions by 2002 A.D. It is also important to note that over two-thirds of items removed from the restrictive list are from the consumer goods category.

To reduce the time and red tape, DGFT office was computerised which was completed by end 1998-99, after that applications on floppy are accepted and paper work is reduced leading to quick disposal of applications. Besides, the exporter and importer will get more time for using the licences, as their export obligation under advance licence has been increased from 12 to 18 months. Finally, the setting up of a green channel facility for export and import consignments for all exporters with good track record will further reduce the hassles and red tape.

The Duty Entitlement Passbook Scheme (DEPBS) is an improvement over the old passbook scheme and value based advance licensing scheme, which are replaced. DEPBS is transparent, easy to operate and the credit is transferable. The scheme gives ad-hoc duty entitlement at 5% of the average f.o.b. value of exports in the preceding three years. This entitlement will enable exporters to import duty free, and this is transferable. The duty free credits are at notified rates for different products.

Payment of duty EPCG Scheme was reduced to 10% from 15% earlier. Threshold limit under Zero duty EPCG scheme reduced to Rs. 5 crores for agriculture and allied sectors Special incentives are given to Agro Sector, Hitech exports and SSI products.

Deemed Export benefits are extended to oil and gas sectors. This category would encourage domestic sourcing of inputs and software exports are encouraged and they are also permitted on line data communication for DTA sales also. Hardware units are allowed to sell upto 50% in DTA. Besides DTA sale for EOU, EPZ goods in Agro and allied sectors are liberalised. To encourage domestic capital goods industry; special import license facility was extended to these suppliers. Anti-dumping mechanism was strengthened and to encourage electronic goods industry, special depreciation norms for them are provided upto 70% in three years.

Exim Policy of 1999-2000

The new policy has further reduced the restrictive list for imports. By bringing 894 imports items into free list, mostly from the sector of agricultural and consumer goods, from the current negative list, and another 414 items being placed in Special Import Licence (SIL), there are only 667 items in the restricted list, as against 2714 items in the restricted list in 1997, when India signed the W.T.O agreement. The removal of restrictions was achieved as per our commitment to WTO.

Besides, in tune with the international practice, Free Trade Zones are created in the place of EPZs. Duty exemption scheme was made more flexible. Exporters with a standing will now be allowed to import any duty free input without approaching the DGFT. The pre-export Duty entitlement pass book credit entitlement has been doubled from 5% to 10% of previous year's export performance.

The threshold limit for zero duty EPCG scheme has been brought down from Rs. 20 crores to Rs. 1 crore in the case of chemicals, plastics and textiles. Besides, there will be no additional customs duty on capital goods import, under the zero duty EPCG scheme in Marine and Electronics sector. The latest policy allowed duty free imports of consumables to leather and handicrafts exports as was allowed to gems and jewellery exports.

The other measures are briefly summarised:

(1) Institution of ombudsman for faster solution to exporters' problems.

(2) Value addition for rupee exports to Russia was reduced from 100% to 33%.

(3) Special green card to exporters exporting 50% of their production, which will allow them to various facilities from the Government.

(4) Net foreign exchange earnings as a percentage of exports was made uniform at 20% to both EOUs, & EPZs.

(5) The entitlement of Domestic Tariff area sale for EOU and EPZ was increased to 50% of f.o.b value of the previous year.

Exim Policy 2000-01

Exports have grown by 11% in 1999-2000 in dollar terms and the target for the next year was set at 20%. The target of 20% was achieved during 2000 to 2007 except in the year 2001-02 (in dollar terms). To achieve this target, the Exim Policy has announced the creation of two special Economic Zones in Gujarat and Tamil Nadu and the existing EPZs in Santacruz, Kandla, etc., will be converted to SEZs.

In tune with the requirements of W.T.O. quantitative restrictions on 714 more items were lifted, to allow free imports. To protect the domestic industry, government proposed to take anti-dumping and anti-subsidy measures in respect of free imports. The states are expected to promote exports and an outlay of Rs. 250 crores for states to spend on export promotion measures was announced.

EPCG Scheme is extended to all sectors without threshold limit. Duty draw back pass book scheme for exporters is also continued. Duty free replenishment certificate scheme is announced for more than 5000 products. Sector specific initiatives for EOUs and EPZs in gems, jewellery, biotech, pharma products, leather, garments, silk and granites is planned. The policy aims at a boost to e-commerce, electronic filing of forms and capital goods imports are subject to only 5% duty. There was no SIL from 2000-01. There was major rationalisation of export promotion schemes in the coming year. By 2003, all trade restrictions were removed to comply with the WTO Agreements.

Exim Policy 2002-07 (Tenth Plan)

This Exim Policy was fine tuned in 2004, with a number of trade facilitation measures so as to promote export of quality goods and services. The procedural and operational methods are simplified to impart greater transparency and reduce transactions costs for exporters.

Under the Duty Free Replenishment Certificate Scheme (DFRC), duty free fuel can be imported with actual user conditionality by manufacturers to offset the high power costs faced by them. Under Export Promotion Capital Goods Scheme (EPCG), the procedures were simplified. Rupee payments received for port handling charges were allowed to be reckoned for the discharge of export obligation under the EPCG scheme.

Measures to boost project exports included: (a) enhancement of equity base of ECGC from Rs. 500 to Rs. 800 crores. (b) Creation of a National Export Insurance Account to enable the ECGC to underwrite high value projects, implemented by Indian Companies abroad. (c) Allowing import of all kinds of Capital Goods under the Duty Free Entitlement Scheme (DFES) for the benbefit of the services sector.

Tenth Plan Agenda for Exports

The Tenth plan has projected a growth rate of 12.4% in India's exports. The medium term export strategy is to achieve the country's share of export trade as one per cent by 2006-07, from the then share of 0.6 or 0.7% in 2002-03. Exports as a percentage of GDP at current prices stood at 15% in 2010-11. Exim Policy for this period has identified the need for market diversification with special focus on the Sub-Saharan Africa and Latin America and to promote quality production of strategic export sectors like gems, jewellery, textiles, IT, Software and focussed on Assistance to States for Infrastructural development for export growth of agro-based products, cottage industries, handicrafts, etc.

As regards, imports, tariffs are reduced for essential goods, needed for investment and for exports. As reported by the Task Force on Indirect taxes, the customs tariff reform is already being implemented. Following the introduction of VAT, the import duties were reduced to 10 to 20% by 2006-07, depending on their nature — namely essential goods, intermediate goods, finished and consumer durables.

Indian Shipping and Other Infrastructure

Another development in India's foreign trade is the increased role of Indian shipping and Indian insurance in carrying our trade.

Indian shipping has grown vastly from 0.39 million GRT to about 7 million GRT over the period 1950 to 1999 and there was also a high degree of diversification of her fleet. The seventies has witnessed the maximum increase in tonnage (3.73 million GRT). By 1992, the shipping capacity of India has increased to 5.91 million GRT, with ships numbering about 422 and this increased to 480 ships in 1999. Of this, public sector shipping companies owned a tonnage accounting for about 56 per cent of the country's tonnage. This was made possible by the availability of deferred payment facilities and foreign lines of credit. The Shipping Development Fund set up in 1958 by the government aided the industry which was later aided by SCICI in the process of expansion. The public sector shipping companies provided effective competition to private sector companies with the result that shipping has grown on healthy lines. The Indian share in world shipping ranged from 1 per cent to 2 per cent but Indian ships could carry about 50 per cent of Indian cargo which fell to 25% at present. There was stiff competition from non-conference foreign lines and inadequate container carrying facilities in Indian ships, stood in the way of further expansion.

The Fourth Plan provided for an expansion of tonnage to 3.5 million GRT with which the share of Indian shipping in foreign trade cargo was expected to go up to 40 per cent. The Fifth Plan target was 8.6 million GRT but the actual achievement was about 5.4 million GRT by the end of 1979. The Sixth Plan Draft provided for a shipping tonnage of 7.7 million GRT to be achieved by 1985, but the actual achievement was 6.32 million GRT. The government has kept a goal of carrying 50 per cent of our trade by Indian ships and the actual achievement was much less. The export policy resolution of the government aims at further encouragement to Indian shipping: "Among the inadequacies of the existing infrastructure for exports, that of shipping needs to be emphasised. The government proposes to intensify its efforts to expand the national merchant marine fleet, to start new services and to strengthen existing ones, as may be necessary for the development of our trade." The Eighth plan tonnage target is 7 million GRT which was not achieved due to severe competition and finance problems. The 9th plan target was 9 million GRT. The government also proposes to secure fair treatment for our export cargo and to provide improved shipping opportunities for it.

Methods for the handling of export cargo in our ports have also been improved. The total cargo handled by Indian ports was increasing with improved handling facilities at ports. Our cargo handling capacity at ports was reported to be about 153 million tonnes at end 1991 and has possibly increased further due to New Bombay Port and better facilities at Visakhapatnam port. Indian shipping both coastal and foreign is worth about $5.5 billion and it has great potential to grow. The fact that shipping carries about 70% of total trade as against airways and land routes shows the importance of shipping in India.

In view of the rising cost of shipping, India would be losing foreign exchange if its trade is carried on in foreign ships. The loss is put at $ 4.4 billion in an year. It is understood that the ratio of freight, insurance to f.o.b. value of exports varied from 1 to 8%, as per the RBI Survey in 2004-05. This ratio varies depending on transport by air, sea or land, nature of commodity and destination, etc.

Problems of Indian Shipping

The main problems are dwindling Indian fleet strength and decreasing share of Indian ships in India's foreign trade. Indian shipping despite our vast ocean coast has never been in a good shape. The Government has not given enough thought to developing Indian shipping industry, as fast as the overseas trade.

During 1999-2003 world trade was in recession and Baltic Freight index and Baltic Handy Index were down to their lowest levels. With no immediate prospects of improvement, Indian Shipping is also at its worst phase. Neglect of the interests of Indian shipping by the Government taxation policy and lack of Non-resident status to its earnings, outgo of manpower and problems of depreciation of vessels are some of the reasons for the poor shape of the Shipping Industry.

The number of ships in 1980 was 375 and it was 422 in 1992 and 480 at end December 1998. During the period of 1980 to 2003, Gross Registered tonnage (GRT) rose from 5.54 million to 6.43 million (a rise of 22.2 per cent, as compared to a rise by several times of foreign trade) by 2003 and to 8.59 million as on 1.5.2006.

The share of India's ships in foreign Trade of the country declined from 35.5% in 1990-91 to 27.8% in 1995-96, but has been rising since then. The major problem in the field of shipping is the lack of indigenous designs of ship building business. We have to import cargo ships instead of making them in India.

Banking and Foreign Sector

Indian banks have sixteen entered the foreign trade business in a big way for a long time. As at end October 2011, sixteen Indian banks had overseas operations, spread across 42 countries with a network of 244 branches, including 6 offshore units, 6 joint ventures, 17 subsidiaries and 30 representative offices — a total of 303 offices. In April 2005, SBI has acquired 51% stake in Indian Ocean International Bank Ltd., Mauritius. Arrangements of services, financial and business services constituted the bulk of the rise in recant years.

Foreign Banks operating in India stood at 38, with 321 branches at end September 2011. These branches are spread over 35 centres in 17 States/Union Territories. Besides 47 banks from 23 countries operated representative offices in India. Thus as in early 2011, a total of 85 foreign banks have presence in India either through the branches or representative offices. All these offices are connected to promote foreign trade of India.

India can increasingly operate in international currency markets through its foreign branch network of banks. Government has recently strengthened the capital base of nationalised banks with foreign branch network so as to enable them to improve their image abroad and facilitate their larger participation in foreign currency markets. Indian banks can also compete more efficiently with foreign banks at home and abroad by improving their expertise and efficiency. At present, only the SBI and a few other nationalised banks such as Bank of India, and Bank of Baroda are able to operate in Euro and Asian currency markets as they have the largest network of offices abroad.

The Government has allowed the IDBI to borrow in the international capital markets Syndicated by the Lloyds Bank International and SBI. In addition to existing 23 private sector scheduled banks, many more private sector banks were licensed since 1992. The ICICI has also concluded arrangement for a floating rate note issues to augment its foreign currency resources for lending to the private sector. The IDBI and other financial institutions are now permitted to enter the Euro-currency and Euro-bond markets. A number of private and public companies are also encouraged to raise funds from non-residents, and since 1992 to borrow abroad through GDRs and FCCBs.

Marine Insurance

The government's policy was throughout for encouraging marine insurance to be covered by Indian companies. As in the case of shipping, increasing production of insurance coverage has come into Indian hands after independence and more so after nationalisation of general insurance.

Marine insurance is intended to protect the interests of the shippers in international trade against the perils of sea, including fire, acts of piracy, stranding of ships, collision or other accidents. There are various risks involved in handling the cargo or in the process of transfer of goods through various hands, namely, forwarding agents, freight brokers, the shipping agents, charterers, clearing agents and the like. But basically three parties are involved in any shipping business, namely, the shipper of the goods, (exporters), the shipping company and the consignee (importer). The insurance policy covers risk generally from the point of handing over the goods to an agent of the consignee or to the port of destination. Insurance business in this line is governed by the provisions of Marine Insurance Act of 1963. In actual practice, insurance in the world over is in the "Lloyds form", and various clauses known as "Institute clauses" are attached to it. These clauses define the scope of the coverage available generally from insurers.

The hazards of insurance have increased in recent years due to increase in size of ships, unsatisfactory conditions in various ports and lowering standards of conduct by human agents in handling of cargo, etc. Oil tankers and bulk carriers involve larger risk elements. Sometimes, frauds are committed on the insurers by collusion between shippers and shipping companies. Reasonable precaution has to be taken by the exporters and importers of frauds by shipping companies. The International Chamber of Commerce at Paris has issued a publication "Guide to Prevention of Maritime Frauds" which would help in this regard.

Latest Exim Policy Trends

The latest thrust of Exim Policy is to boost service exports, such as in the fields of health, hospitality and entertainment. All service exports with a minimum foreign exchange earnings of ₹ 10 lakhs were allowed duty free imports to the extent of 5% of their exports from the year 2003-04.

Agro exports and food processing are another area of focus. Some exports like Paddy, sugar etc. are allowed duty free. Exports of autos and auto parts textiles, gems and jewellery have received a boost. Imports of second hand capital goods of more than 10 years old have been made easier, by waiving the "actual user condition".

Procedures have been simplified and special incentives were provided to EPCG and DEPB Schemes. The export performance criteria was dispensed within favour of criteria of net foreign exchange earner. In general, all service exporters can import 10% of their overseas sales at zero duty. Export obligations under EPCG Scheme were cut to a quarter of current levels; sales to SEZs from DTA was to be treated as export, while sales to DTA from SEZ are exempt from special additional duty. (SAD). Sales from domestic market to special economic zones (SEZ Units) would be entitled to duty entitlement pass book (DEPB), duty drawback benefits and free from central sales Tax. All these tax and non tax sops will cost the exchequer about Rs 30,000 crores in a year.

Now that all quantitative restrictions are removed, the future thrust of exim policy is only on export promotion. Exports in 2002-03 have grown by 17% and those in 2007-08 by 29%, while it was a decline of 2% in 2001-02. The exports from India now constitute only 1.2% of total world trade, while it aims to expand this to 1.5% of total world trade.

Exim policy for the Tenth plan period 2002-07 was announced in March 2002. The policy was oriented to growth of world trade of India. For this purpose, the growth rate of India's trade should be 12% per annum or more. The objective of policy was to make it a vital part of the growth of the economy, employment and poverty alleviation. The growth rate of 8% of the GDP is possible, if both industry, and agriculture contribute through maximization of exports. The growth rate of GDP of 8% or more was already achieved in 2003-04 to 2007-08. It was 15% of GDP in 2010-11. The international environment being dynamic, the exim policy has to be adjusted annually to the tune of changing conditions. In this context, the latest policy shift has been to the growth of service exports and export of agro based products in the coming years. Sector wise, the export thrust has been given to textiles, garments, auto parts, gems and jewellery, drugs and chemicals. Export houses, EOUs, EPZs and SEZs are given greater freedom and incentives by reducing the transaction costs and hassles of Administrative machinery of Government and by simplification of procedures.

In the area of service exports, software exports, has been given the prime importance of growth boosters. Besides, exports of health services tourism, entertainment, media, etc., are the other thrust areas of policy, which got some incentive scheme in the Exim policy. These incentives are in the form of duty free imports, and other tax concessions and augment the flow of credit and finance to these sectors.

In the area of Agriculture and allied products, the policy identified thrust areas as horticulture flowers, fruits and vegetable and dairy and marine products. The measures were intended to help their growth of exports and include the association of corporates with Agri Export Zones, modification of norms for fixing the Duty Exemption Pass Book (DEPB) rates for some inputs and output of agriculture, promotion of special zones with some tax and bank finance schemes, development of towns of export excellence or industrial cluster towns (Ludhiana for woollen knit wear, Tirupur for hosiery, etc.) and special strategic packages for export status holders and diversification of markets into North Africa and Latin America. The policy includes measures for administrative simplification and some modifications of Traditional Export Promotion Schemes. Quality control and Brand Schemes are to be encouraged by the central and State Governments through modernization and upgradation of test houses and by setting up of machinery to investigate complaints by DGFT.

The Exim policy for the Tenth Plan 2002-07 And for Eleventh Plan (2007-2012) has continued the earlier schemes like Duty Entitlement Pass Book (DEPB) scheme, Duty Free Replenishment Certificate (DFRC), Advance licenses, Export promotion capital goods scheme (EPCG), Export oriented units (EOU), Special Economic Zones (SEZ) etc. There was a greater emphasis on promotion of trade to Latin American countries such as Argentina, Brazil, Chile, etc., through Bilateral Trade agreements and to African countries, where India has diplomatic missions. These schemes contain emphasis on promotion of exports and imports of India to these regions. The Focus Latin American countries (LAC) scheme was launched in 1997 and the Focus Africa Scheme was launched in 2002. The trade to these countries stood at around 7-10% of India's total trade and there is good potentiality to increase this share of India's foreign trade in future.

Foreign Trade Policy 2004-09

A comprehensive foreign trade policy was announced in August 2004 which has aimed at the doubling of the foreign trade to increase its share of world trade to one per cent of world trade by 2009, to make foreign trade an engine of growth and to increase employment opportunities in the export sector. The special focus areas are agriculture, handlooms, handicrafts, gems and jewellery, leather and footwear, and marine products.

To accelerate the growth of agriculture and services sector on the export front, the FTP 2004, also revamped the Board of Trade to advice the government on these matters from time to time. To give a real boost to the export sector, policies are envisaged on non-credit tools of aid to the export sector and simplification of procedures and make them hassle free.

In February 2005, certain thrust areas were identified for policy implementation, such as electronic data interchange for on-line filing of returns, electronic data collection, rejuvenating the project exports, reshaping the special economic zones (SEZ) and SOFTWARE TECHNOLOGY

PARKS (STP) in respect of taxation, customs and labour participation etc. This policy change also includes decentralization, simplificiation transparency, accountability and e-governance in respect of the procedures and practices.

Greater flexibility was given to exporters in export realizations, retention of foreign Exchange earnings abroad, and its utilization, Payments in foreign currency to units in DTAs for their supplies to units in SEZs and by project Exporters and service exporters to their Indian suppliers. Exporters in small and medium sectors and large scale trading manufacturing units with good track record were given the eligibility for the GOLD CARD SCHEME, for easy availability of the export credit.

In April 2005 the FTP was fine tuned to provide incentives for agriculture and marine product exporters and those in the service sector for their exports. The state governments and commodity boards were also involved in this thrust area for export promotion through the removal of all cesses and any local taxes levied on these commodities meant for exports. All benefits given under VISHESH KRISHI UPAJ YOJANA operated by the Centre are being extended to poultry, dairy, horticulture, and minor forest products and value added items in the agricultural sector.

In the area of imports also, the procedures and practices are simplified in addition to removing all quantum controls and reducing the tariff and non tariff barriers, Documentation for import remittances made into India has to be provided only for amounts above a certain level of US $100,000. Credit for imports up to $20 million per transaction with a maturity of one to three years was allowed for import of capital goods. A large number of measures were also announced during 2005-06 with a view to facilitate the export and import trade and promote the growth of foreign sector and these policies during the Eleventh Plan Period are referred to later.

Despite such good policy initiatives, the trade balance continued to show a growing deficit, particularly during the recent years. There was however growing volume and value of exports rising by 20 to 27% per annum but offset by a larger growth of imports of about 30% during this period. But with the robust growth of the GDP at 8-9% in the recent past, and with a comfortable exchange reserve position, the growth of foreign trade of the above order was considered good for investments to grow and the corporate sector to expand their operations. The export surplus an account of invariables stood to support the deficit on merchandise trade account.

Appendix I and II present the proforma details of Principal Export Commodities, and Principal Import Commodities respectively.

Eleventh Plan Projections

During the plan period of 2007 to 2012, the GDP was expected to grow at rate of 10% and for this the savings and investment rate should be about 38 to 40% of GDP. For industrial growth, infra structure development is made essential pre-requisite which is to be achieved by public and private partnership. This was not achieved and the economy during 2010 to 2012 was in doldrums due to slow growth of industry, inflation and general slowdown of investment.

Eleventh plan projections indicate a higher rate of growth of exports specially in the services sector and our trade should be more than 1.5 per cent of the world trade. During the year 2007, India's exports were already higher than one per cent of the world exports according to the WTO data, the India's share in the world trade already increased to 1.3 per cent in 2007-08, which is the first year of the eleventh plan period.

The merchandise exports recorded an average growth rate of 20.3 per cent during the period of 2000 to 2010 which is much higher than 8.6% recorded in the previous decade of 1990 to 2000. Beside the export basket has become more diversified and services sector is expected to grow much faster Particularly the exports of engineering goods and petroleum products had increased much faster than other commodities. Already India has emerged as the major exporter of services items particularly in the field of I.T and software services and services exports would be a growth driver.

Recent Foreign Trade Policy Change

In order to support the export sector, in the context of slow down of our exports since Oct. 2008. The RBI has announced the following measures in Nov. 2008.

(a) The aggregate limit of export credit refinance was enhanced from 15% to 50% of the outstanding export credit provided by banks.

(b) The period of entitlement of the first slab of preshipment credit in rupee terms was extended from 180 days to 270 days. The same for the post-shipment credit was extended from 90 days to 180 days.

(c) The prescribed interest rate applicable to post-shipment credit in rupee terms was extended to overdue bills up to 180 days (BPL Rate minus 2.5% points).

The policy statement of 2008 on Foreign Trade Policy for 2004-09 introduced sectorial initiatives and relief to sectors, affected by rupee appreciation and announced measures to reduce transaction costs and procedural simplifications to help exporters. India's duly free Tariff preferences (DFTS) scheme for the least developed countries, announced by the government grants duly tree access on 94% of total tariff lines, to be implemented over next five years from 2008. This share covers 92.5% of global years of all LDCs and covers 49 LDC members.

Various other measures of the government included the extension of duty entitlement passbook scheme (DEPS) beyond November 2008, enhancement duty drawback benefits to certain inflows, like fabrics, bicycle, Agricultural hand tools, and some other items, which are all affected by trade recession since October 2008. The Market Access Initiative scheme (MAI) was started with a surplus of Rs. 5 crores of base fund for export promotional activities by Trade Missions abroad.

In the union Budget 2009-10 measures announced included extension of the Adjustment Assistance Scheme for badly not export sectors, like leather textiles, capital goods, germs and jewellery, larger credit flow to Micro, small and medium enterprises, extension of the period for income tax and customs duty and other measures to help the adversely affected exporters like simplification and easy availability of export credit.

APPENDIX I

Principal Export Commodities

I. Primary Products

A. **Agricultural and Allied Products of which:**

1. *Tea*
2. *Cotton*
3. *Rice*
4. *Oil and Meat*
5. *Marine Products*

B. **Ores & Minerals**

II. Manufactured Goods of which:

A. **Leather & Manufactures**

B. **Chemicals & Related Products**

1. *Basic Chemicals, Pharmaceuticals & Cosmetics*
2. *Plastic & Linoleum*
3. *Rubber, Glass, Paints & Enamels, etc.*
4. *Residual Chemicals & Allied Products*

C. **Engineering Goods**

D. **Textiles** ***of which:***

1. *Cotton Yarn, Fabrics, Made-up, etc;*
2. *Readymade Garments*
3. *Manmade Yarn, Fabrics, Made-ups, etc.*

E. **Gems and Jewellery**

F. **Handicrafts**

G. **Carpets**

1. *Handmade*
2. *Mill-made*
3. *Silk*

III. Petroleum, Crude and Products

IV. Others

Total Exports (I+II+III+IV)

APPENDIX II

PRINCIPAL IMPORT COMMODITIES

I. Bulk Imports

A. Petroleum, Petroleum Products and Related Material

B. Bulk Consumption Goods

1. *Cereals and Cereal Preparations*
2. *Edible Oil*
3. *Pulses*
4. *Sugar*

C. Other Bulk Items

1. *Fertilisers*
   - (a) *Crude*
   - (b) *Sulphur and Unroasted Iron Pyrites*
   - (c) *Manufactured*
2. *Non-Ferrous Metals*
3. *Paper, Paperboard and Manufactured including Newsprint*
4. *Crude Rubber including Synthentic and Reclaimed*
5. *Pulp and Waste Paper*
6. *Metalliferrous Ores and Metal Scrap*
7. *Iron and Steel*

II. Non-Bulk Imports

A. Capital Goods

1. *Manufactures of Metals*
2. *Machine Tools*
3. *Machinery except Electrical and Electronics*
4. *Electrical Machinery except Electronics*
5. *Electronic Goods including Computer Software*
6. *Transport Equipments*
7. *Project Goods*

B. Mainly Export Related Items

1. *Pearls, Precious and Semi-Precious Stones*
2. *Chemicals, Organic and Inorganic*

3. *Textile Yarn, Fabrics, etc.*
4. *Cashew Nuts, Raw*

C. Others *of which:*

1. *Gold and Silver*
2. *Artificial Resins and Plastic Materials*
3. *Professional, Scientific and Optical Goods*
4. *Coal, Coke and Briquittes etc.*
5. *Medicinal and Pharmaceutical Products*
6. *Chemical Materials and Products*
7. *Non-Metallic Mineral Manufactures*

Total Imports (I+II)

PART – III

BALANCE OF PAYMENTS AND RESTRICTIVE POLICIES

14

Balance of Payments Theory

No country is self-sufficient and the interdependence of countries is reflected in international economic and commercial transactions. An economic transaction is an exchange of value or transfer of a title to a good or an asset. A commercial transaction is an exchange of good or service for money which will result in payment in currency or monetary assets leading to financial flows. The resource flows from one country to another due to purchase and sale of financial claims are referred to as financial transactions. The international exchange of goods for goods, goods for services or services for services or goods and services for money are all referred to as international economic and commercial transactions. Besides, there are flows of funds on capital account for working capital (short term funds) or for investment (long term funds)

Definition

Balance of payments of a country is a "systematic record of all economic and commercial transactions between the residents of the reporting country and residents of foreign countries". This account is for a period of time, normally one year. These transactions are as between residents of one country with those of other countries. Residents are to be differentiated from nationals and are normally resident in the reporting country for a greater part of the year. A national is a citizen of a state and may be a resident in his own nation or outside. On the other hand, diplomats, military personnel, temporary migratory workers and branches of domestic companies abroad are regarded as residents of the country, where they come from rather than where they reside because they are not subject to the control of national authorities of the country where they reside. Balance of payments refers to the transactions between the residents of one country with another, rather than as between nationals of two countries. The basic idea is that balance of payments should record economic and commercial transactions flowing from one geographical region to another, constituting the nation states with the domestic incomes and output subject to the control of national authorities. Such records may help the government of the reporting country to measure the flows oi goods and services or resources flows from their country to others and vice versa. Monetary authorities of the reporting country should know the receipts and payments as between the reporting country and others so as to assess the impact of such flows on domestic money supply and on the savings of the economy. Besides, economists would like to study from these data the impact of foreign transactions on national income of the reporting country — their impact on current income and expenditure (current account) and on assets and liabilities of the country (capital side).

The monetary and fiscal policies and foreign exchange policy would be formulated or reformulated on the basis of these data. It would thus be seen that the balance of payments data are very useful from the point of view of formulation and operation of the domestic economic policy.

Accounting of Balance of Payments

Balance of payments is kept on a double entry book-keeping system with credits and debits of equal size. For every transaction, there is a corresponding entry on both the credit and debit sides. Thus, if exports are made, there will be a credit for outflow of goods on Current Account and a corresponding entry of debit for claim on a foreign company or country or increase in foreign assets or claims on foreigners. Similarly, imports will appear as a debit item for the inflow of goods and the credit item for being paid out is shown by increase in foreign liabilities, reduction of foreign assets or outflow of funds or claims on us. Thus, for every credit/debit entry on Current Account, there is a corresponding entry on capital account to match the former. In case of unilateral transfers such as gifts, donations etc., there is no corresponding payment or change in assets or liabilities. The contra entry is donations or gifts on the debit side and for the credit, it is the flow of goods from out of the country. It is not always possible to match all debits which credits due to differences in sources and timing of events. A discrepancy might then arise necessitating a balancing entry, namely, errors and omissions.

Sources of Compilation

In the case of countries which do not have exchange controls, statistical recording of balance of payments data is done by the government with the help of their Statistical Office which in turn depends upon a host of private and government agencies, banks, companies, etc. Each member country of the IMF is compiling these data for onward transmission to the Fund and for their own records and use. In view of the crucial importance of these data for policy-making, planning etc., compilation and timely availability of these data are considered to be utmost importance.

The usual sources of compilation for any country are the government agencies and the monetary authority of the country. These data are collected either on a statutory basis or a voluntary basis from various private and government, etc., agencies, airways ports, etc., banks and financial institutions. Where exchange controls operate as in India, these data are more easily available with the agencies entrusted with the operation of exchange controls such as the monetary authority of the country, the government and the banks.

Limitations in Compilation

A few limitations in compilation of balance of payments may be noticed here:

(1) Not all transactions are reported through official channels, particularly where there are no exchange and trade restrictions.

(2) A time-lag between an actual transaction and its reporting is possible so that the balance of payments do not properly record the transactions during the period.

(3) There could be under-invoicing or over-invoicing of goods and services so that they do not represent the true value of gain or loss to the country.

(4) Not sufficient details of all transactions are available in some cases as, for example, in remittances, short-term capital inflows or outflows, gifts, samples, etc., particularly in respect of services or invisible items.

The item errors and omissions will be a major component of balance of payments if such limitations are substantial and it is always possible that debits and credits do not tally during any period of time.

Components of Balance of Payments

The major classes of transactions recorded in the balance of payments are current account and capital account transactions. On the current account, only transactions of current nature resulting in incomes or expenditure and not leading to asset formation are recorded. There are four sub-categories under this head, namely, (a) Transactions of merchandise or visible items of goods, namely, exports including re-exports and imports, (b) Transactions on invisible account, namely, foreign travel, transportation, banking, insurance and other services, interest, dividends, royalties, Government Embassy expenditures, etc., (c) Unilateral transfers like gifts, donations, charities, etc., (d) Non-monetary gold movements. All the above items can take place on private account or government account and may be subject to government restrictions or controls, if any. Gold is a special category as it can be used both as a commodity and as an international medium of exchange or money. Domestic transactions of gold, namely, sale of gold by residents to monetary authorities are also recorded in the balance of payments, as they affect gold holdings and international reserves of the country. Gold is held as part of international reserves of countries.

The capital account transactions are short-term capital inflows and outflows for private purposes, official purposes or banking purposes. Private flows of capital include private company remittances for working capital purposes to subsidiaries or branches of foreign companies or short-term loans, grants, etc., from foreign banks, international financial institutions, foreign government etc. These short-term flows may be for investment purposes or speculation on private account or for compensatory purposes on government account. These can also be banking funds for short-term purposes.

There are long-term capital movements which may again be private or governmental. The private flows include loans and advances granted to private parties (Buyers' credit), investment in shares, bonds, debentures, etc., by Indians abroad or by foreigners in India, investment in joint ventures, consultancy, turn-key projects, deferred payment credits, etc. Such flows on official account also take place through governments or governmental agencies or financial institutions in India through lines of credit, foreign government loans, credits, grants etc., for private long-term purposes.

The capital account reflects the changes in foreign assets and liabilities of the country and affects its creditor/debtor position. An excess of foreign assets over foreign liabilities indicates a net creditor position and vice versa. Net changes in current account are reflected by a corresponding and opposite change in the capital account, changing the foreign assets and liabilities position of the country. Current account is like an income and expenditure statement with surplus or deficit in it transferred to capital account which is like a balance sheet. If all these accounts do not tally, errors and omissions are added to balance the corresponding column of balance of payments. In an economic sense, a country has a surplus or deficit in its balance of payments, when its transactions other than those merely financing the real transactions are not in balance. Those merely financing are said to be "below the line" while others are "above the line". The selection of items below the line is generally decided by each country, depending upon its requirements for economic policy in the short run and long run. The various concepts used by countries at present are discussed later in the chapter.

In a statistical sense, errors and omissions is a balancing entry to correct any discrepancy between total credits and debits after including all the items in the balance of payments. The balancing item is derived on a net basis so that net current account balance together with "errors and omissions" would equal the net opposite position in the capital account. Suppose the net surplus (credit) on current account is Rs. 60 crores and the net debit on capital account is Rs. 40 crores, the errors and omission would be Rs. 20 crores (+)

The size and magnitude of errors may reflect the sophistication in the reporting system rather than the reliability of the data conceptually. These errors being random variables should reflect movements on both debits and credits (plus or minus) over the long run. A consistent positive sign would indicate that receipts are understated or payments overstated and vice versa.

The last item on balance of payments other than "errors and omission" is the movement in foreign exchange reserves of the country normally shown in capital account. These reserves are in foreign currencies, foreign assets, investments and balances held abroad, or gold of the government, and official monetary agencies like the Central Bank.

Balance of Payments Data

As referred to earlier, there are continuous interactions between the domestic sectors and foreign sectors in every country. The movements in the balance of payments influence the savings and investments in the economy and the national income and expenditure of the country. These data are useful to estimate and plan for the following:

(1) Savings gap.

(2) Foreign exchange gap.

(3) Investment outlays.

Each of the sectors has some savings and investments and while some are net savers, others are net investors. In India, the foreign sector has been a net saver for some time in the past and this promotes investment by other sectors of the economy. Such investment helps the growth of incomes and employment in the economy. Besides, these inflows relieve the balance of payments constraint (or foreign exchange gap) of the developing country due to the absence of adequate import capacity, or the inadequacy of foreign exchange reserves which would stand in the way of growth of income and employment of these countries. Thirdly, such inflows would promote markets, specialisation and larger production in the world as a whole. These data are thus useful for formulation of savings and investment policy, planning the growth of the economy, internal monetary policy, fiscal policy and more directly, the foreign exchange policy. The trends in balance of payments would have repercussions on the internal and international monetary scene and influences the foreign exchange, monetary and fiscal policies of the country and the overall growth of the economy.

Mechanism of Adjustment

When entries are made on a double-entry basis, credits and debits must tally. In this sense, balance of payments must always balance. But it is only in an accounting sense. In an economic sense, what we need to know is the mechanism of adjustment. How are the forces operating towards balancing of inflows and outflows of a country when there can be larger export than imports (a positive trade balance) or a larger invisible exports over imports (or a positive invisible trade balance) or a larger current account balance? Normally, a deficit in current account will be made good (if not due to statistical errors or omissions) by the outflow of monetary gold, short-term credits or a loss of foreign exchange assets or increase in foreign exchange liabilities. If the short-term credits and inflows of funds are autonomous and not induced for financing a deficit on other accounts, then these will be a part of regular balance of payments. Leaving aside such deliberate efforts at balancing due to induced flow of funds, the mechanism of adjustment works automatically through: (a) Price changes, and (b) Income changes or both.

Price Mechanism

In international trade, price mechanism works through price elasticities of demand and supply. Under the classical assumption of perfect competition at home, factor mobility internally and constant factor proportions, elasticities are high and a small price change may correct a deficit of surplus in balance of payments. Here price is used in the micro sense of price of a good or macro sense of prices of all goods and services. International trade takes place due to excess supply at home and excess demand abroad for any product. If these excess supply schedules are price-elastic, small changes in them may bring about quick adjustment, because a small fall in price for example, may increase the demand for or reduce the supply of and clear the market for the good. Elasticity is measured by $\frac{\Delta S/S}{\Delta P/P}$ or $\frac{\Delta D/D}{\Delta P/P}$ in respect of supply and demand - responsiveness of supply/demand to a small change in price.

In real world, these elasticities are low, particularly for a developing country like India, whose production structure is based mainly on agriculture. For price mechanism to work effectively the relevant elasticities should be high. Marshall-Lerner condition for improvement in balance of trade and payment as a result of changes in price is as follows. "The sum of elasticities of demand — the demand at home for a country's imports and the demand abroad for its export — must be greater than one". Depreciation or lowering of the price of a currency in international transactions would then improve the balance of payments. Depreciation or devaluation would mean a lowering of the domestic price in terms of foreign currencies. Devaluation can improve the balance of payments, if the relative elasticities of supply of and demand for goods entering into the international markets are high. Besides, the deficits in balance of payments should not be high or chronic.

The above analysis of the effect of price change suffers from limitations of unrealistic assumptions of perfect competition and constancy of other conditions and is based on partial equilibrium analysis. If the sum of elasticities is less than one, appreciation of currency (or re-valuation) may improve the trade balance. Revaluation means an increase in the price of one currency in terms of another currency. Besides there will be simultaneous income effects — effect on domestic incomes and foreign repercussion of such price changes which may promote or thwart the price effect.

Income Adjustment

If we start with Hume's law of no foreign savings, an increase in exports will increase income at home which in turn would lead to larger imports which would balance the trade and payments. The amount by which an initial increase in exports would lead to an increase in income is called foreign trade multiplier-equal to 1/MPM where MPM is marginal propensity to import. This is the automatic adjustment process through income changes over a period of time. This thesis follows from the postulation that Y = C + X - M; Income = consumption + exports - imports, where no savings are existing. But if savings also exist, the increase in exports will be balanced by increase in imports and in savings, provided that investment is unchanged. In this case the multiplier is 1/ MPM + MPS where MPS is marginal propensity to save. The foreign trade multiplier expresses the change in income caused by a change in exports or investments/savings in an open economy in which income spills over into imports. The above formulation is based on simple assumptions. If complex formulations are necessary, the final outcome would be indeterminate if (1) Price and income effects operate simultaneously as in the real world, and (2) If there is a significant effect from a change in imports on income abroad which again produces a substantial change on its exports, which is said to be the foreign repercussion effect — an income change at home producing income changes abroad and thus on domestic incomes again.

If the accelerator is also at work at home, then an increase in exports would lead to an increase in investment and to further rise in income. If the foreign effects are also operating then the original increase in exports may produce a larger increase in imports and lead to an unfavourable balance of trade or the effect would be indeterminate.

Absorption Approach of Alexander

Adjustment in balance of payments may take place due to "redistribution effect" or "money illusion effect" or demonstration effect". An important mode of adjustment is the income redistribution. If import prices rise due to depreciation or for other reasons, the cost of living of the classes consuming imports would rise and profits may be made in the foreign trade sector, particularly exports which might lead to lower absorption of imports resulting in adjustment in the balance of payments. A decline in consumption or a decline in investment may lead to a readjustment of balance of payments according to S.S. Alexander.[1]

If there is money illusion, called the Pigou effect, with a constant money supply and increase in prices and money incomes, there will be larger savings and investment and lower consumption to keep up savings. Thus, lower consumption and lower absorption might lead to lower imports and to balance the deficit in balance of payments. If there is less than full employment, a rise in prices leads to a larger production, larger income leading to larger savings and investment. Thus, income changes consequent on foreign trade changes would lead to an adjustment in the balance of payments. It should be conceded that these adjustments are possible in flexible economies with free competition and free flow of economic forces which are non-existent in the real world. Adjustment in the balance of payments is also possible through the demonstration effect on production and consumption at home emanating from abroad. Thus, larger exports might induce larger imports through the demonstration effect. It is also possible that larger imports facilitate larger exports through its effect on production and expenditure on goods and on savings and investment at home.

Elasticity Approach vs. Absorption Approach

The elasticity approach postulates that foreign trade changes operate through price and terms of trade changes in a way that income and spending would adjust to trade. On the other hand, the absorption approach works through savings and investment which will determine expenditure and incomes and the trade would adjust to these changes. A deficit in balance of payments would mean that domestic expenditure is more than domestic output. Adjustment would have to work by increasing the level of income to equal to expenditure and domestic investment to domestic savings and foreign savings (X – M). In the short run, elasticity approach may be more suitable while in the long-run income expenditure adjustments are possible and absorption approach may appear to be more apt. In the real world, such simplified approaches may not be appropriate. What happens is a mileu of all forces, including price and income effects, investment and savings changes and a host of other

1. S.S. Alexander, "Effect of a Devaluation on a Trade Balance", in AER, *Readings in International Economics.*

factors operate on balance of payments. Adjustment in the balance of payments on the general equilibrium model takes place through a complete set of forces emanating from all sectors of the economy, including domestic and foreign, and a combination of both the approaches is thus relevant.

General Equilibrium Approaches

The balance of payments disequilibrium may be a monetary phenomenon or real phenomenon or the result of structural maladjustments. In the first case, disequilibrium is the result of difference between aggregate receipts and payments, which is to be made good by monetary adjustments, namely, credit creation or destruction — changes in 'M' or 'V' (Money Stock or Velocity). The deficit may reflect a "stock" decision or "flow" decision of economic units. The stock decision refers to the community's preference for foreign assets and money as against domestic assets and money. Then the direct controls would have to be resorted to. In a flow concept, the reference is to excess payments over receipts which can be corrected by expenditure-reduction policy or expenditure-switching policy. The former leads to anti-inflationary policy and the latter to selective monetary and fiscal policies or controls. Expenditure reduction or increased output or both can be aimed at with expenditure switching from foreign to domestic goods and services.

If balance of payments deficit is due to real factors, then increase in output and income or adjustment in the production structure is necessary. So is the case of India which has persistent Balance of payments imbalances to be corrected by economic reforms since 1991-92. Structural maladjustment is a possible reason for real factors operating adversely on the balance of payments. In that event, long-run structural changes in the economy and in production patterns have to be effected. Devaluation and controls might help only as temporary expedients for adjustment in the balance of payments in such cases. The economic and financial reforms initiated since July 1991 have improved the balance of payments position, of India.

Balance of Payments — Measurement of Deficits

The total of credits and debits in current and capital accounts may not always balance. There can be surplus or deficit which is made good by a corresponding balancing entry, namely, official financing items. These items may be gold, use of IMF assistance or drawal on the country's foreign assets.

For purposes of economic analysis and policy formulation, there are various types of balances arising out of credits and debits in the balance of payments. A few of such concepts of balances may be set out as: (a) Trade Balance; (b) Current A/c Balance; (c) Basic Balance; (d) Balance in regular transactions; and (e) Balance settled by official transactions.

(a) Trade Balance: (X + M = 0): It is the most widely used concept where X is exports and M is imports on merchandise account as the relevant data are the earliest to be available for any period and easy to comprehend and handle. Trade balance is the balance of exports and imports of merchandise goods. It is useful for analysis of flow of goods, sector-wise, and in input-output tables. Price and income elasticities are more easily analysed in terms of merchandise trade balance - exports and imports. But these data are not useful for further analysis in foreign exchange budget or in money supply analysis or in national income analysis.

(b) Current Account Balance: $X + M + X' + M' = 0$: where X1 is exports on invisible trade account and M-1 is imports on the same account.

Exports and imports of both goods and services are considered in this concept and it is a combination of balance on merchandise account plus balance on invisible trade account. A total outstanding balance on the current account is made good by contra balance on short-term and long-term capital flows, excluding errors and omissions. This concept is useful for national income analysis. If $X + M + X^1 + M^1 > O$, meaning that if the current account Balance is positive, the country is gaining from the rest of the world and it stimulates domestic national income if there is unemployment or under-employment of resources. If this positive balance adds to foreign exchange reserves, money supply increases and produces an inflationary impact in the short run. If the foreign savings are productively invested, income, output and employment will be increased under conditions of less than full employment. If all countries aim at a positive current account balance, it will lead to a scramble, undercutting, etc. If some have a positive balance, there must be others with a negative balance as all cannot have a positive balance. But this concept is not very useful for some purposes such as foreign exchange budgeting.

(c) Basic Balance ($X + M + X' + M' + LTC$) = STC where STC is Short-term Capital and LTC is Long-term Capital: This concept was propagated by economists like Ragner Nurkse for the purposes of economic analysis. It assumes that current account balance and long-term capital flows are autonomous and they are counter-balanced by short-term capital flows which are generally induced. There may, however be short-term flows which are autonomous and motivated by investment or speculative gains. The concept helps the analysis of transfer problem in international payments. Thus, if autonomous receipts and payments leave a negative balance, it is to be counter-balanced or financed by short-term inflow in the form of gold, international currencies or credits. This would involve exchange of currencies or credit instruments in the foreign exchange market.

This concept is useful in national income analysis, foreign exchange budgeting, funds flow analysis. etc. Besides by the basic balance concept, equilibrium in the balance of payments can be judged and the pressure on the exchange market and the extent of the transfer problem can be analysed. Briefly, transfer problem relates to the difficulty of exchanging one currency against another. If one currency is more in supply in the exchange market, its value depreciates. So on top of the country's difficulty of finding resources for transfer, the transfer itself would lead to depreciation of currency due to the difficulty of proper matching of currencies.

(d) Balance of Regular Transactions: This concept is a finer version of the Basic Balance in that all short-term capital (STC) is not used for balancing purposes. A part of it is STC(d) or autonomous and domestic and a part of it is STC(f) or induced and foreign. This latter part would be considered as liquid funds whose conversion would create a problem in the foreign exchange markets.

$$X + M + X^1 + M^1 + LTC + STC(d) = STC(f).$$

In the above equation, STC(f) is the liquidity in the international markets which will create problems of transfer and lead to disturbances in international markets, particularly when countries do not have enough gold to enable conversion of foreign funds into gold at the will of the surplus country. When a county is a banker and a trader like the USA or UK, it will have a liquidity crisis due to a run on their currencies. So what is relevant for them is a concept which will include only induced official flows of funds, as on such occasions, private flows cannot be depended upon. Thus, some STC(f) may flow on private account for interest rate gains or speculation or for working capital purposes. Hence, the need for a concept which distinguishes private and official capital flows is felt particularly in countries which are international bankers and traders. Thus, a balance settled by official short-term capital flows has been formulated.

(e) Balance Settled by Official Transactions: The induced short-term flow of funds to finance the balance of payments deficits is further split up into official and private. Thus, STC(f) is of two components - private and official - STC(fp) and STC(fo). STC(fp) is short term capital on account of private agencies, like trade credits STC(fo) is short-term capital on account of official agencies or monetary authorities of the country. This reflects the official funds flowing in or out to balance the balance of payments. These are induced funds as opposed to autonomous flows which are again both official and private. Of the induced flows, it is only officially induced flows which are taken to represent deficit in the balance of payments. These flows include both monetary gold movements and international currency flows. The above distinction between official and private flows under short-term foreign capital flows was spearheaded by a former IMF Chief Mr. M. Bernstein. This distinction is also in tune with the original distinction made by the IMF in its first Balance of Payments Year Book of 1949 between autonomous or private transactions, on the one hand, and official or compensatory movements, on the other. This type of classification has been used by the IMF to measure the disequilibrium in the balance of payments for the purpose of change of par values or imposition of control on trade and payments.

For a country like India, the concept of basic balance is adequate to measure the balance of payment disequilibrium. But there are a number of trader-banker countries at international level like the USA, UK, West Germany or Japan whose currencies serve as international liquidity or reserve currencies. As in domestic banking, the concepts of solvency, liquidity and safety apply to international banking. Countries whose currencies constitute reserve assets in international liquidity may have to observe better caution against run on their currencies which may lead to non-conversion of such currencies into gold. In these cases, disequilibrium in balance of payments should be measured by short-term official foreign capital which is induced to be of a compensatory nature and not by short-term foreign capital (e) above which includes both private and government flows.

15

India's Balance of Payments

Introduction

In India, balance of payments compilation, concepts and techniques are almost similar to those followed by the International Monetary Fund (IMF). These are codified by the Fund in their Balance of Payments Manual given to member countries for their reference and guidance. Although the details of items and the mode of presentation may differ from country to country, the broad framework does not differ as between the member countries who submit periodically their balance of payments accounts to the Fund for their consolidation, assessment and/or publication.

The usual classification of the accounts into current and capital items — the former of income nature and the latter of capital nature — is followed by India also. The items shown above the line are considered to be of autonomous nature and those below the line, of a financing nature. The concept of surplus or deficit as followed by the Ministry of Finance is the sum total of items shown below the line, namely, (1) IMF Net, (2) SDR net, and (3) changes in the country's foreign exchange reserves. The rest of the items of current and capital nature appear above the line. In the presentation of data by the RBI, reserves and monetary gold appear as balancing items, leaving aside "errors and omissions".

In India, balance of payments had been showing consistent deficits which were designed to finance the plan expenditure. Thus, our imbalance in balance of payments is not really of a short-term disequilibrium nature but of a structural nature. Massive doses of foreign aid (official loans, grants and commodity assistance) have been used for financing a sizeable part of our import requirements for planned investment. So the measurement of the deficit is being made in terms of drawal on induced foreign official resources (loans and grants), borrowings from IMF and use of foreign exchange reserves.

Sectoral Breakdowns

India's balance of payments data are presented in a way as to be amenable to sectoral analysis. The details of short-term and long-term nature under both government and private sectors are presented separately. Thus, the contributions to the foreign sector represented by the balance of payments from the government, business and financial sectors are available from these data. In current account, imports and exports are given as debits and credits. Under the category of invisibles, government and receipts and expenditure and government remittances — inflows and outflows — and other items to the extent possible, used to be presented for the government and the private business sector. The transfer payments and receipts used to be presented separately for governments and private sector. Balance of payments data used to be published both in Rupee and US dollar terms. Quarterly data for the recent years and Current Account data are given area-wise, such as Sterling area, Dollar area, etc.

Appendix I presents the proforma, in which India's balance of payments is presented as at present. Credits relate to inflows or receipts while debits relate to outflows or payments. Since exports relate to the inflow of funds, these are credits while imports relate to debits. Sometimes, receipts are shown as disbursements and payments are shown as amortisation in the presentation of data.

The details on capital account are also presented in a way that the government (official), private and banking sectors role can be derived. Private sector represents the business and household sectors in India and primarily the former while the banking sector represents the flows of the financial sector. The government and private sector flows may be of both short-term and long-term nature and are presented as Foreign Investment, Loans and Banking Sector loans include External Assistance, Commercial borrowings and short term capital flow. These details are given in Capital Account. The data also include Rupee Debt Service and other capital. Errors and omissions are shown as part of the Balance of payments while the rest are shown as financing arrangements. But Banking sector flows are definitionally of short-term nature and the amounts involved are also small. The banks are now permitted under the existing liberalised Exchange Control rules to keep some amounts abroad and bring funds from abroad for their owns business. Banks can, normally keep minimum working balances abroad and loans and overdrafts can be secured from abroad upto a limit without the RBI's prior permission. Banking capital excludes payments and receipts on behalf of the RBI. Private loans include foreign, private and official loans received by the private sector in India, either through the government financial institutions or through private sector banks and financial institutions. Since 1992, private and government companies have been permitted to borrow directly from abroad. Government loans are official credits received from foreign governments or governments bodies, foreign central banks or other financial institutions abroad. Foreign Direct and portfolio investment is permitted and so is Indian investment abroad albeit on a limited scale.

Sources of Data — India

In India, the Reserve Bank of India is the sole agency responsible for the compilation of balance of payments data. The RBI in turn collects these data from various sources, namely, banks, corporate units, government bodies and Indian Government missions abroad, etc., and from the surveys conducted by them. As exchange control authority, the RBI gets some data from the banks who are authorised dealers in foreign exchange, from customs and trade authorities who are in charge of import and export licences under the Trade Control Act and from the government and government agencies, including the Ministry of Finance in respect of investment capital flows, joint ventures, etc., and in respect of their receipts and expenditures abroad. Airways, oil companies, shipping companies and post offices also provide information to the RBI on the inflows and outflows of funds. In respect of service payments and receipts, investment income, remittances, etc., companies in the private sector and branches of foreign companies provide the necessary information. The Reserve Bank conducts a survey on unclassified receipts for securing data unrecorded through the normal banking channels such as small inward and outward remittances. It also conducts a survey of foreign private investment and foreign collaborations to collect data on joint ventures, deferred payments and other modes of flow of private capital. The Ministry of Finance provides all the data on capital flows of government account and on account of corporate sector on the basis of their approvals for foreign borrowings and for investment proposals in India. The Post and Telegraphs operate the exchange control in respect of some imports, exports and remittances, etc. They are also a source of information for balance of payments data.

Authorised dealers, who are agents of the RBI in the implementation of exchange control, report to the RBI regularly their transactions with the public — all receipts and payments and transactions of sale or purchase of currencies. Besides, Customs send the export-import licences data as reported in the Trade Control returns submitted by exporters/importers. These are also routed through the ADs. The transactions of the government and some private sector undertakings, which are put through the government agencies abroad such as the Indian High Commissioner in London, India Supply Mission, Washington and Indian Embassy at Tokyo, report the relevant particulars about these to the RBI on a monthly basis. Particulars relating to external assistance received or given are obtained from the Ministry of Finance in the form of monthly statements.

There is still a deficiency in the balance of payments compilation due to the inadequate coverage of private capital movements, which are not on a cash basis. The bulk of the foreign capital flows in the private sector is in the form of retained earnings. The data relating to them are collected through a survey designed for this purpose on a quarterly basis from branches/or subsidiaries of foreign companies. Such details are collected from 1963-64 onwards.

Transactions in imports were also refined as to reflect imports on f.o.b basis instead of c.i.f. and incorporate i.f. elements in insurance and transportation. Deferred payment exports and imports are split up year-wise for changes in foreign assets and liabilities and entries are made in the balance of payments to reflect these changes.

Trends in Balance of Payments

In the post-independent India, regular balance of payments data have been maintained. During 1948-49 to 1950-51, the country incurred huge deficits in the balance of payments amounting to a total of Rs. 629 crores, for the whole period financed by drawal on foreign exchange reserves, which were mostly sterling reserves at that time, built up during the war period. The rupee was devalued in September 1949 by 30.5 per cent following the devaluation of sterling to maintain competitiveness of Indian exports and to improve its earnings.

During the First Plan period, the balance of payments position improved considerably and the overall deficit was brought down to a total of Rs. 348 crores over the period. Both exports and imports were at a low ebb. Export performance was generally good due to a commodity boom in 1951-52 and import demand was effectively kept down by controls. External assistance to the tune of Rs. 221 crores financed a part of the deficit in the balance of payments.

It was only during the Second Plan period that the tempo of planned investment gathered momentum and the effect of this was felt as pressures on the balance of payments. Imports far surpassed exports and the deficit over the period 1955-56 to 1960-61 amounted to Rs. 2135 crores. Such a large deficit, was made possible by large inflows of foreign aid of which the actual utilisation during the period was Rs. 1446 crores. The rest of the deficit was financed by drawing down of our foreign exchange reserves.

In view of the continuous deficits in our balance of payments, it was often misunderstood as a symptom of disequilibrium. But these deficits being planned, no action was taken for corrective adjustment. Only on two occasions, need for action for balance of payments adjustment was felt. The devaluation in 1949 and in 1966 was found imperative. The first one was forced upon us due to the devaluation of sterling and with our close links with sterling at that time, we would have lost a good chunk of our markets denominated in sterling if we had not devalued. Our gain was in terms of maintenance of our exports, continued link with sterling and discouragement of imports. As our reserves were mainly kept in sterling, the devaluation had preserved the sterling values of reserves.

During the Third Plan period, there was a progressive rise in imports on account of foodgrains scarcity and rising investment targets. The trade deficits amounted to Rs. 2295 crores and the total balance of payment deficit to Rs. 3056 crores. As in the Second Plan, this deficit was mostly financed by external assistance (Rs. 2806 crores) and partly by drawal on IMF (Rs. 244 crores). The rest (Rs. 6 crores) was financed by drawing down of reserves which had already reached the rock-bottom level of Rs. 298 crores.

By the end of Third Plan (1966) and with the outbreak of hostilities with Pakistan, there was a set-back to our prospects of securing external assistance, and planned growth was slowed down. Greater emphasis was laid on self-reliance in respect of food and foreign assistance. Besides, conditions forced us to a devaluation of the rupee by 36.5 per cent in June 1966.

During the period of annual plans 1966-69, domestic supply position improved and exports picked up and overall deficit for the three-year period was put at Rs. 2992 crores which was almost entirely financed by foreign aid utilisation and a net drawal on IMF.

The impact of devaluation in 1949 as much as in 1966 is difficult to assess. Trade with rupee payment agreement countries was dislocated as they wanted renegotiation of bilateral trade agreements on the basis of the revised par value of the rupee. No immediate boost to exports was in evidence in respect of its multilateral trade either in 1949 or in 1966. Exports picked up due to a better world demand and improved supply position of commodities at home in 1951-52 and 1967-68. These facts confirm the general presumption that India could not benefit from any price changes or exchange rate changes.

During the first three plan periods invisible trade showed a net surplus with the result that current account deficits were lower than what the merchandise trade deficits would have led to. Subsequently, invisible trade turned into net deficits and its favourable impact on our balance of payments disappeared until a surplus re-emerged gain in the seventies. More recently, the inward remittances from the Gulf countries slowed down with the tapering off of the boom in these countries. But invisibles continued to be positive balance largely due to private unilateral transfers.

During the Fourth Plan period, 1969 to 1974, the net positive balance in balance of payments amounted to Rs. 396 crores. This was made possible by a sizeable utilisation of foreign assistance (Rs. 4184 crores), a drawal on IMF by Rs. 62 crores and a positive balance in invisible trade of Rs. 1664 crores due to remittances from Gulf countries. Our foreign exchange reserves were augmented during this period from Rs. 394 crores at end March 1969 to Rs. 581 crores as at end-March 1974. During the Fourth and Fifth Plan periods there was a general improvement in the food situation and a sizeable buffer stock was built up. The current account continued to present surpluses during the subsequent periods. During the latter part of the seventies, there was a continued inflow of remittances leading to a positive invisible trade balance and a positive balance in current account, with the result that the foreign exchange reserves stood at a record of Rs. 5220 crores at end March 1979. It was only in the Sixth Plan and Seventh Plan period (1980-90) again that there were persistent net current account deficits financed by large doses of foreign assistance and drawal on IMF. During Ninth Plan period (1997-2002), and in Tenth Plan period 2002-07 there was considerable improvement in Balance of Payments and our foreign reserves stood at $ 75 billion early in 2003, and $ 152 billion as end March 2006, and $ 279 billion at end March 2010 and $ 293 billion in April 2012.

Of the various items of current account, the most significant are the merchandise transactions which account for about 70 per cent of the total receipts and payments. Of the invisible items of current account, travel, transportation and transfer receipts constitute not only a positive balance but also account for a significant share in the total invisible account. While in the sixties, net foreign travel receipts were about Rs. 15-20 crores on an average per year, and net transfer receipts around Rs. 50 crores, they have risen sharply in the seventies and accounted for Rs. 5,242 crores and Rs. 23,284 crores in 1995-96 and around Rs. 58,000 crores during 2001 and 2002. Investment income is another significant item which however made negative contribution to the balance of payments in some years. The current Account deficit persisted ranging to the extent of 1.02% of GDP in recent years, and it stood at 2.6% of GDP in 2008-09 and rose to 4% of GDP in 2011-12.

Role of Services in Balance of Payments

In more recent years trade in services has come into greater focus for many reasons. Firstly, the comparative advantage for trade in goods has reached a limit in respect of many developing countries while the need for imports and exchange earnings continued to grow. It is in this context that these developing countries have to divert their attention to the promotion of services sector in international trade. Secondly, the growth of transport and communications and shortening of distance and other barriers due to technological breakthrough, international trade in services such as labour, consultancy, education, professional services, personal services, etc., has grown. Thirdly, some of the non-trade services became tradable and trading in services has increased due to growing restrictions on trade in goods in many countries. Fourthly, revolution in Technology, growth in software services, Biotechnology, media, communications, knowledge based services etc. led to larger trade.

Some of the services have become internationally tradable due to the growing role of transnational companies and technological revolution in the dimensions of time and space. These services can be classified under the following heads:

(i) Those in which the producer moves to the consumer, such as Indian labourers, nurses, doctors, etc. working in Gulf countries or international chain of hotels serving in foreign countries (Hilton Group).

(ii) Those in which consumer moves to the producer such as tourists or students, patients seeking treatment in hospitals, etc., visiting foreign countries for the services.

(iii) Those in which either producer or consumer moves to others such as dancers and singers, artists, scientists visiting abroad for performances or lecturers or foreigners visiting our country to hear them or learning from them.

(iv) Those in which neither the producer nor the consumer moves out such as in banking, insurance or technology transfers, or information flows.

As regards the quantum of world trade in services, the value of trade has grown enormously during the last two decades. Here the terms "services" is defined to include all current account items other than merchandise trade and pure transfer payments. At present gross trade in services is about one-third to one-half of the value of the merchandise exports or imports. It is also interesting to note that this trade in services is more concentrated in industrialised developed countries than the trade in merchandise items, and it will take a long time before developing countries can capture any important segment of the world trade in invisibles.

Non-resident Inflows

Under invisibles, a substantial inflow took place in recent years in non-official flows into India. Since 1982, the Government has been encouraging these inflows through higher rates of interest on non-resident rupee accounts with banks than on domestic deposits. The RBI has kept S.L.R. on them lower at 25 per cent as against the normal requirement against domestic deposits at 31.5 per cent at that time. Such deposits are exempt for wealth tax purposes and interest income exempt for income tax purposes. The rates of interest on foreign currency non-resident accounts were, however, kept lower than on Indian deposits due to lower interest rates in the markets abroad for foreign currencies. The aggregate inflow of funds on all non-resident accounts during 2001-02 was $ 2728 million which was almost three times that of the amount five years ago. The NRI inflows slowed down subsequently, and there was a net inflow of $ 4,289 million in 2008-09 as against a net outflow of $ 980 million in 2004-05.

Services Sector in India's Trade

So far as India is concerned, trade in services has been an important segment of the balance of payments leading to a surplus under invisible account during most of the years. The invisible trade under current account has changed from a negative balance of about Rs. 14 crores in 1970-71 to substantial positive balance of about Rs. 3,849 crores in 1984-85 and stood at Rs. 1,39,597 crores in 2004-05 and Rs. 4,19,800 crores in 2008-09 and Rs. 3,92,494 crores in 2010-11. The bulk of the positive balance has arisen out of private transfer receipts, software exports and other miscellaneous receipts. It would, therefore, appear that trade in the services sector has a potentiality to be an engine of growth in India's foreign trade.

India has a comparative advantage in some services such as skills I.T Software consultancy, tourism, etc., and it should exploit this advantage to the fullest extent.

It is, however, true that if all the developing countries are taken into account, the services sector plays a minor role in the total international trade scenario. While the developed market economies have a surplus in trade in services sector, the developing countries have a large deficit which has been growing year after year.

The poor performance of the developing countries in the services sector is due to lack of infrastructural facilities and technological backwardness. The developed countries, on the other hand, have an advantage due to the growing role of transnational companies in the services sector, and technological revolution in robotics and informatics which has brought success to the efforts to attract receipts into those countries.

The developing countries have a comparative advantage only in respect of labour services. Even this advantage disappears slowly due to technological advancement which replaces labour by capital. The LDCs have a great disadvantage in the field of technological upgradation. They should, therefore, insist on a freer flow of labour services into the developed countries and a freer access of developing countries into the technological progress of the developed world. If the services section in the developing countries has to grow, it would require large lump investments, long gestation periods and low rates of returns in areas of infrastructure, informatics and robotics and a host of related areas. The developing countries lack the finance and the quantum of multilateral and bilateral aid available to them has declined in recent years.

Besides, the restrictive trade practices of a large number of transnational companies which l e a large role in the services sector of the developed countries have stood in the way of LDCs penetrating into the trade in services. It would, therefore be in the interest of the developing world in general and India in particular to insist on a code of conduct by the multinationals in the areas of services sector and freer access to the technological progress of the West. The scope for larger trade in services is no doubt there but a surplus in this sector by the developing countries is a remote possibility. There is potential for expansion of trade in this sector for India also but the extent of the gain will depend upon the co-operation and help given by the developed industrial countries in the years to come, and the role of MNCs and the attitude and policies of W.T.O.

Despite the large growth of invisibles, the current account showed deficits in some years, only up to 2011-12.

Foreign Exchange Reserves

The components of India's foreign exchange reserves which are used for financing our foreign trade are as follows:

(1) RBI balances held abroad.

(2) RBI foreign investments.

(3) Gold held by the RBI.

(4) Balances held abroad by Government agencies.

(5) Balances held abroad by authorised dealers.

Upto 1950-51, a bulk of our foreign reserves was held as sterling balance. In 1950-51 our reserves (including gold) stood at Rs. 1029 crores. During the First Plan, reserves financed nearly 37 per cent of the deficit and they fell to Rs. 902 crores by end of this period. During the Second Plan, about 25 per cent of the deficit was financed by reserves, which stood at a low level of Rs. 304 crores. By the end of Third Plan the reserves touched the lowest level of Rs. 298 crores.

After the devaluation of the rupee in 1966, there was a distinct change in the trends in balance of payments. By the time the Fourth Plan was started in 1969-70, our reserves stood at Rs. 728 crores (excluding SDRs). During the seventies, reserves were built up considerably, following some improvement in trade balance and substantial inflows of funds on invisible trade account and remittances from abroad. Our reserves including gold increased from Rs. 764 crores at end 1973-74 (end of Fourth Plan) to Rs. 5388 cores by end 1979-80 (excluding SDRs). There has been a deterioration in our payments position since then and our reserves including gold stood at

Rs. 3,660 crores at end December 1982 but improved again to Rs. 7,170 crores by end February 1987 and stood at Rs. 9,926 crores in June 1991 and rose to Rs. 2,64,036 crores at end March 2002 and to Rs. 6,19,116 crores by end March 2005, which doubled to Rs. 12,83,900 crores by end March 2009 and stood at Rs. 13,61,000 crores in 2010-11.

The gold component of our reserves rose from Rs. 117.8 crores in 1950-51 to Rs. 182.5 crores in 1966-67 due to revaluation of gold from Rs. 53.58 per 10 grams in 1996 to Rs. 84.39 per 10 grams thereafter. The quantity of gold holdings was augmented by Rs. 5.3 crores each in January 1977, December 1977 and December 1978 and by Rs. 5.2 crores in December 1979 due to restitution of gold by the IMF to India. The increase in gold value in June 1978 was due to purchase of gold under a non-competitive bid at IMF gold auction. At end March 1981, gold held by the RBI was valued at Rs. 224.7 crores and at end December 1981 at Rs. 225.6 crores. There was fresh acquisition of gold by RBI from Central Government in 1984-85 by Rs. 20.25 crores and in 1985-86 by Rs. 28.50 crores with the result that gold stocks with RBI stood at Rs. 274 crores at end March 1987 and at Rs. 19,686 crores at end March 2005. At end November 2009, gold worth of Rs. 3,083 crores was purchased by India from IMF and this augmented the gold component to Rs. 81,200 at end March 2010 as against Rs. 50,718 at end October 2009 before the purchase of gold. At end March 2012 the gold stood at Rs. 1,37,700.

SDRs are a new international reserve asset created since January 1970 by the IMF to supplement the traditional international reserves in the form of gold and convertible currencies. The expansion of world trade has turned out to be larger than the growth of newly-mined gold and the expansion of international liquidity should be augmented to facilitate the growth of world trade. Accordingly, Special Drawing Rights (SDRs) were created, each equivalent to 0.888671 gram of fine gold. These were allocated to member countries on the basis of the member's original quotas with the Fund. The first allocation was done in January 1970 and India's share was SDRs 126 million. This was followed by an allocation of SDRs 101 million in January 1971 and SDRs 100 million in January 1972. The restitution and use of the SDRs is controlled by the IMF through a formula and India has been using them since their inception. From time to time SDRs were allotted to India and the allocation in January 1981 was to the extent of SDR 117 million as compared to SDR 119 million in January 1979 and a similar amount in January 1980. The outstanding amount on SDR account of India stood at a high of 306 million dollars in December 1985 but fell to 197.6 million dollars at end January 1987 and stood at a low of us $ 10 million at end March 2002, and US $ 5 million at end March 2005, due too their extensive use by India during this period. The SDRs of India stood at $ 1 million at end March 2009, whcih rose to US $ 4,46,950 million by end Mach 2012.

Foreign Assistance

External assistance utilised during the First Plan was only Rs. 221 crores. But the role of external assistance had increased during the Second and Third Plans to Rs. 1,446 crores and Rs. 2,805 crores respectively (inclusive of PL 480 and 665 Assistance). During the three years of Annual plans (1967-69), external assistance utilised was Rs. 3,228 crores and during the Fourth Plan (1969-70 to 1973-74), the corresponding amount was Rs. 4,184 crores. In the next five years external assistance utilised had gone up further to Rs. 7,309 crores (1974-75 to 1978-79). External aid in the Sixth Plan was about Rs. 11,000 crores which was the largest amount used in any plan period. Grants and PL 480 and 665 assistance ceased from 1971-72. Grants proportion has come down to 9-10% of the total external assistence, which has dried down in recent years. Net assistance after repayments and service payments are excluded has become negative, in the last few years upto March 2004.

In the Sixth Plan period (1980-81 to 1984-85) the objective of self-reliance was pursued more vigorously and the proportion of external assistance to total outlay was brought down to about 8 per cent. In the Seventh Plan period (1985-86 to 1989-90) the corresponding proportion did not exceed about 10 per cent. The annual debt burden due to repayment of principal and interest was estimated by the Planning Commission (Ninth Five Year Plan Document) at around 18-20 per cent of the current account receipts and stood at 14.1% in 2002. After 1990-91 the policy was one of free market economy and freer trade. The external debt to GDP ratio was 22% at end March 2009 and Debt-service ratio was 44.6% in 2009.

India's external debt declined from $ 99 billion at end March 1995 to $ 92.2 billion at end March 1996 and stood at U.S $ 229 billion at end. March 2009, which was not considered a heavy Burden in terms of the debt servicing ratio and low percentage of short-term debt (21.2%) and a large component of concessional aid (18.2%). Foreign Exchange reserves also reached a peak of US $ 293 billion, which gives a debt reserve ratio of a high of 4.2% in March 2011.

External assistance was mostly in the form of loans and grants had dries and IMF borrowings also stood at zero. In the latest year 2008-09, the total assistance stood at $ 2,098 million this has to be compared to the flow of external assistance of US $ 3,912 million in 2002-03 and US $ 3,225 million in 2003-04. These figures include loans and grants from government and private accounts. Our dependence on external assistance was kept low due to the deliberate policy of the government.

APPENDIX I

The Proforma in which India's Balance of Payments are Presented by the Reserve Bank of India

	Credit	Debit	Net
A. Current Account			
I. Merchandise			
II. Invisibles (a + b + c)			
(A) Services			
1. Travel			
2. Transportation			
3. Insurance			
4. Government not Included Elsewhere			
5. Miscellaneous			
(B) Transfer Receipts/Payments			
(i) Official			
(ii) Private			
(C) Investment Income			
Total Current Account (I + II)			
B. Capital Account			
Foreign Investment (a + b)			
(a) In India			
Direct			
Portfolio			
(b) Abroad.			
Loans (a + b + c)			
(a) External Assistance			
1. By India			
2. To India			
(b) Commercial borrowings (Medium-term and long-term)			
1. By India			
2. To India			
(c) Short-term capital flow			
To India			

C. Banking Capital (a + b)

(a) Commercial banks

(i) Assets

(ii) Liabilities

(iii) Non-Resident deposits

(b) Others

D. Rupee Debt Service

E. Other Capital

Total Capital Account (a + b + c + d + e)

F. *Errors and Omissions*

G. Over all Balance (Total)

H. Monetary Movements (i + ii)

(i) IMF (net)

(ii) Foreign Exchange Reserves.

16 Bilateralism in Foreign Trade

This chapter deals with Bilateralism in Foreign Trade as part of Trade and Commercial policies, influencing Balance of Payments and in particular the current Account of Balance of Payments.

In the post-war world, countries had varying degrees of exchange and trade restrictions primarily to protect their domestic interests. Trade and international economic relations were at a low ebb in such a set up. To restore trade relations and promote trade, some of the countries entered into bilateral agreements with others for exports and imports at mutually agreed quantities and prices. Trading partners settled their trade balances in a mutually acceptable way.

Broadly, trade can take place either by exchange of goods for goods, or exchange of goods for an acceptable medium of exchange, among the trading partners or for an international currency. The first is barter trade and the second is trade in blocked currencies while the third constitutes multilateral trade. It is the last category which is widely accepted in the forums of the IMF and IBRD as it is the least discriminatory and subject to least restrictions. In multilateral trade, exports and imports are paid for in an international currency, convertible into gold (prior to 1973) or US dollar or pound sterling. In bilateral trade, exchange of goods for goods takes place at a mutually accepted price and excess balances are settled in a pre-determined manner.

Why Bilateralism?

Trade with socialist countries is possible on a government-to-government basis only, as private enterprise is not permitted to trade with them. Such trade is possible through barter or on a bilateral basis.

Bilateralism is part of the mechanics of mutual exchange control. In an era of trade blocism and exchange restrictions, bilateralism can be considered as a step in the direction of multilateralism.

As Schelling observed, "the system of bilateral arrangements might well be called the mechanics of mutual exchange control between countries".[1] Advantages of bilateralism are as follows:

(a) Trade with socialist countries is made possible.

(b) Trade with countries closed to trade due to exchange restrictions is opened up through bilateralism.

(c) It would promote trade for developing countries in need of development imports without adequate exchange reserves.

(d) It helps acquire development technology know-how, etc., for growth.

(e) It is possible to make the flow of exports and imports mutually balancing as items of trade, quantities and prices are planned and set out in advance.

(f) Trade equilibrium at higher levels is possible.

Role of Bilateralism in India

Bilateralism appears to have played a major role in India's foreign trade. India needs the assistance of Soviet bloc for political and strategic reasons and trade with them is possible only on bilateral basis. On the one hand, capital is scarce and domestic supplies are limited and outpriced in the international markets and on the other hand, both greater capital and larger imports are necessary for maintenance and development of Indian industries and agriculture. In this context, imports are to be planned for essential requirements and pruned down to the level of foreign receipts through exports and foreign credits. Bilateralism appears to be the right vehicle of planned imports and exports and suited well for India when her exports are outpriced in international markets and her industries are uncompetitive because of sheltered domestic markets and high cost-price parities due to long years of protectionist policy and import substitution. In bilateralism the price factor can be subordinated to politico-economic factors. Another advantage of bilateralism is the self-liquidating character of trade balances under this system.

The export Promotion Committee (1957) and Import and Export Policy Committee (1962) favoured trade agreements as part of foreign trade policy of India. Accordingly, bilateralism has grown in India since the fifties, particularly with Eastern Europe and the USSR. In 1951-52 our trade with Eastern Europe was only 1 to 2 per cent of the total trade, but has grown to 20-25 per cent in the early eighties. We have trade agreements with not only Eastern Europe but with the EEC, Gulf-countries (OPEC) and some Afro-Asian countries. Starting with only 10 countries in 1950-51, we have now about 40 countries on the trading list of this category. All trade agreements together might account for one-third of our total trade.

---

1. T.C. Schelling, *International Economics*, 1958, p. 112.

Types of Agreements

As regards the nature of these agreements, they differ widely. Some are only trade agreements and others are trade and payments agreements. Some trade agreements are linked to credits provided by one to the other. In the case of trade and payments agreements, provisions are made as to the mode of payment for the excess on either side and as to the uses to which these surpluses can be put. Where credits are granted, payment arrangements are linked to these credits.

As a result of these payment arrangements, some of which are in inconvertible currencies or rupees, these accounts would be blocked except for the specified purposes to be used as per the agreements. Some trade agreements are just barter deals, specifying the goods of export and import in their order of priority. Some agreements provide for only mutual balancing of trade with no provision for payments. Under the annual trade plans, the Soviet Union purchases from India jute, tea, sugar and a host of other consumer goods. A few agreements are for bulk purchase such as of wheat with the USSR or rice with Thailand and Burma. Certain agreements are loose schedules enumerating goods to be traded while trade takes its natural course through the private sector.

The significance of bilateralism to the foreign exchange market is that it would reduce the amount of financial flows into these markets. The international media of exchange and liquidity are used less to this extent. Certain trade and payments are diverted from natural channels, and free flows of supply and demand are curbed. The pressure on the exchange reserves is less to that extent. Trade diversion and trade creation would both be possible while discrimination and unnatural flows of foreign trade are not ruled out.

Direction of Trade

Bilateral trade of India depends on the economic and political relations of India with other countries. The trade agreements entered into by India with other countries varied from year to year. Some contracts are renewed year after year. Some agreements contain the MFNC (Most Favoured Nation Clause) for giving tariff and other tax concessions. At present, there are many countries with which India has trade agreements of which agreements with only five countries, namely, Czechoslovakia, Germany, Poland, Rumania and Russia were in inconvertible rupees for many years in the past but not now. Other trading partners in this regard are Afghanistan, Bulgaria, Indonesia, Libya, Syrian Arab Republic, Mauritius, Turkey, Malaysia, Egypt, Iran, Iraq, Jordan and Yugoslavia. Some of these countries, notably Afghanistan and Bulgaria, have opted to multilateralise their payments into freely convertible currencies. Yugoslavia had also preferred to have multilateral trade since the seventies. Sudan has a bilateral trade agreement for import of cotton as against export of tea. India has entered into agreements with China, Pakistan, Ethiopia and Maldives for limited trade. India has similar agreements with Bangladesh, Nepal and Bhutan. In October 1997, India and South Africa have signed agreements to promote trade and co-operation in mining and tourism and hotels. Sri Lanka and India have entered into an agreement for free trade in selected goods in 1999. Trade with OECD countries was declining while that with Asia and developing countries was increasing in more recent years.

FTAs and Direction of Trade

India has entered into Free Trade Agreements with many Asian and African countries and in particular with SAARC. The SAARC includes Bangladesh, Bhutan, Maldives, Nepal, Pakistan and Sri Lanka.

Bilateral trade is mostly with Asian and African countries, in addition to OPEC and Eastern European countries. The relative changes in our export trade with these countries can be seen from the following Table for the decade 1994-95 to 2004-05.

Table 16.1 India's Export Trade

				Destination wise (in percentages to total Exports)
Regions	**1994-95**	**2004-05**	**2007-08**	**2010-11**
OECD	58.6%	44.0%	38%	33.0%
OPEC	9.4%	16.0%	16.4%	21.55
Eastern Europe	4.0%	2.1%	2.1%	1.1%
Developing Countries	26.5%	37.3%	42%	41.6%
of which-SAARC	4.4%	5.4%	5.9%	5.0%
— Asian Developing Countries	21.6%	29.2%	31.6%	25.9%
— Other Latin American and African Countries	20.0%	29.3%	33.4%	13.1%

Note: Totals do not add as the above groups are not exclusive.

Source: RBI: Handbook of Statistics.

In general our imports are more than our exports. But this is true with respect to OECD countries and Eastern Europe in particular imports from Russia, China and other Asian countries, other than SAARC, are more than exports, in recent years. Country wise, our trade is more with China, Japan, Australia and U.S.A. in value terms. Bilateral trade is more with OPEC, Eastern Europe, some Asian and African countries, accounting for one-third to one-fourth of our total trade. Our trade with Latin, American countries continues to be low at 2.1% over the part decade.

Composition of Bilateral Trade

The composition of trade under bilateral agreements is similar to that under multilateral trade. The bulk of the export items are traditional goods like tea, tobacco, cashew kernels, jute and cotton textiles, oil cakes, etc. However, some non-traditional items are also exported under these bilateral agreements, such as engineering goods, machine tools, ores, etc. Imports comprise mostly capital goods, spare parts, non-ferrous metals, chemicals, drugs, fertiliser, etc.

The trade agreements list the acceptable export and import items which each country may trade in their order of importance. As these agreements vary from country to country, there is no uniform pattern of export and import trade, but they normally include exports and imports indicated above and difficult to sell. Each agreement has its own method of payments for these exports and imports and for balancing the trade and financing the deficits. Besides, as major part of this trade is in inconvertible rupees, arrangements are made from time to time to settle any imbalance between exports and imports through credits.

In some of these agreements, a "shipping clause" is included whereby the trading partners agree to use, to the maximum extent possible, the vessels owned or chartered by the shipping organisations of the respective countries. This shipping clause is intended to save the loss of foreign exchange in the event of the goods being shipped by third countries vessels.

Gains from Bilateral Trade

Although bilateral trade is useful to create some trade where no trade exists, it is not favoured by the IMF because the bilateral trading partner balances its payments with each of its partners separately rather than with all the partners together. The surplus with one country cannot be utilised to make up the deficit with another country unlike in the case of multilateral trade. Bilateral trade does not require convertibility *prima facie* of trade balances.

Doubts have been expressed in some quarters about the gains from bilateral agreements to India. Firstly, it is felt that the terms of trade, i.e., the ratio of export prices to import prices, may be unfavourable to India. But in actual practice, these agreements stipulate that the prices of the goods bought and sold should be the same as the prices ruling in the major international markets for these goods. If the goods are not internationally traded, they are valued at the mutually acceptable prices reached at the bargaining table. It appears that India has not lost in terms of trade with its trading partners under bilateral agreements. India has in fact gained by opening up of trade channels where no trade was earlier possible due to the prevailing exchange and trade controls and high level of costs and prices prevailing at home as compared with international markets for our export products.

Secondly, as a specific gain from these trade agreements, mention must be made of the fact that there has been as expansion in the foreign trade of India. But for these agreements, India's trade would not have expanded as rapidly as it did in the recent past. Bilateral trade has opened up new markets for Indian goods, both traditional and non-traditional.

Thirdly, bilateral trade has enabled India to enlarge its import capacity to meet the growing demand for imports for its development requirements at a time when the available supply of convertible foreign exchange is limited.

Fourthly, bilateral trade is planned on a country-to-country basis and in view of its planned nature, there is scope for diversification of trade under bilateralism. This advantage has, however, remained only theoretical, as no significant diversification has been achieved so far in our trade with these countries.

Fifthly, trade with communist countries is generally bilateral and on a government-to-government basis. In this respect public sector institutions like the STC and MMTC in India were meant to conduct bilateral trade with these countries.

It has been alleged these trade agreements encourage "switch trade", i.e., the diversion of the goods imported from India by the trading partner to a third country. Such a diversion to a convertible currency country results in a loss of foreign exchange to India. Government is, however, aware of the possibility of such diversion and have taken steps to prevent its occurrence through mutual understanding at the official level.

The disadvantages of bilateral trade agreements are offset by advantages like wider markets, stable prices, larger exports, enhanced import capacity and lower trade deficits. Some trade contracts have helped us to secure exchange concessions in respect of quotas, tariffs, etc., imposed by our trade partners.

Bilateral trade is also necessary to utilise the economic and other aid granted by the East European countries, which has to be repaid through the export of goods and services from India. Besides, most of the aid is tied to the country granting it and to specific projects in India. As such, India has to import specific goods from the country granting the aid and has to repay it, along with interest, through the export of goods to that country. Loans, other than supplier's credits, are normally long-term, repayable over a period of 10-12 years and carry an interest rate 2½ per cent. Besides bulk purchases through such agreements have allowed us gains of lower prices, economies of scale and other benefits of canalisation as through the STC. Essential goods of consumption and capital goods which could not have been imported due to inadequate foreign exchange were imported through trade agreements. Exchanges of technology, joint ventures and technical collaborations are further possibilities which might flow from trade agreements.

UNCTAD III has appointed a committee to go into the question of advisability of developing countries abandoning bilateral trade. This committee has not been able to come to any conclusion on the issue of bilateral trade of developing countries. But from the point of view of India, bilateralism has still an important role to play and could not be abandoned.

Mechanics of Payments

There is hardly any difference in the payments procedure between transactions with rupee payment countries and those with convertible currency countries from the point of view of the individual importer and exporter. Transactions with rupee payment countries normally involve rupee bills. No foreign exchange transactions are involved, as none of the bills is denominated in any currency other than the inconvertible rupee. There is no need for forward cover or forward transactions either.

For the purpose of financing rupee trade, the central bank of the trading partner maintains a central account with the Reserve Bank of India, and one or more accounts with a few commercial banks in India with the permission of the Reserve Bank. The central account with the Reserve Bank is used for. (1) Depositing excess rupee balances with the commercial banks; (2) Replenishing the latter accounts with balances when needed and (3) Transactions relating to technical credit. The technical credit is intended to facilitate the smooth flow of trade between the trading partners in the event of a short-term imbalance in trade. The surplus country provides technical credit to the deficit country. For example, if exports from India exceed imports into India, the Government of India provides what is known as technical credit for the purpose of payment to the Exporters. When imports exceed exports, the technical credit is repaid by the trading partner. The central bank of the trading partner issues instructions relating to the use of technical credit and authorises the Reserve Bank to repay the overdraft when the central account has excess funds over the minimum working balances. Similarly, in the event of there being a surplus in the central account over and above the working balance, these surplus funds can be invested in the Treasury Bills of the Government of India.

In addition to the central account, the Reserve Bank maintains a special account for some trading partners. It is credited/debited with the amount of technical credit granted from time to time by the Government of India/its trading partner. Funds will be shifted from the special account to the central account and *vice versa* according to requirements and instructions from the trading partners and the Government of India.

Under the Reserve Bank's Exchange Control Regulations, the normal Return Forms have to be completed in respect of these operations (i.e., debits and credits) on the accounts maintained with authorised dealers, which require either prior approval of, or a report to the Reserve Bank. These forms have to be forwarded to the Reserve Bank along with the returns on outstanding balances which are submitted periodically. Besides, the commercial banks which maintain the bilateral trade accounts have to submit periodically to the Government of India and the foreign trading partner special returns relating to the transactions over the period and the outstanding balances at the end of the period.

The accounts of the trading partners with the commercial banks facilitate transactions with exporters and importers. In the case of a deficit in the account with the commercial bank, funds will be transferred to it from the central account with the Reserve Bank. In the event of a surplus with the commercial bank, these funds will conversely be transferred to the central account with the Reserve Bank.

As regards imports or exports under these accounts, there are three categories:

(a) Imports/exports made by the STC, MMTC and other public bodies;

(b) Imports/exports made by private parties whose bills are negotiated by a special account from the bank which does not maintain the trading partner's account;

(c) Imports/exports made by private parties who are clients of a bank which maintains a special account.

If the bills are import bills, the bank may accept them like any other bills for payments under L.C. or for collection. The party has to submit the import licence, and the c.i.f. value of the import should not exceed the amount of licence. Bills accepted for collection have to be accompanied by the bill of lading, invoice, etc. If the bills are for collection, the Indian importer is debited and the foreign correspondent bank is credited.

If they are export bills, they may be sight bills or usance bills. Sight bills purchased from the exporter are sent to the correspondent bank abroad for realisation from the foreign importer. Usance bills are discounted and the exporter is paid immediately and they are sent to the correspondent bank abroad for realisation. The export documents consist of bills of exchange or drafts, bill of lading, commercial invoice, certificate of origin by a chamber of commerce and insurance cover.

From the above, it is obvious that there is no significant difference between bills under bilateral trade and other trade bills, except that as already indicated, most of the bills under bilateral trade are rupee bills. From the point of view of accounting, the Indian bank keeps the account of the foreign bank denominated for this purpose by the trading partner and the latter keeps an account of the former. These accounts are called special accounts. Thus, when exports from India are paid for the foreign importer, the Indian bank credits the Indian exporter and debits the denominated foreign bank. Similarly, when imports into India are paid for by the importer, the Indian bank debits the Indian importer and credits the denominated foreign bank. These credits and debits in the special accounts of the designated banks will indicate the surpluses or deficits in the bilateral trade with that country.

Normally, these agreements are subject to review once a year or so. Attempts are made to equate over the period the total value of exports from and imports into India. Thus, the normal practice is bilateral balancing of trade. Any balance in the rupee account of a commercial bank in India is, upon the expiry of the contract period, to be used during the ensuring six months to purchase Indian goods.

Alternatively, these balances are to be disposed of as mutually agreed upon between the contracting parties. More often than not, the bilateral trade agreement is renewed and these balances are transferred to the subsequent period.

In most of the trade agreements, particularly with the East European countries, a "gold clause" is included whereby the value of the rupee is guaranteed in terms of its gold content. This is intended to ensure that in the event of any change in the par value of the rupee, the funds in special account/ central account and the accounts stated in the trade contracts with these countries will be adjusted in proportion to the change in the par value. Under the "gold clause", the exchange value of the rupee in terms of gold, viz., Re. 1 = 0.118489 gram of fine gold, is to be taken into consideration while settling payments. Thus, if the value of the rupee falls below this parity due to a devaluation of the rupee, the rupee balances under the trade agreements will have to be correspondingly written upwards. Conversely, if the gold value of the rupee goes above parity the rupee balances under the trade agreements will have to be correspondingly written down. The "gold clause" ensures that the trading partners, as also India, are not put to losses on account of a fall or rise in the exchange value of the rupee. In particular, the foreign exporters and importers insist on the "gold clause". In fact, most of the trading partners of India are not satisfied with the "gold clause" because even with no change in the gold content of the rupee, the latter was depreciating along with sterling in terms of a basket of currencies in the international markets. the rupee-rouble exchange rate is changed, for example, many times due to depreciation of the rupee, and the East European Governments accept the notional rates of exchange of the rupee vis-a-vis their currencies to be revised also. The effect of this could be to make it necessary for India to part with more goods than before for a given bundle of East European goods. Large trade balances of Russia were held by them in non-convertible rupees and the rupee rouble rate became a bone of contention for a long time.

In our trade agreements, provision is also made for the trading partners to give a "most favoured nation treatment" to each other in respect of customs and excise duties. This means, that each trading partner will assure the other that the goods imported into the country will be taxed at the lowest prevailing rates.

Normally, there will be a Joint Committee of Government officials of both the trading partners which will meet every year, with a view to reviewing the operation of the agreement and taking such suitable steps as are needed in respect of the technical credits, loans, balancing of trade, etc.

Counter Trade

This is a new technique of promoting world trade and is likely to become more popular in the years to come. About one-fourth of world trade at present is reported to be conducted under this system. Many developed and developing countries are using this method to boost their export earnings or to reduce their need for free foreign exchange reserves.

Counter trade is a method by which two countries can mutually trade, namely, export a commodity up to a given value as against the import of another commodity up to the same value. These are also called link deals, swap arrangements or compensation trade. Both private and public sectors can participate in this system, if there is co-ordination between importers and exporters.

The advantages of this type of trade are as follows:

(1) This would help reduce trade deficits.

(2) This may bring down market uncertainties and provide export outlets for "difficult to sell" items of many companies.

(3) This would eliminate the need for payment in free foreign exchange.

(4) This would promote mutually beneficial trading arrangements, in terms of both export and import requirements.

The Ministerial Conference of Developing Countries held in New Delhi in July 1985 called for a time-bound implementation of the Global System of Trade Preferences (GSTP) with across the board tariff cuts of 10 per cent and creation of a conducive climate for expansion of mutual trade among the countries of the South, namely developing poor countries. India has not made much use of this facility of GSTP so far. Efforts should, therefore be made for mutually beneficial trade through such arrangements as link trade, barter or counter-trade and removal of tariff and non-tariff barriers amongst the developing countries. India has offered tariff concession to SAARC countries, in respect of some items. Counter-trade becomes a relevant vehicle in this context for India as well.

In view of the balance of payments difficulties more recently, many developing countries are shifting to counter trade or bilateral trade. While under the counter trade one export good and a corresponding import good are identified and trade up to a specific value takes place, under barter trade or bilateral trade, the list of export goods and import goods would be specified and trade up to requirements would be permitted, irrespective of the values. The balancing of trade under the latter would depend upon the type of trade and payment agreements.

India has already initiated counter-trade arrangements with some countries when STC, MMTC and other public sector agencies have linked up their import requirements to their export obligations in respect of some commodities like sugar, ore metals and edible oils. One example is that India has entered into counter-trade arrangements with Trinidad and Tobago envisaging an import of urea up to the value of $ 10 million per annum as against an export of power generation equipment from India up to the same value.

This method of trade would be potentially useful means to promote our trade with African and Asian countries. Already Indonesia, Malaysia, Thailand, Kenya, Zaire, Ethiopia, to mention only a few have insisted on counter trade. Libya, Algeria and Iran have imposed counter trade obligations on their exporters. Brazil has reportedly entered into such arrangements with some twenty countries to expand their exports.

Under this system, if any country wants to export their products, their exporters have to co-ordinate with importers to promote the exports along with some imports. If these imports take place under obligation, it is also necessary that we may have to re-export the same with or without value added or other modifications. Some low quality goods can be imported for domestic consumption as in the case of rice or edible oils for export of better quality goods of the same type or of a different type. India has made a start in this new direction of counter trade by matching exports with imports country-wise, in respect of some commodities, like Basmati Rice.

State Trading Corporation

While on the subject of bilateralism, it would be apt to focus attention on government agencies and bodies who act as agents for trade flows under bilateral agreements. One such agency is the State Trading Corporation set up in 1956. Its objective was to organise and effect exports of some commodities which are technically difficult to sell such as small-scale products, groundnut, oils, cakes, silver, sugar, Handicrafts products, etc., on behalf of the government and also to import fertilisers, metals, minerals and raw materials and intermediate products, etc., on behalf of the private trade and industry. The list of the commodities handled by STC has been widened over the years and changed according to circumstances and needs of the economy. It was also intended to handle trade with government agencies abroad or foreign trade monopolies, particularly in the socialist bloc.

The STC succeeded in expanding trade with the socialist bloc by barter arrangements and established contacts with private parties in the West. The share of STC in India's export trade was less than 1 per cent in 1956-57 but has gone up to 20 per cent in 1975-76 before declining to about 5 per cent by 1985-86 and further to 1-2% by end 2009.

On the import side, its share in total imports was 9.4 per cent in 1971-72 which rose to about 10-12 per cent in the early eighties and declined to 2-3% more recently. As export promotion has been the goal, STC should have concentrated more on exports rather than on imports. Besides, it has always played a passive and complementary role with the private sector rather than try to take over the increasing share and responsibilities in the foreign trade field. The product mix either in exports or imports is not stable or consistent, as it has varied according to the requirements or exigencies of the situation in the economy. Edible oils, newsprint, cement, sugar and chemicals, drugs, rubber, etc., were imported usually in large quantities to meet domestic shortages and these are canalised items. The STC also undertakes price support operations in respect of shellac, coffee, spices, tobacco, etc., and entered more recently into jute goods exports and other "difficult to sell" items, which are non-canalised. Canalised exports are sugar, leather, castor oil, molasses, opium, salt, etc. Canalised exports now constitute only about 30-35 per cent of the total exports by STC. The proportion of canalised items was brought down due to agreements with WTO. Its trade pattern has shifted somewhat in the direction of counter-trade more recently. Many items like sugar were taken out of the canalised list of the STC.

The industry and trade were not happy with the STC in its canalised business. It was slow in operations due to delay and red-tapism. Delay in refund of documents from the STC to private trade and in refund of earnest money have created problems for the private industrialists. Many times, purchases by STC are not at competitive price as they are on bilateral basis and the result of bargaining.

Criticism of STC

Criticism was levelled against the performance or STC by the private industry and trade circles and by the various parliamentary committees. As the critics point out, STC has duplicated the channels of trade and supplanted the public agencies by entering into areas which are easy to penetrate rather than enter into difficult areas. Its policies have been criticised as its operations betray lack of marketing expertise. Its entry into internal distribution and trade channels, particularly in respect of cement, fertilisers, etc., has been the particular target of criticism for the inefficient handling of the problem.

The STC now handles, on both export and import fronts, a wide variety of products. Besides, it arranges for internal distribution of some commodities which it imports. It also acts as an agent for the settlement of disputes between parties in India and abroad and secure raw materials and intermediate products for Indian industries which are export-oriented. It is an agency of the government to monitor bilateral trade with some countries like Yugoslavia. It has a joint venture project in leather products with Bulgaria and a shoe uppers unit at Noida. It is also the agency for arranging counter trade.

Some of the points of criticism against STC are as follows:

(a) Excessive inventory holding either in the form of cash or unsaleable products.

(b) Lack of a stable product mix.

(c) Lack of sensitivity to market.

(d) Defective purchase policy.

(e) Lack of aggressive salesmanship as it has inadequate expertise in some fields.

(f) Subordination of commercial and profit considerations.

Despite all this criticism, the STC has widened the trade channels, expanded our trade, particularly with bilateral countries, diversified our trade pattern through its private contacts with the West and governmental contracts in the Communist bloc. The STC has succeeded in the promotional aspects of trade policy and increased the volume of trade and prospects of trade. As regards new markets, it has introduced instant coffee, packaged tea, tapioca chips, etc., into Europe, coffee into Japan, shellac into China, gramophone records into USSR, etc. STC has successfully penetrated new markets and new areas of marketing in terms of countries and commodities.

The STC provides financial, marketing, and technical assistance to the small-scale sector and arranges for the sale of their products abroad such as oils, leather products, fruit juices, footwear, readymade garments etc. The storage capacity of the STC has been considerably augmented so as to expand their role in bulk handling. The buffer stock policy in respect of shellac and price support operations for natural rubber were helpful in augmenting exports and imparting price stability.

The STC has some foreign offices in addition to branches in India with its head office in New Delhi. Canalised imports mopped up the extra profits which private importers would have reaped. In the area of non-canalised imports, the success of STC was doubtful, due to its inadequate corporate planning strategy and lack of manpower expertise. It's marketing strategies lack dynamism and foresight. If the STC is to play a more useful role in future, it should strengthen its foreign offices, particularly in Asia and Africa and mid-West, and reorganise its structure by strengthening its departments with proper training and manpower planning.

MMTC

In 1963, the Minerals and Metal Trading Corporation was set up to carry on export and import trading in minerals and metals, iron, manganese, coal, etc. Our traditional importers of these products are Japan, Bangladesh, Burma and Sri Lanka. As we have to strengthen our trade relations with them and open up new markets, particularly in Africa and Asia, through the setting up of joint ventures, MMTC was given a special responsibility. Mica has a great potentiality in TV, engineering and electronic industries. Manganese, copper, zinc and other metals have good scope for export either as ores or in semi-processed forms. What is needed is a proper thrust by the MMTC and an imaginative long-range marketing strategy. Efficient and quick service to foreign customers is needed. Secondly, research about the market potentialities helps significantly. Thirdly, manpower training and development will be necessary for a thorough reorganisation. Participation in trade fairs, constant dialogue with customers, improvement in quality of services, efficient and businesslike method would go a long way in improving the role of STC/MMTC in the foreign trade field.

Imports comprise mainly fertilisers, non-ferrous metals, stainless steel and industrial raw materials which accounted for three-fifths of the Corporation's turnover. The main items of export are iron ore, manganese ore and coal. New items of export have been added more recently such as chrome ore and concentrates, finished products manufactured out of copper, zinc, stainless steel, etc.

The other agencies set up in the public sector for exports and imports are briefly set out below:

(1) **The Handicrafts and Handlooms Exports Corporation of India:** This was set in 1962 as a wholly-owned subsidiary of the STC for making exports of handicrafts, handloom goods, gold jewellery besides canalising exports of woollen/blended knitwear, carpets, sweaters and related articles.

(2) **The Cashew Corporation of India:** It was set up in 1970 as a wholly-owned subsidiary of the STC to ensure uninterrupted supplies of raw cashewnuts at fair prices to export-oriented domestic units and arrange for the export of processed cashew nuts and its products. It is diversifying its activities into edible nuts, spices, etc.

(3) **The Projects and Equipment Corporation:** It was set up in 1971 as a subsidiary of the STC to effect exports of capital equipment (railway equipment and engineering equipment) and turnkey projects and to import necessary inputs.

(4) **The Tea Trading Corporation:** This was set up in 1971 with the primary objective of exporting value added tea, packaged and bagged teas. It operates some tea gardens and tea warehouses. Some domestic sales of tea to government and government agencies are also undertaken by it.

(5) **The Mica Trading Corporation:** It was set up in 1972 to handle the exports of mica but started operations in 1974. It has been exporting mica since then and has set up plants for the manufacture and export of micronised mica powder, wet ground mica powder and mica paper, etc.

With the economic reforms initiated since 1992, the trend is to privatise and open up the economy. The role of State has been coming down and the barriers to trade are being dismantled. Under these changed conditions of privatisation and globalisation of the economy the role of State trading and canalisation of imports or exports have lost their original significance.

All quantitative restrictions on most of the exports were removed. Emphasis was laid on forging proper trade agreements with Sri Lanka, Bangladesh, African countries. Indian contact with SAARC countries has increased, with emphasis on export of services like I.T. communications, etc.

17 Commercial Policy and Theory of Tariffs

So far we have discussed trade theory as if trade is beneficial to all under conditions of perfect competition, free mobility of factors inside the country and no mobility internationally. Under such conditions, free trade was advocated as ideal by the classical economists. Tariff, duties, quotas etc., are interferences with the free trade and would lead to difference in comparative cost advantages prevailing before and the pattern of trade flows would thereby change. These interferences into free international Trade may be classified as:

(a) Price controls in the form of export or import duties levied by the government.

(b) Quantity controls in the form of quotas imposed by the government.

(c) Price discrimination as between different markets practised by exporters — charging higher prices in markets where elasticities of demand are lower.

(d) Dumping in the form of sending goods abroad at any price in order to maintain monopolistic element at home — reverse dumping is selling goods at home at any price in order to maintain monopoly element abroad.

(e) Cartels in the form of international business agreements to regulate price, division of markets and thwart competition by other methods.

These forms of interference exist in various forms in international trade among many countries and commodities. In the real world, free trade and perfect competition do not exist but only various degrees of imperfection in markets are found. In this chapter, attention is focused on tariffs in international trade.

Definition

Commercial policy can be defined as any policy which influences the commercial relations in respect of exchange of goods and services internationally *vis-a-vis* the domestic trade. Thus, definitionally taxes or duties or restrictions on movement of goods, quotas or incentives and subsidies come under this policy. The instruments of commercial policy are:

(a) **Fiscal:** Taxes on income and sales turnover, taxes on goods (Customs and Excise duties) both direct and indirect taxes.

(b) **Monetary:** Cash subsidies, incentives, price support operations, easy availability of export credit and interest rate rebates, etc.

(c) **Exchange Controls:** Control on direction of trade flows, on method of payments and receipts, etc.

(d) **Quantitative Controls:** Quotas, dumping, etc., would come under this category.

Free Trade vs. Protection

Once the philosophy of free trade is not acceptable due to varying degrees of imperfections in the economy and in the factor and commodity markets, then varying degrees of control on trade and payments are justified as the next best alternatives. The first best method is not suited to the real world as it will not maximise the welfare of all trading nations due to the non-existence of assumptions of free competition. Protection to domestic industries in varying degrees and restrictions on free flow of trade across borders are thus justified in the interests of the national economy. Optimisation at sub-optimal conditions and equilibrium at less than full employment conditions would result from tariff and quota restrictions on trade. Quotas are more suitable when price mechanism is faulty and cannot be relied upon. Similarly, in a socialistic pattern of development when the price mechanism does not play a significant role in growth, tariff and quota restrictions have a justification.

Effects of Tariffs

One of the methods of raising revenue for the government is taxing the goods exported, or imported namely, tariff. The imposition of tariff is an interference with the price mechanism which in turn influences excess supply and demand entering into international markets. The effects of tariff can be studied under the following heads:

(a) Protective effect is the increase in domestic production as a result of the imposition of tariff on imports.

(b) Consumption effects is the reduction of domestic consumption of foreign imported goods as a result of tariff and higher domestic price.

(c) Revenue effect is the additional revenue secured by the government due to the levy on imports/exports.

(d) Redistribution effects is the net producer's surplus derived by subtraction from consumer's surplus, additional economic rent paid to existing domestic producers in the form of additional profits.

The size of the protective effect depends upon the elasticity of supply. The higher the elasticity, the larger is the protection. A tariff is prohibitive when the protective effect is sufficient to expand domestic production to a point where it will satisfy domestic demand fully without imports. A point to note here is that the industry producing an import good subject to tariff may gain but not necessarily the whole country. One country may gain at the expense of others and whether the gain of the former compensates for the loss of the other is not certain. The protective benefit enjoyed by an industry at micro level might only perpetuate inefficiency as its enjoys an assured market at home and is not in the long-run interests of the country from the point of view of allocative efficiency or productivity.

The only valid argument for a tariff from the world point of view is the infant industry argument. If an industry is of national importance and as such it should grow and attract more investment, tariff is justifiable method of achieving the objective. The industry, supposed to be an infant, is expected to grow to an economic size as to reap the economies of scale under the protective umbrella of tariff.

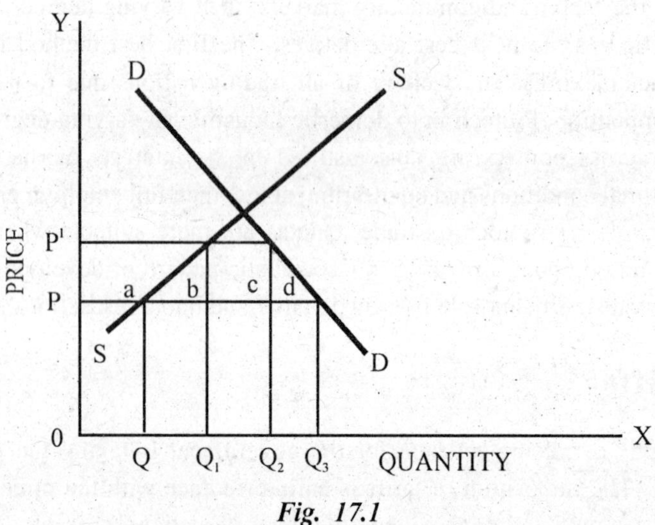

Fig. 17.1

Diagrammatically the above effects can be presented as shown in Fig. 1 in partial equilibrium analysis:

DD and SS are demand and supply curves for the import good. PP' is the tariff and QQ_3 is pre-tariff import of that commodity. Q_1Q_2 is post-tariff import. Protective effect is the increase in domestic production QQ_1 at the new price inclusive of tariff OP'. Consumption effect which is always negative is reduction in consumption by Q_2 Q_3. The revenue effect is the gain in revenue to government on the new level of imports Q_1Q_2 multiplied by the tariff rate (PP') (represented by quadrilateral c in the diagram). The redistribution effect is the additional profits due to higher prices to producers represented by the quadrilateral a. The consumption effect is reduced or eliminated if the tax is entirely met by foreigners exporting the product. The redistribution effect increases the reward for scarce factors and reduces the incomes of the abundant factors which is contrary to the trends observed under free trade when the premium paid to the scarce factors is reduced. The monopoly element of scarce factors and vested interests of a few sheltered producers will weigh heavily in the tariff policy. b is a gain to producers and d is a loss to consumers. Whether b can compensate for d is doubtful and would depend upon subjective factors.

Another reason for the imposition of protection is the high domestic cost price structure whereby the industry is not competitive in the external markets but its development is in the interests of the nation like defence material, ammunition, etc. Planned economic growth and development of domestic industries through import substitution also justifies the granting of protection.

A point may arise when it is advantageous to use quotas rather than tariff. While tariffs produce effects through the price mechanism, they are slow and cumbersome to work. They lead to greater administrative costs of operation. As against these, they give revenue to the government or create producers' surplus or extra profits. Quotas are quick to act and effective in achieving the objective of limiting imports or prohibiting them entirely. When commodities are price inelastic, it is advantageous to resort to quotas. Similarly, in a situation when government revenue is not important but protective effect is, then quotas may be resorted to. Quotas might also lead to extra profits to producers and distributors or lead to deleterious effects on consumption, distribution, etc. From the point of view of production, it may be advantageous to impose tariffs rather than quotas as a semblance of price incentives might work in the former case and allocation of factors and their rewards might still work in the direction of greater production.

Effective Rate of Protection

Internationally traded goods are part of the domestic input-output matrix. The new theory of tariff structure emphasises the resource allocation effect of tariffs. The effective rate is the percentage increase in the value added per unit in an economic activity which is made possible by the tariff structure at the same exchange rate. It depends on the tariff rate on the commodity produced, tariff rate on the inputs of the-commodity and input co-efficients of that output. Thus, effective rate f is given by formula $f = \frac{t - qr}{1 - r}$ where t is nominal tariff on the output, q is the nominal tariff on the intermediate good (or input) used in the final output, r is the proportion of final product represented by that intermediate product. It assumes that the input-output matrix is fixed and is known. If the input is tax-free and constitutes about 50 per cent of the value added, then the effective rate is double the nominal rate. Here q is zero and $f = \frac{t}{1 - r}$ where $r = 0.50$ which gives f as double that of t. It is to be noted that only tariff on inputs is to be considered and not inputs of the inputs which would constitute double counting.

An export tax is comparable to an import subsidy and an import tax to an export subsidy. An export product may use imports as inputs which are subject to import tax although the export product is not taxed. Then the effective protection to the exportables is a negative rate as applicable to inputs.

Similarly, suppose an importable is using as input in exportable which is taxed at say 25 per cent, then this influences the protective effect on the importable. On the same lines, production and consumption taxes on tradables would influence the protective rates, if those goods are used as inputs of exportables or importables. Effective rates of protection can thus be positive or negative if all these influences are taken into account.

Taking such effective rates into consideration one should assess the effect of such rates on production and consumption at home. If the production substitution elasticities are high, production would shift from goods with low effective rates to goods with high effective rates. If a similar analysis is made for consumption effects, depending on expenditure substitution elasticities, consumption would shift from goods with high tariffs to goods with low tariffs. These changes are continuously taking place in the real dynamic world, leading to continuous changes in the equilibrium position.

Any change in tariff on traded goods would bring about changes in the interrelationships between traded and non-traded goods and if aggregate expenditure is kept at full employment income level, changes in expenditure pattern would lead to excess supply or excess demand in the domestic markets and this internal imbalance if not offset by a corresponding imbalance outside the economy would result in exchange rate changes. The existence of free foreign exchange markets and flexible factor prices would facilitate exchange rate adjustments. Effective protective rates are to be estimated to understand their full implications on resource reallocations, changes in productive structures and exchange rate adjustments. For global equilibrium there should not only be internal balance but external balance as well.

Concepts of Protection

The above discussion should lead us to four distinct concepts of protection:

(a) **Nominal Tariff:** An industry is protected if the nominal tariff on its imports is positive. This can tell us the consumption effect but not the production effect as production depends on the tariffs imposed on its inputs also.

(b) **Effective Tariff:** An industry is protected if its effective tariff is positive and if the prices of non-traded input goods are not altered and exchange rates do not change, that is, if input taxes only are taken into account.

(c) **Net Effective Tariff:** An industry is said to be protected if its net effective rate of tariff is positive after taking into account the exchange rate effects of protective structure.

(d) **Total Protection:** An activity is truly and totally protected if the net result of the protective structure combined with the exchange rate adjustments is to raise the value added in that activity.

Some of the assumptions on which the above concepts were formulated are unrealistic. To mention only a few limitations, elasticities of demand and supply are not infinite and the inter-relationship between inputs and outputs and between traded and non-traded goods do not remain constant.

Non-economic Arguments for Protection

Many times political factors and vested interests prevail on the government to impose protection. National interest is the prevailing non-economic general argument for tariffs. In times of emergencies or war, the first axe to fall is on the entry of foreign goods into the country unless they are necessary for war effort. Defence is thus national priority which justifies tariffs. Similarly, socio-economic reasons like the nature of agriculture and their way of life justifies that tariff protection in certain activities. "Beggar thy neighbour" policy is making the best of the selfish interests at the expense of other nations which is generally deprecated.

Economic Arguments for Protection

Some of the economic arguments for tariffs, leaving aside the most popular argument of the infant industry are as follows:

(a) Terms of Trade Improvement: If the foreigner pays fully or partly, the tariff imposing country can gain by lower price for imports and better terms of trade.

There is no guarantee, however, that the foreign country does not impose a countervailing duty. Besides, whether there will be improvement in terms of trade or not, will depend on the relative elasticities of supply and demand. If the domestic demand is elastic and foreign supply is inelastic, and import duty will benefit the country imposing it by improving its terms of trade. If there is any increase in domestic price to the consumer, this is offset by the revenue earned by the government (revenue effect).

(b) Anti-competitive Effect: If a country wants to introduce monopoly in any industry, one of the ways is to impose high tariff walls. But removal of tariffs would introduce a competitive effect and force innovation and technological change in the domestic industry to keep itself abreast of foreign competition. In case any industry is not in a position to do so and if it has also a high cost-price structure and cannot compete effectively but its survival is in the national interest, tariff walls are necessary.

(c) Income Effect: As tariffs cut spending abroad, income not spent abroad is either spent at home or saved. Under conditions of unutilised capacity or less than full employment, it would lead to a rise in output and employment at home through larger spending or investment. In the case of inflation and excess money incomes at home, however, this income effect distorts the distribution of incomes and adds further fuel to inflation and leads to the perpetuation of inefficiency.

(d) Balance of Payments Effect: A favourable balance of payments effect of tariff emerges out of a possible cut in imports, assuming that other things (exports, inward remittances, etc.) remain constant. The money so saved by cut in imports is assumed to be spent at home on other items of consumption or investment and that macro-economic action of the country also supports the micro-economic decision of cuts on imports.

All the above arguments in favour of duties on exports and imports are of dubious validity in the real world. Mostly socio-economic and political factors play an important part in such economic policy decisions as tariffs. Where the price mechanism is faulty and has to be intervened, tariffs are not the best method, as subsidies may stimulate output without restricting consumption. But subsidies are inflationary if they are paid out of government revenues. Direct taxes and transfers are superior to tariffs in that they avoid distortions in the production and consumption patterns. Whatever objective can be achieved by tariffs can be better achieved by other alternatives. But in actual practice, all countries impose tariffs on a variety of export and import commodities, prompted more by the exigencies of domestic supply and demand, international forces, pressure of vested interests and short-term gains.

Arguments against tariffs are many and weighty. They distort the price mechanism and lead to lower trade and lower consumption profile. Protection encourages inefficiency, vested interest, misallocation of resources and higher costs and prices. As between quotas and tariffs, quotas are preferred in some cases as they are neat and effective and do not disturb the functioning of the price mechanism.

Whatever these instruments can do to the economy, can be better done through other methods with less adverse effects. Thus, exchange rate changes (devaluation or revaluation) may be better than a system of tariffs and subsidies. The monetary policy and a proper fiscal policy might promote growth of industries better than protection.

18

International Trade Organisations

GATT

The International Trade Organisation (ITO) was set up in 1947 and subsequently the General Agreements on Tariffs and Trade were concluded between the participating countries laying down the rules and guidelines for conducting international commercial relations. The GATT contained provisions for limiting the reliance on tariff and non-tariff barriers in trade.

The General Agreements on Tariffs and Trade (GATT) came into force in 1948 with an original membership of 23 nations and it has 105 members in 1995 when WTO was started. The signatory members have agreed on a code of conduct in international trade, designed to promote the movement of goods through reduction in tariff barriers and through elimination of discriminatory practices in trade and tariff. The various rounds of tariff reduction in 1949, 1951, 1956, 1960-61 (Kennedy Round) and 1973-79 (Tokyo Round) and 1993 (Uruguay Round) covered a wide area including anti-dumping, non-discrimination, most-favoured-nation clause, subsidies, countervailing duties, customs valuations and government procurement policies.

The GATT is wedded to the principle of non-discrimination and freer trade. It has been more successful in this line in respect of industrial products rather than agricultural products, because most developed countries prefer to use Article 19 which permits safeguards against imports causing damage or domestic injury to agriculture. Protective measures were resorted to many times on a selective and discriminatory basis by the developed countries against the developing countries, despite their membership of GATT. There was, however, a conscious effort to prevent the GATT from becoming a club of the richer nations and procedures have been evolved to draw in developing nations while not expecting them to take on their shoulders the obligations of keeping their markets open to the products of developed countries. Still the benefits flowing to developing countries from lower trade restrictions are not substantial.

. The most-favoured-nation treatment is to be given to all the members of the GATT and this clause empowers the members to bargain for reduction in tariff barriers among members. Two exceptions to the MFN treatment are the customs union and the free trade area. The GATT includes members which are both advanced and developing countries. Under the auspices of this agency, many tariff negotiations were conducted for reducing and eliminating the tariff barriers, particularly with respect to developing countries. Most of these negotiations were aimed at bilateral concessions in tariff with a view to promoting larger trade among the developed countries and between developed and developing countries. There are still many tariff restrictions as well as quota provisions imposed by developed countries on developing countries. While tariffs are preferred, quotas are also frequently found among the barriers imposed by the developed countries.

UNCTAD

The UN Conference on Trade, Aid and Development (UNCTAD) has been championing the cause of development as the objective of all trade and aid, particularly in respect of developing countries. Various international trade agreements and commodity agreements have been promoted by the UNCTAD, which aims at stabilisation of earnings of developing countries and improving their terms of trade. There are international commodity agreements in respect of tin, cocoa, sugar, jute, etc., which are working satisfactorily. There is also a provision for the creation of buffer stocks for reducing price fluctuations to the benefit of both producing and consuming countries. The international buffer stock arrangements encompass a wider variety of commodities identified by UNCTAD (coffee, cocoa, tea, rubber, etc.). The buffer stock arrangements benefit both producer and consumer countries by stabilising the prices.

The various UNCTAD meetings starting with the first in 1964 have tried to promote agreements between producer and consumer countries on the stabilisation of commodity prices. The stockpiles of the various commodities are also being financed by member countries and international institutions under the aegis of the UNCTAD.

Broadly, the trade barriers and the disadvantages of LDCs in matters of trade are being effectively tackled by UNCTAD on behalf of developing countries. The Group of 77 developing countries has pledged co-operation and joint action by the developing countries for securing the full benefits of trade to themselves *vis-a-vis* developed countries the programmes of co-operation include international commodity agreements and buffer stock arrangements and their financing. More recently, the UNCTAD has taken up the case of commodity agreements for tea and jute in which India is keenly interested. Although not much success was achieved in forging an agreement between the producing and consuming countries in the case of tea, some agreement was arrived at in the case of jute and an International Jute Organisation was started with its headquarters at Dhaka in Bangladesh in July 1983.

WORLD TRADE ORGANISATION (WTO)

A new world trade body under the fold of GATT was started in January 1995. India was one of the Founder Signatories of the new body, WTO. The new pact was negotiated for over 7 years under the GATT Umbrella covering 125 member countries. There are more than 150 members as at end 2009.

The main highlights which will help India and other developing countries are tariffication of quota and other trade barriers to highly protected industries like Dairy Products, Agricultural Products, etc. Reduction in export subsides, tariffs on industrial products, opening up further of markets for services, textiles, etc., are the other features of the new pact. In the long run, the reduction to trade barriers is expected to increase global trade. India may benefit due to larger agricultural exports and better access of our textile goods in international markets.

Multinationals can now apply for product patents, in India, for their newly patented products in agricultural chemicals, pharmaceutical chemicals etc. The amendments to Patents Act, and Patent Rules would enable the Government to grant patent rights for seven years in the above product range. Trade in services and intellectual property rights and protection thereof have been brought under the ambit of WTO. It has ruling powers in case of disputes as between members.

Anti-dumping laws are made more precise and specific and Government can impose countervailing duties to prevent subsidised exports from abroad coming into India. Changes in Anti-dumping laws and the power of the Government to impose countervailing duties to prevent subsidised exports are all made in tune with the final act of the uruguay Round of Multilateral trade negotiations.

In November 1995, a Disputes settlement Body of WTO set up as an Appellate Body that will hear appeals from Disputes panel in cases on issues of law covered in the panel Report. In December 1995, the WTO established an Independent Entity (IE) for settling disputes between exporters and pre-shipment Inspection Companies. It started operating since May 1996.

Objectives of GATT

GATT aims at reduction of barriers to trade and elimination of discrimination in matters of trade relations. It promotes free and multilateral international trade which in turn is expected to expand international trade both in value and volume, increase world output and consumption and raise the standard of living of the world as a whole. By freer flow of trade, allocative efficiency of resources will increase and leads to better utilisation of world resources which will again lead to larger output better productivity and higher standard of living for the world as a whole.

In particular, the rules on which GATT is developed are the following:

(1) Avoidance of quantitative restrictions

(2) Elimination of all discriminatory trade practices

(3) Use of consultations as a vehicle of settlement of disputes among member countries, and

(4) Reduction of all tariff barriers.

GATT and MFN Clause

As GATT was based and non-discrimination and reduction of all tariff and non-tariff barriers, as a step in that direction, members may agree to grant to each other most favoured Nation status in respect of tariff barriers. Article 1 of the Agreement deals with MFN clause which states that any advantage, favour privilege or immunity granted by a contracting party to any product originating in or destined for any country shall be accorded to a like product originating in or destined for the territories of all the contracting parties. This means that each member country should be treated as the most favoured nation among the contracting members. Any concessions materialised under bilateral agreements should be extended to all other members on an equal basis.

MFN clause in short, aims at multilateralising the tariff and non-tariff barriers to trade as a step in the direction of reducing and eliminating them. Restrictions are permitted for the following purposes.

(1) When the country has balance of payments (bop) problems and exchange reserves are inadequate.

(2) When a country is underdeveloped and these restrictions are used for promoting economic development on a temporary basis.

(3) When a country wants to restrict any imports which will hurt the country's domestic price supports and production control programmes.

TARIFF NEGOTIATIONS

As GATT is based on the tripod of principles of non-discrimination, elimination of trade restrictions and consultations among members, one venue of achieving the objectives of GATT is tariff negotiations and members are encouraged to negotiate for reduction of tariff. The following guidelines have to be adopted for such negotiations.

(1) Reduction of tariffs to be on reciprocal and non-discriminatory basis.

(2) Reduction of tariffs to be for binding of low tariffs on sustainable long term basis.

(3) Members to negotiate in good faith and mutual confidence.

Originally GATT adopted the technique for tariff negotiations, on a nation to nation basis and on a commodity to commodity basis. This is called bilateral-multilateral technique, because it is bilateral when members agree for tariff reduction on a nation to nation basis and is multilateral when following the MFN clause, tariff reductions agreed upon have to be applied generally to all contracting parties of GATT. The bilateral aspect of negotiations was given up in Kennedy Round of International Trade negotiation (1964-67).

The various Rounds of Tariff Negotiations are summarised below:

No of Rounds	GATT Conferences (years)	Name of Rounds	Brief Results
First	1947	Geneva (Switzerland) Round	GATT agreement was signed, Tariff Schedules formed and some tariff concessions granted.
Second	1949	Annecy (France) Round	Tariffs on specific goods, reduced and some tariff concessions exchanged.
Third	1950-51	Torquay (England) Round	Some tariffs were reduced and tariff concessions exchanged.
Fourth	1956	Geneva Round	Tariffs on specific products reduced and some tariff concessions granted.
Fifth	1960-61	Dillon Round (Geneva)	20% cut in average tariffs, EC Negotiation started for tariff concessions, 35% cut in tariffs a manufactured goods for the first time.
Sixth	1964-67	Kennedy Round (Geneva)	
Seventh	1973-79	Tokyo Round	Agreements covered non tariff barriers, subsidised exports and tropical products.
Eighth	1986-93	Uruguay Round (Punta Del Este)	Agricultural products included for the first time. Trade in services TRIPS, TRIMS and removal of import barriers, tariff and Non-tariff barriers and MFA.

Final Act of GATT, (1994)

The Final Act of GATT was signed at Marrakesh on April 15, 1994. under this, the members entered into an agreement on the Technical barriers to trade, which empowers the importing countries to enforce technical regulations at customs point, debarring goods not conforming to their technical regulations. Technical Regulation refers to the "document which lays down the products characteristics or their related processes and production methods, including the applicable administrative provisions, with which compliance is mandatory".

WTO vs. GATT

After the Marrakesh agreement was signed, the GATT of 1947 was replaced by WTO in 1995 with 77 members which increased to more than 150 members by 2010. WTO is an improvement over GATT, in that it shifted emphasis from negotiation approach to the legal machinery for disputes settlement. Instead of giving veto powers to some like the U.S.A. or weighted voting as in IMF and IBRD all members are given equal voting power. unlike GATT, the agreements under WTO are permanent and binding to the member countries. DSM (Disputes Settlement Mechanism) & WTO is quicker and binding on the members. Its approach is not dilatory as in the case of GATT but is Rule based and time bound unlike GATT, the WTO has wider coverage of goods and services and trade related aspects like intellectual property rights and several issues, not taken up by GATT.

WTO is a legalistic organisation, based in Geneva. Its structure includes Ministerial conference (MC) which is the Supreme governing body for decision making, supported by the general council.

Functions of United Nations Conference on Trade and Development (UNCTAD)

UNCTAD was established as a permanent organ of the General Assembly of the U.N. Its main executive body is the Trade and Development Board. If has four subsidiary organs to assist in its functions, namely

(1) Committee on Commodities

(2) Committee on Manufactures

(3) Committee on Shipping, and

(4) Committee on Invisibles and Financing Related to Trade

The TDB is composed of 55 members elected by the full body of the conference from its members on the basis of equitable geographical distribution. It meets twice in a year.

The main functions of the conference are the following:

(1) To promote international trade and aid among all the countries with a view to propell the economic development.

(2) To frame policies for the international trade and related problems conducive to economic growth.

(3) To formulate proposals for putting into effect the above policies.

(4) To review and facilitate the coordination of activities of the other institutions within the UN, and

(5) To be available as a centre for harmonious trade and related documents on development policies of governments.

It will be seen from the above that UNCTAD is different from the GATT both in functions and operations. While GATT is purely for Trade development, UNCTAD is for trade and aid for purposes of economic development. GATT is for negotiation and commitment of members, while UNCTAD is a formal deliberating and conciliatory body.

UNCTAD has nearly 170 member countries. It meets once in four years and the subjects on which it deliberates and makes recommendations on policies and principles, should promote trade, aid and development. Trade includes both merchandise and invisible trade. The subjects encompass a wide range of areas of interest for growth and development, such as protectionism, transfer of resources to developing countries, monetary reforms, SDR allocation, conditionality of IMF loans. In the matter of trade, the subjects covered are also wide, to include as for example, shipping, tourism, tariff reduction etc.

The main purpose of these recommendations is to urge the governments to adopt policies which are conducive to a new international division of labour keeping the interests of LDCs in mind and make the external sector conducive to growth of developing countries.

It has recommendations to both developed and developing world. The developed world should reduce tariffs and give greater access to exports of LDCs in the markets of DCs; it should promote larger aid and particularly united aid to developing world. It has recommended that each developed country should transfer atleast 1% of its annual income as aid to developing countries. The developing countries were recommended to progressively diversify their economies from primary producing and exporting countries to industrial producing and exporting countries, which means that they should industrialise their economies and start agro-processing and exporting industries. It has recommended international commodity agreements and buffer stock arrangements for many agro products which LDCs export. But the target of 1% of annual income could not be achieved by the developed countries.

UNCTAD Conferences

The following is the list of UNCTAD meetings, conducted so far. Nine meetings were held and the last one was held in 1996 at Midrand in South Africa. Each of the meetings highlighted some specific issues, affecting trade and aid.

Table 18.1: List of Conferences

Conference	Venue	Year
UNCTAD - I -	Geneva	1964
UNCTAD - II -	New Delhi -	1968
UNCTAD - III -	Santiago -	1972
UNCTAD - IV -	Nairobi -	1976
UNCTAD - V -	Manila -	1979
UNCTAD - VI -	Belgrade -	1983
UNCTAD - VII -	Geneva -	1987
UNCTAD - VIII -	Columbia -	1992
UNCTAD - IX -	Midrand -	1996
UNCTAD - X -	Bangkok -	2000
UNCTAD - XI -	Sao Paulo, Brazil -	2004
UNCTAD - XII -	Accra, Ghana -	2008
UNCTAD - XIII -	Doha, Qatar -	2012

The UNCTAD conferences are held every four years.

The last meeting discussed issues, pertaining to WTO, sustainable development and debt relief to developing countries. The earlier conference agreed on the creation of new structure for the UNCTAD Body namely the setting up of the Trade Development Board, which meets twice in a year in regular session in addition to special sessions as and when required and an executive committee of the permanent representatives of UNCTAD in Geneva to meet periodically to guide the UNCTAD work programme. It was also agreed to create export committees on poverty alleviation, economic co-operation among the developing countries and services and *ad hoc* working groups to support the committees and the T.D.B, on a wide range of subjects of interest to developing world, like Aid and Investment, Trade efficiency, Privatisation, etc. Four UNCTAD commissions and one working party do meet more often than the Board and discuss the matters of Policy Programmes and Budgetory issues and related matters.

UNCTAD-X at Bangkok

The UNCTAD held its tenth session in Bangkok in February 2000. This meeting has achieved a measure of consensus on globalisation, which should seek to integrate the weaker and less developed countries into the world economy and promote growth and development. This conference has achieved a narrowing down of the views of member countries on the developmental aspects, particularly in respect to market access, capacity building, and reforms of the world's financial architecture. UNCTAD's concern was voiced in matters of Trade, Finance, Investment and Technology and the responsibility of developed countries to involve the LDCs in matters of policy making globalisation process for the purpose of promoting growth in LDCs.

WTO Origin and Functions

The WTO is a product of Uruguay Round of negotiations of GATT. The old GATT system was allowed to continue under what was known as the "Grand father clause". The members can continue to keep their existing legislation, even if they violated the GATT. WTO has almost the same objectives, but its method of operation is given a legal framework for disputes settlement and their enforcement, by a more powerful body.

WTO has the following four main functions:

(1) It shall facilitate the implementation and operation of Multilateral Trade agreements

(2) It shall provide a forum for negotiations among the members in their trade relations.

(3) It shall provide and administer Trade Review Mechanism, and an understanding on the Rules and procedures governing the settlement of Disputes.

(4) To achieve greater cooperation among world bodies to formulate a more cohesive global economic policy making, and in particular with IMF, IBRD, etc.

The General Council of the WTO will have the following functions:

(1) To review and supervise the operations of the revised agreements, relating among others to the goods, services and Trips.

(2) To act as a Trade Review mechanism.

(3) To act as a Dispute settlement body.

(4) To establish and supervise the working of the goods council, Services Council and TRIPS Council as supervisory bodies.

Only members who accepted the outcome of the uruguay Round of negotiations of GATT can become members of WTO. India is one of such original members.

The functions of General Council were referred to already. It operates through the Disputes settlement Body (DSB) and Trade policy Review body (TPRB). The Director General is the Chief Executive Officer assisted by a secretariat and his tenure is four years. He is also assisted by four Deputy Directors from different member nations. Further, it has three councils to advise on (1) Trade in goods. (2) Trade in services and (3) Trade Related aspects of intellectual rights.

The trade Review body has three committees to assist them namely the committee on Trade and Development (CTD), the committee on Balance of payments Restrictions (CBOPR) and the Committee on Budget Finance and Administration (CFBA), who specialise in policies related to subjects allotted to them and advise the Trade Review Body (TRB).

WTO is concerned more with some neglected aspects of trade barriers, which are referred to below. These were not dealt with by GATT.

(1) Variable Levies which refers to taxes on goods, collected at the customs point.

(2) Export Restrictions based on quantum or value or export quotas.

(3) Consumer protection Legislation, which is a kind of trade barrier to control the entry of goods into the country.

(4) Health and Environmental factors in the Regulation of Trade. Some countries impose controls on imports in the name of health and environmental considerations, such as bananas by the U.S. or agricultural products on the grounds of use of DDT and other chemicals.

(5) Child Labour Regulations banning of imports on the ground of use of child Labour by LDCs.

(6) Shipping and freight carriage restrictions to national carriers by importer countries.

(7) Discriminatory trade balancing arrangements violating multi-national trading pattern.

Main Issues in WTO

The main issues under which discussions were taking place in WTO Ministerial Conferences are set out below briefly.

(1) **Agriculture:**

(a) ***Export Subsidies:*** Removal by DCs and their reduction in LDCs, in a time bound manner. No agreement could be effectively reached.

(b) ***Market Access:*** Improvement in market access to agricultural products of developing countries while allowing them flexibility for safeguarding their interests. There was no substantial progress on this issue.

(c) ***Domestic Support:*** Reduction in trade distorting domestic support programme for Agri products, with special and differential treatment for developing countries. The DCs are supposed to do more in this respect, as per the Doha mandate, but not much progress was made in this respect.

(2) **Professional Services under GATS:** India has large commitments in the areas of health, financial services, telecommunications, tourism and travel. Here the commitments are based on imperatives of domestic policy on FDI.

(3) **Market Access to Non-agricultural Products:** The extent and mode of tariff reductions varied among countries. But India has moved very much close to the requirements of WTO with tariff reductions, and removal of non-tariff barriers.

(4) **Trade Related Intellectual Property Rights and Public Health:** TRIPS Discussions centred around the methods of patent protection in pharmaceuticals and yet provide medicines at low cost to LDCs and ensure incentives for R&D efforts in LDCs.

(5) **Singapore Issues:** These include Trade and Investment, Trade and Competition Policy, Trade facilitation and Transparency in Government procurement. No agreement was reached on these issues so far.

(6) **Trade Rules:** Anti-Dumping, Subsidies and RTAs are the issues discussed under this head. India is reported to have taken a stand of its own in the interests of all developing countries and sought amendments to the Trade Rules permitting negotiations.

(7) **Disputes Settlement Body:** This issue is subject to negotiations and Doha declaration stated that these negotiations are a continuing process and provisions of Disputes Settlement Understanding (DSU) will not be a part of success or failure of other negotiations. Negotiations are continuing for an agreement on the role of and working of DSB.

(8) **Trade and Environment:** Trade obligations under WTO Rules and those under Multilateral Environmental Agreements (MEA) have to be co-ordinated and liberalisation of trade in

Environmental goods and services. Presently, DCs have been objecting to some imports on environmental grounds which are to be sorted out.

(9) **Trade, Debt and Finance:** Solutions are to be worked out to strengthen the coherence of International Trade and Financial Policies with a view to safeguard the multilateral trading system and problem of external indebtedness of developing countries.

(10) **Trade and Technology:** Need to take steps within the mandate of WTO to increase flows of Technology to developing countries.

(11) **Electronic Commerce:** Facilitation of E-Commerce and co-ordination with traditional terms of Commerce Development related issues - Fiscal and Monetary implications of E-Commerce - imposition of customs duty on electronic transmissions-competition within Electronic Commerce-legal issues and jurisdiction and applicable law.

No consensus could be reached on many of the above issues, particularly on subsidies to Agriculture by the D.Cs. The U.S-EU Framework for freeing farm trade was unacceptable to the G-22 member governments. Besides, the developing countries are united in their opposition to the inclusion of Singapore Issues. The process of negotiations of the WTO after Cancum was very slow. The Cancum Ministerial meeting was mainly of stock taking nature and only resulted in lengthening the negotiating period, rather than their abondonment. It may be noted that Uruguay round took eight years to complete rather than the originally mandated three years. This was the same time-consuming process that the previous trade rounds of WTO took to finish negotiations. The consensus was to continue negotiations under the aegis of WTO.

WTO-TRIPS — Uruguay Round

Before June 1993, the Director General of GATT was Arthur Dunkel and Dunkel Draft was considered and accepted at Uruguay Round of Negotiations, held in June 1993, when peter Sutherland succeeded Dunkel. The Dunkel draft .was rated high as promising welfare gains to members worth hundreds of billions of dollars. That these estimates were all extravagant was shown by a study published by the World Bank on "The uruguay Round and Developing Countries," containing 13 well written Research papers, edited by will Martin and Alan winters.

The uruguay Agreement contains well over a dozen wide ranging agreements. of these four are more important, namely Agreement on Agriculture, Agreement on Textiles and clothing (ATC), Agreement on Market access in Industrial products and agreement on Trade Related Aspects of Intellectual Property Rights (TRIPs).

The Agreement on Agriculture achieved a great deal in defining rules for agricultural trade, but it achieved little in terms of immediate market opening. It will have nil or negligible impact on Agriculture Production. In Industrial field, the agreement to phase out the multifibre Agreement (MFA) under the ATC constitutes a major achievement. The commitments by developed countries amount to a reduction in their import weighted average tariff from 6.3 to 3.8%. the developing countries could not commit much barring a few exceptions, which means that this agreement does not mean much in terms of actual benefits to world trade. As regards the TRIPS agreement, it's effects are likely to be adverse to developing countries. The agreement promises to extend monopoly rights to the patent holders to the entire world for 20 years. This provision will result in a transfer of income from developing countries to developed countries, where in are located innovators and R&D efforts to a large extent. Some Researches have estimated the losses from Trips to the developing countries at well over several billion dollars (*viz;* Arvind Subramanian, with the IMF, who worked on this scheme under Arthur Dunkel).

The result, in a nutshell is that UR commitments mean nothing to developing countries. The removal of Trips and MFA however, could generate some favourable effects to developing countries. The benefits of TRIPs are negative to developing countries as by giving patent rights for 20 years, mostly to MNCs in DCs, there will be net outgo on royalty payments, fees and charges from the LDCs to DCs. The benefits estimated from MFA and TRips at $ 200 billion for the world and $ 50-90 billion for the developing world are biassed estimates arising out of research by the Developed countries. India should therefore develop its own patents and research capabilities. The impact of Trips will therefore be negative and nil for India in particular. The experience of UR negotiations shows that the capacity to effectively negotiate by the developing countries is badly damaged by their inability to produce their own Research documents and the production of biassed research results and pressures generated by such research from the vested interests from the Developed world. More importantly the dissenting voices of the LDCs could not be heard before the powerful lobbies of the DCs in such Forums.

Trade Related Investment Measures (TRIMs)

As part of urugray Round trade negotiations, an Agreement on Trims was entered into whereby no member shall apply any TRIM, which is inconsistent with the WTO Articles. TRIM refers to certain conditions and restrictions, imposed by the government in respect of foreign investment in the country. These conditions inconsistent are given below for illustration.

(1) A certain amount of local imputs to be used.

(2) A certain proportion of output to be sold locally.

(3) Imports not to exceed a given proportion of exports or exports and imports should balance.

(4) Foreign exchange outflow should be a certain proportion of foreign exchange inflow or they should balance each other.

Any such conditions are to be phased out in a period of 2 years for industrial countries, 5 years for developing countries and 7 years in the case of least developed countries. Provision is also made for extension of the periods given above in case of genuine difficulties by developing and less developed countries.

India is one of the signatory members of the WTO and as such it is required to observe these conditions. But these conditions are not good for unequal members, as the developed countries can afford to allow no conditions. Countries like India can be exploited by the MNCs of developed countries if these conditions are removed.

China and some other developing countries did gain from larger flow of foreign investment (FDI) and their growth has been faster due to the removal of all conditions and restrictions imposed on foreign investment. India is moving in that direction but not as fast as in China, as it is done in a systematic and slow manner as not to upset the balance between domestic investment and foreign investment particularly since 1993.

Indian Intellectual Property (TRIPS)

The potential for Research based intellectual property is great in India. But Indian companies do not spend much on R&D and hence they have no intellectual property, worth the name. Besides, there is no protection to intellectual property rights in India. There is a huge time differential in the launch of new products in India and the launch abroad, due to lack of intellectual rights protection in India. In a study made by Daniel M. McDonald, Managing director of SmithKline Beecham Pharmaceuticals India Ltd., it was found that with respect to top 10 products world wide and the top 10 products being sold in India, there is a time difference of 10 years. The most recent launch in India was ten years old abroad in U.S. and UK.

In order to overcome the above disadvantage the Government of India have introduced a new scheme of Exclusive Marketing Rights (EMR) recently which will enable foreign MNCs to market their latest products in India. But this is only transitional stage towards patent protection. In the absence of the latter, the EMR is going to have only peripheral impact on the foreign MNCs, and their operations in India.

Besides, even granting of patent rights will help only if there are no price controls or production or distribution controls on the products. In India some products, particularly in the area of pharmaceuticals, suffer from some control or other. The controls are one of the reasons why the FDI flow into India is low, as compared with a similar country like china. During the last 8-9 years, India could attract only US $ 10 billion as compared with $ 35-45 billion in China. Controls on ownership is another reason why India could not attract as much FDI as in the case of china.

WTO — Disputes Settlement Body

The difference between GATT and WTO is that the latter was given legal powers through the disputes settlement Body, which has become vital for the smooth functioning of the multilateral trading system. There is now a Rule based Dispute settlements mechanism. WTO members are given equal voting rights with no veto power to the U.S.A., as in the case of GATT. The GATT system was based on negotiations, which was found to be not effective and binding.

Being Rule bound, WTO may be able to compel the members to abandon many health and environmental standards, if they are contrary to International Trade Rules. The panel Reports are voted as per the rules and the decisions of the whole body are binding on members. The critics say that the Appellate body and Dispute settlement panel vote in secret, which means that they can authorise nations to retaliate against violations of Trade agreements. As the power and sovereignty of the U.S.A is now terminated, the U.S.A alongwith some other developed countries have asked for a full review of the Disputes settlement mechanism and to improve the transparency in WTO operations.

In the recent disputes between U.S and Japan with regard to U.S access to Japanese market for photographic film and U.S ban on import of shrimp caught without safeguards against turtles, the WTO Rules went against U.S decisions. But developing countries are also criticising the WTO as a wholly legalistic structure without any regard, as GATT has, for sensitivity for need for equity and environmental concerns. Unlike GATT' the WTO has binding disputes settlement undertaking, which does not allow blocking of any complaints. Some LDCs as Banana producing countries suffered due to the rigid posture of WTO and lack of flexibility or even concern for the interests of LDCs. Besides the legal cost of disputes settlement system of WTO are too heavy and cannot be afforded by them and they may not have the expertise for it.

There is need for reform of WTO. It has to be made more responsive to the considerations of equity and justice to the developing countries. It should set up a legal cell within its secretariat to advise the LDCs on legal matters and to reduce the cost burden. The developing countries should have a right of benefiting from such panel proceedings in the absence of non-governmental legal and other experts with it. Many developing countries suffer in the hands of WTO, due to the financial muscle power of MNCs based in leading industrialised world. The WTO failed miserably in the first test in which the interests of the developing countries were pitted against those of the transnational corporations, from the developed world. WTO could not protect the LDCs from the powerful vested interests of MNCs and the DCs.

In August, 1999, an appellate Body of the Geneva based WTO delivered the ruling upholding the final Reports of Disputes settlement panel, which has rejected India's stand, justifying quantitative restrictions on imports of 2700 items on B.O.P. grounds in its Trade dispute with the U.S.A.

Similarly, there is concern about the public accountability of the D.S.U demands. The current rules of WTO are too rigid and need redrafting with a view to make the WTO more responsive to non-economic ends and justice to the less powerful group of LDCs. The alleged leaking of interim reports from panels emphasises the need of revising the Rules on publication. There should be a right of one complainant to attend the consultations of another complainant on the same matter and there should be a third party for securing the implementation of the panel recommendations.

WTO recommendations on intellectual property rights, patents, etc., are taken full advantage by the MNCs of the developed countries, but not the LDCs. The interests of Agriculture of LDCs is also not protected, as it should be. In short, the WTO should be remodelled to be flexible and responsive to the special needs of LDCs.

WTO — Trade Policy Review Body (TPRB)

As part of the obligation of India to WTO, easing of import restrictions was started in 1997. As on April 1,1998 there were quantitative restrictions on imports of 2714 commodities. As per the current plans, these restrictions would be removed in about six years from 1997. Accordingly, nearly 340 items of import were shifted from restricted list to O.G.L in April 1998. Easing of import restrictions continued in 1999 to 2006 policy statements, on Exim policy. By 2006, most of the import restrictions were removed.

During April 1998, the Trade Policy Review Body (TPRB) of the WTO undertook evaluation of India's Trade Policy. This review included in addition to conventional areas, new areas of services, trade and trade related intellectual property rights. Its last Review was in 1993.

The TPRB has noted the sharp tariff reductions undertaken in India since 1993. The simple average of all tariffs came down from 71% in 1993 to 35% in 1997-98. During the same period average tariffs on imports of manufactures had declined from 73% to 36%. The applied rate and peak tariff for agricultural imports during 1997-98 were 26% and 45% respectively. The overall import weighted average tariff declined from 87% in 1990-91 to 20% in 1997-98, even after taking into account the temporary duty of 5%. The Peak rate of Customs duty reduced to 25% in 2003-04 and further by stages to 10% by 2006.

The TPRB has noted that since the last Review (1993), India has made significant progress in the reduction of non-tariff barriers as well. During the 1998 review, the list of freely importable goods and goods under S.I.L covered about 68% and 10% respectively of the total tariff lines. Between 1995-96 and 1997-98, India has increased the coverage of SIL by one-third. The share of imports on which the STC has some monopoly has been reduced from 27% at the end of last decade (1990) and to an insignificant proportion by 2009.

TRPB was however not happy with the pace and quality of reforms in India. The direction of reform was more in export-orientation rather than a more general outward-orientation. This has happened because the reforms in tariff and non-tariff barriers were not accompanied by similar reforms pertaining to export subsidies and incentives. The exemption of the profits from export earnings from income tax was questioned. The TPRB pointed out that many exporters in India are entitled to SIL. Since these licenses are freely transferable and fetch a premium in the market, they argued that facility can be looked at as an export subsidy. The TPRB has noted that India has yet to make good progress in the reduction of export subsidies.

India cannot remain a mute spectator of the world bodies like GATT and WTO. India is now committed to a market oriented economy where trade liberalisation is one of the main planks as also the foreign investment in India. In an era of emerging regional trade blocks, such as EFTA and NAFTA, in Europe and North America respectively, there are similar opportunities for India with Asia and pacific Regions.

India may benefit from the Agreement on Agriculture and Multifibre agreements (MFA). If the quota restrictions of DCs are given up India will stand to benefit under both heads. As per the agreement DCs will have to import atleast 3% of their agro products and exporting countries have to reduce their Agro subsidies as not to exceed 10% of the value of production. India is already on the move to reduce the Agricultural subsidies. Assuming that there will be improvement in quality of Agro-products and textiles products in India, our country stands to gain and we have to go along with W.T.O.

Trade Policy under WTO

Under Agriculture, India submitted detailed proposals for maximizing export opportunities for agricultural products by seeking reduction in the high tariffs and subsidies, prevalent in developed countries. There is a greater emphasis on bringing Indian standards to international levels. Given the lack of technological development in all spheres in developing countries, comparable to that in developed countries, India feels that special measures need to be taken by developed countries to give effect to the clauses extending special and differential treatment to developing countries in the implementation of WTO agreements.

As regards the intellectual property rights, India's obligations under the Trips Agreement have been implemented by passing the necessary legislations such as the Geographical Indications of Goods (Registration & Protection) Act 1999, and the protection of plant varieties and Farmers' Right Act with the objective of giving a significant thrust to protection of plant varieties and farmers' rights. India seeks to provide protection to intellectual property rights through changes in specific legislative provisions in the existing laws.

As regards trade in services, government had laid greater emphasis on efficient performance of services sectors, like Telecommunications, banking insurance, shipping, roads, ports and air transport. India participated in the Uruguay Round Services Negotiations and made commitments in 33 sub-sectors as compared to an average of 23 for developing countries. In tune with the General Agreement in Services (GATS) negotiations should be allowed through request and offer approach. Movement of natural persons is to be allowed as one of the modes of supply of services which is not allowed freely by developed countries. The export interests of developing countries should be taken a special care by developed countries.

Recent WTO Operations

During 1997, the pace and direction of WTO activities were mainly influenced by the negotiations on trade and Information Technology (IT) products, telecommunications and financial services. In the area of goods, 43 members countries of WTO agreed in March 1997 to the elimination of tariffs on I.T. products. Further a group of seven countries and the E.U agreed to accord duty free treatment to 465 pharmaceutical products.

The use of Disputes settlement Mechanism (DSM) continued to be high. During 1997-98 the Disputes settlement Body (DSB) of the WTO received 40 notifications of formal request for consultations under Disputes Settlement undertaking (DSU). Ten new panels were established during the period and five Appellate Body and panel Reports were adopted.

The relations of WTO, IMF and World Bank have now been based on two agreements between these organisations. During the year, 1998 cooperation on technical assistance with the IMF, World Bank and other international agencies including UNCTAD and the International Trade centre has been reinforced. In addition, many non-governmental organisations were brought more closely into contact with W.T.O activities.

WTO Seattle Conference

As referred to, already WTO has 148 members which is likely to increase further. The latest WTO ministerial meeting was held between November 30 to December 4, 1999 at Seattle. The agenda for the meeting includes:

(1) Review of three-existing agreements namely DSU, TRIPS and TRIMS.

(2) Consideration of new agreements, on which consensus is not reached, namely industrial tariffs, market access, e-commerce, social clause (environment and labour) transparency in government procurement, multilateral agreement on investment, trade and competition policy and trade facilitation.

The expanded agenda was referred to working groups for eliciting a consensus on the above issues. In the absence of consensus among members these should not be included in the agenda. The Seattle Conference ended in a fiasco as no worthwhile business could be agreed upon.

The areas where India is interested in, are agreement on industrial tariffs, Agreement on Agriculture and the agreement on services (in particular financial services). Seattle negotiations will go beyond the plurilateral to a multilateral level. India will be interested in particular in the inclusion of labour movement in services and agriculture as India has professionals in their core competence, and agriculture is a core sector.

India may lose by the use of countervailing duties and inclusion of the development subsidies among the export and import subsidies to which DCs are opposed. GATT has allowed some of these subsidies for development purposes. Textiles constitute a major export item of India and it is kept outside the free Trade Laws.

India is opposed to some clauses of TRIMs agreement, which impede the development objectives of trade policies of LDCs. TRIMs agreement does not allow indigenisation and local area content. India is yet to assess the gains and potential gains from the existing agreements of uruguay Round before committing for more. Rectification of some clauses of the present agreement is what is called for in the interests of India and LDCs.

The DCs are having barriers to our exports of textiles, ready made garments and agriculture which are vital to the economies of developing countries. Market access to developed countries is vital for India.

India has a time period of 10 years to bring down their Aggregate Measure of Support (AMS) to 10%, which is being pursued. The Developed countries are expected to reduce their export subsidies by 36% by 2000 and their domestic support to 13%. India has to bargain for greater access for its agricultural exports in U.S.A., E.U. and Japan, in particular. As regards services, it has to bargain for greater access to consultancy, professional services and labour movement. While Technology is included in the Agreements, labour is not included and India and China are interested in it. It is understood that China has also joined the WTO. It is to the advantage of China and India along with smaller countries and SAARC countries in particular to take a common stand in the WTO conferences, as against the interests of MNCs of developed countries. This has been done when India's position was accepted by Group 22 LDCs.

Uruguay Round — AOA

The Agreement on Agriculture (AOA) was brought into the world trading system, for the first time by WTO. The three basic clauses of AOA are the market access through tariff reduction, domestic support or subsidies to Agriculture, and export competition.

As regards the tariff, India has bounded tariff for almost all agricultural products and so the question of giving market access of minimum of 3% of consumption level does not arise in India. The bound tariffs range from 100% for raw-materials to 150% for processed agricultural products and 300% for edible oils. The products with zero tariff are rice and skimmed milk powder with less than 1.5% fat content. The negotiation in this regard may reduce the tariff binding to less than 50%. As regards domestic support to agriculture, in India, both the product specific and non-product specific supports are below the 10% level permitted to a developing country. The highest level of support of non-product specific nature was 7.5%. The implication is that India is not obliged to change its support to agriculture.

On export subsidy front, there is hardly any agricultural commodity that gets any such subsidy on worthwhile scale, except the income tax exemption to export earnings for all products including agriculture. There is nothing that India stands to lose on the negotiating Table. India should insist on all major trading partners to reduce export subsidies. India should suggest a cap of 50% maximum tariff on all agro-products.

Doha Ministerial Conference

The Fourth Ministerial conference of the WTO took place in Nov. 2001 at Doha, Qatar. The Declaration recognized the need for safeguarding the interests of the developing countries. Agreement has been reached to strengthen such provisions which concern the developing countries, particularly in the field of environmental protection and The Labour Standards. The declaration also mirrors the concerns of the developing countries in the context of government action for maintenance of public health, and extension of the scope of norms on geographical indicators and protection of the traditional knowledge. It was agreed to maintain customs free status of electronic commerce through electronic transmission.

The high level of protection provided to Trade in agriculture by developed countries should be removed as they stand in the way of exports of farm products by developing countries. Non-trade related issues have to be kept out of the agenda of WTO. India is opposed to the extension of WTO jurisdiction on issues of trade and labour standards and trade and environment. The TRIPS agreement is to be interpreted in a manner supportive of members right to protect public health and ensure access of medicines to all, in the developing countries.

The WTO provisions on geographical origin of wines and spirits should be extended to other products and there should not be any misuse of biological and genetic resources and traditional knowledge of developing countries. The market access to products of developing countries in the developed countries has to be improved by removal of trade barriers and tariff peaks in the industrialised developed countries. In services, the movement of natural persons has been given focus, apart from reaffirmation of the guidelines and procedures of negotiation. The implementation proposals on these subjects will also become part of the negotiations. It will thus be seen that most of the concerns of India have been taken note in the Doha conference.

WTO Consultations

The Fifth Ministerial meeting of the WTO was held at Cancum in Mexico during September 11 to 14, 2003. It has deliberated on the progress of work programme, adopted in the Doha Declaration. The deliberations ended without any fruitful outcome. They could not reach any agreement on the major issues before them, due to differences between the Developed EU and American Countries on the one hand and G-20 developing countries on Agriculture and G-16 developing countries on "Singapore Issues," on the other hand. On Agriculture, the issues involved are Export Subsidies, Domestic Support and market access to agri products. Singapore issues related to trade and aid and investment flows across nations and related items like competition.

India's Post Cancum Consultations

India has actively participated in these consultations. It has played a crucial role in forming alliances among developing countries in the WTO negotiations-namely G-20 on Agriculture and G-16 on Singapore Issues.

It may be recalled that the Fifth Ministerial meeting of the WTO was held at Cancum in Mexico during September 2003. The post-Cancum consultations focused on four negotiating areas namely Agriculture, Market access to Non-agricultural goods (NAMA), Singapore Issues and Cotton. Agricultural exports and market access were most crucial. Many proposals for tariff reductions were proposed. At the "Agricultural Week", held during March 2004, delegates agreed on the need for according special treatment for developing countries but differences arose on the condition that would apply.

Subsequently, negotiating papers were put forward by G-20, G-10 and G-33 to bridge the gap between the positions of U.S. and EU and that of developing countries. The EU promised to phase out farm export subsidies, on the condition that other forms of export subsidisation are also ended. The Framework agreement adopted at WTO General Council in August 2004 brought the negotiations back on the track. The major decisions taken by the General Council included elimination of all forms of subsidies on Agriculture by an "end date", in a phased manner, reduction of all trade distorting domestic support programmes, and continuation of the flexibility available to developing countries and for providing certain subsidies for export of some agricultural products for a reasonable period, after phasing out of all forms of export subsidies and removal of other forms of trade barriers.

PATENTS AND TRADE MARKS

The TRIPS Agreement of uruguay Round of Trade negotiations contain seven areas namely intellectual property rights, copy rights, trade marks, trade secrets, industrial designs, geographical appellations, integrated circuits and patents. Of these seven areas, India is not in conformity with the TRIPS Agreement in respect of patents only. India is far behind in protection of patents, as conceived by WTO.

A patent is a monopoly right, granted by law to the commercial use of an invention, that is new and is useful to the public. The patent is protected in many countries, giving the inventor an opportunity to recoup his costs and earn a profit to reward the invention and encourage the R and D effort.

Thus, the main objectives of patent protection are the following:

(1) to reward research and invention.

(2) to induce the investor to disclose the details of its commercial use, so as to make it useful to the public.

(3) to allow his monopoly use for a specific period so as to enable him to reimburse his expenses, and

(4) to help him earn extra profits to induce investment of capital in Research and Invention.

Indian Patents Law

Under the Indian Patents Act 1970, in respect of food, pharmaceuticals and agro chemicals, there is only process patent and no product patent and that patent protection is for 7 years for the above products and 14 years for the other products. But according to the Uruguay Round, there should be both process patent and product patent and protection shall be for 20 years.

The Indian Patents Act excludes methods of Agriculture, horticulture and biotechnological processes and products for patentability. These are patentable as per the WTO Agreements. The Patents Act is now amended to include product patents.

The use of neem and turmeric and other agro-products used in Ayurveda for medicinal purposes, not patented in India are finding way by research into Allopathic medicines, which are patented. There is thus a lacuna in our patent system.

Uruguay Round agreement does not compel a country to extend patentability to plant varieties. Instead a country can opt for an effective Sui generis system, which is not well defined by WTO. However, the Government of India is proposing to bring out a Sui generis system's legislation to protect plant varieties, like Basmati Rice. Under the uruguay Round final Act, a country may exclude from patentability, plants and animals other than micro-organism and essentially biological processes for the production of plants and animals other than non-biological and microbiological processes.

Trade Marks

Brands and Trade marks used extensively for marketing products help promotion. Tata Tea and Nestle Instant coffee are some examples. Brand is a name, term, sign, symbol or design, which is used to differentiate it from its competitors, like Colgate Toothpaste. Brand name is that part of the brand which can be vocalised or utterable. Brand mark is that part of the Brand which can be recognised but not utterable, like Agmark, a symbol, a design or distinctive colouring. Trade mark is a part of the Brand, that is given legal protection because it is capable of exclusive protection and appropriation. It gives the product seller, the exclusive rights to use Brand name and/or Brand mark.

Trade and Merchandise Marks Act

This Act of 1958 governs the registration of Trade marks, so that the proprietor of the Trade mark enjoys the legal right to the exclusive use of it and make monopoly profits on it.

The objects of this Act are to provide for registration and better protection of the rights of holder of trade mark and for prevention of the fraudulent use of it by others.

According to the Trade and Merchandise Marks Act, a trade mark is a mark which establishes a connection of certain goods and the proprietor or the registered user of the trade mark. It may also include a certification trade mark.

Procedures

The applicant for Trade Marks has to approach the Trade Marks Registry office of the Government of India. The Registrar of Trade Marks is the controller General of patents, Designs and Trade Marks. Besides the Head office, there are number of branch offices, with specified geographical jurisdiction to each of them, as decided by the Central Government.

To be eligible for registration, the good should be distinguishable from others, and trade mark should be distinctive. It should not be similar to any other registered, trade marks nor have similar description. The Act laid down some prohibited list for registration, such as those which are contrary to any law or may cause deceit or confusion, scandals or obscene, or hurt the religious feelings, commonly used words, names of persons, etc.

The applications are to be made in prescribed form and are scrutinised by the Registrar, for compliance with the Act and may or may not grant registration. If not granting, the reasons therefore have to be recorded. If accepted, the Registrar shall cause an advertisement to be issued inviting any objections and reasons therefore. After going through all the formalities, relating to any possible objections, the Registrar shall issue applicant a certificate in a prescribed form and manner. This is valid for a period of 7 years, under the Act.

A registered trade mark is assignable and transferable for consideration along with or without the goodwill of the business concerned. The Registered proprietor has the power to assign trade marks and give receipt for consideration. The proprietor and the registered user may be different if the proprietor has assigned for use to the Registered user. The user's name can also be registered, for any product which is registered.

The Act prohibits infringement of trade mark rights by anybody in the course of trade and business. An unregistered trade mark does not enjoy any of these privileges.

The Act has also provided for several other matters such as penalties for offences of infringement or falsifying or misuse and there are special provisions for textiles goods, and other products.

Patents (Amendment) Act, 1999

The Patents (Amendment) act 1999 mainly deals with the grant of patent/ exclusive marketing rights (EMR) to sell or distribute in India the substances, used or intended for use as medicine or drugs. This act has incorporated an article (157 A) to protect national security. The article empowers the central Government not to disclose any information relating to patentable invention or any application relating to the grant of a patent which it considers prejudicial to the interest of security of India. It can also revoke any patent already granted in the interests of security of India. This article is however in consonance with the WTO agreement (Article 73 on security exceptions). This Act was amended later on also to suit the emerging conditions in the economy.

The 'security of India' is a vague term and the effect of this article depends on how it is interpreted. The act has however defined this expression as anything that relates to the fissionable materials or material from which they are derived or materials like arms, ammunition and implements of war or those supplied to military establishments or those used in times of war or other emergencies in the matter of international relations. These in short relate to drugs, fissionable substances used in biological and chemical warfare.

Some micro-organisms and bio pesticides have dual use as in pharmaceutical industry and biological warfare. These are hazardous to human, animal and plant life. EMR allows the import of such hazardous materials for storing and distribution. But this facility can be misused by importing such dual purpose materials and storing for use in biological and chemical warfare. But the definition of security of India has not included the banning of such dual purpose materials or substances. The drafting of the article requires thus modification in the interests of security of India.

Patent Norms Revised 2006

The Patents (Amendment) Rules of 2006 were notified on May 11, 2006. The new rules bring in more transparency, decentralisation of the operations of the Patent Offices and simplifications of the procedures to grant of Patents and disposal of applications within a time frame.

Product patents are brought in line with India's commitment to the WTO. Patent applications are now to be published within one month after the expiry of the statutory period of 18 months. In case an application is received for early publications then the application is to be published within one month from the date of such request.

The patent offices at Kolkota, Chennai, Delhi and Mumbai can perform 'all patent' related activities and the time frames stipulated for these activities have to be observed. The time for granting permission to file patents abroad has been reduced to 21 days. And the normal period for a decision to be taken by the Controller after submission of the examination Report by the Patent examiner, is one month. Time frames have been set out for each of the activities of the patent office.

WTO and Policy Changes

India's trade policy review was conducted by WTO at Geneva in June 2002. To boost the electronic hardware industry. Some changes were made in the Electronic Hardware Technology Park (EHTP) Scheme to enable the sector to face the zero duty regime under the Information Technology Agreement of the WTO. On the basis of the principle of real comparative advantage 220 commodities were identified as potential export products and 25 focus markets were identified. Service sector is given special export thrust. Strategies are formulated at the commodity level and market level for export focus. Besides, 15 key macro policy issues were identified for attaining overall competitiveness, such as FDI flows, exchange rate changes, tariff issues, infrastructural and procedural issues.

The next meeting of WTO was held in Mexico (Concum) to discuss the internationally acceptable accounting standards and agriculture in the member countries.

The group of 77 of the UN is a loose coalition of 77 LDCs was founded in June 1964 and their first meeting was held in Algiers in 1967. The group was formed to protect the coalition of collective economic interest and promote the negotiating power of the LDCs against the developed world in matters of trade and development.

India was a member of this group since the beginning.

19

Commercial Policy in India

The trade policy is announced every year based on the past trade performance, projected foreign exchange budget and developing trends in the economy. But the basic tenets of the policy are the progressive rise in export earnings, conservation of foreign exchange reserves and import licensing for the purpose of export promotion, import substitution and fuller utilisation of capacity in Indian industry and to meet the essential requirements of capital goods for investment.

Trade policy is to be viewed in the general equilibrium model as part of the overall economic policy geared to promote growth of output, incomes, etc. Trade policy is one of the controlled expansion in India but not of free trade as under the laissez-faire philosophy.

Trade policy comprises both export policy and import policy. The commercial policy is an adjunct of trade policy. The objective of promoting growth of investment in tune with the priorities set in the plan is pursued in respect of these policies.

Tools of Commercial Policy

To achieve the above objectives under a policy of controlled growth, the tools used are tariffs - import and export duties and licensing, quotas and cartels or payment restrictions and prohibitions on some items. The positive aspect is encouragement of some exports and imports through offering fiscal and other incentives and other forms of assistance or concessions and canalisation of imports through State agencies.

Control on Trade

Restrictions on trade are imposed under Import and Export Trade Control Act of 1947. This Act was originally for a period of three years and extended from time to time and was placed on a permanent footing in 1971. Several notifications and policy announcements are made under this

Act. In 1975, Import and Export (Control) Amendment Ordinance was passed to make provisions for stringent action against offenders in export-import trade. The restrictions take broadly the following forms:

(a) Tariff or price controls or export and import duties; and

(b) Quantum restrictions or quotas.

Tariffs have the twin objectives of revenue to the government and protection to the industry or both. These objectives are difficult to distinguish and may overlap. Tariffs work within the overall framework of the price mechanism. Most of our export duties which are few in number are for revenue and a large proportion of import duties is for revenue or protective revenue and not for pure protection. These duties are useful as a retaliatory measure against foreign governments which impose duties or as an anti-inflationary measure at home.

The present chapter deals only with tariffs and subsidies. The other restrictions are dealt with in a separate chapter under Licensing and Procedures of Export and Import trade.

The annual publication of the Government of India on "Customs Tariff" publishes data, in a detailed manner, on the nature, extent of the duty, etc., in respect of each of a wide variety of commodities, both under imports and exports. The commodities subject to export duty are relatively few and are designed to mop up excess profits of exporters or to take advantage of the near monopoly supply of some commodities. But these duties are varied according to the supply and demand conditions and changes in the international price situation of dutiable goods.

Trends in Export Duties

Starting with the year 1954-55, our export duties were reduced on many commodities with a view to encouraging our export performance and to bolster up our foreign exchange reserves. By 1965-66 only three commodities, namely, raw cotton, cotton waste and mercury, were subject to export duty.

With the devaluation of rupee in June 1966, export duties were reimposed on a large number of commodities to mop up their excess profit arising out of devaluation.

Exports of gold, silver, coins and currency are prohibited except with the special permission of the RBI. Similarly, import of these items are controlled by the RBI under the Foreign Exchange Regulation Act, 1973.

The policy in respect of export duties is to keep them to the minimum and at a stable level generally so as to avoid international repercussions. Only a few commodities are subject to export duty at present.

Trends in Imports Duties

As regards import duties, the commodities subject to duty are many in number. These duties are meant for revenue, protective revenue, or protection. Imports whether on OGL or subject to licence would attract duty except in the case of those free of duty. Most of these duties in India are, however, for revenue purposes rather than for protection. Over the last three decades, the duties for protective purposes have come down, while those for revenue have increased. This trend is in tune with the growing requirements of government over decades. Total revenue from customs had risen from about Rs. 230-250 crores in 1951-52 to about Rs. 550 crores in 1965-66 and further escalated to Rs. 9296 crores in 1985-86 and stood at Rs. 66,792 crores in 2009-10. The importance of revenue accrued through customs had increased from about 25 per cent of total revenue in 1965-66 to 36 per cent in 1990-91 but declined thereafter to 28% by 1998-99 and to 10% by 2009-10 due to rationalisation and simplification of taxation. A bulk of the customs revenue is accrued to government from import duties (about 98 per cent). Due to our obligations under GATT and WTO and due to bilateral agreements with some countries, import duties are either reduced or removed in more recent years which explains the relative fall in its revenue.

Subsidies are the reverse of tariffs. While tariffs are levies imposed on exporters and importers, subsidies are cash and non-cash benefits passed on to these sections. Tariffs and subsidies are thus the negative and positive aspects of the government policy in relation to the foreign trade sector. Peak import tariff rate was reduced to 30% by 2002-03 and further to 5 to 10% by 2009-10 by stages from more than 100% before 1991.

Subsidies and Incentives

In India, subsidies and incentives are broadly of four categories:

(a) Fiscal incentives such as duty drawback, income-tax and sales-tax concessions, etc.

(b) Financial incentives such as cash compensatory assistance, export credit concessions, etc.

(c) Special incentives such as S.I.L import entitlements, Green form allotments, etc., and

(d) Other forms of assistance.

Many of these subsidies and incentives are being withdrawn since 1992 following the fiscal reforms.

These are dealt with in detail below:

(a) Fiscal Incentives

In the case of income-tax assessment, a rebate and allowance were provided for specified expenses incurred out of business income for delegations going abroad, for business trips and for promotional activities in connection with export markets abroad. Some rebates and allowances are announced in the Budget from time to time. For income tax purposes, 1 per cent of f.o.b. value of exports or 5 per cent of the incremental exports in any year is deductible from income. This is considered a very significant concession for export business, which is since withdrawn.

A scheme of customs duty drawback and excise duty drawback is operated in respect of goods exported but on which both these duties are paid. In respect of specified commodities exported from India, the exporter on application is entitled to refund of up to 95-100 per cent of the duty paid on an imported article which is reexported or the whole of import duty on intermediates, spares etc., used in the goods manufactured and exported from India. Excise duty paid on indigenous materials used in the manufacture of export products is also refunded after export on application by the exporter along with the specified documents and certificates. The goods eligible for such facilities and rates of duty drawback are given in the schedules to the scheme.

Following the government decision to refund duty through commercial banks, the RBI had introduced a scheme for the grant of advance by banks to exporters against their duty drawback entitlements. Under this scheme, effective from February 1976, the RBI provides refinance up to a maximum period of 90 days to all authorised dealers in respect of advances made by them to exporters against their duty drawback entitlements, as provisionally certified by the Customs authorities. RBI has now withdrawn all such schemes for exports to make them more competitive globally.

In respect of some goods, which are subject to excise, an exporter may enter into a "bond-for-export" of specified quantities of these goods and claim exemption from payment of excise or claim refunds in respect of duty paid on materials used in export products. In the case of "manufacture-in-bond", the exporter is under a bond to manufacture and export his goods in respect of which the inputs are exempt from both excise and import duty. Such manufacture of duty-free goods is kept under excise or customs supervision and surveillance. These schemes of export-under-bond or manufacture-under-bond or exports from free Trade Zone (such as Kandla or Santacruz Zones) would enable the exporter to export commodities without payment of any central excise or customs duties, provided none of their goods is diverted to domestic sales.

Some state governments like Gujarat and Maharashtra are also allowing sales tax exemption in respect of goods exported from their states, provided they are clearly distinguishable as export products. In some cases, refunds are granted by state governments also in respect of sales tax paid on the products which are subsequently exported by the manufacturers.

Customs and Excise Duty Drawback Scheme

For the purpose of export promotion, the Customs and Central Excise Duties Drawback Rules were framed in 1971 providing for drawback of both Customs and Central Excise together. The rules as amended from time to time envisage that drawback may be allowed on the goods specified in the schedule to the said Rules at such rates as may be determined and announced by the government from time to time. The drawback depends on the average quantity of the imported goods going into the production of the export good (raw materials and intermediates) including the wastages involved in the process and the rates of duties on them. The rate of drawback so fixed is called brand rate and is based on the information on the particular product of the applicant or in respect of the industry as a whole supplied through their Association.

The exported goods in respect of which duty drawback is to be claimed must be specifically based on imported goods which are exported after some processing and duty should have been paid earlier on imported inputs. When such export goods are presented to the Customs they must be clearly marked as under duty drawback claim. F.o.b. value, specification of the goods, marking, weight etc., are to be indicated. Copy of AR. 4 issued by the Central Excise authorities, insurance cover, freight invoice, export sale contract, letter of credit, GR form, pre-shipment inspection certificate etc., are to be submitted to the Customs for claiming the drawback. The customs would issue, after satisfying themselves about the actual export and bonafides of all statements made, a duty drawback payment order. This is the procedure where the industry drawback rate or brand rate is fixed already by the government for that product or for the exporter. Where no rate is so fixed, the manufacturer exporter may apply to the Director, Drawback, Ministry of Finance, Department of Revenue, for determination of such rate giving all the relevant particulars such as the specification of goods, ports of destination, duties paid on imported goods or export duty paid, etc. In the latter case, a provisional application may be made to the Customs for duty drawback claim and other formalities observed.

(b) Financial Incentives

These incentives comprise cash assistance for meeting the price and quality disadvantage suffered by Indian producers in the foreign markets and financial assistance for meeting the promotional activities of exporters. The cash compensatory assistance is designed to compensate the producer for the disadvantages suffered in respect of duties, taxes etc., paid by them and for higher shipping or transport costs, etc., incurred by them as compared to their foreign competitors. In order to enable exporters to plan their export efforts on a long-term basis, such cash assistance was announced for three years at a time in respect of specified commodities such as marine products, processed food items, leather and leather goods, engineering goods, sports goods, plastic goods, silk and rayon textiles, jute and cotton textiles woollen and coir products, handicrafts, chemicals, project exports etc. The cash assistance varied from 5 to 20 per cent of f.o.b. value of export depending upon the export product and the cost disadvantages suffered by them. The government expenditure on export promotion mainly in export subsidy had escalated from Rs. 160 crores in 1975-76 to Rs. 425 crores in 1980-81 and to an estimated amount of Rs. 2811 crores in 1990-91 which includes all forms of assistance; following the reforms this expenditure was reduced to Rs. 500 crores by 1998-99. Our exports to Nepal, Bhutan and a few other countries are not eligible for such assistance. About 420 commodities enjoyed this facility. All these subsidies on exports were removed under WTO Agreement.

Other forms of assistance under this head are cash payments out of Market Development Fund for meeting in part or full the expenditures of export promotion of the following types:

(a) Market and commodity surveys;

(b) Export publicity and advertisements abroad;

(c) Participation in foreign trade fairs and exhibitions;

(d) Sending Delegations and Study Teams;

(e) Establishment of offices or branches abroad for export promotion.

(f) Grants-in-aid to Export Promotion Councils and Trade Development Bodies; and

(g) Quality control and pre-export inspection which has been made compulsory in respect of a few commodities like jute and tea products.

The export promotion activities of the above type are to be sponsored by the respective Export Promotion Councils, Commodity Boards, etc. The quantum of assistance varied from 50 per cent to 100 per cent of such expenditure. Every exporter to be eligible to these incentives should register with the appropriate government body like the Engineering Export Promotion Council for engineering exports and has to make a proper application also with the necessary certificates from the Customs and other agencies in proof of the actual export.

A reference may be made here of the scheme of blanket release of foreign exchange for export promotion by the RBI. Although export promotion measures involving export finance are referred to in a separate chapter, it may be pertinent to point out here that export houses can, effective from October 1977, get blanket release of foreign exchange from RBI up to Rs. 1 lakh (or 2.5 per cent of the f.o.b. value of their exports) for undertaking promotional activities abroad through delegations, deputations, exhibitions, trade fairs, sales-cum-study teams, etc. The RBI has also launched a new forward cover policy to cover exchange risk of exporters. These have been further liberalised after 1991 financial reforms and dilution of FERA.

(c) Special Incentive Schemes

The scheme of import entitlement was originally introduced in 1957 to assist Indian exporters in procuring imported raw materials, components, intermediates etc., not domestically available, from abroad, with the least trouble and at international prices. The scheme is applicable to specified engineering products, chemicals, sports goods, carpets etc., which are non-traditional manufactured exports. The exporter has to make an application on a quarterly or half-yearly basis as specified in the scheme in the prescribed form to the Import Licensing Authority at the port in whose jurisdiction the exporter is operating. The application should be accompanied with the requisite fees, bills of lading invoices, certificate regarding the receipt of foreign exchange and insurance policy of ECGC.

The import entitlement is available up to 70-75 per cent of the f.o.b. value of exports or export value at international prices. This is to be used for import of inputs, raw materials, spare parts, etc., usable in the export production. This entitlement is transferable to another manufacturer but not to a merchant-trader. Besides exports made to rupee payment countries are also entitled to this system of imports from the general currency area.

Exporters of some specified products such as engineering goods, garments, etc., have been given what is called "Green Form Allotment", This allotment refers to the guaranteed supply of indigenous raw materials needed by registered exporters in the manufacture of their export products. Such supply is based on their actual export performance or committed exports. Import replenishment in respect of some export commodities such as iron casting products, etc., is given up to 133½ per cent of steel materials consumed by them in their export products of which 100 per cent is at concessional rates and the rest at normal controlled rates.

With the free convertibility of the rupee on current account since 1994-95 and liberalised trade policy, many of these incentives were given up.

Advance Licensing System

Under this system, the exporter is exempted from the payment of all duties for the import of inputs, raw materials etc., for the export production. Under the simplified procedure introduced in February 1987, the licence holder can import such items directly or obtain the supplies from the stocks of the canalising agencies like STC, SAIL, etc. The public sector units and canalising agencies are allowed to import raw materials and components needed for exporters for supply under advance licensing system or export-import pass book scheme. The import of consumables is also allowed duty free for the manufacturer exporter. In the case of transfer of such licences from the manufacturer exporter to trader or merchant exporter the need for bank guarantee is dispensed with. The regional licensing authorities have been given power to enhance the monetary limit of imports in case variation in exchange rates necessitated the upvalidation of the import value of the goods.

(d) Other Incentives

Over and above such fiscal and financial incentives, the public sector bodies such as STC, MMTC or foreign embassies or Missions abroad are available to exporters to provide the following services or assistance:

(a) Collection and dissemination of foreign market information by DGCI &S, IIFT, ECGC, ITDA, Exim Bank, etc.

(b) Market studies and surveys made by the Indian Trade Commissioners, Commercial Secretaries abroad, IIFT Export Promotion Councils and Commodity Boards etc.

(c) Generic export publicity and advertisement, as in the case of tea and jute goods.

(d) Exhibitions and Trade Fairs through the Trade Development Authority.

(e) Training of foreign trade personnel, provided by the Directorates of Exhibitions and of Commercial Publicity, Export Promotion Councils, Commodity Boards, Indian Institute of Foreign Trade, etc.

Aid to Export by SSIs

Under the scheme of Export Aid to Small Industries (EASI), the STC assists the selected small and medium-scale manufacturer-exporters to export their products abroad, under one window. Starting with the exploration of markets, collection of market information, the STC helps these SSI units in their export efforts until their export proceeds are received. Thus, STC provides all types of assistance to small-scale units in their export efforts.

Import-Export Policy

In the new Import-Export Policy announced after the economic reforms started in July 1991 there was a further thrust at export promotion. Export of gold jewellery of purity of not less than 9 carats as against 14 carats earlier was permitted. The category of deemed exports was expanded to include all goods supplied to Free Trade zones and 100 per cent export-oriented units as well as supplies and materials meant for the fertiliser projects set up in the country against global tenders. A new scheme of C.C.S. — cash compensatory scheme providing for rationalisation of rates and classes of commodities and addition of new products under eligible category has been introduced from July 1986 which was replaced by Exim Scrips in 1991. The payment procedure for C.C.S. as well as for duty drawback scheme was simplified to facilitate quick payments. The C.C.S. and Exim scrips, and many other export incentives were given up since 1992-93 when India adopted Trade account convertibility of Rupee. An Export Market Development Fund was started by the government with the Exim Bank for helping techno-economic research surveys and technical assistance for exports of new products and to new markets.

There was a provision for deduction of 50 per cent of export profits for tax exemption if it is transferred to reserves for development from 1985-86. For 1986-87 this concession was further liberalised to allow an additional 4 per cent of net foreign exchange earnings as exempt from tax. Tax concessions in the form of reduced duties or abolition of duties were granted for a wide variety of export and imports. special facilities like subsidies and income tax exemption up to 5 per cent of profits are granted. Exim Scrips were also given up as export promotion measure when the rupee was made partly convertible in March 1992 and exporter is allowed to retain some portion of export earnings abroad.

Export Processing Zones (F.T. Zones)

With a view to promoting exports, a number of Export Processing Zones were set up in the country. Such Zones in Kandla and Santacruz have been operating for over a decade. In more recent years, such free trade zones were also set up in Falta, Chennai, Cochin, Noida, (U.P). etc. Except in the case of Santacruz, they are all multi-product zones, manufacturing and processing a vast variety of products for exports. In Santacruz, it is only electronic and related products.

By exempting these units from all formalities, taxes and tariff hindrances, they are made more efficient and cost-competitive in foreign markets. They have also been given encouragement in the form of investment subsidies, input supplies at international prices, duty-free imports and tax holidays for a period of 5 years. Foreign investment was more liberally permitted in those Zones, for either equity participation or technical collaboration. The performance of these zones has been improving year after year.

100% Export-Oriented Units (EOU)

The scheme of 100 per cent Export-Oriented Units was started in India in December 1980. This scheme envisages production for entirely exports by the units set up for the purpose. About 193 units were approved for the purpose and commenced operations by 1992. Green cards were issued to all the approved units to entitle them to priority in supply of raw materials for construction purposes, transportation, etc.

A number of concessions were granted to them to enable them to increase their exports such tax rebates and exemptions. The government has granted reduction in customs bonding charges, free transfer as between EOUs or EPZs etc. The financial institutions were giving a rebate of 1.5 per cent in the interest rate applicable to these EOUs for various purposes for the first five years. A part of their production up to 20% which was raised to 50% in certain cases is permitted to be sold in the domestic markets also.

A single Board of Approval for export processing zones and EOUs and SEZs etc. was set up in 2001 for simplification of procedure.

The prevailing export promotion schemes operating now are briefly set out below:

(1) Export Promotion Capital Goods Scheme: The EPCG scheme was widened to include not only manufacture, but mining also. This allows duty free imports for manufacture of capital goods for export. The maintenance spares importable under EPCG has a limit of 20% of the value of export goods, with imports being allowed during the validity of the period for fulfilment of export obligation. The threshold limit of zero duty EPCG scheme has been reduced from CIF value of 5 crores to Rs. 1 crore and above in 1998.

(2) Duty Exemption Scheme (DES): Goods under this scheme for exports are entitled to duty free imports of spares, raw materials etc. Exemption from payment of additional customs duty earlier available to manufacturer exporter has been made available to merchant exporters as well. Deemed exports under Advance Intermediate licence have been brought under the category of special Import Licences. The duty free import of raw material is also available for exports to U.N. bodies and other multilateral agencies if they come under special import licence category.

(3) EOUs/EPZs: Supplies from one EOU/EPZ to another and exports of supplies after undergoing some further processing are counted as exports for the purpose of fulfilling the export obligation. Besides if the EOU/EPZ units have acquired the ISO 9000 (Series) or any other internationally recognised certification of quality it is now entitled to a special import licence at a rate of 2% of their exports.

(4) Passbook Scheme: The facility of passbook to exporter is allowed giving the exemption entries in the book for payment of normal and additional customs, through debits or credits for future claim of MODVAT or duty drawback as the case may be. Exporters can get the credit in the passbook for payment of duties against import of capital goods as well as imports against SIL meant for exports.

(5) Re-exports: Goods imported including those from the Negative List have been allowed for re-export without a licence subject to some conditions, such as a minimum value addition of 10%, importation under customs bond and kept with the bond premises.

(6) Regional Advance Licensing Committees have been set-up to provide licences to exporters at various regional centres like Chennai, Kolkata, Bangalore etc. to expedite the procedures for licences below the value of Rs. 5 crores. The Zonal Joint Director General of Foreign Trade can now dispose some cases and the Zonal Advance Licensing Committee can issue licences upto Rs. 5 crores. The rest will have to go to the Headquarters.

During 1997-98, the government initiated certain measures to mitigate many infra-structural constraints. Firstly, the government established a system of single window clearance for setting up of inland container Depots/Container Freight stations, in various parts. Secondly, Electronic Data interchange (EDI) and Electronic Commerce systems are approved and electronic media is used for submitting applications, by exporters and quicker disposal of cases by the concerned Departments.

Thirdly, reduction of interest rates was effected on certain types of export credit effective April 1998 and by two and a half percentage points in respect of Rupee credit.

The new schemes announced during 1997 to 2002 are as follows:

(1) Setting up of bonded warehouses for exports.

(2) Provision of Automatic Advance licensing to export houses and various trading houses under Duty exemption Schemes.

(3) Uninterrupted movements of export consignments, from anywhere in India.

(4) Setting up of Special Economic Zones.

Special Economic Zones (SEZ)

The rationale of setting up of many SEZs in some states is to support the shift in economic policy from import substitution to export promotion. Eight existing export promotion zones have been converted into SEZs and approval has been given in 2001-02 for setting up of 17 SEZs in states with prospects of export promotion.

The SEZ Scheme was announced in March 2000 to promote export production in a hassle free environment. It was incorporated in the Exim policy for the five year period 1997-2002. These are duty free zones meant for export production manufacture of goods and rendering of services including banking and insurance, production, processing, assembling, trading, and remaking reconditioning and reengineering including the gold, silver, platinum jewellery, etc

The incentives offered under this scheme include duty free importation or domestic procurement of goods for the setting up of units, 100% FDI in manufacturing sector under automatic route income tax exemption for these units for the first five years and 50% tax for two years thereafter central sales tax is exempt on domestic purchases and 100% retention of foreign exchange earnings in the EEFC Account (Exchange Earners Foreign Currency Accounts).

In March 2002, Overseas Banking Units (OBUs) were permitted to be set up with facilities of exemption from CRR and SLR requirements. The banks would give access to SEZ units to the international banking facilities, borrowing of lower international notes, being exempt from the ECB restrictions. They are allowed overseas trading investment and carry out commodity hedging. They are exempt form Income Tax Act and Customs Act. Transactions between SEZs and Domestic Trade areas would be treated as exports or imports, as the case may be. The objective is to develop these units in SEZ as purely export led units to promote export led growth.

Many existing schemes were also modified to ease infrastructural constraints to exporters during 1998-99, following a severe setback to export performance. These included permission to use legal undertaking, in place of bank guarantee by the established manufacturer-exporters, improvements in incentives, and facilities, given to EPZs and EOUs and enhancement of scope for EPCG scheme. A special fiscal package was also announced for the software sector, with a threshold limit of Rs. 10 lakhs.

Trade Development Authority (TDA)

The Trade Development Authority is an institution set up by the government to act as a catalyst for export promotion. The manufacturers and exporters can be regular members of it.

Apart from traditional services such as buyer-seller meets, contact promotion programmes, participation in trade fairs, the TDA has been attempting to break through into new markets and introducing new products into the existing markets. The major activities of TDA, thus, include arranging trade fairs in India and abroad, campaigns of Buy-India, publicity and generic trade promotion. It has also arranged sales-cum-marketing missions to various countries for different product groups.

The TDA also arranges for importers to meet foreign product suppliers. It has led a number of delegations for purchases abroad and arranged for display of foreign samples at selected Indian centres. It has organised seminars and conferences for promotion of sales, technological upgradation etc. The TDA has set up a technology cell for promoting technology transfers, joint ventures and collaboration agreements.

The TDA has been active also in the field of consultancy and market research, supply surveys, forecast studies, interfirm comparisons, etc. A number of studies were prepared and distributed to the members. The TDA has done pioneering work in the field of dissemination of information and market intelligence through bulletins and hand outs.

The important export promotion measures of TDA, now called India Trade Promotion Organisation (ITPO) are given briefly here:

(1) India Promotion Programme in Department stores abroad.

(2) Buyer seller meets organised.

(3) Arranging Trade Fairs and Exhibitions.

(4) Integrated Marketing Programme and Product Development Programmes.

(5) Arranging samples to be sent abroad and procuring them from abroad.

(6) Carrying the supply studies for domestic products, making forecast for export, arranging product and country data, provide training, etc.

Other Institutional Agencies

In the field of foreign trade, in addition to Trade Development Authority (TDA), There are a number of other institutional agencies like Indian Institute of Foreign Trade (IIFT), Trade Fair Authority of India (TFAI) and Indian Institute of Packaging (IIP). The IIFT has been rendering service in the field of foreign trade for more than twenty years. The activities of the Institute include commodity studies, overseas marketing surveys and conducting of seminars, research studies and training. The IIP is concerned with research and development in packaging, laboratory testing, training and publications in the area of design for packages and packaging technology. The TFAI conducts fairs and exhibitions in India and abroad and organises commercial publicity through mass-media and promotes foreign trade of India. Indian Embassies abroad help in securing contracts conducting fairs and for supplying commercial information with export thrust.

The Guhan Committee, set up to examine the role of IIFT, TDA and TFAI, was reported to have recommended the continuance of the separate identities and cross representation on their Governing Bodies to provide connections and interfacing between these bodies. The report is released early in February 1987. It is reported that the Committee preferred the setting up of a national information centre for dissemination of trade information. It was also suggested by them that TDA should remain the co-ordinating agency for export promotion in India. About TFAI and IIFT also, the Committee has made useful suggestions for co-ordination, promotion of exports, sharing of trade fairs, exhibitions, etc.

The above framework for export promotion continued even today with the stagnation of the export performance during 2009 to 2012 due to global recession. The thrust for exports of services was made by the government urging the above agencies to be more proactive, but no major policy changes were made.

20

Theory of Customs Union and Regional Economic Cooperation

In the theory of international trade, free and unfettered multilateral trade is the most favoured situation which would maximise world welfare under certain assumptions. But in actual practice, these assumptions do not hold good due to imperfections in international markets and controls on international trade and payments which would result in less than optimal conditions. In such a world, a measure of promoting greater welfare through larger trade is the regional economic cooperation in the form of trade and payment union or customs union. This would mean that two or more countries would agree to cooperate in such a way as to increase their economic and commercial transactions among themselves and to promote freer trade and payments inter se. While in bilateral trade agreements only two countries agree to channel and promote their trade in a particular direction, in regional economic unions or in common markets, a set of countries with a geographic contiguity or common interests would agree to promote trade and payments among themselves by reducing or eliminating tariffs and other barriers among themselves.

What is Customs Union?

Customs union is an agreement among a group of countries to cooperate in international trade, to reduce trade barriers and to promote trade among them. It is an example of regional economic cooperation. The theory of customs union postulates basically that under certain conditions, the customs union would promote greater welfare among the trade partners in the union. These conditions were laid down first by J. Viner and later developed by R.G. Lipsey. Broadly, the effects of customs union are two-fold — trade creation and trade diversion. These two work in opposite directions, the former increasing the welfare and the latter reducing it. The net effect is positive if the economies of countries involved are complementary at least potentialy, but in actual fact competing.

Trade creation occurs if a reduction in trade barriers through the union would bring about some trade where no trade exists. Trade ipso facto is not desirable unless a high-cost country imports from a low-cost country in respect of any commodity. In such a case, if trade takes place, resource allocation in both the trading partners would be more efficiently carried out and the overall costs of production would be lowered.

Trade diversion takes place if one member of the union imports from another in preference from a country outside the union, as it is possible that the latter is producing more efficiently than the former which is in the union but diversion takes place by virtue of lowering of tariff restrictions as between member countries of the union.

Suppose the union is set up among three countries, A. B and C, who are geographically close like the European Common Market countries. There are three possibilities in respect of trade. Commodity "X" is not produced by any of the three countries. So it is imported and it will continue to be so even after the union (no change). Second possibility is that one of the three is producing "X" commodity more inefficiently than other countries which are outside the union. Then after the union, trade diversion takes place from the more efficient country outside the union to the less efficient country inside the union (less welfare). A third possibility is that all the three countries produce "X" good and as a result of the union, only the country with the lowest cost would specialise in it and export to others. In this case, trade creation takes place and it would lead to greater welfare and lower resource costs for all the three countries (more welfare). If there are possibilities of substitution in production and consumption and elasticities are high, then the scope for gains is good.

Trade Creation and Trade Diversion

Trade creation and trade diversion can be explained diagrammatically using the partial equilibrium approach in Fig. 1 DD and SS are domestic demand and supply curves. WH is the tariff. OW is the world price, MM is imports. If tariff is lowered (or eliminated) to partner countries and price will be OP, and the tariff to the rest of the world is still WH, but WP for the partner country, then the partner's supply would replace the world supply to that country. Trade expands from MM to

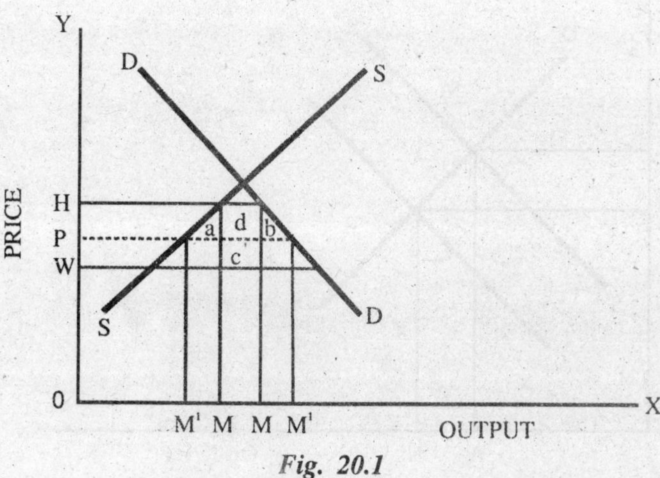

Fig. 20.1

M_1 M_1 and trade creation is represented by triangles a and b. Trade diversion is measured by c. A part of this loss is gain to domestic consumers by lower priced and part is a gain to foreign producers in partner countries. But whether the world as a whole gains or loses depends upon measurements of a, b, c and how big is the gain to producers, consumers and the government as tariff revenue is income of the government which is lost if tariffs are reduced to partner countries. Compared to the country's position before the customs union but with the existing world tariff rules, in the domestic country, home production is replaced by imports to the extent of M^1 M, and government revenue is reduced by d in the diagram.

Gains

What happens in the case of trade diversion is that, firstly, a deterioration in the terms of trade implying a lowering of welfare and secondly, an increase in consumption implying an increase in welfare. The net result is indeterminate. The deterioration in terms of trade occurs due to the lower priced imports being substituted by higher price imports. Increase in consumption may take place by lowering of tariff due to customs formation. We should note here that some of the factors on which gains from customs union would depend:

(1) The higher the pre-union tariff walls, the greater is the gain from such union. The gain from tariff removal on the welfare can be shown in Fig. 20.2 as follows.

The lower the tariffs to the outside world, the smaller are the losses on trade diversion but greater the gains on trade creation. DD is demand and SS is supply curve for wheat. Imposition of tariff can be conceived as a shift of SS curve S' S' due to rise in price to consumers (cost + tariff). The new equilibrium price is at c and cb is the tariff (cb/AB is the tariff rate). If tariff is removed, consumption will increase by AN and price is lowered by PP^1.

(2) Economic cooperation in the union would benefit the countries if the countries are geographically nearby, so that the transport costs are the lowest.

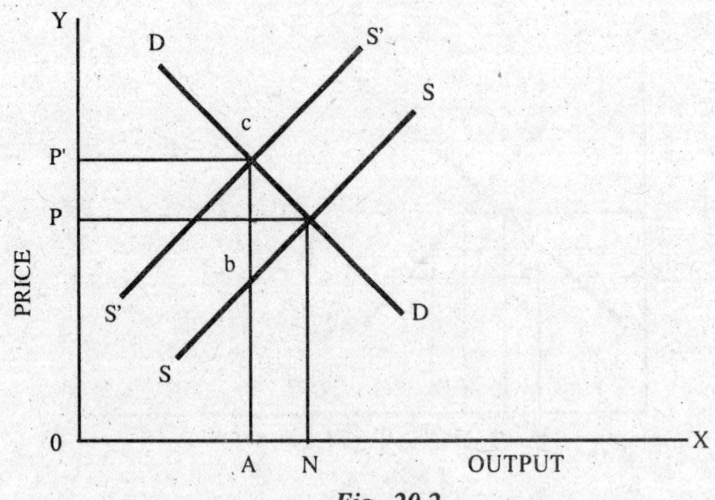

Fig. 20.2

(3) The countries would also gain more if the partners are actually competitive but potentially complementary so that the scope for specialisation and lowering of costs would be greater.

(4) The greater the cost differentials as between the partner countries the greater is the gain from lowering of tariffs and customs union.

(5) Countries whose foreign trade constitute a small part of their national income gain more than others due to less distortion on the domestic price structures.

(6) If the union leads to realisation of dynamic benefits such as economies of scale, or enforced competition, better allocative efficiency in investment, the effects of trade creation might outweigh the reverse effects of trade diversion. These dynamic effects would have to be added to the comparative static picture.

Dynamic Effects

Dynamic effects of customs union refer to effects on production and distribution and to changes in investment and income. Economies of scale through specialisation are made possible by larger trade and larger production and would lead to lower costs and prices. The competitive effect is the result of lower tariffs when bigger companies and smaller companies have both to compete on equal terms which leads to better competition and less monopoly. Among other dynamic effects, mention may be made of a relative change in prices. Competitive forces stimulate investment, particularly in areas where markets are expanding due to trade creation. It is also possible that some investment is diverted from lines which are less profitable due to trade diversion to lines which are more profitable due to trade creation. Larger net investment is possible if trade creation effects are more than trade diversion effects and would lead to larger national income and output. In addition to larger domestic investment, it is possible that larger foreign investment may take place to exploit the foreign markets, opened up due to lowering of tariffs and barriers to trade.

Economic Cooperation among Developing Countries

The developing countries can have a strategy of development through formation of customs union or free trade area or common market which are the major forms of regional economic and monetary cooperation. Some other forms of cooperation is commodity marketing schemes, regional development banks or payments, unions. If the economies of the developing countries have diversified structures, regional economic cooperation or customs union among them would promote trade and lead to an export biased growth. Reduction in or elimination of trade barriers among such countries is a necessary condition for coordinated industrialisation. There should also be coordinated planning and move to a common market as in case of EEC (European Economic Community). The East African Common Market, Latin American Common Market, Central American Common Market, Andean Common Market, etc., are expected to provide gains of trade creation and economic integration. Such schemes favour member countries as against non-member countries. Economies of scale can be achieved by negotiating industry by industry tariff removal or by some coordinated trading arrangement or production programmes or development planning. Such cooperation under the supervision of a Regional Development Bank like Latin American Development Bank or Asian Development Bank or a U.N. body like ESCAP may promote coordinated programme of action. But such attempts have not succeeded to any significant extent so far in developing countries. Only a few trade agreements or payments, unions are working with some degree of satisfaction. There are a few commodity agreements, buffer stock arrangements or payments, unions but not much progress could be made in the direction of producers' cartels or production control programmes due to opposition from developed countries and lack of consensus among producing countries as in the case of jute, tea, etc. It is only in 1982 that an agreement was entered into under the auspices of UNCTAD to set up an International Jute Organisation at Dhaka (which was done in July 1983) to promote the interests of jute-producing countries.

Regional Cooperation

There are different types of regional bodies in Europe, America, Africa and Asia. Some of them are for simple economic cooperation, some for trade promotion, a few trade and payments facilities and others for promoting investment flows and accelerating economic growth. Thus, African Development Bank, Inter-American Development Bank and Islamic Development Bank are examples of bodies for promoting investment and economic growth. European Free Trade Association and Association of South-east Asian Nations are bodies for mutual economic cooperation and trade promotion. There are bodies for promoting payments facilities like Asian Clearing union and Council for Mutual Economic Assistance. On the same lines the SAARC is a body for promoting economic and cultural ties. Like Islamic Bank and Arab Bank for Economic Development in Africa, Asian Development Bank is also a regional body for providing financial and technical assistance with a view to relieving poverty and promoting growth in Asia. India is involved in SAARC, ACU and ADB and these are dealt with elsewhere.

Asian Clearing Union

So far as India is concerned, it has joined the Asian Clearing Union formed in December 1974 among the following six member countries of ESCAP - Bangladesh, Pakistan, Nepal. Sri lanka, Iran and India. Burma has since joined the Union in April 1977. This Union was designed to facilitate the settlement of current international transactions among the member countries on a multilateral basis. This is an example of regional economic cooperation.

Purposes

(1) It would provide facilities for settlement of mutual transactions on a multilateral basis.

(2) The use of members' currencies is encouraged for settlement, thereby saving the use of foreign exchange reserves by them.

(3) It would facilitate international cooperation for expansion of trade and payments and bring closer the monetary and banking systems of these countries.

Constitution

The agreement came into force in October 1975. The head-quarters of the Union and the secretariat is kept at Teheran (Iran). There is a Board of Directors to guide the Union on policy matters. Each participant country is represented by its monetary authority, from which one Director and an alternative Director would represent on its Board of Directors. The members would elect a Chairman and Deputy Chairman for a term of two years. Rules have been formulated for the regular conduct of meetings of the Board, voting and for other procedural matters. A general Manager would carry out the decisions of the Board and is assisted by a Secretariat. The Board would meet once in every six months or earlier as may be desired and take such decisions as may be necessary for the conduct of operations through ACU..

Unit of Account

The unit of account is Asian Monetary Unit (AMU) which is equal to one SDR. All transactions of members are put through the SDR or in the currency of any member and the regular rates of conversion of SDR into members' currencies and the rate of one member currency against another are published from time to time. Any change in the currency value of a member is notified immediately and corresponding changes in exchange rates of members are effected as from the date agreed upon.

Eligible Transactions

Only current account receipts and payments are made through the clearing and are passed through the Secretariat at Teheran through the monetary authorities of the member countries. Payments through the clearing are prohibited in respect of oil, gas and gas products. Also capital account transactions are not permitted through the ACU. Trade can flow in the normal channels for being eligible to be put through the clearing. Bilateral trade as between India and Nepal and between Iran and Pakistan are not to pass through the clearing as other facilities are already arranged for them. From July 1985, Iran agreed to route through A. C. U. the trade receipt/payments for oil.

Use of clearing facility was voluntary initially in respect of payments permitted but made compulsory since January 1984. Such eligible payments are to be put through by the banks in member countries which are called designated banks (authorised dealers in India). Only travel payments and transactions under deferred payments by trading partners were kept out of the compulsion.

Eligible Instruments

The normal instruments of payment for export, import or other current account receipts and payments which are accepted through the clearing are Telegraphic Transfers, Mail Transfers, Bills of Exchange, Cheques and Money Orders. These instruments are to be denominated in AMU or in the currency of the trading partner who is a member country. The AMU is replaced by SDRs as a unit for trade and payments afterwards.

Settlement of Accounts

Accounts of receipts and payments as between members are kept in AMU and settlement is done on a regular basis. The designated banks advise the central bank of the country of such transactions daily and the central bank in turn sends daily telex of all such transactions to the Secretariat at Teheran. Each member country's accounts are kept separately and balances are calculated once in ten days which is the accounting period. Interest is paid on net credit balances by the debtor country to the creditor country on the daily balances outstanding between settlement dates. The rate of interest is determined by the Board of Directors on the basis of daily inter-bank lending rates (LIBOR) in the Euro-dollar market over the preceding accounting period. This rate is applicable during the next period and the excess of credits over debits is settled by this method once in two months by payment in an internationally accepted currency (SDR $, £ etc.). Credit in the above fashion is limited up to 1/12th of the visible exports (excluding oil, petrol and natural gas products) of the country with its trading partner in the last calendar year. If a participant's net debtor position at the end of the accounting period exceeds the limit of 1/24th of the visible imports (excluding petroleum, etc.) from other participants for the year, it shall pay the excess to the participants with net creditor position in proportion to the absolute net creditor position of each. Such credit or debit balances will be advised by the General Manager of the Union to member countries from time to time and accounts are kept in AMU by the Secretariat at Teheran. These accounts are maintained on the basis of daily telegraphic advices from member central banks on their payments and receipts from other members.

Benefits of ACU

ACU is an effort at regional economic cooperation and a step forward in the promotion of multilateral trade and payments. It would encourage foreign trade expansion among the member countries. It will save in transaction costs, reduce unnecessary delays and provide credits up to specified limits. As only net balances are settled, it will save in the use of foreign exchange reserves. Banking and monetary systems in member countries could be more directly linked and greater monetary cooperation can be expected. It is a right step in the direction of regional economic integration.

In India, the Reserve Bank had denominated only selected authorised dealers to deal in AMUs initially in 1975. The list has since been expanded and from September 1978 all authorised dealers are designated Banks to deal in AMU and through the Clearing Union. The RBI would publish every fortnight or as often as there is a change in exchange rates, the rates of conversion of AMU into member currencies for the purposes of clearing. Since October 1980, the RBI has not been purchasing AMUs but has authorised the banks to buy and sell AMUs among themselves to promote inter-bank transactions.

AMU Rates

The RBI used to purchase spot and sell spot AMU, at rates under the old procedure. These rates were, changeable from time to time.

Every fortnight the rates applicable were declared and published. Under the new procedure introduced in August 1985, the RBI announced on a daily basis the purchase and sale rates for ACU currencies. The rates are quoted as for any foreign currency for Rs. 100. The principle followed is buy-high and sell-low, as the quotations are in foreign currency units per given domestic currency unit.

It was reported by the RBI in 1991, that the ACU mechanism has been withdrawn for the time being, pending discussions with member countries following the move to rupee convertibility from March 1992. Indian exporters are allowed to receive payments through ACU dollar Accounts, effective from January 1, 1996, and the RBI has withdrawn from the scheme, as ACUs are no longer relevant to India due to Current Account convertibility of the rupee effective from 1994.

SOUTH ASIAN ASSOCIATION FOR REGIONAL COOPERATION (SAARC)

Attempts at regional economic cooperation in Asian region were not very fruitful for a long time. Their economic and political systems are different and their production patterns are not complementary. However, economic growth can accelerate only through such regional groupings and through cooperation.

One such grouping, which has taken shape in 1985 is the South Asian Association for Regional Cooperation which has its member countries as India, Pakistan, Bangladesh, Bhutan, Nepal, Maldives and Sri lanka. This group held its first summit in Dhaka and covers about one sixth of the world population.

The main objectives of the SAARC may be set out as follows:

(1) To strive for socio-economic welfare and cultural development of the people of the region.

(2) To work for the common goal of economic and social development.

(3) To promote cooperation through cultural exchanges, participation in common cultural activities, arts, entertainment, etc.

(4) To encourage collaboration and exchange of information in the fields of culture, social, technical and scientific research.

(5) To stimulate freer trade and larger investment flows to accelerate the pace of economic development.

(6) To facilitate optimum utilisation of human and material resources among the participating countries, through common ventures.

The SAARC members have been earlier competing in world trade and investment but there is ample scope for cooperation in all directions. For example, India and Bangladesh can cooperatee in the sale of jute and India and Sri lanka in the sale of tea and India and Pakistan for ready made garments, etc. Competition can be reduced and by common marketing strategy improve their terms of trade.

Benefits of Regional Groupings

SAARC members can take foreign trade as a lead sector and promote intra-regional trade first. Secondly, they can have a common strategy for sale of their goods which are competing earlier. Thirdly, they can plan joint ventures for promoting trade and investment in the region. Fourthly, they can have co-ordination in scientific and technical fields and promote research and share the knowledge for common benefit. Fifthly, they can cooperatee in supply of inputs in production and for marketing of their products.

At present the progress of the regional cooperation movement was poor due to ethnic problems, border conflicts, differences in political systems and ideologies, but the potentialities for mutual cooperation and joint ventures and joint marketing strategies are vast. There is an effort in exchange of cultural information at present through the exhibitions, films and visits of delegations. Participation in sports, arts and cultural information at present through the exhibitions, films and visits of delegations. Participation in sports, arts and cultural fields is one area in which some progress was shown.

The real breakthrough will be, when they can cooperatee in the field of trade and payments including joint investments in the infrastructural fields in the countries which are geographically contiguous. They have yet to show the will and consensus for joint efforts at trade and investment for economic development.

The bilateral trade flows among the participating countries are continued on the basis of trade agreements, but this does not go far enough to: (1) promote intra-regional trade, and (2) expand and diversify the composition and direction of global trade flows across the borders. The participating countries have to bury the differences in the common interest and even for self-interest for the purpose of promoting their trade and world trade. The common interests should overweigh the petty differences and regional economic growth can be faster through cooperation rather than competition among the participating member countries.

Regional Cooperation and India

India has been pursuing a policy for greater regional cooperation in trade and Aid, with neighbouring Asian and South Asian countries. thus, it has played an active role in promoting regional cooperation among South Asian countries. India has offered tariff concessions on 911 commodities to South Asian Association for Regional cooperation (SAARC) member countries. The objective is to establish a free Trade Area in the region (South Asia free Trade Area) by year 2001. In continuation of the efforts in this direction, import restrictions were removed for all import items in respect of SAARC members in August 1998. Trade with Sri Lanka and Bangladesh was made free from any tariffs. India is pursuing trade agreements with African countries, China and Russia to Promote trade and investment. Some political constraints are noticed in India's trade with Pakistan and Iran, which are sought to be overcome by mutual consultations.

India is a member of South Asian Preferential Trade Agreement (SAPTA) the Indian ocean Rim Association for Regional cooperation and the BIM ST-EC, which is the Bangladesh, India, Myanmar, Sri Lanka, Thailand Economic cooperation. India did not benefit from these agreements. India's exports to SAARC stood at 5% of total exports in 2010-11 as against 26% to other Asian developing countries, which do not have any trading agreement. Although India's trade with other developing countries is increasing, OECD countries continue to be largest market for both exports and imports of India, accounting for as much as 33% of over total trade.

Regional Trade Agreements

The global trading system has seen a sharp jump in Regional Trade Agreements (RTAs) over the past decade. Most of those are in the form of trade arrangements and Free Trade Agreements. With collapse of the COMECON, and departure from MFN based trade, even Russia, USA and Japan have gone for FTAs since 1990s.

Preferential Trade Share of the Intra RTAs Trade in Merchandise imports of the world has gone upto around 51%, as per a WTO Report. In Asia, it was expected to be around 16%. India has also relied on many FTAs as with SAARC, (Preferential Trade Agreements) and a number of bilateral trade agreements with Thailand, Singapore, Malaysia and other Asian countries. India has also trade agreements with China, Japan and Australia, among others. A Framework agreement for a Comprehensive Economic Cooperation was signed in October 2003 between India and ASEAN countries. But India continued to pursue the goal of multilateral trade liberalisation under the Roadmap of WTO. ASEAN FTA has to take off in 2007 with a smaller negative list of 850 items, which are outside the Free Trade Agreement.

India has not gained much from these RTAs with Asia and Africa in particular, as their economies are very much similar. The RTAs', as pointed out by Viner and Meade (International Economists), have both trade creation and trade diversion effects. A country can gain only when its Trade Creation effects outweigh those of trade diversion. The conditions under which this could happen are the divergence of factor endowments and economic structures among trading partners and the extent of the complementarity in their economies. Asian and African countries being similar in their structures, RTAs among them and India did not benefit much.

21

Exchange Management in India

Introduction

Controls on foreign exchange dealings involving foreign receipts and payments are an adjunct to the controls on foreign trade. These controls were first resorted to during the Second World War for the purpose of conserving limited foreign exchange reserves and mobilising them for war effort. The war-time controls were put on a statutory basis soon after the war by the Foreign exchange regulation Act of 1947. This act was replaced by a more comprehensive legislation "Foreign Exchange Regulation Act of 1973" (FERA) incorporating wider powers of control to the RBI and better enforcement through Inspecting Officers and Enforcement Directorate with a view of plugging all the loopholes or leakages noticed in its working since 1947. But the basic framework of controls remains the same under the new Act as under the old. As a member of the IMF, India is under an obligation to collaborate with the Fund to ensure orderly exchange arrangements and to promote stable exchange rate. Although current account controls are not permitted by the Fund, India secured their permission under Article XIV to keep these controls as transitional measure. In March 1992 limited convertibility of rupee was launched and on the basis of experience gained, full convertibility of rupee on trade account was announced in March 1993, followed by full convertibility of rupee on current account since March 1994. Now India is under article VIII of IMF Articles of Agreement. A new Bill on the Foreign Exchange Management Act was passed by the Parliament to replace Foreign exchange Regulation Act. Thus, FERA has been replaced by FEMA, in 1999, and became effective in June 2000.

RBI as the Exchange Control Authority

One of the important central banking functions of the RBI is maintenance of external value of the rupee. As such it has been given the custody of foreign exchange reserves and sole agency for administration of exchange controls in India. All receipts and payments in and out of India require general or special permission of the RBI. The dealings in foreign exchange and foreign securities in India, payments to person resident outside and export and import of currency notes, bullion or precious stones, etc., are subject to general or special permission of RBI or are prohibited. The administration of controls is carried on by the RBI with the help of ADs, and money-changers.

The types of transactions which are controlled by the RBI and the government are in general, those having international financial implications and include inter alia the following important items. Many of them are liberalised and some of them withdrawn since 1991 economic reforms.

(1) Purchase and sale of and other dealings in foreign exchange and maintenance of balances at foreign centres by residents.

(2) Procedure for realisation of proceeds of exports of goods and services.

(3) Payments to non-residents or to their accounts in India for imports and others.

(4) Transfer of securities as between residents and non-residents and acquisition and holding of foreign securities.

(5) Foreign travel (with or without foreign exchange).

(6) Export and import of currency, cheques, drafts, travellers' cheques and other financial instruments, securities, gold, jewelleries, etc.

(7) Trading, commercial and industrial activities in India of foreign firms and companies (including branches of foreign firms and companies) and foreign nationals, as well as acquisition of business undertakings or holding of shares in Indian companies by such firms, companies and persons.

(8) Appointment of non-residents and foreign nationals and companies as agents or as technical and management advisers in India.

(9) Employment, profession, etc., undertaken in India by foreign nationals.

(10) Acquisition, holding and disposal of immovable property in India by foreign nationals and companies.

(11) Acquisition, holding and disposal of immovable property outside India by persons resident in India.

Authorised Dealers (ADs)

Authorised dealers are the scheduled commercial and co-operative banks who are authorised by the RBI to deal in foreign exchange which include all scheduled commercial and co-operative banks at present. The regulations under the FERA governing the banks are contained in the Exchange Control Manual and in the various circulars and notifications issued thereunder by the RBI. The ADs can deal in foreign currencies and for that purpose open and maintain accounts abroad in such currencies, approve applications from the residents for purchase of foreign currencies and maintain rupee accounts in the names of non-residents and pass debits and credits to such accounts. The ADs can deal directly with the public and the RBI with the ADs in putting through these transactions.

The ADs have an association called Foreign Exchange Dealers' Association (FEDA) which fixes the rates for dealing in sterling with rupee on the basis on RBI's declared rates for buying and selling and the middle rates. The ADs are free to quote their own rates for other currencies on the basis of cross rates quoted in London as between sterling and other currencies and on the basis of RBI's buying rates for D.M., the US dollar and Yen. The RBI buys and sells sterling under Section 40 without limit while it buys only £ $ DM and Yen under Section 17 (3) of the RBI Act. The RBI used the Pound Sterling as its intervention currency for keeping the exchange rate of the rupee stable. The RBI has also started selling US $ from February 1987. Since 1992, RBI is quoting a Reference Rate in terms of US $ and intervenes in the market to stabilise the rupee in terms of dollar. Dollar replaced sterling as an intervention currency.

As agent of the RBI, the ADs have to scrutinise applications from the public and implement the rules and regulations of exchange control under power delegated to them by the RBI. They have to satisfy themselves that all receipts and payments are in accordance with the Exchange Control Manual. It is obligatory for ADs under Section 74 of FERA to comply with all general or special directions and instructions given by the RBI. They can keep Non-Resident Accounts (Nostro and Vostro) and operate on them subject to the over-all control and reporting to RBI. They can deal in permitted methods of receipts and payments, keep minimum working balances in foreign centres, operate in the inter-bank market and maintain a square or near square position in each currency which means that their purchases (spot and forward) and sales should be matched as far as possible.

Money Changers

Money changers are authorised by the RBI to deal in foreign currencies and coins. Restricted money-changers can only purchase while others can do both purchases and sales in foreign currencies and coins. Some hotels, firms and establishments, etc., have been given licences by the RBI to act as money-changers.

Permitted Method

All exporters have to get a code number from the RBI for which an application in form CNX has to be made in duplicate. This code number has to be quoted in all subsequent correspondence with banks and RBI. The inward remittances are freely permitted except that they are to be reported to the RBI. The export receipts are to be declared in the prescribed form and should represent the full export value of the goods and the transactions should be put through the ADs. The method of receipt should be permitted currencies (listed in the Exchange Control Manual) and in approved forms. The proceeds should normally be realised with six months and in the case of Pakistan and Afghanistan within three months (extended to six months in October 1985), except in the case of exports of engineering goods under deferred payment arrangements when permission is generally given for extended periods of receipt. Trade discounts and agency commissions are permitted normally up to 5 per cent of the invoice value.

The object of control in respect of exports is to ensure that the export earnings are duly and promptly repatriated back to India in full, within the stipulated time and in the currency of the importing country or a convertible currency. No under-invoicing or over-invoicing or any measure to earn foreign exchange, with a view to keeping it abroad is permitted. Blanket exchange permits and exchange release for sales promotion are permitted up to certain limits. Exporters are now permitted to keep some part of their earnings abroad for their requirements of imports of inputs or other genuine needs.

The prescribed methods of receipt and payment are as follows:

(A) External Group Countries: Include all countries who are not in Group 'B' - Bilateral Group. Export receipt should be in the currency of importing country or of any country in this Group. Import payment from India should be in rupees to the account of the resident of the exporting country or of any country in this Group.

(B) Bilateral Group Countries: Include countries in bilateral trade with relative trade and payment agreements. Any receipts or payments in respect of these countries should be in non-convertible rupees or as per the relative agreement on which ADs are advised from time to ime, or as per the relative agreements on trade and payments.

In respect of Nepal and Bhutan the receipts and payments are to be effected in rupees without reference to the Exchange Control formalities.

Other Receipts

All receipts whether current or capital are to be channelised through ADs. Any unauthorised use of foreign exchange is not permitted. The foreign exchange earned should be repatriated home at the earliest possible time through the ADs into the official channels. The purpose of remittance and the beneficiary of remittance and other details are to be recorded and reported to the RBI by the ADs. All inward remittances for investment of foreign capital in India should be made to the Ministry of Commerce and Industry, while those for repatriation after such clearance are to be made to the RBI. All flows on current account are now free while those on capital account are liberalised.

Payment for Imports

Authorised dealers are permitted to open letters of credit or make remittances abroad for imports, if they are covered by import licences or are under OGL. If the goods are covered under deferred payment terms, prior approval of RBI is also necessary for opening of letters of credit or giving a bank guarantee. The method of payment should be in terms of permitted currencies and advance payments require prior approval of RBI and are granted in respect of engineering goods or capital goods. Payment to bilateral account countries should be in non-convertible rupees, as per the relative trade agreements. Payments are freely allowed and at free market rates of exchange since March 1992.

Other Payments

Payments for travel, education, medical treatment, etc., are permitted as per scales laid down by the RBI from time to time, depending upon the purpose and the country of visit. These payment restrictions are advised to the ADs from time to time and have been fairly liberalised more recently due to comfortable foreign exchange position of India. Remittances of freight, profits, dividends, insurance etc., are permitted to actual beneficiaries abroad. Family remittances of foreign nationals are permitted but not of Indian nationals or Indian residents for maintenance of their families abroad. Similarly, transfer of assets by Indian nationals emigrating abroad is also not allowed except in small quantities or in special circumstances. Some of these items of flows of funds on current account are now freed.

All applications for transfer of funds for investment abroad are to be made to the Ministry of Commerce and Industry for clearance first and then to the Ministry of Finance and RBI. These are now granted freely in view of comfortable foreign exchange position and liberalised policy. An automatic route for flow of funds for investment abroad is allowed to exporters and foreign exchange earnings subject to some limits.

Delegation to ADs

Ads have been delegated some powers to approve and to make remittances for dividends, profits, subscription to magazines, membership fees, correspondence course fees, examination fees, etc., up to prescribed limits without reference to the RBI. Similarly, remittances out of income for family maintenance abroad for non-nationals are permitted upto some limits. Payments for samples for trade and laboratory testing upto some limits of value are permitted by the ADs. But prior permission is required in case of reduction in proceeds over invoice value, change in terms of sale or penalties, quality claims or any other deductions in invoice value. Since 1992 FERA was diluted very much and many controls were removed.

Forward Covers

Exchange control permits ADs to enter into forward sales and purchases with customers for genuine trade transactions provided they are in permitted currencies and in prescribed methods and corresponding foreign country's exchange control does not prohibit such transactions. The Ads can in turn cover them in an inter-bank market in India or abroad or with the RBI. The AD has to satisfy himself that the importer has an import licence with an exchange control copy, except when the imported goods are on OGL. The customer must have also entered into a purchase contract, opened a letter of credit or produced other documentary evidence in that direction. Banks can normally enter into sale contracts up to six months except in the case of deferred payment imports in which case RBI's permission for long periods is secured. Where an export is made on consignment basis, a forward sale is given only after shipment is effected and upto the extent of the value declared in the shipping bill. The contract should be based on the value expected to be received minus agency commission. Any extension of contract beyond six months normally requires prior permission of RBI. Cancellation of forward contracts should also be referred to RBI for approval. The RBI has introduced many changes in December 1995 to expand the spectrum of forward cover facilities such as for overseas projects, contracts, commissioning charges, consultancy fees, cross currency imports etc. Banks are now permitted to cover such risks in foreign markets. In 1994-95, RBI has permitted banks and companies to trade freely in the forward market and stopped giving the cover and without prior permsision of RBI forward contracts on interest rates are also permitted.

Securities

There are no restrictions on import of securities, Indian or foreign. Export of securities is prohibited except with the prior approval of the RBI. Similarly, issue and transfer of securities to non-residents require the general or special permission of the RBI as also the Foreign Investment Board of the Ministry of Industrial Development. Indian residents require prior permission to hold foreign securities or export or send out of India Indian securities. Now these transfers are freely permitted and both direct and portfolio investments by NRIs and FFIs are now permitted.

Foreign Currency Accounts

The RBI has granted general permission to persons resident but not domiciled in India to maintain and operate foreign currency accounts. Such of the accounts of residents as existed before 1947 were continued but fresh credits to such accounts are to be approved by RBI beforehand. Normally, residents of India are not permitted to open or maintain such accounts in foreign currency abroad, except those permitted in connection with technical collaboration or joint collaboration agreements. More recently banks and export earners are permitted to keep some amounts abroad for their immediate or short-term requirement. Indians who are resident outside India had to close such accounts when they return to India on a permanent basis, but it is not necessary at present due to recent liberalisations.

Non-resident Accounts

The terms resident and non-resident have been defined in the Foreign Exchange Regulation Act of 1973. A non-resident is one who resides outside India for the whole or a substantial part of the year, Indians who are working abroad, and offices and branches abroad of Indian or foreign companies in India (excluding residents of Nepal and Bhutan). Two types of non-resident accounts are clearly discernible:

(1) Private non-resident accounts (of individuals, firms, companies and organisations).

(2) Non-resident bank accounts.

The private non-resident accounts are again of three categories:

(1) Ordinary non-resident (rupee)accounts (NRO) are opened without reference to RBI in respect on non-Indians and Indians residing abroad but holding a passport of a country other than that of India with funds from abroad but others require prior permission of RBI.

(2) National Defence Remittance Scheme Special Accounts were opened during 1965-66 with the rupee proceeds of inward remittance received under the NDR scheme from non-resident Indians abroad. These funds are not repatriable from India under any circumstances but can be converted into rupee accounts and used in India, if the circumstances of the account holder warranted it.

(3) Non-resident (External) Accounts Rules 1970 permit the opening of such accounts (FCNR) in the names of persons of Indian origin or Indian nationality but resident abroad provided the funds are transferred into India from abroad through banking channels. Such funds can be paid back in foreign currency for repayment of principal and interest without prior approval of the RBI after the maturity of fixed deposits. Non-resident (ordinary) accounts can be converted into non-resident (external) accounts or transfers from one to the other are permitted. The operation on these accounts are no longer subject to earlier controls.

In more recent years, foreign investment in India is encouraged. Non-residents of Indian origin are given liberal facilities for investment in shares, debentures and units of the U.T.I., both on repatriation basis and non-repatriation basis. There are provisions for non-resident investment in new issues up to 40 per cent in the case of some industries and even 100 per cent in respect of a few priority industries such as hospitals and hotels, which are foreign exchange-earners and in sick units. Funds have thus flown in through the non-resident accounts for remittances and investment. Foreign investment in Indian Companies is now permitted up to 51% of equity capital.

The operating Non-resident Deposit categories were as follows:

(1) Foreign Currency Non-resident (Banks) Scheme — This is for banks' borrowing [FCNR(B)].

(2) FCNR (A) Scheme was discontinued with only outflows of maturing deposits upto 1998.

(3) Non-resident Non-repatriable Rupee deposits [NR (NR) RD] scheme has facility for repatriation of interest amount only and not principal. This was discontinued in 2005, effective 2006.

(4) NR(E) RA is deposits in foreign currencies by foreign individuals and institutions or NRIs.

(5) NRO accounts are opened from 2006 for the NRID to keep ordinary accounts in rupees with banks in India.

The total outstanding balances on these accounts stood at $ US 17,435 million at end March 1996 and at $ US 32,975 million at end March 2005. There funds stood at $ 41,554 million at end

March 2009 and $ 58,608 million at end March 2012. There are only two accounts which are active and operative at present, namely FCNR(B), and NR(E) RA. Most of the funds are flowing in through FCNR(B) and NR(E) RA.

Non-resident (Banks) Accounts

All accounts kept in India by foreign banking companies including foreign branches of Indian banks, are designated non-resident bank accounts. ADs can open accounts in Indian rupees for their correspondents, branches, agents, etc., abroad subject to the advice to the RBI. The operations (credits and debits) on these accounts have to be reported to the RBI. They have the same implication as operation in foreign currency accounts kept by Indian banks abroad with their agents, correspondents and branches. The operations on these accounts are freely allowed now.

Loans and Overdrafts

ADs can grant temporary loans and overdrafts to their agents, correspondents and branches etc., abroad other than from bilateral group without prior approval of RBI up to a limit. They can also receive similar financial assistance from abroad. Such facilities are for current operations and of working capital nature and not for investment in term capital and loans to private parties. Such operations are to be reported to the RBI.

Blocked Accounts

An account is blocked if operations on it are not permitted without the prior approval of the RBI. Any account of a person, firm or company, resident abroad may be opened a blocked or may be declared as blocked by the RBI under the Exchange Control Rules. Thus, assets in India, including bank accounts and securities, etc., of Indians emigrating to foreign countries, are set out as blocked accounts. Balances in blocked accounts can, however, be invested with RBI's permission in fixed deposits with banks, or other approved categories of shares, debentures, etc. The rules governing the blocked accounts are laid down in the Exchange Control Manual and have been liberalised more recently allowing more liberal use of these funds for local payments or investments by accounts having less than Rs. 50,000. The operations on such accounts are normally governed by rules of the RBI and subject to scrutiny of RBI and to be reported to it in Form A-4. Blocked accounts have disappeared with the liberalisation in FERA and permission given to free use of all such funds, since 1992-93.

LIBERALISATION OF EXCHANGE CONTROL

Since 1992, deregulation and liberalisation were pursued by the Government and the RBI in respect of foreign exchange and exchange controls. The basic framework of controls remained, except for liberalisation in some directions; Rupee was freed on trade account in 1993 and on current account in 1994. Consequential and supplemental to these measures the RBI has diluted many provisions in FERA.

ADs were given more powers, through delegation of authority in respect of both Trade Account and Invisibles Account. ADs were allowed to export surplus stocks of foreign currency notes and coins, keep balances and short-term investment abroad for their working requirements. The ceiling of ₹ 15 crores, imposed in 1995, on AD's over night position was removed, in January 1996. ADs can use their discretion in releasing foreign exchange for foreign travel for business seminars, conferences, medical treatment and studies. Banks have to maintain Tier I capital funds at 5% of foreign exchange open position.

Exporters were permitted to keep Exchange Earner Foreign Currency accounts, (EEFC) to utilise them for all purposes connected with trade Promotion and other current Account purposes. ADs were given freedom to fix their own Aggregate Gap Limit (AGL) for more efficient management of their assets and liabilities. They were also allowed, if they have the expertise, to initiate positions overseas in cross currency dealings. They can give forward cover to overseas investors on account of dividends due or returns on foreign investment in India or to Shipping Companies in respect of foreign collections.

ADs are allowed to offer hedges, interest rate swaps, currency swaps, caps/collars, and forward rate agreements to corporates, without prior permission of RBI or government. RBI has been providing single window clearance under fast track within 21 days for proposals of joint ventures and foreign investment by Indian companies up to a limit.

Interbank deals account for about 80-85% of total transaction in forex market and the RBI has initiated the process of setting up clearing house facilities for settlement and clearance for the operations of ADs. The RBI has set-up a Market Intelligence cell to study and monitor the developments in Forex Market, on a daily basis.

CAPITAL ACCOUNT LIBERALISATION

Throughout nineties, the role assigned to foreign capital is guided by considerations of financing a level of current Account deficit that is sustainable by other economic criteria. The capital Account convertibility is to be slow process, subject to many prior conditions to be achieved. There has been policy shift in favour of non- debt capital flows into India in the nineties, and the first decade of the 21st century.

India is following a gradualistic approach to capital Account liberalization, as it is fraught with dangers to the economy. So FDI and Foreign portfolio investment are being encouraged. Many developing countries have liberalized capital controls in the seventies and eighties but having faced many banking problems, have reversed the policies. These liberalisations require complete sequencing of many prior developments and macro-economic stabilization programmes are necessary for successful experiment of freeing of capital account.

The main recommendations of the Committee on Capital Account convertibility are as follow:

(1) Fisical Consolidation – Gross fiscal deficit to be brought down by stages to 3.5% of GDP

(2) Mandated rate of inflation to be 3 to 5 % per annum

(3) Strengthening of the financial system – flexible interest rate regime to be deregulated – CRR to be brought down to 3%. Statutory limit – Gross NPAs of banks to be brought down to 5% and 100% marked to market valuation of investments.

(4) Best practices for forex risk management

(5) Banks to follow international Accounting norms and disclosure norms.

(6) Capital prescription to be stipulated to market risks

(7) Debt service ratio to be brought down to 20%; it is now 17.3% in 2011-12.

(8) Adequate foreign exchange reserves to cover not less than 6 months' imports.

RECENT LIBERALISATION MEASURES

Exporters are permitted to extend trade related loans/credit to overseas importers out of their exchange earners foreign currency balances (EEFC). Advance remittance facilities for import of goods with out bank guarantee were liberalised. Indian Companies are allowed to retain abroad funds raised through ADRs/GDRs. They are also permitted to acquire property outside India for their business purposes and their offices abroad. Traders are allowed to hedge their foreign exchange exposures without any limit. There was further simplification of procedures in foreign exchange transactions and in the banks' reporting system.

Indian residents and companies and the mutual Funds are permitted to invest in certain listed companies abroad. Banks are allowed to invest their unimpaired Tier I capital in overseas money market or debt instruments. Funds raised through FCNR (B) route or ADRs and GDRs are allowed to be invested abroad in CDs/TBs and other money market instruments, pending their targetted utilisation.

Residents are allowed to open Resident Foreign currency (RFC) accounts without limits. They can remit foreign exchange for acquisition of foreign securities under Employees stock option scheme (ESOP). They can acquire ADRs/GDRs and sell them for foreign currency by way of credit to their EEFC/RFC domestic accounts or their rupee accounts at their discretion. ADs can issue International credit cards.

As regards foreign investment in India FIIs are allowed to hedge the market value of their entire investment in equity at any time. ADs are authorized to offer forward contracts to non-residents/ FIIs to hedge their investments made in India. Foreign banks in India are allowed to hedge their Tier I capital in Indian books without any restrictions. NRIs and PIOs are permitted to remit upto US $ 1 million a year out of their NRO accounts for specified purposes.

Sodhani Committee Recommendations

Following the recommendations of this committee the RBI implemented the following measures:

(1) General permission for sale of shares, required under Portfolio Investment Scheme given to NRIs was extended to OCBs,

(2) NRIs and not OCBs have been permitted to invest in MMMFs, set-up for money market operations in India.

(3) General permission to NRIs for subscribing to Articles of Association of Indian Companies engaged in Industrial activities to cover other companies engaged in other permissible activities.

(4) Granting of housing loans to NRI staff of Indian companies.

(5) ADs are permitted to remit sale proceeds of shares kept under pledge for liquidation of loan outstandings.

(6) General permission for crediting interest on delayed refunds of share application money.

(7) Extending the scope of safe custody of securities on behalf of NRIs to institutional custodians.

In short, consideration was given to NRIs for more liberal treatment of their repatriation and operations of them under Portfolio Management. Funds mobilised by banks through the NRI deposits (FCNRCR, EEFC and NRERA) can be invested abroad by banks in short-term investment, in addition to their lending at home.

ADs can effect remittance up to US $ 10,000 or its equivalent for importers to settle disputes abroad on trade account. Hotels and Airline companies are allowed to receive payment in Indian rupees from foreign tourists without insisting on their encashment certificates.

Software exports were permitted, since September 1995 without receipt of advance payment and software exports are put on par with any other exports. Since Oct. 1995, RBI has stopped announcing dollar buying and selling rates, but specific quotes are given for a deal with RBI, by any AD. Since Nov. 1995, ADs are allowed to provide US $ 5,000 or less in any year to the close relatives abroad for their maintenance by any resident Indian if the beneficiary abroad is a permanent resident abroad and has insufficient income and unable to return to India. Authorised dealers are permitted since February 1996, to effect remittances towards import of designs and drawings, up to Rs. 25 lakhs on production of suppliers' invoice postal wrappings and exchange control copy of Bill of Entry as documentary evidence in support of import.

Norms for investment abroad were eased in May 1997. Indian companies are now allowed to freely invest in overseas market up to $ 15 million raised through GDR or EEFC without RBI prior permission, provided they are invested in overseas projects. Corporates are allowed since June 1997 to raise funds abroad up to $ 15 million as short-term finance useful for even rupee expenditure on their projects, if they are export earners and EPCG licence holders. Other corporates are allowed to rise up to $ 3 million for their foreign currency requirements or for their rupee expenditure. These limits were raised later on.

Exchange Rate Management

Since 1994, when the rupee has declared convertible, Exchange control in the strict sense was not operated. What the RBI did is better called Exchange Rate Management (ERM). FERA was replaced by FEMA in 1999.

The RBI policy in this regard was guided by market conditions, current account deficit, and capital inflows/outflows. Excess demand and supply pressures of Rupee versus dollar were absorbed by RBI intervention. The Rupee value was maintained within a narrow range between Rs. 36 to 40 per US $ at end Dec. 1997 and at around Rs. 44 in 1999. The RBI had to maintain a delicate balance between price stability or control of inflation and the required Exchange rate stability. Even at Rs. 36, per US dollar, rupee depreciated by about 15%, during the Eighth Plan period (1992-97). From March 1993, there was a temporary appreciation of the rupee due to the adoption of convertibility on trade account followed by convertibility on current account in March 1994.

There was relative stability of the Rupee during 1994-95 and up to Sept. 1995; in 1995-96, the RBI allowed the rate to fall from Rs. 31 to Rs. 35 and started supporting it between Rs. 35 and 36. It has stabilised around Rs. 36 by May-June 1996. The RBI intervention in the Forex market since October 1995 helped the rupee rate to remain around Rs. 35 - 36, until Nov. 1997 when it fell to Rs. 39. It has purchased dollars, when there are larger inflows into the country and also sold when there is large demand for dollars, from its foreign exchange assets. The exchange rate has since fallen to Rs. 47-48 per us dollar at end March 2003 and stood around Rs.45 at end March 2010. Excluding gold and SDRs, India's foreign currency assets rose from a low of $ 29 billions in March 1991 to a peak of US $ 241 billion in March 2009. This sharp rise in exchange reserves was due to foreign confidence in Indian Economy and large foreign inflows of funds from abroad. This enabled India to repay some of its foreign debt obligations including those to IMF and the RBI to intervence in the forex market to stabilise the rupee, which is necessary for sustained growth of our exports.

RBI on Exchange Control Norms

In June 9, 1999, the Reserve Bank of India has announced the relaxation of exchange control guidelines. There is now more freedom for remittances — of commission on exports, by shipping companies to protection and indemnity clubs and on investments by NRIs and OCBs.

In addition, the RBI has given general permission for several transactions.

Authorised dealers (ADs) have been allowed to remit casual gifts up to $ 1,000 per calendar year to the corporate clients and other applicants to relatives and friends abroad.

ADs are allowed to make remittances up to $250 or its equivalent per transaction in respect of post parcel imports without insisting on the parcel receipt.

ADs may also allow remittances towards import of drawings and designs received by e-mail or fax, subject to production of documents prescribed for software imports.

ADs have been allowed to remit commission on exports within the prescribed limit of 12.5 per cent of the invoice value, even in cases where the amount of commission has not been declared on export declaration forms.

Foreign embassies, missions and diplomats in India who could earlier open foreign currency accounts only with the main offices of the State Bank of India have been allowed to open foreign currency accounts with any bank with an AD status, subject to the accounts being funded by inward remittance in convertible currencies.

ADs can allow remittances by shipping companies which are their constituents towards subscription to protection and indemnity (P & I) clubs in accordance with the approval granted to shipping companies by the Government under the General Insurance Business (Nationalisation) Act, 1972.

Exim Bank can directly receive, consider and approve project export proposals up to a value of Rs. 100 crore, provided all facilities required for the execution of such contracts are provided by it.

ADs have also been empowered to allow remittances by recognised international, national and state level sports organisations towards prize, sponsorship money for sports events up to $ 100,000 in each case as against $ 25,000 earlier.

Credit card issuers can issue rupee credit cards valid in India, Nepal and Bhutan. These may be issued to non-resident Indians (NRIs) and persons of Indian origin (PIOs) also. Remittance from India will, however, not be allowed in settlement of bills in the event of use of such cards in other countries.

Indian residents are now allowed to hold international credit cards (ICC) provided by overseas organisations subject to the condition that the liabilities arising from the use of such cards in India as well as outside India are met by the organisation issuing the card, without any remittance from India.

ADs and full-fledged money changers need not submit a copy of the letter from the applicant giving particulars like name and address while applying for exchange under basic travel quota (BTQ), along with a statement in form FLM 8.

ADs can now renew the general permission granted by the RBI not only to NRIs but also to overseas corporate bodies (OCBs) under the Portfolio Investment Scheme. The permission may be renewed for a period of five years at a time.

Domestic mutual funds have been given general permission to issue units or any other similar instrument under the schemes floated by them to NRIs, PIO and OCBs on non-repatriation or repatriation basis, subject to SEBI approval.

Proprietorship concern or a firm in India have been given general permission to accept deposits from NRIs and PIOs on non-repatriation basis. Indian companies (including non-banking finance companies registered with the Reserve Bank) also have the general permission to accept deposits from NRIs, PIO and OCBs on a non-repatriation basis, subject to certain conditions.

Domestic companies have been given general permission to issue shares or convertible debentures up to 100 per cent of paid-up capital to NRIs, PIO and OCBs subject to certain conditions.

NRIs and PIO have been given general permission to transfer, by way of gifting any rupee security, shares, bonds or debentures of a company registered in India held by them to a registered charitable trust or organisation.

Resident individuals, proprietorship concerns and partnership firms can now avail interest-free loans from NRIs and PIO on a non repatriation basis.

Non-resident PIO have been given general permission to transfer immovable property held by them in India to relatives and registered charitable trusts or organisations by way of a gift.

Non-resident holders have been exempted from the operation of provision of Section 29(1) (b) of Fera 1973 to acquire the underlying shares released by Indian custodians of ADRs and GDRs upon the surrender of these. General permission has also been given to the company or depository concerned under Section 19(4) of Fera 1973 for entering an address outside India in its register or books in respect of such shares.

NRIs, PIOs and OCBs have been given general exemption for the sale and transfer of shares, bonds or debentures of Indian companies through stock exchanges in cases where such transfers are made in favour in Indian citizens, PIO or in favour of a company or body incorporated under any law in force in India.

The FEMA 2000

The FEMA has given a shift in the objectives of Foreign Exchange resource management from one of conservation to facilitation of transactions. It has categorised the contraventions as civil offences and not criminal. FEMA provides for only monetary penalties and a separate Administrative mechanism for dealing with any offences. An Adjudicating Authority, Special Director (Appeals) and Appellate Tribunal were set up to deal with cases within a time frame. The concept of compounding introduced in FEMA is its distinguishing feature as opposed to investigation by Enforcement Directorate under FERA. The Compounding Authority is the RBI, under the Act and it has to dispose off the application within 180 days.

The 1997 Asian crisis has brought to light the shock, that the banking and monetary systems of Asian countries have suffered by moving to the Capital Account convertibility as a single event.

India was absolved from this shock due to its caution and measured steps taken after the initiation of Economic and Financial Reforms since 1992.

The broad reform agenda encompassed the moves to market competition, integration and sophistication in the financial architecture and privatisation of economic activity. These measures have brought in a higher degree of productivity, and efficiency, better obsorption of technology in the industrial sector, whereby they could export more, and become global players. Many MNCs of Indian origin have appeared on the scene through mergers and acquisitions of domestic and foreign companies. The Indian producers have proved their mettle by competing on equal terms with the foreign counterparts and Indian export growth rate at around 20% in dollar terms proves the expertise and efficiency of Indian entrepreneurs.

Reform measures in the external sector have been a major contributor to the above developments. The process of economic and financial liberalisation will be the backdrop towards globalisation and a further reform process in the fiscal field will help in this move towards Capital Account convertibility.

Road Map to Capital Account Liberalisation

In April 2006, the Central Government have announced that a road map is being prepared for moving into full Capital Account convertibility for the Rupee, in the context of globalisation and privatisation of the economy. But it is not a one-shot measure and is a process, with a number of prerequisites to be grounded in the economy. In its way, it is vulnerable to shocks, potential or real, there are the external factors like oil prices, interest rates abroad, in addition to internal factors like monsoon, fiscal and monetary policies, etc.

The capital account liberalisation aims at a gradual move towards the removal of all restrictions on free movement of capital across borders and elimination of all hassles in the integration of domestic and foreign sectors and globalisation of the economy and the markets. The harmonisation of the these forces has to be achieved, namely the movement of free capital across borders has to developed with a free flexible exchange rate with relative stability and the pursuit of an independent monetary policy. So measured steps are being taken towards capital account convertibility.

The RBI has taken various initiatives in the direction of Capital Account convertibility. The Exchange Control Department of RBI has been christened as the Foreign Exchange Department, highlighting the intent of avoiding controls and facilitating the foreign exchange transactions. A separate department of external investment and operations was started to oversea and operate in the external markets and to manage RBI's investments abroad and other related matters. There is greater transparency in data monitoring and information dissemination and to move away from micro-management to one of macro-management of forex flows and forex markets.

The other moves and measures include liberalisation of FDI and FII flows into direct and portfolio investments, some automatic routes for External commercial flows borrowings, issue of ADR and GDRs by Indian Corporates, and freeing NRI deposits from interest rate regulations by linking them with LIBOR. Similarly, outflows of capital are allowed in the form of limited investments in foreign listed companies by MFs, and individuals and corporates, along with liberalised remittances on Capital Account by Indian residents to outside the country.

The passing of Fiscal Responsibility Act in 2003 has given the needed pressure to the governments, both central and state to move towards reduction of fiscal deficit and of economy in the unproductive expenditures.

Recent Foreign Exchange Policy Changes

(1) The aggregate limit to overseas investment by mutual funds has been enhanced from US $ 5 billion to US $ 7 billion in April 2008.

(2) The limit for direct receipts of import bills and documents was raised from US $ 1,00,000 to US $ 3,00,000 in case of import of rough precious and semi-precious stones by non-status holder exports.

(3) Foreign direct investment was allowed in credit information companies upto 49%.

(4) Foreign direct investment in commodity exchanges was allowed with an overall ceiling for FDIs and FIIs.

(5) ECB policy was modified for borrowers in Intra-structure sector by raising the limit from U.S $ of 20 million to US dollar 50 million. The act in cost ceiling for ECB was raised as follows in May 2008.

Average Maturity	Existing	Raised
3 years up to 5 years	150 bps over six months LIBOR	200 bps over six months LIBOR
More than 5 years	250 bps over six months LIBOR	350 bps over six months LIBOR

There was further liberalization in All-in-cost ceiling from 200 bps to 300 bps for ECPs upto 3 to 5 years, and from 350 bps to 500 bps for ECBs of 5 years to 7 years and above.

(6) The foreign currency exchangeable borrowing scheme of 2008 was operationalised from September 2008. The definition of infra-structure for the ECB purposes was extended to include running, exploration and refining, in addition to existing list of the power telecommunication, railways and roads, sea and airports industrial plants water and sanitation and sewerage projects, etc.

Greater flexibility to operations of FIIs in the Equity and debt markets in respect of the ratio of their investments in equity and debt instruments and exemption from the ratio of 70:30 which were the restrictions operating as in October 2008.

From January 1, 2009, participants in Asian clearing union (ACU) have the option to settle their transactions either in ACU dollar or ACU Euro. Accordingly, AMU or Asian monetary unit has been realisigened as ACU dollar or ACU euro, which shall be equivalent to one US dollar and/or on euro.

While on FCCBs the RBI has put the Buy Back on approval route in October 2008 provided the buy back was arranged through their foreign currency resources held in hand or abroad and/ or out of fresh ECBs raised in conformity with the prevailing norms. There is automatic route for those whose buy back is at a minimum discount of 15% of Book Value (BV). For those whose buy back at a minimum discount of 25% of BV, the RBI will consider them for the approval route, if the buy back is out of internal accruals.

At present, units in service sector like hotels, hospitals, and software sector, are allowed to avail of ECBs upto US $ 100 million per financial year for import of capital goods. In April 2009, the total amount of permissible buy back of FCBs out of internal accruals put under approval route was raised from present level of U.S $ 50 million to U.S $ 100 million subject to certain conditions. In June, the period of realization and repatriation to India of the amount representing the bulk export value of goods and software exported was raised form 6 months to 12 months. This was operative upto June 30, 2010; subject to review with effect from July 22, 2009, the eligible companies resident outside India were permitted by RBI to issue Indian depository receipt (IDRs) through the domestic depository and to permit persons resident in India and outside to purchase retain, possess, transfer or redeem such IDBs, subject to compliance with the companies (Insurance of Deposit Receipt) Rules 2004, and subsequent amendments to it in the SEBI.

PART – IV

INTERNATIONAL MARKETING AND TRADE PRACTICES AND PROCEDURES

22

International Marketing

Marketing Concepts

One of the important managerial functions in a company is marketing, which refers to the policies and decisions relating to purchases of inputs, sale of output, servicing of the sales, distribution, transportation, storage, etc. In the corporate world, marketing is generally defined as the performance of the business activities relating to the flow of goods and services between the business sector and other sectors of the economy in relation to buying, selling, storage, distribution, etc.

Marketing is closely related to other operations of the company such as production and financing of the enterprise. The operations relating to production of goods and services in a particular mix and the conversion of inputs into flow of outputs are the functions of the Operations' Manager. The financing aspects relating to investment as well as working capital and the optimal use of finances in the process of such production are the functions of the finance manager. The cash inflows and outflows, sources and uses of funds and the optimal mix of the various types of funds for a least-cost combination to produce a given product mix are the concern of the finance manager. In short, the operations' manager is concerned with production of goods and services while the finance manager plans and controls the flow of finances for these operations. The marketing manager provides the outlet to the operations in the form of flow of goods and services with particular reference to the end use at the consumers' level. These three functions of a corporate entity are to be integrated and performed in a co-ordinated manner. In this sense, marketing management is an important segment of the total managerial concept.

The plan of marketing in respect of both intermediates and final outputs is to be carried out by the marketing manager in the form of a programme of action. The marketing programme is thus a plan of action setting out the objectives and the mode of achieving the objectives over a defined period of one year. The activities generally involving marketing are pricing, logistics of the product movement, promotion of sales, distribution channels, marketing research etc. The market research provides the feedback of the company's effort and is the basis of further managerial decisions. In the system of management by objectives, the company sets out its objectives and a plan of action is prepared to achieve these objectives. A product mix is accordingly decided each year. There are the functions of top management. Once the production-mix is fixed, where to sell, when and how to sell are the other aspects of the marketing activity. A marketing programme is drawn up then to apportion the effort among various alternative market segments and relates to a plan of action.

Foreign vs. Domestic Markets

International marketing relates to international finance as marketing activity in value both inputs and outflows of funds and their tuning, etc., are all intricately connected to finanace.

Marketing management has two parts, namely, domestic and foreign, in so far as the company has foreign operations. Although policies in one area impinge on those in the other, we confine here to export marketing. The term "export marketing management" may be defined as that part of corporate management concerned with decisions and policies relating to marketing of products, inputs and outputs abroad. The export marketing programme to be drawn up by every company dealing in export of goods and services, envisages a plan for guiding the company's activities for promotion of their export revenue over a period, normally one year.

As in domestic marketing, the export marketing policy should also envisage pricing, product-mix, promotion, channels of distribution, stocking and marketing research. Even so, there are some basic differences between these two markets.

International markets are more competitive in the sense that a larger number of competing suppliers of the same or closely linked goods are active in the market. Cost consciousness and quality awareness would be greater than in the domestic markets. Besides, designs, packaging, stricter adherence to standards, after-sales service, warehouse stocking, etc., are more important. Customs, habits and environment play an important part.

Distance being an important factor in foreign trade, transport, shipping, insurance, proper packaging and warehousing are relatively more vital than in domestic trade. Due consideration is to be given to delays in transport handling and storage problems, etc. Uncertainty in the market trends on top of legal and political uncertainties also play a significant role. The export manager has to be in constant touch with the foreign agents for market information. This information should comprise the market trends, changes in consumption, pattern and tasks of people, imports and domestic production of the product in question, tariff and non-tariff barriers, local and foreign exchange controls, laws and regulations of the government affecting the sale and distribution of imported goods in the concerned country. The availability of any preferential treatment, incentives, tax concessions or rebates, etc., also play a significant part in foreign trade, as well as in foreign investment. Normally, anti-dumping rules, minimum quality standards and packaging requirements are found in almost all countries. In addition to dumping, trade diversion and under-cutting in prices are some of the unethical practices in foreign trade. Another major risk of foreign marketing is the possible fluctuations in the exchange rates of the rupee, which might upset the original cost-profit calculus.

Market Information

At macro-level, the Government of India has proposed the setting up of a National Centre for Trade Information, which will co-ordinate the collection and dissemination of all trade information from foreign centres, trade consuls and embassies abroad. This will go a long way in filling up a wide information gap in the present marketing system. The commercial wings of Indian Embassies abroad and the Directorate of Commercial Intelligence in India play a role. The Trade Development Authority (TDA) and a number of organisations in India conduct trade fairs and lead the trade missions to exhibit their products abroad market information is also got from the industry discount. The export houses and the multi-national companies could be given a freer hand in exploring the new markets for existing exports and for new products. In dissemination of market information from foreign countries, banks, multinationals, trade and business associations and chambers play an important part. In the case of new products, the Government may offer free feasibility studies on a selective basis and in selected countries. Project exports, joint projects, long-term collaboration plans for both technology and marketing and a host of other devices can be adopted to explore and maintain the foreign markets on a long-term basis. Market Research and R & D efforts of a number of companies play an active role in this endeavour. Exim bank provides technical and financial help to exporters and importers, in India.

Evaluation of Market Research

Market information is also collected through Market Research which can be defined as the process of collection, recording and coding of the market data and of analysing the information and data on inventories, sales and revenues from the product-mix marketed. The company can have its own R & D department or may engage an outside agency for the purpose. Research is designed to throw light on the market trends and changes in tastes, preferences and consumers attitudes to their products *vis-a-vis* those of competitors, on market sales involving the forecasting of sales, dealer-wise or market segment-wise, analysis of sales and costs and benefits of advertisement, etc. The problems of marketing, sales and distribution are studied on a continuous basis to build up an information system for the top management to enable them to take right decisions on the changes needed on the product-mix, channels of distribution, sales strategies, etc. The R & D department of the company would also aim at improving the quality of product designs, lowering of costs, increasing productivity and improving technological inputs.

Export Marketing Policy

The subject of export marketing policy has two aspects, prima facie, namely, macro-policy and micro-policy. The former relates to the economy as a whole comprising a mix of trade policy, fiscal policy, foreign exchange policy and other relevant policies influencing foreign trade in quantum, composition and direction. The latter relates to the export marketing strategies at the firm level, influencing the product-mix, pricing, sales promotion, advertisement, distribution channels, market intelligence and a host of other decisions and policies at the firm or corporate level.

At the macro-level, trade policy comprises again export promotion policy and import substitution policy or a combination of both as to suit the changing economic scenario of the country. Fiscal policy also influences trade through various incentive or disincentive schemes, tariff rate changes; customs, excise and other taxes affecting the trade flows. The foreign exchange rate is the single largest factor influencing trade flows as the cost-price parities are affected by the exchange rate variations. Valuation of the currency over-valuation and under-valuation — alter the price parities as between domestic and foreign products and as between the products of two countries in a third market. These policies at macro level are discussed in appropriate chapters in the book. Micro level policies have to be tuned to and altered as per the changes in Macro-levels policies.

Macro-level Marketing Strategy

At the macro-level, exports constitute less than 15 per cent of the total GDP at current prices. While, on the one hand, the foreign sector is vital for the economic growth of the country, on the other, exports constitute an insignificant part of the total production. In view of this, the Committee on Trade Policies* set-up by the Government of India in 1985 has opined that there is no possibility of an export led growth in India but there can be growth led exports in the future. The Committee has recommended reliance on both export promotion and import substitution. In the field of export promotion, the Committee recommended that export production and marketing should be an integral part of the production and sales programme for the domestic economy. Export promotion policy should provide an environment for growth of exports in which the micro units would be able to expand production for exports. The integrated national policy for the development of exports is to plan a product-mix containing some exportable items in most of the industries. Such items should have competitive advantage as judged by the comparative costs and should be labour-intensive. The value-added component of exports should be higher than in respect of domestic sales. Such selected items should be entrusted to the respective export promotion bodies either in the private or public sector. The Government and the public sector bodies should also help the identification of markets for the selected commodities. The various export incentive schemes should be related to foreign exchange earnings from these industries and should have a time-bound schedule. There should be an annual plan for export marketing listing the old and new export products in the order of importance of their contribution to foreign exchange earnings and laying down the strategies for their promotion. In each of these exportable industries, a certain amount of export surplus is to be generated and ear-marked for foreign markets. The government has to strengthen infrastructural facilities such as shipping, port facilities, insurance and credit, etc., which would improve the logistics of movement of export goods. The government has already liberalised imports necessary for export growth. Better demand management in the domestic economy for the goods having an export market, particularly in respect of agricultural products, is also attempted. The trade policy is being co-ordinated with the exchange control policy and appropriate exchange rate policy is pursued for promotion of trade and for other service items of the balance of payments. The fiscal policy also promotes exports

---

* Report of the Committee on Trade Policies, Ministry of Commerce, Government of India, 1985.

through various incentive schemes such as reduction in or drawback on excise customs, sales-tax, etc. These policies have been already rationalised and simplified, so as to reduce the procedures and formalities, and the liberalisation process was carried further since July 1991, following the economic and financial reforms.

Search for Markets

Unlike in the domestic markets, exports would depend on various extraneous factors, such as chill winds of competition, changing scenario of market tastes and preferences and a host of other factors. The export marketing strategy would, therefore, depend upon a prior appraisal of the market forces abroad. The company having exports should have an export house or export department. After a preliminary investigation into the potential markets abroad, the marketing manager prepares an export plan. Research into markets would involve potentiality studies of various foreign markets. The necessary information is secured by the market research studies of which the following are the most important: (i) The product studies should analyse consumer preferences for products of a similar nature, including the company's own product and brand preferences with regard to packaging designing and other characteristics of the product; (ii) The consumer studies would identify the potential consumers, their preferences in terms of the income, habits and attitudes of the people etc.; (iii) Sales studies try to measure the sales potential of various segments of the market and analyse the sales trends and forecast the future sales. Distribution and sales analysis are conducted to analyse the impact of various sales policies in terms of the distributor and dealer preference and their performance in terms of geographical segments and market segments; (iv) The market research studies are also undertaken with respect to cost and benefits of the various sales strategies and marketing programmes; (v) Sometimes, advertising studies are also undertaken to measure the effectiveness of each of the campaigns of advertisement and sales promotion.

Such studies are to be undertaken on a continuing basis as foreign markets are subject to greater vagaries. Legal and political differences as between the countries and the differences in the tastes and preferences of the markets abroad would produce greater uncertainty on the foreign markets than in the domestic markets. The recent growth of consumerism — the movement to protect the interest of consumers — involve greater responsibilities on the marketing manager. The spread of information and sophistication in the taste and health consciousness of people have imposed rigorous restrictions on the quality and packaging standards in the international markets. Besides, the movement of environmentalism has also given rise to social consciousness of consumer protection from air and water pollution, health hazards, etc. Environmentalism considers the interests of society in terms of safeguarding their interests. Therefore, the standards of product quality, designing and packaging have all become more important. The laws of foreign countries, economic and political uncertainty, the rapid changes in the habits of foreign consumers and multifarious competitive forces operating on the markets lead to greater burdens on the export market strategies. The economic uncertainty resulting from inflation and recession and exchange rate changes, or other major economic trends in foreign markets has also added a further dimension to the marketing problems. The shortages and surpluses in respect of the competing products or closely connected products have an important bearing on the marketing prospects of a company's product. Besides, many foreign governments have their own laws and rules regarding the import of foreign goods and imposed rigorous standards in respect of quality, storage and packaging of the products sold in these markets. Many times, many pharmaceutical products proposed to be exported to the markets in the US by Ranbaxy and Dr. Reddys had to face legal hurdles from FDA, in the US and Europe. Federal Drug Administration (FDA) of the US has to permit legally import of generic drugs from India or other countries. According to this legal practice many importers by other countries form India are subjected to legal hurdles and regulatory procedures. The export marketing strategies are, therefore, subject to an array of forces, some of which are unpredictable and in such circumstances, the task of export manager is made very risky and troublesome.

Micro-level Marketing Strategy

At the micro-level, marketing management assumes importance for the purpose of export promotion. This relates to an aspect of company management involving the decisions and polices in the field of marketing of goods abroad. The principal marketing policies should contain aspects of pricing, advertisements, servicing, warranty, credit, etc. One of the important aspects is designing a product-mix or product differentiation suitable for foreign market segments' so as to promote the goods in demand abroad. In addition to designing a product-mix, the marketing programme should envisage branding or trade marks, distributing channels, sales personnel, geographical market coverage, reciprocity and terms of sales, etc.

The export marketing manager has to be doubly cautious and alert for the reason that foreign markets are bridled with greater uncertainties and risks, and costs of marketing are higher abroad than domestically, as referred to earlier.

The market research division provides the necessary information on the markets and feedback from consumers, regarding product-mix, pricing, promotion of sales, etc. The agencies for purchase abroad such as wholesalers, retailers, departmental stores, agency houses, merchant-importers, etc., are to be located. The appropriate marketing strategy would fix the design and packaging and network of storage and service points. The cost and benefits of each of the alternative policies are also estimated and a suitable product-mix, marketing strategy and distribution channels, etc., are decided.

Product-mix and Brand Patenting

In the selection of right product-mix, the suitability of the same for foreign markets, their environment, habits, etc., have to be borne in mind. Here product refers to the satisfaction to be accrued to the consumer. The product line keeps the link between the company and the consumer. The task of developing products or product lines to satisfy the changing needs of the consumer is called merchandising. The strategies available for merchandising are product differentiation, market segmentation, and planned obsolescence.

Product differentiation attempts to create a new demand for the same product by the introduction of certain modifications and new packaging. Market segmentation seeks to adjust the physical product and total product to consumer demand by recognising the various sub-markets for the parts, ancillaries, etc. Planned obsolescence creates new products by allowing the old ones to die and by creating minor and superficial variations in the old products to create new ones.

Brand promotion is a strategic device for export markets. The same company can have different brands to suit the different segments of the market as in the case of Brook Brond Tea, Colgate, etc. Brand Promotion is by advertisement and propaganda. A combination of media is adopted say T.V., newspapers, banners, etc.

The product programme draws up the optimal product-mix and the flow chart for various products and distribution outlets for the same. Product design and packaging are important aspects of the same. Designs and brands are to be patented in the respective countries.

The design is to be consumer-oriented and as foreign markets are different from domestic markets in respect of tastes, habits and environment, foreign designs have to be adopted to make products attractive and competitive. Brand name or a trade mark is also an important aspect of the marketing programme. Either the producer's own brand or the foreign agent's brand is being used depending on the popularity and reputation of the concerned parties. Besides, registration of trade brands with the concerned governments is also an indispensable pre-requisite.

The right channel of distribution is also vital for promotion of foreign sales. Depending on the nature of the product, habits in the country in question and peculiarities of foreign markets, the channels of distribution are to be chosen. Consignment sales, brand name sales, departmental stores or agency sales are some examples of the distribution channels. Depending on the policy adopted such as either intensive distribution or selective distribution or exclusive dealership or the policy of leasing, the foreign warehousing arrangements and logistics of the movement of goods are arranged. New channels of sales are a house-to-house distribution TV channels and newspapers, etc.

Pricing

The theoretical fixing of price according to demand and supply forces does not always operate in the export markets. In the case of marketing by multinational corporations, price is a strategic determinant. Sometimes, it is not related to the cost of production but to what the market can bear.

In making price decision, the company may adopt different criteria for different market segments. Basically, the marketing manager takes into account the cost of manufacturing and selling the product which is a combination of manufacturing and distribution costs. But the nature and extent of the consumer demand competitive forces operating in the market, constraints of distribution and customary trade margins and company's own promotional strategy impose limitations on the simple use of the cost plus formula. As the most important factor in the foreign markets is the consumers' preferences and their ability to pay, the marketing manager would decide the price structure in the foreign markets on varying considerations. This is what is called the strategy of charging what the market can bear. The availability of fiscal rebates, duty drawbacks and cash compensatory support and other export incentives may also alter the price structure in the foreign markets. Many multinational companies sell their products at below their costs in some market segments and with exorbitant margins in other segments of the market. Dumping and international sales at throw-away prices of some of the companies are examples. The various trade discounts and consumer discounts are all a part of this game of having a varying structure of prices of the same product instead of having uniform foreign prices.

Pricing is crucial to the company as it is the major source of revenue to the company. The company would try to secure the maximum revenue from a given basket of products from the various market segments by aiming, firstly at covering costs and secondly, by charging what the market can bear. Very often, the companies cannot follow a uniform procedure of covering the marginal costs or average costs. Some companies follow the cost-plus principle and some others the full costs, namely, variable and fixed costs. There are some companies which follow incremental cost pricing policy in which case only the variable costs are covered but not the fixed costs. It would, therefore, be difficult to pinpoint in theory the pricing policy of the product-mix in the foreign markets. But the company would generally ensure that in the overall sale of its products in all the domestic and foreign markets, there is always a margin of profit. The extent of the margin may however, vary depending upon the characteristics of the various segments and other forces operating in the market referred to earlier. Some pharma MNCs were reported to have exhorbitant margins of profit on some drug patents, sold in developing countries. "Some companies change what the buyer's market case pay" or "What the market can bear".

Promotion Measures

Promotion refers to non-price incentives or selling activities designed to promote sales of a company abroad. Such promotion measures may be of generic nature such as promoting consumption of tea in preference to coffee. Alternatively, such promotion may relate to specific country products like Darjeeling tea or a company's product like Kirloskar Engines, Colgate, or Cola or Nescafe or Tajmahal Tea.

Three important types of promotion are advertising, personal selling and sales promotion. In foreign markets, personal selling is the least important. Advertising which is a mode of presentation of the availability of a product appeals to many potential buyers in the markets. In practice, sales promotion is the most important medium of promoting a product abroad which is done through either generic promotion or specific promotion, referred to above. Such promotion may adopt devices as trading stamps, dealer aids, premiums or discounts and so on.

Advertising has become a sophisticated art and is pursued aggressively by MNCs on their foreign products sold in India as in the case of the Coke, Pepsi, pizza, etc. All promotion involves costs and the marketing manager has to weigh each means of sales promotion and adopt the right means suited to the particular market segment. In the case of foreign markets, the foreign agents or export houses abroad may advise the right method suited to each market segment and to each product-mix.

The sales promotion measures also differ depending upon the object in view, namely, initial penetration into markets, or maintenance of the market share or counter the increasing competition from cheaper substitutes or increase the market share of this company's product. The trade brands and other insignia of some products to indicate the origin of the country and company accompanied by proper advertisement are generally adopted in foreign markets. In most cases of existing markets, the maintenance of high quality and consistency in standards, followed by storage of inventories in foreign centres and after-sales services are the best guarantee for any sales promotion strategy. The dependability of supply and availability of spares and parts are added attractions for foreign markets.

Evaluation and Control

The results of any marketing programme should be evaluated at regular intervals — half-yearly or quarterly — through a process of control mechanism. The essence of control lies in checking the existing actions against the desired results listed in the marketing programme.

After clearly defining the objectives and desired results, some mode of measurement of the activity such as the quantum of sales or revenue or any other indicator is to be designed for the control system. There should also be a method of comparing the current activity with the past activity as well as the desired level of activity. The actual performance is to be measured and the results are flashed back to the top management by the marketing manager. It is also necessary to change the policies or make modifications to rectify the defects and improve the results. Such policy changes again flow from the top management to the marketing manager from time to time. Corrective action is taken for any such errors or shortfalls in results. Taking action at the right time and in the right dose is also an important aspect of the control mechanism. Control is exercised through periodical reports from agents, inspections by salesmen and occasional studies.

Any effective system of control should be flexible, strategic at selected points, rather than exhaustive and have a built-in feedback system. The means of communicating the feedback information and the corrective changes in policy, as a consequence of that should be meaningfully designed. The export department or the export manager should have a system of direct control on all the market segments through a two-way information system at some strategic points for control, namely, the warehousing or stocking points, or selected retail outlets at various market segments. The means of measuring the actual performance, comparison of their performance with the desired objective, etc., should also be standardised. The export manager should have a quick means of communicating with the top management on the corrective action to be taken for any deviations from the desired results. This would ensure a continuous process of evaluation and control on the marketing activities.

Risk in Export Markets

If the invoices are in local currency the depreciation of the currency is a risk to be hedged. Exchange and trade controls in the countries concerned is another risk, for which correct information flow is necessary. Political risks of the foreign country to be expected are to be covered by Foreign Investment Guarantee by the foreign government. The rating of country risks from international credit rating agencies are available. Sudden changes in tastes and preferences of consumers in foreign countries can be taken care of by market research and planning. The risks of transport, shipping and airways are to be insured.

Risk in export marketing depend on the proportion of export sales to total sales, the nature of the product mix and elasticity of demand for the product. If export sales are a small proportion of total sales, the MNC may keep its prices unchanged in the hope of keeping its market share but if competition dictates, it may even lower prices to hold its share on the market. If the product is produced to the requirements of the client, the price is not disturbed. If the product is a consumer good and product mix can be changed at short notice, product differentiation will be introduced and price is maintained.

An MNC can use its foreign subsidiary as an export platform and will benefit by local currency devaluation. Devaluation benefits exports and import substitutes. The income and price elasticities of goods, exported will determine the extent of gains. Export sales and the impact of exchange risk on it will depend also on its ability to shift production and change the product mix, market shifts and changing of the sources of inputs, among countries.

Finally, the actual impact of a currency change on a firm depends on whether the exchange rate change is fully offset by differences in inflation rates or whether the real exchange rates and relative price changes are different. In the latter case, only real effect of exchange risk on export sales of a firm, has to be considered. The exchange risk can also be hedged in the Forex market, which is now possible in India as well, through Forward Rate Agreements or Currency Futures, or Forward Exchange Cover.

23 Government Regulations and Procedures

Both exporters and importers have to investigate first whether the commodity they wish to export or import requires a licence under any law for the time being in force. Under the Import and Export Control Act of 1947, the Central Government is empowered to prohibit, restrict or otherwise control imports and exports. Under this Act, the Import Control Order (1955) was passed and Schedule I to this order contains the list of articles subject to control which cannot be imported except with a licence. The commodities on Open General Licence (OGL) can be imported without a licence. The rationale for licensing is to keep exports and imports in conformity with the current government policy.

Imports and exports of gold, silver, currency notes, coins, etc., are prohibited, except with prior permission of the RBI, as they are subject to FERA rules. The current regulations with respect to imports and exports are found in the latest Hand Book on Import Policy and Export Policy respectively. Under the Imports and Exports Control Order 1977 and rules made thereunder, all exporters require a licence for specified commodities. Export control extends to all commodities included in Schedule I to the Export Control Order 1977 or as announced from time to time.

Licensing Policy

Generally, licensing policy is framed on the basis of a foreign exchange budget prepared periodically by the government. The budget is based on the expected export earnings and other inward exchange receipts. After allocating for expenditure on debt servicing and maintenance of our embassies and other expenditures abroad, the balance is allocated among different users of imports. The requirements food, fertilisers, petroleum and its products get priority allotment and they are all in public sector. The following agencies get allotment:

(1) Public sector undertakings for their requirements of raw materials, capital goods, etc.

(2) The Iron and Steel Controller for Steel.

(3) Ministry of Finance for private sector allocation.

Licensing Authority

There are many Regional Licensing authorities with specified geographical coverage and a few of them can cover REP licences. The list is given in the Handbook of Import-Export Procedures. For an import/export licence, an importer or exporter has to approach any of the following agencies:

(a) Chief Controller of Imports and Exports (CCI&E), New Delhi or Joint Chief Controller of Imports and Exports, Kolkata, Mumbai, Chennai, Cochin, New Delhi, Rajkot.

(b) Iron and Steel Controller's Office.

(c) Development Officer, Tools, Development Wing, Ministry of Commerce.

The licences issued by the CCI&E fall into the following categories:

(A) Actual Users (AU) either industrial or non-industrial. Actual user is a person who secures a licence required for his own use and not for trade.

(B) Registered Exporters, i.e., those who import under the import policy for registered exporters and are registered with an Export Promotion Council or Commodity Board, etc.

(C) Others.

Sponsoring Authority

In addition to the licensing authority, there is a sponsoring authority for each category of importers as to its essentially and a clearing agency for indigenous clearance. Sponsoring authorities are the concerned Ministries, DGTD, the Departments of Government, Commodity Boards, etc. There are about 35 sponsoring authorities recognised by the Government. They have to certify that the proposed commodity is indigenously not available and has to be imported and if available indigenously, they give reasons as to why it has to be imported.

In respect of small scale industries, priority allotment is given on the basis of the sponsorship of the State Directorate of Industries.

Procedures

The importers should get a code number from the CCI&E and no import is permitted without a licence. The application for a licence should be made in a prescribed form for the purpose, duly signed by the applicant or by his duly authorised agent under law, along with a fee for the purpose. The application is to be made within a specific time, namely, end-October or end-February. The fees, application format and other details are given in the Handbook of import and Export Procedures. The applicant should also submit an income-tax clearance certificate in the form specifically set out for the purpose. This is to be sent to the appropriate licensing authority connected with the region to which he belongs. The procedures for importing by public sector enterprises and Government Departments, imports of gifts and procedure for actual users, REP licences and for canalisation of imports through STC or other agencies are also set out in the above handbook.

The import licences of two categories are issued:

(1) General currency area licences which are valid for the import from all countries, except those from which import is not permitted, namely, South Africa, South West Africa, etc and

(2) Specific licences which are valid for import from a specified country or countries.

The exporter gets an export licence in his own country but makes sure that the importer has also got clearance from his own country for its import. These licences should be currently valid. The validity period is stated in the licence as two years to six months depending on the nature of the commodity and shipment should be made within 15 days from the expiry date. A grace period of 30 days is allowed for negotiation of drafts after the expiry date. The normal licence period is April to March. The licences are granted in duplicate — one to be presented with the bill of entry to the Customs and the other (the Exchange Control copy) to be presented with the application for establishing a credit or for the remittance of foreign exchange in payment for imports. The Exchange Control copy is retained by the bank until fully and finally utilised and then forwarded to the RBI. But when they are only partially used or when they have to be resubmitted to the Trade Control Authority for revalidation or extension, they are returned to the importer. The banker must endorse these copies in rupees with the amount of credits opened and used and the balance available. The banker should also endorse any foreign currency purchased or drafts paid under this licence and show the unutilised portion on the back.

Import Licences

Import licences are granted to various categories such as actual users — industrial and non-industrial — DGTD units (for raw materials) SSIs, registered exporters, capital goods and Heavy Electrical Plants, STC, etc. The bulk of the import Licences is given to Registered exporters and capital Goods categories and those requiring raw material components, accessories, machinery etc., The major categories of actual users are scheduled industries covered by the DGTD, other industries scheduled and non-scheduled are not covered by DGTD and small-scale industries.

Majority of items are listed in the open general licence which is subject to change from year to year and of which the bulk is in capital goods items. The actual users would get automatic licence for import up to an additional 10 per cent over the certified actual consumption in either of the previous two years provided they export at least 10 per cent of their annual production of the selected items. The existing facilities of supplementary licences to existing units and the new units in exceptional cases would continue. Some imports of capital goods are banned; some capital goods are available to actual users under a licence and some are available under OGL. There are items in the banned list, absolute banned list, restricted list or canalised entry list etc. Import licences granted for capital goods and heavy electrical plants are valid for two years and for others 18 months.

The actual users of a non-industrial category belonging to laboratories, hospitals, Central and State bodies, etc., are permitted to import their requirements provided the goods are under OGL subject to the condition that they are required only for their consumption. The imports of capital goods are permitted under OGL after the indigenous availability of that commodity is examined and certified. The public undertakings including the railways, could import goods under OGL as required by them for consumption after being cleared by the concerned technical authority and exchange for the purpose is released by the Ministry of Finance.

The registered exporters are those export houses which are registered with various registering authorities as specified in the Handbook of Export-Import Procedures. these export houses are allowed the facilities of import replenishment against export, where under import of relevant banned or canalised items is permitted. The statement of import policy for registered exporters is also set out there. For every export product variety, import of materials permitted and percentage of import replenishment, etc., are also laid down. The REP licences are transferable and direct imports of canalised items under REP licences are permitted. There are three categories of REP licences: (i) Those issued ex poste where the licences and goods imported are both transferable, (ii) Duty free advance licences which are issued ex ante before exports but with an export obligation are non-transferable, and (iii) Licences to export houses and trading houses are not transferable but goods imported are transferable. Even the imports of banned items are permitted, subject to a monetary limit of 20 per cent of the face value of REP licences. In 1980-81, a new feature was introduced permitting imports, free of customs duty of raw materials against REP licences for export of certain specified products, such as stainless steel utensils, steel pipes, tubes, etc.

The import policy encourages the availability of imported goods more easily for export purposes. These import licences are granted (without duty exemption) if they are used in export products, provided the minimum value added to the imported product is at least 25 per cent which is subsequently brought down to 20 per cent. Provisions for advance licences, extension of validity, supplementary licences, etc., are all laid down in the three books referred to above. Duty Exemption Scheme and the details thereof are also contained in the Import Policy Handbook. This scheme is applicable to those export products in which the minimum value added to imports is 25 per cent and the amount of customs duty payable by the party is not less than 5 per cent of f.o.b. value of the export product.

Data on import licences over the last few years show that the bulk of them (65-70%) are for Registered exporters, followed by capital goods category (20%) and raw materials for scheduled industries (5-10%). Amounts granted to actual users, SSIs and STC, etc., are negligible.

Special facilities are provided to non-resident Indians importing capital goods, etc., into India for the manufacturing process and also for project exports for bringing back to India certain unused equipment, machinery, etc.

Public sector agencies have been assigned an increased role in the import of raw materials and their supply to actual users, particularly from the list of OGL. The canalised items are increased or decreased from time to time, depending on the requirements. The more recent addition to the canalised list are tin plates, raw petroleum, coke, DDT, stainless steel, etc. The Inter-Ministerial Monitoring Committee reviews the import programmes and also arranges for the canalising agencies to meet the registered demand of the actual users and would oversee the canalising scheme in respect of selected items.

Export Licenses

The Policy statement contained in the Export Policy Handbook gives the details of policy with regard to items in Part B of Schedule I to the Exports (Control) Order 1977. Annexure I gives a list of items such as onions, groundnuts, shellac, seeds, potato, cement, etc., canalised through a government agency. The list of canalising agencies is given in Annexure V. In respect of some export items such as mica, shellac, coir yarn, carpet backing, minimum export prices are set out.

The commodities subject to export control are listed in Schedule I of the export policy. Part 'A' contains a list of items the export of which is normally banned; Part 'B' has a list of items which are permitted subject to prevailing conditions from time to time. Scheduled III contains lists of commodities subject to OGL under four categories, namely OGL - 1 to OGL - 4. OGL - 1 relates to all land-borne trade with neighbouring countries; Ogl - 2 with samples, gifts, etc., of various commodities, OGL-3 gives a list of about 85 commodities which are permitted to be exported subject to certain fulfilling conditions as to quota allotments or minimum prices, etc. OGL-4 contains export items which are to be canalised through a public agency such as STC, MMTC, SAIL, JCI, etc. Many items have been taken out of canalisation in recent times.

In the case of some commodities like jute, tea, etc., export contracts are also registered with a government agency like the Jute Commissioner or Tea Board, etc., on a voluntary basis or under prevailing rules for securing recognition and acceptability for government rebates, concessions and cash assistance etc., and for imparting a sense of confidence to the importer. Most export subsidies and concession on export credit were removed due to changed conditions under WTO.

A new import-export policy was announced in April 1985 mainly based upon the recommendations of Abid Hussain Committee. This Committee was set up by the Government in July 1984 to suggest measures for rationalisation and improvement in trade policy. Its report was submitted in December 1984. As a background to this, the earlier policy, based on Alexander Committee recommendations, may be referred to briefly.

Alexander Committee

In 1978 the Alexander Committee gave its recommendations in the field of import-export policy. Inter alia, its recommendations include the discontinuance of protection to domestic industries and liberalisation of licensing and other policies. Subsequent to this, there was considerable liberalisation of imports and introduction of export promotion measures. Despite these, India continued to face trade deficits and export stagnancy.

Abid Hussain Committee

It is in this context that the Abid Hussain Committee had been requested to have a fresh look at the import-export policy. Accordingly, the new import-export policy announced in April 1985 contained drastic policy changes towards liberalisation and rationalisation based on this Committee's Report. The main objectives of the new policy are to maintain continuity and stability in the trade policy, to facilitate and expand export production through freer access to imported inputs, to promote import substitution and to facilitate modernisation and improved efficiency in the export sector.

Major recommendations of the Abid Hussain Committee are set out below:

(1) The import-export policy should be framed and operated for 3 years at a time so as to maintain stability and certainty as to the policy measures.

(2) The duty drawback scheme should be rationalised and simplified by avoiding multiplicity of rates and uncertainty as to the period.

(3) The CCS scheme should also be rationalised to compensate exporters in respect of indirect taxes paid by them and CCS should not form part of a taxable income of the exporter.

(4) The REP scheme should be reformulated along the lines of "advance licensing" system for manufacturer-exporters and an export-import pass book to be introduced to serve as a permanent import replenishment licence.

(5) The real effective exchange rate should be maintained at a level that ensures competitiveness to Indian exports.

(6) About 50 per cent of the profits of exporters should be exempted from income tax which can be utilised for the development of export business.

(7) Export production should be free from the restrictions of licensing capacity in respect of imports of capital foods and technology.

(8) There should be an exchange entitlement scheme for exporters to use a part of their export earning for market development abroad.

(9) Channelisation of imports should be an exception allowed as a special case.

(10) Quotas and other restrictions should gradually be replaced by tariffs in future.

(11) Capital goods needed for modernisation should be allowed to be imported under OGL with a zero or negligible import duty.

(12) The various categories of import licences should be merged into a simplified list of "OGL", "limited permissible category" and "prohibited" list.

(13) The level of protection to existing industries should be reduced and de-escalated over time, so as to encourage efficient import substitution in the economy.

Import-Export Policy (Exim Policy)

In the import policy, the items are classified into "banned", "restricted" and "OGL" lists. The Exim policy is valid for a period of 3 years to ensure stability. Regional advance licensing committees were set-up at Mumbai, Kolkata Chennai and New Delhi to grant import licence to exporters under the duty exemption scheme. The automatic licensing category has been abolished and OGL list has been expanded and an import-export pass book has been introduced for operating the import replenishment scheme for manufacturer-exporters. Besides, special facilities have been provided to export trading houses and 100 per cent export-oriented units. Many items under the channelised list have been brought under the O.G.L.

The import-export pass book scheme, introduced during the Sixth Plan tries to eliminate procedural delays in respect of granting licenses to the REP exporters and to enable them to have duty-free imports for export production. It will serve as a single all-purpose duty-free import licence. The validity of the pass book is for 27 months for exports and 18 months for imports. Under the advance licensing scheme which exists simultaneously, the registered exporters get the benefit of duty-free import on an advance basis to effect exports. This licence is meant for actual users and is not transferable and has an export obligation based on the value of the licence.

The special facilities offered to the 100 per cent export-oriented industries are to allow them to import their requirements under OGL. Similarly, the special facilities offered to export trading houses are allocation of some foreign exchange which they have earned for use in their market and product development measures. Import of machinery for them or supporting producers is allowed under special facilities. Additional foreign exchange allocation was also made to them for setting up warehouses and offices abroad.

Among other measures of export promotion, mention may be made of the exemption for export production from the capacity limits licensed and from restrictions on import of capital goods and technologies. Hike in the MRTP limit from Rs. 20 crores to Rs. 100 crores and exemption of 27 industries from the scope of MRTP Act have provided a further fillip to export production and export growth. The subsequent abolition of MRTP Act in July 1991, in respect of asset limit growth helped the export growth. Besides, the government has also announced several concessions in respect of excise duty paid, income tax on exporters, particularly in respect of small scale units. Concessions are also granted in respect of customs duties payable by some of the export units.

In August 1985, the Finance Ministry has announced further measures of export promotion, viz., extension of international price reimbursement scheme for steel to alloys, reduction of excise and customs duties on synthetic fibre and reduction of customs bonding charges for export-oriented units from 250 per cent to 150 per cent. The extension of the cash compensatory support scheme beyond December 1985 and other measures taken were designed to lower the costs for export production and allow them to update the technologies. It will thus be seen that many recommendations of the Hussain Committee were implemented by the Government, by 1991-92, when economic and financial reforms were started. As part of structural Reforms, Customs duties were either rationalised or reduced. The maximum rates was brought down to 5-10%. As per the requirements of WTO, trade barriers were reduced or eliminated during 1997-2006.

Thrust on Export Promotion and Import Substitution

Under the new policy, both export promotion and import substitution have been given equal importance. A number of constraints on both have been removed and productive efficiency has been given a premium. The role of market forces and increased competition have been encouraged. Simultaneously, protection measures have been de-escalated by replacing quotas and other restrictions by tariffs to expose Indian products to foreign competition. This was in tune with the recommendations of the Hussain Committee Report. The objectives of the new thrust in policy are to promote export competitiveness and to replace the policy of import substitution at any cost by import substitution meanings in an efficient manner. Special emphasis is laid by the Hussain Committee Report on continuous technological upgradation which is necessary for rapid and efficient industrialisation. With these objectives, the policy has provided for liberal access to imports of technology in selected areas of the economy and special mention has been made of the need for modernisation in some sectors such as jute and cotton textiles automobiles, steel, coal, electronics, etc. Lastly, the Hussain Committee has also laid emphasis on the need for co-ordination of the tariff policy and industrial policy with monetary and fiscal policies with a view to improving competitiveness of export products and increasing the indigenisation of import production. The monetary policy aims at controlling inflation and keeping the cost of export credit at cheap rates to be comparable with those of foreign competitors. The industrial policy aims at the expansion of industrial production without constraints, while fiscal and trade policies should go hand in hand for the purpose of promoting the production and expansion of exports.

Exim Policy (Continued)

The recent Exim Policy was already referred to and the items in Free list were increased in such a way that only 667 items are on the restricted list. This number of items was further reduced later on. The other major changes relate to the creation of free trade zones on the lines that exist elsewhere in the world, liberalisation of the Duty Exemption Scheme, special green cards for exporters, who export 50% of their production, entitling them to special facilities, etc.

Other measures include the following:

(1) Increase from 5 to 10% of previous year's export in respect of pre-export DEPB credit entitlement.

(2) Value addition for rupee exports to Russia was reduced from 100% to 33%.

(3) Threshold limit for zero duty exports for EPCG scheme was brought down from Rs. 20 crores to Rs. 1 crore for chemicals, plastics and textiles. The additional customs duty

on import of capital goods, under the above scheme was removed in respect of marine and electronics sector.

(4) Duty free import of consumables in respect of gems, handicrafts, textiles and leather sectors, which are good export earners.

(5) Entitlement of Domestic Tariff area sale increased to 50% of FOB value of the previous year, and Special Economic Zones were set up for manufacture and export of goods and services.

(6) Net Foreign exchange earnings, as a percentage of exports made uniform at 20% to both E.O.Us and EPZs.

(7) Institution of ombudsman for further redressal of the exporters' problems.

(8) EPCG scheme was further liberalised.

Export Credit Guarantee Corporation (ECGC) and Exporters

An exporter has to compete in the world markets and has to offer highly competitive terms, including short-term credit to the buyers. The ECGC helps him in the process by providing guarantee to the financing bank so that the exporter gets credit from his bank for purchase of goods for export or manufacture of goods for export and thus to expand his business. The ECGC helps to carry the credit risk for the commercial banks and guarantees payment from the buyer's risks — those relating to buyer, buyer's country for his funds. All export transactions carry heavy risks — commercial and political — those relating to buyer, buyer's country and unforeseen contingencies. If these risks are insured by an agency, the banks would be more willing to lend to the exporter. There risks are borne by ECGC.

ECGC's Role

The ECGC has a major role in insuring against the risks inherent in foreign trade and helping the growth of our foreign trade. The ECGC has about 10 branch offices with its Head Office at Mumbai. It is a government company and its administrative control is with the Ministry of Commerce and has a Board of Directors representing government, industry, trade, banking and other interests. It provides services which are not normally provided by commercial and insurance companies. The degree of risk involved by the coverage of ECGC is very high due to the nature of foreign trade, unknown creditworthiness of the foreign buyers and unpredictability of foreign political and commercial factors abroad and on sea. The services rendered by the ECGC are, therefore, highly valuable from the point of view of promoting India's foreign trade and foreign investment abroad.

The ECGC provides cover to various types of risks, namely, risk of not receiving payment from foreign buyers, trading on short-term credit, of not receiving payments in respect of deferred payment exports and in respect of services rendered and construction projects undertaken abroad.

The ECGC gives financial guarantees to the banks in respect of provision of credit to exporters in addition to its special schemes, such as transfer guarantee, buyers' and sellers', government line of credit, credit for joint ventures and overseas' investment.

Standard Policies Terms and Coverage, etc., are Subject to Change

On all standard policies, the ECGC bears up to 90 per cent of commercial and political risks. The commercial risks covered include insolvency of buyer, protracted default of buyer and non-acceptance of bills or failure of buyer. The political risks covered include changes in government policies, war, civil disturbances, etc., restrictions in the buyer's country, changes in import policy or export policy either in buyer's country or seller's country and any other losses in shipping due to changes in routes or accidents. Risks not covered by ECGC are due to disputes in quality, mechanical or inherent defects, failure of buyers to obtain proper government authorisations and defaults of the exporters and their agents and against exchange rate fluctuations.

Types of Policies

The ECGC has three major types of policies, viz., contracts policies, shipment policies and consignment export policies. The contracts policy starts from the date of entering into the contract with the foreign buyers and the shipment policy starts from the date of making the shipment from India. In the case of consignment exports, the policy would cover political risks from the date of shipment and comprehensive risks (all risks) from the date of sale of goods abroad to the foreign buyer.

The policy of the ECGC is to share risk with the exporters and the premium rates are accordingly fixed for each of the policies on a case-by-case basis.

Settlement of Claims

Generally, settlement of claims are made as early as possible after four months of the occurrence of the event of loss or due date. The date of occurrence of the event relates to the default of the foreign buyer or non-payment of claims on the due date. In case the buyer is insolvent the claim should be paid four months after the due date or one month after his loss is admitted in the insolvency court. Claims in respect of additional handling, change of route, interruption in transport or accidents would be paid on the production of proof of loss.

In case the exporter and the foreign buyer have gone into a court of law/for any non-fulfilment of contract terms, the ECGC could offer to pay claims only after the buyers' liability is established and the amount of the claim is also established by the court. Such claims would be paid direct to the financing bank of the exporter. When the exporter is at fault as per the contractual terms in respect of quality or time of delivery, the ECGC does not cover the loss involved.

Procedure for Insurance

There are application forms with various Regional Offices of the ECGC which are to be submitted to the nearest Regional Office with a policy fee which may be subject to changes. in the case of shipments policies, the exporter undertakes to submit monthly returns in respect of shipments made and the progress of the contractual terms. In the case of contracts policy, the exporter undertakes to send a declaration monthly on the contracts entered into during the preceding month, in addition to shipment made over that period. The ECGC should also get a monthly statement of all overdue payments so that it can take steps to avoid possible losses. The ECGC may charge additionally in case they require the bank reports on the foreign buyer.

Specific Policies*

While the above are whole turnover policies for regular and continuing exports, there are certain special policies designed for specific categories of exporters, such as services policy and construction works' policy. These two cover again only political risks or commercial and political risks (comprehensive risks) either with the private parties or with the government parties. The specific services contract policy covers both commercial and political risks (comprehensive policy) in respect of private party and only political risks in respect of contracts with foreign governments.

In respect of construction works policy, there are again two types of policies, viz., to cover — private parties and the government employers. The ECGC covers 85 per cent in respect of government employers and 75 per cent in respect of contracts with private parties. Generally, the ECGC encourages short and medium-term credits appropriate to the size of the order and type of goods.

In respect of all contracts involving exports on deferred payment terms such as capital goods, turn-key projects or construction works, services of consultancy, etc., the above specific policies are suitable. Such contracts of a value exceeding Rs. 50 lakhs are to be cleared by a Working Group consisting of RBI, IDBI and ECGC before the banks can take up the case. The exporter bank itself would send such proposals to the Working Group for clearance before proceeding further, as the ECGC clearance would be a pre-condition in many cases for extending bank finance.

In respect of these contracts, two types of covers are available, as referred to earlier, namely, Comprehensive Risks policy or Political Risks policy. The Comprehensive Risks policy covers insolvency of buyers, delay or protracted default in payment, restrictions on remittances or other restrictions in buyer's country, war or civil disturbances in buyers' country and government policy either in exporter or buyer country. The Political Risks policy covers only such of the above which are of political or civil nature. All the above policies covers up to 90 per cent of the loss of the seller in the case of services and up to 75 per cent — 85 per cent in the case of construction works. Premium rates and other terms depend upon the value and duration of the contracts, parties involved and assessed risks involved.

---

*Terms and Coverage, etc., are subject to change. These Include Short, Medium and Long-term Insurance Coverage.

The Berne Union

Reference may be made here in passing, to an international organisation designed to promote better coordination of national policies on export credit and insurance.

India is one of the member countries of the Berne Union started in 1934 whose basic objectives are as follows: (i) International acceptance of sound principles of export credit insurance and establishment of discipline in the terms of credit for international transactions, and (ii) International cooperation in fostering a favourable investment climate and in developing and maintaining sound principles of foreign investment insurance. Credit terms and insurance terms were extended and liberalised over the years and the Berne Union has only tried to limit competition and encourage understanding and promote standardisation of terms and conditions of export credit and insurance provided by countries.

Financial Guarantees

The ECGC guarantees also protect the banks from losses due to non-repayment of their advances from exporters although the benefits are accrued to both exporters and banks, covering the pre-shipment and post-shipment credit. They give protection to the banks against loss of money due to insolvency or default by exporters. This would encourage banks to provide liberal credit to exporters with a view to promoting foreign trade. Five types of guarantees have been evolved for this purpose — Packing credit guarantee, Post-shipment export credit guarantee, Export finance guarantee, Export production finance guarantee and Export performance guarantee. The ECGC pays the banks three-fourths of the loss in the case of Export finance guarantee, Post-shipment export credit guarantee and Export performance guarantee and two-thirds of the loss in the case of the rest.

Packing Credit Guarantee

Any advance given to an exporter for the purpose of purchase, manufacture, processing or packing of goods meant for export against a firm contract of sale, irrespective of the fact whether it is against a letter of credit or on credit terms qualifies for this guarantee. The risk covered is the loss suffered by a bank due to failure of the exporter to repay the insured debt because of his insolvency or protracted default, non-payment due to non-shipment of goods, non-delivery of valid shipping documents by the exporter to the lending institution. Two-thirds of the loss is paid by the ECGC.

Post-shipment Export Credit Guarantee

This guarantee is issued to banks to protect them from any loss from purchase, discount or negotiations of an export bill. It is normally given in respect of exporters who have taken an appropriate shipments policy. It protects the bank against protracted default or insolvency of the exporter and the coverage is up to three-fourths of the loss.

Export Finance Guarantee

This enables the bank to offer discounting facilities up to 125 per cent of the value of shipping documents in case the domestic costs are higher than the export price. This provision enables the exporter to cover all his domestic costs and not merely the export value by bank finance. The coverage is up to 75 per cent of the loss due to insolvency or default of exporter. Normally, this cover is up to the amount of cash assistance/customs/excise duty drawbacks admissible to the exporter from the government.

Export Production Finance Guarantee

In case the f.o.b. values of exported commodities are lower than the domestic prices, certain incentives are granted by the government to the exporters. As they will take time to realise, bank finance is needed in the intervening period. The guarantee seeks to fund needed finance up to 50 per cent over and above the f.o.b. value of exports at the pre-shipment or post-shipment stages. The coverage is up to two-thirds of the loss if any, incurred by banks due to insolvency or default by the exporter.

Export Performance Guarantee

This has been evolved to help exporters to secure on easier terms, bank guarantees they have to furnish in the course of export business. Bank guarantees are needed for exporters in the case of many government contracts or services/construction contracts. Exporters need not have to deposit cash of huge margins for securing bank guarantee if this ECGC cover is available. This guarantee is issued to the bank if bank guarantees are required for: (a) Exporting goods without payment of Central excise duty; (b) For importing raw material without payment of customs duty or indigenous raw materials without payment of excise duty for the manufacture of exports in bond; (c) For import of raw materials or capital goods with an export obligation; (d) In case foreign buyers make advance payment to the exporters; (e) If exporter has to give bank guarantee for performance of an export contract; and (f) If exporters have to pay earnest money to participate in foreign tenders.

There are also special schemes which are offered by the ECGC such as transfer guarantee which seeks to insure the risk which the banks get exposed to on confirmation they might add to the letters of credit opened by them in favour of Indian exporters due to certain political risks. Insurance is also given for finance granted to foreign buyers (Buyer's credit) and foreign governments (lines of credit) by Indian banks and these are export credits granted to foreign buyers for the purpose of enabling them to buy from Indian exporters. Besides, the joint venture insurance policies of the ECGC would cover the risk involved in the Indian parties' involvement in joint ventures up to the value of the special contracts placed outside the country. The Indian exporters having joint projects with advanced countries for investments in third countries would be able to utilise this service and the coverage of insurance is to the extent of liability of the Indian investor in the third country or a percentage share of the total contract. Similar coverage is also available for Indian investment abroad in respect of Indian participation in the third party countries, or Indian joint ventures, construction projects or turnkey projects. The cover would be available to the extent of the principal amount invested or to the amount of loans made available by Indians abroad and to the dividend or interest payable thereon. This cover is available for a period from 15 to 20 years on a sliding scale. Lastly, there are certain special schemes for small exporters whose turnover is not more than Rs. 10 lakhs. There have been some relaxations in respect of each of the policies to small exporters by offering them higher percentage of cover or lower charges, etc.

24 Export-import Procedures and Documentation

The starting point of an international commercial transaction is an enquiry from a party abroad about the terms of sale of any commodity. The exporter then sends his quotations for various types and qualities of his products either in rupees/dollars or other currencies along with samples, if necessary. These quotations may be on cost ex works basis or cost plus freight (C&F) or cost, insurance plus freight (c.i.f.) basis which are explained later. When the importer and exporter agree on the terms, then a sale contract is entered into. This can be a formal legal contract or informal written agreement or even an exchange of correspondence evidencing the intention to buy and sell. A sale contract incorporates the terms and conditions, quality and quantity of the goods, packing and specifications, the place and mode of delivery, the period of delivery, payment terms, prices accepted, etc. Normally, the exporter has to add to his ex-works price the cost of: (a) Transport from his factory to the port; (b) Port Commissioner's charges; (c) Shipping, freight and other forwarding agents' fees, handling charges, etc.; (d) Insurance from warehouse, etc.

Foreign Enquiries

Exporters and importers would first get to know of foreign offers to buy or sell from the Indian Trade Missions abroad, Indian Embassies, Trade Development Authority in India, various Chambers of Commerce, government bodies such as the Export Promotion Councils, Commodity Boards, Development Councils, etc. The global or regional tenders and trade enquiries are published in the Financial News Bulletins, daily papers, Weekly or Monthly Bulletins of the Ministry of Commerce, DGCI&S, Chambers of Commerce or TDA, etc. Sometimes, the exporters get in touch with importers through their own agencies, correspondents and branches abroad. They may also get to know of the enquiries from the Trade Missions or Trade Consuls to various countries in India and Joint Chambers like Indo-American Chamber, etc. Exporters and importers would keep in touch with these agencies and their publications, bulletins, etc. Lastly, often, participation in foreign exhibitions, trade fairs, visits abroad and business contract abroad also help secure foreign contracts.

Sale Terms

Sale terms should be clearly stated whether ex-works, f.o.b., c.f. or c.i.f. In international trade, disputes can be avoided by clearly specifying the rights and obligations of both parties to the contract, viz., seller and buyer. The International Chamber of Commerce provides guidelines regarding these rights and obligations, some of which are referred to in the Appendix.

In an ex-works quotation, ownership of goods is transferred at the octroi itself from the seller to buyer. The buyer or his agent arranges for transportation to the port, its loading, shipping, insurance, clearance, etc. The examples are the purchase of jute goods, tea, etc., in Kolkata by the agents of the USSR, Syria and Iran.

In an f.o.b. quotation (free on board) or f.a.s. (free along side) the seller delivers the goods on board the ship named by the buyer while the subsequent responsibility lies with the buyer or his agents. In a c.f. quotation, the seller is responsible for transport to the ship, loading and shipping, etc., while the insurance is borne by the buyer. In the c.i.f. quotation, even the insurance is borne by the seller and he includes in the price quoted, the cost of goods, packing handling, loading, transport, shipping and insurance. C.i.f. and c quotation includes cost, insurance, freight and commissions.

The terms of sales depend on the custom of trade, nature of the product sold, profit margins in the trade, legal and government controls in the respective countries, organisation of the firm and the circumstances of the buyer and seller.

Role of Freight and Insurance

During the new millennium so far 2000 to 2010, exports from India have grown at a sharper rate than before, namely at around a simple average rate of 20%. This should have led to a similar rise in our transportation and insurance income. The pattern of invoicing, as seen in a sample study of RBI (RBI Bulletin, Feb.2006) is as follows for the above years:

Method of Invoicing	%age to Total (Range)
FoB	46 to 54%
CIf	18 to 25%
Cf	26 to 31%
CI	Around 1%

The study relates to the period 2001 to 2005. The component of freight and insurance depends on the method of invoicing basically. But behind this facade, there are many influencing factors like the mode of transport, nature of commodity exported, size in terms of value of goods, the destination of exports, geographical distance between exporters and importers and the policy of the Governments of the concerned countries, accessibility of ports of sea, land routes or Air routes, etc. To elucidate, exports of high value but low size are generally sent by air, while those in bulk size, like wheat, cement, paddy etc. are sent by sea. Those sent by land are to adjacent nations like Pakistan, Nepal, Bhutan, etc. The high value goods like gems, jewellery, perishable commodities are preferred to be sent by sea/air depending on the destination. Thus fruits, vegetables, flowers, marine products (shrimps) are generally sent by air, due to the urgency of time element to the buyer in such cases.

As per the RBI Survey, the ratio of freight and insurance is around 6% of the value f.o.b. of exports if sent by Air, 5% if sent by sea and around 2% if sent by land. But these ratios depend more importantly on the destination of exports. Thus in the case of U.S., UK, Canada, Australia, EU countries, this ratio is the highest at 7 to 8%, if sent by Air and at 5 to 6% if sent by sea. The element of insurance in particular is invariably less than 1% of the f.o.b. value of exports, whatever is the destination, although there are minor differences as between exports sent by sea and Air and they also vary with the commodity, its nature, bulk, value and destination, etc. As between Air and Sea, the difference is between one or two percentage points. As per the RBI Survey data, the highest ratio of 8.8% was noticed in the case of exports to UK by Air, for 2004-05. The next highest ratio is in the case of South Africa whether sent by Air or Sea.

Another point noticed in the survey data is that the insurance component of the f.o.b. value of exports came down over the years due to privatisation of insurance sector, and the prevailing competitive market environment in the insurance field following the recent reforms in privatisation and liberalisation of foreign investment in Indian industrial and manufacturing sector.

Generally, the Government Policy is to encourage the inflows through their own shipping and insurance and this leads to exporters preferring their own shipping and insurance agents, who are forced to quote competitive rates due to globalisation and prevailing market competition. But if the buyer-importer prefers to carry the goods by their own transport agencies, the exporter will have no significant role in the invoicing method.

An examination of dependence of freight and insurance on the value of goods exported showed that whether sent by Air or land route, the freight cost is inversely proportional to the value of goods exported. When sent by sea, the ratio of freight to the f.o.b. value of exports is high in the lower and upper size classes. This is to be explained by the fact that the requirement and availability of the number of containers to be shipped. More number of containers are required, when the value and bulk of the goods to be shipped exceeds a certain level in general. Cargo handling by ships and by Air differ widely and this explains the difference in the freight component of the f.o.b. value of exports.

Payment Terms

The terms relating to payment should also be clearly stated in the sales contract itself. If payment is arranged within a period of six months, this is called short-term payment and the exchange control rules in India necessitate in general, all receipts to be secured within six months of the date of shipment. This was relaxed after effecting free convertibility of rupee on trade account in March 1993. Payment terms depend upon the commodity sold, position of the buyer and seller, trade practices and availability of bank credit. Some of the important terms of payment leaving aside the letters of credit involving bank credit which will be discussed later are cash with order, consignment sales and open account.

(1) Cash with Order: Cash with order or advance payment is the best term possible which is accepted by the buyers only in extraordinary circumstances when the goods are to be the buyer's specifications and no other buyer may be willing to take them. Exchange Control regulations now permit advance payment in certain cases.

(2) Consignment Sales: Goods like tea, coffee, wool, etc., which cannot be standardised and where the produce should be available in the foreign market physically to be sold are sent on a consignment basis. The consignment is to an agent or representative abroad whose integrity and credit worthiness are known to the exporter. Sometimes, the consignee executes a bank guarantee to the effect that as and when goods are sold, the sale proceeds will be duly remitted. In this case, banks enter into the transaction either as remitting agency for importers or collecting agency for exporters.

(3) Open Account: Goods are sold on open account when there will be no drawing of bills or other documents to negotiate by banks. "On payment" is made at periodical intervals by DDs, TTs, etc., as and when the sales are made. Such terms are limited only to subsidiaries, associate firms or closely connected firms such as foreign collaborators.

Buyers' Credit

If credit is granted to the buyer by a financial institution in the seller country or a financial institution in the buyer country, then it is called buyer's credit. The buyer enters into an agreement with the financial institutions to pay the supplier on cash basis or document basis and credit granted to the buyers for the purpose. The financial agreement between the buyers and the financial institution lays down the conditions to be fulfilled by the supplier before payment is made to him such as the form, values and maturity of promissory notes, the form in which the supplier must present the claims and bills to the financing bank, interest rate applicable, credit repayment terms, taxes, commission and other charges to be paid by the borrower, and the procedure to be followed in the case of defaults. Such credits are generally granted by the supplier country's financial institution like EXIM Bank for periods ranging from 5 to 10 years. The supplier in such cases gets the government and the central bank's clearance for arranging this type of credit.

Lines of Credit

A line of credit is granted by a foreign government or an international institution in the buyer country so that a larger number of buyers could benefit from it. This generally is available for a programme such as Railways, Roads, Electricity, Water Supply, etc., and the responsibility for assessing the creditworthiness of the buyers or of the project is passed on to the buyer country's financial institution. Such credit lines are granted to cost while ICICI in India by the German banks and UK banks for purchase of capital goods and machinery in respect of plastics, drugs, etc., and by the IDBI to Bangladesh, Malaysia, Mauritius, etc.

Letters of Credit — Documentary and Non-documentary

Letter of credit is the most important mode of payment for trade throughout the world. As the buyers and sellers are often not known to each other and the bankers are well known for their credit standing, the bank's creditworthiness is substituted for the creditworthiness of the buyer under this method. The documentary L/C is an undertaking given by the bank to pay or accept the bill provided the beneficiary (exporter) fulfils the terms and conditions of sale as set out in the application made to the bank by the importer (buyer). Generally, banks follow in India uniform customs and practice code in the issue of the documentary credits which will be binding as between banks and between banks and customers. The documentary credit protects the seller from the risk of loss of funds due to the uncertain credit position of the buyer and promotes foreign trade and foreign investment. The bank charges from the buyer-importer at the interest rate admissible for the credit so granted and may or may not ask for a margin deposit of funds for the purpose. The banks also charge for the handling of documents in the process of negotiation or collection. In the case of non-documentary credits, no documents need accompany the Bill of Exchange in which case the exporter bank only arranges to collect the amounts involved and no handling charges may be levied.

Net to Replace LC

Globalisation is bringing about many changes in the pattern of trade and pattern of financing. The terms of Global trade are changing by dropping some old antiquated instruments like Letter of Credit. Indian suppliers might find it difficult to insist on the formalities of L.C. and other documentation. The US Global buyer might find the LC a botheration and time consuming.

The new system is "Open Account Trading" which involves both buyer and seller consumating their transaction through the Net. The terms are accepted by the parties and an international banker acceptable to both, say Stanchart, HSBC or Citi- Bank will get involved in financing of it. The Buyer in US is a large MNC and a global player and wants to buy from a small or medium size supplier in India.

The buyer in US uses the technology to send a purchase order directly to its bank, after the buyer and seller agree on terms on the internet. The bank notifies electronically the seller in India to prepare for shipment and its readiness to provide preshipment credit through its Indian Branch. The Bank should have been convinced of the credentials and credit worthiness of buyer/seller through his bankers. Both the buyer/seller and banker should be using the same software. The seller prepares the documents which can be verified, electronically, by the buyer and his banker. The shipping company and insurance company who are part of the supply chain will confirm their commitments on the same electronic platform. Once the buyer's banker is satisfied that the shipments are made and insurance is valid, he makes the final payment on the orders and as per terms of the credit with the buyer MNC.

This new system through the internet, saves the time and work involved by outsourcing a number of steps in the supply chain by the buyer and the banker also saves time and work involved in the physical scrutiny of the documents.

Types of Credit

Documentation in respect of credit will depend upon the type of credit available from banks.

(a) Revocable or Irrevocable: While revocable credit can be cancelled at any time without the concurrence of the beneficiary, the irrevocable credit cannot be so revoked.

The revocable letter of credit, according to the International Chamber of Commerce, is "not a legally binding undertaking between the bank or banks concerned and the beneficiary". Irrevocable letter of credit is a definite undertaking on the part of the issuing banks and constitutes an obligation to the beneficiary to honour bills or drafts under the credit, provided the terms and conditions of the credit are complied with. Even the revocable credit is good until it is cancelled and the cancellation is notified to the beneficiary and/or his bank and proves the bonafides and the intention of importing by the buyers.

(b) Confirmed and Unconfirmed Credits: A documentary L/C which is irrevocable can be confirmed or unconfirmed. The confirmation of the importer bank is communicated through its correspondent or agent or branch in the exporter's country. If it is an irrevocable credit, the latter bank — correspondent, agent or branch — confirms the credit to the beneficiary. The confirmation adds further strength to the exporter in his own country by his own banker. If the local bank advises the credit without confirming, it, it is called "unconfirmed credit". While the confirming bank has an obligation to negotiate bills under this credit drawn by the beneficiary, the advising or notifying bank has no such obligation.

(c) Transferable Credit: It is one which contains an express provision that the benefits under it to be enjoyed by the beneficiary can be transferred from the latter to a third party who supplies him raw materials for this manufacture or supplies manufactured outputs if he is a merchant trader.

(d) Back-to-back Credits: There are the secondary credits opened by a bank on behalf of the beneficiary of an original credit in favour of the domestic supplier. This is a formal opening of another credit line on the basis of credit to the beneficiary. Suppose a London importer of tea opens a confirmed irrevocable Letter of Credit through the Barclays Bank in London to the Bank of India in Kolkota. As the tea merchant has to buy tea from a tea producer, the former may arrange with the Bank of India to issue a confirmed letter in favour of the tea producer for his use in the manufacturing process. This is known as "back-to-back credit".

(e) Red Clause or Green Clause: This is incorporated only in irrevocable credits and authorises the negotiating bank to make advances to the beneficiary to enable him to manufacture or purchase the goods from the local suppliers. When relations between the exporter and importer are close or they are connected as collaborators or suppliers of long standing, then the red clause is incorporated in the L/C at the request of the importer buyer for the benefit of the exporter. Such clauses are used in packing credit arrangements in wool exports, tea exports, etc.

(f) Revolving Credits: These credits are granted on a revolving basis to suit the requirements of suppliers who are doing this business on a continuing basis. This credit obviates the need for opening fresh letters for each shipment. As soon as the negotiated drafts under the credit are reimbursed by the importer to the bank opening the credit, fresh credit is available to the foreign negotiating bank.

It will thus be seen from the above discussion that the parties to the L/C besides the buyer, beneficiary and the issuing bank are the notifying bank which advises the credit to the exporter in his country, confirming bank which confirms the credit to exporter in his country, the negotiating bank which negotiates the drafts, bills of exchange, etc., and the paying bank which finally pays to the exporter. If the notifying bank also confirms the credit and negotiates the bills, then all the three parties are merged into one bank. The paying bank may be the original issuing bank in the buyer's country in which case, the bill is drawn in the foreign currency (from the point of view of exporter) or by the notifying or confirming bank in which case the bill is drawn and paid in the local currency of the exporter.

Main Documents of Foreign Trade

The documents used in foreign trade are broadly of two categories, namely substantive documents and auxiliary documents. In the first category are included: (1) Bill of Lading, (2) Marine Insurance and (3) Bill of Exchange. The auxiliary instruments are commercial invoices, consular invoice, custom invoice, certificate of origin, inspection certificate, packing list, etc.

(1) Bill of Lading

The Bill of Lading is an important document issued by a common carrier, namely, the shipping company or Airways, stating that the goods mentioned therein have been received for shipment or airlift and that it has undertaken to deliver the goods at a named destination on payment of freight or for which freight has already been paid (c.i.f. or c.f.). The Bill of Lading is a document of title to goods, transferable by endorsement and is a receipt from the shipping company regarding the number of packages with a particular weight and markings and a contract for the transportation of the same to a port of destination mentioned therein. The shipping company is governed by the carriage of goods by the Sea Act which provides protection to shippers and obligations on the shipping companies.

A Bill of Lading stating "Received for shipment" is not adequate if the sales terms are "on board". The Bill should specify that goods have been "on board" or "shipped" to satisfy the terms of c.i., or c.i.f.

Bills of Lading are the following types: (a) Freight paid or freight payable. In the case of c.i.f. or c.f., the freight should be paid by the shipper and in case of f.o.b., it may be payable by the consignee or importer or his agent. The Bill of Lading "Freight collect" is, therefore, not proper tender for c.i.f. terms of sale; (b) Clean or claused bill. In the case of any adverse remarks such as "damaged bags" or "bill torn" or "Drums dirty or old", such bill are called "claused" or dirty bills as against clean bills which do not mention anything adverse on the condition of packages, (c) Stale bills of lading. If the bills are kept for too long with the shipper and by that time goods might have reached the destination port, the importer has to pay demurrages for non-acceptance of the goods which is due to delay in the receipt of shipping documents. Such delayed bills of lading are called "Stale Bills".

Mate's Receipt: When goods are delivered to the agent of a shipping company for shipment by a specified vessel and he agrees to do so, then a Mate's Receipt is given to the shipper. This is exchanged for a regular Bill of Lading from the Master of the ship or the shipping company. Mate's Receipt is, however, not an acceptable document to the Bank from the point of its negotiation. For such terms as "on board" or shipped or c.i.f. or c.f., this is not adequate delivery.

Through or Transhipment Bills: If the transportation involves more than one mode, namely, ship, rail, road etc., then a "Through Bill" is issued. Such bills are not accepted by some bankers as they are not certain about the state in which goods will reach the consignee after all the transhipments. If the sale terms are specific about "on board" or "shipped" only such terms are to be used and transhipment bills are avoided. There has been more recently cases of exports using more than one means of transport, in India which gave rise to combined transport documents. In the case of inland container depots in Bangalore, Delhi, Guntur and Coimbatore, for example, export cargo may be loaded direct at these dry ports' involving transport by land/air/sea leading to the use of combined transport documents. India was making efforts to get these documents officially recognised by the International Chamber of Commerce and U.N. bodies.

Charter Party Bill: When goods are in bulk, a shipper or a group of shippers charter a complete vessel for transport of those goods. Such bills arising out of Charter Vessels are called "Charter Party Bills". If a charter agreement is not known to a third party who has booked on this vessel, the Bills of Lading arising out of this are not so attractive to bankers as they do not know their route and destinations and the time periods involved.

Negotiability of Bills of Lading: All Bills of Lading are negotiable if the terms used are "consignee or his order" or the "party or his order". The Bills are issued in triplicate — all in original and signed by the Master of the ship. When any one is used for taking delivery of goods, the others become invalid.

Airway Bills: Airway Bills is specifically designed for quick transport; it is a document of title to goods but not negotiable. They are generally made out in the name of the consignee who takes delivery and makes payment. Three parts of the Airways Bill are issued — the first part marked for "Carrier", second for the consignee and the third for the consignor. While the first is signed by the consignor and the second is signed by both the consignor and the carrier, the third is signed by the carrier or his agent.

(2) Marine Insurance Policy

As the banks are lending against goods in transport, they wish to avoid risks of loss and invariably insist on insurance. Marine insurance is done through a policy of insurance taken at a stated premium and is quasi-negotiable instrument. This policy indemnifies the party-shipper against the normal marine losses or perils of the sea, such as damages to the vessel, or cargo by accidents or casualties, fire, jettison, natural calamities, etc. Marine insurance policy generally has a legal standing and not a certificate of insurance. The bank has to scrutinise whether there are any added clauses on the policy, the amount covered, voyages and goods covered and the risks covered and the extent of the coverage. The "Institute Clauses" are the standard policy clauses which are included and attached and amplified in the policy to avoid misunderstanding. Such clauses are accepted by the Institute of London Underwriters.

Types of Losses: (a) Total loss. (b) General average loss borne proportionately by all interests at risk. (c) Partial loss on particular average loss but not of a general type if the ship is sunk, burnt or stranded. (d) Losses attributed to fire, explosion, collision, etc. (e) Discharge at a port of distress. (f) Special charges for landing, warehousing, forwarding, etc.

(FPA) Free of Particular Average Policy: This policy covers losses or damages falling under a particular average clause. This is a minimum liability insurance and gives only partial cover for losses.

Particular Average (WPA) Clauses: This widens the range of partial losses covered above at a slightly higher premium. WPA clauses generally cover all marine losses plus General Average losses plus particular average losses if the loss is above a specified value of shipped goods and up to a percentage value of goods. This gives fuller protection than the FPA clauses.

All Risks Clause: This gives 100 per cent protection in respect of risks covered but not cover risks due to war, strikes, riots, inherent vice or damage in the goods, etc. Sometimes, arrangements are made for more than 100 per cent coverage of risks at a extra premium. As none of the above policies covers war risks, strikes, riots, civil commotion, etc., if any, the party desiring to have them, has to have additional cover for them.

Warehouse to Warehouse Cover: This is a comprehensive cover called transit clause covering protection from the commencement of transit to the final destination.

Action for Claiming Indemnity: The concerned bank holding the policy should give prompt notice to insurers, carriers and all parties concerned in the event of damage of loss. A survey of the loss should be got done to assess the extent and the degree of damage and send a claim to insurers accordingly in time. The documents required to be submitted for claim either for partial loss or full loss coverage are the insurance policy, packing list, weight list, bills of lading, invoice, Master's

Protest certifying any unusual happening on the voyage, survey report on the nature and extent of damage, etc.

Types of Insurance Documents

There are various types of insurance policies such as floating policy, open cover policy, specific policy, etc. Of these, specific policy is most acceptable, from the point of view of the banker.

(a) Floating Policy: A floating policy is a contract of insurance to cover a number of shipments the maximum value of which is given but the details of which such as the name of the vessel, destination, weight and specification of cargo, etc., are not declared. These details are expected to be filled in or endorsed on it later. This is not, however, valid from the point of view of the banker unless the sale terms include the tender of such an insurance certificate.

(b) Open Cover Policy: This is an insurance contract open for a period of time or on a permanent basis for cover of a number of shipments of which the value and type of cover are all pre-determined. Like the floating policy, its coverage is not for any specific goods, but unlike the floating policy, the details of shipment, value of goods on voyage, conditions of cover etc., are all known beforehand. Like the floating policy, an open policy is also not legally acceptable document of title to goods from the point of view of bankers in many countries, including India.

(c) Certificate of Insurance: Insurers issue certificates of insurance stating that certain specified goods are covered under an open policy or floating policy. In such cases, the policy is retained in the custody of the shippers. Unless such certificates are authorised in the sale terms, bankers are reluctant to accept them due to non-negotiability of the documents in the absence of policy of insurance.

(d) Specific Policy: A specific policy is a contract of insurance which covers a specific shipment. Such a policy is most acceptable to the bankers due to its negotiability as it is available for attachment with the relative documents.

(3) Bills of Exchange

As the bill of exchange is an important document used in foreign trade, it is pertinent to know about its nature and content here in detail. A Bill of Exchange is according to the Indian Negotiable Instruments Act, 1881, "an instrument in writing containing an unconditional order signed by the maker, directing a certain person to pay a certain sum of money only to or to the order of a certain person or to the bearer of the Instrument".

Legal Requirements

The bill is a legal document. It should satisfy the following requirements:

(1) It must be an unconditional order, not containing any clauses or conditions.

(2) It must be an order in writing.

(3) It must be addressed by one person, drawer, to another person, drawee, whether he be individual/partnership firm or company or any legal entity.

(4) It must be signed by the drawer who is giving the order and in the case of a firm or company by the person authorised to sign.

(5) It must be payable on demand or at a determinable future date — "on sight or usance of 30 or 60 or 90 days after sight". "Sighting the bill" means the formal acceptance by the drawee.

(6) It must be payable to order or to bearer. In order to be able to negotiate, the bill must be a bearer bill with words "to order".

(7) It must be for a specified amount and must be written in both words and figures.

The parties to a bill of exchange are the drawer, the drawee and the payee, the endorser and the endorsee. The drawer is the person who draws the bill while the drawee is the person on whom it is drawn. The payee may be the drawee or his bank or the person specified therein or bearer. The endorser is the bank who has acquired the rights of payment to itself from the payee and he has placed his name and signature at the back of the bill signifying that he has acquired the title to the bill and payment is due to him. The endorsee is the person to whom it is endorsed and can secure payment from the drawee. In the case of a correspondent bank who has secured the right of receipt, it can be an endorsee to the bill. The endorsement may be of different types; (i) Blank endorsement which is a mere signature on the back of the bill; (ii) Special endorsement which mentions the name of the person to whom it is payable; (iii) Restrictive endorsement such as "Pay to Barclays only" which prohibits further endorsement; (iv) Qualified endorsement which has some qualifying conditions such as negotiated "without recourse". Qualified endorsement as well as restrictive endorsement would not be acceptable for further negotiation.

The advantages of a bill of exchange if it is not restrictive or qualified are as follows: (1) It is negotiable and the holder in due course gets the right of receipt of money under it; (2) It is protected under law and the rights and obligations of parties are clearly specified under law; (3) The title is passed on by mere endorsement and is easy to handle or negotiate; (4) The trader has an advantage in that, he can get his funds without tying them up for long from a financial institution through negotiation, purchase or discount, etc.

The bills of exchange can be classified as follows:

(1) Clean Bills and Documentary Bills: While clean bills are not accompanied by shipping documents, documentary bills are accompanied by them. Collection charges for the latter are more due to the responsibility and expense of handling the accompanying documents.

(2) Documentary Bills: May be those against payment (DP) or against acceptance (DA): Documents on acceptance are released to the drawee on his acceptance of the bill. Documents on payment will require the importer-drawee to pay before obtaining the possession of documents.

(3) D. P. Bills may be sight bills or payable against documents. Sight bills are payable at sight or on demand but a grace period of two days is normally allowed for the drawee to scrutinise the documents and arrange for payment. All D.P. bills are normally sight bills, payable on demand. Usance bills are payable after a period of time counted from the date of sighting (signature of the payee) or from the date mentioned by the drawer on the bill. The former are called "After sight bills" and the latter "after date bills". As D.P. bills are payable on delivery of documents, the terms of payment are also called "cash against delivery" (c.a.d.).

Other Foreign Trade Procedures

In foreign trade, a number of other documents arise out of the essential nature of the transaction involved. As soon as a sale contract is entered into, the goods are manufactured as per the specifications required and would be kept ready for quality control and pre-shipment inspection.

Quality control and pre-shipment inspection are carried out in accordance with the Export Quality Control and Inspection Act of 1963 by the Export Inspection Council. This inspection could be arranged at the factory premises or at the warehouses kept by the port authorities, and is designed to protect the interests of our country vis-a-vis other countries.

The shipper-exporter would get in touch with the forwarding and clearing agents who work for a commission to get the shipping space allocated for the exports. The exporter formally applies for space in the ship for his destination in a ship destined to reach the mentioned port. The shipping company issues a shipping order or a shipping advice giving an allotment of space in the export cargo. In the case of shipping advice, it is only an intimation about the availability of space in a ship while the shipping order is an instruction to the commanding officer of the ship that the goods would be received on board a specified ship mentioned therein. The goods are sent from the factory through a lorry with a lorry ticket along with a form called dock challan giving the details about the consignment, its marks, number, description, weight and measurements, etc. The goods meant for a particular ship are then sent to the shed with a landing slip along with a payment called "the landing charge".

The cargo will be weighted and measured prior to shipment on the basis of which freight is charged. This is done at the time of loading at the shed vessel or at the time of overside loading. These details about measurement, weights, etc., are recorded in the dock challan or boat note. Dock challan is an intermediate note or receipt for goods in the dock pending shipment if the ship is berthed at the yard. Boat note is a receipt of goods on boat for transhipment to a ship stationed in the mid-steam. The exporter would pay the following charges to the Port Commissioners before the goods are sent to the ship: unloading and loading, river dues, surcharge, toll charge, rent, etc., except the dues to the boatman or bargeman.

The next step is customs checking at the shipyard. The objectives of the custom check are to see that the goods sent out are permissible and to ensure that all the formalities required by the law of the land are complied with and where a licence is required the same has been obtained. The customs check can be done either at the factory by sending a customs appraiser to check to consignment at the factory premises or in the shed of the shipping company or shipyard before it is loaded on the ship. The customs appraiser has to satisfy himself that the real value of the goods declared is the f.o.b. value, that there is no under-invoicing and that the shipping bill has been properly prepared as to the number, quantities and other details about the cargo. The Preventive Officer on board the ship would check a proportion of the packages before the shipment is allowed as to the admissibility of the exports. After the customs appraiser and the Preventive Officer are both satisfied, they will endorse the dock challan, if goods are sent for shed vessels and on the boat note if the goods are sent for overside loading.

A number of ancillary instruments such as certificate of origin, consular invoice, commercial invoice etc., are also required by the exporter. The certificate of origin is given generally by a Chamber of Commerce, Board, etc., authorised by the government to issue such certificate and it would indicate that the country from which the goods are exported is the country in which the goods have originated.

Invoice is a statement of account sale rendered by the seller to the buyer indicating the quantity and quality of the goods sold and debt owed by the buyer to the seller on that account. The major types of invoices are: Customs invoice and Consular invoice. The customs invoice indicates the value of the goods declared by the customs in a special form to be filled by the shipper. The consular invoice relates to a certificate recording the volume, value, quality grade, source, etc., of the export as certified by the Consular office of the importing country located in the exporter's country. Such certificates are required by some countries, particularly the USA, Canada, Philippines and Mexico and are granted by their Consular offices.

All the above invoices may not be required in all cases and normally only commercial invoice as originally submitted by the exporter would be required. This invoice is duly filled in and submitted by the seller in a set of 3 copies giving the details about the unit price, value of goods, contents of each of the packages, quality and specifications etc. In most cases, the buyer may ask only for commercial invoice unless the government of his country has laid down rules with regard to certificate of origin, consular invoice, etc., without which goods cannot be imported.

In the case of some exports, the importer might ask for a weight note or an analysis certificate or any other special documents. The weight note can be secured at the time of loading a ship or boat from the customs/shipping companies while the analysis certificate can be got from the Quality Control Agency or pre-shipment Inspection Agency.

APPENDIX

Uniform Customs and Practices for Documentary Credits

In order to enable banks in all countries to follow uniform practices with regard to the handling of documentary credits the International Chamber of Commerce has published a document embodying these customs and practices adopted by banks (International Chamber of Commerce Publication No. 290). These customs and practices relating to documentary credits are binding on all the parties. The expression. "documentary credits", "transferable credits", "revocable credits" and "irrevocable credits" are all clearly defined in this document. The obligations and responsibilities of the issuing bank, negotiating bank and accepting bank are also set out here. Credits by their nature are separate transactions from the sales or other contracts and credit instructions must be clear and separate from the sale and other contracts.

Articles 1 to 6 of Uniform Customs Rules clearly describe the form and notification of credits, revocable, irrevocable, confirmed and unconfirmed credits, etc. Articles 7 to 13 state the liabilities of the banks and the care to be taken by them in handling these documents. Banks have to examine all documents with reasonable care to ascertain that they are in accordance with the terms and conditions of the credit. The banks assume no liability for the form, sufficiency, accuracy, genuineness etc., of any documents or for delay in transit or mutilation or loss in transit or for acts of God or for any acts done in good faith in accordance with the term and conditions of credit.

Among the documents to be handled by bank, shipping documents evidencing the shipment or despatch are referred to in the Articles 15 to 18. All instruments should be clear and precise. The instructions to issue, confirm or advise a credit must state precisely the documents against which payment, acceptance or negotiation to be made. The banks can accept all documents as tendered when such vague terms as "first class" or "well known" are used.

The date of bill of lading will evidence the date of shipment or despatch and bill of lading must show that the goods are loaded on board a named vessel. Mere "delivered to deck" or "loaded on deck" would not be adequate. If prepayment of freight is indicated by an appropriate stamp, that is evidence of the payment of freight.

A clean shipping document is one which bears no superimposed clause declaring a defective condition of the goods or packaging. Banks can refuse to accept such documents unless the credit terms authorise them to do so. Bills of lading by the forwarding agents or issued under a charter party or covering shipment by sailing vessels will not be accepted. Transhipment bills and through bills covering transhipment en route or travel through several modes are accepted. The banks will accept a combined transport document involving more than one mode of transport and other shipping documents such as inland water way bill or consignment note, postal receipt, certificate of mailing or air consignment, etc.

Insurance documents must be specified in the credit terms and must be issued by insurance companies or their agents but not by brokers. The insurance document must be expressed in the same currency as the credit and the cover should be effective at the time of shipment or despatch.

Commercial invoices must be made in the name of the applicant for the credit and the amounts involved should not exceed the credit limits permitted by the issuing bank. Under Article 35 partial shipments and shipments in instalments are allowed unless prohibited in credit terms. Under Article 37 the credits must stipulate the expiry date for presentation of documents. The expiry date includes the date mentioned in the words "up to", "to", "until", etc., and if it falls on a holiday; extended up to the next following business day. Expiry date either for shipment or presentation of documents may be extended by mutual consent of the parties, but banks paying, accepting or negotiating under such extended expiry date must add to the documents the fact of such extension and presentation within the expiry date extended in accordance with Article 39 of the "Uniform Customs".

The terms used in credits are to be as clear as possible. For example, the words "departure", "despatch", "loading" will be construed by banks as synonymous with shipment. The expression "on or about" and similar expressions would be construed as a period falling within 5 days on either side of the specified date. If no date for presentation for payment is stipulated, banks may refuse documents presented after more than 21 days of the issuance of bills of lading or other shipping documents.

The "Uniform Customs" also specifies the practices of banks and the terms to be used. It clarifies the terms such as first half or second half of a month or middle or end of a month. Where an issuing bank does not specify the date for the currency of credit available, the confirming or advising bank may confirm the date.

Article 46 of the "Uniform Customs" deals with transferable credits. A credit is transferable if it is expressly designed so by the issuing bank. Partial or full credits are transferable as per terms of credit by which the beneficiary can give instructions for transfer to third parties the benefits under the credit.

Uniform Rules of Collection

The International Chamber of Commerce has laid down in their Publication No. 322 uniform rules for collection by banks. Collection means the handling by banks of documents on instructions received from their correspondents or principals in order to obtain acceptance or to deliver documents for acceptance or payment. There are two types of documents — financial documents, namely, bills of exchange, Promissory notes, cheques, etc., and Commercial documents. namely, invoices, shipping and insurance documents, etc. While clean collection refers to collection of financial documents, documentary collection means collection of financial documents along with commercial documents or only of commercial documents.

The banks have to act in good faith and verify that the documents are all as per the collection order. The collecting bank will act as per instructions from the principal or the remitting bank and is to be indemnified by the latter for all liabilities or obligations imposed by foreign laws or usages. The collecting bank has no responsibility for transit delays, errors in transition or interpretation of technical terms or for acts of God or nature.

Documents are to be presented by the bank without delay and in the accepted form in which they are received, after affixing their stamp, if necessary. In the case of documentary collection, in the absence of specific instructions, documents must be delivered against payments only.

Payment is to be received in the local currency or currency of payment accepted by the parties in the agreement. If part payment is accepted, documents will be released only after full payment. The amounts partially collected should also be made available immediately to the bank issuing the collection order.

The presenting bank is responsible for seeing that the form of the acceptance appears to be complete and correct, but is not responsible for the genuineness of any signature or for the authority of any signatory to sign for acceptance.

The collecting bank is under no obligation to have the documents protested for non-payment or non-acceptance, unless the collection order contains specific instructions in this regard. If the principal nominates a representative to act as a case of need, there should be clear instructions regarding the powers of the case of need, failing which the collecting bank is under no obligation to consult this case of need.

The collecting bank has to advise immediately the instructing bank of any action taken, in case of non-acceptance or non-payment or of any action taken for the protection of goods etc. The advice has to be in an accepted form and mode regarding the payment or non-payment or acceptance or non-acceptance.

The advice of the payment or non-payment should give the details of amounts received or reason for non-payment and other relevant details thereof. If the collection order contains provision for collection of interest charges or collection charges/expenses, the same have to be collected, failing which reference has to be made of the same immediately to the issuing bank or remitting bank, as the case may be.

New Global L.C.Norms 2006

The UCP 600 is ready for vote in October 2006, and is a successor to UCP 500, which governed the working of the L.C. Documentary. The new UCP contains only 39 Articles instead of 49 Articles in UCP 500. The convention is stricter than before as there is a time limit for the bank to decide on whether shipment documents are compliant with the L.C. Conditions. The transport documents are redrafted and definitions of all terms like honour and negotiation are specifically clarified. The electronic transfer of funds is taken cognisance of.

The Banking Commission meeting is not open to the users-exporters and importers, but only banks have voting power and China the world's No.3 trader is not a signatory to UCP. This convention was held under International Chamber of Commerce and no legal sanctity. But in India RBI and IBA and FEDAI have the power to enforce them on banks in India through their Instructions and Guidelines. The RBI and ICC have the power to attend and vote for the Norms under UCP 2006.

25

Operations of Banks, IDBI and Exim Bank

Commercial banks are an important category of institutions operating in the international financial markets. They play a vital role in the financing of foreign trade and in effecting payments and receipts in the foreign exchnage markets. They provide credit to the exporter from the date of shipment to the date of receipt of funds from the importer. They negotiate bills and collect funds from the importer. They also provide guarantee on behalf of the exporter, arrange for inward and outward remittances, help in the travel facilities through travellers' cheques in foreign currency, issue of drafts, etc. They are the channels through which international indebtedness is settled or capital funds can come in and go out. They are scheduled commercial called Authorised Dealers. Banks also provide foreign market intelligence, credit information service and a host of other services. Sheduled Commercial Banks alone are authorised to deal in all transactions, foreign exchange and foreign currencies in India under the Foreign Exchange Regulation Act of 1973. They are called Authorised Dealers:

Organisation

The Foreign Department of commercial banks is so designed as to perform the above functions, both at the head office and at the branches which have foreign exchange business. The Manager in-charge of the Department is responsible for the operations in tune with the policy of the Board of Directors as laid down by the Chairman/Managing Director.

The organisational structure of the foreign departments of the banks varies from bank to bank. Broadly, some of the important sections of the foreign department of any bank are as follows:

(A) Export Section: (i) Advising and confirming Letters of Credit; (ii) Negotiation of bills under Letters of Credit (L/C); (iii) Foreign bills purchase; and (iv) Foreign bills under negotiation or collection.

(B) Import Section: (i) Opening Letters of Credit and paying for imports against Letters of Credit on behalf of its customers; (ii) Arranging for collection of inward bills (import) sent by banks abroad for collection; (iiii) Execution of deferred payment guarantees covering the import of capital goods by its importer customers.

(C) Foreign Remittance Section: (i) Arranges for issue of travellers' cheques, drafts etc., in foreign currency; (ii) Encashment of foreign currency notes and coins; (iiii) Encashment of foreign drafts and travellers' cheques, etc.

(D) Exchange Section: This section deals with maintaining of exchange position and control, keeping of accounts (Nostro and Vostro), entering into forward contracts, purchasing and selling of currencies, operating in the foreign currency or foreign exchange markets and reconciliation of bank's foreign account.

The sections of the Foreign Department and its structure varies from bank to bank and things have changed with automation in banks. There are various programmes for various purposes of the Bank's operations and the computer aided programmes help the banker to keep a track of the foreign operations.

Import Credits

In the case of consignment sales, banks enter into transactions as remitting or collecting agents. In the case of documentary credits, they act either as paying agents or as collecting or negotiating agents for the exporter abroad. So far as the importer is concerned, the bank issues the L/C, either revocable or irrevocable, confirmed or unconfirmed. The buyer makes a request on an application form for opening of L/C in favour of a foreign party. The buyer is a customer of the bank and if the foreign party is not known to him, the former requests his bank to make enquiries about the party's credit standing abroad. This service is rendered for a nominal charge. The banker has to see before opening the L/C: (i) Whether import is covered under the Import licence, which is current and unexpired; (ii) Whether the import value is within the limits set by the import licence, inclusive of c.i.f.; (iii) Whether arrangements are made for warehousing and storing of goods in good condition until sold; (iv) Whether specific mention is made of the documents to be collected from exporter such as invoice, weight certificate, certificate of origin, Bill of Lading, insurance policy, etc.

The bank issuing the L/C has an obligation to pay in terms of L/C agreement to the exporter's bank, if all the necessary documents are received. In case if it is payment against documents accepted, it is paid immediately on sight or within a grace period of two days. If the bill is a usance bill, on the expiry of the period, the payment is made by the importer's bank. As the bank has an obligation that all formalities are observed before payment, the bank observes all these formalities before debiting the importer.

Export Credit

For the exporter, if the issuing bank of the importer is of good standing, that is, adequate to go ahead to prepare export documents even without an Indian bank confirming it, provided the credit is an irrevocable credit. The negotiating bank or collecting bank will buy or collect the bills after a careful scrutiny of them such as the following:

(1) Drafts are drawn on the issuing bank.

(2) Buyer's name and seller's name are correctly entered and proper endorsements are made.

(3) The date is within the time limit of the credit.

(4) The amount is within the credit limit granted.

(5) Exporter has an export licence, if that is necessary and the value of shipments falls within the limit set by the licence.

(6) The tenor of bill is correct.

(7) Credit number is given.

(8) Stamps as required by law are attached on usance bills.

(9) All required documents are submitted. Insurance policy but not certificate of insurance is acceptable. Bill of lading in full set must be submitted and fully examined as to the negotiability, correctness and accuracy to the satisfaction of the conditions of credit in respect of all documents submitted.

Exporters and bankers should carefully avoid discrepancies between the terms of credit and the actual shipment and documents given to the bank. Indemnities have to be taken by the banks in respect of duplicate documents, discrepancy on shipment of goods, leading to claused bills or discrepancies in weights and measurements, etc.; there are other discrepancies which can be avoided by an exporter through careful preparation.

Post-shipment credit is a type of lending against book debts of the exporter. Generally, an indemnity guarantee is taken from the exporter in negotiating the bills by the banker. Along with the bills of lading and all other export documents, a letter of hypothecation of goods to the banker is also taken.

Pre-shipment or packing credit requirements are first assessed by the banker on the basis of balance sheet and income-expenditure data along with their cash flow and funds flow statements. The banker generally fixes the limit as peak level and non-peak level limits on the basis of projected requirements of the borrower in the manufacturing process. These requirements are for payments to raw material purchase, wages to labour and for other current expenditure or for working capital purposes. These limits are based on the projected requirements agreed to by the banker and his customer after the bank examines the company's accounts and funds flow statements etc.

Parties Involved In Foreign Trade

International Trade involves many parties other than exporter and importer. All of them have a role to play in the flow of trade.

(1) Shipping and Airlines Companies, transporting the goods and services and providing the bill of lading or Air way bills.

(2) Local or foreign Insurance Company that provides insurance cover and issues a certificate to that effect to the exporter.

(3) Governments and Embassies who grant permission or licences to exporters or importers.

(4) Bankers to the exporters and to the importers and their correspondents in the respective countries outside.

(5) Central banks of the concerned countries who impose or remove any exchange controls or restrictions on receipts and payments or provide exchange risk cover to banks on behalf of exporters.

(6) ECGC or Export Credit Guarantee Corporation in India provides risk coverage for bank credit issued by the exporter bank to the exporter. This may involve customer and country risk coverage of the importer also.

(7) Exim Bank: Exim bank provides refinance to the banks issuing credit to exporters under its various schemes of re-discounting. These cover both short and long-term advances, pre-shipment and the post-shipment credit, etc. The currency risk is covered by the banks and credit risk and country risk are covered by the ECGC. Thereby, the banks can get refinance facilities from Exim bank for the export credit, they provided to the exporters, on behalf of the importer or importing country. Exim bank also helps the exporter with direct finance in some cases and provides guarantee for bank finance, forfeiting, etc.,

Mode of Bank Finance to Exporters

(1) Running an overdraft to cover miscellaneous expenses of exporters and their production costs.

(2) Pre-shipment loans for specific requirements of exporter relating to a specific order — example is packing credit for exporter to buy raw materials and up to the stage of manufacturing.

(3) Purchase of bills of exchange after shipment and providing cash against credit sales.

(4) Negotiating, accepting and collecting the bills and documents of trade, which involve examination of documents, transmitting them to the importer or his banker for collecting the proceeds, when they are due.

(5) Banks provide information on foreign countries, their markets, their currencies and about the credit rating of the importer and his country.

(6) Banks extend introduction to parties and safeguard and protect the interest of the concerned parties.

(7) Banks provide risk coverage and safeguard the parties from currency rate fluctuations.

(8) Bank would help importers in the form of overdraft, loan facilities for shipments, overseas finance (buyer credit) from exporter country or another country.

Method of Payments

There are four methods of payment by importer to exporter:

(1) Advance Payment: For specific goods manufactured or provided for specific need of the importer.

(2) Open Account Trading: Payment in areas for regular flow of shipments: payment at the end of the month or quarterly payments, applicable to agencies or subsidiaries.

(3) Documentary Collections: Here the bank acts as an agent for the exporter customer to collect the proceeds of export. The documents after export are surrendered to his banker who in turn scrutinises the documents and send them to the correspondents abroad for collection of proceeds from the importer.

(4) Documentary Credits: This is a written undertaking by the issuing bank on the request of importer of goods, for a charge to provide credit to the exporter or make payment for goods shipped once the documents are submitted to them. This is in other words a credit to importer to pay to the exporter for the goods shipped as he needs time to sell and get money.

BANKS' EXCHANGE TRANSACTIONS

Sale and Purchase

Each exchange transaction involves a sale and a purchase. It is a sale of one party and one currency and a purchase of another. From the point of view of a bank, sale of foreign currency against rupees is a sale transaction. The same transaction involves also a purchase of rupees by the bank. For the exporter, it is a sale of foreign currency against rupees. Outward foreign currency remittances — foreign currency drafts, air mail transfers (MT), Telegraphic Transfers (TTs), payment of Import Bills (Inward Bills), expressed in foreign currencies and Bills for collection (BC sales) are examples of sale transactions. Purchase transactions are purchase of foreign currencies for Indian rupees. These relate to inward remittances, foreign currency drafts, Mail Transfers (MTs), Telegraphic Transfers (TT) and payment of Export Bills (outward bills) expressed in foreign currencies.

Spot and Forward

For an Indian bank, actual conversion of foreign exchange or currencies should take place at its end before it becomes a foreign exchange transactions. For this the bills should be denominated in foreign currency or if denominated in rupees, reimbursement thereof should be in foreign currencies.

A spot or ready transaction is one where exchange takes place immediately or on the same day. A forward transaction is one which is put through at some future date, 30 days or 60 days of 90 days hence. In the latter case, it is a contract to buy or sell a foreign currency at some future date. An export bill for $ 5000, for example payable on sight drawn by a Canadian importer under an irrevocable letter of credit is purchased outright by the Indian Bank and the exporter is paid in rupees. This is a spot transaction. If, on the other hand, the bill is a usance bill (of say, 30 days) payable after thirty days and the bill is a B/C bill, the bank takes it for collection and it would take 15 days to send the bill to the drawee bank and the proceeds remitted by the latter to the Indian bank. If the exporter does not want to wait until then and wishes to take no exchange risk, he would sell it to the bank and get the rupees on the bill immediately. The conversion of the currency will take place at a future date and it is a forward transaction. The bank would buy it or discount it and the loss of interest and other charges are loaded in the exchange rate quoted for such transaction by the bank.

Nostro, Vostro and Loro Accounts

Any bank dealing in foreign exchange keeps foreign currency accounts with correspondent banks, branches and agents abroad. If an Indian bank has to deal in UK sterling, it deals in Nostro Account (our Account with you) kept by it in London with its correspondent Bank, say Barclays. If Barclays Bank keeps a Rupee Account with Indian Bank in Kolkota for a similar purpose, it is called Vostro Account (your Account with us). If a third bank's account is referred to, it is called Loro Account (third party account — their Account with you). The Vostro accounts in India are designated as non-resident Rupee accounts of foreign banks and branches.

These accounts are kept on the mirror principle. As Nostro account is our stocks of foreign currencies abroad, our sales of foreign currencies would be debits there and our purchases are credits there. If an Indian bank issues a draft in foreign currency (£), then it is made by a debit to its Nostro Account in London. An export bill purchased by Indian bank will be credited to this Nostro account there. As the foreign banks keep an Indian bank account (Nostro account) all purchases and sales of foreign currencies are credited and debited there. But the Indian bank keeps a mirror or shadow account (corresponding proforma account) with itself in its General Ledger. If the Nostro account is with Barclays in London, the proforma account is designed as "The Barclays Bank Ltd." (our Account).

Principle of "Valuer Compensee"

Any foreign exchange transaction based on Valuer compensee (value here and value there) should not involve any loss of interest or principal for either party. If any instrument is passed with this clause, deliveries of two currencies at our end and at their end are done simultaneously and no blocking of funds is involved. Such transactions are put through by telegram, cable or telex. If a clause "Value date" is used, the deliveries of currencies at two centres should take place on the same date simultaneously as a result of which no interest is lost to either party. Alternatively, interest has to be paid if the date of entry is not the same in the account of the receiver as in the account of the payee. In the case of any transaction with "Value date" added to it, no interest should normally be collected and credit will be given on the same day of presentation or receipt of advice. This is now more common with electronic transfer of funds, with funds crossing in the borders with in seconds on the same day.

Rate of Interest

An interest is charged on bills which involve a transit time of a usance period to maturity. In cases of transfer through instruments other than TTs, sometime period is involved. The time taken may be the time necessary for air mail or sea mail — during which proceeds at the foreign centre are realised and the advice comes to the paying centre. In the case of usance bills which have a maturity to run, the bank may charge the exporter interest for the period, if the exporter is paid the proceeds before final maturity. Thus, an exporter is paid rupees on presentation of a sight bill, but the bill has to be sent to their foreign correspondent to collect the proceeds from the importer bank and then advise the bank at this paying centre. These formalities would take about 10 - 20 days during which time the bank would be out of funds and lose interest which would be charged to the exporter by the bank paying in our country. This interest element is sometimes charged separately and sometimes loaded in the exchange rate quoted by the bank. Thus, the rate quoted by the bank depends on the nature of the transaction, namely, (1) Whether it is a buying or selling transactions; (2) The country to which or from which the transaction has arisen which will determine the transit period during which interest is lost to the bank; (3) The type of instrument used, namely, bank draft, M.T., cheque, bill of exchange, etc. and (4) Whether the bill is purchased outright or is sent for collection. In the case of a bill for collection, no credit is passed to the exporter until the proceeds are realised and no interest is involved but only collection charges are levied.

Buying and Selling Rates[@]

Every bank will quote both buying and selling rates. If the exchange rate is quoted as so many units of foreign currency for one unit of domestic currency, (Indirect rate or foreign currency quotation such as Rs. 100 = £ 1.4511), then the principle that the bank observes is "buy-high and sell-low". Then the buying rate, for example, will be Rs. 100 = £ 1.4758 and selling rate Rs. 100 = £ 1.4370.

@ Rates in July, 1999. As it is an example, the date does not matter.

The pound sterling exchange rates are fixed by the Foreign Exchange Dealers' Association of India (FEDAI) based on RBI's buying and selling rates for sterling up to 1975 and for dollar later. The other currency rates are worked out by banks on the basis of cross London rates for the respective currencies vis-a-vis sterling. Thus, if the RBI selling rate is £ 5.5432: (example only).

Then deduct the exchange margin	£ 1.4470
(Sell-low rule).	– .0100
Our Bank's Selling rate	£ 1.4370
Thus, if the RBI Buying rate is	£ 1.4758
Then add exchange margin (Buy-high rule)	+.0100
Our Bank's buying rate	£ 1.4858

If the quotation is Direct rate, then domestic currency units are given per one unit of foreign currency unit £ 1 = Rs. 67.9975 as at end March 2010. This method of quoting was not in practice, particularly since the devaluation of rupee in 1966. This direct method of quotations was allowed from Aug. 1993 and is now in operation. Prior to that for example in June 1992, RBI buying rate £ 3.8720 and RBI selling rate £ 3.8530 per Rs. 100. Now all rates are quoted in US dollars, as also the RBI's reference rate for its operations. Euro currency rate was announced by RBI from January 1, 2002. Banks follow the FEDA rates announced on a daily basis.

Types of Rates

The selling rates are quoted separately for (a) TTs, (b) B.Cs and other instruments. The Bank would apply the TT rate for all clean sales for transfers, remittances etc., irrespective of whether they are put through by means of TTs, drafts or MTs. The bank would quote BC selling rate for import bills other than clean sales. The TT rate is definitely better to the customer than the BC rate. Example, TT selling £ 5.4995 and BC £ 5.4895 spot. Quotations of 1985-86 were used for illustration when there was stable exchange rates due to RBI controls.

In the case of buying rates also, the bank quotes TT rate to all non-export transactions: (a) TT clean when no documents are involved; and (b) TT documentary in which banks handle documentary bills. The first one is better than the second as the latter includes charges for handling documents. Besides, there is OD rate (on Demand Buying rate) which is quoted for bills payable on demand or without documents. These relate to export receipts or other non-export receipts which require that the receipts are effected on presentation of documents at the other foreign centre. These involve an interest element for the transit period, which is included in the rate of exchange. Even in the case of cheques or drafts, the interest element is added if the cheques or drafts are to be sent to the foreign centre before they are credited to our Nostro Account abroad. Examples are TT clean, £ 5.5450, TT documentary £ 5.5735, OD Bills £ 5.5820, all spot.

In the London, Singapore and major international markets, the banks quote both bid and offer rates for each other currency against their own currency. In London, for example, the banks quote

US Dollars per Pound Sterling in two forms — LIBID (London Inter-Bank Bid Rate) and LIBOR (London Inter-Bank Offer Rate).

Long Rates

Long rates are the rates applicable to purchase of foreign exchange arising out of the discounting a long bills (usance bills). These long rates are of various maturities from 30 days to 180 days. They are arrived at by loading to the OD rate, the interest factor for the usance period plus grace (or transit) period. The interest factor is theoretically determined by the rate prevailing in the foreign centre to which the currency relates. The premium for one month, 3 months and 6 months are quoted on a daily basis.

Tel Quel Rates

Tel quel rates are the rates quoted for bills with a broken period of usance such as 40 or 45 days. The long rates, referred to for specific usance periods such as 30, 60 or 90 days are adjusted to suit the bills such as they are when offered for discounting or rediscounting. Thus, a bill of 90 days maturity might have been presented after a lapse of 15 days with a maturity of 75 days to run. The rate quoted by banks for such bill is called Tel quel rate.

Prior to January 1984, FEDAI used to fix the Sterling rate schedule which was mandatory for all banks to adopt and quote to their customers. This schedule was fixed after providing for the maximum interest permitted and a fixed margin of profit.

In January 1984 following the prevailing international practices, Sterling rate schedule was abolished and banks in India began to quote exchange rates on the basis of the going market rates. The era of fixed margins and fixed interest elements was replaced by open competition among banks in charging for the services. The interest element for transit period, grace period and usance period is now charged separately by banks and the exchange margin is also variable.

Forward Rates

Forward rate is the rate of exchange applicable to a future exchange transaction in respect of which the rate applicable is fixed right away by means of forward exchange contract but the transaction would take place at some future date fixed now. Forward rates are based on the spot rates with a discount or a premium on the former depending upon the expected future interest rates. The forward rates are quoted for each type of instrument, corresponding to which there is a spot rate. Thus, forward rate for selling TT/BC and buying rate for TT, TT documentary, OD Bills etc., are available from banks. These are advised by the FEDA from time to time to banks in respect of sterling now dollar and the banks would work out the rates on the basis of London cross quotation in respect of other currencies. The rates of exchange for Rupee against D.M., French Franc etc., are arrived at by taking the Rupee-sterling rate as given by FEDA and sterling -DM rate/Sterling-

Yen/Sterling-franc rates as quoted in the London market. The rates so arrived at are called cross rates.

Rates for forward transactions are adjusted with a premium or discount on the spot rate. The factors which determine theoretically the premium or discount are the rate of interest, demand for and supply of forward currency and likely appreciation or depreciation of the currency in future. Suppose the method of quotation is foreign currency units or indirect method: Rs. 100 = £ 5.4100. The premium on that spot rate is thus deducted as follows to derive forward selling rate:

Spot rate	£ 5.4100	for TT	£ 5.4000	for BC
Premium	- 0.0100	& DD	- 0.0100	
	£ 5.4000		£ 5.3900	

The above is based on the principle of Sell-Low applicable to indirect method of quotation. In the case of buying, the principle is Buy-High and the following example illustrates the case:

Rs. 100 =	£ 5.4545	for TT clean	£ 5.4735	for TT Documentary	£ 5.4880	for O/D Bills
Premium	+ .0060		+ 0.0060		+ 0.0060	
	£ 5.4605		£ 5.4795		£ 5.4940	

The concept of premium or discount has to be carefully understood and appreciated as the same premium has resulted in deduction for selling rate and addition for buying rate. A premium results if excess demand over supply is present for forward currency, if the rate of interest at the home centre is higher than abroad and if there is likely appreciation of spot rate in future. In July 2003 with convertible rupee, the quotation is in terms of Rs. per unit of foreign currency say Rs. 76.25 buying Rs. 77.78 selling per £, and Rs. 46.44 buying Rs. 46.90 selling per $.

Inter Bank Trading

Foreign exchange trading of international banks has become a major source of income for them. The inter bank trading becomes the most significant component of total trading in the exchange market accounting for as much as 80% of the total volume. The inter bank payment system is paper based, using bankers' cheques. Electronic inter bank transfer system in New york is through the clearing house Inter bank payment system (CHIPs) and in London through the Clearing House Automated Payment System (CHAPS). The net amount payable or receivable is conveyed through a Society for World wide Inter bank Financial Telecommunications (SWIFT). This method is being used in India as well. Swift is for communicating messages as between the trading banks.

The netting of the trade contracts and fixing of the net amounts due either of credits or debits is done through a system called FXNet for bilateral netting of the spot and forward trade contracts (for exchange rates, refer to chapter 27).

Exchange Rates and Forward Premia

The Table below presents the data of Inter bank Forward premia for 3 months and 6 months respectively month-wise during 2004-05 and from March 2008 to July 2009. This illustrates the point that various national and international factors influence the forward premia of a currency, in addition to the interest rates and the domestic inflation rates in the respective countries. The basic factors continue to be interest rates and purchasing power of the currencies. Forward rates depend prima facie on the demand and supply for forward dollars, while the underlying factors continue to be future expected interest rates and expected inflation rates in the respective countries, say India and US for the dollar quotations.

The premium has gone down in 2004-05 as compared to 2000-01 and in fact there was a discount in certain months which indicates that the future is much less uncertain. When it is at a discount, the spot market is much better than the futures market. The uncertainty of future increased between March 2008 and March 2009 and then declined by July 2009, but rose again from March 2011 due to economic turbulance.

Table Forward Premia (Monthly Average)
Inter Bank Forward Premia

Year	Month	3 Months	6 Months
2004	March	0.62	0.51
	April	0.35	-0.10
	May	-1.33	-0.69
	June	0.93	0.69
	July	2.25	1.86
	August	2.85	2.60
	September	2.20	1.88
	October	2.87	2.50
	November	2.16	1.90
	December	2.03	1.70
2005	January	2.50	2.08
	February	1.99	1.76
	March	1.82	1.62
	April	1.96	1.76
	May	1.57	1.47
	June	1.40	1.31
2008	March	2.75	2.50
2009	March	3.69	3.66
2009	July	2.74	2.74
2011	July	6.94	6.63

Source: RBI Handbook of Statistics.

Note: Negative signs, indicate discounts on Forward rates.

Option Deals

If the delivery date is not certain, the buyer may ask for an option forward delivery such as within a period of 3 months. Option is a right to buy or sell a specified currency on or before a specified date. Then the buyer may take the currency any time up to that period and bank quotes a rate with the maximum premium permissible for a three-month forward sale. If it is at a discount, then the least discount for a three-month period is taken into account. That is, any quotation will be to the greatest disadvantage of the customer and greatest advantage to the banker.

Swap Transactions

A swap is a budlee transaction which is a simultaneous purchase and sale, namely, purchase of spot currency against sale of the same forward currency sometime later. It may be that it is a sale of spot for a purchase of forward currency or sale of forward currency of one duration against the purchase of forward currency of another duration (forward-forward). Such deals are put through by banks at agreed discount or premium, mostly among themselves in the inter-bank market. Swaps may be effected for keeping the bank's Nostro accounts with funds, for short-term investments in foreign countries or as a means of covering outright forward transactions. In India exchange control regulations are relaxed to allow of swap transactions, particularly in dollar, as it is the RBI's intervention currency. The banks can do them only when supported by the definite trade transactions with their correspondents and branches abroad. The principle of swap is useful in arriving at the least cost extension or cancellation of forward exchange transaction and in adjusting exchange positions by banks. In Currencies as in shares and commodities, there can be future contracts for delivery of a specified currency at a future date.

EXPORT FINANCE AND BANKS

Importance of Export Finance

Export finance is a part of global finance given to the corporates. Importance of credit to exporters cannot be overemphasised. India has to compete effectively with other countries in the export markets in order to penetrate into new markets and widen its hold on the existing markets. Since many countries have been pursuing policies geared to the promotion of exports through adequate export credits at low rates of interest, India has also pursued the same policy in regard to export finance.

In all major industrialised countries, banks and other financial institutions are deeply involved in financing of exports on special terms. Some of them are granting "mixed credits" that combine export credit with foreign aid to developing countries. In all such cases, the governments and/or central banks of those countries are directly involved in subsidising exports. Examples of the institutions involved in such credits in foreign countries are Exim Banks of USA and Japan, Export

Development Corporation of Canada, Banque Francoise Paur le Commerce Exterior of France and Kreditanstalt for Wiederaufbean of West Germany. There are also Export Credit insurance agencies and schemes operating in all these countries for the benefit of exporters.

In India, starting with the Export Bills Credit Scheme of 1963, the refinance provided by the Reserve Bank has always been at concessional rate. Export Credit Refinance limits have been provided by the RBI for banks on the basis of export credit, granted by them. A similar facility has also been given under pre-shipment or packing credit scheme of 1968 by the Industrial Development Bank of India (IDBI).

During the Sixth and Seventh Five-Year Plans greater importance was given to the export promotion measures in view of the continuing stagnancy of our exports and declining flow of foreign aid from international financial institutions. A number of fiscal and monetary measures were taken with a view to promoting exports. In 1982 the Exim Bank was set up for the purpose of providing all the services, financial and otherwise, to exporters under one window. The Exim Bank now provides a host of services to all categories of exporters, which will be dealt with later.

In this chapter, attention is focused on the provision of bank finance to exports. Both commercial and co-operative banks provide pre-shipment and post-shipment credit to exporting units while the RBI and IDBI provides refinance facilities. IDBI had also been providing direct medium and long-term export credit, in addition to its other facilities.

Pre-shipment credit relates to the finance required up to the stage of shipment of goods for manufacture, transport, packing, etc., which is also called packing credit. Post-shipment credit relates to the finance needed from the stage of actual shipment until the time of realisation of proceeds.

Medium-term export credit is provided both by banks and non-bank financial institutions like IFC, SFCs and erstwhile IDBI. While short-term credit is normally up to 90 days and 180 days in respect of specified categories of capital goods, medium-term credit is normally up to a period of 5 years, extendable up to 10 years in the case of some categories of engineering goods, for which deferred payment terms are offered.

Quantum of Export Finance

The outstanding export credit provided by scheduled commercial banks at end June 1970 was only Rs. 320 crores which constituted about 7.6 per cent of non-food bank credit. This had increased to Rs. 2,409 crores by end March 1986 which constituted about 5 per cent of the non-food credit. During the decade of the seventies, exports rose in India by about four times, while export credit rose faster, namely five times. During eighties exports rose by five times and export credit rose faster than that. Export credit outstanding constituted about one-fourth of the total exports during the recent years Export credit outstanding at end March 2009 is Rs. 1,28,940 crores; Export credit target as percentage of total bank credit is 12% but the actual ratio is only 5% in 2009 and it varies from year to year. In the year 2010-11, export credit stood at Rs. 1,20,200 crores.

The IDBI's export refinance granted was also equally impressive. It was only Rs. 7.5 crores in June 1965 which rose to Rs. 116 crores in June 1980. Starting only with refinance of medium-term credits IDBI has expanded its activities into a full-fledged international finance wing since 1976 comprising direct finance, refinance, overseas buyers' credit, foreign lines of credit, overseas investment finance in addition to its guarantees for export performance. Direct finance to exporters as well as buyers' credit and foreign lines of credit have since grown significantly. Since January 1982 the Exim Bank has taken over this work from the IDBI.

RBI Export Credit

The RBI has been pursuing a policy of encouraging exports through prescription of lower interest rates on export credit and also charging lower rates for export credit refinance. As early as in October 1958, the RBI had extended the Bill Market Scheme to export bills to help banks secure refinance at Bank rate on the security of these export bills. As the use of this scheme by banks was not significant, the RBI Act was amended in September 1962 to enable it to purchase and rediscount export bills maturing within 180 days. Following this, in March 1963, the RBI introduced Export Bills Credit Scheme under which advances would be made to banks against promissory notes of their constituents repayable on demand and upon declaration of holding of usance export bills drawn in foreign currencies or Indian rupees.

Through exports bank credit was refinanced to the extent of 1-2 per cent. Bank credit to GDP is less than one per cent of GDP. The growth in export credit was declining, although exports are growing at a faster rate. The growth in export credit was 14-17%, while exports are growing faster at about 20-25%.

Since, 1969 the RBI has provided refinance at a concessional rate of 4 per cent — 6 per cent to banks, against pre-shipment credit advances to exporters up to 180 days or even more, provided the banks do not in turn charge more than 6 per cent — 8 per cent to their constituents. There was liberalisation of these facilities from time to time and export credit was treated as a priority category. Even during times of credit stringency, export credit continued to receive priority treatment with no curtailment in quantity of credit or in refinance facilities. The export credit refinance rates varied from time to time with effective from April 1999, this refinance is provided by the RBI at Bank rate. Now export credit is granted at below PLR of banks by 2.5 percentage points less (viz., PLR-2.5). RBI's export credit refinance was at around Rs. 34,000 crores as in 2008-09 and remained stagnant.

Export Credit (Interest Subsidy) Schemes

The Export Credit (Interest Subsidy) Scheme was started in 1968 with a view of providing a partial compensation to banks for the loss of interest earnings on their advances to exporters arising out of ceilings fixed on interest rates on export credit by the RBI. The subsidy was to the extent of 1 per cent of the cost of lending granted by the banks in respect of exports. In 1972, the State and Central co-operative banks catering to export credit were brought under the scheme. In September

1980, the scheme was extended to buyers' credits as in the case of Bangladesh imports from India. The subsidy was raised to 3 per cent in respect of some export credits early in 1986.

The ceiling rate on advances for exports was stepped up by stages from 6 per cent in 1969 to 10.5 per cent in 1974 when the minimum lending rate for general categories was itself raised to 12.5 per cent. Similarly, the maximum rate for deferred payment export credit was also raised from 6 per cent to 7 per cent in 1974. In September 1974, following the introduction of tax on interest earned by banks, the maximum rate for deferred payment exports was raised from 7 to 8 per cent and for other export credits from 10.5 per cent to 11.5 per cent.

In 1975, a Standing Committee on Export Finance was set up by the RBI with the representatives of IDBI, ECGC, FEDA and commercial banks, Finance Ministry and Commerce Ministry. This Committee would look into the problems of export credit as they arise and suggest remedies to ensure adequate availability of credit to the export sector. The benefit of concessionary export credit was also made available to export of consultancy services and for meeting the expenses of technical staff and other project staff or purchase of raw materials etc. Similar extension of concessionary credit was announced in respect of goods sent for exhibition-cum-sale or trade fairs.

In 1998-99, the maximum rate on all pre-shipment credit (other than for engineering goods and constructions projects) was at a concessional rate of 11 per cent to 13 per cent when the general rate on bank advances was 16.5 - 17.5 per cent. The post shipment credit rates are also kept lower to encourage exports. Interest rates fell after 2000 AD under flexible rate policy. With reforms, interest rates were freed and made move flexible and interest subsidy schemes were given up in 2000-01. Export credit interest rates were linked to PLR and lower than PLR by a margin, of 2.5 percentage points.

Duty Drawback Scheme

In January 1976, the RBI initiated a new credit scheme called "Duty Drawback Credit Scheme". Under this scheme, banks could advance to exporters against their duty drawback entitlements on export of goods, free of interest. Such advances are to be refinanced by the RBI up to a maximum period of 90 days, also interest free. The banks could grant such advances on the basis of export performance of the party, duty drawback entitlement as certified by the Customs authorities and accompanied by other relevant documents. Although they are interest-free advances, banks might charge for their incidental expenses from the parties. Refinance from the RBI is given until the moneys are received from the government to be paid direct to banks.

Export Credit Terms

Consequent on lowering of interest rates on lending, in March 1978, the ceiling rate on export credit was reduced from 11.5 per cent to 11 per cent for credit up to 90 days and from 13.5 per cent to 13 per cent for credits beyond 90 days. The ceiling rate on post-shipment credit for deferred payment exports for a period exceeding one year or engineering and capital goods remained unchanged at 8 per cent. The interest rates on Rupee export credit ranged from 10 to 13% in April 1999 as against 11 to 14% in April 1998. The refinance rate of RBI was also reduced from 10.5 per cent to 10 per cent at the same time. The availment of refinance from the RBI could be up to 50 per cent of the increase in export credit in the proceeding calendar year either under the Export Bills Credit Scheme or under the Preshipment Credit Scheme. In May 1998 the limit of 50% was raised to 100% of the increase in export credit granted by banks. In 2001-2002 export credit interest rates were kept lower by 2.5 percentage points as compared to the PLR of banks, which was itself lower at 10-11%. Ceiling rates were kept separate for pre and post shipment credit.

In February 1979, the period of post-shipment credit for exports was enhanced from the existing 120 to 180 days in order to make exports more competitive.

In March 1986, the period of pre-shipment credit was also extended to 180 days along with a lowering of interest rates for export credit. The exporters from Kandla, at Santacruz and other free trade zones are also given working capital finance at concessional rates and are exempted from production of letters of credit or firm orders for export at the time of availment of pre-shipment credit from banks.

With the general hike in leading rates in July 1980, the pre-shipment credit rate for exports was pushed up from 10 per cent to 11.85 per cent for 180 days and 14 per cent for further periods of 90 days in respect of medium and heavy engineering goods and construction contracts. These were raised further in March 1981 along with a general levelling up of all interest rates. But in March 1986, export rates were again brought down to encourage exports from India. In 1995, when the general level of interest rate on advances was 15% export credit at pre-shipment and post-shipment stage was 13% but post-pre-shipment credit in foreign currency was kept lower at 6.5 to 8.5%. RBI continued to provide refinance for a large proportion of export credit even now. The rate of interest on export credit is PLR –2.5% points, and PLR is also lower at 11 to 12% as at early 2010.

IDBI — Export Finance

One of the objectives of the setting up of the IDBI was to take over the refinance facilities, provided earlier by the Refinance Corporation for Industry, such as refinance of medium-term export credit. The goods eligible for such refinance through the co-operative and commercial banks and through SFCs are capital goods, producer goods and consumer durables. The scheme provided for refinancing of pre-shipment credit where it is combined with post-shipment credit but the period of credit, excluding pre-shipment credit should be not less than six months and not more than 5 years, as originally started. This refinance was provided at a concessional rate of 4 per cent, provided the banks charge not more than 6 per cent to their customers. The refinance rates were revised upwards from time to time in tune with the general interest rate policy.

IDBI provided a host of services, both funded and non-funded aid takes the form of direct assistance and refinance, (Bill finance, support to other FIs, etc.) Direct assistance took the form of Rupee loans, foreign currency loans, underwriting, guarantee and equipment leasing, etc.

The IDBI operated many export finance schemes which have been widened and deepened so as to promote the growth of exports. Since 1976, the IDBI has a full-fledged International Finance Department, geared to provide direct assistance, refinance facilities and other forms of export assistance. The direct assistance is to suppliers of export items of engineering and capital goods on deferred payment terms. The IDBI has been granting overseas buyers' credit to foreign buyers and foreign lines of credit to selected buyer countries and has been operating the Overseas Investment Finance Scheme for facilitating Indian participation in joint ventures located in other countries, particularly in developing countries. Pre-shipment credits are also granted where they involve manufacture on specific orders from foreign countries in the category of capital and producer goods. Besides, export guarantees are also granted in collaboration with banks for over-seas construction jobs secured by Indian contractors and for equipment supply and turnkey contracts won by Indian exporters.

Despite the fact that the general pattern or interest rates had been hiked up many times, the refinance rate for medium-term export credits remained unchanged at 6.5 per cent, provided the banker does not charge more than 8 per cent to the customer. The rate for participation Export Finance Scheme and Buyers Credit Scheme remained at 7.5 per cent. From 1980 the rate on medium-term export credit was, however, pushed up to 8.6 per cent and the Overseas Investment Finance rate to 11.85 per cent. Effective March 1981, while the medium-term export credit rate remained unchanged at 8.6 per cent, participation export credit rate was moved up to 7.75 per cent and overseas investment finance rate to 12.5 per cent. Since end 1981, the export finance schemes of IDBI were taken over by the Exim Bank.

Export Market for Small Scale Industries

Trading companies operating in the private sector have taken care of the export markets of small scale industries in Japan. In USA, such work is undertaken by Export Management Companies. In India, no separate institution has been set up to take care of the problems of export finance and export marketing of small scale industries. The STC which is acting as a canalising agency was taking care of the requirements of the SSIs. There have been many proposals for setting up of a separate financial institution for small scale industries. The requirements of SSIs were taken care of by the banks and the SFCs supported by refinance from Exim Bank/IDBI, and recently by SIDBI.

Exim Bank

In 1967 there was a proposal by the Commerce Ministry for the setting up of an Exim Bank in India and it did not get wide acceptance at that time. The Banking Commission (1972) was also against the duplication of institutions in the field of export credit and recommended against setting up of such a body. The idea was later revived and spelt out in a report by the Committee headed by Shri B. D. Kumar in 1974. The idea was not accepted at this time also as the government felt that the IDBI could take care of the functions of the Exim Bank through the creation of an International Finance Wing. This was done in March 1976 with the objective of providing export finance (including

Overseas Buyers Credit and Foreign Lines of Credit) counselling services to Indian exporters, collection of credit intelligence on importers and negotiation of import loans or lines of credit from International Finance Bodies like the IBRD, IDA, etc. The IDBI has been co-ordinating the activities, in this regard, of banks, SFCs and other financial institutions.

With urgency given to promotion of exports for fostering economic development under the Sixth Plan and for stepping up the rate of growth of exports, exporters have been demanding all assistance at one window and simplification of procedures. The government finally accepted the idea of setting up an Exim Bank in 1979. The necessary legislation was passed in August 1981.

Exim Bank Objectives

Exim Bank is a service institution set up to serve the foreign trade sector in the form of finance, advice, consultancy, market intelligence, credit information services, etc. It has both developmental and finance functions. The objectives are clearly set out as "granting loans and advances in India solely or jointly with commercial banks and other financial bodies to persons exporting or importing or intending to export from India goods and services including export of turnkey projects, joint ventures and civil construction services".

It will not duplicate the services of banks or the ECGC as both short-term finance and insurance have been kept out of its purview. It would lay greater emphasis on term finance, information system on foreign markets and foreign buyers, etc., and encourage the export of capital goods, turnkey projects, construction services, consultancy and deferred payment exports. Joint ventures abroad and joint ventures in third countries in particular are also encouraged by the Exim Bank. In short, it is an Apex institution providing finance and refinance in connection with the foreign trade of the country, comparable to NABARD in respect of agricultural finance and IDBI in respect of industrial finance.

Organisation

The Exim Bank of India was set up as a wholly-owned corporation by the government with an initial authorised capital of Rs. 200 crores which may be increased to Rs. 650 crores by the Central Government as may be necessary and with a paid-up capital of Rs. 50 crores. Government would also give an initial loan of Rs. 20 crores at a concessional rate of interest of 5 per cent and may grant such loans from time to time as required. It can borrow from the RBI under National Industrial Credit (Long-term Operations) Fund and from abroad up to certain limits. The corporation can also accept deposits from the public or raise funds from the capital market. A special fund is proposed to be set up by the corporation called Development Fund through loans, gifts, donations, etc., from government or other sources for research, training and development.

The policy-making body is a 15-member Board of Directors with a Chairman and Managing Director. There will be five representatives from the government, one each from the RBI, ECGC and IDBI, 3 from commercial banks and four from the exporting community.

The corporation has taken over the International Finance Wing of IDBI along with its guaranteed liabilities of Rs. 150 crores executed by the IDBI and outstanding assets of Rs. 115 crores in respect of their export transactions. The exchange control functions of RBI and insurance functions of ECGC are not touched by the Exim Bank. The short-term finance will continue to be given by commercial banks. The corporation will concentrate on medium and long-term credit, deferred payment credits, issuing guarantees or other long-term financial arrangements. The corporation will have the additional responsibilities of financing imports, merchant banking, development banking financing of promotional activities and rendering all services on the above accounts. It started operations in March 1982 with its Headquarters at Mumbai and representative offices at Chennai, Kolkota, New Delhi, Washington and Abidjan (Ivory Coast).

Functions of Exim Bank

The operations of EXIM Bank includes funded assistance and guarantees. Funded assistance takes the form of supplies' credit, pre-shipment credit finance for EOUs and export marketing finance. Besides it provides lines of credit, buyers' credit, refinance of export credit, bulk import finance, export product development finance, pre-shipment finance, bridge loans, overseas investment finance, production equipment finance, finance for leasing, etc.

The Exim Bank performs the following functions:

(1) Granting loans and advances in India solely or jointly with commercial banks to persons exporting or intending to export from India goods including export of turnkey projects, civil construction contracts or other contracts and services including consultancy services.

(2) Granting loans and advances solely or jointly with commercial banks to persons outside India for import from India of goods, including turnkey projects, civil construction contracts or other contracts and services, including consultancy services.

(3) Granting lines of credit to governments, financial institutions and other suitable organisations in foreign countries to enable persons outside India to import from India, goods including turnkey projects, services, including consultancy services.

(4) Handling transactions where a mix of government-to-government credit and commercial credit for exports is involved.

(5) Issuing bid bonds and guarantees and other similar facilities in India or abroad solely or jointly with commercial banks on behalf of persons exporting or intending to export from India goods including turnkey projects, consultancy, etc.

(6) Purchasing, discounting and negotiating export bills, etc.

Incidental Functions

(1) Maintaining of foreign currency accounts with banks and correspondents abroad for purposes connected with the business of Exim Bank.

(2) Buying and selling currencies or foreign exchange and undertaking such other functions of authorised dealers as may be necessary for the discharge of its functions.

(3) Undertaking and financing of research surveys, studies, etc., in connection with promotion and development of international markets.

(4) Providing technical, administrative and financial assistance to any exporter in India or any other person who intends to export goods from India for promotion, management and expansion of any industry with a view of promoting international trade.

(5) Planning, promoting, developing and financing export-oriented industries.

(6) Forming or conducting subsidiaries for carrying out its functions.

(7) Acting as an agent of the Centre and State Governments, RBI, IDBI, etc.

Operations

There are two types of operations by Exim Bank, namely, funded and non-funded operations. Funded operations involve financial outgo while non-funded operations include various types of guarantees such as advance payment guarantee, performance guarantee, guarantee for retention of money and guarantee for borrowings abroad, guarantee required for execution of export contracts and for issue of Bid bonds.

The Exim Bank's funded facilities may be set out under the following programmes, operated by it.

Programmes

(i) Direct Financial Assistance to Exporters: Under this head, funds are provided on deferred payment terms to Indian exporters of eligible goods and services which enable the Indian exporter to extend deferred payment credit to the overseas buyers. Commercial banks can participate in this programme directly or under Risk Syndication Facility, when risk of non-payment by supplier is shared by banks with the Exim bank.

(ii) Consultancy and Technology Services: Indian companies can avail themselves of Exim Bank's financial facility against deferred credit extended to overseas buyers of Indian consultancy, technology and other services.

(iii) Pre-shipment Credit: While pre-shipment credit up to six months is provided by banks, that beyond six months is given by Exim Bank jointly with banks to facilitate the provision of rupee funds for expenses in construction exports and turnkey project exports, enabling them to buy raw materials and other inputs.

(iv) Facilities for Export-oriented Units: There are two categories of exporting units: Firstly, 100 per cent export-oriented units which get green cards for securing easy access to their inputs and secondly, units set up in the Free Trade Zones such as Kandla, Santacruz, Falta, Chennai, Cochin and Noida (UP). The Exim Bank provides term loans or deferred payment guarantees for them to acquire Indian plant and machinery or foreign plant and capital goods.

(v) Overseas Investment Facility: The Bank provides funds to Indian promoters of joint ventures overseas for equity participation over a period of 1 to 10 years to set up projects abroad or in third countries.

(vi) Buyers' Credit: This credit takes possibly three forms, namely: (a) Direct credit to importers for Indian capital goods, consumer durables and others; (b) Lines of credit to foreign governments as in the case of Mauritius or foreign financial institutions as in the case of Bangladesh for provision of term credit to importers of Indian goods and services; and (c) Re-lending facility to overseas banks or multinational banks to enable them to provide them finance to importers of eligible goods and services from India.

(vii) Refinance of Term Loans to Indian Banks: This again is of two types: (a) Refinance of export credit provided by Exim Bank up to 100 per cent in respect of deferred payment loans granted by authorised dealers; and (b) Export bills not exceeding 90 days rediscounted with the Exim Bank by Authorised dealers for reimbursement of their funds.

(viii) Facilities for Deemed Exports: Deemed exports are those as defined by the Ministry of Commerce which result in a saving in foreign exchange or which contribute to foreign exchange earnings such as supplies to export-oriented units or to IBRD-financed projects, etc. These deemed exports are also provided with the same facilities, both funded and non-funded, as in the case of others, by the Exim bank. The definition of deemed exports has been changed by thé govt. as per the requirements.

(ix) Small Scale Industry Export Bills Rediscounting: This facility is designed to help the small scale industry to have more easy access to commercial banks' credit for export purposes. This new scheme was started in 1985 under which the ADs can rediscount with Exim Bank, the export bills of SSIs arising out of post-shipment export credit granted to them.

The latest new schemes in operation since 1992 are the following:

(1) Production Equipment Finance programme for financing equipments, purchased by export-oriented units.

(2) Export Marketing finance to export marketing activities both as loans and grants for strategies marketing in industrialised country by Indian manufacturing companies.

(3) Export vendors Development Finance — The focus under this scheme is to help exporters develop strategic vendor development plans and enhance the export capabilities through creation and strengthening of backward linkages with vendors.

The Exim bank operated schemes as per the requirements. Indian exporters of capital goods, producer goods, engineering goods, turnkey projects, construction projects and consultancy services are all eligible for term finance — funded and unfunded assistance from the Exim Bank. Proposals of more than Rs. 1 crore value are scrutinised by an inter-institutional working group, consisting of Exim Bank as leader, RBI and ECGC as members. Exports on deferred payment credits are eligible for finance and refinance from the Exim Bank, for periods beyond six months and up to 100 per cent of finance required and granted by commercial banks. The rates of interest and margins for various schemes vary from time to time. Normally, periods of credit vary from 1 to 10 years and margins from 10 to 20 per cent. Finance in rupees as well as in foreign currencies depending on the needs is made available by the Exim Bank.

As referred to earlier, the interest rates for export credits were kept considerably lower in more recent years. The Exim Bank rate was reduced to 8.5 per cent since February 1986 for buyers' and sellers' credit. The pre-shipment and post-shipment rates for banks were also lowered to 6.5% if it is foreign currency credit. In February 1987, a new scheme was announced by the Government, whereby exporters would get an interest rebate of 20 per cent of the total interest payable subject to a floor rate of 10 per cent chargeable, if the exporter can sell abroad at least 25 per cent of his production. Interest subsidies were given up since 1994 when current account rupee transactions were freed from controls.

Following deregulation and liberalisation since 1991, the export credit interest rates were hiked up to reduce interest subsidy but since 1998, they were again reduced and concessional interest rates are applied to export credit granted by banks, due to slowing down of export growth and widening trade balance and balance of payments deficits. This trend was reversed in 2002, when for the first time, there was a Current Account Surplus in 2001-02. The export subsidies and interest rate subsidies were all removed or reduced in tune with India's commitments under WTO Agreements after 2002-03. Tariffs and other barriers to trade were reduced or eliminated by 2009-10 and interest subsidy was also brought down to 0.1% of the GDP by 2008-09. As in June 2010, there is only banks' export credit at reduced interest rate of PLR – 2.5 percentage points.

26

Banks and External Sector

Problems of Balance of Payments

The deterioration in balance of payments was visible during the later half of eighties due to sluggish growth in exports and continued rapid growth of imports. There was also a deterioration under many items of current account receipts. This deterioration has worsened during the years of 1989-92, leading to heavy and exceptional drawing from the IMF. India had also to resort to the exceptional financing from the World Bank to the extent of US Dollars 1 billion, including from ADB and Japan. Drawings from the IMF took the form of second drawal equivalent to $ 221 million, in July 1991 and a third drawal of $ 637 million in September 1991 under Compensatory and Contingency Financing Facility and $ 117 million in November 1991 and $ 264 million in January 1992 under the Standby Arrangement. During that critical period of 1989 to 1992, India has drawn heavily from the World Bank and IMF, as the current account deficit during these four years was of the order of Rs. 43,079 crores in total. Our foreign exchange assets including gold stood at a low of Rs. 5,843 crores in June 1990 and Rs. 9,926 crores in June 1991. Subsequently, there was some improvement due to reforms. This improvement was noticed on both, on account of trade and also invisibles due to pick-up of exports and inflow of foreign funds and remittances. During 1994 to 2010, there was again deficit in the current account balance except in 2001-02 to 2003-04. The deficits were growing during 2006-07 to 2009-10 due to global recession in 2008 and 2009. The current account deficit varied from 1 to 2% of GDP.

Inflows increased due to NRI funds following the incentives of fiscal and tax nature and inflow of $ 863 million under Foreign Exchange Immunities Scheme 1991. The scheme of India Development Bonds issued by SBI garnered $ 1,627 million, during 1991-92. During 1992 to 1994, there was a favourable turn of the B.P. position due to faster rise of exports and slow-down of imports and improvement in current account receipts. Foreign exchange assets rose sharply to around $ 20 billion. The strong growth in reserves was essentially due to rising portfolio investment from abroad, inflows on account of GDRs and FCCBs issues by Indian companies and continued current account improvement, following the structural reforms initiated since July 1991. The deterioration after 1994 was due to world economic recession, slow down of exports and larger growth in imports. The U.S. sanctions on India following the pokhran blast of Nuclear Bomb in May 1998 was another setback to growth. The SBI mobilised about US $ 4 billion as Resurgent India Bonds in August 1998 to augment the reserves partly. As a result, the reserves stood at a high of $ 33 billion in June 1999 and $ 76 billion at end March 2003 and $ 141 billion at end March 2005. There was again a deterioration during 2007 to 2010 due to global recession and financial crisis in Europe. The foreign inflows continued with the result that forex reserves grew to around $ 280 billion by March 2010, and $ 291 in May 2012.

Industrial and Trade Policy Changes

Under the recent Economic Reforms initiated since July 1991 Industrial licensing was dispensed with to a large extent. The Capital Issues Control Act was repealed with the result that domestic borrowing by companies in the Capital Market was completely free. The MRTP Act with regard to Asset Limit was amended so that the FERA and Multinational Companies can expand and diversify without limit. Indian Companies are now allowed on a selective basis to borrow abroad. Foreign exchange restrictions were relaxed and FERA was diluted with the result that the exporters are now free to earn and retain foreign exchange abroad. Companies including FERA Companies are free to enter into any industry, expand and diversify without restrictions, export and import freely with minimum restrictions which are imposed in the national interest for defence or strategic reasons.

The Exim Policy announced in March 1992 for the Eighth Plan period 1992-97 eliminates licensing, quantitative restrictions and other regulatory controls. Under the new policy, exports and imports are allowed freely subject to the restrictions of a negative list for exports and one for imports. These negative lists contain goods which are prohibited to be exported or imported, or subject to licence for restricting the trade or for canalisation.

As for quality of exports, the Government have announced special incentives in October 1992 to exporters to attain the internationally accepted standards of quality, for which they should secure the ISO 9000 certification or BIS 14000 certification. They would ensure that our exports can grow on a sustainable basis. Incentives are also provided for export of capital goods, and other items through concessional duties or duty exemption for imports, used in exports. "Deemed Exports" category has been widened and the duty exemption and duty drawback facilities have been extended to them. The benefits of Refund of Terminal excise duty and special import licence have been extended to "deemed exports" category.

Special import licences which are transferable are granted to the following categories on the basis of Net Foreign Exchange (NFE) earned by them:

Exporters to ACU	—	20% of NFE
Deemed Exporters	—	15%
Star Trading Houses	—	10%

Trading Houses	—	7.5%
Export Houses	—	5%

The definitions of trading house, export house, and star trading house have been changed as follows: Export houses = Net Foreign Exchange (NFE) earned Rs. 12 crores. Trading Houses = NFE Rs. 60 crores and Star Trading House = NFE Rs. 150 crores.

Import Policy up to February 92 was one of import compression and since February 1992 it was one of import liberalization. The liberalization was a part of the wide ranging reforms initiated in July 1991 and due to strengthening of foreign exchange reserves. Minimum cash margins imposed on imports in October 1990 was done away with capital goods, raw materials, intermediate components, consumables, spares, parts, accessories, etc., can be imported without a licence. Many items are also put on the canalised list, as for example petroleum products, fertilizers drugs, vegetables oils, seeds, fatty acids and oils and cereals. The customs tariff has also been reduced on many items and were subject to a maximum of 110% only, which was further reduced during later years, to 40-50% (1999), and 5 to 10% by 2004-05.

Plan Achievements

The Current Account deficit as a proportion of GDP was 2.4% in the Seventh Plan but was projected to decline to 1.6% in the Eighth Plan (1992-97). Exports were projected to grow by 13.6% in volume terms in the Eighth Plan. The share of exports in GDP grew to 7.8% during this period, as against 5.2% in the Seventh Plan (1985-90).

The import growth was estimated at 8.4% per annum in the Eighth Plan and the proportion of imports to GDP would be 11.6% as against 8.3% in the Seventh Plan.

During 1985-90, the export growth rate was good even in US dollar terms. For example, it was 15.6% in 1988-89, and 19% in 1989-90 but fell to 9.1% in 1990-91 and led to a negative growth of 1.5% in 1991-92.

During Eighth Plan, exports grew at an annual average of 18% and imports by 20%, with the result that the trade gap widened. More or less the same picture prevailed during the Ninth Plan and Tenth Plan period of 1997 to 2007. During 2009 to 2011, exports grew by about 20%, despite a fall in 2007-09.

Export growth rate during nineties was 8.6% as against 8.1% during eighties. On the other hand, import growth rate spurted up from 7.2% during the eighties to 9.6% during nineties, thus widening the gap between exports and imports. Export growth decelerated during the years 2000-03, due to world economic recession. India's share in world exports continued to be less than 1%. There was again a global recession from 2007 to 2009, but India's share in world exports continued to be around 1% to 1.2%.

The significance of planning has however declined in view of the current economic and financial reforms, the trend to globalisation and privatisation and opening of the economy to foreign forces.

Export Credit

In continuation of the discussion under this head in the last chapter, recent developments are dealt with here. Total export credit by all scheduled commercial banks outstanding at end June 1999 was around 10.3% of bank credit against the target of 12%. The target for 1994-95 and 1995-96 fiscal year at a level of 12% of bank credit was achieved. But this fell to 10-11% in subsequent years was due to decline in growth rate of exports. Exports have grown by about 20% in dollar terms in fiscal 1993-94 and growth was maintained in 1994-95. As end June 1999, export credit stood at Rs. 34,504 crores of which nearly 50% was given back to banks as RBI refinance limits, and this proportion varied from 25% to 50% normally. In absolute terms, export credit declined in 2001-02, as against a significant growth in 2000-01. Export credit continued to rise In absolute figures year after year. Export credit as a percentage non-food gross bank credit was 8% in 1990-91 before the reforms started, but rose to 12% by end of Eighth Plan (1997) but declined to 7% by 2004-05 and further to 5% by 2009. The decline was only in relative terms and the absolute figures are continuing to show a rise. The relative fall as a percentage of non-food gross bank credit was due to greater flow of credit to non-food and non-export sections in the economy. The scheme of Rediscounting of Export bills abroad was introduced in October 1993 and the Scheme of Pre-shipment Export Credit in Foreign Currency in November 1993. Both the Schemes were well received by the exporters. Banks have found that exporters prefer post-shipment export credit denominated in dollars as it is relatively cheaper.

Since July 1991, the Government and the RBI have taken a number of measures to promote the export growth through the banking policy. However, with partial convertibility of rupee since March 1992, some schemes like CCs and Exim scrips etc., were withdrawn. Earlier in August 1991, the Export Credit (Interest Subsidy) scheme 1968 was also withdrawn. Effective October 1992, interest rate on rupee export credit was reduced by one percentage point and in March 1993, by a further one percentage point to 13%. Effective April 1993, Government have exempted the export credit from the levy of interest tax, which resulted in a relief of 0.5% in the interest rate to exporters. Exporters do not need any further incentives when rupee was made fully convertible on current account since 1994-95. Export refinance from RBI is however continued.

Authorised dealers were allowed to rediscount the export bills abroad at rates linked to interest rates abroad without reference to RBI. The banks can draw on the foreign currency balances abroad (Nostro Accounts) or in Foreign Currency Non-resident accounts, Exchange Earners Foreign Currency accounts, Residents' Foreign currency accounts etc. Importers can secure funds in foreign currency from any of the above accounts at LIBOR related interest rates abroad.

In order to provide the exporters bank credit at international interest rates, a scheme has been started in October - November 1993, called Pre-shipment Credit Foreign Currencies is (PCFC). This provides credit for imports by exporters for their inputs and for export as well. These credits are available in foreign currencies at the international market rates and LIBOR related rates. For these credits, the RBI refinance, is not however, available, as per the latest credit policy. But the scheme has been liberalised effective May 1994 by making available the running account facility to all exporters having a good track record. Bank credit for exports stood at Rs. 33,442 crores as in June 2011

Exports recorded a negative growth in 1998-99. The trade deficit has widened as a result. Export growth picked up in 1999-2000. Export growth became negative again in 2001-02, after which there was a continuous growth in exports by more than 20% each year.

The Table below shows the data of post reform period. The exports picked up immediately after the trade liberalisation since 1992 and this growth received a set-back in 1997-98 and continued in 1998-99. The trade deficit started widening in 1995-96 and in 1999-2000 and again from 2004-05 to 2009-10.

Table 26.1: Trade Data

(in U.S billions)

Year	92-93	95-96	97-98	98-99	99-00	2001-02	03-04	04-05	08-09	10-11
Exports	18.5	31.8	35.0	33.7	36.8	43.8	63.8	85.5	182.8	254.4
Imports	21.8	36.7	41.5	41.9	49.7	51.4	78.1	111.5	298.8	352.5
Trade Deficit	3.3	4.9	6.5	8.2	12.9	7.6	14.3	28.0	–116	–98.2

Net invisibles have grown during the last decade by six times, while exports have grown only by three times. Current Account turned surplus in atleast three years out of ten years.

Export Credit Refinance

Export credit has been growing rapidly over the last few years with the result that the target for export credit at 10% of the total bank credit fixed for June 1993 was achieved much earlier. As already referred, the target has since been revised upwards to 12% of total bank credit. Simultaneously, the utilisation of RBI refinance facility has come down as the banks have been flushed with funds. During March 1993, export credit refinance limits have reached historic high levels of 69.2% of export credit. But as referred to earlier, utilisation of the limits has come down in later years. The RBI has therefore brought down the refinance limits by stages in May 1993 and again in May 1994 to lower level as compared to before. With the comfortable liquidity position of banks, the moderation in export refinance limits did not affect the lending by banks for export purposes after 2000-01.

The scheme of post-shipment Export credit denominated in US dollars proved attractive to exporters; but the amounts involved do not qualify for refinance from RBI. However, the scheme of Pre-shipment Export credit in Foreign Currency (PCFC) which was introduced in November 1993, proved very useful and the amounts involved have gone up.

Export and Import Bank of India

In continuation of the discussion under this head in the last chapter, the Exim Bank continued the financing and refinancing activities in relation to foreign trade. It provides the funded assistance to both exporters and importers as also the non-funded assistance in the form of guarantee to banks on behalf of both Indian and foreign parties. It is the agency for promoting exports and foreign investments.

At present it has been operating the following five schemes:

(1) Foreign Currency Pre-shipment Credit: It is a short-term pre-shipment credit in foreign currency and enables exporters to avail of financial assistance from commercial banks to meet the cost of imported inputs required for export production.

(2) Production Equipment Finance Programme: It ensures rupee finance of medium and long-term nature to eligible exporters for acquiring small equipments and parts under one umbrella agreement.

(3) European Community International Investment Partners: (ECIIP) It aims at promoting joint ventures in India with private sector, small and medium enterprises in the E.C. It also ensures financial support for such ventures.

(4) Forfeiting: Under forfeiting programmes, facilities are provided to Indian exporters for discounting their medium and long-term export receivables without recourse basis with international forfeiting agencies. This will help export sales on credit to be on cash basis, in effect, through the discounting of export bills, by forfeiting agency.

(5) Business Advisory and Technical Assistance Programme: (BATA) This would provide services of technical assistance to Indian exporters to the IFC sponsored BATA Programme for the Caribbean, Central America, South Pacific, Poland and other East European countries.

Export Assistance

Exim Bank/ECGC Counter Guarantee.

The Export performance guarantee is given by the ECGC, against the credit guarantee by banks. The expert assistance granted by Exim bank is in the form of refinancing of export credit granted by eligible authorized dealers, and in the form of long-term finance guarantee, and long-term finance for the export of capital and engineering goods and project exports on deferred payment basis in participation with the scheduled banks.

The RBI provides also refinance facilities to Exim bank and to authorised dealers. By this refinance facility, the Exim is in a position to disburse foreign currency lines of credit to exporters. Due to the global recession in 2008-09, there was a decline in export growth and exporters were in troubles. To relieve these difficulties, RBI has announced a rupees 5,000 crore refinance to the

Exim bank to be passed on to exporters. The RBI has also promised to help exporters as and when need to tide over difficult times in 2008-09.

Export credit insurance is also provided by ECGC, so that exporters can get the timely and adequate finance from banks. The ECGC provides guarantees to banks to protect them from the risk of loss in financing exporters which facilitates greater funds from banks to the export business. The insurance covers the country risk and shipment risks, buyers' risk and socio-political risks of the counter-party. ECGC policies are tuned to provide risk insurance to exporters and guarantors to banks against these risks. The policies by the ECGC are in the form of standard policy, specific policy, financial guarantors and special scheme guarantees. These guarantees and schemes of the ECGC aim at covering the commercial risks, political risks, and in-transit risks of shipments, war natural calamities, etc.

BANKS AND INDIAN COMPANIES

In recent years with privatisation and globalisation of the economy, the Corporate Sector began to increasingly depend upon the new issues market and domestic and foreign capital markets. Their dependence upon banks and financial institutions including the Public Sector Banks began to decline, but their reliance on the domestic capital increased to Rs. 29,578 crores during 1993-94 as against Rs. 21,651 crores in 1992-93. This has gone up to Rs. 72,061 crores in 2001-02 (including private placements). Now that the Indian Companies are having access to foreign markets through Indian and Foreign banks abroad and foreign financial institutions, they started borrowing abroad since 1992. Given the low interest rates of 4% in international markets, the Indian companies with good credit rating would benefit through foreign currency issues and convertible bonds, and global depository receipts. Although GDRs are issued in foreign currencies either in the form of shares or bonds they will be denominated in Rupees upon conversion into shares of the issuing company. Banks have a crucial role in the above process. GDRs are traded abroad and are mostly on discount in the foreign market. The GDRs were issued for 918 million US Dollars during 1996-97 by the corporates and their borrowing abroad through GDR and FCCBs has increased after 1994[@] due to liberalisation of conditions. In 1997-98 seven issues were floated for a total of Rs. 4,387 crores as compared to 16 issues for a total of Rs. 3,275 crores in 1996-97. The amount raised fell later due to depressed market conditions and lower credit rating of India following Pokhran nuclear testing.

As per the notification of the Government in May 1994, a company or a group of companies will not be allowed to borrow more than two times during the financial year, and a minimum gap of 12 months is necessary between two issues. Out of the proceeds of the issues, 85% has to be used for imports of capital goods, plant, machinery, etc. The rest of the amount of 15% can be used for general purposes including corporate restructuring. The companies have to submit quarterly returns on the use of these funds to the Government, Ministry of Finance. The GDRs have no lock

@ There was also borrowing in the form of ECBs which reached a peak in 1998-99 but declined to a net outflow of us $ 1.1 billion due to prepayments of many high cost earlier borrowings in 2001-02. They reached a peak of $ 22.6% billion in 2007-08.

in period, they are traded as if they are shares in foreign markets until conversion or redemption. The interest payments and dividends are subject to deduction of tax at source at 10%. Besides, capital gains on account of all these transactions outside India are free from any Indian tax. The GDRs are the resulting instruments of credit from overseas depository banks, which are authorised by the issuing companies in India to issue outside the country. GDRs to non-resident foreigners and NRIs against the deposit of shares of the Issuing Company in India. These shares are held by denominated domestic custodian bank. The GDRs are negotiable and all transactions in GDRs are exempted from Indian taxes so long as they are executed outside India. Fresh guidelines were issued by the Government in October 1994 removing the stipulation that Euro issue funds should be used within one year from the date of issue and other conditions were also liberalised in 1996. The amount of ECBS, raised abroad amounted to us $ 22.6 billion in 2007-08 before falling to $ 8.1 billion in 2008-09.

BANKS AND FOREIGN CAPITAL

Under the present liberalised financial scenario and globalisation trends, banks' role has become more important in the economy. Banks help the external sector by financing of exports and export production, financing of imports and providing foreign exchange for outward and inward remittance, and funds flow both for current and capital account transactions. They take more foreign exchange risk, foreign credit risk and provide necessary funds to public, business and government. They facilitate the growth of exports and import financing and provide hedge against foreign currency risk. Among banks, the multinationals and foreign banks are more involved in the external sector and with their contacts and counterpart agencies abroad, they are in better position now to provide services in the external sector and in foreign exchange. They are helping Indian corporate Sector to raise funds abroad as equity or debt in the Euro currency market and through foreign financial institutions in the form of GDRs and Euro bonds and foreign currency convertible bonds. The banks and public are now allowed to deal in foreign exchange more freely than before, due to relaxation of FERA and keep accounts abroad or borrow from abroad. Some public financial institutions and banks, including UTI have floated offshore funds to raise finance in foreign currencies, of which atleast 20% should be invested in Indian Corporate Sector. In the issue and marketing of these bonds, as much as GDRs and offshore funds, etc., the major Investment and Security Firms like Merril Lynch, Robert Fleming, Morgan Stanley, Baring Securities, etc., have acted as the lead managers.

As many as 50 giant companies of India have borrowed abroad over the recent years in the form of GDRs. The largest amount of borrowing namely of $ 450 million was raised by the Reliance Industries, followed by Grasim Industries with $ 190 million and Hindal company $ 172 million. The underlying shares for each GDR may vary from 1 to 10, depending upon the market price of share in India converted into foreign currency. The issue price per share (GDR) will thus, be decided by the issue managers, depending upon the domestic market price of the share, converted into the relevant foreign currency, credit rating of the company and country and foreigner's perception of the issuing company and country, etc. Indian banks and foreign banks play a major role in arranging these issues.

Exchange Rate and Banks

Rupee was first devalued by around 18% in July 1991, in two instalments. This was followed by abolition of cash compensatory support scheme, earlier made available to exporters as an incentive, but to keep incentive for exports to grow, a new scheme of exim scrips to exporters was introduced. These were made transferable and tradeable and entitled the holder to freely import foreign goods needed for domestic production. This export incentive scheme became unnecessary when in March 1992, the rupee was made partially convertible on trade account up to 60% of the export proceeds. The rest of the 40% was to be sold to the banks at the official rate of exchange by exporters. This led to the introduction of Liberalised Exchange Rate Management System (LERMS) where in the RBI manages the stability of the exchange rate through limited intervention. The experience with this by banks has proved to be beneficial to trade and encouraged the Government to move to more liberalised system. Later in March 1993, rupee was made fully convertible on trade account to boost the exports, with 100% of exports converted at the market rates. The export incentives such as Exim Scrips were withdrawn. In March 1994, full Rupee convertibility on current account was also announced with the result that the banks in India have to operate in a free foreign exchange market, exposing themselves to greater risks.

Recent Changes in Bank Activity

Banks have been given more freedom of borrowing and lending both internally and externally and the recent measures of financial deregulation have freed the controls on the interest rates to a large extent and facilitated the freer functioning of the banks in lending and investment operations. Besides, since 1994 banks are also permitted to enter directly into leasing, hire purchase and factoring services, instead of through their subsidiaries, as before. Banks are now free to enter or exit into any fields depending on their profitability and commercial considerations. Banks can borrow from abroad and enter into forward covers abroad on interest rates and exchange rates. Even now they are allowed to operate them on a limited scale. Of course these activities are subject to certain guidelines from the RBI.

Invisible Trade and Banks

India has a surplus in invisible trade account since 1973-74. But again in 1990-91, it had a net deficit. After the economic and financial reforms were started in 1991-92, the trend to privatisation and globalisation was initiated. Since then, there was a continuous net surplus in invisible trade account. As compared to a surplus of US $ 31,232 million in 2004-05 in invisible trade, there was a larger deficit on merchandise account of $ 33,702 million, leading to Current Account deficit as against surpluse in the earlier three years. As compared to 1991-92, the net invisible surplus in 2004-05 was higher by twenty times. During the same period, the merchandise exports rose by only 4.4 times in dollar terms. What emerges from these trends is that, India has better comparative advantage in services which led to an unprecedented rise in net surplus in invisible trade account as against continued and rising deficits in merchandise trade account. After 2004-05 there was a continued risk in net invisible account surplus which stood at $ 89.6 billion in 2008-09.

In the national economy also, the role of services sector has seen unprecedented growth during the last one decade. During the above period of post economic reforms (1991-92 to 2004-05) services under GDP have grown by nearly three times, while the overall GDP at constant prices grew only by two times. While the GDP growth rate during 2001 to 2005 was about 6 to 8%, that of the services sector was 9%. Similarly, while during the nineties the services sector accounted for only less than 50% of the GDP, the same during the latest period 2005-2009 accounted for about 65% of the GDP. This clearly evidences the relative importance of the services in the GDP in the Indian economy. The same is reflected in the growth of invisible trade of India, vis-a-vis the merchandise trade.

Exports of merchandise as a percentage of GDP grew from a mere 5.8% in 1990-91 to 9.9% in 2000-01 and 11.7% in 2008-09. The imports grew from 8.8% of GDP in 1990-91 to 12.7% in 2000-01 and 29% in 2008-09. Import growth rate was not only higher throughout but it has grown faster than the growth rate of exports with the result that the gap between them widened and merchandise trade balance has been negative and was growing.

A reverse picture was presented by the invisible receipts and payments. Thus, the invisible receipts as a percentage of GDP was only 2.4% in 1990-91, which was the same for the invisible payments in that year. But the invisible receipts as a percentage of GDP grew from 2.4% in 1990-91 to 2.9% in 2004-05 and to 4.8% in 2008-09. The invisible receipts growth was higher than that of merchandise exports growth. Besides, the invisible receipts grew at a faster rate than that of invisible payments with the result that the net surplus on invisible account was growing. The invisible payments rose form 1.6% of GDP in 2004-05 to 2.1% of GDP in 2008-09.

The net invisible surplus grew by nearly 33 times by 2004-05 as compared to the Pre-Reform period of 1991-92. Between 2004-05 and 2008-09 net surplus rose by three times. As compared with 1994-95, a decade ago, the net invisible surplus grew by only 8 times. Even so, the growth of invisible trade was by faster rate in some years particularly between 1991-92 and 2000-01 (the decade of nineties), which was mainly attributed to growth of new knowledge based services, Telecommunications, I.T., media Travel and Transportation, etc., which has brought about a revolution in economic and financial scenario. Sub-sectoral analysis of the performance of services sector shows that Trade, Hotels, Transport and Communications contributed to about two-thirds of the growth, followed by Finance, insurance and Business Services (about one-fourth to one-fifth of the growth of services sector).

The services sector remained the key driving force in the economy and its contribution to GDP growth has been more than 50% since 1997-98. The share of services sector in the GDP at 57.6% in 2004-05 and 64.5% in 2008-09 and was higher than in other developing countries in general. In particular the contribution of I.T. software and I.T. based services (BPO) has been significant for the growth of services sector and for exports of these services.

Banks' role in financing of invisibles trade and in facilitating the inflows and outflows is equally important. The one mode of rising influence of the banks is the Road map drawn up by the RBI for the presence of foreign banks in India and of Indian banks abroad, through opening of foreign branches or wholly owned subsidiaries. (WOS) The W.O.S. would have minimum capital of Rs.300 crores and sound corporate governance and as per the commitments to WTO foreign bank branch expansion is permitted in India, according to the prevailing policy, in underbanked areas.

The Indian branches of foreign banks and foreign branches of Indian banks would help in the travel and transportation segment of service sector exports and imports. Business and professional services and IT related services would all go through the banks' clearing and settlement system. In the acquisition and mergers and in setting up of joint ventures for construction projects, hospital and hospitality business services, the banks provide the guarantee and foreign finance and access to the foreign markets for commercial borrowing and for arranging for ADRs and GDRs, etc.

All Current Account transactions are now free from RBI controls in addition to a few capital account transactions. All these have to flow through the ADs and with greater delegation of powers to them to operate for the portfolio investments of FFI and FIIs in addition to NRIs and OCBs, the role of banks in invisible trade account has vastly increased and this in particular has facilitated the unprecedented increase in invisible trade and in receipts and payments on this account. The dealings in foreign exchange are a necessary part of these inflows and outflows under Current Account, referred to above.

Factoring

In addition to other services which banks provide to export sector, mention must be made of the Factoring and Forfeiting Services. Factoring refers to lending against book debits and receivables which are taken over from the customer company by the bank. Factoring and forfeiting have not taken off in the Indian soil due to lack of expertise and experience in this line. The risks involved in this context in India are high and banks are conservative. Even after setting up the subsidiaries for this purpose in 1991, the actual business was started only in April 1994.

Factoring services rendered are the following:

(1) Purchase of book debts and receivables.

(2) Administration of sales ledger of the clients.

(3) Prepayment of debts partially or fully.

(4) Collection of book debts or receivables with or without documents.

(5) Covering the credit risk of the suppliers.

(6) Dealing in book debts of customers without recourse.

Mechanics of operation of factoring:

(1) Assess the credit standing of the client.

(2) Set a credit risk limit and open a line of credit.

(3) Factor fixes the limits to credit exposure and time periods.

(4) Client sells the goods to the customer and invoices the bills assigning them to be paid to the factor.

(5) Copies of invoices and receipted delivery challans are handed over to the factor for further action.

(6) Factor provides the payment up to 80% of value of invoice after scrutiny of the documents.

(7) Customer who purchased has to provide the rest of 20% of the value.

(8) Factor sends statements for the bills purchased and collections made and charges debited to the client.

WHAT IS FORFEITING?

Forfeiting is the conversion of credit bills into cash by discounting them. Only foreign bills are involved in the transactions:

Bills for the supply of raw materials include:

- of inputs
- of capital goods

Earlier consortium lending and government to government lending is replaced now by the forfeiting. It is discounting at fixed rate for foreign bills of trade and involves providing finance for any type of and duration of international trade flow.

FACTORING VS. FORFEITING

(1) Forfeiting applies to international trade only, while factoring refers to domestic bills - purchase and discount.

(2) Risks taken are risks of debtor, debtor country, currency risk, goods at sea, etc. - These are specific to forfeiting.

(3) Forfeiting may be through Exim Bank or in collaboration with Foreign Forfeiting agency, in Foreign country.

(4) Forfeiting involves accepting the above risks and discounting the bills/promissory notes and other documents in international trade thereby making a credit sale by exporter only cash sale in practice.

(5) Forfeiting is either with recourse or without recourse. Mostly, the preference of exporter is for forfeiting without recourse, in which risk is borne by the forfeiting agency.

(6) Conversion of credit bills to cash — only foreign bills are used through foreign agencies, or importers in the importing country or in a third country.

(7) R.B.I. permission was granted to Exim Bank for forfeiting, along with other services it renders to exporters.

Problem Areas in Forfeiting

(1) There is no legal framework to protect the banker or forfeitor except for the existing covers for the risks involved in any foreign trade transaction.

(2) The forfeitors suffer from lack of reliable data on credit rating of foreign agencies or importer or foreign country. As such, even EXIM bank may not cover some countries like Nigeria which are high risk countries.

(3) High country and political risks dissuade the services of factoring and banking to many clients.

(4) High costs are involved due to high risks in this area.

(5) There is need for some changes in Law for developing a secondary market in them.

(6) Forfeiting can be separately provided for any single shipment or a series of shipments for a deal involving many shipments, but the rates will vary depending on the risks involved. These risks vary very widely depending on the time period, distance, nature of the trade and contractual terms etc. The commodities and countries involved determine the degree of risk that the Factor has to bear in the transaction and whether it should be made with recourse or without recourse.

Factoring and Forfeiting

Banks do provide non-bank financial services in the form of leasing, hire purchase, housing finance, factoring and forfeiting. By an amendment to the Banking Regulation Act in 1983, banks have been permitted to provide these services either through their own Departments or divisions or through their subsidiaries, set up for the purpose. Banks have set up merchant banking and mutual fund subsidiaries and have been undertaking direct and indirect lending for housing purposes. Other services such as leasing and hire purchase were undertaken on a limited scale and more so through their subsidiaries. In fact, the services of factoring and forfeiting were only a recent developments following the recommendations of the Kalyanasundaram Committee, set up by the RBI in 1988. Since then considerable work has been done, preparatory for the successful operation of these services by banks.

Vaghul Committee Report on Money Market reforms has also suggested the developments of new instruments of factoring and forfeiting services for trading in the Money market, in 1989. Later the first factoring company was started by the SBI in 1991, followed by Canara Bank and PNB, setting the subsidiaries for the purpose. While the SBI would provide such services in the Western region, the RBI has permitted the Canara Bank and PNB to concentrate on the Southern and Northern regions of the country respectively, for providing such services for the customers.

The distinction between factoring and forfeiting has to be borne in mind at this juncture. Both are similar in that they relate to the purchase of book debts; while the factoring refers to purchase of domestic book debts and receivables, etc., the forfeiting refers to the foreign bills, book debts and receivables etc., in foreign currencies. Both relate conversion of credit to cash transactions of clients. Credit risk and collection troubles are the responsibilities of the factoring agency. In the case of forfeiting there are country and currency risks also in addition to the credit risk of the party. On the basis of the statement of the bank, providing the factoring services, the client can draw funds up to the limits, which in turn depend on: New book debts factored, old book debts factored and collected and amounts realised and charges debited to the client. Factoring can be with recourse or without recourse. Normally, it is without recourse, when risk is borne by the forfeiting agency.

Other Services

The Factoring agency, being generally the banker or its subsidiary knows the client and his creditworthiness. The other services provided depend upon the banker-customer relationship, his requirements and the circumstances of the case. The Factor may give a sanctioned limit, on the basis of their assessment of the book debts and receivables and this position is reviewed periodically. The Factor provides his client with a periodical statement on sanctioned limit, utilised credit and balance outstanding, etc. The data includes the list of book debts taken over, realised, age-wise classification of them, collected and due for collection and those with recourse and without recourse etc.

Impact of Forfeiting

Both factoring and forfeiting are alike so far as the bank's services are concerned. Both purchase bills for cash or accept for collection. The attendent risks and return are different in these cases and the method of credit assessment and risk and examination of documents will all be different.

Another aspect of these services is the effect of them on the Balance sheet of the Factor and the client respectively. So far as the Factor is concerned, it is an off-balance sheet item in the case of bills with recourse. But if the bills are taken without recourse, they will appear as contingent liability in the footnotes. The reverse is the case of the client, whose balance sheet will now be devoid of such burden on the debts or receivables and give a better and healthy picture. So far as the client is concerned, the changes in the balance sheet due to factoring and forfeiting are brought out in the example given below:

Factoring and Balance Sheet

Impact of factoring on the balance sheet entries is shown below:

In (Rs. Crores)

Current Liabilities		Current Assets		
Bank Borrowing against		Inventory	100	
Inventory	70	Receivables	80	180
Against Receivables	40	Other Current Assets		20
	110			
Other Current Liabilities	40			
Net Working Capital	50			
	200			200

Original Current Ratio 1.33:1 - (200: 150)

Assets of receivables of 80 are purchased by the Factoring Agency. Factor pays 80% of this (64) to the client. Due from factor remains 16. The new balance sheet will appear as follows:

Current Liabilities		Current Assets	
Bank Borrowing against		Inventory	100
Inventory	70	Receivable (Due from Factor)	16
		Other Current Assets	20
Other Current Liabilities	16		
New Working Capital	50		
	136		136

New Current Ratio is 1.58:1 - (136:86)

The new current ratio is better for the client and his credit rating goes up before the public eye.

Bills purchased by the Factor will be off balance sheet item for the factor.

If it is with recourse, it appears as a contingent liability for the client.

Effects

This leads to reduction in debts and less collection problems. It is an off-balance sheet item. Reduction in bank finance, improvement in current ratio of the client, higher credit standing, reduction in costs, time saved and more efficiency in production and distribution and better planning, etc., are the major effects, beneficial to the company, in the investors' perception.

PART – V

FOREIGN MARKETS

Definition

Foreign Exchange as a subject deals with the means and methods by which rights to income and wealth in one country's currency are converted into similar rights in terms of another country's currency. It involves the investigation of the methods by which the currency of one country is exchanged for that of another, the causes which render such exchange necessary, the forms in which exchange may take place and the ratios or equivalent values at which such exchanges are effected.

Such exchanges may be in the form of one currency to another or of conversion of credit instruments denominated in different currencies such as cheques, drafts, airmail transfers, fax and telegraphic transfers, cable transfers, bills of exchange, trade bills, banker's bill or any promissory notes. It is through these instruments and foreign currency accounts of banks that the banks are able to effect such exchange of currencies or claims to currencies.

Every exchange of goods and services is having a corresponding exchange of remittances involving two currencies, as depicted in the Chart below.

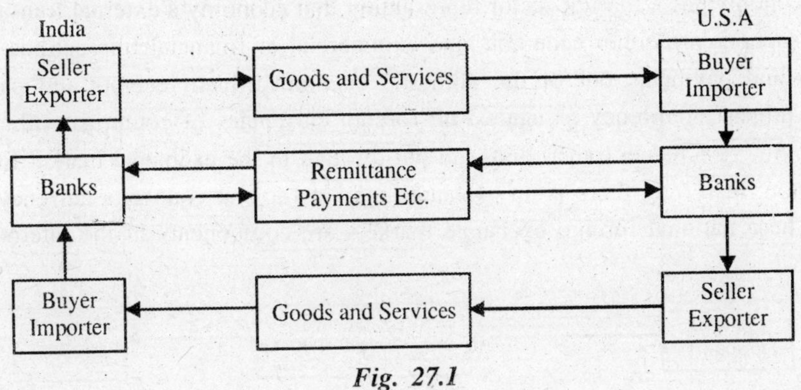

Fig. 27.1

No currency will be physically exchanged as it is not legal tender in any country other than in the issuing country. So exchanges take place through book entries and/or through credit instruments by banks. The instruments through which exchanges of currencies take place are Cash in physical form, Telegraphic Transfers (TTs), Mail Transfers (MT), Demand Drafts (DDs), cheques, Bills of Exchange, etc. In the absence of banks, the buyer-importer who has to pay in dollars has to hunt for an exporter-seller who received an equivalent amount of dollars from the foreign importer. Bank facilitates, such transactions by acting as intermediaries between buyers and sellers or importers and exporters.

International Financial System and Foreign Exchange Market

One of the important components of the international financial system is the foreign exchange market. The various commercial and financial transactions as between countries result in receipts and payments as between them. The items of balance of payments leading to receipts and payments have been referred to in an earlier chapter, namely, trade, travel, transportation, royalties, fees, investment income, unilateral transfers, short-term and long-term capital receipts and payments etc. Such receipts and payments involve exchange of one currency for another. Thus, rupee is a legal tender in India, but an exporter in UK will have no use for these rupees. He, therefore, wishes to receive from the importer in India only in pound sterling. Then the importer will have to convert such rupees into pounds, in that transaction; the foreign exchange market provides facilities for such operations. The demand for goods and services from one country to another is the basis for demand for currencies in the exchange market. Such merchandise and invisible trade items constitute nearly 70-80 per cent of the total transactions in the market with the public. Conversion of currencies is also necessary for short-term capital flows or long-term investment in financial or physical assets of another country. It will thus be seen that the exchange markets are necessary not only for trade transactions but for any financial receipts or payments as between countries. Any receipt and payment of foreign cash, coins, claims in currencies or credit instruments involve a foreign exchange transaction.

Foreign Sector and Foreign Exchange Market

Each economy has a foreign sector representing that economy's external transactions. All such external transactions are either economic and commercial or financial transactions. These result in receipts into and payments out of the domestic economy. Such receipts and payments involve exchange of domestic currency as against all foreign currencies of countries with which economy has dealings. Such exchange transactions are put through in the exchange market for that currency. For each nation, therefore, there is an exchange market for that country's currency vis-a-vis other currencies. These national foreign exchange markets are components of the international financial system.

There is thus, as for any other currency, a market for the rupee. If an Indian bank buys dollars, it will pay rupees for dollars and if it sells dollars, it will receive rupees for dollars. The origin of these transactions in an export or an import, inward or outward remittances or any similar transactions between Indian residents and foreign residents. An exporter in India receives dollars from say, USA and he surrenders the bill of exchange along with other documents to his bank. The bank would have bought that currency from the exporter. The Bank has since been on the look-out for selling those dollars in the foreign exchange market for those in need of dollars. Let us say an importer in India importing from the USA is in need of dollars to pay to the exporter. Another bank is approached by the importer with a demand for dollars and the former must have sold dollars to the importer. Having sold dollars that bank would then buy the dollars to cover up their position from the former bank.

Thus, basically demand for and supply of foreign currencies arises from exporters or importers or the public having some receipts from or payments to foreign countries. These receipts or payments may give rise to foreign credit instruments which the banks buy or sell at specified rates. There are different rates for buying and selling in which an interest element is included and quoted by the banks if the bill or promissory note or any instrument of exchange is not a demand or sight bill but a usance note involving some period to run to maturity for payment. Even in the case of sight bills, some grace period of 2 days and transit period of 10 to 20 days are allowed as fixed by the Foreign Exchange Dealers' Association, depending upon the place on which it is drawn and interest element for these periods is also included in the rate quoted by banks.

Banks generally cover up these positions in currencies by corresponding purchases or sales from other banks. Such a market as between banks is called inter-bank market. There are reputed brokers who act as intermediaries for banks in these transactions. They give bid and offer rates for purchase and sale of currencies and the margin between bid and offer rates is the profit for the bank or the intermediary wholesaler. In the retail market banks deal with their clients or customers. On an average daily turnover in the inter bank market is nearly four times that in the retail trade or merchant trade with the public in the Forex Market in India (as per data published by the RBI).

Banks' Purchase and Sale

Every foreign exchange transactions involves a two-way conversion — a purchase and a sale. Conversion of rupees into dollars involves purchase of dollars and sale of rupees or vice versa depending upon the angle from which we are looking. If it is looked at from the country having rupees (India), then the transaction looks as follows:

(a) Sale of rupees for dollars (importer) — conversion of home currency into foreign currency.

(b) Purchase of rupees for dollars (exporter) — conversion of foreign currency into home currency (see the chart below)

As an Indian banker has to keep his accounts in rupees, he buys and sell foreign currencies like any commodity for money (Indian rupee).

Instruments of Credit Traded

In addition to conversion of foreign currency notes and cash for domestic currency notes/coin, a number of instruments of credit are used for effecting conversion of one currency into another. These instruments are discussed below.

(1) Telegraphic Transfers (TT): A TT is a transfer of money by telegram or cable or telex or fax from one centre to another in a foreign country. It is a method used by banks with their own codes and correspondent relations with banks abroad for transmission of funds. As it involves the payment of funds on the same day, it is the quickest means of transmission of funds. As there is no loss of interest or capital risk in this mode, it enjoys the best rate for the value of receipts.

(2) Mail Transfers (MT): It is an order to pay cash to a third party sent by mail by a bank to its correspondent or branch abroad. It is issued in duplicate — one to the party buying it and the banker — correspondent or agent abroad. The amount is paid by the agent bank to the third party mentioned therein in the transferee country by its own cheque or by crediting the party's account. As the payment is made after the mail advice is received at the other end, which will take a few days, the rate charged to the purchaser is cheaper to the extent of the interest gain to the seller-bank. MT rates are cheaper than TT rates.

(3) Drafts and Cheques: Draft is a pay order issued by a bank on its own branch or correspondent bank abroad. It is payable on sight but there is always a time lapse in the transit or in post between the payment by the purchaser of the draft to his bank and the receipt of the money by the seller in the foreign centre. As in the case of MT, there is risk of loss of the draft in transit, delay in effecting payment to the beneficiary and loss of interest during the intervening period. The rate charged by the bank for this is less advantageous to the buyer of the draft than in other modes.

(4) Bills of Exchange: It is an unconditional order in writing addressed by one person to another, requiring the person to whom it is addressed to pay a certain sum on demand or within a specified date. If it is payable on demand, it is a sight bill and if it is payable after a period, it is a long bill or a usance bill. Such bills can be banker's bills or trade bills. Bank bills are drawn on a bank abroad. While the bank bills carry better rates due to their greater security, the trade bills drawn on private parties my not fetch good rates. Sight bills are paid on sight but allow a transit period of 10 to 20 days for which interest is lost. In the case of usance bills, the purchase price is adjusted on the basis of maturity date of the bill for the interest lost, adjusted in the rate quoted for such a bill.

Foreign Exchange Market Components

There are three major components of this market, depending upon the level at which transactions are put through:

(1) Firstly, transaction between the public and the banks at the base level involve receipts from and payments to the public or purchases from and sales to public.

(2) Secondly, transactions as between the banks dealing in foreign exchange involving conversion of currencies taking place in the same centre or as between centres in the same country (inter-bank market) or as between countries involving the correspondent or agent banks abroad or branches of the domestic banks abroad.

(3) Thirdly, transactions between banks and central bank involving purchase and sale of foreign currencies for cover or final disposal of excess foreign balances. The central banks may in turn deal with the foreign central banks or foreign governments.

Basically, the above exchanges involve no physical exchange of currencies except in small denominations when travellers and tourists carry them across national borders, but through exchange of credit instruments or book entries in the books of banks in various centres. The banks are linked together by phone, cable, telex, post or other means of communication. The transactions are put through directly by the banks or through the brokers located at various centres where these transactions are concentrated like Mumbai, Kolkota, Chennai, etc. All the dealer banks in foreign exchange in India have an Association called Foreign Exchange Dealers' Association.

Exchange Rate Mechanism

As in the case of any commodity, there is a price for any purchase or sale of a currency. Such a price in the exchange market is called the exchange rate. This is defined as the number of units of one currency that will be exchanged for a unit of another currency. The exchange rate of any currency can be expressed in two ways one in terms of the number of foreign currency units against a given unit of domestic currency (Thus, ₹ 100 = £ 1.4734 as Indirect method) and the other in terms of the number of domestic currency units against a given unit of foreign currency. Thus, £ 1 = ₹ 75.60 as direct method as at end June 2003 and ₹ 72.85 as at end March 2009.

It is pertinent to ask what factors normally determine the exchange rate in the market. Prima facie, if the market is free and rate are allowed to fluctuate, the exchange rate would depend on the supply of and demand for a currency. Thus, taking dollars vis-a-vis rupees, the rate is determined by the demand for dollars and supply of dollars in relation to the rupee. Those who demand dollars are primarily importers from the USA to India who have to pay the US exporters in dollars Similarly, those who supply dollars are primarily the exporters to USA who are paid in dollars by importers in USA.

The rate of exchange is determined at any moment by the forces of demand for and supply of a currency which in turn depends on the demand for and supply of commodities and services as between India and the USA. They also depend on arbitrage and interest rate speculation, currency speculation and short-term capital flows if these are permitted. This can be represented diagrammatically as follows:

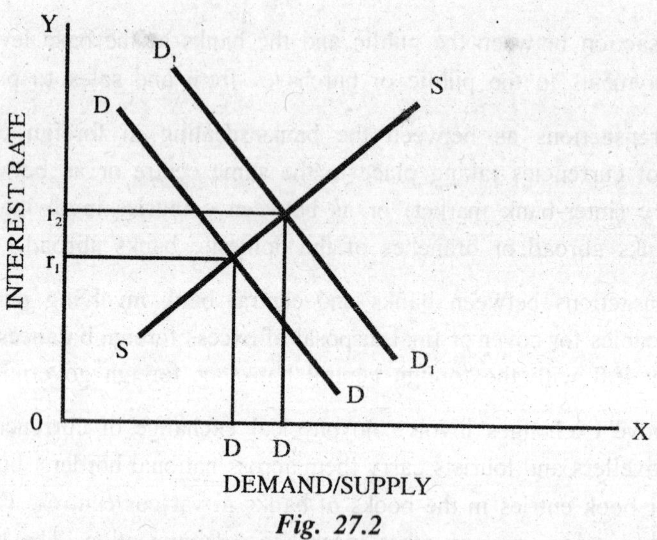

Fig. 27.2

Given the supply (SS), if the demand increases from DD to $D_1 D_1$ the rate will rise from r_1 to r_2 and vice versa. A rise in the rate for rupee means more foreign currency units are given for a given unit of domestic currency.

Gustav's Theory

The basic factors which determine the exchange rates are the intrinsic purchasing power of the currencies in their own domestic economies. In the era of paper currencies, which are not backed by gold or gold exchange standard, currencies of different countries are not based on their intrinsic worth in terms of gold, but in terms of what Prof. Gustav Cassel, the renowned classical economist, called the Purchasing Power Parity Theory. According to this theory, exchange rates are determined by what each unit of a currency can buy in terms of real goods and services in its own country. The rate of exchange is the amount of currency which would buy the equivalent basket of goods and services in both the countries. Such an exercise in real world is based on comparison at two periods of time, with one year as the basis of comparison, but no absolute comparison as between two currencies is possible as the pattern of goods and services produced varies from country to country. It is assumed that the base year prices in both the countries are at equilibrium and the exchange ratio at that time represents the ratio of their purchasing powers. Thus, if the base period exchange rate is 1:1 a doubling of prices in the domestic economy of B with A's price remaining constant, would lead to a new exchange rate of 1:2. This ratio would set the bounds or limits to day-to-day fluctuations in the exchange rates based on the supply or demand forces for each currency.

Limitations

This theory of Gustav is criticised on the ground that the quality of goods and services in both the countries is not the same and that a comparison of them is not realistic. The markets are not free due to trade and payments restrictions such as tariffs, quotas etc. Besides the base period exchange rate may not be the equilibrium rate which distorts the comparison of their purchasing power parities at the current period. The index number technique used for such comparison is also criticised as defective due to changes in the composition of goods, their qualities over a period of time, etc.

Under the exchange rate system prevailing in the world, before 1971, under the aegis of the IMF, exchange rates were fixed in terms of gold or US dollar and a fluctuation on either side by 1 per cent was permitted. Any changes in exchange rate parity, as fixed with the Fund, could be changed up to 10 per cent by consultation with the Fund. Any change beyond 10 per cent is to be justified on grounds of fundamental disequilibrium in the parities. The system prevailing after the breakdown of the Bretton Woods system in August 1971 is one of a wider band of margins and floating currencies with varying degrees of controls. such floating system is one of a wider band of margins and floating currencies with varying degrees of controls. such floating system favoured stable but adjustable par values and fixation of par values of currencies in terms of SDR which is represented by a basket of currencies and intervention in the exchange markets in terms of a multi-currency approach.

Spot and Forward Rates

If an importer is paying on receipt of documents, then he can buy dollars spot and the bank sells him spot dollars. But if the importer agrees to pay three or six months hence, his demand for dollars might arise only after three or six months hence. These dollars are called forward dollars and the market is the forward market. The existence of a forward market provides cover or hedge against fluctuations in the spot exchange rates. This exchange risk falls on the banks who are buying or selling dollars forward. The banks in turn can pass on the risk to the central bank of the country or to a foreign bank at another centre.

Just as banks are buying and selling spot, they also do business in forward currencies. Corresponding to the spot rate of exchange, there is a forward rate for various periods. If any bank succeeds in matching forward purchases with forward sales of the same currency, it avoids "taking a position" and assumes no risk. If they do not match, the bank may have an uncovered position which it may cover with another bank which has a contrary position. If it fails to cover with a bank, it may still do so with the central bank of the country or with a correspondent bank abroad. If a bank takes a position uncovered, it may take a calculated risk in the hope that the rate may move in his favour or he has failed to secure a proper cover in which case he would adjust uncovered position against a spot deal or against a future sale or purchase.

Currencies purchased or sold in forward would be subject to the influences of interest rates at home and abroad. A forward currency will be at premium (higher than the spot expressed in foreign currency per domestic unit quoted as Rs. 100 = $ 4.7555), as at end June 1991. Later rates were quoted as $ 1 = Rs. 31.3283 in June 1993, and $ 1 = Rs. 46.48 at end June 2003 and Rs. 50.94 at end April 2012, if interest rates abroad are higher than at home. The premium or discount will depend on interest rates and expectations of interest rates and exchange rates. Forward premia for US dollar is around 3 to 4% per cent per annum at end June 2003, depending upon the time periods involved. The forward premium fell to 1.5 to 2% per annum by end June 2005, but rose against to 3 to 4% by end March 2009.

Speculation

Speculation and hedging operations are taking place in free markets to take advantage of interest rate and exchange rate differentials. In the case of India, such hedging and speculation are not possible as banks are not allowed to take position in any currency beyond the minimum working balances to be kept in various centres. In a free foreign exchange market, short-term capital flows take place to take advantage of interest rate differentials and will be quickly reversed, leading to instability in the exchange rates. One-sided speculation is also very destabilising which generally the central bank of a country would not allow unchecked. Controls on capital account, particularly to counter such destabilising short-term flows, are in tune with the spirit of the International Monetary Fund. Speculation on a limited scale and if it is on both sides of purchase and sale is healthy and welcome to keep the balance in the market and absorb the excesses of demand/supply of currencies in the foreign exchange market.

Arbitrage

When foreign exchange markets are free to fluctuate, the exchange rate of a currency should be the same in almost all the centres. Thus, if the dollar rate per sterling is different in New York and Frankfurt, then funds would flow in either direction to take advantage of the rate differential. It is, however, possible that slight differentials might be still there due to carrying costs of moving funds from one place to another. Such operations in terms of movements of funds from one centre to another are called arbitrage operations.

Such operations can take place only if there are no exchange controls in both the countries and if funds are free to move. Thus, if either New York or Frankfurt is subject to exchange restrictions involving central bank supervision of funds inflow and outflow and ban on free movements, arbitrage cannot take place and differentials in rates between two countries might exist.

Arbitrage is not limited to two centres or two currencies along. Three-point and multi-point arbitrage can also take place if the respective currencies are free. Thus, in a three-point arbitrage, the dollar-sterling rate and the dollar-franc rate are considered and the cross rate between sterling and franc should be in conformity with the above two rates. Otherwise, three-point arbitrage can take place by moving funds from dollar to franc and franc to sterling and back to dollar from sterling. Suppose the dollar-sterling rate is £ 1 = $ 2.80 and franc 350 = $ 1 and £ = 1020 francs. Starting with $ 100, one can buy up pounds, move from pounds to francs and then to dollars back, making a gain of about $ 5 per $ 100 in the above example. Thus, arbitrage can take place as between centres or currencies at more than two centres and currencies at a time. Such arbitrage operations may be for gain in exchange rate differential or in interest rate differential as between centres. The former are called currency arbitrage and the latter interest arbitrage. An operation of simultaneous purchase and sale in each of the two markets to take advantage of interest differential is called interest arbitrage. Such deals are put through by swaps or forward deals.

The operations in the foreign exchange market are exposed to a number of risks which are difficult to foresee and forecast. These risks may be credit risks arising out of lending to a foreign borrower whose credit rating is not known for certainty. Secondly, there may be currency risks of trading in a currency whose stability and strength is known to fluctuate. Thirdly, there are country risks involved in lending to a country whose political and economic strength is weak and is uncertain. Fourthly, there are risks of fluctuating interest rates in various currencies in the inter-bank market and anticipations may sometimes go wrong. Fifthly, there are risks of illiquidity due to mismatch between current assets and current liabilities with the result there may be sudden need for borrowing and difficulties may arise in securing funds at short notice. Lastly, the dealers sometimes take risks by exceeding the limits of prudent trading in a currency with the result that they may find it difficult to cover the transactions and incur losses in such a position. Such risks are more marked in international lending and borrowing and in foreign exchange and currency markets. Further details of risk are discussed in a separate chapter.

For a country like India, with a wide network of controls, arbitrage operations are not possible. Indian rupee was insulated from world free currency markets as the banks' operations in India were strictly controlled and monitored by the Reserve Bank of India, until 1992, when the trend to freely convertible rupees was started. As capital account controls are still prevailing, most hot money flows are controlled. But arbitrage and Exchange risk cover are possible for current transfers.

INDIAN FOREIGN EXCHANGE MARKET

In India there are many commercial and co-operative banks who are authorised to deal in foreign exchange called Authorised Dealers and are eligible to operate in the foreign exchange market. However, not all co-operative banks are authorised to deal in foreign exchange. These banks cover their open positions in currencies in London through their correspondents or branches abroad or in India in the inter-bank market. However, banks finance thousands of crores of foreign trade, and put through crores of foreign remittances and a host of other purchases and sales. In the process of such purchases and sales directly with the public, the authorised dealers would have various currencies which they try to dispose of by matching demand with supply in the inter-bank market. It is only the unmatched net requirements that are purchased from the RBI, or excesses sold to the RBI.

Exchange Dealers

The foreign department of every bank draws up a position sheet for each currency daily in which purchases and sales of the currency are recorded. As the banks generally avoid taking any exchange risk by keeping uncovered balance and are not permitted to do so under the previous regulations, they try to cover their position by the end of the day. When the purchases exceed sales, the credit balance is plus (or long) and overbought. This is to be covered by equal sales of that currency. When the sales exceed purchases, the debit balance is minus, short or oversold position and is to be covered by equivalent purchases. These sales and purchases would include both spot and forward, import bills or export bills negotiated or purchased, clean sales or purchases (other than through bills, namely, by TT, MT, cheques, drafts) BC sales, etc.

Before entering into the inter-bank market, the banker decides how much to cover and what is the outstanding balance position in his books. Banks operate in the inter-bank market through the foreign exchange brokers. In every important market centre, some brokers operate in these dealings. The banker keeps some minimum balances in his Nostro account to meet the customer needs as they accrue. The more exactly he synchronises the delivery dates of his purchases and sales, the greater is his profit. The finer the rates he quotes, the better in his position. The better he foresees the trends in exchange rates and interest rates in various centres, the more efficient he is and the better is his profitability.

In the inter-bank market, banks put through the dealings of purchase and sale of currency through authorised brokers. Brokers in each centre are in contact with other centres in India and in foreign countries for effecting matching transactions in various currencies. In all centres, export bills, import bills and various remittances are daily purchased and sold by banks. Imports give rise to payments abroad and purchase of foreign currencies. As the bulk of the imports in India is on government account and the SBI keeps the account of the public sector undertakings and of the government, the SBI enters the foreign exchange market mostly as a buyer of foreign currencies. Exports are more concentrated in the private sector, in which all banks are involved in varying degrees. Hence, sales of foreign currencies in the exchange market are more evenly spread among the banks in India. Many times, brokers cannot match in the local centres for odd currencies like Austrian Shilling or Nigerian naira or Libyan dinar, which are to be put through in a more sophisticated market like London or Singapore.

In India, some financial centres are more developed than others in the foreign exchange market. Thus, Mumbai, Kolkota and Chennai are more developed than others. Some of the foreign exchange transactions being seasonal, the markets are also seasonal.

RBI and Exchange Market

The RBI operates in the market as the last recourse agency. The RBI purchases and sells sterling spot and buys and sells forward sterling up to six months but since June 1966, forward sales have been stopped. Since the abandonment of convertibility of the US dollars in 1971, the forward cover for a longer period was felt necessary due to greater exchange risks and it was provided by the RBI up to 9 months at a rate of £ 0.005 per month fixed extendable up to one year in total, at a nominal charge of £ 0.0075 per month for the extended period.

The other currencies in which the RBI started operations during the seventies were dollars, DM and Yen. The RBI started purchases spot and forward dollars from July and August 1966 respectively and with brief interruptions from August 1971 to October 1972 and February 1973 to September 1973, the RBI continued to purchase spot and forward dollars. Similar purchases of DM and of Yen were started from March and May 1974 respectively. The period of forward cover was up to three months initially but was extended up to six months from September 1975. Thus, the RBI provided cover for 4 currencies which are our major trading partners, namely, sterling, dollar, DM and Yen. The Bank purchased and sold spot £ bought forward Sterling and bought dollar, DM and Yen both spot and forward, at that time.

Thus, the RBI was operating in four major currencies, namely, UK £ US $ Japanese Yen and DM. Early in 1987, the RBI has started selling spot US Dollars with the result that it used to buying and selling two currencies, UK £ and US $ (now only in US $), in addition to its purchases of DM and Japanese Yen. It has also adopted recently the practice of changing the rates quoted by it in the course of the day if the conditions in that market warranted it. The RBI used to quote both the spot and forward rates in the currencies it transacts with the banks and in ACU* on a daily basis.

The RBI was providing cover for a fairly long period of up to 10 years in respect of long-term contracts for engineering exports and construction projects. Since November 1975, the RBI has also offered the cover to ADs against exchange rate fluctuation in respect of deposits received in foreign currency from non-residents. Most of the facilities which the RBI offers are intended for exporters in terms of cover of purchase and sale. This is justified in view of the national importance attached to exports. But they have not offered similar facilities for importers for two reasons. Firstly, the bulk of the imports into India is by the government or public sector agencies who do not need such facilities. Secondly, the inter-bank market is designed to develop to provide cover as and when needed by the importers in this regard. The RBI is maintaining itself as a last resort institution of foreign exchange as in domestic finance. The policy of RBI in this regard is very flexible and designed to promote self-reliance by banks and greater resort to the inter-bank market. The RBI has, however, responded to emerging situation in the foreign exchange market quickly and promptly. Since rupee convertibility was launched in March 1992, RBI is publishing a reference rate around which it operates in the market, to stabilise the rate of exchange of rupee in terms of US dollar. RBI operates in the Forex Market both directly and indirectly and tries to stabilise and influence the market.

Exchange Rate System in India

India was formal member of the sterling area from September 1939 to June 1972, during which period the external value of the rupee (exchange rate) was kept stable in terms of sterling. Since

---

* Asian currency unit which is now replaced by SDR, referred to in another chapter. (20)

the establishment of IMF, of which India was a founder member, the external value of the rupee was declared in terms of gold and US dollar (Re. 1 = 0.268601 grams of fine gold or Re. 1 = US $ 0.3022) and its value was maintained stable in terms of £ by purchases and sales of sterling by the RBI (the sterling rupee rate was Re. 1 = 1 S. 6d). Rupee was devalued twice, namely, in September 1949 by 30.5 per cent and in June 1966 by 36.5 per cent to maintain parity with £. Since June 1966, the new rate has been Re. 1 = 13.3 US cents. This link with sterling which was maintained by keeping the rupee stable in terms of sterling and using the sterling an intervention currency was justified on the ground that the bulk of India's trade was either with the sterling area or was denominated in sterling and that India's foreign interests lie with sterling which was considered at that time a stable and strong reserve currency.

With the breakdown of the Bretton Woods system in August 1971, and the flotations of various major currencies, the Indian rupee was temporarily kept pegged to the US dollar at Rs. 7.5 per US $ 1, and this rate was kept stable by intervention in the market by purchases and sales of sterling. Rupee-dollar peg was used to determine the rupee-sterling rate. This position continued up to December 1971, when under the Smithsonian agreement, the exchange rate of sterling was fixed in terms of US dollar and the rupee was again linked to sterling thereafter. This sterling link proved short-lived up to June 1972 when sterling and other major currencies started floating. Between June 1972 and September 1975, rupee was kept stable in terms of sterling but was allowed to fluctuate against all other currencies. During this period, rupee was effectively devalued against all major currencies other than £ by as much as 18-20 per cent. Since the effect of such depreciation was not favourable to India with her inelastic supplies of export goods and growing debt burden, along with the rising import bill, India decided to delink itself with £ completely in September 1975. Since then, the external value of rupee was determined by the market value, as quoted in London, of a basket of currencies. The currencies included in the basket and the relative currency weights as well as the method of compilation of the exchange rate were kept confidential. Since then the rupee valuation has been based on a mix of international currencies with which India has trade relations and this has resulted in changes in its value very frequently and a net depreciation in terms of sterling. Since September 1975, the value of rupee has been maintained stable within a wider margin of 2.25 per cent on either side up to 30th January 1979 and 5 per cent thereafter. A middle rate, as between selling and buying rates is fixed in terms of sterling which continued to be an intervention currency. The cross rates for the rupee against other currencies are calculated and fixed by banks in terms of the cross quotations in London. Whenever there is a change in the market value of the rates of the currencies in the basket by more than $2^1/_4$ per cent against the standard unit of account, namely, SDR, the rupee-sterling rate is altered suitably. The external value of rupee was kept relatively stable within the permitted band of 5 per cent on either side of the middle rate. Minor fluctuations on either side evidence the fact that India does not need the support of any currency, namely, sterling or dollar. But there was, however, a net depreciation in terms of sterling. The wisdom of using the sterling as an intervention currency was doubted and advocates were not wanting in demanding the use of dollar for the purpose, at that time.

Floating vs. Fixed Exchange Rates

In the post-Smithsonian era, the currencies have been on various types of floating systems due to the abandonment of the convertibility of US dollar. Single float, joint float, managed float etc., are examples of such floats. The system of fixed exchange parities (par values) was given decent burial following the breakdown of the Bretton Woods system in August 1971.

Floating rate is a rate which is allowed to fluctuate freely according to supply and demand forces. Such float is a free float if no intervention takes place by the central bank of the country. In the real world, some degree of intervention exists which leads to a managed float. Such managed floats are either single or joint. Dollar, sterling and Yen were floating with varying degrees of intervention within a band of 2.25 per cent on either side and they are single floats. The European Common Market countries (West Germany, France, Belgium, Netherlands, Luxemburg and Ireland, Denmark and Sweden) are under a joint float within a narrow band called "Snake in the Tunnel". The new IMF policy is to keep relatively stable exchange rates within a wider band of fluctuations. Indian rupee is kept relatively stable with the help of a basket of currencies, up to July 1991, when the rupee was devalued and LERMS' was adopted later. (Limited Exchange Rate Management System).

Advantage of Basket Currencies

With the existing system of exchange controls in India, a free floating rupee was out of question in the eighties. The rupee is not strong enough to withstand the speculative onslaughts. Our trade would have suffered. Alternatives left to the monetary authorities in India were, therefore, to link it with $ or £ or a combination of some major currencies like the SDR. Since both $ and £ were having their own problems, the choice has fallen on a basket of currencies but unlike the 16 major currencies in the case of the SDR, at that time only 5 major currencies having good trade connections with India in 1975 were chosen in its basket. The SDR valuation would have been unrealistic for India as some of the currencies represented in SDR have no relations with India's trade. The basis of SDR valuation was itself changed to a bag of five currencies in 1981. It was felt that it would be advantageous for India to link the rupee to a mix of currencies properly weighted as this would give greater stability and more certainty, so that India's trade and investment abroad would not suffer. The import bill and debt servicing burden are heavy for India and it would be necessary to have relative stability in the exchange rate. The fact that moderate depreciation took place in effect as against $, DM, etc., would have probably helped our export trader in particular.

Present Exchange Rate System

With the initiation of economic and financial reforms, in July 1991, far reaching changes were introduced in the foreign exchange policy and exchange rate management. FERA was diluted and banks have been allowed greater freedom of lending and their deposit and lending rates have also been freed to a large extent. Foreign exchange release is mostly left to the banks, for many purposes, subject to an upper limit for each purpose. Rupee was made partially convertible first in 1992, followed by full convertibility on trade account in 1993 and thereafter full convertibility on current account, inclusive of invisible account in 1994. The era of decontrol on foreign exchange has started with these reforms. We have now a System of Exchange rate management adopted by the RBI since 1994, and the FERA was replaced by FEMA in June 2000.

RBI Policy Applied to Banks

RBI continued to delegate more powers to ADs in dealing in the forex market and in effecting receipts and payments.

RBI has been publishing the Reference Rate of rupee against dollar and Euro on a daily basis. The RBI is dealing in buying and selling of Rupee for the dollar only both spot and forward. On the basis of the RBI's Refinance rate, Foreign Exchange Dealers Association (FEDAI) is giving the rates for banks, but banks are free to adjust their rates depending upon their currency positions.

Examples of RBI and FEDAI Rates are given below:

$ 1 = in Rupees

	RBI rates	FEDAI Rates
March 4, 1994	31.3800	31.3790
March 3, 1995	31.5725	31.5659
June 30, 1995	31.3940	31.3940
July 1997 (End)	35.7100	35.7150
May 1999 (End)	42.8400	42.8500
March 2003 (End)	47.5000	47.5100
March 2005 (End)	45.7500	45.7600
March 2008 (End)	40.3600	40.3500
March 2009 (End)	51.2300	51.2400
March 2010 (End)	45.1400	45.1300
March 2012 (Ends)	51.15	51.16

In the forward exchange market, RBI allowed free functioning following the current account convertibility of the rupee since March 1994, particularly after deregulation of lending rates in October 1994. The swap premia seemed to adjust to real interest rates, i.e., interest rates adjusted for inflation rates. Another factor affecting the swap premia is the call money rates in the respective countries.

RBI has been persuading banks to develop forward market in India by dealings with interbank and in foreign market. There is however need to develop foreign exchange derivatives for providing hedge through forward contracts, swaps and cross currency options. It is possible to develop Rupee based options if international quotes for rupee are available which is not the case at present.

Currency Deals

The quotations may be called direct quotes or indirect quotes. The principle the banker follows is to give two way quotes — based on "give less and take more". The spread between the buying and selling rates is the banks' profit. The interest component for any period is shown separately from the currency position. The spread depends on the cable cost, brokerage cost and administrative cost leaving only a small margin of profit to the banker.

If the quotation is $1 = Rs. 35.750 - 35.780, then the banker is prepared to buy dollars at Rs. 35.750 and sell dollars at Rs. 35.780. Here the principle is buy low and sell high. Let us take a quote of $ to pounds say pound £ = $ 1.5200 - 10, the quoting bank wants to sell sterling at $ 1.5210 and buy at $ 1.5200. The price of dollar to D.M. at $ 1.5810/20 means that for every dollar, the quoting bank will pay 1.5810 DM and would receive 1.5820 DM for dollar. In the quotation, the bank always wants to gain.

Method of Quotation

There are two methods of qucting the exchange rate of any currency. One is the direct method which gives the number of currency units of a domestic country to one unit of foreign currency. The second method is indirect method, which gives the number of foreign currency units for one unit of domestic currency.

Some banks give the quotes under the Indirect method, as shown below for illustration. As it is only for illustration, the date and time of the quotation may not be material. These quotes are for Rs. 100 — a fixed domestic currency unit and the number of foreign currency units for a fixed domestic currency unit of Rs.100 are given for each of the major trading partners of India.

For Rs. 100 =

US	—	2.29
UK	—	1.21
Euro	—	1.76
Pakistan	—	136.1
Bangladesh	—	145.16
Sri Lanka	—	228.51
Hong Kong	—	17.87
Thailand	—	89.89
Malaysia	—	8.7
Singapore	—	3.79
Indonesia	—	21.703
China	—	18.97
Japan	—	245.6
UAE	—	8.41

Egypt	—	13.28
Israel	—	9.99
Turkey	—	3.06
S.Africa	—	14.11

The official method of quotation is the RBI Reference rate as so many rupees for US \$, on the basis of which the FEDAI gives the buying and selling rates for the major currencies in India. Thus on May 24, 2006, the rupee was quoted at Rs. 45.75 for US \$ (US \$ 1 = 45.75). The official quotations published for the four major currencies by RBI, namely \$, £, Euro and Yen as on March 31st, 2010 are as follows:

This is the Direct method of quotation, namely the number of units of domestic currency (Rupees) given for one unit of foreign currency.

As on March end 2011

(in Rs. for foreign currency unit)

	June 30th, 2005	March 31st, 2010	March 2011
per US \$ =	Rs. 43.5150	Rs. 45.1400	44.64
per UK £ =	Rs. 79.6988	Rs. 68.0400	71.91
per Euro =	Rs. 52.6425	Rs. 60.6050	63.23
per 100 Yen =	Rs. 39.5200	Rs. 48.4450	54.40

Source: RBI Handbook of Statistics.

Trading by Banks

In some banks, the dealing rooms are located also in Chennai and Bangalore. In fact foreign banks concentrate their deals mostly in Mumbai, while SBI has its Central Dealing room at Kolkata. The largest component of inter bank market operations is concentrated in Mumbai.

SPOT Trading Operations

One bank has classified the trading operations as shown below:

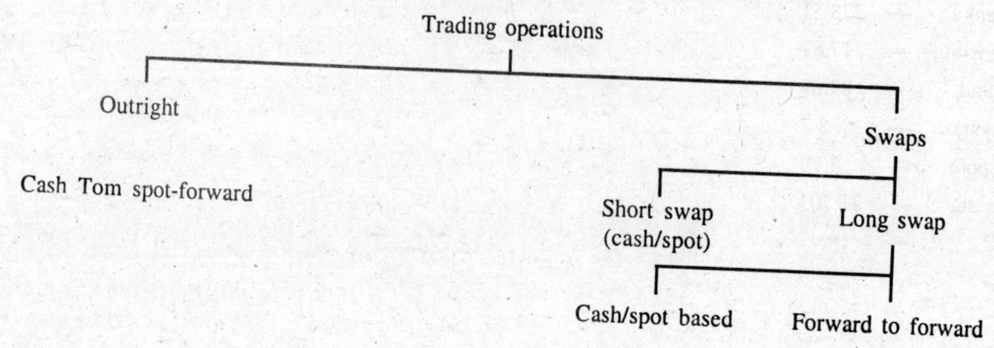

Tom means To-morrow here. Spot is settled on the same day (cash), value tomorrow (tom) and forward (beyond spot date); spot deals are less risky while forwards are more risky. The forwards may be for a few months, say 1 to 6 months.

Spot trading has two types of deals:

(1) In and Out Trading: The number of deals are many but the profit/loss in each is minimal. Minimal exposure and minimum risk is involved in this.

(2) Position Trading: There will be fewer deals with large exposure being held for some time for profit to be booked.

The portfolio dealer in foreign currency has to go in for a judicious mix of these two strategies. Examples of these two strategies of the Trader in Mumbai is given below. For in and out trading the exposure, pound 1 million.

1 million pounds bought @ 1.5270, sold 1.5272 profit: 2 pips

1 million pound bought @ 1.5274, sold 1,5277, profit: 3 pips

and so on; he made 10 deals, each with a profit of 1 to 3 pips. For 10 transactions of million 1 pound, he has made a profit of say 20 pips, exposure is only pound 1 million total.

In position trading, the trader takes a big exposure say of $ 5 million hoping DM will improve against dollar. He sells $ 3 million first at DM 1.5840 and if the trend assumed is correct, he sells another $ 2 million at DM 1.5780. When the DM rose 1.5700, he sells all the DM for dollars back to make profit on his total position. Say the average sale price of dollars is 1.5780 and now purchase price is 1.5700. He made a profit of 80 points for dollar, which is a large amount, for deals involving, millions of dollars.

Exchange Rates in India

The Table below gives TT rates of various currencies in terms of Rs. TT means Telegraphic transfers which is next best means and quickest method of transferring funds from one currency to another currency. It is next to physical delivery of currency on spot. The rates for TT buying and selling for major currencies in the world are given in terms of rupees for each of the foreign currency units. The margin between buying and selling rate is the profit to the wholesaler.

Exchange rates for the latest date possible are given below in the Table. These are Inter bank rates quoted by the Axis Bank for 28th June, 2010. As the US dollar is RBI intervention currency, both buying and selling rates for US dollar are given separately for spot. For three major currencies namely US $, Euro and British Pound Sterling, quotations for yesterday and a month ago are also published by the RBI for comparative purposes of the performance of rupee *vis-a-vis* those currencies.

It will be seen from the Table that the principle of "Buy Low and Sell High" is observed in this method of quotation as so many units of Domestic Currency for one unit of foreign currencies.

The exchange rates (spot) are given for major currencies of India's trading partners for both buying and selling for TT, Travellers' cheques currencies and Bills, etc.

As compared with a year ago or a month ago, the rupee has depreciated as against the dollar and dollar itself is depreciating against major convertible currencies. As in early June 2009 the rupee dollar rate was Rs. 46.83 per dollar while the same was about Rs. 43.7 in June 2005, a depreciation of about 7%.

Exchange Rates 28th June, 2010

Source: AXIS Bank

Currency	TT Buy	Bill Buy	TT Sell	Bill Sell	TC Buy	CCY Buy	TC Sell	CCY Sell
Australian Dollar	40.0725	39.9925	40.8225	40.9050	39.6500	39.4500	41.2500	41.4500
British Pound	68.7325	68.5925	70.0000	70.1400	68.0500	67.7000	70.7000	71.0500
Canadian Dollar	44.1075	44.0175	44.9300	45.0200	43.6500	43.4500	45.4000	45.6000
Danish Krone	7.5775	7.5625	7.7400	7.7550	7.5000	7.4500	7.8500	7.8500
Euro	56.5725	56.4600	57.6225	57.7375	56.0000	55.7000	58.2000	58.5000
Hong Kong Dollar	5.8600	5.845	5.9875	6.0000	5.8000	5.7500	6.0500	6.1000
Japanese Yen (*100)	51.0575	50.9550	52.0075	52.1100	50.5500	50.2500	52.5500	52.8000
New Zealnad Dollar	32.4850	32.4200	33.0975	33.1650	32.1500	32.0000	33.4500	33.6000
Singapore Dollar	32.9900	32.9225	33.6100	33.6775	32.6500	32.5000	33.9500	34.1500
Swedish Krone	5.8975	5.8850	6.0275	6.0375	5.8000	5.8000	6.1000	6.1500
Swiss France	41.7225	41.6375	42.5025	42.5875	41.3000	41.1000	42.9500	43.1500
UAE Dirham	12.3000	12.2750	12.8175	12.8425	12.1500	12.1000	12.9500	13.0500
US Dollar	45.8325	45.7425	46.2475	46.3400	45.3500	45.1500	46.7500	46.9500

Source: *AXIS Bank*, E.T. 29.6.2010.

London Inter bank offer rate (LIBOR) for one month, 3 months and 6 months for various currencies are also available. These are the interest rates for deposits kept in those currencies in the Euro-Currency market, for the respective maturities. Cross currency rates are given in a separate

Table, in later pages which will be useful to calculate the cross-currency rates for the Rupee. We know the rupee rate in terms of dollar and dollar rates in terms of each of the other currencies and we can work out by crossing, the rupee values of the other currencies from the given Table.

Cross Currency Deals

Dealings in Forex market depend on the availability of rupee funds as also the foreign funds. Therefore, the surplus funds or floating funds of the banks are used for the dealing vis-a-vis the foreign currencies.

In India, premium or discount depends on the demand and supply position and not much on the interest rates. Movements in the spot currency rates also influence the forward premium or discount. Suppose, a large import payment in dollars is due 3 months hence, the premium for 3 months is higher than 6 months premium because of demand and supply factors, although in terms of interest rate gain, 6 months premium should be higher than 3 months premium as per normal interest rate structure.

Let us take a simple crude example;

Suppose the pound Rs. rates are as follows:

	$ - Rs.	Rs. - pound	pound - $
Spot	31.25-28	47.50-53	1.5260-70
1 month,	15-20 points,	13-16 points	36-32 points

Suppose you have a deficit in pound, what is the best way to cover it? Rupee is at discount over pound. If we buy pound or sell pound, we receive less (13 paise). Instead of going directly to sterling, if we go through $ - rupee route and $ to pound; on one $, we gain 15 paise by this method. We bought spot $ at 31.28 and sold one month forward at 31.43 (discount added 31.28 + 15). Then take the pound - $ forwards 36-32 points. Pound is at a discount and dollar at premium. Here we sell spot dollar at 1.5270 and bought one month forward dollar at 1.5234 (36 points deducted from spot rate 1.5270 - 36).

Combining the above two deals we bought $ at 31.28 and sold at $ 1.5270 to acquire pound. The Spot £ is at Rs. 47.7645 = (31.28 × 1.5270). We sold forward $ at 31.43 and bought forward $ at 1.5234 for one pound. We sold one month forward pound at 47.8804 Rs.= (31.43 × 1.5234). Thus, we bought spot pound for Rs. 47.7645. We sold one month forward pound at Rs. 47.8804. We gained 12 paise in this swap deal. Whereas we would have lost in direct deal as the rupee was at a discount on pound.

MISMATCH - NEED FOR MATCHING

In export and import deals and other purchase and sale deals, the dealer gets short dollar purchase, 1,000 million — not convered. Forward dollar sold 2,000 million — not matched. If the purchases and sales of the same currency and the same maturity are done on the same day, they are said to be matched. Otherwise matching is to be done through inter bank deals or with foreign branches and foreign correspondents abroad, so that open position is minimal. The uncovered open position in any currency overnight should not exceed a limit as set by banks' own Top Management guidelines. The cover can be through swap - Spot to forward or forward to forward. However, risk matching or risk reduction has to be adopted by the dealers through any derivative products.

When you expect premium to go up or swap differentials to rise, pay now and receive later — sell now and buy later. When you expect premium to come down in any currency, buy now and sell later.

FOREX MANAGEMENT

If we have extra Nostro funds keep them in call market, in that currency and earn some interest abroad. If German interest rate (6%) is higher than in US rate of 4%, buy DM spot and keep in the call market at the higher rate of 6%, in Frankfurt and convert back to dollar by selling forward DM one month to three months hence. Here the currency rate expectations play a major role. If the DM is becoming dearer and its interest rate (6%), higher than in New york (4%) then the above operation in funds management will earn profit. Such operations should maximize profits with minimum risk.

Similarly, payments are due to come to India in $ three months hence from US. Three months dollars will be in demand. So buy spot dollar and keep earning interest in Europe at 6% more than in US and sell them to those needing dollars three months hence.

There are a host of other methods of gaining in Forex market due to interest rate differentials and expectations regarding them and exchange rate changes and their expectations or cross rate differentials in exchange rates. The illustration of cross rates is provided below. These are regularly quoted and published.

Explanation of Cross Rates

Cross rates are rates quoted through a third currency. Thus, Indian rupee can be quoted through dollars at US $ 1= Rs. 43.07, but US $1 = D.M. 1.8334. The rupee D.M rate can be quoted on the basis of the above two rates, calculated as follows:

Rs. 43.07 = 1.8334 DM

Rs. 100 = $\frac{1.8334}{43.07} \times 100 = 4.2568$

or one DM = $\frac{43.07}{1.8344} = \text{Rs.}23.49$

Each foreign Currency, say US $ or British pound is quoted against each of the other currencies in the form of a matrix. These other currencies are the major trading partners of India, such as US $, AU.$, CA $, GBP (£), FR F (franc) and so on. The bank can calculate the cross rates against say Singapore dollar or Swiss franc or Italian lira from the quotation of Rs. versus dollar and dollar versus any other currency, which is required to be quoted.

These cross rates were published in the financial press, on a daily basis, by the Foreign Exchange Dealers Association at one time. But now the cross rates are got from London Quotations and are given by any of the foreign banks in India like Standard Chartered or American Express. They are published as a matrix in the press. (shown in the Table below).

Derivative Products

One of the methods of risk coverage by the Treasury Manager is the use of derivatives, either in the Bond market or in the Forex market. The risk in the cash market can be hedged in the derivative market. An example of such deals in the Forex Market is the forward contract to cover the risk of currency fluctuation in the spot contract. Swaps and options are other examples of risk covering instruments. There are discussed in later chapters, under part VI.

Forward Contracts

It is a contract for delivery of foreign currency at a specified future date at a fixed exchange rate. Only genuine trade and invisible transactions can be covered in India, as per the RBI guidelines. These forward contracts for foreign currency can be delivered at a fixed date or within a specified range of dates and penalty provisions may be laid down for breach of contract by either party. These depend on the terms of the approved contracts, usage and practice. The data on forward and swap contracts as also the Inter bank turnover, forward premia, RBI deals etc., are published by the RBI in their Annual Reports and other reports.

Swaps

A swap is a deal in which a bank buys a specified foreign currency and sells the same at different maturity dates, like simultaneous purchase of dollar on spot and sales of forward dollars for the same amount. Here the risk is possible due to adverse movement in exchange rate which is covered by prior fixing of the rates. Forward to forward deal is the purchase of two months dollars, followed by a sale of three months dollars. Swap deals are used as a tool to cover arbitrage operations namely buy in Frankfurt and sell in London of the same currency (dollars), Swaps are also required to cover a mismatch in forex deliveries to the genuine clients of the bank. Use of swaps or even Repos for speculative purposes are not permitted by the RBI. Arbitrage of risk cover or genuine marching of demand with supply are permitted by RBI. Repos are repurchase agreements, covering a currency, gilted security or Bond, etc.

Cross Currency Rates 28th June, 2010
Rates as of 6 PM IST Monday 28th June 2010

Country	INR	USD	AUD	GBP	CAD	JPY	SGD	CHF	AED	AUR
India	–	0.0216	2.4767	0.0144	0.0224	1.9340	3.0025	0.0235	0.0795	0.0175
US	46.2125	–	1.1443	0.6640	1.0347	89.3600	1.3876	1.0871	3.6730	0.8102
Australia	40.3762	0.8738	–	0.5803	0.9042	78.0900	1.2126	0.9500	3.2097	0.7081
Britain	69.5859	1.5060	1.7235	–	1.5584	134.5800	2.0897	1.6372	5.5316	1.2203
Canada	44.6473	0.9665	1.1059	0.6417	–	86.3600	1.3407	1.0506	3.5492	0.7830
Japan	0.5171	0.0112	1.2806	0.7430	1.1578	–	1.5527	1.2164	4.1103	0.9066
Singapore	33.3051	0.7206	0.8246	0.4785	0.7459	64.4100	–	0.7834	2.6471	0.5839
Switzerland	42.4991	0.9199	1.0526	0.6108	0.9518	82.2000	1.2764	–	3.3788	0.7453
UAE	12.5800	0.2722	0.3115	0.1808	0.2818	24.3300	0.3778	0.2960	–	0.2206
Euroland	57.0210	1.2341	1.4123	0.8195	1.2771	110.2800	1.7124	1.3416	4.5331	–

Rates as on 28th June, 2010.

Note: This table presents the cross currency rates as on a specific date and time, giving the INR (Indian Rupee) and other currencies of major trading partners of India as against other currencies. These rates are indicative and banks may quote their own rates, depending on their perception of party risk.

Source: E.T., dated 29th June, 2010.

Market for Rupee

In daily foreign exchange market, rupee is purchased and sold by banks and FIs and RBI does open market operations. Rupees are traded shortly against dollars. RBI announces its reference rate of rupees for dollar and Euro, on a daily bases, on the basis of which, the Foreign Exchange Dealers, Association of India (FEDAI) publishes its rate around when the ADs can fix their own rates for dealing in foreign currencies with the public. The Public includes the exporters and importers, Corporates, mutual funds, individuals and others. There are called merchant trades. As a second tier of trade, there are inter-bank dealings, as between banks - public and private banks and foreign banks. In the foreign exchange market, inter-bank dealings are more important constituting for about $^{2}/_{3}$rds of the total turnover. There is also a segment of forward trade as against spot purchase and sale transactions. The forward trade component varies from 60-65% in the case of spot trading in the merchant transactions as opposed to only 10 to 20% in the inter-bank trading in the forex market. Swaps are more important than the forwards in the inter-bank market in India.

The rupee rate against dollar in daily trading depends on many factors, including the supply and demand forces, for dollars. More importantly, it depends on flow "sensex fares" which in turn depends on FII inflows. As can be seen from the following extract, the foreign investment in stocks is a major determinant of the demand forces and supplying of liquidity on the domestic factors including the fiscal deficit of the government the rupee rate moves up and down around the reference rate announced by the RBI – RBI in turn depends on the past performance, and market expectation of the demand and supply of dollars and against the rupee.

Re rise as FIIs increase stock holdings

Mumbai: The rupee appreciated against the dollar for a second day after overseas investors increased holdings of the nation's shares to a record. The currency touched its strongest level in a week as foreign investment in stocks rose $6.6 billion this year to an all-time high of $79.4 billion on June 24. "The important thing for the rupee is how the Sensex fares," said Philip Wee, a Singapore-based senior currency economist at DBS Group Holdings Ltd. "The rupee is a capital - flow story due to its twin deficits. The fiscal deficit is doing well as the economy is doing well. But the problem is that stock flows are needed for the current account.

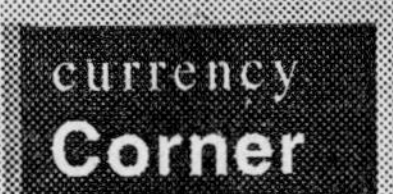

Source: ET. 29th June, 2010.

Options

Currency options are contracts with a right to buy or sell a stated currency without any obligation, at a fixed rate on a future date. If the future rate moves against expected line, the holder of the option can exercise the right to buy or sell as suits his earlier position.

Futures and Options

While forward contracts can be entered into by any parties outside the stock exchange or in any organized system, the futures contracts are regulated by a proper authority with fixed terms, involving an obligation to buy and sell or give and take delivery. Delivery is compulsory in futures. A currency future contract is an agreement to buy or sell a foreign currency at a fixed amount at a stated price or rate at a specified future time. The obligations rest on both the parties and their deals are regulated and supervised by a properly constituted authority. The holder of the option can exercise the right to buy or sell. For this right to cover the risk, the party has to pay a price called premium. Under the American options, the customer can exercise the option at any time during the currency of the contract but under the European contract, the option has to be exercised only at a specified date mentioned. As it is only a right, but no obligation, it need not be based on genuine transactions and no delivery may be there and may lead to speculation.

Forward Rate Agreements (FRA)

Major foreign banks are offering FRAs to depositors and borrowers. Here the bank guarantees the depositor or borrower the difference between the agreed rate and the LIBOR. If the six months

LIBOR under the FRA is say 9% but the actual rate happens to be 10%; the difference will be reimbursed by the bank to the customer for a premium or price. If the actual rate of LIBOR is 8%, the customer will have to pay 1% to the Bank. As per the terms of the agreement, this is a type of hedge measure provided by the bank.

Forward and Future Contracts

The difference between forward contracts and future contracts is as follows:

In forward contracts the delivery is compulsory but not in futures. In forward contracts the amount and maturity period are flexible but in futures it is organised trading in the Exchange with standard contracts, standard maturity dates and contracts trading is regulated by the authorities through down payment margins and other margins which are marked to market values. Forward contracts are traded over the counter, telex, telegram, etc. These can be contracts for various amounts and periods of maturity, say, 1 month to 12 months.

Currency Futures

Futures contracts based on the dollar-rupee rate were introduced in the country on the MCX stock exchange and NSE in August 2008. Since then till the end of 2008, their turnover was high at Rs. 29,000 crores per day, as against the range of Rs. 60,000 to 70,000 crores in the case of the equity futures. RBI and SEBI have yet to the give their clearance for other pairs of currencies say dollar-yen or dollar to sterling or rupee to yen and rupee to sterling or euro, etc.

There were unprecedented volumes at the time when the rupee climbed to Rs. 45.86 to the dollar, in December 2009. Among the various factors influencing these currencies, the strength of various traded currencies or their weakness or expectations about their status or common factors behind the currency rates are more important.

On the NSE for example, the volume of turnover range from an average of Rs. 2,674 crores in the month of March 2009 to more than Rs. 8,225 crores in December 2009. Similar was the trend in MCX market. It is reported that the exchange traded futures market was more efficient than over the counter inter bank forex market. While the over counter market is decentralized, the exchange traded futures are more cost effective and regulated. Hence, the RBI and SEBI are likely to announce the well traded market in currency in a full-fledged manner on the BSE or USE (a partly owned outfit of the BSE) also, in all the traded currencies in India.

Currency and Interest Rate Swaps

Swap is simultaneous sale and purchase of identified amounts of one currency against another for different maturities, for different interest rates (from fixed rate to LIBOR and vice-versa). It is a finance transactions in which two parties agree to exchange streams of payments or cash flows over time. There are three main types of swaps: (1) Coupon Swaps — fixed or floating rates.

(2) Basis swaps — exchange of one bench mark for another — say from LIBOR to Treasury Bill rate. (3) Cross Currency Swaps — flows from one currency to another.

Sodhani Committee Report (1995)

This Committee has come out with two reports one on the details on various schemes and incentives available to NRIs and the other for development of active exchange market system. The major recommendations are set out below.

NRI investments are not freely flowing in due to the following constraints, which have to be removed; namely administrative red tape, tax hurdles, government interference, rampart corruption, Infrastructure and inadequate access to bank credit by NRIs. The time taken for allotment of new issues to NRIs is very long; despatch of certificates or statements should be faster and there should be quick transfer of shares from one to other and for payment of dividends, etc. The issue of shares to NRIs by company is to be left free without prior permission of RBI but the companies have to report the holdings of NRIs and the details of these holdings as per the Committee's recommendations.

NRIs should be free to buy not only in new issues but from existing shares from Indians directly. Only the ADs should have the powers to scrutinise and effect the payments. There should be no lock in period for shares, in sick units acquired by NRIs, OCBs and they should be brought in on par with all FFIs. Most of these recommendations are implemented in stages since October 1996.

As regards the measures for the development of Forex Market, the following are given as a few examples:

(1) To increase the number of participants by inclusion of companies, and merchant exporters.

(2) To allow the ADs to lend and invest or borrow abroad and to allow them to keep cross currency positions abroad.

(3) To allow development of modern products and derivatives such as futures, options etc. in the Forex market.

(4) To develop proper accounting practices and disclosure standard for such operations, as per international standards.

(5) Companies and exporters can keep funds abroad and take positions.

(6) The RBI and tax authorities should clearly bring down their restrictions and relax these controls and formalities regarding the abolition of withholding tax and derivative transactions.

(7) Legal and regulatory framework should be simplified and even reduced.

(8) Risk management techniques should be expanded and developed through the introduction of futures and other derivative products.

(9) RBI's attitude should change from regulatory angle to developmental angle.

Although the wording of the Sodhani's report is different from the words used above, the substance of the Report's recommendations was set out here. The most important pre-requisite for developments of the Forex Market in India is the reduction of controls and restrictions, delegation of more powers to ADs and expertise in RBI and banks to be improved and banks to be empowered to deal with risk management techniques and for development of derivative markets. The government and tax authorities should be either liberal or free for such foreign transactions with a low withholding tax of not more than 10% as applicable of FFIs in some respects at present. The treatment given to NRIs by banks has to be improved and OCBs and NRIs should be treated on par which is now implemented. The role of the treasury Manager in banks and Companies, therefore becomes critical, needing a multi-disciplinary expertise, in the forex market, as it is more volatile and complicated by national and international factors.

Capital Account Convertibility Measures

Recent Capital Account Liberalisation measures were already referred to in chapter 21. Banks have been authorised to deal in foreign exchange markets abroad — say borrow and invest abroad up to 15% of their unimpaired Tier I capital. ADs were delegated powers to release foreign exchange for opening offices abroad and other expenses. Loans for periods beyond 10 years were kept outside the ECB ceilings. The exporters were entitled to use abroad upto 50% of their EEFC accounts, subject to some conditions. ADs are permitted to deal in forward markets and provide cover to holder of FNCR\NRE accounts and to FIIs. They can trade in foreign currency in some cases without prior approval of RBI. They are allowed to provide credit and non-credit facilities to Indian companies or WOS abroad and to NRIs. They are allowed to import gold and deal in gold, if they satisfy certain conditions. Companies are allowed to borrow abroad through ECB, ADRs, GDRs, etc.

Banks dealing in foreign exchange have been given freedom in some operations or capital account. Prior authorisation of RBI is dispensed with in some cases. They can provide buyers credit and acceptance of finance facilities to exporters. The SEBI registered Indian Fund Managers and Mutual Funds are permitted to invest in overseas markets in accordance with SEBI guidelines without RBI permission.

Free capital inflows for FDI and portfolio investment, subject to some guidelines were also allowed. Joint ventures abroad and Indian investments abroad with WOS, or for manufacture was allowed subject to some restrictions.

28

Euro-Currency Markets

Euro-dollar or Euro-currency markets are the international currency markets where currencies are borrowed and lent. Each currency has a demand and a supply in these markets. Thus, dollar deposits outside USA or sterling deposits outside UK are called off-shore funds and have a market so long as they are convertible and readily usable in international transactions. Convertible currency is defined as one which is widely accepted in international payments and whose country does not have current account controls under Article VIII of the I.M.F. Agreements. Thus, Euro-currency market is a market principally located in Europe for lending and borrowing the world's most important convertible currencies, namely dollar, sterling, DM, French franc, yen, etc. On the same basis, the Asian currency market or the African currency market can also be defined.

International Money and Capital Markets

In general, international money and capital markets are for lending and borrowing moneys or claims to money in various currencies in demand outside the country of origin. By far the most important of such money markets are located in Europe called the Euro-currency markets. Next in importance comes the Asian currency market located in the East. Although US dollars are most frequently traded in these markets, any internationally convertible currency which has a demand and supply can also be traded.

As in the case of international money markets represented by Euro-currency markets or Asian currency markets, there are international capital markets as well, represented by Euro-bond or Asian-bond markets, which reflect the lendings or borrowings at the long-end of the liquidity spectrum of five years and above. While such international money markets have developed in the fifties, the corresponding capital markets have grown in the sixties.

Both the money and capital markets of this type for off-shore funds were of recent vintage when the old sources of funds under the pre-war system of borrowing from the domestic money and capital markets of New York and London etc., had dried up. Domestic money markets in the post-war world were greatly insulated from foreign money markets in most cases due to the prevailing exchange controls in the interest of pursuit of independent domestic monetary policy, but the interactions and effects of one on the other could not be completely ruled out. Trading in these currencies is both for short-term and long-term and in any of the currencies which are convertible. The bonds or certificates can be denominated in any convertible currency in which the borrower and the lender have confidence, in terms of the stability of the currency, its future value and intrinsic strength of the economy.

Exchange Markets vs. Currency Markets

The international currency markets are an adjunct of the foreign exchange markets. While in the latter, currencies are exchanged, one for the other, in the former, the currencies are borrowed and lent for varying maturities. In the foreign exchange market, one currency is exchanged for another currency at a rate of exchange which is the price in terms of the number of units of one currency exchanged for one unit of the latter. On the other hand, the price paid for borrowing or lending a currency in the international currency market is the rate of interest. The purpose for which currencies are exchanged in the foreign exchange market or borrowed in the international currency market may be the same, namely, for meeting trade and payment requirements, or for short-term or long-term investment in working capital or fixed capital or for meeting debt or other obligations.

These two markets are inter-related in the sense that operations in the one impinge on the operations in the other and that arbitrage and speculation take place in both and that exchanges of currencies in the exchange market are involved in most or all operations in the international currency markets. When a currency is borrowed, it is possible that this currency is exchanged for another, before it is used for payments or a loan may be granted with a multi-currency clause with the result that a number of currencies are borrowed in the same transaction and one is exchanged for the other.

Origins of the Euro-Currency Markets

After the Second World War, a number of European and US banks used to take deposits out of USA to place them in free centres in Europe like London, Zurich, Frankfurt etc. These US dollar deposits with the outside banks were used for short-term lending to the countries in need of dollars for balance of payments purposes or for investment. Such activity in dollar deposits gathered momentum with the sterling crisis in 1957, which encouraged European and British banks to depend more upon dollars. More particularly, the introduction of non-resident convertibility throughout Western Europe in the early sixties gave a fillip to the use of dollars in the financing of world trade. The imposition of controls in the domestic economies on interest rates on time deposits (Regulation 'Q' in USA) and on free flow of funds across national boundaries and on US banks' lending abroad had added stimulus to the Euro-dollar market. But more importantly, lack of any controls on banks operating in these markets for offshore funds as those imposed on the domestic money markets and absence of any reserve requirements for these international deposits and lendings of the type of domestic deposits enabled these Euro-banks to operate at least cost and at lowest margins. These factors led to highly competitive rates being offered by Euro-banks compared to national banks. Thus, Euro-banks are more competitive and their rates for deposits and lendings are relatively finer as compared to domestic money rates, as the former work on lower margins. Finally, the surplus dollars flowing through persistent deficits in balance of payments of the USA gave life-blood to this market. The foreign owners of these dollars got a good investment outlet in these markets. The domestic monetary and foreign exchange controls in some countries aided the development of the market for off-shore funds.

Dealers in the Market

International banks or multi-national banks and foreign branches of domestic banks, private banks, merchant banks and other banks are the main dealers in this market. In fact, most of the US banks deal in this market. The market is of a wholesale nature, highly flexible and competitive and well-connected in the world over by a wide network of brokers and dealers. London is the focal centre for the Euro-dollars as Singapore is the focal centre for Asian-dollars. There are a number of centres in both West and East, namely, Zurich, Luxembourg, Paris, Tokyo, Hong Kong, Manila, etc. London has grown in importance because of its historical connections with international banks, its link between European and American interests, its expertise in banking field and freedom from controls in their dealings. On a similar basis, Singapore has developed as a centre in the East due to its geographical strategic position in between the London market and Tokyo market. When London is still working, Singapore opens and as such this market provides a link to their dealings, particularly in the inter-bank dealings.

Besides, Singapore has other advantages like an excellent telecommunication system, a tradition for free banking, representation for all nationalities, expertise in banking services and positive incentives from the government for its growth in the sixties and seventies.

EURO-BOND MARKETS

This is an international market for borrowing capital by any country's governments, corporates and institutions. The centre of activity of borrowing and lending is London and Europe. But borrowers and lenders come from all over the world.

A bond market is a long-term funds market. Banks of multinational character called international banks or investment banks organise those transactions. The supply of deposits in dollar or other convertible currencies come from the exporters with foreign currencies, mostly in dollars and countries with balance of payment surplus with the USA. Although called Euro-dollar, it can be Asian market (Asian dollars) Gulf-market (petro-dollars), etc.

It was developed since 1960s, following the huge surpluses of US dollars to countries other than U.S. The reasons for the offshoot of such dollars outside USA, are of the following:

(1) Continued deficits in trade payments of USA.

(2) Use of such surpluses by the owners to lend outside in London and Europe.

(3) Lack of funds in the capital markets of New York and London for the traditional type of borrowing from national capital markets.

(4) Regulation 'Q' in U.S. which controls the interest rates in U.S. Time deposits.

It is a telephone and telex market and called the OTC market and thus, depends upon the infrastructure for financial services like telecommunications, telex, phones, etc.

While bonds refer to long and medium dated securities and debt, the Euro-currency notes refer to short dated debt of a few months to one year.

Magnitude of Trade

The magnitude of trade in this market runs into trillions of dollars, particularly in the inter bank deal. In 1987 the amount of Euro-bonds were 150 billion dollars, while the same in 1964 was 500 million dollars. This amount now runs into billions of dollars. These are mostly fixed rate issues, (60%) warrants, convertibles and floating rate notes or bonds, etc. The borrowers and the issuers of Euro-bond loans are Banks and other financial institutions, corporations, governments and some government bodies and supernational organisations. The investors in the bond market are central and commercial banks, government agencies, international financial organisations like ADB, IFC, etc. Investment and Pension Funds, Insurance Companies and Corporations.

Market Features

(1) Both investors and borrowers are well known names in the international markets. Banks and top level corporates and governments can borrow.

(2) These loans are unsecured and no government guarantee either. Only creditworthy borrowers are generally approaching this market.

(3) Country's credit rating and borrowing party's credit rating are being looked into; ratings by Standard and Poor or Moody's are popular for assessing the creditworthiness of the borrower.

Regulations

The market is functioning outside the countries and is offshore in nature. No regulation of any national and international nature exists. SROs regulate the investment industry. Thus, the market practices in the secondary market trading are based on the rules laid down by Association of International Bond dealers. The issues are mostly for medium term for 5 to 10 years.

Some parent companies and some foreign governments do guarantee the interest and payment of principal. The interest payment is provided in the agreement itself and stricter controls are exercised in the collection of interest, although these rates are lower than those on national bonds of any country. Many countries notably U.S. and Germany removed the withholding tax to attract bond market to the national level. But Euro-bond market has been kept out of the jurisdiction of any nation.

Bearer Status

These bonds are negotiable and transferable as they have the bearer status. There are no restrictions on transfers, and the right to receive interest and payment of principal is for the bearer of the bond. The bonds are printed on special security printing paper and terms and conditions are printed on the back of the paper. There is also authentification of the individual bonds by the staff of Lead Manager. The Security and safe custody of the bond and avoidance of fake certificates are all the responsibilities of Managers to the issue and banks dealing in this market.

Instruments Issued and Traded

(1) **Fixed Rate Bonds:** Here the company gets a fixed rate of say 10% coupon bond for a maturity of 5 years and above.

(2) **Convertibles:** Issuers of bonds are eligible for conversion into shares of the company after a date, at a fixed conversion price.

(3) **Floating Rate Notes:** This coupon is changed every 3/6 months depending on the LIBOR or any other standard rate, as laid down in the agreement.

(4) **Swaps:** Interest rate swaps — borrowing at a fixed rate but swapping it for floating rate or vice-versa.

Currency swaps can be depicted as shifting of one bond of dollars into some other currency, either at fixed rate or at a floating rate.

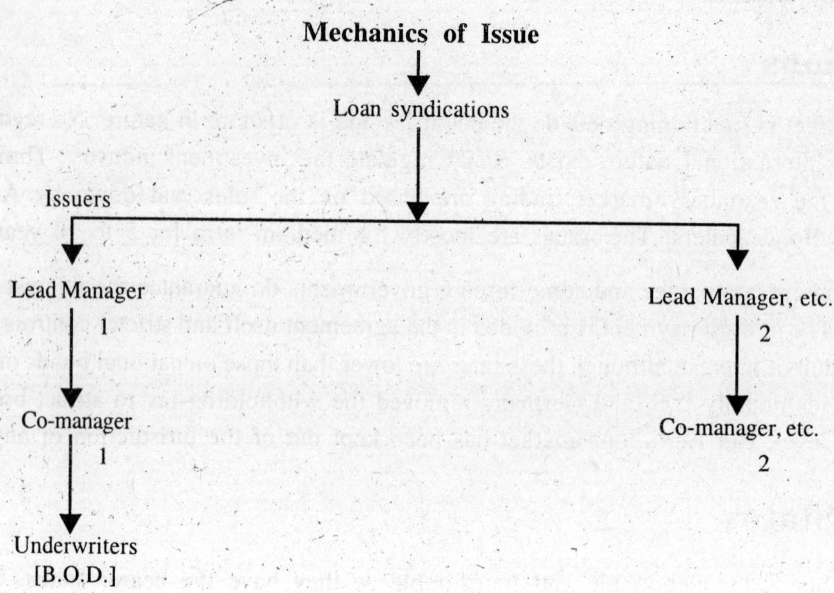

Brought out deals occur when the lead manager offers to launch the issue at a specified price. There will be trustees and paying agents in different countries and agents are appointed in various commercial centres in different countries. They take care of the sale of these notes or bonds.

Lawyers and Auditors

They are needed for proper documentation of offer circulars and prospectus and preparation of the agreement and signing of the same before the money is released to the borrower — Issue of Tombstone in the press at the end of the issue. The fees are payable to all these parties namely, the lead manager, co-manager, underwriter, the solicitors, lawyers, auditors, etc.

Euro Bond Clearing and Settlement System

Buyer and seller exchange the notes of what they owe to each other, the buyer the number of securities and the seller the money he is due. All the trades are automated and transactions in primary and secondary markets are kept in the form of book keeping entries in the books of traders — Before automation, contract notes were issued to the parties to the trade. They are checked manually and transferred to computer system for matching and confirmations.

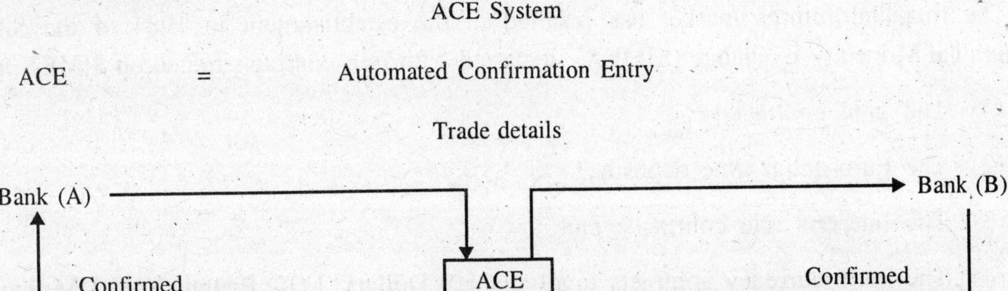

Rules of AIBD or Association of International Bond Dealers and their code of conduct will apply to these entries.

ASIAN CURRENCY MARKET

Just as Euro-dollars have been popular in the currency markets in the sixties, Asian dollars have come into prominence in the seventies. Asian dollars are the same current account surpluses in dollars used in the Asian continent. Singapore has developed as the centre for this market, particularly after 1968.

This market facilitates the use of dollar balances in the Asian continent for balance of payments purposes as well as for investment in development projects. It has imparted greater liquidity to the Asian economies whereby larger trade and larger investment became possible in this region. There was also greater co-operation in economic and financial matters, as a result of the Asian dollar market in many centres in the region such as Hong Kong, Sydney and Manila.

Singapore acts as a bridge between the Asian market in Tokyo and Hong Kong and the western market in London, Paris and Frankfurt. Singapore has both time and location advantages in keeping contact with the western and eastern markets. Besides its strategic geographical location, Singapore has the necessary financial infrastructure, expertise and other facilities for developing into an international currency market.

The scheme of market operations and the techniques used by the agents and operators as well as banks in the market are the same either in the Euro-market or the Asian-market. The rates of interest on various maturities, the pattern of financing etc., may vary. The demand and supply forces operated in the Asian zone are different from those in the European zone. The socio-economic factors and the political forces are also different in Asia and the resulting market forces and the operations are, therefore, different. Although the markets are all inter-linked, the Asian dollars are thus distinguished as a separate entity.

The growth of off-shore syndication, off-shore funds management and the financial futures are the main developments in the Singapore Asian Dollar market more recently.

The financial futures market has resulted in the establishment in 1984 of the Singapore International Monetary Exchange (SIMEX). It started with four contracts traded on SIMEX, namely:

(1) The gold contracts;

(2) The Euro-dollar time deposits;

(3) The interests rate contracts; and

(4) The multi-currency contracts involving US Dollars, U.K. Pound, Yen, DM, etc.

PETRO-DOLLAR MARKET

One of the important developments in the international currency markets in the last two decades has been the hike in the oil prices in 1973 which led to a larger flow of funds into these markets. Many petroleum-producing countries have since started accumulating foreign funds due to current account surpluses in their balance of payments. The second price hike in 1979 had also considerably augmented the current account surpluses leading to a larger increase in their foreign assets. These off-shore funds of the oil-producing countries have been designated as petroleum dollars and the market in such currencies as a petro-dollar market.

In more recent years, the deregulation of domestic banking and removal of restrictions on the capital accounts of many countries like Switzerland, France and Japan and the repeal of the withholding tax on interest income of non-residents in the USA, Germany and France in 1984 have given a further fillip to the international currency markets and attracted petro-dollars into these markets. There has been an increase in the number of financial instruments, and the methods of floating the instruments have also been diversified. These developments have increased the competitiveness in the international currency markets.

Petro-dollar flowed first into the traditional financial centres as off-shore funds such as the USA, West Germany, UK, Japan, and France. In more recent years, Switzerland, Beirut, Singapore and Hong Kong have also attracted these funds in an active manner. The recent removal of restrictions on the capital account in Switzerland and the existence of banks' secrecy and political neutrality aided the development of the international financial centre in Switzerland in the early eighties. The geographical position of this country in the middle of Europe and the well developed banking system in the country have also added attractiveness to this financial centre.

The initial hike in oil prices has resulted in a large inflow of funds into the industrialised countries for investment. Some of the surpluses have been used by the Arab countries to purchase luxury consumer goods and essentials from the international markets. Subsequent flows began to move into the physical assets, dams, railways etc., inside the country and real estate inside and outside these countries, Later, there was investment in short-term or long-term assets of a financial nature. The rest of the current account surpluses has found a place in the international financial centres. These funds were kept with foreign banks or national banks as off-shore funds, and have given rise to petro-dollars which are recycled for purposes of relending, investment and use in various developed and developing countries of the world for growth.

The oil-producing countries referred to as "OPEC countries" in the BIS data, include Iraq, Iran, Nigeria, Qatar, UAE, Bahrain, Saudi Arabia, Syria, Oman, Libya, Kuwait, Algeria, Ecuador, Gabon, Indonesia, and Venezuela. The liabilities to oil-producing countries (OPEC) reported by banks to the BIS have increased from 44 billion US dollars in 1974 to 160 billion dollars in a decade. Of this, the share of Swiss Banks has been about 14 per cent.

The petro-dollar market has started developing since 1974. In addition to the use of the current account surpluses for current consumption and imports, assets have been built abroad by these countries. The use of currencies of these petroleum-producing countries has also been increasing since then. Thus, since 1978, there has been an increase in the share of their currencies in the total identified financial holdings of foreign exchange of the countries from a mere 4.3 per cent in 1978 to 11 per cent at the end of 1984. The second oil price hike in 1979 has given a further boost to the use of their currencies in international financial markets and the increase in their assets abroad. Thus, net assets of the oil-exporting countries rose from US dollars 257 billion at the end of 1979 to US dollars 380 billion at the end of 1983 according to the Bank of England estimates.[1] Of the assets held in industrialised countries, about 60 per cent of the oil-producing countries' assets are held in the UK, USA and Germany and the rest are distributed among the other industrialised countries. These were initially concentrated in liquid assets such as bank deposits and short-term money market instruments and later diversified into long-term investments such as bonds, equities and loans.

European centres like London, Paris, Frankfurt, and Beirut in addition to New York have been the main centres attracting petro-dollars since 1974. Subsequent to the second hike on oil prices in 1979, there has been an increase in financial flows to Asian centres like Singapore, Hong Kong and Tokyo. However, after 1984, the current account surpluses of these oil-producing countries have dwindled due to the consistent fall in oil prices and this resulted in deficits or reduced surpluses of these countries in foreign accounts. The major industrialised countries continue to be the main suppliers of savings to the financial centres.

The petro-dollars like other Euro-currencies affect the volume and geographical pattern of capital flows among countries. These in turn influence the interest rates in the markets and exchange rates as between the currencies. A larger flow of short-term capital across borders could be destabilising sometimes. On the other hand, a higher degree of capital mobility might have facilitated the functioning of the floating rate system. These funds have also eased the balance of payments pressures of deficit countries like the oil-importing countries. The long-term capital flows on account of Euro-currencies have helped the LDCs in view of the recycling of the petro-dollars for investment and for correcting the balance of payments disequilibria. During the latter half of seventies when petro-dollars flooded the markets, a larger volume of development finance had flowed to the developing countries. A part of these oil surpluses has been multilateralised through regional and international institutions for

1. Bank of England Quarterly Bulletin, March 1985, BIS, International Banking Statistics, 1978-83.

assistance to the LDCs. IMF oil facility is an example of how petroleum-producing countries aided the oil-importing countries to correct their balance of payments imbalances. Such larger flows of funds for investment in the seventies have in fact given rise to debt repayment problems in respect of LDCs.

Impact on Exchange Markets

The impact of Euro-currency markets on the foreign exchange markets is multi- dimensional. Not only the demand and supply of various currencies are influenced through pressures from the Euro-currency markets but the exchange rates are altered by speculation and hedging in currencies. Larger international capital mobility due to the operations in the currency markets, influences the volume and geographical pattern of capital flows. These flows can be both stabilising and destabilising depending upon the conditions. The geographical asset preferences of nations also influence the exchange rate variations and the role of the financial intermediaries in the currency markets rather than that of the final economic agents became more important. The impact can be either positive or negative or neutral. The impact has to be analysed from the point of view of both sources and uses. As sources, new types of outflow in the form of deposits or investments are possible by lending to Euro-currency markets. This outlet has another dimension in that funds (dollars) can be kept outside the US system. As uses, it is now easier to borrow in dollars as also to obtain dollar credits from banks outside the US. Taking the above points into account, if there is a net capital outflow from the country, the impact on the exchange market is negative. If there is net capital inflow, the effect is positive and in all other cases the impact is neutral.

Segments of the Market

The business in Euro-dollars starts with the acceptance of dollar deposits of any maturity with fine rates for each maturity. There are two segments in this market, namely, inter-bank and non-bank public. In terms of the number of transactions and amounts involved, the bulk of them, namely, about 80 per cent, is accounted for by inter-bank transactions. Firstly, banks use this market as a buffer — to absorb the excesses of supply and demand — in their transactions of deposits and lendings with the non-bank public. Secondly, this inter-bank market is a means of adjusting their liquidity position to the requirements. Thirdly, banks do arbitrage and speculation in the market depending upon their view of how the future movements of interest rates and exchange values of currencies would be. Apart from these, the basic purpose of banks' involvement in the Euro-currency markets is to satisfy the genuine demand for currency in the commercial operations of the borrowers which is the market for non-bank public.

Sources and Uses

The main sources of funds for the market came from varied groups individuals, corporations, commercial banks, international institutions, multinationals, the central banks, the governments, etc. In view of the controls in the domestic market, many respectable corporations, banks, etc., keep their deposits abroad. Thus, a part of the dollar deposits is owned by the US banks and US nationals. Besides, the official agencies, governments and central banks also keep their deposits in this market which not only gives an official stamp of approval but an encouragement to the market. Originally, the market had grown without any official favour and as an off-shoot of pure private enterprise. Subsequently, when it reached a state of significant dimensions which no single nation could control, all governments and international institutions began to consider it respectable and partake in its operations. Borrowers and lenders in the market are only banks insofar as the inter-bank segment is concerned. Among the non-bank public, companies in export and import business or in investment business or multinationals in need of funds and governments or central banks for balance of payments purposes figure prominently in the non-bank markets. Among borrowings, bulk of it is for commercial operations by non-bank public and business corporations.

The Euro-currency market has no geographical limits or a common market place. Business is done by telex, telephone and other communication systems. Internationally reputed brokers put through the transactions for the banks. Deposits are secured for the banks operating in the market by the general guarantee of its parent or holding company and in some cases, by its central bank and/or government of the concerned country. Similarly, loans to commercial parties are guaranteed by their respective governments. Deposits and loans to banks are, however, not guaranteed except by the bank's parent companies or their exchange control authorities.

The amounts of loans and the periods of maturity vary over a wide range from a few thousands to millions of dollars and from call loans to maturities extending up to 10-15 years. Some of the loans may be syndicated and jointly sponsored by a number of banks. There are also varied interest rates on floating rate notes.

The purposes for which loans are taken from this market are very varied — from balance of payments requirements of governments or monetary authorities to commercial short or long-term investments in the private sector. The market has very little scope for follow-up of the end-use of credits. But terms and payments schedules are tight so that strict financial discipline is imposed on the borrower with penalty clauses. The syndicated loans have a leading bank as the manager, who assesses the worthwhileness of the project financed and insist on a time schedule of drawals and repayments which impose a sense of discipline on the borrower.

Size and Growth of the Market in Euro-dollars

The Euro-currency market has grown enormously since its inception in 1958. The principal agencies for collection of data on operations in this market are the Bank for International Settlements and the Bank of England. Starting with less than $ 1 billion in 1958, the market has grown to $ 100 billion (net size) by 1972 and further to a few thousand billion early in nineties.[2] The bulk of the rise was accounted by the OPEC and developed countries.

---

2. Total Foreign Currency Positions or Liabilities of BIS reporting banks. For further details and latest data; please refer to Bank of England Reports.
Source: BIS Annual Reports.

About two-thirds to three-quarters of these funds are in dollars and the rest in various other convertible currencies. In the seventies, the relative importance of non-dollar currencies had increased due to the decline in confidence in dollar and the abandonment of the old Bretton Woods System. The importance of the Bond market has also been growing in recent years. Loans of more than 3 years now constitute a larger portion of total loans than before.

Techniques of Operations

Deposits of currencies are made against a certificate given by the bank. These certificates of deposits are bearer bonds and transferable by endorsement and a market has been developed in them. This is the secondary market which imparts liquidity to the depositors as these certificates can be discounted with the banks dealing in this market.

The loan operations are concluded mostly for short-term duration and if necessary on a revolving basis. Some loans are transacted on a floating interest clause which enables the rate to be varied depending upon the daily interest rates prevailing in the market or on a quarterly or six monthly interest rate review. The long-term loans or bond issues are facilitated by the introduction of revolving credit facility. The increased use of floating rate of interest clause and revolving credit facility and improved performance of the US dollar in the foreign exchange market were responsible for the increase in bond issues in recent years. Multi-currency clause and floating interest rate clauses afford protection to both the borrowers and lenders in the market against a sharp fall or rise in interest rates as well as exchange rates in any currency which influences the Euro-currency market. Basically, short-term funds in the form of deposits are converted into term loans in this market.

Internationally reputed brokers are constantly in touch with the banks dealing in Euro-currencies. Their quotations for borrowing and lending rates of interest in each currency are advised to the banks early at the start of the trading hours of the day. These quotations given separately for each of the maturities and for each currency are the starting point for offer and bids in the inter-bank market which is the centre piece of Euro-currency market mechanism and which accounts for 80 per cent of the total transactions in the market. The commercial market consisting of loans to the public — both short and medium-term — is arranged on a syndicated or a consortium basis if the loan is for large amounts. The syndicated loans have become an important segment of the market in more recent years.

In addition to the revolving credit facilities, fixed term facility extending up to 5 or more years has subsequently developed. In such cases, banks are mostly intermediaries taking in deposits for the same maturity as fixed term loans which they are offering to borrowers. Many times banks take a view of the likely trend of interest rate in various currencies before granting such term loans.

Another type of facility granted by banks is standby facility which gives the borrower greater flexibility. Companies in need of funds at a future date can negotiate such a line of standby credit. The borrowers pay a commission of ½ per cent to 1 per cent for such a commitment. These are called the Notes Issuance Facilities (NIFs).

Such large scale credit arrangements are made possible by banks' operations in the inter-bank market — one bank helping the other banks — or by the syndicated or consortium arrangements among banks. The bulk of growth of the Euro-dollar market must be attributed to be revolving nature of the credits and the gearing ratio on which banks operate.

With the growth of sophistication in operation and rising competition in the market, the margins between the lending and borrowing rates have been reduced considerably in recent years. The margins are anything ¾ th per cent to 1½ per cent and in some cases, they are as low as $^3/_8$th per cent to ½ per cent. The fact that these margins are low reflects the efficiency of their operations and the high degree of sophistication and competition in the markets.

The interest rate in the market is the London inter-bank offer rate (LIBOR) which is the average of rates offered by the leading banks in the inter-bank market in London. The lending rate is adjusted up to 1/8th of the one per cent of the LIBOR along with a margin to the bank for lending to the non-bank public. The margin or spread depends upon the market conditions of demand and supply and the interest rates in various centres ruling and expectations.

In addition to interest charges, the borrowers have to incur incidental expenses in the form of charges for syndication, management of the issue, negotiation charges, commitment fees, etc. These fees would aggregate to anything from ½ per cent to 3 per cent of the amounts borrowed. The fees which the banks collect also influence the spread they keep between their borrowing and lending rates. This market is vastly dependent on confidence of the banks and in the banks operating here. The country risk and credit rating of the country influence these operations.

The more recent developments are a lengthening of the maturity period, lowering of margins, growing competition and increased size of loan operations. If the reputation of borrowers is high, no security is taken. Many times it is against a government guarantee and the cases where this security is not taken may be few, mainly accounted for by the reputed multinational corporations. Although, the credit risks are rising and costs of management of the Euro-currency department are growing and inflation is further eroding into their margins, the increasing size of the market and the growth of the deposit and lending operations along with sound banking practices have been responsible for keeping the margins low. The Euro-currency market is thus developing fast in the international financial scene on healthy competitive lines.

Importance of the Market

The growth of Euro-currency market has produced far reaching effects on the international financial system and the monetary scene. Firstly, these floating funds have augmented the official international liquidity and helped the financing of deficits in the balance of payments of countries. Secondly, these Euro-currency funds are found useful for private corporate investments and for funds and for working capital purposes. Thirdly, the quick and efficient source of funds provided by this market has helped the easing of pressures on the international monetary system, particularly on the dollar and other currencies under strain. Fourthly, it has provided a channel for profitable investment for excess funds of governments, central banks and business corporations. This market has finally opened up avenues for greater international monetary co-operation and integration.

India and Foreign Currency Markets

The operation of Indian banks in the international currency markets has been allowed since 1969, particularly in Singapore and Hong Kong. In the seventies, the State Bank of India was permitted to enter the market. Over the past few years, the SBI has raised funds for the public sector units such as the Shipping Corporation of India and later for units in the private sector also (Orissa Aluminium Project). So far loans raised in these markets were well within $ 50 billion such as for purchase of aircraft by Air India or drilling equipment by ONGC. The SBI has also been instrumental in raising loans for the Birlas for their project in Indonesia and for the TISCO from the US and UK banks. In 1980, a $ 680 million Euro-dollar loan was raised for the Orissa Aluminium Project. It is thus clear that private parties and banks in India are increasingly allowed to either borrow from this market or operate in this market. The recent decline in flow of funds from IBRD and other world bodies had an added impetus to the growth of these operations.

Euro-dollar loans were raised for the Bombay High for its fourth and fifth stages (200 million dollars). The rate at which the loan of $ 680 million was raised for Orissa Aluminium was 17 per cent — slightly above the prevailing London inter-bank offer rate of 16.5 per cent. This rate could float up or down depending upon the LIBOR. But even so, it is cheaper than that at which some countries have borrowed (Brazil, for example) namely, at 2 per cent above the LIBOR. The rates have fallen steeply later and the private sector in India is allowed commercial borrowing abroad, called External Commercial Borrowings (ECBs).

The fact is that, we have refrained from resorting to this market for a long time because of its high cost and the commercially-going rate charged therein. In addition to the high cost of borrowing in it, India was deterred from this market because of uncertainty of interest cost due to its variability every six months, under floating interest rate clause and shorter maturities on Euro-loans unsuitable to developmental need of India. We continued to enjoy until recently the benefit of soft loans from IDA, IBRD and IMF. But now a stage is reached when we have almost exhausted these resources, as their own funds were getting attenuated. Then the only alternative appears to be to allow the private sector to borrow from these markets, compete with their counterparts abroad effectively in both the output markets and input markets as much as in financial markets. When private companies borrow at commercial rates, they have to make enough foreign exchange earnings to pay for the servicing charges on them. The projects must then be of long life but a short gestation period and investment should lead to productive asset creation and enlarge the export potential of the country to repay instalments due on the loans. India has also problems of identifying projects with a short gestation but a long life duration and commercially viable projects. Besides the commercial fees and strict adherence to schedules of repayment, etc., of there borrowings were the further deterring factors.

The Indian banks and ICICI have been borrowing in international capital markets and from financial bodies abroad for commercial and industrial purposes. The Government of India has been encouraging more recently the use of Euro-dollar funds in a flexible and yet discretionary manner for commercial enterprises such as Orissa Aluminium. Rastriya Chemicals, etc. A number of companies such as Gujarat Narmada Fertilisers, Telco, Tata Power, J.K. Synthetics, etc., were able to raise funds from non-residents or foreign capital markets. The government has permitted the IDBI, ICICI and other financial institutions to raise foreign resources through syndicated loans in Euro-currency markets. After making rupee convertible since March 1992 on trade account, a number of private sector companies like Reliance and Essar, have been allowed to borrow in these markets abroad. Details of these latest developments are dealt with in a separate chapter.

International Financial Centre in India

Can India host an international financial centre? What are its repercussions on the domestic economy? The financial centres at Singapore, Hong Kong, London, etc., have been evolved historically by natural advantages, convenient locations and deliberate planning. Questions are often asked about the feasibility of developing such centres in India. Efficient manpower and competent bankers, network of communications, computer facilities and other infrastructural facilities are necessary for the development of a financial centre. India has to go ahead further with its reforms to develop such facilities and a set of dedicated secondary markets in broker firms, discount houses, bill market etc., before such a financial centre can be set up. Many needed reforms are already taken since late Nineties and offshore markets can emerge in the Special Economic Zones.

The other essential pre-requisites are:

(1) Reduction in rigours of exchange restrictions so as to free the current account transactions; this has been done, in 1994.

(2) Allow free inflow and outflow of funds at least for genuine-investment and not for speculation, which was allowed to a limited extent.

(3) Rupee to be strengthened further by greater cost consciousness of producers, greater efficiency and productivity of factors.

(4) Rupee holdings abroad to be liberalised and allowed freer trading in it.

(5) Necessary fiscal concessions, exemptions and simplification to be made in corporate income-tax, withholding tax on income earned by non-residents, etc., which are in the process of being done through on going structural reforms.

Offshore banking is already in place in the SEZ centres and limited capital outflows of Current Account are also taking place. Indian Corporates are keeping funds abroad, and are operating and investing in foreign money markets. The next step is to prepare for full capital account convertibility, for genuine trade and investment purposes which is yet to be done. This will have to be preceded by strengthening of the economic fundamentals which will make the rupee stronger. That should increase the demand for rupee in International Financial Centres. There is need for elimination of corruption and bureaucratic red tapism and reduce fiscal deficit to 3% through enforcement of Fiscal Responsibility and Budget Management Act of 2003. Increased productivity and efficient use of capital will have to be ensured. These will be pre-requisites for moving to an offshore centre in India along with Capital Account convertibility. As in 2012-13, the rupee was weak and was depreciating. This is due to rampant inflation lack of fiscal discipline and sagging economic growth. Rupee has to be strengthened and the economic growth has to be ensured on a continuous basis.

29

Foreign Aid and Term-Lending (Bond Markets)

Introduction

One of the important methods of financing trade is through aid and credits. Larger trade is possible through larger aid and it is in this context that a study of the mechanics of aid is relevant in international finance. Foreign resources are, however not an unmixed blessing as some costs are involved such as amortisation, interest payments, political and economic interference of donors, etc. But economic development of any country depends on the rate of investment and pattern of allocation of funds. The rate of investment depends on the available domestic savings and foreign resources. The latter in turn depends on the foreign aid, loans, grants and other forms of assistance, including technical collaboration and assistance. In the initial stages of development, domestic incomes and savings would be low and hence the reliance on foreign assistance. Historically, even the USA and Soviet Russia and a host of other countries have depended upon foreign aid for economic development of their countries at one stage or the other. In the modern industrialised world, flow of technology as between countries may partly depend upon the flow of foreign aid and foreign private investment.

The importance of foreign aid is emphasised in connection with easing of foreign exchange constraint in a country with sluggish export growth and exiguous state of foreign exchange resources. Firstly, foreign aid fills in the savings gap (investment minus savings at home); and secondly, it releases the foreign exchange constraint in the sense of making available input without having to pay for it immediately in foreign exchange. In more recent past, when the domestic investment rate was as high as 26-28 per cent and the domestic savings rate was lower than that, we had to depend upon foreign savings, and the contribution of the foreign sector to the domestic economy cannot be over-emphasised in this context. Compared to eighties and seventies the investment rate was higher in the nineties. But the savings rate was not rising at the same rate in the domestic economy. The reliance on foreign resources was felt necessary, during plan periods upto eight plan.

Theory of Foreign Capital Flow

The general theory of capital movement applies to autonomous private capital flows but not to the flow of foreign aid which are induced flows and it is particularly true in the case of developing countries. According to the traditional theory, private capital of a long-term nature moves across borders to take advantage of differences in yield and diversification and opportunities for investment. The latter would depend upon differences in factor endowments and in factor proportions employed in the various productive process in different countries. Thus, capital from capital-rich countries would flow to the capital-poor countries where the return is high, and where there are investment opportunities. The pattern of flows under foreign aid does not depend upon the pure economic factors nor on pure commercial considerations as referred to above, but more on politico-economic factors.

There are various theories on the subject of aid for development, such as Balanced Growth Theories (Nurkse and Lewis); Unbalanced Growth theories (of Hirschman and Streeten) or Dualistic Theories (of Higgins, Ranis, Fey, etc.) or Bottleneck Theories (of Wickesell and Singer) or Two-gap Theories or Single-gap Theories (of H.B. Chenery, Strout, etc.)[1]

The effect of aid on the foreign exchange market is to increase the supply and ease the pressures of demand, to facilitate the transfer mechanism in the currency markets and to obviate the need for frequent changes in the exchange rates, pending the process of structural adjustment in the domestic economy. The inflow of foreign funds would, however, increase the money supply which may not lead to inflationary pressures so long as funds are efficiently and productively used in the development process.

The effect of aid on the economic development can be explained through a macro production function which includes imports, exports and/or foreign investment as a function of development or vice versa. The contribution of foreign sector is felt in the product market — input and output markets through expenditure on products at home and abroad. It is also felt in the factor market by the "augmentation effect" on domestic resources, the "bottleneck-relieving effect" so far as the foreign exchange constraint is concerned and the "acceleration effect" through the inter-dependence of the factors in the factor markets.[2] Thus, the availability of foreign resources for the purpose of investment would accelerate growth by helping the co-operating factors at home to be fully deployed and by accelerating the rate of investment. This would enable the necessary technical innovation and accelerate the entrepreneurial function. Imports and foreign resources augment domestic economic growth theoretically by a multiplier process through any of the effects referred to above. The mechanism may work either through input markets or output markets or through interactions of all the product markets and factor markets. The basic postulate is that foreign resources fill in the gaps, make available non-available and complementary resources and augment the investment process. The argument that imports supplant the domestic resources and compete or replace domestic factors has

1. Vide, V.A. Avadhani, Imports and Capital Formation in Under-developed Countries, Sudhir Prakashan Publications, 1978.
2. Ibid.

been discarded by the above arguments. Technology is brought in along with foreign capital, aid or credit, which will help the growth process.

Aid Requirements

The amount of aid required is estimated either by the savings gap approach or by the foreign exchange gap approach. Under the former, given the warranted investment and the domestic savings rate, foreign resources required are derived by deducting one from the other. The foreign exchange gap, namely, the difference between exports and imports, is also used for assessing the foreign resources needed for development. A third approach is spill-over gap to be filled in as it arises due to inflation, time-lags and faulty estimations. The actual amount of foreign funds required would depend upon a host of politico-economic factors. The important economic factors are available domestic savings, targeted rate of investment and incomes, incremental capital-output ratio and the estimated gap in resources.

The criteria for granting aid by the donor countries are the available exports surplus of those countries, domestic savings, investment rates, their national incomes and their own requirements at home. The donor countries have firstly the problem of transfer of resources in the foreign exchange market as large scale transfer of resources involves the movement of the exchange rate against them. Secondly, such aid flows would also affect the domestic money supply both in the donor country and the donee country. The outflow of funds from India would reduce the money supply while the reverse holds good for the inflow of funds. Such inflows and outflows effect the expenditures at home and outputs and incomes of the people. They also produce redistribution effects, shifting incomes from one sector to another with different average and marginal propensities to consume and save.

Criteria Governing Aid

The donor countries look not only into their own capacity to grant aid but at the recipient country's capacity to absorb aid. The latter is judged by the efficiency and productivity in the resource allocation in the pattern of planning and investment and in priorities of allocation, the methods of raising resources and the overall performance of the economy. The other criterion is to judge on the basis of needs of the recipient country which are examined in relation to the relative population, average standard of living, natural resource endowments, planning efforts, etc. The self-efforts of the country at raising domestic savings and investment, long-term prospects of growth of output and of exports and repayment capacity of the recipient country, its allocative efficiency, etc., are also looked into.

There are certain adverse effects as well as beneficial effects of transfer of funds through aid. The beneficial effects arise out of increased foreign investment, increased output incomes and employment, etc. These effects are experienced in varying degrees both by the donor and donee countries. With a view to increase the effectiveness of aid, the donor countries insist on a correct measurement of the absorption capacity of the donee country. The absorption capacities are measured in various ways, including the level of productivity, the marginal and average propensities to save and capital-output ratios in the recipient country, import substitution and export promotion policies adopted at home and the planned and actual marginal investment ratios.

The criteria for donor countries to give aid are their level of per capita income, availability of domestic savings and balance of payments surpluses. The donor country should have a comfortable resource position in the domestic capital market and an easy foreign exchange reserves position without heavy balance of payments pressures.

Trends in Aid to India

India's economic development had relied heavily on foreign assistance in the initial stages. During the successive Five-Year Plans, the proportion of external assistance to total financial resources of the plans increased up to 1969-70 and reached a maximum of about 36 per cent in the annual plan periods (1966-67 to 1968-69). It was only about 10 per cent in the First Plan, 24 per cent in the Second Plan and 29 per cent in the Third Plan. After 1969-70, the reliance on external aid declined as part of the government's deliberate strategy of reducing our reliance on foreign sources. In the subsequent two Five-Year Plans of 1969-74 and 1975-80, the proportion of foreign assistance to total plan outlay was brought down to 13 per cent and 10 per cent respectively. In fact, during the Fifth Plan period of 1975-80, amortization and interest payments on foreign debt worked out to about 50 per cent to 60 per cent of the gross aid during that period. The importance of net foreign aid in the planning process has declined thereafter. During the Sixth and Seventh Plan periods (1980 to 1990), the proportion of foreign aid to total plan outlay was not more than 8 per cent to 10 per cent. During eighties, aid flows from bilateral and multi-lateral sources financed up to 35% of current account deficit. But during nineties, net inflow of external aid was declining. There was a large stock of unused aid with India; the composition of resource inflow changed into more private trade credits and commercial borrowing abroad, due to drying up of aids from multilateral agencies during nineties and later on.

Types of Aid

Various types of aid were granted to India, depending upon their nature and purpose. Two major types of aid are tied and untied. Tied aid is that which is linked to a country or project for specific use in the project and the country mentioned therein and untied aid is one that is not tied to any project, programme or country. Untied aid constitutes about one-third of the total in the case of India. Tied aid works out to be a major component of foreign aid granted. The tying may be to a project specified in India or to a specific programme of the Government of India or to a currency or country for import of the corresponding goods and services mostly from the donor country.

There can be single or double tying of aid. Single tying relates to tying only once to a project or programme or currency of a country. If tying is to both currency and project, it is called double tying.

Another broad classification of aid may be military aid and economic aid. Military aid is given by a friendly country for strengthening the political ties with the recipient and is not solely based on economic or commercial considerations. Thus, the US aid to NATO countries and to Pakistan is based on military considerations. Economic aid for development by the developed countries is also partly based on political affinities with the recipient country. Such aid can be bilateral or multilateral. While bilateral aid is from one government to the other, multilateral aid is through international financial institutions for use in the import of goods and services from any country.

In the case of India, bilateral aid constitutes the bulk of the total aid. The aid utilisation depends upon the type of tying, the form and nature of the aid. Tied aid and bilateral aid are usable only for specific purposes or projects and in specified countries. This would lead to a lower rate of utilisation of such aid. On the other hand, multilateral aid is usable anywhere and hence its rate of utilisation will be high. In India, the degree of utilisation of foreign assistance is about 75-80 per cent of the total aid which is mainly due to the big component of bilateral assistance in it. Major donor countries are the USA, France, West Germany, USSR and the UK, Japan in the bilateral group. The international institutions which provide multilateral assistance to India are IMF, IBRD and IDA. For some time, assistance from petroleum-producing countries in West Asia had increased. The multilateral assistance from institutions worked out to about 20 per cent of the total external debt of the Government of India, as reflected in the composition of external debt, in recent years.

Forms of Aid

Among the various forms of aid, loans account for the bulk of it, namely, 80-90 per cent and the rest is accounted for by grants. Until 1970-71 commodity assistance in the form of PL 480 and PL 665 Aid (laws of USA for disposal of excess foodgrains) used to figure as aid to India and constituted about 20-25 per cent of the total aid. Part of the PL 480/665 assistance was repayable in rupees and part in convertible currencies. In the seventies India had not relied on any aid for foodgrains but had built a sizeable buffer stock of foodgrains at home by itself. Until the Third Five Year Plan (1965-66), loans accounted for 60-65 per cent, grants for 5-10 per cent and commodity assistance for 25-35 per cent. At present about 85-90 per cent of the total aid to India is on loan basis and 10-15 per cent in grants. Some of the loans are from the international bodies on a multilateral basis. Assistance from the IDA is on soft terms, namely, at lower rates of interest and on long repayment schedules, which is ideally suited to economic growth for a poor country with low per capita incomes like India.

Desirable Pattern of Flows

Aid and trade are linked together and trade is better than aid for allocation of resources and their productive use at home. If aid facilitates the larger flow of trade, particularly on a multilateral basis, it is desirable to depend on aid. For the purpose of development long-term aid on soft terms and in particular untied aid would be most beneficial for the receiving country. Internationalisation and institutionalisation of aid are desirable for the benefit of the receiving countries, so that donor countries do not feel the political hegemony over the recipient. As such, UNCTAD was advocating institutionalisation of aid, increasing aid flows up to at least 1 per cent of GNP of developed countries and aid on softer terms. More recently, such aid has dried up due to increasing domestic economic problems of donor countries. Besides, as trade is better than aid, the long-term strategy of growth of the aid recipient country should be such that aid utilisation is effective, and productivity and output are increased so that the country can grow on its own momentum without foreign aid after a time. It should be possible for the country to service foreign debt (for amortization and interest payments) through their normal export performance annually. For this purpose, trade has to expand more than aid after a point, by which servicing of foreign debt could be facilitated. The long-run interests of a country would, therefore, be in greater trade or exports and imports and growth of the economy and not in continued dependence of foreign aid.

Indirect Aid

Aid channelled through a third country is called indirect aid. Thus, USA might provide India with technical and financial assistance with a condition that India should pass it on to Nepal. Third country currency assistance is also passed on if the loan is through the currency of a third country, who is neither the donor nor the recipient, and such aid would benefit the third country also by easing the pressures on its foreign exchange, as the loan is utilised in that third currency and country.

Advantages and Disadvantages of Aid

Aid is not an unmixed blessing. It has both advantages and disadvantages and the extent of reliance on aid is to be decided by each country on its own merits. Advantages of aid in general are many, if used productively and efficiently by the recipient country. Firstly, it would provide larger imports than possible by exports or country's foreign exchange reserves. Secondly, import of essential consumption requirements can be met by aid and this would promote domestic consumption and inflationary pressures are kept under control. Thirdly, by facilitating the import of capital goods for investment, growth in the economy is accelerated. By proper planning and investment, debt burden can be kept under control and enough export potential can be generated to service the debt burden. Aid also facilitates fuller utilisation of capacity, through imports of spare parts, raw materials, etc. If, on the other hand, aid is frittered away in ostentatious consumption or unproductive enterprises, then the burden becomes heavy. Similarly, if aid is tied, the project costs would be higher as supplies cannot be got from the cheapest markets and the recipient country would lose. The same is true if aid is on a bilateral basis, when the alternative avenues of supplies of goods or services are cheaper and the recipient country has to pay a higher price for the goods imported and for the services rendered from abroad with the result that the debt burden becomes heavier.

The type of aid and terms of aid are, therefore, crucial variables for determining the debt burden and the advantages and disadvantages of aid. Debt servicing become a burden if aid is tied or the terms of aid are onerous. Aid is no doubt a necessary but not a sufficient condition for growth. Doubts are cast on whether foreign funds would really supplement domestic savings rather than supplant. Foreign funds might not always lead to investment and growth if used for balance of payments purposes, delaying the process of adjustments in the economy. It is important, therefore, that aid is phased out and is productively used so that after a period of time, dependence on aid is reduced and debt servicing would not be a burden.

During the last few years, repayment of principal and interest exceeded the gross external aid with the result that there is net outflow on this account. Net capital flows to emerging market economics of the world for the period 2000 to 2010 here become negative.

Debt Burden of Government

The outstanding external debt of the Government of India is around $ 305.9 billion, as on March 31, 2011. The servicing of such debt involves two burdens — money burden and real burden. (1) Money burden is in finding the resources for payment of interest and repayment of loan instalments and (2) Real burden involves the transfer of such resources abroad involving the foreign exchange loss or outflow from the country. Real burden is the loss of physical resources, on top of the transfer burden leading to adverse movements in its foreign exchange rates. As per World Bank Debt Tables, India's foreign debt is mostly of long-term nature from private non-guaranteed sources. Debt stock GDP ratio was 17% and Debt service ratio was 4.2% in 2011 (for total external debt). Short-term debt as percentage of our total debt stood at only 21.5% in March 2009. Our reserves cover up to 10 months of imports into India. These factors show that our foreign debt burden is not heavy.

Foreign Investment in India

An adjunct to aid is the private foreign investment and foreign participation in domestic ventures. Foreign investment in India takes the form of (i) Direct investment of capital in India by branches of foreign companies or subsidiaries of foreign companies, or (ii) Creditor capital, or (iii) Portfolio equity holdings by non-residents. All these three forms can be found in official as well as in private account in India. But foreign investment on official account constitutes the bulk of our net foreign liabilities. Besides, such investment was mostly in long-term loans from foreign governments. There is also direct investment by branches of foreign companies of foreign-controlled rupee companies or creditor capital (supplier's credit or loans). Private foreign investment in India took mostly the form of suppliers' credit to commercial and industrial enterprises and long-term loans or credit. The data on foreign assets and liabilities of India are published from time to time by the RBI in its bulletins,[3] in respect of Banking sector.

The foreign investment policy of the Government of India was to encourage foreign capital inflow and foreign technical know-how into areas clearly demarcated for them as desirable. Where the country has adequate technological know-how, foreign investment is discouraged. No foreign investment is permitted in strategic industries like ammunition, atomic energy, defence items, etc. In areas of key industries such as chemicals, fertilisers, cement, paper and pulp where there is scope

3. "International Banking Statistics in India", *RBI Bulletin,* June 2005.

for foreign investment and technological know-how, foreign investment is permitted for the purpose of encouraging import substitution. More recently, foreign investment by all countries has been encouraged to flow into India, provided such investment does not exceed 49-51% per cent of equity of the Indian venture and takes the form of loans, equity participation of foreign collaboration. This norm is relaxed in the case of 100 per cent exporting units. The industries which are export-oriented such as hotels, hospitals, etc., are the permitted avenues of investments for all countries. The government has also given consent where necessary for foreign technical collaboration with Indian industry and for investment by non-residents in Indian enterprises, up to some limits. Purpose-wise and agency-wise or country-wise external assistance provided by foreign countries to India is published yearly by the RBI. FII inflows/outflows are also published regularly by the RBI, and reported by SEBI.

Foreign investment in India is also encouraged as a vehicle of transfer of technology not indigenously available or to promote export-oriented production in India. Investment in India by developed countries is encouraged (1) in the form of portfolio investment (a) in the export-oriented units, (b) in priority areas of cement, fertilisers, petroleum product, paper, etc., (2) Investment in hotels and hospitals, etc., and (3) Investment in portfolio form in some other activities, (4) Foreign direct investment in selected sectors.

Latest Foreign Investment Policy

Foreign investment in India is encouraged by many methods:

(1) Through NRE accounts and FCNR accounts, which bring in deposits in foreign currencies or external rupees for use by banks in India.

(2) Direct investment and portfolio investment by NRIs in the shares and securities of Indian companies.

(3) Investment by foreign institutions and OCBs is permitted up to 51% of equity of Indian companies.

Under the liberalisation policy of July 1991 and thereafter automatic approvals are granted for foreign investment in high priority industries up to 51% useful for import of capital goods or for foreign technology agreements. Trading Houses engaged in export business are also allowed foreign investment up to 51% of equity. Even existing companies whose foreign holding is less than 51% are permitted to issue fresh equity, if foreign holding is less than 51% and permitted to issue fresh equity to foreign companies/nationals. Procedures for granting permit by the RBI and by the Secretariat for Industrial Approvals and by Foreign Investment Promotion Board have been streamlined and simplified. Foreign Investment Promotion Council was also set-up in 1977 to help promotion of foreign investment into India.

Since 1992, these measures were further liberalised. The earlier stipulation that dividend payments outflow by companies with 51% equity must be balanced by export earnings over a period of seven years was dispensed with. FFIs are permitted by the SEBI to invest and operate in the Indian Capital and stock market. The holding by any FFI in any single company is subject to a ceiling of 5% and all FFIs together in any single company can hold up to 24% of equity later raised to 40%. Foreign banks and foreign security firms are now allowed to operate in India subject to necessary approvals form SEBI and RBI. The investment by NRIs and OCBs is permitted up to even 100% in the new issues of capital or in convertible debentures of private or public limited company in the specified priority sector industries. FFIs and FIIs are already operating in the Indian Financial markets.

There will be no lock in period for any of these investments except those which have been allotted on a firm basis under the preferential quotas to FFIs. The NRIs have been granted repatriation facility as well. The FFIs investing under the 24% quota are given the benefit of a flat rate of tax of 20% on dividend and interest income and 10% on long-term capital gains, before taking out the funds. NRI investment in sick companies and in 100% EOUs will continue to be allowed up to 10% to which was added the investment of 100% in power generation in 1992.

The FERA was diluted by removing the Sections 26 (7) 28, 29 and 31 whereby FERA companies are put on par with the Indian companies. They can undertake any activity in India and acquire and dispose of property, etc. They are allowed to use their trademarks in India.

The investment and disinvestment under portfolio investment were made easy and automatic if they are put through the Stock exchanges in India. FFIs can have lower tax rate of 10% instead of 20 to 30% as earlier on short-term capital gains. To keep pace with technological revolution in computers, an Electronic Hardware Technology Park was set up for foreigners to have 100% equity participation duty free import of capital goods and a tax holiday for 5 years.

NRIs are allowed to invest in any venture, firm, company or partnership up to 100% on non-repatriation basis without prior approval of the RBI. Liberalisation was also seen in the RBI exchange controls on the ADs. They are permitted to borrow abroad up to limits and release foreign exchange for remittance of dividends, interest, etc., to NRIs/OCBs and for Indian nationals going abroad for medical purposes or education, travel, etc. Foreign investment is of two types – Direct and Portfolio investment. The Portfolio investment is made through stock and capital markets. Foreign Direct Investment (FDI) is now defined to include equity capital of unincorporated enterprises, reinvested earnings of foreign companies, intercorporate debt transactions between entities, in addition to equity capital investment in related entities. Foreign inflows reached a peak in 2007-08 at US $ 61.6 billion and stood at US $ 21.3 billion 2008-09. As against thus, the outflow of Indian direct investment abroad was US $ 18.7 billion in 2007-08 and US $ 6.8 billion in 2008-09.

The table below gives an idea of the impact of new policy on foreign investment inflows since 1991, following economic reforms.

Table 29.1 Foreign Investment in Inflows

In US dollar millions

Item	1991-92	1995-96	1997-98	1998-99	2001-02	2004-05	2008-09	2010-11	2011-12
Direct Investment	150	2133	3557	2462	3904	5536	35168	30380	46847
Portfolio Investment	8	2748	1828	–61	2021	8909	–13855	31411	17410
Total Inflows:	158	4881	5385	2401	5925	14445	21313	61851	64257
of which GDRs/ADRs	—	683	645	270	477	613	1162	2049	597

Source: Annual Reports RBI.

NRI Schemes

From time to time, the rates of interest and the terms of acceptance, maturity periods, etc. of NRI deposits are amended to suit to the changing international money market conditions. After the launching of economic reforms, almost many FERA conditions have been diluted. In May 1993, FCNR scheme was amended to give more freedom to banks to borrow under the scheme. Under the FCNR (BANKS) Scheme, banks can borrow through deposits of "6 months and above but less than 1 year". The regular FCNR scheme will continue to operate for deposits of one year but less than 2 years", and "2 years but less than 3 years" and "3 years only". The depositor under the scheme continues to have exchange cover in the sense that he can take back the funds in the currency and the rate at which he has deposited. This cover was given up by the RBI later on, when there was no need for it due to current account transferability of the rupee.

New Foreign Currency (Non-resident) Accounts (Banks) Scheme

This new scheme was introduced in April 1993. As in the existing scheme, repatriation of funds will be freely permitted under the new scheme. The exchange risk cover will be provided by the banks and not by the RBI. However, the banks are now freed from the regulations of CRR and SLR requirements and from controls on the rates and quantum of lending. The other terms and conditions including the deposit rates will be identical with the existing FCNR scheme. The present NRI deposit schemes in operations are FCNR(B), NR(E)RA, and NR (NR)RD, which as now replaced by NRD (Non-resident Ordinary Rupee Account).

GOVERNMENT GUIDELINE ON PRIVATE FOREIGN INVESTMENT

(Rules Regarding NRI Investment)

Direct Investment without Repatriation Benefits

(1) General permission for all NRIs (not OCBs) except for investment in a concern engaged in agriculture/plantation activity or real estate business.

(2) Investment permitted in both primary and secondary market issues without limit.

(3) Interest and income allowed to be repatriated up to US $1000 or its equivalent in full and one-third of the balance income earned during any financial year, up to US $ 1000 or its equivalent in full and two-thirds of the balance income earned during the financial year 1995-96, and the entire income earned during the financial year 1996-97 and onwards. Repatriation is possible after payment of income tax. No lock in period for repatriation of sale proceeds of immovable property. Remittances out of NRO accounts permitted upto US $ 1 million per calendar year for specific purposes. ADs are permitted to issue international credit cards to NRIs.

Direct Investment with Repatriation Benefits

(1) There are two direct investment schemes: the 40 per cent scheme and the 100 per cent scheme.

(2) Under the 40 per cent scheme, NRIs are allowed to invest in shares and debentures of companies with repatriation benefits to the extent of 40 per cent of the new issue. There is no ceiling on remittance of interest or dividend.

(3) Under the 100 per cent scheme, NRIs can invest in high priority industries listed in Annexure III to the statement on Industrial Policy up to 100 per cent of the new issue. Dividend and interest can be freely remitted.

Other Investments

(1) NRIs can invest in sick industrial units up to 100 per cent by subscribing to existing shares or new issues. The investment has a lock-in period of three years.

(2) In certain high priority industries in which foreign investment up to 51 per cent is permitted on repatriation basis, NRIs can pick up the balance 49 per cent on repatriation basis.

(3) NRIs can invest up to 100 per cent in shares or convertible debentures of companies engaged in real estate development. Dividend can be freely repatriated, but the investment carries a lock-in period of three years.

(4) Permission for investment in non-convertible debentures has to be obtained from the Reserve Bank.

(5) 100 per cent investment in export-oriented units and export trading activities is permitted.

(6) Under the Portfolio Investment Scheme, NRIs are allowed to acquire shares and debentures through the stock exchanges in India by making an application to Reserve Bank. There is a ceiling of 5 per cent of the paid-up share capital of the company which can be raised to 24 per cent or 30% if the company concerned passes a resolution to that effect in its general body meeting. Individually, NRIs can invest up to 5 per cent of the paid-up share capital or the series of convertible debentures. The earlier lock-in period of one year has been withdrawn.

RBI LIBERALISATION OF NRI INVESTMENTS

With effect from April 15, 1999, the NRIs are allowed to open new Non-Resident (Special) Rupee Account which they can operate like Residents on their rupee accounts. In such cases, NRIs who were normally not allowed to invest in real estate, agriculture and plantation business can do so through the above account. The existing facilities for NRIs and PIO (person of Indian Origin) to maintain and operate NRO account, NRE account and FCNR account will continue. The repatriation facilities under these accounts will continue to be liberalised.

Besides, NRIs and PIO s have been allowed to lend to resident individuals, partnerships or proprietary firms and also transfer shares by way of gifts to residents. PIOs are also allowed to gift away immovable properties to charitable trusts and organisations.

All expatriate categories namely NRIs, OCBs and PIOs will also be allowed to invest in government securities and treasury bills, and they were earlier permitted already to invest in shares and debentures under the portfolio scheme. They are also permitted to sell shares, acquired through direct investment schemes without RBI prior permission.

The latest RBI liberalisations include general permission for investments by NRIs, OCBs and PIOs in deposit schemes of companies NBFCs and Mutual Funds. The RBI has also allowed the repatriable investments by NRIs and OCBs in Air Taxi Projects and operations subject to clearance by the Director General of Civil Aviation.

The above liberalisations have simplified investments by NRIs and opened up the floodgates for any operations in India by NRIs and PIOs like the domestic residents. They should help in flow of larger funds from NRIs.

BORROWING ABROAD — GOVERNMENT GUIDELINES ON DOMESTIC COMPANIES

Following the launch of the economic liberalisation programme in mid-1991, with an open door policy on foreign investment, there has been a far reaching change in the entire gamut of rules and regulations governing industrial and external sectors. Foreign investment is encouraged even with majority equity participation and direct and portfolio flows are welcome.

The converse of this policy thrust is that Indian companies are permitted to access global markets to tap funds for modernisation, meeting the import requirements and a host of other purposes. In the aftermath of this sweeping transformation, almost 50 companies have raised funds from foreign investors mainly through the instrument of global depository receipts while a few have opted for bonds issues.

In the first set of guidelines on Euro issues, the salient features were:

(1) Prior permission of the Government of India.

(2) Good track record of issuing companies for a minimum period of three years.

(3) No lock-in period.

In the second set of guidelines issued in May 1994, the government announced a few changes. They are as under:

(1) No more than two issues in a year.

(2) A minimum gap of 12 months between two issues by a single company.

(3) Out of total proceeds, 85 per cent to be utilised within a year for financing of capital goods imports, domestic purchase/installation of plant and machinery, pre-payment or scheduled repayments of external borrowings and internal investments.

(4) Quarterly statements on the use of funds.

In view of the monetary impact of huge inflows of money abroad, the government tightened the regulations on Euro issues on October 1994. The highlights of the policy changes are:

(1) It is mandatory to keep the money abroad till the funds are actually utilised. They can invest in bank deposits and money market instrument abroad.

(2) No need to utilise the capital within 12 months of raising it.

(3) An auditor's statement on the deployment of funds to be furnished every three months.

(4) Issue of warrants with GDRs/FCBs is banned.

(5) Companies allowed to park their funds in foreign stock markets and real estate abroad. Resident individuals, companies and MFs are allowed to invest in listed companies abroad.

(6) Selected financial institutions allowed to access Euro market on behalf of small and medium companies.

In December 1994 and later, the Government had second thoughts on granting permission to all companies indiscriminately, in view of the growing foreign debt problem of the country. Thereafter, the Government has slowed down the process of granting such permission. But the broad policy of globalisation of the economy has however continued. The restrictions on banks on the use of FCNR(B) funds and their unused Tier I capital have been liberalised. Foreign Equity Investment in India was continued to be encouraged.

Policy on Euro-Currency Borrowing

External commercial borrowings include bank loans, buyers' credit, supplier's credit, securitised instruments, such as F.R.Ns, credit from official Export credit agencies, or from multilateral and regional financial institutions like IFC, ADB, etc.

Consistent with maintaining the external debt burden at a tolerable level, access to ECB is allowed by corporates subject to an annual ceiling. The projects for which such borrowing will be permitted are in infrastructure, power, oil exploration, Telecom, Railways, Roadways, Bridges, ports, and export sectors.

ECB will have the following maximum average maturities:

Table 29.2

Borrowing Limit/Agent	Average Maturity Limit
Less than US $ 20 million	3 years
More than US $ 20 million	5 years
100% E.O.US	3 years
Others	3 to 5 years

All corporates are allowed to raise up to U.S $ 15 million at a maturity of 3 years. There are no end-use restrictions except that these funds cannot be deployed in stock market and real estate investment. Corporates with export earnings are permitted to borrow up to three times the average annual earnings during the last three years, subject to a ceiling of $ 100 million and subject to the some restrictions as above. These borrowings are kept for mostly short term purposes with short maturity periods.

Holding company or promoter can borrow up to $ 50 million to finance equity investment in a Joint Venture/Subsidiary.

Borrowings with maturity of 8 years and above are allowed subject to the following ceilings. There were subject to change as and when required:

Maturity period	Amount as ceiling
8 to 16 years	US $ 100 million
Above 16 years	US $ 200 million

Besides, long term debt instruments should not have "put and call" options. D.F.Is can borrow under this window in addition to their normal allocation, made by the government annually.

ECBs are to be used for import of capital goods and services and project related Rupee expenditure in all sectors subject to some conditions.

All infrastructure and greenfield projects are permitted to borrow up to 35% of the project cost. All Telecom projects are allowed to borrow upto 50% of the project cost. In all cases, no investment in stock market and real estate is allowed with these funds. Interest payable on these borrowings by all industrial undertakings is eligible for withholding Tax-exemption. All approvals for less than 3 years are granted by the RBI and the rest by the Ministry of Finance.

Refinancing of outstanding amounts under the existing loans by raising fresh loans at lower cost is permitted on a case by case basis, subject to the fact that outstanding maturity of original loan is maintained. Roll over of an existing ECB or inter corporate swapping of ECB is not allowed.

Corporates can undertake asset liability matching exercises for hedging interest or exchange rate risk on their underlying foreign currency exposure without prior approval of the authorities through

(a) Interest Rate Swaps;

(b) Currency Swaps;

(c) Coupon Swaps; and

(d) Forward Rate agreements (FRA)

Foreign Currency options were also permtited in the mid 2003. Foreign currency hedge contracts were already allowed to banks and corporates, to cover their currency exposures.

The above guidelines are periodically reviewed in the light of the prudent management of external debt by the government. Changing domestic market conditions and domestic requirements and foreign market conditions, etc., are taken into account in any review of these guidelines for Euro currency borrowing and External commercial borrowing.

Latest ECB Trends

The External Commercial borrowing by Indian Corporates was higher in 2004-05, as against a net negative figure in 2003-04, which was due to larger repayments than fresh borrowings. The net resource transfers under external assistance to India turned positive in 2004-05 after a long negative trend during 1995-2004.

The net external inflow under ECB during 2004-05, was due to good investment demand domestically and favourable liquidity conditions in overseas markets. Global investors particularly pension funds and insurance companies showed a clear preference for Bonds of Indian Corporates of good credit rating. Indian companies used these funds for investment in capital goods, new projects, modernisation, expansion, and diversification as the investment climate and capital market were booming in the year 2005 and 2006. The outstanding ECBs in India's External Debt was $ 26,942 million, working out to 22% of the total, in 2006, which went up to $ 62,676 million in 2009.

Indian Aid to Other Countries

India also extends assistance to other countries in the form of loans and grants. The loans are in the form of suppliers' credit or trade credits mostly of a long-term nature. These loans and grants are mostly to neighbouring countries like Nepal, Bhutan, Sri Lanka, Bangaldesh, etc.

More recently, Indian private investment abroad is permitted by the government either in the form of technical and consultancy project exports, construction projects or turnkey projects. Indian ventures abroad are of three categories:

(i) Direct investment by Indian companies or suppliers' credit by Indian exporters;

(ii) Joint ventures along with some developed countries in a developing country or even in a developed country; and

(iii) Consultancy and project exports.

Magnitude of External Assistance

India is emerging as one of the major donor countries to developing Asian neighbours. External assistance provided by India rose from US $ 247 million in 2000-01 to US $ 412 million in 2008-09. India's assistance took the form of technical co-operation, and training. Grants constitute 90% of the total external aid by India. The major beneficiaries are Bhutan, Sri Lanka, Nepal, Myanmar and some African countries. External assistance took the form of grants and loans, under plan and non-plan expenditure of the Central Government.

Joint Ventures

Joint ventures are joint collaborations in the field of manufacturing processing and marketing by two or more countries. A joint enterprise can be brought about by an agreement at joint ownership, control and management of a venture located at home or abroad between a local firm and a foreign firm. Such contracts involve also a common licence, or sharing of a trade patent or manufacturing formula or management contract.

In the case of India, such joint ventures by foreign companies are obliged by government policy to share with Indian equity a proportion of ownership capital extending from 25 per cent to 75 per cent depending on the nature of the manufacturing activity and its importance to the Indian economy. Even without joint venture, foreign individuals, firms and companies (of Indian origin) are now permitted to invest in Indian companies. This was designed to encourage private foreign capital inflow into India. NRIs can now invest up to even 100% in Indian ventures on a non-repatriation basis.

Indian joint ventures may also result in our investment in foreign countries. Such investment may take the form of equity participation in share capital, sharing of technical and managerial expertise, setting up of a turnkey project or export of capital goods, plant and machinery. Indian joint ventures extend to both developed and developing countries and investment in a third country also.

Government Policy Guidelines

For Indian entrepreneurs to enter into joint ventures abroad, they require the prior approval of the Indian government. There is an Inter-ministerial Committee on Joint Ventures abroad. The Committee, comprises the representatives of Ministries of Commerce, External Affairs, Finance, Industry, DGTD and the Department of Company Affairs. Applications have to be made in a prescribed form for the purpose under Section 27 of the FERA and Section 372 of the Companies Act, to the Ministry of Commerçe which provides secretarial assistance to the Inter-ministerial Committee. This Committee is guided by certain norms, referred to below:

(1) Exchange Control and other governmental rules of the host country should be complied with.

(2) Indian participation in the venture should be in the form of export of know-how, consultancy, plant, machinery and capital goods.

(3) Granting of Rupee loans by Indian participating companies and raising of foreign exchange loans abroad are permitted.

(4) Generally, cash flows for equity participation are not permitted, except in special cases.

(5) Necessary project reports, cash flow and profitability projections should be submitted to prove the technical and financial viability of the project undertaken by the joint venture.

(6) RBI clearance of foreign exchange release would then follow depending on the terms on which the project is cleared by the government.

The plant, machinery and other goods exported under the above scheme would be entitled to all export incentives which are currently available to exporters. These exports are permitted on deferred payment basis or under loans, or lines of credit. Inward receipts for service fees, royalties, consultancy, etc., are to be as per the Exchange Control guidelines or capitalisation if that is permitted by the terms of government approval.

Indian investment centres abroad help the prospective entrepreneurs in formulating such schemes of joint venture or other forms of foreign investment. They help to locate foreign participants, disseminate market intelligence and act as intermediaries between Indian entrepreneurs and foreign participants.

But it is understood from the studies conducted by the Indian Investment Centres abroad that many approved projects could not be fructified. Some of them were abandoned before the projects were launched, due to late realisation of the difficulties and non-viability of the project or due to inadequate financial support. A few were also given up after launching due to differences with collaborators, objections from the host country or non-fulfilment of agreed conditions by the foreign collaborators. It would thus, appear that the mortality rate of the Indian ventures abroad is rather high.

India became a member of Multi-lateral Investment Guarantee Agency, set-up in 1988. It provides investment assurance and advisory services for foreign private investment. Reference was made to this in an earlier chapter.

India's Direct Investment Abroad

India's Direct investment abroad is aimed at providing access to new markets and new technologies including research and development. Bulk of this took the form of mergers and acquisitions of foreign companies. This process started with IT Companies and spread to related services, in PC and Computer software. During the period 2000 to 2006, the process of M&A has shifted to manufacturing industries also, such as steel, viscose fibre and copper, by acquiring companies in resource rich countries namely, Canada and Australia with the objective of backward integration. IT and pharmaceutical companies have also come forward for investing abroad — some by acquiring existing companies and some by setting W.O.S. in those countries. Public sector oil companies have acquired equites in selected oil exploration companies, retailing and refining.

Sector-wise analysis shows that India's investment abroad was mostly concentrated in manufacturing, followed by services, particularly financial services, trading and others. The magnitude of this investment was put at US $ 706 million in 2000-01, which increased to US $ 1547 million in 2004-05, and to US $ 18.7 billion in 2007-08 and US $ 16.8 billion in 2008-09, and to US $ 18.7 billion in 2007-08 and US $ 16.8 billion in 2008-09.

Country-wise, US has attracted the largest amount of FDI from India, followed by Russia, Mauritius, etc. Indian Firms have about 440 joint ventures or investment projects in the UK. There are more than 1400 Indian companies operating in Singapore. A large number of those companies are listed on New York, London, NASDAQ Stock Exchanges. This expansion of Indian enterprises across the world increased their market access, led to diversification and larger R&D effort.

The policy of the Government of India in the area of foreign investment by Indian enterprise is to encourage joint ventures by Indian entrepreneurs and help them joining with foreign entrepreneurs in setting up turnkey projects and construction projects in partner countries or in third countries, particularly in the Middle East and Gulf countries and to encourage Indian private enterprises to invest in these countries in terms of project exports, technological transfers and consultancy exports. Some of the less developed countries are in need of Indian technology and know-how, and joint ventures along with or without third country assistance are to be promoted.

The countries where such investment was made include both developed and developing countries in the East and West, including the UK and USA, South East Asia, Africa, Middle East, Europe and South Asia. Nearly one-half of it is in the East Asian countries. Industry-wise, the highest number of collaborations were in the field of industrial machinery followed by electrical industry and automobile and auto-ancillary industries. Joint ventures are mostly in the manufacturing sector, particularly in light engineering, chemicals, drugs, iron and steel products, paper, glass sugar, leather and rubber products.[4] Among non-manufacturing activities, Indian direct investment abroad is found in business of hotels, consultancy, I.T., multi-media, Telecommunication construction projects, trading, shipping, etc.

Multinational Corporations (MNCs)

The role of multinational corporations in the pattern of world production and trade has been increasing over the decades. As estimated by the Brandt Commission, they now control about one-third of the world production and the intra-national branch transfers of these MNCs would work out to about one-fourth of the world sales. The bulk of private investment is accounted for by the MNCs. The induction of latest technology and exploitation of the natural resources in the developing countries may be mainly due to the enterprise of multinational corporations. The oligopoly situation in their operations can be gleaned from the concentration of their productive capacity in the big 50 MNCs.

Definition

By definition, a multinational corporation is an enterprise which has "managerial headquarters located in one country while the enterprise carries out operations in a number of countries as well."[5] Either ownership is held in one country and control in another country or both in one country and the operations in many countries. The corporations have operations and sales extending to various countries with some of them exceeding the Gross National Product of even the advanced developed countries. the strategy of expansion is through private direct investment abroad through setting up of subsidiaries or branch offices or in joint ventures. As most of the companies have reached their limit of expansion in their own countries, the scope for expansion lies in foreign countries. For horizontal expansion, setting up conglomerates and integrating dissimilar activities, they arrange a holding company to have a number of subsidiaries in a number of countries. By vertical integration

4. For detailed discussion, see Sanjaya Lall, *The New Multinationals*, John Wiley and Sons, 1983, Chapter on "Multinationals from India".
5. I.L.O. "Multinational Enterprises and Social Policy", 1973.

with forward and backward linkages, expansion takes place through branches and setting up of factories in other countries, for parts, spares, ancillaries, etc. Another method of expansion is re-investment and self-financing of the various diversified activities of the corporation in the existing countries. The transfer of technology, enterprise and sometimes managerial talent also go along with direct foreign investment by these corporations.

Nearly 50 per cent of the MNCs are based in the U. S. and the rest in the UK, France, Japan and West Germany, which are the major industrialised countries in the world. Industry-wise, the concentration of multinationals is in airlines and extractive industries, such as oils, minerals, etc. Now they are spread over a wide variety of industries and services.

Rationale of the Dominance of MNCs

The key to the success of the MNCs lies in their broad-based operations, secrecy of their accounts and vast technological research base. They have control of not only the capital but also technology with which they seek investment avenues and markets in other developed and developing countries. The rationale for their expansion is both offensive as to capture new markets and defensive in the sense of retaining their share of the market in the teeth of competition. Their expansion is mostly in fields of minerals, oils and plantations, where foreign investment was welcomed historically. The scale of operations increases and costs per unit go down significantly. Similarly, larger technological transfers permit larger research and development costs, as they are now spread over a larger scale of operations.

The establishment of their units in foreign countries is based on the availability of cheaper labour, managerial talent or other inputs or to reduce the transport costs or to expand their market and scale of operations. Secondly, they have the controlling interest in technology as well as capital which enables them to wield political as well as economic power in more than one country. They seek unexploited resources, natural as well as human in the developing countries for exploitation and to capture the markets. Besides, the foreign governments encourage the inflow of foreign direct investment, for the purpose of expansion of economic activity, income and employment. With the increasing tariff barriers and protectionism in most of the developed countries, MNCs have found a method of circumventing them by establishing their own factories, processing units and joint ventures in under developed countries. They also take advantage of tax-concession in some of the LDCs. They secure benefits of lower costs through technology-sharing, economies of scale, marketing and managerial expansion and a further boost to technological upgradation and R & D.

Merits and Demerits

Admittedly, it is to the advantage of both the MNCs and their home countries to have their activities expanding in many countries. However, the host countries have both advantages and disadvantages due to flow of investments from the MNCs. The merits are briefly, the promotion of investments, larger income and employment in the host country, provision of latest technology with a productive capacity at low costs of production, increased competition with the domestic enterprise, and larger world trade which result in better all-around specialisation. The MNCs have also started adapting themselves to the requirements of the LDCs which are their host countries. Restrictions with respect to the direction of investments as well as the quantum, location and capacity and other regulations are generally complied by them in the host countries.

There are also disadvantages in the operations of the MNCs. Motivated by profit, they exploit natural resources as in the case of oil resources without replenishment, undermine the national interest by charging exorbitant prices unrelated to costs, ignore all standards of quality, health precaution and pollution control which they could not do in their own home countries. They could manipulate their accounts with transfer price mechanism and avoid showing excess profits and escape from the tax net. They have the money power with the result they wield their influence on political and administrative system of the governments of the host countries. Many of the MNCs are reported to be unscrupulous to violate all canons of equity and justice and promote their own self-interest through expansion of their activities and making super-profits.

Re-assessment of the MNCs' Role

In more recent years, the role of MNCs has been accepted as inescapable. They have an important part to play in the transfer of private resources for investment and technologies which very few developing countries can afford to miss. The vast natural resources and the underdeveloped nature of the technologies in many LDCs require the services of MNCs. The governments of the host countries have also regulated their inflows and outflows and the pattern of their operations. Many countries have now established their own multinational corporations albeit on a small-scale, as in the case of India, in the field of banking, hotel services and consultancy services. Besides, in the future, the smaller-sized multinationals are going to capture the market of the vast growing multinationals as the latter are getting unwieldy. Even in India L & T, ONGC, Tatas and Ambanis, among others have become MNCs. Mittals and Mallayya's have become transactional Rainboxy and Dr. Reddy Labs have turned to be MNCs. This development is taking place in both developed and developing countries, although MNCs have readjusted their future role on a different pattern from that in the past, a new category of multinational corporations is coming up from the LDCs to reap the monopolistic advantages and higher benefits from technological intensity and advanced marketing techniques.[6]

The motives of foreign investment would continue to dominate in the future world and the need for capital and advanced research technology is indispensable for the growth of the poorer countries as Asia and Africa. The MNCs bring in certain definite advantages to both the host countries as well as home countries referred to earlier. They increase employment, expand the flow of goods and services and improve the living standard of the people across the world. Thus, had it not been for the MNCs, the developing countries would not have been able to acquire these inputs necessary for development and this assures the continuance of the importance of the MNCs in the future world pattern of production and trade.

6. Sanjaya Lall, *The New Multinationals*, John Wiley and Sons, 1983.

The liberalised policy of foreign flows into Indian industries and dilution of FERA, encouraging MNC to operate and expand in India are promoting the competition and make our economy more competitive market-oriented and efficient.

The multinational corporations have revolutionised the system of world production and sales. Their activities have brought to question the traditional trade theory, based on comparative costs and locational advantages. The transnational company may produce at one corner of the world and supply the finished goods at another corner of the world at a cost lower than that when produced locally with its traditional comparative cost advantage and locational superiority.

The growth of MNC activities has changed the patterns of trade based on skill endowments and transport cost. Some more recent theories such as "Neo-technology" and "Neo-factor proportions theories" base their explanation of trade patterns on market imperfections, differences in technology, skill levels, economies of scale and product differentiation. These take into account the role of MNCs and technological dynamism in LDCs. Professor Gray's generalised theory also incorporates the effects of MNC's operations on world production and trade.

International Long-term Lending — World Bank

In the post-war world, international capital markets have dried up as a source of finance due to war ravages on the domestic economies and various degrees of exchange and trade controls imposed by the respective countries on domestic economic considerations. But the need for finance was also great for rehabilitation of the productive system in the case of developed countries and for economic development of the poorer countries. To start with, government-to-government loans, grants and other bilateral assistance gained ground soon after the war. At this time, multilateral institutions for promoting trade and aid were designed by the founding fathers of the Bretton Woods Conference in 1944 in the form of International Monetary Fund for short-term lending and International Bank for Reconstruction and Development for long-term lending. Both these institutions started functioning in 1946. In this chapter, discussion is concentrated on IBRD and other term-lending institutions in the international financial system. The original largest subscribers to these institutions are the US, the UK, China, France and India.

Leaving aside their structural and organisational aspects, their functional aspects involved both lending and guaranteeing. The World Bank (IBRD) guarantees in part or whole loans made by private investors through private channels and make direct loans out of Bank's own funds or out of borrowed funds from governments or private investors or banks. If the bank lends to a private party, that party's government is expected to guarantee the loan. The basic objective of World Bank was to relieve poverty and provision of basic social services and then promote economic growth.

The sources of their lendable resources are the members' subscription paid in gold and their own currencies and borrowing from the private capital markets by issue of its own bonds such as in the US, Canada, Switzerland, the UK etc. These funds in the members' currencies or in the borrowing country's currency are to be used with the concurrence of the concerned country. The main object of the World Bank is to facilitate the flows of long-term aid in the form of loans at low rates and promote economic growth in developing countries. The Bank accordingly borrows and lends at low rates, keeping only a small margin for its own operations thereby keeping down the interest rate burdens for the borrowing country. Secondly, the Bank is promoting multilateralism in aid flows and thus in trade flows by institutionalising these flows through itself. Thirdly, the Bank by imposing conditions for assistance, developed a tradition for efficient allocation of funds in the recipient country, pursuit of right policies and proper management of the economies. Fourthly, it is helping the balanced growth of the economies of developing countries and of world trade through multilateral channels. Fifthly, it is aiding the member countries with technical and managerial help and training their personnel in their Economic Development Institute. Sixthly, it is helping to create an international stake in the borrowing and non-borrowing members in the regular servicing of loans, as the members have to share the risk of loss as well as actual losses in the Bank's lending operations. Prompt and regular repayments and servicing of loans are thus the responsibility of all members.

The Bank has been making programme and project assistance to member countries, both developed and developing. The bulk of its assistance is going to the developing countries at present. Its principal emphasis is on basic public services and infrastructural facilities like Railways, Communications, Electric Power, Agriculture, Industry, etc. In Fiscal 1998, a new policy specifying the minimum size of liquid asset portfolio was implemented.

The International Development Association (IDA)

The International Development Association is an affiliate of the World Bank set up in 1960 designed to promote economic development and productivity by extending softer loans than the World Bank could to the poorer low-income member countries. Most of the IDA loans are long-term, extending up to 50 years and at low interest rates of 2 per cent to 4 per cent. The repayment terms are also designed to suit the borrower and moratorium is granted up to about 25 years. These loans are for important development projects in the developing countries on flexible terms as not to adversely affect their balance of payments position. As these loans are of multilateral nature, they can be used in any country. IDA may unlike IBRD not insist on government guarantee in advancing to private parties. IDA may provide both technical and financial assistance required for development projects.

The resources of IDA are from the initial subscriptions, additional subscriptions if any and borrowings from members of supplementary resources. Only 10 per cent of the subscriptions of the members are paid up and the rest of the 90 per cent in respect of the developed countries (Group I) was paid up over a period of 5 years in freely convertible currencies. In the case of developing countries included in Group II, they paid 90 per cent of the subscription in national currencies which cannot be used without their consent.

In 1975, IBRD had started a third window for long-term loans to developing countries on terms, intermediate between soft loans of IDA and World Bank. This assistance is for 25 years at a rate of 4.5 per cent for developing countries with per capita incomes under \$ 375. An interest subsidy fund was also started with contribution from some oil-producing and developed countries in order to lend funds at subsidised rate.

International Finance Corporation (IFC)

The International Finance Corporation was set up in 1956, as an affiliate of the World Bank. Its membership and management are kept separate. The object of IFC was to promote flows of private capital without government guarantee. Thus IFC would lend capital in the form of investment in debentures or other senior securities along with private parties in the member countries. It will encourage private management of such concerns and encourage domestic entrepreneurship. To keep the funds rotating, it may sell off its investments in any company of a member country in favour of some domestic investors in that country. IFC has not been investing in venture capital (equity), but only in loan capital.

The IFC has been encouraging the flow of private capital and growth of private enterprise in member countries. It is on the lookout for promising firms in these countries or for commercially viable proposals for investment. It would encourage domestic management and private domestic and foreign capital to flow into the selected ventures in the private sector through its involvement in its technical and financial help for the projects. This was channelised through private financial institutions like ICICI in India.

The Bank for International Settlements (BIS)

The Bank for International Settlements (BIS) was set up in 1930 consisting of the European central banks as members. In 1970, Japan and Canada joined as members. New members could be admitted only on invitation from BIS. The objectives of the BIS are to promote co-operation among the central banks in their international financial operations and to act as a trustee or agent in regard to international settlements entrusted to it by the member countries.

One of the original tasks entrusted to it was to co-operate in carrying out of the "young plan" under which it was entrusted with the duty of receiving and distributing the German Reparation Payments to member countries. The statutes under which BIS was set up had laid down the transactions which it may undertake such as purchase, sale, exchange of gold, bills of exchange and short-term financial obligations of member countries and acceptance of deposits from central banks. The Bank was prohibited from issuing its own notes, accepting bills of exchange, making advances to governments or to acquire ownership of any real property, etc.

The Bank's main sources of funds are the short-term and sight deposits of member central banks. Its dealings are mostly with the central banks of member countries with its interventions in the various exchange markets. Its arrangements with commercial banks of member countries are incidental to its main dealings with the central banks.

The services provided by it to member countries are as follows: (i) Gold operations in international markets; (ii) Foreign exchange purchase or sale operations; (iii) Purchase and sale to central banks of the short-term marketable government securities of member countries; (iv) To act as trustee and agent of the member country; and (v) To act as fiscal agent for the European Payments Union and European Coal and Steel Community.

It provides a forum for exchange of information as between central banks. It would extend credit and help ease pressures on any member's currency and promote co-operation among member countries. Since, 1964 multilateral surveillance of the balance of payments adjustments of the Group of Ten was carried out through the BIS. The BIS extends highly qualitative and confidential service to member countries of a very valuable nature. India has joined the B.I.S. on invitation recently.

Asian Development Bank (ADB)

ADB was originally sponsored by the ECAFE, a body of the U.N. for the Asian and Far East region. It was set up by subscriptions from many countries in Asia and outside and started operations in 1966 as a development bank for helping the poor nations of Asia in their development efforts. It aims at raising funds from private and public sources for development purposes and assist the member states in the region with financial and technical aid, loans, and equity participation, etc. It is located in Manila, Philippines. It has held 39th Annual General Body meeting in India during May 2006.

The main donors are Japan, Australia, U.S.A. etc., and India is also a member receiving assistance. It has Ordinary Capital Resources (OCR) and Asian development Fund (ADF) for providing financial assistance and the latter for soft loans to poorer countries. India is second largest beneficiary of soft loans from ADB.

The assistance of ADB takes the following forms:

(1) Government and Government guaranteed loans to private and public companies and corporations.

(2) Direct private sector lending.

(3) Equity investment in private sector corporate units.

(4) Equity underwriting in member countries.

Loans take the form of project loans, programme loans, sector loans, credit lines, technical assistance loans and unguaranteed private sector loans.

Financial assistance has gone to the following sector of the economy in the order of importance:

(1) Energy sector, power and electricity generation.

(2) Transport and communications sector.

(3) Social infrastructure.

(4) Agriculture and agro-based industry.

(5) Financial Sector.

(6) Industry and non-fuel minerals.

The ADB has also provided technical assistance and loans for this purpose to various projects and programmes. India has been one of the major beneficiaries of assistance from ADB. Its assistance has been a great help for the economic development of the poor Asian countries. This is particularly so, in respect of aid from the soft loan window of the Bank namely Asian Development Fund, which has been replenished from time to time from the rich donor countries like Japan and U.S.A.

30

Foreign Exchange Arithmetic

Introduction

Foreign exchange is a two way transaction involving two currencies or more and in particular home currency and one or more foreign currencies. Rates at which they are exchanged are called exchange rates. There are various rates for various purposes, instruments and periods of payment and receipt. Cross rates will apply when there are more than two currencies in the transaction. In case, the delivery or receipt is postponed, or purchase or sale takes place for a future period, forward premium or discount is there for those forward rates for various periods of say one month to six months over the spot rates. Besides, the bank deals with the customer as an intermediary. It has to buy from the wholesale inter bank market and sell in the retail to its customer. It has to sell to the wholesale market, if it has purchased from the customer. These are called cover transactions. The Bank has therefore a cover rate, applicable to its original deal in the wholesale market to which it adds or deducts its own margin, which is normally 0.5%.

Exchange Arithmatic deals with the subject of customer's deals with banks of purchase and sale of foreign currencies. The sale of foreign currencies is like sale of any commodity, spot or forward. In the case of foreign exchange, a sale is accompanied by a purchase — a sale of foreign exchange means sale of foreign currency and the purchase of domestic currency. As those transactions are based on some principles, these principles and practices are dealt with in this chapter. As this book deals with the subject from the student point of view and not that of banks, the accounts and books of banks are not dealt with, but only the mechanics of the operations in the form of exchange arithmatic is presented here, however briefly it may be.

Factors Influencing Bank Margin

The margin charged by the bank between buying and selling rate varies from bank to bank, customer to customer, depending upon the volume of transactions, customer relationship and the purpose for which foreign currencies are required, etc.

Good credit rating of the customer and his awareness of the market mechanics would get a better rate. A sale of a very large amount running into millions would however attract a worse rate than that for a modest amount of $ 1000 to 10,000. So is the case with very small amounts of $ 100 to $ 1000, due to the difficulty of making cover operations.

The banks quote the rates on the basis of the rate at which they can cover it in the inter bank market and then load it with an appropriate margin before giving a quote to their customers. The cover for sale of foreign currency (say $) will be the purchase price at which it can buy in the wholesale market, which will be the sale price of the market. Similarly, if the bank is buying a foreign currency, it will quote a rate, at which it can sell in the wholesale market, which will be the market's buying rate.

Since the market rates are changing from day-to-day and from time to time within a day, the bank always gives the worst quote to the buyer and the best quote to the seller of the foreign currency; thus the buying rate is Rs. 43.65 per US $ and selling rate is Rs. 43.90, which means that when bank buys $, it will give less rupees (43.65) but when it sells dollars, it wants to take more rupees (43.90).

Generally the quotation is given up to four digits such as Rs. 43.3050/43.3150, which are the bank's buying and selling rates for US dollars, in the wholesale market which are quoted daily in Financial press. In the case of quotation of foreign currency for one unit of domestic currency, Indian banks quote for Rs. 100 equivalent of US $ 2.3094. (Rs. 100 = US $ 2.3094)

Similarly, one Euro is quoted as Rs. 23.41/23.87 which are T.T. buying and selling rates respectively. If quoted in the reverse direction for Rs. 100, the quotation is Euro 4.2716. Rupee has depreciated so much as compared to the major currencies that no quotation is given for one Rupee, but only for Rs. 100/-. Now the practice is to give rates as so many rupees for each unit of foreign currency under this system, purchase of foreign currency is always at a lower rate than sale of the same.

The following rates are quoted by a bank for illustration:

Table 30.1

		Draft/Cheques		Currency	
		Buying	**Selling**	**Buying**	**Selling**
US Dollar	Rs.	46.00	47.35	45.75	47.60
Pound Sterling	Rs.	69.57	70.44	68.10	71.50

(as on 1st July 2010).

Currency rates are worse rates than those of drafts or cheques as in the case of latter, the bank does not part with currency immediately but with a time gap of about 10 days for which it gets interest on that amount which is given as credit to the customer in the case of drafts, cheques, etc., in their quotation.

The relation of sale and purchase rates to the market rates is given by some margin which is bank's own profit.

The relationship of purchase and sale prices is depicted below:

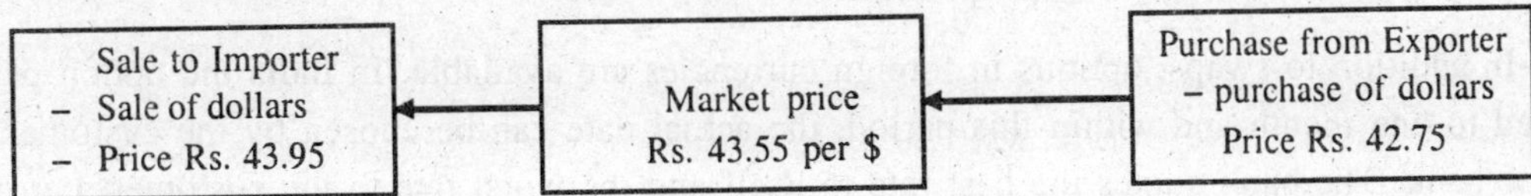

Forward Rate

Forward exchange rate is available from one month to 6 months quoted by the banks. The rate is basically a function of demand and supply for forward dollars of any duration. Banks generally cover their transactions with the public in order to avoid taking any exchange risk. The forward margin over the spot rate is called forward premium or discount. A sale forward of any currency is covered by the bank by forward purchase of the same duration, if it has to avoid taking any risk. Similarly, a spot transaction with the customer has to be covered by a forward cover. Thus, there can be coverage of spot by forward or forward by forward. Thus, the demand and supply for forward dollars arise.

The Reserve Bank purchases and sells foreign currencies, both spot and forward. To regulate the demand and supply pressures on the market and keep stable rates these purchase and sale deals are put through by the RBI. The banks can deal with the RBI or inter bank market. Swaps are readily available in the inter-bank market as between currencies, spot and forward, etc.

For illustration, the table below gives the Forward premia for US $ in terms of monthly averages.

Table 30.2

		1 month premia	3 months' premia	6 months' premia
January	2002	5.70	6.00	5.99
February	2002	5.05	5.49	5.46
March	2002	6.91	6.46	5.93
March	2003	3.81	3.60	3.50
March	2005	2.28	1.82	1.62
March	2007	6.99	4.51	3.80
March	2009	5.22	3.99	3.20
March	2011	6.99	6.99	6.85

Source : RBI Reports.

Note : The premium varies from time to time, depending on the expectations of spot rates then. They were high in 2007 and 2011 due to grater uncertainty in the rupee market following global financial crisis.

The forward premia are available on a daily basis. For illustration, the premia for March 16,2000 for one month is 5.30 per cent annualised and for three months 4.31 per cent and six month 3.71 per cent. For June 30, 2005, one month premium is 1.96 — for three months 1.65 and for six months 1.48 respectively. Monthly averages are also available in RBI publications. For the month of March 2009 are month premium was 5.22 per cent per annum 3.99% for three months and 3.20% for six months respectively.

For purchase of an option currency, which is at a premium in the forward market, the premium applicable at the beginning of option period is applied and for sale, the premium applicable at the end of the period is loaded to the spot rate.

In addition to swaps, options in foreign currencies are available. In India the option period is limited to one month and within this period, the actual date can be chosen by the customer vis-a-vis the bank. The bank quotes the best rate to itself and the worst rate to the customer. Let us take the one month fixed date delivery rates as Rs. 42.98. Then the one month option forward customer rates are quoted as Rs. 43.22/42.93, assuming a margin of 24 ps. and 5 ps. respectively which means that its selling rate is 43.22 and buying rate is 42.93 and the margin will be less for buying by the bank.

The bank's principle for quoting forward rate is the same as that of the spot rates. Take the wholesale market rate and load a margin. If say the inter bank spot rate is Rs. 43.03/06 and one month discount is 5/6 ps. then one month forward dollars in the wholesale market will be 43.08/12.

If a currency is at a discount, the worst rate rule will apply, the highest discount will be loaded to the purchase rate and the lowest to sale rate.

Purchase (bid) rate = Highest discount or lowest premium is loaded.

Sale (offer) rate = Lowest discount or highest premium is loaded to spot rate.

If a bank is quoting for intervening periods falling in between one month or three months, etc., the rates will be the worst rates quoted, say for the end period of one month or two months, etc. These are called broken periods and Tel quel Rates will apply.

Role of Interest Rates

In free markets, in which the interest rates and exchange rates are determined by free forces of demand and supply, the forward margins are governed by the interest rate parity principle. This means that forward margin on the exchange rate will be equal to the interest differential between the respective countries, whose currencies are exchanged.

If we consider two countries and their exchange rates and interest rates in them, then the example can be set out as follows:

US $	German D.M
Interest Rate	Interest Rate
4%	6%

Suppose Exchange Rate is given as $ 1 = D.M 1.50

Forward margin between dollar and D.M is the difference between their interest rates (6% - 4%) namely 2%. In other words, forward D.M will be cheaper by 2% per annum. Should the margin be higher or lower, arbitrage transactions will bring about their equality to interest rate parity. One can borrow dollars at 4% and then exchange these dollars for Marks and invest in Germany at an interest rate of 6% and bring back dollars at the end of the contract period, say 3 months, instead of buying forward dollars.

Assumptions for interest rate parity to be valid are as follows:

Free markets, no intervention or regulation on the markets, arbitrage transactions are allowed and no exchange controls by the central bank, no unforeseen conditions like wars or other calamities, when expectations change.

Maturity Period

If a contract is expiring on a Friday, the payment may be made on Monday, as Saturday and Sunday are holidays. Similarly, if any holidays coincide with the maturity date of the contract, the contract will be executed on the next working day. The number of days is taken as 360 days in a year for calculations in Exchange arithmatic and a month is taken as 30 days. The actual number of days for the currencies to change hands will have to be worked out under each contract. Sometimes, banks take 365 days in a year.

How to Calculate Forward Rate

Given the spot rate of euro as $ 1 = 1.6610 D.M (1.6610/20) and the one month forward margin is quoted at 0.54/57 pennings. If it is a premium on the spot, the forward rate will be euro 1.6556/63, which is got by deducting the margin (0.0054) from 1.6610 D.M which comes out as 1.6556 in the case of bid rate. We get the offer rate by deducting 0.0057 from 1.6620 D.M which comes out as 1.6563 in the case of offer rate. If on the other hand, it is a discount on the spot rate, the margin has to be added and the rates quoted will be D.M 1.6664/77.

Bid rate is the purchase rate and the offered rate is the sale rate. In the money market parlance, if you are short in dollars (represented by borrowing), the counter party has to pay you and if you are long in dollars (represented by the deposit or lending) you have to pay out. The amounts paid or received have to be taken into account along with interest (that is principal + or - interest). For the calculation of interest rates, generally the Euro-market interest rates in each currency are taken into account.

Exchange Arithmetic

Example

(1) X has sent an export Bill for collection and the payment is expected sometime in April 2010 from the present time of 31st January 2010. X would like to have a forward cover from B for the amount of the contract Euro 1,00,000.

B will have to go through the route of US $ to Euro to Rs. as there is no direct Euro/Rs. price quotation. The bill is due sometimes in April and he assumes the worst scenario of end April for collection proceeds to come.

The Dollar – Euro Rate is $ 1 = 1.8152 – 1.8162

The Rs. – Dollar rate is $ 1 = 44.00 – 44.05 (TC)

The market gives buy sell rates for three months hence — 1.8262 Euro

Spot rate for U. S $ to Rs. — 44.00 Rs. to $

Cover Rate will be (44.00 ÷ 1.8262) =	24.09
Bank Margin 0.5% of the cover rate	0.12
Total Rate	24.21

The US $/Rs. rate at the end of April will be 44.0639 taking the premium three months hence as 6.39, annualised. Consequently, the cover rate will be 44.0639 ÷ 1.8262 = 24.1287.

Total rate is cover rate + or - Bank Margin

Total rate 24.1287 – 0.11 = 24.0187

The Rs. per Euro during April is 24.0187

Euro 100,000 × 24.0187 = 24,01870 Rs.

Note: The Bank gives less rupees when buying and takes more rupees when selling. Thus, TT buying rate in April 2010 for US dollars is Rs. 44.42 and selling rate is 44.84. The difference is the margin of gain to the Bank for its services.

Example

(2) X has bought US dollar 100,000 for delivery this month (Spot) at a rate of Rs. 44.84 As the supplier has expressed his inability to ship the goods, the contract is cancelled and X wants to sell back the dollars (in April 2010).

This transaction will be for the Bank 'B' to buy back US dollars. This will be done at the TT buying rate namely 44.42 Rs per dollar - B will cover the exposure by selling the Us dollar to the market for value spot. The buying rate for TT Spot is Rs. 44.42.

Cover rate is	Rs. 44.42
Margin (deduct)	0.21
Total rate	44.21

The contract rate is Rs. 44.84 but the cancellation rate is Rs. 44.21 for the US dollar. Thus, the cancellation charges are 0.63 Rs. per dollar, or Rs. 63,000 in the above deal.

Example

(3) A has already sold Euro 5,00,000 to B against US\$ for delivery on 2nd February 2010 at 1.8162 Euro = 1\$. The export is delayed by one month up to 2nd March. A is required to extend the contract for delivery on 2nd March 2010.

The Bank B has covered the above exposure in the inter bank market for delivery on 2nd February. B's contract in the market remains. So he will take delivery of U.S dollars and give Euro and simultaneously enter into another transaction for one more month by selling Euro for US \$ for an extended date of March 2nd.

B will do a swap where B will buy Euro value for 2nd February both against US \$. For this the Bank will pay the Swap difference to the market, which he will collect from A, along with the interest normal for the bank for one month on the difference between the amount due on 2nd February and the amount due on 2nd March in US dollars. A in effect pays for two transactions costs for cancellation and rebooking. The above rates are not the exact rates as that time as it is only for illustration.

Problem on Interest Rates

Given the Euro market interest rates prevailing on 6th August (with 7th and 8th as Saturday and Sunday) as US \$ $4^{1}/_{4}$ $/^{3}/_{8}$, Euro 7-$^{3}/_{4}$ $/^{7}/_{8}$ the delivery date in the spot market is Monday 9th August. It will be delivered after 30 days and that 30th day from 9th being a Friday it will be delivered on the next Monday — total period of 34 days after the Spot rate.

Borrow one month dollars in the spot market on 6th August at $4^{3}/_{8}$ % (offer rate) Note that for borrowing and buying marks we have to use the offer rate and for deposits we use the bid rate.

Then buy marks in spot at Euro 1.6610 and deposit them for 34 days at $7^{3}/_{4}$% (on the basis of 360 days in a year).

Assuming one U.S dollar is borrowed, the principal and interest to be repaid on maturity is calculated as follows:

$$\text{U.S \$ } 1.00 + \text{US \$} \left(\frac{1.00 \times 4.3750 \times 34}{100 \times 360}\right)$$

$$\text{U.S \$} = 1.00 + 0.00\ 413 = 1.0041$$

Similarly the deposit of Euro at 1.6610 with an interest rate of $7.^{3}/_{4}$ % , the amount coming in is shown below.

$$C\ 1.6610 + \text{Euro}\left(\frac{1.6610\times7.75\times34}{100\times360}\right)$$

$$= \text{Euro } 1.6610 + 0.0122 = \text{Euro } 1.6732$$

The offered one month forward rate for Euro is worked out as follows:

$$\frac{1.6732}{1.0041}=1.6664$$

A contract can thus be worked at sale of Euro 1.6732; for delivery one month hence at Euro 1.6664 per \$ or for \$ 1.0041. The forward quote is Euro1.6664/77.

Cross Rates for Non-dollar Currencies

Rupee is mostly quoted now in terms of dollars, as it has been used in India's foreign trade as most easily convertible currency. If we want rupee Euro rate, or rupee franc rate, we have to go through the route of via Dollar Euro rate and dollar franc rate. If dollar Euro rate is Euro. 1.8252 per \$ and rupee dollar rate is 44.5200 Rs. per \$, then the rupee Euro rate can be worked at by crossing Euro to \$ route.

Thus, \$ 1 = Euro 1.8252

\$ 1 = Rs. 44.5200

$$\text{one D.M} = \frac{44.5200}{1.8252} = \text{Rs. } 24.3918$$

In the same way if the forward \$/Euro rate is known and Rs./\$ exchange rate is given, the forward rate of Euro/Rs. can be worked out. To that rate an appropriate loading margin is added or subtracted depending on the nature of the quote. Banks in India quote on the basis of the cross rates with dollar vis-a-vis other currencies. These cross rates are presented in the last chapter.

The base rates for each currency are the spot buying and Spot selling rates. The Spot cover cost, brokerage and overhead costs are included in these rates. The various quotes given in India are is follows:

TT Purchase or TT Sale : Applied to inward remittances and export bills sent for collection, the minimum and maximum margins are 0.025 and 0.08.

Bills Purchase and Sale : The rates apply to purchase/discount/negotiation of export bills and remittances in payment of import bills.

The minimum margin and maximum margin are 0.125 and 0.150 for purchase respectively and 0.300 – 0.350 for sale transaction.

Inter-bank market is a wholesale market and Inter-bank transactions are in large quantities and the margin quoted is also a finer rate at four decimal points as Rs. 43.5212 per $, while the same is given at Rs. 43.52 for customers (up to 2 decimal points) with of course some margin added to it. The spread between spot merchant TT buying and selling should not exceed 0.75% to 2.5% for major currencies. The margin for U.K. pounds is 0.75% and for US dollars it is 1.0% and D.M and other major currencies it is at 2.5%. These margins are variable from time to time and bank to bank.

In the case of import bills, for which no forward contract has been booked, the exchange rate will be the one ruling on the date that the customer pays the bill. In the case of sight bills, with letters of credit the customer has to pay the bill within ten days of the receipt of the bill. The quoted rate includes an element of interest for this period of 10 days, as the bank pays the bill immediately while the importer pays after 10 days. In the case of usance bills, the period of waiting is more, say one month to 3 months, for which interest is added separately to the exchange rate.

In the case of export bills, purchased interest has to be received for the period that the export credit facility is given, which is from the date of purchase to the date of payment of bill. When the bill is finally paid, the currency is purchased by the bank at the then prevailing rate. If the bank negotiates or discounts the bill, the interest element for the days that the bill is due is added to the forward exchange rate for the period of maturity of the bill.

Example of a Swap

A contract of purchase of $ 1000 purchased for delivery June is to be extended to August delivery. This can be done by a Swap transaction, which involves the following steps: (Swap of spot to forward)

(1) Sell at the current rate the dollars bought for June delivery. (spot)

(2) Buy at the current rate the same account of dollars for August delivery (forward)

(3) If the current inter-bank rate is Rs. 43 and forward dollars for August delivery Rs. 43.40.

Selling $ 1000 you will get Rs. 43,000 and buying $ 1000 for August delivery will cost Rs. 43,400 The swap cost is Rs. 400/-

If on the other hand, at the time of June delivery, August dollars are at a discount rather than premium, the Swap would lead to some profit.

If the contract rate is better than the current market rate, it may be better to cancel and rebook the forward dollars at any time during the contract period. If the customer is in this position and not the bank, then the bank would lose and customer gains. If the customer wants to cancel and sell dollars $ 1000 in the contract, early in July and not August, then the Swap would involve the following for the bank:

(1) a purchase of dollars for delivery July.

(2) a sale of dollars for August delivery

The cost/benefit is passed on to the customer leaving only administrative costs and concellation fees. Each inflow or outflow to the bank is thus accompanied by some costs/benefits. Costs are invariably passed on to customers, but not all the benefits.

Examples:

(1) When the Bank sells US dollars spot Bank covers the exposure by buying from the market at the buying rate of the market say 43.3700, which is called the cover rate.

Then cover rate	Rs. 43.3700
Deduct margin for sale	0.1569
Then TT Spot rates	43.2131

Rounded up to Rs. 43.21 the buying rate is lower than selling rate for the type of quotation given here namely direct method.

(2) Sam wants to remit Euro 25,000 by TT value spot to his friend in Germany. The bank will sell Euro but cover it in the market. The cover rate is not quoted directly from Rs. to Euro. So the bank buys dollars and then converts into Euro cover rate for dollars Rs. 43.3700 per $ 1 and U.S $ = Euro. 1.8340

Then cross rate for Rs. to Euro is

43.3700/1.8340 = Rs. 23. 6477.

Each D.M will cost Rs. 23.6477

Then cover rate in the market	23.6477
Add: margin for selling Euro	0.0899
T/T Rate for Euro.	23.7376
Rounded for	23.74

(3) A has exported and the export bill for $ 10,000 is a sight bill. How much the Bank will pay to A, immediately.

If Bank has to sell dollars by end of the month (August) the last day of August will be the earliest, delivery date for the bank.

So that bank takes the cover rate as the dollars for August delivery say Rs. 43.3725.

Cover rate	43.3725 (buying Rate)
Less: Deduct Margin	0.1569
Total Rate is Rs.	43.2156

Rounded up to 43.22 Rs. per dollar will be given by the bank; for $ 10,000 it will give Rs. 4,32,200.

(4) A has bought US $ 1000 for delivery in October, 2006 at the rate of Rs. 43.60 per $. As the supplier expressed non-availability of goods, A wants to cancel the contract with bank.

Here cancellation will mean that A will sell back dollars for October to the bank. This transaction is done at the reverse TT rate which means the buying rate instead of selling rate. Let the buying rate be Rs. 43.3675 and selling rate is 43.3725. Take the buying rate as the cover rate

cover rate =	Rs. 43.3657
minus – margin	0.1568
	43.2107
Rounded to	Rs. 43.21

The transaction involves a loss to A as he bought dollars at Rs. 43.60 and cancelled the contract at Rs. 43.21. It is a loss of Rs. 0.39 per $ namely Rs. 390 in the transaction of US $ 1000.

(5) An exporter A sold Euro 50,000 to bank B against U.S $ for delivery at end October 2010 at the rate of 1.8200. The export is now delayed by one month. A wants to extend the contract.

The bank might have already committed in the inter-bank market for sale of Euro for US $ at end October. The banker has to give delivery of Euro and take delivery of US $ at end October 2010. It has to buy Euro against US $ again on 1st November'2010 and sell D.M back to exporter again for the extended period of end November 2010. The involved Swap transaction is shown below.

B will be buying Euro value at end October with dollars. He will sell back the same Euro at end November against US $. For this Swap, there will be a transaction cost — difference between buying and selling rates of the market plus the interest cost on the float for one month at the bank's lending rate and any other incidental expenses.

Under the Original Contract	**End October 2006 Dated**	**Euro Flow 50,000**	**Rate Euro/$ 1.8200**	**$ Flow 27,473**
1st Step of Swap	31st October	50,000	1.8450	27,100
2nd Step of Swap	30th November	50,000	1.8490	27,042
Delivery from A	30th November	50,000	1.8200	27.473

Swap charges 27100 – 27042 = 58.

Bank will recover the Swap charges from the customer as also the interest charges on the rupee equivalent of the float 27473 – 27100 (373) for the period of one month. These charges will be merged into the new contract rate entered into with the customer by the bank.

Problem:

(6) An importer bought goods from Germany and booked forward D.M 5000 for delivery one month hence from his bank. what is the rate quoted by the bank for this. Given, spot rate of US dollars, US $ 1 = Rs. 43.4200 and one month forward $ 1 = Rs. 43.4250 Spot rate of US dollar to Euro; $1 = Euro 1.8125 and one month forward Euro $ 1 = Euro 1.8100. It will be seen from the above data that there is a forward premium for dollar against Rupee and forward dollar is at discount as against Euro In booking the forward one month D.M the bank uses the cross rates.

Given one month forward $ 1 = Rs. 43.4250

Calculate one month forward as Euro 1 = $ 0.5524

As the bank is selling Euro it will use the cover rate for buying the required Euro in the inter-bank market. Using cross rate calculation the rupee rate for Euro is Rs. 23.99 (0.5524 × 43.4250)

Cover rate	23.9879
Add: margin	0.1572
T Rate	24.1451

Rounded off 24.15 Rs. per euro.

If it is Euro 5000, then the importer will have to pay 5000 × Rs. 24.15 = Rs. 1,20,750.

Interest Factor in Exchange Arithmetic

A foreign exchange transaction involves buying in one centre a particular currency and delivering it at another centre. A sale of one foreign currency results in debit to bank's Nostro Account. A purchase of foreign currency leads to a credit to bank's Nostro-account. In theory the sale of one currency is purchase of another currency. Thus, if you purchase dollars in India, you sell Rupees for dollars. A purchase or sale may involve some time lapse, due to the use of credit instruments.

Valuer compensee means value compensated, also called "value here and there". This transaction involves the purchase of one currency and delivery of another currency should coincide. Value received in one currency in one centre is compensated by giving almost simultaneously the counter value in another currency in another centre. In such transactions, no interest is involved.

"Value date" is used to denote the actual date on which delivery of one currency in one centre against delivery of another currency in another centre should take place in a given foreign exchange transaction. If some time period is involved between the deliveries of the two currencies concerned, then some credit element and interest payment are involved. The instruments by which foreign currencies are purchased or sold normally are the following and they involve some time. The only exception is Telegraphic Transfers (TT). In this case no interest is involved but delivery takes place on the same day or next day.

Under TT rates, there will be both buying and selling rates, with a margin between them which is the profit for the wholesaler or bank. Besides, there are two kinds of TTs, namely TT clean and TT Documentary. TT clean is the best rate as it has no documents and no administrative costs of scrutinising them. Those that involve some interest element are the following:

C/D Rates are those where receipt and payment is on demand. OD stands for on demand. These rates are applied to clean instruments like personal cheques foreign currency, travellers cheques, etc., wherein the receipt of domestic currency takes place immediately, while the beneficiary is paid at a later date and involves a transit interest, included in exchange rate.

Long bills. These are for some specific periods, of long time, arising out of usance bills. This involves both transit interest as well as interest for a grace period as in the case of bills for collection. Bills discounted, or purchased will also take into account the interest factor from the date of discounting or purchase to the date of maturity of the bill.

Tel quel rates. The rates offered for broken periods such as 45 days for bills having a broken period of usance to run. These rates are slightly higher than the normal long bills of 30, 60 or 90 days. Long bill rates are higher for those accompanying bills with documents than for those without documents. Long rates are also higher than O/D rates as they have not only a transit period but time period to maturity or usance of the Bill.

The O/D Buying rate is built up by loading transit interest on the TT Buying rate:

$$\text{Interest, } I = \frac{P \times N \times R}{100 \times 365}$$

Where p is the principal, N will be number of days and R is the rate of interest per annum.

Example:

Calculate OD buying rate given T.T. buying rate for Euro as Rs. 23.74 Transit period (N) is 15 days and R is 9% per annum. (Take year as 365 days)

$$I = \frac{23.74 \times 15 \times 9}{100 \times 365} = \frac{320.49}{365.00} = 0.88$$

$= 0.88$

TT. Buying rate = 23.74 for Euro.

Transit Interest + 0.88

O/D. Buying rate is Rs. 24.62 for Euro.

The basic principle is that the bank will take more rupees when it sells foreign currency. It will give less rupees when it buys foreign currency. When TT buying rate is given, it will mean that the bank will take more rupees and hence the Transit interest has to be added. This principle is applicable when the foreign currency unit is fixed say $ 1 or £ 1 and the home currency units are variable or the domestic currency units are expressed in terms of a standard foreign unit (Direct method). The other method of quoting for the currency is to give quotation in foreign currency units for a fixed or standard unit of domestic currency. This is called Indirect method of quoting, used in India before 1992-93 Reforms.

Examples:

Direct Method $ 1 = Rs. 43.5400

Indirect Method Rs. 100 = $ 2.2967.

The method of adjusting interest component or the profit margin to the exchange rate will change with the method of quoting of the rates.

When Quotation is in Direct Method

TT Buying for $ 1 = Rs. 43.15

TT Selling for $ 1 = 43.58

When Quotation is in Indirect Method

TT Buying for Rs 100 = $ 2.2967

TT Selling for Rs. 100 = $ 2.2717

In the first case of Direct method, which we use normally in India now, the selling rate is always higher as more rupees are to be given for selling a dollar by the bank. If the quotation is in Indirect method less foreign currency is given for selling the foreign currency. These principles are basic to the understanding of the Techniques of foreign exchange arithmatic and calculation of forward rates and margin adjustment.

Forward Rates

Forward margin is difference between the Spot and Forward rates. This margin is quoted in terms of premium or discount over the spot rate. Premium means the currency is dearer and discount indicates cheaper rate.

In the foreign currency quotation (that is quotation in so many units of foreign currency for a fixed unit of domestic currency) The principle is "Buy-high and sell low". Then premium in forward is deducted from the spot rate and discount is added to the spot rate.

Example:

Rs. 100 = $ 2.2972 spot rate

Deduct premium

(1)		(2)	
Buying premium		Selling premium	
$ 0.03		$ 0.05	
Given the Buying TT rate spot		Selling TT rate Spot	
2.3072		2.2972	
Deduct	03 margin	Deduct	.05 margin
$	2.2772		2.2472

[Note that the margin on buying and selling are not the same].

Case (1) Foreign Currency Quotation

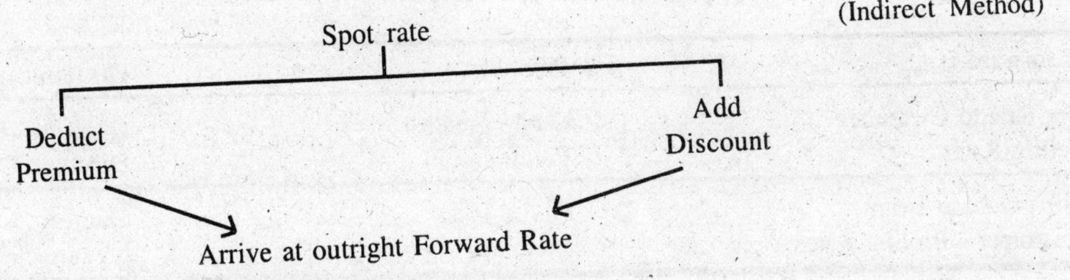

Case (2) Home Currency Quotation

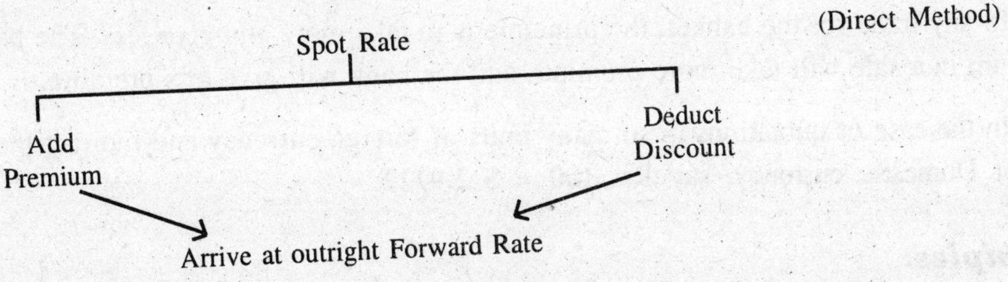

Example:

	TT Buying	TT Selling
$ 1 =	Rs. 43.1500	Rs. 43.5800

The principle in the case of Home Currency quotation is "Buy low and Sell high". In the above case premium is to be added and discount is to be deducted.

$ 1	=	Rs. 43.1500	$ 1=		Rs. 43.5800
Buying margin premium		0.03	Selling Margin Premium		0.05
		43.1800			43.6300

If Forward rates are at premium over spot rate, the Forward rates are dearer. If the forward rates are at discount over the spot rates the Forward rates are cheaper.

Factors Responsible for

Premium	Discount
(1) Excess demand of forward currency	(1) Excess supply
(2) Higher rate of interest at home centre	(2) Lower rate
(3) Lower rate of interest at foreign centre	(3) Higher rate
(4) Likely appreciation of spot rate	(4) Likely depreciation
(5) Rosy expectations of home currency	(5) Pessimistic expectations

The Holgate's Rules for quoting forward Rates

If forward is at;	Premium;	Discount
For Sale to Customer Selling Rates	Quote greatest Premium	Quote least Discount
For purchase from Customer - Buying Rates	Quote least Premium	Quote greatest discount

Note: Holgate is a noted author on Foreign Exchange.

In any trade for the banker, the principle is to take more and give less. The bank, while taking premium in a sale will take more premium and the bank will give less premium in a purchase deal.

In the case of quotations in so many units of foreign currency and indirect method for a given unit of Domestic currency, say Rs. 100 = $ 2.9722.

Examples:

Buy high and sell low are the principles

Selling Rate	**Buying Rate**	
Rs. 100 = $2.9722	Rs. 100 = $ 2.9972 if margin is, the buying rate becomes $ 2.9972.	.0250

1. Problem

(1) Miss Saitha, a customer of your Bank wants to remit $ 1,000 to her cousin in New York. If your bank has no office in New York how will you deal with this transaction?

Given the TT selling rate of dollars as on that date as Rs. 43.75.

Answer: If it is a ready remittance involving conversion of Rupees into dollars and it is a clean transaction as no documents are involved. The TT selling rate will apply and no transit interest or forward margin is involved.

$ 1= Rs. 43.7500,

$ 1000 = Rs. 43,750.

This draft is given on the bank's correspondent or Agent Bank namely American Express in New York for an amount of $ 1000 to debit the customer's account with Rs. 43,750. If the customer has no account with your bank, she has to bring bankers' cheque or pay order or cash. Some banks insist on their owns bank's pay order as in the case of SBI. If it is a pay order of some other bank, clearing charges or interest for the period of clearing at cash credit or clean lending rate of 19% or any other rates as applicable are charged on Rs. 43,750 for a period 4 days although local clearance takes only 2 days, (which may be due to intervening holidays).

2. Problem

An exporter has submitted a D/P bill payable in 90 days to your bank. P wants you to discount it or buy it. The bank quotes the following rates on that day.

TT. Buying OD	Long Bill D/A 90 days
$ 1 = Rs. 43.1580; Rs. 43.1500	Rs. 42.1500

As the bank is buying, the rupees given for dollar will be lower for longer periods due to forward discount (interest component).

The invoice value is $ 50,000. The rupees that the bank will give on discount is

$ 50,000 × 42.15 = Rs. 2107,500 (The rate includes the interest component for 90 days).

In case the exporter waits until the maturity of the bill and asks the bank for collection, then the rate applicable will be the Spot TT buying prevailing at that time (90 days hence). As that rate will be higher say 43.1580, exporter will get more rupees (43.1580 × 50,000) = Rs. 2157900.

If the Bill is in Fr. Francs and our bank's quotations are for home currency for one unit of foreign currency say Fr. Franc = Rs. 7.01/7.34 Buying and selling rates respectively. (Rule/Buy Low and Sell high)

The Bill for Francs 50,000 multiplied by its OD Buying rate is 50,000 × 7.34 = 367000 Rs.

QUOTES AND DEALINGS OF INDIAN BANKS

In the Indian Foreign Exchange market, the present day quotations are in terms of so many units of domestic currency for one unit of foreign currency (Direct method.) The main currency and the intervention currency remains US dollar. The daily inter bank quotations are published in the Financial press and banks get from their head office, early in the morning their quotations for major currencies, based on the quotations of FEDA (Foreign Exchange Dealers' Association) sent by Telex throughout the BANK NETWORK.

Take an Example

Sport rates	Buying	Selling	In short
for $ 1	Rs. 43.15	Rs. 43.55	43.15/55
$/ Rs. 1 month	43.1550	43.55 75 -	FEB Swap points 50/75
$/ Rs. 3 months	43.2125	43.6200 -	FEB Swap points 625/700

The forward margins are quoted for one month to 6 months to be added to the Spot quotation on that day. The forward margins for inter-bank cover operations are quoted on a daily basis and these vary from currency to currency, and from bank to bank.

In general, the Swap points for each month forward are published and each bank has those swap points received in advance from their Head office.

The minimum and maximum margins forward for each kind of transaction for Indian banks are shown below, for illustration.

Kinds of transactions	Minimum margin	Maximum margin
TT. Purchase	0.025	0.080
TT. Sale	0.125	0.150
Bills Purchase	0.125	0.150
Bills Sale	0.300	0.350

Purchases apply to inward remittances, export bills for collection, sent for purchase/discount etc. Sales apply to outward remittances and payment for imports, royalties, fees etc payable abroad.

A Real Case of Exchange Quotations

The rates quoted by one Bank for the public are given below for illustration. The rates are received daily from their Head office, Forex Dept. the branches get them by about 10.30 AM, when they start transactions with the public. The rates quoted below are at 10. AM when the market opened (on 19-8-1999).

MSG TO: AUTHORISED BRANCHES

TODAY'S CARD RATES – 19 08 99 (10.00 AM)

	TTB	BB	CQB	TCB	CURB	TTS	BS	TCS	CURS
USD	43.28	43.25	43.21	42.90	42.40	43.71	43.80	43.90	44.15
EUR	45.51	45.48	45.44	45.10	——	46.01	46.10	46.25	——
GBP	69.35	69.30	69.23	68.70	67.00	70.07	70.21	70.40	70.75
DEM	23.26	23.25	23.23	23.05	21.90	23.51	23.55	23.60	23.75
YEN	38.73	38.70	38.67	38.40	36.50	39.15	39.22	39.35	39.55
FRF	6.93	6.93	6.92	6.85	6.20	7.01	7.02	7.05	7.10
CAD	29.08	29.06	29.04	28.80	27.40	29.40	29.45	29.55	29.70
SGD	25.84	25.83	25.80	25.60	24.35	26.12	26.17	26.25	26.40

The rates are only indicative. For sale/purchase reports confirm with dealer for the exact prevailing rates. Rates quoted for per unit of Franc and for Japanese Yen, the rates are for 100 units of Franc. As the data are for illustration, the time and date do not matter.

All Rates Subject to Confirmation

Notes:

TTB	:	Telegraphic Transfer Buying and
TTS	:	Selling rates'
CQB	:	Cheques for clearing Bought rates
BB	:	Bills Buying and
BS	:	Bills selling Rates
TCB	:	Travellers Cheques Bought and
TCS	:	Sold Rates
CURB	:	Currency Bought Rates
CURS	:	Currency Sold Rates

The currencies covered are in the order, US dollars Euro currency, British pound, German Euro Japanese Yen, French Franc, Canadian dollar and Singapore dollar, which are the major currencies in which Indian banks are keeping Nostro Accounts abroad. For bills with documents and those D/A and D/P, Usance bills, etc., will get quotations on request and are negotiable. As in 2010 the currencies covered frequently are U.S dollar, U.K pound, Euro and yen.

Example:

An exporter has an export bill maturing for $ 1,00,000 for the period January-March 2010. He has locked into forward difference of 25 paise for this period. If he now submits to the Bank for negotiation what will the bank do?

Market Buying Rate for spot is Rs. 43.3675 the forward cover difference is 25 paise which makes the rate 43.3675 + 0.2500 = 43.6175. Thus, the inter-bank cover rate is Rs. 43.6175 Deduct Margin (normal) 0.1581 (deduction is because banks give less when it has to give rupees on purchase) Rs. 43.4594

Rounded off Rs. 43.46.

The maximum charged by banks as margin is 0.5 per cent.

Besides there will be a float either in favour or against the exporter in the books of the bank, depending on the rates at which the cover up Swap was done while locking into forward. Assuming that the earlier Swap was done at Rs. 43.7500 and 44.000, Cash flows in the books of the bank will be as under:

Date	Rs. Flows	Rate	$ Flows
Spot sale 31st January, 2010	43,00,000	43.00	100,000
First Leg of Swap, 31st January,	43,75,000	43.75	100,000
Second leg of Swap, 31st March,	44,00,000	44.00	100,000
Maturity of Bill 31st March,	43,62,000	43.62	100,000

In the above case the float is the difference between spot sale and first leg of swap 43,75,000 - 43,00,000 = 75,000. This float will appear in the bank books for the period of 2nd February to 31st March. The bank will recover the interest on this float from the exporter, at the then prevailing cash credit rate or overdraft rate. The above example shows how the Swap is effected by the Bank in its books.

PART – VI

FOREIGN EXCHANGE RISKS MANAGEMENT

31

Foreign Exchange Risks Management

Introduction

With the Indian rupee being convertible, since March 1994, the risks in the foreign exchange market have become more pronounced and the need to take risk or protect oneself from these risks has become more relevant. Many countries have already made their currencies convertible and some are in the process of doing so. In the context of such scenario of free foreign exchange markets, uncertainty of currency rates and their volatility has made it imperative for the dealers in foreign exchange to expose themselves to the risk. Risk is inherent in the foreign dealings due to the following reasons:

(1) Trade across countries involve dealings with parties - exporter or importer - who are unknown and whose creditworthiness is uncertain.

(2) Foreign dealings also involve countries whose credibility and creditworthiness is not certain.

Many countries are having political and economic problems, racial, and communal riots, terrorist activities or other disturbances and there is no certainty about their economic and financial policies and their willingness and capacity to repay the loans or service them, through their exports and inward remittances. Fundamentals in the economy may be in doubt and inflation and other problems of the country, such as unemployment, poverty, low rates of growth or no growth in the economies, etc., may be plaguing the country, when they may default in their external obligations, as in the case of some African and Latin American countries. Their capacity to borrow on commercial lines will be then poor and they depend on donations, gifts and concessional aid from Governments and international bodies. They are not able to service and repay the debts to foreigners.

Exchange risk is due to fluctuations in the rate of exchange in conversion of one currency into another and likely changes in interest rates which might effect the forward rates. Forward cover of any currency which the banks provide will take into account the possible changes in interest rates, inflation rates and the intrinsic strength of country and the currency. Exchange risk will basically depend on the economic strength of the country and its foreign exchange reserves, as the volatility of the exchange rate depends on them.

Strength of Currency

Exchange risk depends on the strength or weakness of currency which in turn is a reflection of the degree of strength of the economy. Thus, a country whose productivity is low and its competitive strength in international markets is poor, cannot export enough of the domestic products abroad and its foreign exchange earnings will be poor. Such a country will have a week currency and its rate of exchange will be uncertain.

A strong country like U.S.A. or Japan will have good export performance resulting in trade surplus and good inflow of foreign funds for investment because of its high productivity, low costs of production, latest technology and good investment climate, leading to high rates of growth of output, employment and income. So economy, its strength and its rate of growth and its competitive strength along with a host of other factors will influence the currency rates. The exchange risk is thus dependent upon an array of economic and extra economic factors which will lead to an unpredictable rate of exchange. The risk and uncertainty of exchange rate is a multi-dimensional phenomena and requires an expert to fend and manage the risks involved. Genuine trade and investment require a stable and fixed exchange rate which is not possible in free and competitive world, where trade and receipts and payments abroad are all free and market determined. There is thus need for risk management for all dealings in foreign exchange, particularly so for exporters and importers.

Exchange Risk Defined

Exchange risk simply means that the rate at which a currency is exchanged for another currency may be uncertain and volatile and the amount that an exporter receives in domestic currency or an importer has to pay in terms of domestic currency will be unpredictable and uncertain. Similarly, if funds are transmitted from one country to another, the amounts to be sent or to be received will not be certain, if exchange rates are not fixed. But in the present global economy, free market forces operate to determine the exchange rates depending upon the supply and demand for the currency. This will lead to fluctuating rates, which may result in profits or losses to the holders of foreign currency.

The fluctuating rates result in uncertainty and risk, which will have to be managed by the genuine traders and investors in foreign countries and dealers in foreign exchange and banks. Under free market forces operating, no individual dealer in foreign exchange can influence its price, but the supply and demand pressures for any currency in total lead to its appreciation or depreciation. The totality of receipts either for exports or inward remittances or inflows of funds will decide the demand pressure while the supply pressures emanate from those who have to make payments outside for imports, outward remittances or outflow of funds etc. Such demand and supply pressures influence the exchange rates on a daily and hourly basis and from time to time and lead to uncertainty, in exchange rates. The only way to create some certainty is to enter into fixed forward rate agreements.

Factors Affecting Exchange Rates

Foreign exchange rates, being freely determined, the following factors influence the exchange rates and enhance the risk in particular.

(1) Hot money flows as between countries and currencies will take place to take advantage of short-term economic and political factors or disturbances or fears of such developments leading to changes in currency rates and interest rates.

(2) Speculative attacks on currencies in anticipation of exchange rate changes and interest rate changes through short-term flows of funds.

(3) Exchange rate volatility emerges out of erratic fund flows as between countries, short-term flows of funds in either direction and inflows of funds followed by immediate reversals, etc.

(4) Freely fluctuating exchange rates across countries do sometimes lead to erratic movements of rates on either side, unless countervailed by Central Bank of the country to off-set such excesses.

(5) Present international monetary system under the IMF imposes the burden of adjustment on the deficit countries to change their exchange rates rather than on the surplus countries. In the absence of adjustment on both sides, balance of payments adjustment is delayed and partial with the result that exchange rates remain uncertain and fluctuating and sometimes even unpredictable.

(6) Limited powers of IMF to discipline the Surplus countries also lead to partial adjustment or lack of adjustment as between currencies of countries with the result that currency rates may fluctuate very widely and requires central bank intervention to stabilise the rates.

Basically exchange rates as between two currencies should reflect the true fundamentals of the concerned countries, such as domestic purchasing powers, relative strength or weakness of the economies in terms of their productive power and trends in output, employment and income. In the absence of stabilised and equilibrated rates, the actual prevailing rates may fluctuate widely which will lead to uncertainty and risk. In order to avoid such destabilising fluctuations in rates; many developing countries maintain exchange and trade controls to reduce such risk and promote trade and investment in their own countries.

India has also moved to current account convertibility in March 1994, with the result that rupee exchange rate is now freely fluctuating in either direction. But to reduce undue fluctuations, the RBI has been announcing a reference rate for rupee in terms of dollars and the Foreign Exchange Dealers Association (FEDA) has been fixing the major currency rates in terms of rupees for banks to adopt them to the extent possible, as warranted by the foreign funds position. Even so, the risk and uncertainty is not eliminated in the foreign exchange market in India. It is still the demand and supply pressures on rupee that determines its exchange rate. The RBI is intervening to see that the fall of rupee is slow and even to prevent undue fluctuations due to hedge deals and speculation. During, the early years of 21st Century, Exchange reserves were built up and many foreign debts of the Govt. to IMF and other agencies were paid off. The RBI was in a better position to stabilise the market and prevent speculation, as in 2009-10.

Types of Risk

The risks in foreign exchange market in India are of the following nature and include transactions in both trade and non-trade items of balance of payments:

(1) Risk of creditworthiness of the other party in trade in concerned countries.

(2) Risk of credit control and exchange control rules in concerned countries.

(3) Risk of economic and political policy changes in the other country.

(4) Risk of interest rate changes in the respective countries.

(5) Risk of loss of goods shipped in transit or theft, damage, or destruction.

(6) Risk of market changes in the concerned countries or changes in the costs or in duties or levies imposed by the trading partners on others.

(7) Risk of war or epidemics, or riots or any untoward events like increasing terrorist activities and internal war like activities affecting trading relations as between the trading partners.

(8) Risk and uncertainty of exchange rates of one currency against another.

(9) Risk and uncertainty due to change in forward rates for the currency following the changes in interest rates as between countries.

(10) Risk of changes in cross currency rates for any unpredictable changes in the currency markets and in foreign exchange markets.

Foreign exchange markets are very sensitive and volatile as they are influenced by all and sundry developments in economic, political, social and financial factors among the countries. Events across borders and domestic and international forces operate on the markets to force volatility in rates and attendant risks in the exchange markets.

Exchange Rate Management in India

The rupee was devalued twice in July 1991 and the depreciation of the rupee continued in the free market thereafter. The rupee dollar rate was Rs. 17.1274 in March 1990 which fell to Rs. 32.6456 in February 1993, and thereafter it stabilised around Rs. 31.3727 since March 1994 when current account convertibility was introduced by the Government. Since then the rupee depreciated slowly and reached Rs. 48 per dollar at one time and is stabilised around Rs. 46 to 48 by mid-2010. After some appreciation in 2003 to 2005, it has weakened again to Rs. 46 in June 2006. It was strengthened again in 2007-08 to Rs. 39.99 at end March 2008 before it has there depreciated to Rs. 54-55 per dollar by June 2012, rising to Rs. 50 at end March 2009.

After the structural reforms undertaken since July 1991, the rupee exchange rate management assumed all the importance and attention from the RBI and the Government. The Liberalised Exchange Rate Management System (LERMS) introduced in March 1992 is a step in that direction of a freely convertible rupee at a future date. Under this system, rupee can be freely converted with a free market rate up to 60% of exports, while official rate still prevailed for the 40% or rest of the exports. This system called Liberalised Exchange Rate Management System (LERMS) helped to stabilise the rupee and the official rate remained unchanged except for a downward adjustment of 1.12% in the rate effected on December 4, 1992. The market determined rate remained also stable and the spread between the official rate and the market rate remained in a narrow range except for short and extraordinary periods.

The experiment with limited convertibility was successful and the Government was emboldened to launch the full convertibility on trade account in March 1993 and on current account in March 1994. Since then there was unification of the dual exchange rate into a single floating rate which imparted considerable strength to the rupee. Now the external value of the rupee is determined by market forces fully. As this is on the current account, it only meant that the A.Ds did not have to surrender to the RBI the exchange proceeds at fixed rate as before. The exporters can sell their earnings at the free market rates to the banks as the importers have to buy the same from banks at the prevailing market rates from time to time.

Since mid-January, 1995, the RBI has banned the roll-over of forward contracts, and as a step in the direction of liberalisation, allowed the customers to book forward contracts in any permitted currency. Now the companies will have to book forward contracts matching with their foreign exchange exposure. This facility to hedge in any currency will permit the corporates to take positions in currencies and develop the foreign exchange market and the forward market in particular.

Full Convertibility of Rupee

As referred to earlier the convertibility on trade account was launched on March 1993 and exports have become convertible at free market rates up to 100% of them. The experiment on convertibility on trade account proved a success in the sense that no untoward fluctuations in the rupee rate were noticed during 1993-94 with the result that the Government has announced in March 1994 the full convertibility on current account also which means that all invisible receipts and payments have to be effected at market related rates. Thus, not only trade items but all invisible items or services are paid and received at the free market rates since March 1994. This has increased the risk in foreign exchange market and for exporters and importers.

In the Budget 1994-95, the Government of India have also announced a package of further measures to promote and facilitate exports. Exporters are allowed to retain 25% of the foreign exchange earned in dollar denominated accounts abroad. Export Oriented Units (EOUs) are permitted to retain up to 50% of their exchange earnings in dollar terms abroad. These measures would help reduce conversion costs in payments abroad for their import requirements and other service payments. These measures were further liberalised later.

The foreign exchange receipts and payments are now freer than before under all current account items, particularly for travel, tourism, medical expenses and education. The Government have introduced amendments to the FEMA to do away with many controls on foreign investments in India, inflow of foreign technology, employment, etc. India is now on a path of full convertibility of the rupee on both current and capital account. Preparatory to that, foreign investment in equity of Indian companies is permitted up to 51%. Much of this investment which requires to be cleared by the Government, Ministry of Finance, Investment Division has been flowing more freely into priority sector industries. Foreign direct portfolio investment has been freely allowed without limit and foreign financial institutions, FIIs and foreign security firms have been permitted by the SEBI to operate in the Indian stock and capital markets.

Multilateral Investment Guarantee Agency

The MIGA is an international agency set up in 1988 for the purpose of promoting and encouraging the flow of foreign direct investment. It offers investment insurance and advisory services for foreign direct investment in developing countries. It provides protection to international investors against losses arising out of non-commercial risk of currency transfers, expropriation, war and civil disturbances. It provides promotional and advisory role to Governments in framing and implementing foreign investment policy. India signed the MIGA convention in fiscal 1992 and with this the member countries who signed this convention increased to 85. India has also opened up bilateral negotiations for extending the investment guarantee with many other countries for promoting the foreign direct investment in India. Thus, it has entered into bilateral guarantees with many countries, including the U.S.A., Germany, Russia and China, among others. This is intended to reduce risks in foreign Investments, for the member countries of the MIGA convention.

FERA Liberalisation

FERA companies which are companies incorporated in India but in which non-resident interest is more than 40% have now got freedom from many restrictive provisions under Sections 26 (7), 28, 29 and 31 of FERA.

FERA companies are now permitted to do the following:

(1) To borrow money or accept deposits from persons resident in India.

(2) To acquire an undertaking, carry on any trade, commerce or industry, or purchase shares of any company.

(3) To allow trade marks of theirs to be used by any person or company.

(4) To accept any appointment as agent or technical or management advisers.

(5) To acquire hold, transfer any immovable property in India.

Trade and Exchange Risk

In dealing with international currencies, risk is inherent in both trade and finance. These risks arise out of dealings as between countries: (1) In terms of exchange of goods for money, (2) In terms of sale of services and payment thereof in foreign currencies, (3) Lending and borrowing in foreign currencies, and (4) Capital inflows and outflows from foreign countries. Risks arise out of all these transactions and due to unpredictable market related forces which determine the supply and demand pressures on foreign currencies and speculative forces. Demand and supply for currencies emanate from corresponding demand and supply for goods and services and needed receipts and payments to and from abroad.

The instruments involved in foreign trade and in foreign exchange dealings have also a component of risk in them. Briefly, these instruments are: (1) Currency dealt with in small quantities and involve loss or theft or cheating for counterfeit notes, etc. (2) M.T., T.T, D.D. cheques, etc. — risk is in transit loss, time in transit and delays involved, etc. (3) Commercial and trade bills: bills of exchange and other foreign trade bills and documents have risks involved in the parties, drawer, drawee, banker and the goods involved in these bills. Sight bills are having a grace period during which payment can be delayed. Usance bills have a period to maturity of 30 to 180 days usually. These bills and documents are given to banks for collection or for outright purchase, which are again full of risks. The risks arise out of defective documents, time for waiting, problems with goods in transit, shipping or air freight, etc., party risk and country risk and risk of default or non-payment. Besides, there is the currency risk during the conversion of foreign currency into domestic currency and *vice versa*.

The exporters and importers have to bear some risks. Some risks like party, country and currency risks are passed on to the banks, ECGC and Exim Bank. Insurance agencies cover some risks like those in transit loss, shipping and air freight, etc. Banks in turn pass on some risks to central Bank of the country, or cover them with foreign correspondents, international markets or inter-bank market.

Exchange Rate and Currency Risk

Exchange rate is determined by free flow of demand and supply forces for one currency against another. Receipts and payments on trade account, for services and capital flows would influence the demand and supply forces which are in turn determined by the following factors: (1) Relative quantum of exports and imports and other remittances; (2) Cost and price differences in goods and services as well as their quality; (3) Relative purchasing power parity of domestic currency vis-a-vis foreign currency; (4) Interest rates at home and abroad; and (5) Inflation rates at home and abroad.

Spot rate is decided by the demand and supply pressures, which are influenced by the above factors. Besides, the demand for a currency is also influenced by the hedge and speculative forces and by interest rate changes. The forward rates are at discount or at premium depending on the current interest rates and expectations about them, present rates of exchange and expectations about their movements, future arbitrage and hedge deals and short-term speculative flows of funds etc. Some discussion on forward rates is also found later in the chapter.

Types of Exchange Rates

The exchange risk depends on the type of rate. In this context, it is relevant to know the types of rates which are common in the foreign exchange market. The major types are set out below: (1) Spot rate: The rate for immediate exchange of currency or receipts. Thus, the rate for exchange of currency notes, T.Ts., M.T.s, cheques, and D.Ds which are clean and unaccompanied by documents is called the spot rate; (2) Short rates: The rates for short periods of 30 to 90 days; (3) Long Rates: The rates for long periods of 90 days and above; (4) Tel quel Rates: the rates for broken periods of 15 days or 45 days etc. The risk varies with the rate dealt with. The longer the period of rate, the larger is the risk, The tel quel rates are generally higher than for rounded periods of one/2/3 months due to more administrative work. Short rates for those with documents carry higher risk than clean credits or instruments, for the same reason. Similarly, the forward rates are having more risk than spot rates.

Risk also varies with the country and the currency, in which the instruments are drawn. The political and economic factors, stability or otherwise of the political system and economic policies and a host of non-economic factors play a role in deciding the risk and the rate charged.

Forward rate is generally at a premium due to larger risk involved in it than the spot rate. It is assumed here that the rate is quoted in direct method say $ 1:1.58 euro. The forward premium will indicate the larger number of euro per dollar to be given in each transaction. Applying the principle of "buy high and sell low" for the indirect method of quotation, as in the case of rupee until August 1993, the forward rate for the rupee will be at a premium, in the sense that more rupees are to be given for a dollar. Take an example, say $ 1: Rs. 31.2100 for TT buying spot. The forward premium for one month is 10 points which means that the rate will be $ 1: Rs. 31.2110 for one month forward and so on. The means that you have to give more, say Rs. 31.2110 for buying a dollar forward one month, as against Rs. 31.2100 for spot buying. If you are selling dollars, you will only get Rs. 31.2090 for dollar forward. The basic principle is that the longer the period, the larger is the risk.

Arbitrage and Speculation

In addition to the financing of the genuine trade and payments on merchandise and invisible trade account, banks do finance capital flows of both short-term and long-term. Funds move in and move out for hedging and speculation as between currencies. While sometimes the hedging transactions help stabilise the rates, the same cannot be said of the speculative flows of short-term nature. The excesses of such flows destabilise the exchange market and lead to violent fluctuations in exchange rates. The greater the volatility, the larger is the risk in foreign exchange market and premiums on forwards will go up abnormally. Arbitrage is dealing in foreign exchange to take advantage of the difference in cross rates as between centres or currencies or as between quotations in two or more centres. Thus, if dollars are cheap in one centre and dear in another centre, arbitrage takes place to buy in the cheap centre and sell in dear centre with the result the rate quotations will tend to get equalised as between centres. Thus, to an extent, arbitrage has a stabilising influence on the foreign exchange market.

Types of Risk in Foreign Exchange

There are different types of exchange risks in the foreign exchange market which are set out briefly below:

(1) Credit Risk of Customer: Credit rating by international banks and international credit rating agencies will help reducing this risk. In India, ECGC and banks do take this risk for the exporters.

(2) Country Risk: This is different slightly from the currency risk and arises out of the policies of economic and political nature and their external payments position and their export earnings to service the foreign creditors, convertibility or otherwise of their currencies, etc.

(3) Currency Risk: This risk arises out of the volatility or otherwise of the currency and its strength or weakness in terms of other currencies and interest rates and relative degrees of inflation in the respective countries which influence the exchange rates. It also depends on the hot money flows and speculative short-term flows as between countries which will destabilise the exchange rates. The currency risk is generally covered by banks on the guarantee of the ECGC. The country risk may be covered by the ECGC in some cases or by the Exim Bank.

(4) Market Risk: Risks of commodities, their quality and the change of government policies of taxation, etc., are borne by the exporters or the ECGC in some cases. It will thus be seen that some risks cannot be avoided or passed on by the exporters and in fact many more risks are to be borne by the importers than by the exporters, as the Government policy in India wants to encourage the exports from the country.

Coverage of Risks

In India both exporters and importers face risks of foreign exchange market, referred to above, but risk coverage to exporters is more than to importers. The reason is that the Indian government has to enable exporters to compete effectively with their foreign counterparts, where exporters get many facilities, particularly credit at low rates of interest and lower tax rates.

The RBI cannot impose controls in foreign exchange market as hitherto as FERA has been replaced by FEMA but it has been entering the market to stabilise the rate and more recently it has been announcing a reference rate for its operations, to stabilise the market. FEDA is fixing the rate for major currencies around which banks are free to operate in the Indian foreign exchange market. Banks continue to cover the currency risk and Exim Bank provides the credit and country risk cover for long duration export contracts. ECGC extends the risk coverage by insurance-country and party credit insurance — for banks to lend to parties of unknown credit rating. But banks and firms are allowed to keep funds abroad and take risk in currencies and even trade in foreign currency markets. They can hedge, swap currencies enter into arbitrage deals, secure/provide cover abroad, and even take open positions in currencies. Options and futures are also open to banks and firms to cover their risks and trade in the markets. These terms are explained in later chapters.

Market Makers in Foreign Exchange Market

A market maker is one who takes the risk and gives a two way quotation for any currency — bid and offer rates — and deals in given currencies. As the RBI deals only in dollars, the banks who act as market makers, which are generally foreign banks, concentrate deals in dollar, yen, etc. The market makers are generally prone to take positions or hold uncovered currency holdings in strong currencies such as dollar, yen or euro as their rate fluctuations are minimal and risk is lower. The risk manager in a company or in a bank, plans his holdings of uncovered currencies into a diversified portfolio, to reduce risk and maximise returns. He may invest in short-term assets or money market instruments of countries whose currencies are strong. Such currencies are unlikely to fluctuate violently and are stable, but returns may be lower, due to lower interest rates. The risk manager has a trade off between risk and return. If he takes a higher risk, he get higher returns.

A market maker has to forecast not only the currency rates but the interest rates in the respective countries, which will influence the forward rates. He may cover the risk in some currencies but keep open positions in others. He takes calculated risks to maximise his returns. Leaving the uncovered positions, he may cover by the following methods:

(1) Swap forward to spot; (2) Swap forward of one maturity to another maturity, (3) Swap one currency against another of same maturity or a different maturity, (4) Buy spot for future liability, (5) Buy strong currency and sell weak currency, (6) Buy forward of one maturity against sale of another maturity or of another currency and a host of other techniques. Derivative products for hedging and risk coverage like those of options swaps, caps, collars are being developed in India.

Market makers in foreign exchange market are authorised dealers, and the Reserve Bank of India. In markets, well developed the Central Bank intervention is minimal and the market making is left to reputed foreign exchange dealers and international banks.

RISK IN FORWARD MARKET

As refered to earlier forward exchange rates are more risky than spot rates. These refer to rates which are quoted for the currencies of delivery in one month to six months ahead. During 1991 to 1994 the exchange markets were undergoing many changes due to the on going reforms in India.

During major part of 1994 following the full convertibility of rupee on Current Account, forward markets turned more volatile and listless conditions prevailed in the spot market. Again in September to December 1995, the forex market was very volatile and rupees depreciated to Rs. 36 per US $.

During August 1997 to February 1998, again the exchange rate was very volatile due to the Asian currency crisis and rupee depreciated to Rs. 42 per dollar by July 1998 and stood at around Rs. 44 per dollar in March 2000, and Rs. 46.3 in July 2003. It stood at around Rs. 46/– early in June 2010, and Rs. 50 to Rs. 54 per dollar in 2012.

The forward exchange market is generally influenced by many factors, in addition to spot market conditions, like:

(a) Perception regarding US dollar rate and Indian Non-resident Rupee exchange rate against dollar and in general currency markets.

(b) Current position and forecast of domestic and foreign money market conditions. Expectation of forthcoming short-term rates in the months ahead.

(c) Arbitrage, hedge and speculative deals effecting the market.

(d) Currency risk manager's strategies of the proportion of forward cover effected to total exposures.

Forward market cover was as high as 18% in 1992 just at the time of introduction of partial convertibility of the rupee in February 1992 but fell to less than 10% by February 1994, when the rupee gained in strength.

The exporters and importers are able to cover their forward risk with the banks for their receipts and payments, but in times of currency stability such covers are less in demand and the traders chose to take some risk themselves. Similarly, the currency Risk manager will also keep some open positions. Since January 1995 firms are allowed to trade in currencies and in forward exchange as referred to earlier. The currency risks of short-term of 3 to 6 months are generally lower. The currency risks, involved in medium and long-term Foreign exchange exposures of companies are unpredictable and difficult to cover. But these risks are high in India at present. The earlier practice of covering such risks by Exim Bank and ECGC will have to be turned into developing a long and medium-term forward market. Now banks as well as firms can keep foreign currencies abroad and trade with the attendent risks. The RBI policy is to encourage a well developed forward market in foreign exchange.

The factors of interest rates and money market conditions are important determinants of forward market. The banks started covering their positions of exposure under FCNR Scheme, when the market was volatile. The market was more stable in 1994-95, but turned volatile again in the latter half of 1995-96.

The risk of currency manager is higher or lower depending on a host of factors. The proportion of risk covered by him to total exposure will depend on his perception of money market rates in India and abroad and volatility of the currency market and number of financial and non-financial factors. When the US dollar interest rates are high, exporters prefer to keep their earnings abroad. If the rupee dollar rate is stable, exporters can take a view on the future exchange rate and lock in a forward to forward Swap arrangement with banks to obtain a better cover on their receivables.

The forward market is however illiquid beyond 6 months as the banks find it difficult to foresee the coming trends.

The risk that the currency Manager takes will vary from manager to manager depending upon the conditions in the money market and currency market. He generally covers his risk by taking forward to forward cover by adopting appropriate Swap techniques and calculated risk management through diversification and proper investment strategies. The currencies in which he takes a position should be stable as US dollar or Euro or Yen. The same can be said of the currencies held abroad by firms and companies in India.

Hedge cover of exchange risk for the trader is common. Besides, banks resort to currency Swaps, options and futures in foreign currencies to cover their exchange risk. The risk manager generally keeps an open position only in strong currencies, which are likely to be less volatile. Highly volatile currencies are generally less traded, and their risk is invariably covered. But the cover rates are higher. The terms of hedge, Swaps and options as applied to foreign exchange markets are explained in other chapters.

The recent attempts of the RBI to develop a rupee exchange market and a forward exchange market were already referred to. The companies are in a position to trade in the market and take position in currencies which need not be in the currency in which their foreign trade contract lies. They can keep foreign exchange earned abroad and trade in the currencies permitted by the RBI. The foreign currency option market is also expected to be developed well due to the measures, taken recently by the RBI, as also the forward exchange market in India.

Portfolio Management in Foreign Assets

Banks keep their foreign funds in various forms: cash on hand, balances with other banks, deposits with banks of various maturities, foreign Government bonds, treasury bills, short-term commercial bills and Treasury paper, etc. These assets are of various maturities and risks. The maturities may vary from ready cash in foreign currencies to various durations of short and medium nature.

Management of the above assets involve the same principles of risk and return, as applicable to domestic assets. Risk is more in foreign assets than in domestic assets. The foreign currency and funds managers have to plan to maximise the returns and minimise the risk through proper diversification into country and currency combinations and the use of Beta for long-term assets. The currency manager has to choose a proper coverage of risk and reduce his risk in currency positions, through various options open to the trader in foreign exchange market.

In general, the principles of portfolio management in domestic market will apply to management of foreign assets as well. The special risk to be covered in the foreign markets were referred to in other chapters.

32

Derivatives Futures and Options

The derivative markets are for those assets or instruments, which are synthetic financial products derived from the real assets or stocks or commodities. These new financial products have combinations of features of the existing real products and can be traded separately independent of the instruments or stocks, from which they are derived.

The major derivative products have been classified as options, futures and hybrids, which are all widely used in developed countries and in some developing countries. These products are increasingly becoming popular and traded volumes in these products are increasing, year after year.

Why Derivative Markets?

In emerging markets, there is a greater need for these markets for risk reduction from the high volatility of financial markets. Portfolio managers, particularly FFIs and FIIs may face market risks, commodity price risks and foreign exchange risks that can be properly controlled through the prudent use of these derivatives for hedging. Increasing globalisation and operations of foreigners in domestic markets make it necessary to develop certain facilities like hedging which in developed countries, they are used to.

The domestic markets will improve asset diversification, deepen the financial structure and promote the sophistication of the markets through the route of the derivative markets, offshore markets, etc. These new financial products deepen the structure and promote the superior allocation of resources so as to maximise return and minimise risk and ultimately to promote capital formation and higher economic growth.

Absence of derivative markets makes the domestic firms less competitive locally and globally and the domestic markets less attractive and imperfect. There will be unfilled gaps in the financial structure. Increased inter linkages of markets due to globalisation make it necessary to promote the derivatives, which lead to sophistication of these markets by filling up the gaps.

Pitfalls

The experience of developed countries with the derivative markets was not all that rosy. Without adequate safeguards trading has been taking place, in these markets with a speculative objective, with the result that there are instances of spectacular debacles in the derivative markets. There were failures of Barings Bank, and Metall Gesclschaft due to speculative over exposures and financial difficulties of Orange County and Bankers' Trust due to operations in these markets and for lack of proper comprehension of the risks involved.

In view of such failures or difficulties, what is wanted is education of the pitfalls of trading in derivative markets and provision of training facilities for traders and investors alike.

Role of Regulator

Too much regulation and too little regulation are both bad in respect of these markets. Too much regulation will have a throttling effect and prevent the entry and growth of the market. Too little regulation will lead to lack of enough protection to investors and fear of failures in the market.

The role of regulator has many objectives. The purpose of regulation is to protect the interests of investors, infuse confidence in the market and prevent unfair trade practices. Next regulatory objective is to promote smooth functioning of the market and prevent undue speculation and trade defaults.

Regulatory role on the market has its impact in many ways, namely, through the throttling effect on growth, minimising incentive to gaming and abuse, and promoting a healthy growth. It is now well accepted that only optimal level of regulation promotes a healthy market. This is particularly relevant to developing countries and emerging markets. The control effect operates through imposition of margins and prevention of over speculation and leading to gaming failures of the dealers and traders.

Trading in Derivatives

Trading on healthy lines necessitate adequate disclosures of open positions of traders, and trading by companies, and proper reporting. Disclosure of the covered positions, open positions, volume of trade and net losses and gains, etc. would help the market to grow in right directions. The disclosures are to the investors by all the players in the market and the companies and to the regulators for enforcing proper controls, and margins and by imposing trade restrictions. All the trading firms should have their own internal controls and by observing standards of capital adequacy and prudential norms, real hedging purpose can be served. A well capitalised clearing house improves the confidence in the market. The regulators and the Exchange authorities have to impose and implement an optimal level of controls.

Problems

One of the major problems of these derivative markets is over speculation which has to be controlled by a right degree of regulation. Developing countries have to promote them in a meticulous manner, through education, training and with all necessary infrastructure, a right degree of regulation with a fair degree of self regulation of the exchange authority and trading and dealer members. Derivative market depends on the observance of the rules of the game, like disclosures and transparency, maintenance of capital adequacy standards and avoidance of monopoly positions (undue long positions) and unfair trading practices.

The regulation of these markets is an important factor, as the confidence of investors is to be built in these markets. Market integrity and investor confidence are the major issues to be dealt with in earnest for promotion of the market. This confidence is dependent on the right degree of regulatory rules, exchange procedures and by member actions. Trades in the derivative markets unlike in the primary markets or cash markets, have zero sum consequences which means that for every deal the gain of one is the loss of another. The losses are therefore inherent in the market operations itself.

Although some degree of speculation is necessary and tolerated in any of these markets, a strict control through margins on these deals is necessary. This market is also sensitive to rumours and trading positions of numbers. It has to be nebulously protected from these problems to promote its growth.

Currency Futures and Options

The best examples of derivative markets are currency futures and options in U.S. and other developed countries. Futures contracts in currencies are contracts tradeable and contracts for specific quantities of given currencies, the exchange rate being fixed at the time that contract is entered into and delivery dates set by the controlling authority. The International Money Market Division of Chicago Mercantile Exchange (IMM) sets the terms of the contracts and contract specifications. The currencies in which they are available relate to most convertible currencies.

Although the volume of futures market is still smaller than the forward market but is growing at a rapid pace. Inter-bank call market and International Money market are all parts of the foreign Exchange Market. Here the traders charge commission which may work out to 0.05% of the value of the contract. There will not be bid — and ask spreads as in the Euro-currency markets. Deals are struck by brokers on the trading floor and trading on Telephone and Telex is much less. In India, options in currencies have become tradeable from July 2003. Earlier to that, only forward contracts were permitted for hedge and risk management. Currency futures were started in 2008 on the NSE and MCX and have taken off well unlike the interest rate futures introduced in June 2003, on the NSE.

Futures and Forwards

The futures have standardised specifications and trading takes place in an organised market. As contract sizes and maturities are standardised, all participants in the market are familiar with them and trading is well organised. The smaller size of a futures contract and freedom to liquidate the contract at any time before its maturity will differentiate them from the forward contracts.

Forward contracts are private deals, mostly confined to between any two parties who can sign a type of contract they agree on. The amounts involved and maturities and other terms are specific to the individuals/parties concerned. They are not standardised as in the futures contracts.

In IMM, contract lots are all fixed and terms standardised. The trading volumes are large as default risk is eliminated. In contrast, private deals are forward contracts as between two specific parties and run the risk of default. As it is a contract, the law of contract will apply for any defaults or violation of the terms of the contract.

Futures trading is organised on a regular basis with a clearing House and default risks are reduced. Profits and losses of futures contracts are settled at the end of each day on a daily settlement basis with a practice called marking to the market. Every day, futures investors must pay for any losses and receive any gains from the day's price movements. This process of marking to the market on a daily basis goes on until the maturity date. A forward contract is not settled on a daily basis but at the time of maturity. Futures contracts are closed by taking delivery or with an off-setting trade. A long position in D.M., can be offset by a sale of a futures contracts of a like amount. The distinction between forward and futures contracts can be seen below:

Forward Contracts	Future Contracts
1. Traded on phone or Telex.	Traded in a competitive arena.
2. Self Regulating.	Regulated by an authority like IMM.
3. Tailor made sizes.	Standardised sizes.
4. Delivery on any date and as per the requirements of the party.	Delivery on specific dates fixed before hand.
5. Settlements on the due date.	Settlement on a daily basis.
6. Margins are not required.	Margins are required.
7. Credit risk is borne by each party to the contract.	The clearing house is the counter-party which reduces risk.

In forward contracts, more than 90% of all contracts are settled by delivery. On the other hand less than 1% of all futures are settled by delivery. The quotes are in European style in forward contracts (local currency units per US dollar). Futures contracts are quoted in American style (dollars per foreign currency unit). The transaction costs are based on bid — and ask spread in forward contracts; the same are based on brokerage fees for buy and sell orders for futures contracts.

An example of contract specifications of foreign currency futures is given below in Table 1.

Table 32.1

Contract Currencies		British Pound		Canadian Dollar		Euro		French Franc		Japan Yen
Contract Sizes	£	62,500	C$	100,000	Euro	1,25,000	ff	250,000		12,500,000
Margin Requirements										
Initial	$	2000	$	700	$	14000	$	700	$	1700
Maintenance		1500		500		1000		500		1300
Minimum Price Change		.0002 (2 pts)		.0001 (1 pt)		.0001 (1 pt)		.00005 (5 pts)		.000005 (1 pt)
Value of one point	$	6.25		10		12.5		2.5		12.5
Months traded		January, March,		April, June,		July, Sept.,		October, December month.		
Last day of trading Third Wednesday of the Delivery month.										

Source: Chicago Mercantile Exchange Publications. There were prevalent in Nineties and could have changed since. This is only for illustration.

Both Forward contracts and futures contracts, have their own advantages and disadvantages. Futures do not offer any sizes and any currency that we desire to have. They offer a well organised mechanism for speculation and hedge in currencies. It offers a risk free contract, with freedom to liquidate the contract at any time before the maturity. It is only by chance that corporate clients will get future contracts to their exact requirements. If forward contracts are entered into they can have size, maturity and other specifications to their requirements. But these contracts carry a great risk which has to be covered again in futures market.

There is a regular arbitrage between the forwards offered by banks and IMM contracts offered by Chicago Mercantile Exchange. In practice, the arbitrage operations bring about parity in terms offered or price of these contracts in forwards and futures. They will bid up futures price and bid down the forward price and approximate equality is brought about. Because of these arbitrage operations on a daily basis regularly, the futures and forward prices do not differ significantly.

Currency Options

Currency futures and forwards protect the holder against the risk of adverse exchange rate changes, but they also deny him the possibility of windfall gains. One can hedge against the risk of a possible loss, but the risk taking itself might reward the risk taker. An option would be profitable to exercise in certain situations when the option is in the money at the current exchange rate. As applied to currencies, call options give a right but no obligation to buy while put options give a right but no obligation to sell, the contracted currencies at the exercise price. The option can be exercised at any time up to the expiration date under the American type of option, while the same can be exercised at the expiration date only under the European type of option.

How to use the option

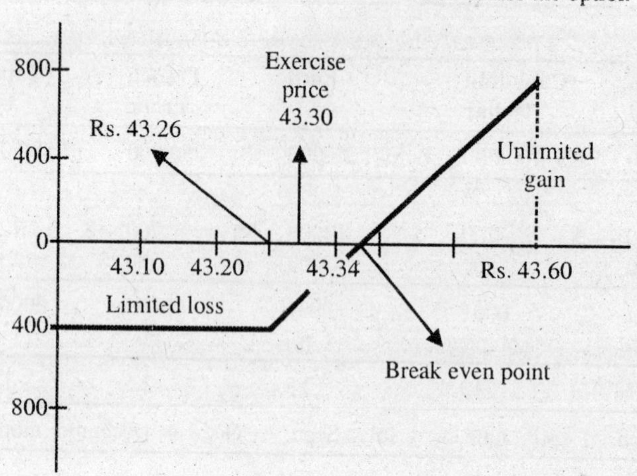

Examine the following graph.

U.S. dollars 10,000 contract size option premium Re. 0.04 per dollar

Exercise price = 43.30 Rs. per $

Spot price = 43.30 Rs. per $

Break even point:

43.30 + 0.04 = 43.34

If an Indian importer has to pay three months hence $ 10,000 to U.S. exporter, he has purchased a call option at a price (Premium) of dollars 0.04 per dollar or $ 400 for $ 10,000, contracted for. In this case he has hedged his currency risk for his payment due in US $. If by chance the spot price at the time of his payment is Rs. 43.60 per $ he is in the money. He would exercise this option and buy $ 10,000 at the option Exercise price of Rs. 43.30, when the spot price is 43.60 a gain of $ 3000, which more than offsets the premium of $ 400 that he paid. If at the time of payment, the spot price is less than Rs. 43.30 the option is out of money and he will not exercise the option; he will buy the required dollars from the spot market and his loss on the contract is $ 400 only. The importer will exercise the option only when the spot price is more than Rs. 43.34 per dollar inclusive of the premium paid for option ($ 0.04) (spot 43.30 + 0.04 = 43.34).

The reverse is the case of put option. The exercise price and premium paid may remain the same. Here the exporter wants to sell his $ 10,000 due to be received at the end of 3 months. The put option would be "in-the-money" at any price of Rs. 43.26 or less. Break-even point is Rs. 43.26. At any price of Rs. 43.34 and above, the option would be out-of-money. If the spot price at the time of expiration date and the date of receipt of dollars, is Rs. 43.10, he will exercise the option and sell $ 10,000 to the writer of the option at Rs. 43.30. That means that he will receive Rs. 4,33,000, but if he has sold in the spot market at that time, he would have received only Rs. 4,31,000. His notional gain is the difference between the above two figures, adjusted for the premium price paid for the put option. This means that he would have gained Rs. 2,000 minus Rs. 400, viz., Rs. 1,600 in the options contract. If on the other hand, the spot price has gone up to Rs. 43.60 he would not exercise his option but sell in the market and get Rs. 4,36,000 instead of Rs. 4,33,000, which he would have got under the option. From this gain, he would have to deduct the option premium paid for the contract, namely, Rs. 400. Either way, he does not lose but may gain, if at all, the loss may be only the premium paid for the option.

Currency options serve two purposes. They provide a hedge against a possible adverse moment of exchange rates. Secondly, they can be used by pure speculators whose presence in the options market adds breadth and depth to those markets.

The chart below presents the operation of the put options in the currency market.

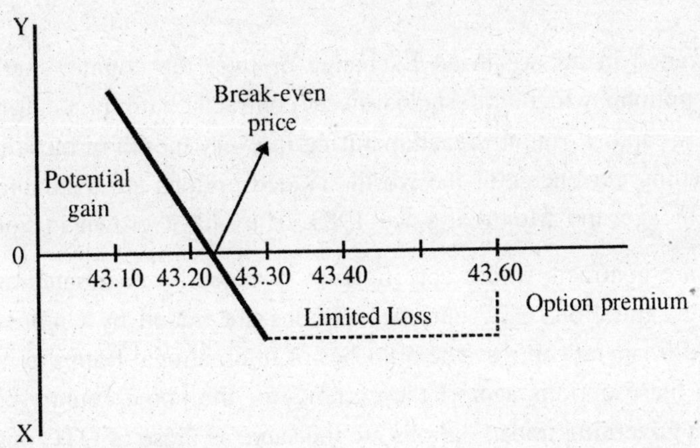

Contract size = $ 10,000

Option premium = Re. 0.04 per dollar

Exercise price = Rs. 43.30 per dollar

Premium paid Rs. 400 for the contract

The option holder's profit, net of the option premium paid is higher, the larger is the fall in the spot rate. If the spot rate rises above the Exercise price, the option becomes valueless as he would better sell in the spot market after that, where he would get a higher price than at the Exercise price.

The main users of currency options for genuine hedge are traders — exporters and importers. Many MNC affiliates buy these options if they want to be certain of how much to receive or pay in the future when the exchange rates may be uncertain. Investors or bidders for overseas firms or joint ventures or takeovers, whose requirement for funds, comes on the acceptance of bids, buy call and put options which are safer hedges than the futures and forwards. Many speculators find it better to operate in the options market where they can get better returns than in the futures and forwards.

Differences between Futures and Options

Futures hedge offers the closest offset to the loss due to the decline in Rupee value. With rapidly rising exchange rates, the company would benefit most from hedging with a long position in an option market as opposed to a futures contract. Conversely with rapidly falling exchange rates, the company would benefit most from hedging a futures contract. Each of them, namely, futures and options have their advantages and disadvantages and each has a role in providing product differentiation in the financial markets. They deepen and widen the market and improve the liquidity and volumes in the market.

Market Structure

Options are traded in an organised Exchange or over the counter market. Exchange traded options are listed options which are standardised contracts with predetermined Exercise price, standard maturities — upto 12 months each maturing in every month in most convertible currencies, which are major trading currencies of the world. Traded options are available in major Exchanges like Amsterdam, Chicago and Montreal since 1983. They have grown in volume year after year.

OTC options are contracts whose specification is generally negotiated as to amount, exercise price and rights and expiration. OTC currency options are traded by Commercial and Investment banks in many world financial centres. The branches of International Banks in major financial centres are willing to write these options against the currency of the home country as per the demand for them. The principles governing traded options are the same as those of OTC options. American types of options are widely used and options in major international currencies are available for corporates from the multinational banks operating in Euro-markets and international Capital markets and having subsidiary branches in many countries.

OTC options market has two segments, namely, wholesale segment for inter bank deals and retail segment for non-bank customers. The inter-bank market in currency option is similar to the interbank market in spot and forward exchange. Banks provide the needed currency options to customers in retail market and cover them up in the wholesale-inter-bank market. Many MNCs and affiliates turn to the banks for hedges through options in order to find precisely the terms that match their needs. It is this retail market which is most useful to the multinational corporations. But the writers are also the multinational banks in respect of OTC options. Unlike in the spot and forward exchange, the options market exposes the writers to more risk and there is an asymmetry between the demand and supply in the option market.

Futures Options

These are options written on futures contracts. Here the option gives the right to buy or sell the standard futures contracts, in a currency other than its currency. When exercised, the holder receives a short or long position in a currency futures contract that expires one week after expiration of the option contract. The future contract is delivered exactly like the delivery of a currency, if the option is exercised. If it is not exercised, trading is done on a daily basis and profit or loss is booked from time to time. The introduction of the futures options has been hailed as an important landmark in the development of the financial markets and provides the traders, investors and speculators a wider variety of instruments to reduce the risks, or take risks for speculative instinct.

This wide variety of instruments has improved the breadth and depth of the financial markets in the world over.

Risk Management in India

RBI has announced its intention of developing interest rate swaps and forward markets for currencies. Forward Rate agreements are also being provided by banks. Strips and Asset backed securities have a greater role to play and a beginning has been made in India for residential mortgages and auto loans. Strips are explained later and these are all derivative markets.

Credit swaps offers advantage of hedging risk and some institutions like IDFC can take over credit risks and banks can lend against guarantee of other banks.

Active use of derivatives require the existence of Term money market for 6 months to one year, which the RBI is trying to promote. Freeing of interest rates, in the Money market, deregulation of Term deposit rates and lending rates, freedom given to banks to determine their own rates of penalty for premature withdrawals, exemption of inter-bank liabilities from the CRR and SLR requirements are some of the steps that the RBI has taken for banks to develop their own methods of Risk management.

Banks have to develop the system of ALM or asset liability management by identifying mismatches for various periods of time. Some banks can quote bid and offer rates for various periods of Time Money to initiate the growth of this market. FRAs (Forward Rate Agreements) and Interest Rate Swaps (IRS) would provide good hedges against interest rate risk. The development of forward currency market would also provide hedge against currency fluctuations. Such derivative markets already exist in stock index and equity markets and in currency markets these are being developed at present (2008-09). Derivative markets, short selling options and futures, etc., are the next steps which the banks should be encouraged to adopt as techniques of risk management as much as corporates in India.

MANAGING FINANCIAL RISKS IN INDIA

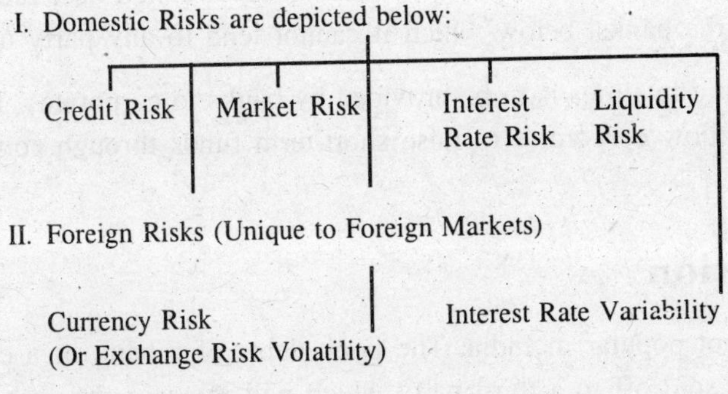

Methods of Meeting these Risks

(1) Insurance for credit Risks.

(2) Asset liability matching or exposure liability to be matched by Asset changes.

(3) Matching the inflows with outflows for liquidity risk management or use of Repos.

(4) Hedging the risk such as interest rate risk or currency risk.

(5) Use of Derivative Products like options, futures, forwards, swaps, switches, etc.

Repos

Repos are repurchase agreements involving sale and repurchase. Currently banks, and primary dealers (PDs) can create liquidity through Repos. Repos in the PSU bonds and corporate bonds have not grown but only in Government securities. Repos are used by RBI to control liquidity in the economy. Repo is the base purchase rate of RBI for LAF for banks to expand liquidity.

Repos in foreign exchange market were at a low ebb during 2001-2003. A Study by B.I.S. in 2001-02 showed that derivative market in India was at an insignificant level of less than 1% of the total world level. World economic recession in 2002-04 and again in 2007-09 was the major cause of this.

Short Positions

Short positions are prohibited or restricted by the RBI and SEBI, in the debt market. But once the short sale is allowed atleast by PDs they can hedge the position without having to offload the securities in the market.

P. L. R.: Banks fix PLRs — one for short-term advances and the other for term loans. Now the banks are free to fix their own rates. Suppose there are no fixed PLR and banks offer floating deposit rates and accordingly change the P L R as per the deposit rate changes, then the asset liability mismatches will be less. As in 2009-10 the RBI has asked the banks to declare their base rates which are the minimum cost of funds for the banks, below which it cannot lend to any party or sector.

R. U. F.: Revolving underwriting facilities is to be provided by banks to corporates. This will increase the fee based income and allow corporates to raise short-term funds through commercial paper and other methods.

Asset Based Securitisation

The securitisation of asset is not popular in India. The book debts of a bank or a company can be converted into securities and sold off to a third party which will increase the cash flow to this company. This will remove the fluctuating stock of receivables from the company. It will remove from the Balance sheet these assets, some of which may be of doubtful character and thereby Balance sheet will look healthier. Securitisation replaces receivables with funds. This will lead to better management of credit risk and asset backed securitisation enables originators to remove market risk from the interest rate mismatches by transferring it to investors, who may be institutions and F.I.s.

Prohibitive stamp duties and lukewarm participation of investors and lack of secondary market in them and inadequate foreclosure laws have hindered the growth of this market in India. Asset backed securitisation has great scope in India, if there are no hurdles to its growth and there is a secondary market in them. Now, there are signs of developing securitisation market in India, after the setting up of Asset Reconstruction Corporation of India, and authorisation for setting up of more asset reconstruction companies by the Govt and the RBI.

Strips

The strips are separated instruments for interest payments as against principal amounts. This is particularly relevant to government bonds and corporate bonds. A ten year gilted bond is strippable for example into 20 half-yearly coupons for interest, separate from that of repayment of principal. Strips facilitate a risk free zero coupon yield curve, which can be used for pricing other instruments. The principal amount is separated from interest flows in there strips.

If strips have fixed interest coupon it has no reinvestment risk and the investor could get desired pattern of cash flows with certainty. Another major advantage of strips is that it helps development of a zero coupon risk free yield curve. This could act as a benchmark for pricing of derivative instruments. Strips also offer banks a trading instrument for duration management.

A market for strips is yet to be developed in India. The gilted securities have no uniformity of dates for payment of coupon interest. There is no standardisation of strips for trading. The infrastructure in the form of clearing and settlement is yet to be developed, for the strips to be traded on a standardised basis. If the coupons fall due on fixed dates in a year and an auction system is developed with a proper cut off yield, the prices of strips are determined and strips become fungible for trading.

Credit Risk Management

The traditional methods of credit risk management are operational limits to loans, loan provisioning, portfolio diversification and collateralisation. The more innovative methods are loan securitisation and capitalised derivatives, which are available internationally to manage credit risk.

Credit derivatives have flexibility and reduce costs. They allow banks to hedge the credit risk of a loan without having to assign the loan and with no deterioration in customer relationship.

Credit Derivatives fall into two categories — swap based and option based.

The Swap based versions include the credit swaps, basket credit swaps and total return swaps. The option based versions include spread options and sovereign risk options.

Credit swaps allow to take over the credit risk without having to grant loan. Banks with resources may not have the risk appetite. Hence, international banks can guarantee and take the risk while the funding can be done by a domestic bank. The present practice of the bank is that if it is appraising and taking the risk it should also grant the loan. But Risk of credit and granting of credit can now be dissociated and credit risk can be guaranteed or insured.

Interest Rate Risk

RBI has suggested that the traditional gap analysis — gap in maturities of assets and liabilities is a suitable method to measure Interest rate risk. Moreover, there are some interest sensitive assets and liabilities. A positive gap indicates that more assets than liabilities will reprice in a given time period. A negative gap indicates that more liabilities than assets will reprice in a given time period. Rate sensitivity is more in short-term instruments than in longer term instruments. Duration analysis can be added to gap analysis to get better insight into the interest rate exposure of an institution.

There are two methods that banks can use for meeting this gap in Assets and liabilities — direct restructuring of balance sheet items and the use of synthetic instruments, like swaps, futures, options etc. As balance sheet restructuring is difficult in the short run, banks have to have recourse to synthetic methods to the asset-liability gap management. Forward rate agreements and Interest rate swaps are more frequently used. It is reported that the interest rate futures and options trading are also allowed by banks and F.I.s, which are not yet well developed in India,

Forward rate agreements (FRAs) allow a borrower or lender to lock in an interest rate for a period in the future, which thus effectively extend the maturity of its assets and liabilities. It is an off balance sheet contract between two parties say the bank and customer, wherein one party, agrees on the start date that on a specified future date (settlement date) that party will lodge a notional deposit with the other for a specified sum of money, for a specified period of time at a specified rate of interest.

FRAs are products which banks can market to their corporate customer as part of their cash management services. The bank is left with an open interest rate position that it can close with an FRA in the inter bank market. The customer is protected from an upward movement in interest rate by the process.

If gap analysis shows that in a particular period risk sensitive assets (RSA) are greater than the risk sensitive liabilities (RSL) and the bank expects downward movement in interest rate, it can sell FRA for an amount equal to (RSA — RSL) corresponding to the time period. If interest rates fall, the squeeze in net interest income will be approximately compensated by FRA. On the other hand, if the RSL > RSA and the bank expects the interest rates to rise, the banks will buy FRA for an amount equal to (RSL — RSA).

By using FRA, the bank can lock in its costs. The bank can sell FRAs when the loan demand does not pick up, in order to lock in a targeted return. It may buy FRAs if it is funding longer term loans by rolling over the shorter term liabilities. In a number of situations, the banks can buy FRAs to match the maturities of its assets and liabilities from an interest rate perspective.

Interest Rate Swaps (IRS)

The interest rate swaps are over the counter contracts between two counter parties for exchanging interest payments for a specified period, based on a given principal amount. The principal amount remains unchanged but the flows of interest payments are exchanged, say from floating rate to fixed rate and so on and only cash flows are exchanged and not the principal.

IRS has the following advantages:

(1) Banks use swap transaction for trading and hedging purposes.

(2) Bank can act as intermediary for arranging IRS as between two other parties.

(3) Banks can use swaps as an integral part of their management of interest risk.

(4) Alter the cost of the existing borrowing from fixed to floating rate and *vice versa*.

(5) Convert the rate of return on asset from uncertainty to certainty.

(6) Generate profits or avoid losses from interest rate fluctuations.

(7) Banks can use swap deals to hedge existing assets and liabilities, and for ALM operations.

(8) Depending upon the interest rate expectations, the bank may use swap transactions to hedge, to avoid losses and to adjust the duration of assets and liabilities.

The Bank uses prudential norms and sets limits for unmatched positions. The capital to be maintained under capital adequacy norms will be decided, by risk exposure and hence the need for cover on such exposures. Prudential norms are required to determine the extent of leverage, used. Tax implications of swap payments and receipts are also to be looked into, depending whether it is interest income or other income.

Derivatives Trading in India

Derivatives are traded in India both on BSE and NSE since June 2000. First index futures were introduced in June 2000 and Index options in June 2001. Stock options were allowed in July 2001 and Stock Futures in November 2001, both on the BSE and NSE. But interest rate futures were introduced on NSE in June 2003.

By legislative amendments, options and futures were made tradeable by treating them as securities, by Amendment to the Securities Contracts (Regulation) Act. Derivative trading has picked up faster on NSE than on the BSE, due to institutional support there and better regulatory framework. Secondly, the turnover in derivatives has far surpassed the turnover in the cash market, due to larger speculative fervour and greater participation by FIIs and MFs in the derivative market for hedging and speculation.

Presently traded derivatives are Index Futures, Index Options, Stock Futures and Stock Options and Daily quotations of them are published in the Financial Dailies. They give data on open, high, low, close, for each of the Contracts — Open position and number of contracts and their value in each of the instruments — Index and Stocks, etc. The data on total turnover is also published by BSE and NSE and on a monthly basis by the RBI in their Handbook of Statistics.

In terms of volume of turnover, the most widely traded are the Index Futures and Stock Futures followed by Index Options and Stock Options. But in terms of hedge, as seen earlier, in this chapter options provide a better hedge, covering both the long and short positions of traders. In terms of stocks traded, only most widely traded securities like ACC, Tisco, Reliance, etc., are included for derivative trading. Contracts upto three months are now available for trading in the Index Futures, and Index Options.

33

Swaps and Switches

Swaps and switches are derivatives and synthetic markets among the financial markets. These can be seen in gilt-edged markets, money market, forex market, interest rate and currency markets. These are derived from the existing instruments through exchange of one instrument for the other. Swap in defined as an exchange contract between two parties for two instruments of different yields, interest rates and currencies for the same amount. Switch is also similar to swap. In gift-edged market, banks and FIs, exchange one loan of a definite maturity and yield for another of different maturity and yield. The asset portfolio is adjusted from time to time for changes in yield, liquidity and maturity and in the process, banks requires a short-term loan of two or three years and they have too many loans maturing between 5 to 10 years but less between 1 to 5 years. Switch is not exchange of a security for cash but an exchange of one security for another both in the spot market, for differences in yield and duration.

Swap is an agreement for exchanging of forward dollars for spot dollars and *vice versa* or of floating rate instrument for a fixed rate instrument. Swap is of different varieties say coupon swaps, basis swaps and currency swaps from one currency to another. It can also be an exchange of forward for spot currency. Some swaps will hedge both interest rate risk and currency risks.

Swaps and switches reduce the risks, and costs involved. They are hedge instruments, used as risk management instruments. They widen the market, increase depth and width of the market and sophistication of operations in the financial markets.

Motivation for Swaps

The need for swaps arose out of felt need of the corporates to hedge the under-lying risk and uncertainty of financial outlays and outflows. The risks may arise out of trade in merchandise items or invisible items of balance of payments. Even in capital account, foreign borrowings require both interest rate risk coverage and currency risk coverage.

In respect of domestic financial markets also all the risks mentioned above are there except for the currency risk. The swaps in the domestic markets are required for risk coverage in interest rate changes, yield adjustments, timings of inflows and of outflows to be synchronised, asset liability matching, and adjustments for duration of the portfolio. In trading in the financial markets, particularly in the gilted market, yield and price differences as between loans attract Swaps. Swaps from fixed interest to floating interest rate loans is an example to adjust the yield pattern. Similarly, portfolio adjustments require the change of the portfolio composition to tune the expected inflows to come at the timings of expected outlays. This is called portfolio duration adjustments, this can be in international portfolio adjustment as in domestic portfolio adjustments.

Risk and uncertainty hedge is also an objective of swaps. For example, risk hedging can be done by a swap between floating rate loan and fixed interest loan and for swifting the basis of interest rate fixation from Libor based (as Libor plus) to one based on U.S. Treasury Bill rate or a Government bond or Bank Rate. Lastly, there are two basic objectives, namely, income and capital gains in addition to hedge against risk. Swaps will enable the parties to the contract to exchange the principals at maturity at the current spot rate or predetermined exchange rate or swaps of coupon rates only are also possible.

Economic Advantages of Swaps

Swaps provide real economic advantages to both the parties to the swap. Otherwise swap will not take place. If Arbitrage functions fully and the markets are perfectly efficient, there will be no advantage in swaps. But imperfections in the markets do exist leading to differential in risk-return characteristics. The impediments to perfect markets exist in the form of legal restrictions on spot and forward deals in the forex market, different perceptions of risk and credit worthiness of two parties, and tax differentials, etc.

A U.S. MNC operating in Germany wanted to hold dollars although D.M. was more stable than dollars at that time, because the operator was more familiar with US dollar than with D.M. Both parties received a cost advantage because they borrowed initially in the market where it had a comparative advantage and then swapped for its preferred currency and interest rate liability.

Currency swaps save in costs, promote liquidity and depth in the markets and/or provide a hedge to the risk that the party is exposed to. currency swaps are used to help financing the long-term requirements of funds for the projects of MNCs. In many foreign countries, long-term capital forward foreign exchange markets are absent and not well developed. In this scenario swaps are useful as special purpose vehicles for meeting the financial needs of MNCs and for providing liquidity to these markets. Imperfections and absence of perfect arbitrage system help the growth of the swap markets.

Currency Swaps

A swap contract can be entered in two or more currencies, involving two or more parties. More often than not , banks are intermediaries between two parties to the swap. An MNC, say Suzuki has borrowed in Japanese yen at a fixed rate. It wants dollars for its operation in India. It can swap its exchange risk by entering into a contract for giving dollars at a floating rate or fixed rate, for yen, it has got at a fixed rate. If it wants both exchange risk hedge and interest rate hedge, Suzuki might surrender its yen loan at a floating rate to a dollar loan at a fixed rate. Many banks — domestic and international — arrange these swaps for a charge or commission.

If they do not wish to take the risk themselves they can cover it in the inter-bank market.

Currency swap is a contract or agreement and is not a loan by itself. Currency Swap gives to the parties the right to offset, namely, a non-payment of principal or interest with corresponding non-payment in the other currency. In currency swap there is always an exchange of principal amounts at maturity, based on the original amounts of currency at the pre-determined exchange rate. This means that a swap contract behaves like a long dated forward exchange contract, where the forward rate is the then current spot rate. Forward rates of a currency are a function of spot rates and expected interest rate differentials, according to Interest Rate parity theory. The differences in forward exchange rates between say US dollar and German D.M. is due to differences in interest rates between USA and Germany. If a swap in interest rates in taken between D.M. and US dollars, it will automatically protect from the changes in forward rates.

Debt-Equity Swaps

This is something similar to exchange of debt for equity of the domestic companies. Financial Institutions are given the right to convert their loans given to a company into equity of that company, if it has failed in repayment of instalment of debt and interest payment. This right is used very infrequently and under some conditions, when the management is recalcitrant and proved inefficient and company will go into further red, if things are not set right.

The LDC debt equity swaps relate to the debt of the domestic corporates given to international banks. Six major debtor nations, namely, Chile, Brazil, Mexico, Venezuela, Argentina and Philippines have initiated these debt-equity swaps. The debt of defaulting countries is sold as junk bonds to be converted into equity at a discounted rate.

During the eighties, many Latin American countries were in a debt trap unable to repay their loans to MNCs and international banks. Then the European and U.S. banks found a way of settling their debt at a discount which ranged from 20% to 50%. These debts are sold in the secondary market comprising of big commercial banks, investment banks and even MNCs.

Sometimes, an international bank acts as an intermediary for sale of this discounted debt in the secondary market. Suppose the Nissan Motors, an MNC operating in Mexico wanted to invest an additional $ 60 million to expand its truck factory. Citi Corp offered to get a debt equity Swaps for Nissan. Citi Corp. combed the area and observed all the formalities and got a debt of $ 70 million to be given in the form of peso for an equivalent of $ 60 million — a write off of $ 10 million. The Citi Corp. gave Nissan $ 60 million in pesos for an equivalent US dollars of $ 40 million, of which $ 2 million is taken away by the Citi Corp. as its fees for the deal.

Debt swaps allow investors to acquire the domestic country's currency more cheaply than official exchange rate allows. The domestic currency is given for investment in the country as equity in investment in exchange for the debt in foreign currency due by that country. The foreign currency debt is discounted by 10-50% and sold to a foreign bank in the secondary market and equivalent amount of local currency is given to the MNC, for the surrender of dollars by the MNC. This is done at a highly discounted price. In the above example Nissan paid only $ 40 million to acquire $ 60 million worth of pesos of Mexico for investment as equity in the subsidiary of Nissan in Mexico.

MNCs get a cheaper method of financing their operations in a developing country through debt equity swaps. A firm buys a country's dollar debt in the secondary loan market at a discount and swaps it into equity in the local market. The major international banks like American Express or City Corp. do the intermediation for the sale of debt in the secondary market at a discount in dollars. These dollars are sold to MNCs, who want dollars to invest as equity in those countries. It benefits both the giver and the taker. The Mexico government got $ 70 million loan paid off for $ 60 million — a gain to the Mexican Government. The debt is repaid. The purchasing MNC buys these dollars for conversion to local currency of the indebted country for the operations of its subsidiaries, at a rate cheaper than the official exchange rate.

Nature of Swaps

A swap in international parlance is an agreement between two or more counter parties to exchange the obligations arising from two or more debt instruments. These swaps are restructuring agreements of obligations from any of the debt instruments. Assume that parent company A (USA) has a subsidiary in UK called A (UK). Similarly, there is a parent company B (UK) which has a subsidiary in USA, B (USA) The present company A USA wants to invest in its subsidiary in U.K. and needs Sterling for this purpose. And B (UK) wants to send funds to its subsidiary in USA called B (USA) and requires dollars for this purpose. Then with or without the help of an international bank to act as an intermediary, the parties can enter into a swap deal of the loans in sterling and dollar; without US company sending sterling to its UK subsidiary, B (UK) provides dollars to B (USA). These transactions can be shown in the following chart as flow of funds or swaps of loans.

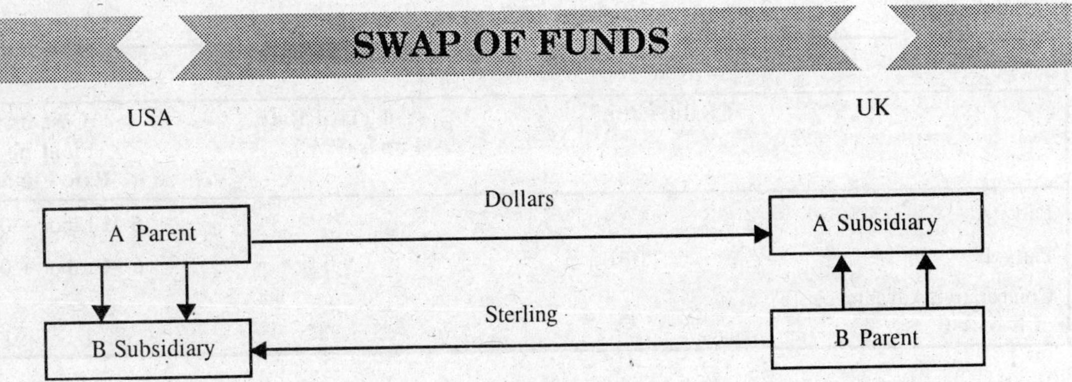

In the above chart A parent has to borrow sterling as a loan and B parent has to borrow dollars as a loan. These loans can be swapped so that A parent gives dollars to B subsidiary and B parent gives sterling to A subsidiary as shown below:

Types of Swaps

There are different types of Swaps, namely:

(1) Interest Rate swaps

(2) Fixed Rate Currency Swaps

(3) Cross Currency Interest Rate Swaps

(4) Basis Swaps

Interest Rate Swaps

Suppose a party has an obligation to pay a fixed rate of interest on a bond and another party has a floating rate debt instrument. If these parties exchange their interest obligations, then the principal amount remains with the original parties. The principal amount should be the same in the case of both the parties. The principal amount is not swapped, as it is in the same currency and for the same amount. Only interest rate payments are swapped.

Both the parties should gain, otherwise they will not agree to the swap. The gain will be in the form of lower costs. Consider Party A and B as shown in the following chart:

Table 33.1

	Credit Rating	Cost of Fixed Rate Funds (P.A.)	Cost of Floating Rate Funds
Party A	AAA	7.5%	6 M Libor + 0.25
Party B	BBB	9.0 %	6 M Libor + 0.75
Comparative Advantage of A over B		1.5	0.50

A is rated Tripple A and cost of funds is lower for A than for B. These two parties enter into an agreement of interest Rate Swap. A borrows fixed rate and lends floating rate to B and B borrows floating rate and lends fixed rate. This should be a win-win situation when both parties stand to gain. For B company to do a swap, its cost of funds should be lower, below what it would have to pay, if it had to directly enter the market.

The principal amount remains with the original parties and only the cash flows due to interest payments are exchanged.

Cash Flow on Interest

	Company A	Company B
A borrows directly fixed rate funds	7.5%	-
B borrows directly floating rate funds		- 6 m LIBOR + 0.75
A pays B floating rate interest at only Libor	- 6m Libor	+ 6 m Libor
B pays A fixed rate interest at 8%	+ 8.0%	- 8.0%

Company 'A' borrows at fixed rate and pays 7.5%, but pays to B Libor + 0; 'B' company borrows floating and pays 6M Libor + 0.75 but pays to A fixed interest at 8%. Here B got rid of the uncertainty of floating rate and hence reduced the risk. A takes the risk but gets the funds at lower rate than it can get directly in the market, i.e., Libor + 0.25. The gain for each of the parties is as follows:

	Company A	Company B
Overall cost of funds (as shown in the above chart)	6 m Libor -0.50	8.75
Comparable direct Cost of funding	6 m libor + 0.25	9.00
Gain	+0.75	+0.25

The gain is there for both the parties, but the gain is more for the company A than company B due to its higher credit rating and its lower cost of borrowing.

Fixed Rate Currency Swaps

Fixed Rate Currency Swaps are transactions between two parties with fixed rate interest liabilities but in different currencies. Each exchange takes its fixed rate interest liability in one currency for fixed rate interest liability in another currency. For this exchange to be effected the initial exchange rate at which the principal and fixed interest payments are to be exchanged and the subsequent exchange rate at maturity when the principal amounts have to reexchanged are to be agreed upon. Whether the actual exchange takes place physically or it is done on a notional basis, it has to be agreed upon what are the principal amounts due at maturity and the interest amounts to be paid as per schedule. This will result in an effective transformation of debt raised in one currency into a stream of flows of fixed amounts in another currency. To be more specific A has a natural advantage of borrowing in Swiss franc, while he needs the US dollars. There is another party 'B', who has borrowed in dollars and his stream of dollar payments can be swapped to 'A', in exchange for a flow of Swiss franc payments to 'B.' If B does not have inflows of Swiss franc; he has to hedge these payments through the forward exchange market. These deals are put through the reputed international bankers. 'A' gets U.S dollars flows and 'B' gets swiss franc flows - their desired flows.

The advantages are obvious: one prefers a currency in which he wants the loan and he wants a hedge so that he knows how much funds he has to set apart periodically. Lastly, these swaps provide major cost savings. The swap enables the counter parties to arbitrage to have access to markets in which they are strong or have a preference. Each gets the currency which he wants and the market to deal in which he has relative strength of advantage. Unless both parties to the swap stand to gain, such swap does not take place. It has to satisfy the relative preferences of each party.

Cross Currency Interest Rate Swap

The cross currency interest rate swap is a swap of both the currency and the interest rate. A company has borrowed through a US dollar denominated fixed coupon rate bond; but the company's requirement is a D.M. denominated floating rate bond to be used for its German subsidiary. His fixed rate US dollar bond is now exchanged for the floating rate D.M. denominated bond. This can be assigned through an intermediary or a bank. This should be suitable and gainful to both the parties.

The currency swap market has grown rapidly, due to the growth of local capital market and the respective Euro-Currency market in a wide range of currencies. The most frequently used currencies are US $, Japanese yen, German D.M., pound sterling, Canadian dollar, Swiss franc, etc. In the 21st century currency to be used is euro, instead of D.M. and franc.

Multilegged Swap

In this swap market there are more than two parties and notably an intermediary bank of international operations. The bank acts as a counter-party to each company and takes the risk for each company and is rewarded by a return for taking the risk. The bank provides company with what it wants, say Floating rate interest bond in D.M. and takes its Fixed rate interest bond in US $. Similarly, for another party, it takes its Floating rate interest bond in Swiss francs in return for its fixed interest bond in US $. This process goes on and this may lead to the bank having uncovered risks while the companies are all hedged by the cover facilities provided by the Bank. This is called Multilegged Swap.

Basis Swaps

This is a Swap of interest rate basis from one of floating on U.S. Treasury bill rate to that of Libor or from that of floating on commercial paper to U.S. Treasury bond rate etc. This refers to the basis on which the floating rate is linked. Basis Swaps also apply to cross currency swaps, where interest is on a floating basis in each currency.

Interest Rate Swaps in India

Despite the halting progress of the convertibility of the Rupee, the deregulation of domestic interest rates is progressing steadily. Until 1994, the RBI set the rates at which banks borrowed money and lent and the spread between them is their profit. Since 1994, the RBI has been dismantling the controlled interest rate regime. Banks can now set their own borrowing and lending rates. The only remnants of regulation is the interest rates on savings accounts and on deposits of 1 to 15 days. Similarly, on the lending side, the left over controls are on the lendings below Rs.2 lakhs, export credit and loans for housing and to weaker sections. The banks are still controlled for monetary control purposes by the CRR, SLR, and repo and reverse repos.

The RBI has asked the banks to set up a system under which they will be forced to recognise their cash flows and interest rate risk exposures through the Asset-liability management process. The banks will now have to grapple with interest rate and liquidity risks. The interest rate swap is one instrument through which anybody can hedge risk of interest rates. Banks are already taking credit risks, which they try to reduce by better appraisal, greater care in lending and emphasis on quality lending which will reduce the bad and doubtful debts. On top of this, the flexible interest rate policy and fluctuating rates have forced banks and all players in the financial markets to run for a cover for interest rate risk.

An Interest Rate Swap (IRS) is a transaction between two parties, whereby there is a notional exchange of and reexchange of flows of interest and /or principal. It involves the receipt and payment of interest during the life of the Swap. This exchange may involve one from fixed rate to floating rate interest payments and vice-versa. similarly, one can hedge the rise in interest rate. One can also go short on interest rates, if he expects a fall in rates. Once the bank can hedge on interest rates they are sure of the payments and they can accordingly adjust the receipts through the lending rates. The transaction in IRS market will not attract CRR and SLR.

There is no inter-bank term money market now due to the CRR and SLR provisions. This market will help the growth of debt and derivative markets in India. RBI has allowed banks to develop IRS market in India, and has been encouraging the growth of term money market.

Banks will have to seggregate the credit risk and interest rate risk. Credit risk can be insured by ECGC and interest rate risks will have to be eliminated in risk management. In making any financing decision, it is now easier to come to a conclusion of credit risk that they can take and credit policy they should adopt.

IRS will reduce the spreads between banks' lending and borrowing rates and between bid and offer rates in gilts trading. The benefits that follow from this derivative market are many to both bank and non-bank participants in financial markets. IRS will develop the debt market and impart liquidity to NCD market.

One example of the benefits of this derivative market can be given by the low cost of flexible mortgage loans that the Americans enjoy. These are available to them because of a large market in Mortgage backed securities and the existence of a sophisticated interest rate derivative market there.

Accounting and documentation treatment and removal of stamp duty on such contracts of IRS will have to be accepted for IRS to grow in India. Standard futures and options contracts are allowed and developed, in India. So, IRS will have to be further developed in India through proper incentives.

Interest Rate and Currency Swaps

Corporates use the interest rate and Currency Swaps as special financing vehicles for reducing costs and risks in financing their foreign investments. In the deregulated and free markets, there are wide fluctuations in currency rates and interest rates. Swap has led to a refinement of risk management technique which in turn led to MNCs greater involvement in the international capital market.

An interest rate Swap is an agreement between two parties to exchange interest payments in a foreign currency for a specific maturity upon notional amount. This notional amount is the principal against which interest is calculated and which does not change hands. The main types of Swaps are Coupon Swaps and Basis Swaps. The coupon Swaps refer to the exchange of payments of interest from a floating rate basis to a fixed rate basis, and vice versa. The basis Swap refers to one wherein two parties exchange floating interest rate payments, based on two different reference rates, one say on Treasury bond and the other on Treasury bill or on Libor.

A floating rate loan can be 50 basis points on the Libor rate. The basis point is 0.01% of the quoted rate. The Swap is as between A and B.

A	B
Fixed rate is 13.25	Libor + 0.50
Libor = 11.35	is the floating rate = 11.85
	11.35 + 50 = 11.85 Libor + 50

basic points

Net lock in period	differences is
1.40	13.25 – 11.85 = 1.40

Fixed rate payment is 13.25

Floating Rate Payment Libor + 0.50; 11.35 + 50 = 11.85

This is only an example and the actual rates are much lower now.

If Libor goes up to 13.00, then 13.00 + 50 = 13.50 will be payable by him instead of 13.25. The hedge is set at an upper limit of Libor.

The banks will be counter-party to provide this hedge by Swap to the exporters and importers traders and manufacturers and to any debtors in general. The banks take the risk and cover it up in the inter-bank market. In the Swap segment in the currency market forward premia ranged from 4 to 7% during the years 2001-2003, reaching a peak at about 7% in March 2002, and even to 8 to 10% in April 2007 and October 2008 in more recent years.

Advantages

Interest Swaps reduce the risk when they are acting as a hedge. They also reduce costs when different parties have different credit rating and their cost of borrowing is accordingly decided. The differences in terms of borrowing in different markets arise due to the risk and creditworthiness of the borrowing party. Party 'A' is having a low rating (BBB) and cannot secure at floating rate market at the rate of libor. But a bank with a high credit rating (of AAA) can borrow at Libor. B (the Bank) then borrows at Libor and Swaps with 'A' who borrowed in a fixed rate of 12.5% or at Libor + 0.50. When the Libor is 11% and the Swap is at 11.5%, then there is no gain to A, as he can borrow at Libor + 0.50. If the Swap is at 11.25%, and he can borrow at 11.50%, then 'A' stands to gain and reduces his cost by 0.25%. If one has to borrow at fixed rate of 12.50%, but he can borrow floating rate of 11.50% and Swaps for a fixed rate of anything from 11.50% to 11.75%, he gains in costs.

'B' also gains as he has borrowed at 11.00% from the floating rate market and exchanged it for 11.75% fixed rate which is still lower than what he can borrow from the fixed rate market (12.50%).

RBI Scheme of Interest Rate Swaps

Scheduled commercial banks, excluding the RRBs, primary dealers (PDs) and all India financial institutions (FIs) are free to undertake interest rate Swaps. The purposes for which they can undertake Swaps as a financial product are for trading, hedge or balance sheet management or for market making. They can offer these products to corporates who wish to hedge the loans on their books. Once these institutions undertake these transactions on a regular basis they have to inform the RBI.

These transactions for hedging and trading have to be recorded separately. Those for hedging purposes shall be accounted for on an accrual basis. Those for trading purposes should be marked to the market (value at the ruling market price). The fees or income and expenses relating to Swaps should be recognised in the Income and Expenditure statement at the time of settlement.

The participants should have to maintain the capital adequacy norms in the case of banks and FIs, in respect of these assets. The PDs have to maintain additional capital at 12% of risk weighted assets towards credit risk on interest rate contracts. They have to disclose all the details in their balance sheets on the outstanding contracts, their notional principal amount, nature and terms, etc., including information on credit and market risk and accounting practices adopted for Swaps.

The fair value is the estimated amount that they would pay or receive to terminate the Swap. There are no restrictions on the size or tenor of any interest rate Swap. The RBI wants the market to develop and did not lay down any bench mark interest rates like money market or debt market rates.

34

Outsourcing and BPO

Theory of Outsourcing

International Trade Theory is based on different factoral endowments and their international immobility across nations. It is possible that factors like Technology are mobile and similarly knowledge based services and intellectual property rights are mobile across borders, although their origin is national. Generic forms of drugs, patented in one country are transferable. Patents and copy rights are usable across borders and transferable for a fee or royalty.

Some factors are thus national in origin but transferable in their usage and services across borders. Thus, factors may be immobile but their services are mobile across borders MNCs are multinational corporations and their goods and services are originating in one country or more but are used in many other countries. Thus, factoral services are mobile and these services are transferable across borders due to advanced technology and telecommunications and IT related services. There are many companies, including banks which are using the services of skilled persons, specific technology, and software programmes of another country — other than that of the outsourcing country.

There are strong grounds and visible advantages of saving in time and costs by outsourcing some services from another company outside the country of the outsourcing company. The server company doing outsourcing business is specialising in this business or processes and has the expertise and experience in providing quality services and at lower costs than that of outsourcing company. The MNC for example can use the services of Research and Development, market penetration through retailing, clinical tests, etc. in China or India, although its home country is USA or UK. Both outsourcing MNC and server company stand to gain by specialisation and cost saving.

Outsourcing or Business process outside (BPO) is the latest development in the trade theory and practice. In this case, the factor is mobile, instead of being immobile as under the traditional theory and its services are also mobile; but what has created the background for this practice is that the national trade policies, and artificial barriers to the movement of these factors, namely on the entry of skilled labour and technology, into the DCs/LDCs.

It first ushered in the form of Call Centres for the back office work of foreign banks and Financial Institutions in US and UK to be carried in India or in any their asian country. Thus, Banking and Financial Services work led the initial BPO change, aided by technology. Now healthcare, media, retail, logistics and telecom related work are the next big opportunities for outsourcing. BPO firms are building specialist skills in those verticals, in an attempt to differentiate themselves. Even insurance is an area, where there are ample opportunities, particularly in health insurance. Thus, Banking and Financial Services along with insurance will continue to lead the growth of BPO business in the world accounting for about two thirds of this total BPO globally. According to BPO sources, next in importance is the retail and healthcare verticals which are the fastest growing ones.

Accordingly, BPO firms are preparing their personnel and HRD skills in these areas of business for specialisation and for future expansion. It was however noticed that work in the healthcare business is dominated by Captive BPOs of Insurance Companies, themselves.

Indian BPO business is expanding at a rapid rate, due to quality of service and for saving in costs and time advantage. The income of BPO will be income under invisibles from abroad, under the Current Account of Balance of Payments. During the last quinquennium of 2001-2006, three out of 5 years have seen the Current Account surpluses due to growth of invisibles trade only.

Outsourcing as Extension of Foreign Trade

Outsourcing refers to raising value additions through the help of outside agency — inside or outside the country of origin. This can be Business Process outside the country for reasons of availability of necessary skilled manpower and cheaper costs of such value addition. IT based professional services have been the starting point of outsourcing. Many US firms and UK firms started the use of this facility of the work of skilled manpower in India in the fields, amenable to outsourcing, namely, IT computer software programmes, Data Processing, etc. The back office work in banks is also outsourced. These fields have been added to printing, medical transcription, clinical tests, Accounting and Auditing and so on down the line.

Some Indian companies are also outsourcing abroad, such as Wipro, Ranbaxy, etc. Mortgage business in respect of real estate, housing, etc. involve a lot of paper work, which is being outsourced by many US firms. Some companies specialise in this job of undertaking outsourcing work in various fields both in the US and India. Servicing Housing loans is a full time job in the mortgage business in the US, undertaken as BPO by some specialised business firms or independent BPO, like Clear to Close (CTC), Visionet Systems (VS) and String Information Services (SIS).

The majority of US firms are reported to be happy with the BPOs in India. But there are some others among US, IT firms who are unhappy with the quality of the work being done in India. The hassles include the safety and security or privacy of the data in the IT based industry. Nasscom wants to create a global Regulatory Body — an SRO which will help the IT and BPO industry to create and enforce a code of conduct and to maintain certain standards of privacy and security.

BPO industry has grown in gigantic proportions recently in the service industry and has become an extension of foreign trade through movement of services of factors immobile across borders. There are both advantages and disadvantages of the growing field of BPO.

Strength of BPO

The years 2004 to 2006 was a boom time for the Indian Business Process and Outsourcing Sector. The impetus for this boom came from the strong fundamentals of the economy with a GDP growth rate of 7 to 8% and exports crossing a growth rate of 20%. The boom in the economy is reflected in the fastest growth of the Sensex of BSE, which is a window of the economy. The BSE Sensex (Base 1978-79=100) rose from a low of 2,924 in 2003-04 to an all time high of above 12,000 in May 2006 (12,671 on May 11, 2006). Many foreign countries have evinced increasing confidence in the ability of BPO Sector in India to deliver quality services. The companies the world over are today looking at the ways to increase efficiency and lower the costs by any possible method. The Business process outside India has come in handy with the skilled manpower and lower wage returns relative to the US, UK and all countries covered by EU.

Outsourcing business in India has captured just about 10% of the world's market in this regard, which is estimated at around US $ 300 billion. The IT services go alongwith BPO services. The Business Professional Services in the form of IT is estimated at around $ 150 billion and the BPO services at around another $ 150 billion. This outsourcing business is expected to grow, in the years ahead, as it has proved its worth both to the giver and the taker (namely the exporter and importer). The BPO sector will surely expand in India, but the main road block, are the shortage of skilled persons, and the rapid turnover of these persons on the job, after being trained for this purpose. BPO is taking place in many service industries like banking, hotels, travel and tourism not to speak of customer service and IT software services.

Advantages of BPO

The generally accepted advantages of BPO are lower costs, increased efficiency and strengthened strategic focus. These advantages are based on the factor endowments and immobility of factors and mobility of factor services. The company using these services can give greater focus on its core competencies and outsource the peripheral and ancillary items of work from another agency inside or outside the country. There is a great cost saving in this process, in addition to better quality and efficiency due to specialisation in business processes.

To achieve above the objectives, there is need for better planning and integration of the process, impart better transparency and management of information. There is need for not only intra enterprise data integration, but inter-enterprise integration, as the outsourcer may have a different pattern of data analysis and interpretation from that of the outsourcing company. These are issues of data access;

it can be in any shape, or format and in different files and building them together is a formidable task and the companies do underestimate the complexity and quality of the outsourcing work. Many times, access and integration and maintaining the quality of work are difficult to achieve and the outcome may fall short of the target.

Disadvantages

The major hurdles to outsourcing work are the quality maintenance and speed of performance and timeliness. Integration challenge is not merely consolidation of data from various sources but to deal with them in an effective manner. Tremendous amount of data are flowing back and forth between the customer and outsourcer. To send all the data all the time means lots of expensive, band width, and more hardware. Much time is wasted in sorting out the data and timeliness of the outcome is doubtful. In addition to quality and speed of work, security and prevention from misuse of the data are also connected issues. The company and its data can be left to unlawful and unintentional access. They have to find ways to keep data encryption at both ends in the process of movement. There are a number of other challenges in the data transmission, analysis and moving data across the firewalls.

ITES-BPO

IT enabled services recorded a strong growth during the recent years. India continues to enjoy the status of BPO destination (Business Process Outside), despite increasing competition from other countries. India contains the skilled manpower, experience in IT related services and relatively lower costs to attract offsharing by firms in US and Europe. Additionally, a favourable time zone difference helps the organisations to maintain internal operations and customer's service round the clock. When the US and Europe stop operations, India can take over as it is day time here, when it is night in the US and Europe. Besides, most of the call centres in India work in the night time to do customer service and takeover the work from them during their day time operations, there in US and UK.

The category of business services emerged as an important driver of service exports from India. India's software industry has been able to increase its market share from 1.5% in 2001-02 to 2.6% in 2007-08.

The global market for software and BPO services is projected to grow by 8.6% per annum over 2004-2010. Many companies in India have entered this BPO service industry for providing end-to-end service offerings. The structure of software exports including ITES-BPO reveals that financial services, including banks, insurance companies, security firms account for the largest share 41% of Indian Software Services. This is followed by manufacturing and telecom sector (20%) with an ITES; customer care and finance have been the fastest growing segments.

India has here able to maintain a steady growth of software and BPO exports in recent years, despite a global slow down and increasing competitive pressures. According to NASSCOM, this industry's vertical market was well diversified across several mature and emerging sectors and the strategy of geographical diversification into all continents with a strong focus on productivity, benchmarking and enhanced operational efficiencies will help the industry to retain its competitive edge as the global leader in software and BPO services exports.

Despite a major global recession in the years 2008 and 2009, exports of software and I.T-enabled services exhibited a steady growth of 16% in 2008-09 of the total software exports, I.T services contributed 57.2% followed by BPO exports at 27.4% and engineering services and product exports at about 15.3% during the year 2008-09. But competitive pressures may force cost cutting measures and improved efficiency of this sector. Even so, NASSCOM has projected the India's software exports would grow by 4-7 per cent in 2009-10. Besides, the NASSCOM projections despite the global slow down in global spending in the near term, and secession in America and Europe, invite that India's Technology and Business services exports may remain in the range of U.S $ 65 billion to U.S $ 75 billion by 2011-12.(Source NASSCOM, "perspective 2020, Transform Business, Transform India", April 2009.)

Six Sigma Methodology

India has become most favoured destination for outsourcing in the world. It has the necessary pre-requisites for this business such as a pool of talented persons, infrastructure, good telecommunications, suitable environment in the form of apt Government policy and above all the cost advantage. India has to face competition from Australia, China, Ireland and Philippines. If India could offer superior quality and cost advantage, it can stand the competition and get the business from the developed countries. For this, it has to retain its edge by adopting Six Sigma methodology, which is the implementation of a measurement based strategy that focuses on process improvement and variation reduction. The statistical techniques have to be fool proof. Six Sigma integrates various strategies and tools from statistics, quality control, business and engineering and from various other disciplines as the need arises. It is used in healthcare, military and general manufacturing. The leading companies like Motorola, GE, American Express, Dupont etc. use these techniques of Six Sigma.

For the success of Six Sigma methodology, one has to widen its reach and application, involve the employee participation and initiative at an organised level. It is a tool for driving excellence at all levels and unleash the collective intellect of the quality personnel towards innovation. The quality of their products, services and output to the customers is kept under continuous watch, under BPO, which ultimately depends on the employee participation and their innovative spirit. The company has to integrate quality into their offerings.

The basic steps to embark on Six Sigma Methodology in any outsourcing agency are:

(1) Define the competitiveness for their business.

(2) Delineate the customer expectations.

(3) Estimate how the competitors are performing.

(4) Bridge the gap between yours and competitors and that with the customer expectations.

Then final roadmap for improvement of quality can be checked out and implemented, after the above steps.

New Trends in Outsourcing

New to Trends are emerging in outsourcing. One is the increasing competition because of new entrants into this business. Secondly is the quality consciousness among the outsourcers and the outsourcing companies, as quality standards have been reported to have fallen as per the companies' feedback from outsourcers. Thirdly, with increasing volumes of data, the question of compatibility of systems and processes has increased. Lastly, there are reports of piracy and misuse of data inputs for the purpose of divesting funds or swindling or cheating in the BPO industry in India.

HERO-ITES is one of the Indian business process outsourcing companies which has a large American client base, particularly in Finance and Telecom sectors, due to its joint venture partner with the American customer service company **"Livebridge"**. As at mid-2006, it was reported that **HERO-ITES**, has entered into a partnership with the Australia's largest call centre, **"Sales Force"**, which will bring in with it about 70 Australian clients. This partnership may flower and grow into a joint venture in the near future and **HERO-ITES** will have first Indian presence in Australian BPO market, with an advantage of expertise and experience.

In the Indian IT Infrastructure outsourcing, two emerging features are noticed, namely multiple sourcing and shift to short term from long term contracts. New comers like HCL Comnet, Infosys, Wipro and TCS are challenging ventures like EDS, CSC and IBM in infrastructure outsourcing. Multiple outsourcing to many players is fast replacing contracts awarded to single players before. Besides, the long term deals have become outdated and short term selective outsourcing has become the order of the day. Remote Infrastructure outsourcing (RIM) model is the fastest growing segment of BPO industry and is expected to hit $ 7 billion mark by 2010. Infrastructure outsourcing will continue to grow as an on-shore cum off-shore mix model with global delivery system and disaster recovery management.

Outsourcing by Banks

Banks have a lot of routine work of a repetitive nature, which can be outsourced inside the country or outside the country. Here outsourcing refers to the use of a third party to perform certain activities on a continuing basis, that would normally be undertaken by the Bank itself. There are many areas where outsourcing by banks are feasible and advisable, like the door to door home banking - collection of cheques and cash and delivery of them at the door of the customer, data processing on cheques/drafts for collection - in station or outstation, TT, MTs, and Bills, etc., sent for collection and attending to customer enquiries, collection of receivables, recovery of loans, etc. Financial inclusion by banks can also be promoted by outsourcing to a profit or non-profit making body as per the latest guidelines of the RBI.

The IT Vision Document: 2011-17 IT envisaged better vendor management and outsourcing practices. The RBI department of IT would work as a nodal point for evolving a centre of excellence for developing and serving the technical and technological needs of the banking sector. The better use of IT and BPO was aimed at in this area.

There are many risks in outsourcing, such as strategic risk, reputation risk, compliance risk, operational risk, exit policy risk, counterparty risk, country risk, contractual risk, access risk and systemic risk. Both the outsourcer and the service provider have to ensure the effective management of these risks. Inter-country systems and privacy maintenance are the other aspects to be taken care by both the parties to the outsourcing contracts.

Any failure or lapses on the part of either party may have serious repercussions on the outsourcing bank and the whole banking system in the country. So the Board of Directors and Management have to provide strict rules and guidelines to outsourcing process and to the service provider. They have to take care of all the above risks and avoid any lapses.

The bank has to analyse how the arrangement will fit into its organisation and reporting structure; and conduct appropriate due diligence of the service provider's financial soundness, integrity, quality of service, and its past experience and expertise. When performing due diligence, the bank has to consider laws, regulations and guidelines of the top management, of the Government or the Central Bank and its regulatory and supervisory requirements. If the service provider is in another country, the bank is exposed to country risk, legal and regulatory risks and privacy risks. Care has to be taken in the original contract itself to provide for all such risks and contingencies and course of action left for the aggrieved party.

The Bank planning to outsource any activity has to check whether it is "material outsourcing", which will promote, quality and efficiency of service and reduce the cost and increase profits. In other words, outsourcing should have material benefits to the outsourcer, whether it is a bank or any other company. LIC and Post Offices have a wide network of agents who extend their services to far off places, remote villages and towns. Such organisations have a role to play in improving customer service. Some Internet sales companies are planning to use these agencies for outsourcing their door to door delivery work. So is the case with banks. Already banks like Kotak Mahindra have been outsourcing the work of Customer Service, home delivery service and other banking services, particularly for cash pickup and cash delivery, etc.

Many private Insurance companies and even banks like ICICI are using the services of agents, marketing executives and sales persons for marketing their services and recovery of loans. Like Insurance and postal services, banks may have to use the outsourcing services for marketing their products, like home and automobile loans or personal loans or consumer loans, in addition to their deposit mobilising schemes or loan recoveries.

Outsourcing, if it is done for a foreign bank or a foreign agency or MNC, outside India it comes under the category of foreign trade in services and is beneficial to the country's balance of payments on Current Account. In the recent past, the trade in invisibles, into which category outsourcing abroad falls, has increased by leaps and bounds, in the whole world trade as also in India's foreign trade. The proportion of invisible trade has increased and also the Current Account surplus has emerged in some years in the recent past.

Data Importance in BPO

Data is the material which is to be handled by the outsourcing company and to be provided by the outsourcer. Outsourcing can become effective only if data is integrated into process management. Data process management in the outsourcer should be compatible with that in the outsourcing company. Data access and data integration are essential inputs in the BPO industry.

First the data storage is a problem, after accessing from various sources. Storage space has become one major problem, as data is increasing by leaps and bounds. The next problem is to keep this data from privacy and misuse by interested third parties. Thus, data encryption has become the next big problem in BPO business.

Data integration, access and processing are some of the steps involved after storage. Quality Issues arise as data are consolidated from various sources and moved from outsourcer to outsourcing company. Besides, the speed of movement and analysis of the quality data become a formidable job at both sending and receiving ends. During the process of movement of data and time involved in the process, safety and security of data from pilferage and misuse have to be ensured. So, they have to figure out the way to encrypt the data fully with the right mechanism on both sides handling the data.

With increasing competition among the servers for outsourcing, each company in the BPO service has to maintain a pool of talented people, retain them after suitable training and drive towards excellence by promoting initiative and innovation among the talented people working for the company. The success or failure of the company depends on the contribution of its people, the measurement based strategy that focuses on process improvement and variation reduction, which in turn improves the quality of service and output of the outsourcer company - the company providing outsourcing service.

Present BPO Companies in India

The year 2005-06, saw a growth of ITES-BPOs by 37%, contributing $ 6.3 billion to the total software and services exports of $ 23.6 billion according to Nasscom. BPO industry in India has the potential to grow by nearly 12 times the present revenue from this source. There will be consolidation through M&A activity in the BPO industry.

Genpac is at the top in business followed by **WNS**, and **Wipro.** Among the top ten companies there are also **HCL, ICICI one source, IBM Daksh, Progon, Aegis BPO Services, EXL Service Holdings, and 24/7 Customer.** This ranking was given by Nasscom as per the business revenue for 2005-06.

Steady growth was observed in Finance and accounting, Customer Service and HRD Management sectors. Banking and Finance Services Segment accounts of 35-45% of offshore ITEs-BPO while pharmaceuticals and life sciences sector are the other sectors which have potential, but not fully penetrated by Indian BPO industry. In the Automobile industry, many Japanese and US Companies have the opportunity to outsource from India for their ancillaries and parts, at lower costs, due to specialisation and lower wage bill.

It will thus be seen that outsourcing in India has come to stay and is growing at a fast rate with good potential. It is a part of our invisible exports and add to our Current account surplus and ease the Balance of payments pressures of the country, if it is doing outsourcing service for a foreign country.

Services have growth both in output and exports Net services surplus expanded from US $ 37.6 billion in 2007-08 to US $ 49.8 billion in 2008-09, led primarily by software and BPO service exports. The structure of India's service exports shows that software and related services contribute the bulk (42-47%) of total service exports. BPO exports have thus a great role to play in India's export profile in the years to come, and BPO services are part of the software and I.T related services total service exports grew by 4th times between 1990-91 and 2000-01, and by 6th times between 2000-01 and 2009-10. Software exports constituted 39% of the total service exports in 2000-01, which shot up to 46.4% in 2008-09. Such is the importance of the software exports and BPO services in particular.

Select Bibliography

1. Agarwala,P.N., *India's Export Strategy*, Vikas Publishing House, 1978.
2. Avadhani,V.A., *Imports and Capital Formation in the Underdeveloped Countries*, Sudhir Prakasan Publications, 1979.
3. Baldwin, Bhagwati, *et.al.*, *Trade, Growth and the Balance of Payments*, Chicago, 1965.
4. Bhagwati, J.N., *Trade, Tariffs and Growth* (London, 1969).
5. Bhagwati, J.N., *Anatomy and Consequences of Exchange Control Regimes*, Ballinger Publishing Co., 1978.
6. Bela Balassa, *Changing Patterns in Foreign Trade and Payments*, W.W.Norton & Co., 1979.
7. Corden,W.M., *Recent Developments in the Theory of International Trade*, Princeton, New Jersey, 1965.
8. Datta, B., *et.al.*, *Economic Development and Exports*, Calcutta, 1962.
9. Das Gupta, A.K.(Ed.), *Trade Theory and Commercial Policy*, Asia Publishing House, 1965.
10. David Denoon (Ed.), *The New International Economic Order*, New York University Press, 1979.
11. Deb Kalipada, *Export Strategy in India*, S. Chand & Co., 1976.
12. De'vries, A.B., "The Export Experience of Developing Countries," World Bank Staff Papers, 1967.
13. Haberler, G., *International Trade and Economic Development*, Cairo, 1959.
14. Harrod, R. & Hague, D.C., *International Trade Theory in a Developing World*, Macmillan & Co., 1963.
15. Irudayam, Y., *Techniques of Export Marketing*, Asia Publishing House, 1967.
16. Johnson, H.G., *International Trade and Economic Growth*, New York, 1961.
17. Johnson, H.G., *Economic Policies Towards Less Developed Countries*, Washington, 1967.
18. Keshkamat, V.V., *Finance of Foreign Trade in India*, Bombay, 1971.
19. Kindleberger, C.P., *International Economics*, Richard D. Irwin Inc., 1968.
20. Krauss, M.B., *The New Protectionism*, New York University Press, 1978.
21. Linder, S..B., *Trade and Trade Policy for Development*, Frederick A. Praeger, New York, 1967.
22. Mikesell, R.F., *Exchange in the Post-War World*, The Twentieth Century Fund, New York, 1954.
23. Meade, J.E., *The Balance of Payments*, Oxford University Press, London, 1951.
24. Nurkse, R., *Patterns of Trade and Development*, Stockholm, 1959.

25. Panchmukhi, V.R., *Trade Policies of India*, Concept Publishing House, Delhi, 1978.

26. Pearce, I.F., *International Trade, Macmillan & Co.*, London, 1970.

27. Rosenthal, M.S., *Techniques of International Trade*, McGraw-Hill Book Co., London, 1970.

28. Sodersten, B.O., *International Economics*, Macmillan & Co., London, 1970.

29. Vadilal Dagli (Ed.), *India's Foreign Trade*, Vora & Co., Bombay, 1973.

30. Verghese, S.K., *Foreign Exchange and Financing of Foreign Trade*, Vikas Publishing Co., Bombay, 1976.

31. Wolf Martin, *India's Exports*, Oxford University Press, London, 1982.

32. AMA, Management Handbook, Russel F. Moore (Ed.), Taraporevala Publishing Industries Pvt. Ltd., 1978.

33. Joseph, L.M. Massie, *Essentials of Management*, Prentice-Hall of India Pvt. Ltd., 1979.

34. Wadhwa, C.D., "Export Development Policies and Plans", Chapter 4 in IIM (Ahmedabad) Publication. "Strategy for Industrial Development in the 80", 1981.

35. RBI, Reports on Currency and Finance (Annual) and Annual Reports.

36. Government of India, Economic Survey (Annual).

37. World Bank, World Development Report (Annual).

38. IMF, Annual Report.

39. World Bank and IMF, Finance and Development (Quarterly).

40. IMF News Survey.